T0292570

Advances in Computer Vision and Pattern Recognition

Founding editor

Sameer Singh, Rail Vision, Castle Donington, UK

Series editor

Sing Bing Kang, Microsoft Research, Redmond, WA, USA

Advisory Board

Horst Bischof, Graz University of Technology, Austria
Richard Bowden, University of Surrey, Guildford, UK
Sven Dickinson, University of Toronto, ON, Canada
Jiaya Jia, The Chinese University of Hong Kong, Hong Kong
Kyoung Mu Lee, Seoul National University, South Korea
Yoichi Sato, The University of Tokyo, Japan
Bernt Schiele, Max Planck Institute for Computer Science, Saarbrücken, Germany
Stan Sclaroff, Boston University, MA, USA

More information about this series at http://www.springer.com/series/4205

Lauro Snidaro · Jesús García
James Llinas · Erik Blasch
Editors

Context-Enhanced Information Fusion

Boosting Real-World Performance
with Domain Knowledge

 Springer

Editors
Lauro Snidaro
Department of Mathematics and Computer
 Science
University of Udine
Udine
Italy

Jesús García
Department of Computer Science
 and Engineering
University Carlos III
Colmenarejo
Spain

James Llinas
Center for Multisource Information Fusion
 and Department of Industrial and Systems
 Engineering
University at Buffalo
Buffalo, NY
USA

Erik Blasch
Information Directorate
Air Force Research Laboratory
Rome, NY
USA

ISSN 2191-6586   ISSN 2191-6594   (electronic)
Advances in Computer Vision and Pattern Recognition
ISBN 978-3-319-28969-4   ISBN 978-3-319-28971-7   (eBook)
DOI 10.1007/978-3-319-28971-7

Library of Congress Control Number: 2015960833

© Springer International Publishing Switzerland (outside the USA) 2016
This work is subject to copyright. All rights are reserved by the Publisher, whether the whole or part
of the material is concerned, specifically the rights of translation, reprinting, reuse of illustrations,
recitation, broadcasting, reproduction on microfilms or in any other physical way, and transmission
or information storage and retrieval, electronic adaptation, computer software, or by similar or dissimilar
methodology now known or hereafter developed.
The use of general descriptive names, registered names, trademarks, service marks, etc. in this
publication does not imply, even in the absence of a specific statement, that such names are exempt from
the relevant protective laws and regulations and therefore free for general use.
The publisher, the authors and the editors are safe to assume that the advice and information in this
book are believed to be true and accurate at the date of publication. Neither the publisher nor the
authors or the editors give a warranty, express or implied, with respect to the material contained herein or
for any errors or omissions that may have been made.

Printed on acid-free paper

This Springer imprint is published by SpringerNature
The registered company is Springer International Publishing AG Switzerland

Dedicated by Lauro Snidaro to his wife Ingrid and son Luca

Dedicated by Jesús García to his family, friends, and colleagues

Dedicated by James Llinas to his wife Sarah for her unending patience

Dedicated by Erik Blasch to his wife Jitka for her continuous support

Dedicated by the editors to the International Society of Information Fusion (ISIF) from which the forums, discussions, and ideas established in this book were crafted

Preface

This book brings together two topics which themselves are complex and multi-disciplinary: the concepts of "Information Fusion" and "Context" both of which have long histories of research and development. In this Preface, we offer our perspectives on the motivations and rationales for the development of this text, and then provide our thoughts that have led to the particular organizational framework of the book.

History

The concept of *information fusion* can be said to have begun with the writings of Aristotle which acknowledged the integration of the human senses. With the advent of technology, the nature of sensing evolved into an understanding that data were being collected not only by the human (e.g. receptors in the retina) but also derived from physical sensors (e.g. pixels). *Context*, as for information fusion, has its own origins in philosophy. From the early Greeks, there were various debates about the interaction of the human on, within, and outside the world. The mental perceptions and physical senses were a means to integrate the mind–body based perspectives in processes that are similar to those for contextual understanding.

The Role of Context

Three demarcations of context-enhanced information fusion include the contextually influenced functions of perception, information systems, and computing. One of the key issues associated with context is *ecological perception* as defined by Gibson. During the 1950s, there was the notion that the human consciousness constructs perceptions strictly from the senses; however, Gibson challenged this notion by noting that the mind can directly interpret stimuli from the world in his 1966 work *The Senses Considered as Perceptual Systems*. Additional work included assertions that the world affords actions and ecological perception in which the notion of own-self to the world, i.e. contextual framing, conditions perception; these works constituted a milestone regarding the role of context in perception. In the 1990s, a second milestone included the large-scale physical collections of information from the world from various sensing data including weather, terrain, and roads which has become known as the **Geographical Information System** (GIS). From the large amounts of data being collected, researchers in information began to use this information to improve estimation accuracy. Recently, the methods of **Context-aware computing** demonstrate that global information can be used to modify or augment local estimation processes regarding parameters or states of interest. With the Internet, there are many possibilities enabling distributed processing, cloud-based access to information, and cognitive autonomy. Today, that information is widely available from databases, wireless connections, and cloud technology. Being able to access relevant GIS data and a broad range of other types of data has popularized the ability to use contextual information for an extensive range of applications.

Table 1 brings together these general themes of information community-established milestones. Looking at the general contributions which are rooted in the historical thoughts of the time, there are three developments of concepts and philosophy, mathematics and data integration theory, and architectures and applications. These three areas facilitated the editors' organization of the material of this book submitted from the top scientists, researchers, practitioners, and leaders in information fusion.

Table 1 Context exploitation capability evolution over time

Information perspective	Time period			
	Ancient times	1960s	1990s	2010+
Fusion	Sensing	Estimation	Multi-sensor	Information
Context	Mind–body	Ecological	GIS	Aware computing
Contextual fusion	Philosophy	Theory	Applications	Architectures

Modern Information System Applications

Modern information fusion systems must consider the specific characteristics of the application domain in which they have to operate, showing robust, and context-sensitive behaviour. Likewise, a system designer must take into consideration different sources of contextual knowledge in addition to immediate sensory data in order to develop an effective, efficient, and useful approach to situation assessment. For applications in a wide variety of domains, contextual knowledge may include structural models of the scene, known a priori relationships between the entities and the surrounding environment, dynamic scenarios necessary to interpret or constrain the system output, and user preferences, social norms, and cultures when estimating the situations of interest for the domain. Context includes conditions which augment otherwise bounded estimates, and results in estimates of enhanced meaning. This book provides a broad framework of discussion for system designers on the use of contextual information for fusion-based estimation that, to our understanding, has not as yet been offered in the literature.

The development of information fusion (IF) systems, to include data-, sensor-, and feature-level fusion, is a necessary engineering process in diverse applications, and new domains require an increasing degree of contextualized solutions and situation–adaptation mechanisms. The potential development of IF systems inclusive of contextual factors and information offers an opportunity to improve the quality of the fused output, provide solutions adapted to the application requirements, and enhance tailored responses to user queries. Contextual-based strategy challenges include selecting the appropriate representations, exploitations, and instantiations. Context could be represented as knowledge-bases, ontologies, and geographical maps, etc. and would form a powerful tool to favour adaptability and system performance. Example applications include context-aided tracking and classification, situational reasoning, ontology building, and decision updating. Contemporary discussions of context are domain and sensor specific for which information fusion enhances performance. For example, context-aided target tracking seeks to determine kinematic movements with domain-constrained sensitivities (e.g. roads), whereas context-aided information fusion solutions utilize not only the road information, but also the social norms of the same geographical information (e.g. traffic rules).

Book Tenets

This book presents the foundational reasoning, theories, and methods for including contextual influences in fusion process design and implementation, along with the most recent results in exploiting contextual information for real-world modern applications. A balance between high- and low-level information fusion problems is highlighted to showcase performance improvements in highly demanding conditions. Holistic approaches integrating research results in different communities, which are relevant for readers outside the information fusion community, have been selected, emphasizing the need to combine different techniques to overcome limitations of a single perspective, legacy computing, or programs traditionally applied to domain-specific data and information fusion problems. Recent advances in information fusion include context exploitation, multi-level fusion performance, and hard/soft fusion. Finally, a selection of representative application domains requiring the injection of contextual knowledge is presented in the book (e.g. vision systems, harbour surveillance, robotics, and ambient intelligence) to illustrate the process, where sensor-based data and contextual information synergistically yield more robust and informative results.

Book Outline

The book comprises six areas for which we have explored and developed relevant contributions: foundations, concepts, systems philosophy, mathematical theory, hard-soft fusion, and applications:

Fundamentals introduces the necessary terminology and key elements in information fusion and context. The main concepts are conveyed with the support of the JDL/DFIG data fusion model, helping the reader to frame context-enhanced fusion in a well-known setting.

Concepts of Context for Fusion presents central themes and issues for context-aware information fusion. A formalization of context is presented along with topics derived from context-enhanced target tracking, decision support, and threat assessment.

Systems Philosophy of Contextual Fusion discusses design issues and challenges in developing context-aware fusion systems. Several architectures are proposed where a pivotal role is given to a middleware layer dedicated to context access and discovery.

Mathematical Characterization of Context provides mathematical grounds for modelling the contextual influences in representative fusion problems such as sensor quality assessment, target tracking, and text analysis.

Context in Hard/Soft Fusion deals with the fusion of device-generated data (hard) with human-generated data (soft). Context brings together hard and soft data as an emerging topic.

Applications of Context Approaches to Fusion offers an array of applications where the exploitation of contextual information in the fusion process boosts system performance. Application domains include maritime and ground target tracking, surveillance, robotics, and assisted driving.

We hope that the information presented can be useful to various practitioners, researchers, readers, and academics pursuing applications to real-world problems where information fusion offers a solution. We have brought together the leading experts in the field to showcase their techniques of using context to enhance information fusion results.

2015   Lauro Snidaro
                                                                   Jesús García
                                                                   James Llinas
                                                                   Erik Blasch

Contents

Contributors

Myriam Abramson Naval Research Laboratory, Washington, DC, USA

José María Armingol Intelligent Systems Lab, Universidad Carlos III de Madrid, Leganés, Spain

Alex J. Aved Air Force Research Lab, Rome, NY, USA

Giulia Battistello Department Sensor Data and Information Fusion, Fraunhofer FKIE, Wachtberg, Germany

Joachim Biermann SDF, Fraunhofer FKIE, Wachtberg, Germany

Erik Blasch Air Force Research Laboratory, Rome, NY, USA

Domenico D. Bloisi Department of Computer, Control, and Management Engineering, Sapienza University of Rome, Rome, Italy

Genshe Chen Intelligent Fusion Technology, Germantown, MD, USA

Joseph Coyne Naval Research Laboratory, Washington, DC, USA

John L. Crassidis Department of Mechanical and Aerospace Engineering, University at Buffalo, State University of New York, Amherst, NY, USA

Jonathan W. Decker Naval Research Laboratory, Washington, DC, USA

Arturo de la Escalera Intelligent Systems Lab, Universidad Carlos III de Madrid, Leganés, Spain

Adam M. Fosbury Space Exploration Sector, Applied Physics Laboratory, Johns Hopkins University, Laurel, MD, USA

Fernando García Intelligent Systems Lab, Universidad Carlos III de Madrid, Leganés, Spain

Jesús García Applied Artificial Intelligence Group, Universidad Carlos III de Madrid, Colmenarejo, Spain

Jemin George U.S. Army Research Laboratory, Adelphi, MD, USA

Antonio Gilliam Naval Research Laboratory, Washington, DC, USA

Geoff Gross Osthus Inc., Melbourne, Florida, USA

Juan Gómez-Romero Department of Computer Science and A.I., CITIC-UGR, Granada, Spain

Riad I. Hammoud BAE Systems, Burlington, MA, USA

Steven A. Israel Raytheon, Chantilly, VA, USA

Anne-Laure Jousselme NATO-STO Centre for Maritime Research and Experimentation, La Spezia, Italy

Michael Kandefer Applied Sciences Group, Inc., Buffalo, NY, USA

Wolfgang Koch Fraunhofer FKIE, Wachtberg, Germany; Department Sensor Data and Information Fusion, Fraunhofer FKIE, Wachtberg, Germany

Ksawery Krenc C4I Research and Development Department, OBR CTM S.A., Gdynia, Poland

Eric Leadbetter Naval Research Laboratory, Washington, DC, USA

Ji-Woong Lee Pennsylvania State University, State College, PA, USA

Tatiana Levashova St. Petersburg Institute for Informatics and Automation of the Russian Academy of Sciences, St. Petersburg, Russian Federation

Peiyi Li Department of Computer and Information Sciences, Temple University, Philadelphia, USA

Pengpeng Liang Department of Computer and Information Sciences, Temple University, Philadelphia, USA

Haibin Ling Department of Computer and Information Science, Temple University, Philadelphia, PA, USA

Mark A. Livingston Naval Research Laboratory, Washington, DC, USA

James Llinas Center for Multisource Information Fusion and Department of Industrial and Systems Engineering, University at Buffalo, Buffalo, NY, USA

David Martín Intelligent Systems Lab, Universidad Carlos III de Madrid, Leganés, Spain

Michael Mertens Department Sensor Data and Information Fusion, Fraunhofer FKIE, Wachtberg, Germany

Ranjeev Mittu Naval Research Laboratory, Washington, DC, USA

José M. Molina Applied Artificial Intelligence Group, Universidad Carlos III de Madrid, Colmenarejo, Spain

Ira S. Moskowitz Naval Research Laboratory, Washington, DC, USA

Leo Motus Research Laboratory for Proactive Technologies, Tallinn University of Technology, Tallin, Estonia

James Nagy Air Force Research Lab, Rome, NY, USA

Daniele Nardi Department of Computer, Control, and Management Engineering, Sapienza University of Rome, Rome, Italy

Benjamin Newsom Next Century Corporation, Columbia, MD, USA

Vincent Nimier Department of Information Processing and Modelling, ONERA, Châtillon, Palaiseau CEDEX, France

Miguel A. Patricio Applied Artificial Intelligence Group, Universidad Carlos III de Madrid, Colmenarejo, Spain

Shashi Phoha Applied Research Laboratory, Pennsylvania State University, University Park, PA, USA

Aurelio Ponz Intelligent Systems Lab, Universidad Carlos III de Madrid, Leganés, Spain

Jurgo-Soren Preden Research Laboratory for Proactive Technologies, Tallinn University of Technology, Tallin, Estonia

Asok Ray Department of Mechanical and Nuclear Engineering, Pennsylvania State University, University Park, PA, USA

Kellyn Rein ITF, Fraunhofer FKIE, Wachtberg, Germany

Francesco Riccio Department of Computer, Control, and Management Engineering, Sapienza University of Rome, Rome, Italy

Galina L. Rogova State University of New York at Buffalo, Buffalo, NY, USA

Stephen Russell Army Research Laboratory, Adelphi, MD, USA

Soumalya Sarkar Department of Mechanical and Nuclear Engineering, Pennsylvania State University, University Park, PA, USA

Miguel A. Serrano Applied Artificial Intelligence Group, Universidad Carlos III de Madrid, Colmenarejo, Spain

Stuart C. Shapiro University at Buffalo, Buffalo, NY, USA

Dan Shen Intelligent Fusion Technology, Germantown, MD, USA

Xinchu Shi Department of Computer and Information Sciences, Temple University, Philadelphia, USA

Nikolay Shilov St. Petersburg Institute for Informatics and Automation of the Russian Academy of Sciences, St. Petersburg, Russian Federation

Ciara Sibley Naval Research Laboratory, Washington, DC, USA

Tarunraj Singh Department of Mechanical and Aerospace Engineering, University at Buffalo, Amherst, NY, USA

Alexander Smirnov St. Petersburg Institute for Informatics and Automation of the Russian Academy of Sciences, St. Petersburg, Russian Federation; ITMO University, St. Petersburg, Russian Federation

Lauro Snidaro Department of Mathematics and Computer Science, University of Udine, Udine, Italy

Alan N. Steinberg Independent Consultant, Woodbridge, VA, USA

Dirk Tenne Varian Medical Systems, Seattle, Washington, USA

Francesco Trapani Department of Computer, Control, and Management Engineering, Sapienza University of Rome, Rome, Italy

Martin Ulmke Department Sensor Data and Information Fusion, Fraunhofer FKIE, Wachtberg, Germany

Nurali Virani Department of Mechanical and Nuclear Engineering, Pennsylvania State University, University Park, PA, USA

Ingrid Visentini Department of Mathematics and Computer Science, University of Udine, Udine, Italy

Chun Yang Sigtem Technology Inc., San Mateo, CA, USA

Part I
Foundations

Chapter 1
Context and Fusion: Definitions, Terminology

James Llinas, Lauro Snidaro, Jesús García and Erik Blasch

Abstract This chapter attempts to cover two topics which themselves are complex and multidisciplinary: the concept of "Context" and the concept of "Information Fusion", both of which have long histories of research publications. This chapter thus attempts to provide the reader concise introductions to these two topics by providing a review of an established framework for data and information fusion that derives from the well-known functional model of the fusion process called the Joint Directors of Laboratories or JDL model of fusion. The latter part of the chapter introduces two frameworks for how information fusion and contextual information can possibly be joined together that would allow for improved exploitation and inferencing in a variety of applications; these frameworks should be viewed as suggestions of notional processing concepts for these purposes. The chapter also provides numerous references for the reader to follow up and explore any of the ideas offered herein.

Keywords Data fusion · Information fusion · Process model · Fusion functions · Architecture · Focal premises · Contextual premises

J. Llinas (✉)
Center for Multisource Information Fusion and Department of Industrial
and Systems Engineering, University at Buffalo, Buffalo, NY, USA
e-mail: llinas@buffalo.edu

L. Snidaro
Department of Mathematics and Computer Science, University of Udine, Udine, Italy
e-mail: lauro.snidaro@uniud.it

J. García
GIAA Research Group, Universidad Carlos III de Madrid, Colmenarejo, Spain
e mail: jgherrer@inf.uc3m.es

E. Blasch
Air Force Research Laboratory, Rome, NY, USA
e-mail: erik.blasch@gmail.com

© Springer International Publishing Switzerland (outside the USA) 2016
L. Snidaro et al. (eds.), *Context-Enhanced Information Fusion*,
Advances in Computer Vision and Pattern Recognition,
DOI 10.1007/978-3-319-28971-7_1

1.1   An Introduction to Information Fusion

Information fusion is an area of research and development that is but also an area of study that is expanding in certain ways as well. As was experienced in its early development (in the 1980s), and is perhaps typical for emerging areas of science and technology, normalizing the language of this then-new field was an initial complexity, and the status of that language still remains somewhat inconsistent and ambiguous. Here we will not concern ourselves with some of these terminological issues but point out that while there are for example argued boundaries between "Sensor Fusion," "Data Fusion,", and "Information Fusion" (as well as "Knowledge Fusion"), we will use only the information fusion phrase and permit ourselves to cross possible conceptual boundaries implied by these other terms. Our choice here is in part motivated by the focus of this book, which is on the concepts, techniques, and application of Information Fusion that employs contextual material, since we argue that the categories of subject matter that fall into the class of contexts are generally broader and more informative than "data," that term considered as more narrow in meaning and implication, especially "sensor data" that generally comprise very discrete numerical measurements.

1.1.1   Definition of Data (Information) Fusion

The initial Data Fusion Lexicon, produced by the U.S. Joint Directors of Laboratories (JDL) Data Fusion Subgroup in 1987, defined data fusion (DF) as

> a process dealing with the association, correlation, and combination of data and information from single and multiple sources to achieve refined position and identity estimates, and complete and timely assessments of situations and threats, and their significance. The process is characterized by continuous refinements of its estimates and assessments, and the evaluation of the need for additional sources, or modification of the process itself, to achieve improved results [1]

A simpler version might be "a process of combining data or information to develop improved estimates or predictions of entity states." The point is, data henceforth "information fusion" (IF henceforth) is an automated information process, which involves combining data in the broadest sense to estimate or predict the state of some aspect of a problem space of interest, and to do so to improve those values beyond what could be done with lesser input. The notion of estimation should also be clearly understood. Few would argue that the inputs into an IF process are random variables; sensor responses are quite typically modeled using statistical concepts to represent the imperfections in sensing operations and in the resultant observables or measurements. If in the broadest sense then the IF process, whatever it does, can be conceptualized as a function, then clearly any function of a random variable yields a random variable; in other words, the fused estimate, no matter how elegantly calculated, is a random variable having a statistical distribution. A major focus of IF processing then is to develop techniques that optimize the resultant estimate, based on the multisource input, usually in some statistical sense, such as minimum variance.

As noted above, it is an endless debate to argue whether "data fusion" or some other term is an appropriate label for this very broad concept. There is no body of common and accepted vocabulary to which we can appeal for such specialized terms. The important point is that this broad concept is an important topic for a unified theoretical approach, and therefore deserves its own label.[1]

1.1.2 Information Fusion "Levels"

Of the many possible ways of differentiating among types of IF functions, that of the Joint Directors of Laboratories Data Fusion Subpanel has gained the greatest popularity. This "JDL Model" differentiates functions into fusion "levels" (depicted in Fig. 1.1) that provides an often useful distinction among IF processes that relate to the refinement of estimates for parameters of interest related to "objects," "situations," "threats," and "processes" [3]. Note that the figure is meant to depict either a single IF node or the aggregate processing of a suite of IF nodes that would each have similar structure; the model is strictly a discussion aid and *not* an architecture or processing diagram, etc. In 1998, revisions of the number of and definitions for the "levels" were proposed in [4, 5] to (a) provide a useful categorization representing logically different types of problems, which are generally (though not necessarily) solved by different techniques; and (b) maintain a degree of consistency with the mainstream of technical usage. It should be explicitly noted that much of the material included from here on is drawn, either directly or somewhat modified, from "Revisions to the JDL Model" by Steinberg and Bowman [5].

The proposed new definitions are as follows:

- **Level 0—Sub-Object Data Assessment**: estimation and prediction of signal/object observable states on the basis of pixel/signal level data association and characterization; this is a new Level added to the process model, not shown in the Figure 1.1;
- **Level 1—Object Assessment**: estimation and prediction of entity states on the basis of inferences from observations;
- **Level 2—Situation Assessment**: estimation and prediction of entity states on the basis of inferred relations among entities;
- **Level 3—Impact Assessment**: estimation and prediction of effects on situations of planned or estimated/predicted actions by the participants (e.g., assessing

---

[1]Some people have preferred terms like "information integration" with an attempt at connoting greater generality than earlier, narrower definitions of "data fusion" (and perhaps, to distance themselves from old data fusion approaches and programs) but such manipulations do not contribute toward better representation or understanding.

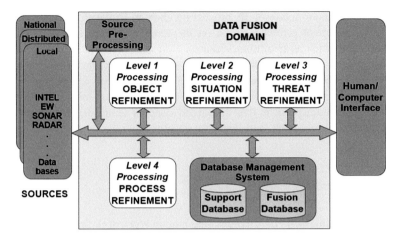

Fig. 1.1 Classical JDL data fusion process model [2]

susceptibilities and vulnerabilities to estimated/predicted threat actions given ones own planned actions);

- **Level 4—Process Refinement (an element of resource management)**: adaptive data acquisition and processing to support mission objectives.

To explain a bit about Level 0, a Level 0 example could be the preprocessing typically done in imagery as a first signal processing step such as noise reduction, equalization/contrast enhancement, etc. These steps are all directed to improving the raw data coming from the sensors in order to facilitate next elaboration phases. Remote sensing [6] applications typically perform Level 0 fusion by combining multi-spectral images at the pixel level.

To recall some of the aspects of the other levels, Level 1 is that level where single-object kinematic and identification (ID) estimates are developed; this is of course done within the resolution limits of sensors and can involve group or "raid" tracking, i.e., of multiple objects, whether this is known or not. It is in this highly mathematical and statistical area that much of the research in IF has been done. Today, capabilities for Level 1 fusion are relatively sophisticated, employing so-called "Multiple Hypothesis Trackers," "Interacting Multiple Model" trackers, among many others. For object ID, reasonably robust Assisted Target Recognition techniques ranging from sophisticated feature-based techniques to model-based techniques have been developed and deployed. Level 2 involves situational estimation, a more abstract and complex informational product, and is usually done by a mixture of symbolic or knowledge-based methods and mathematical techniques. Level 3 involves forming estimates of what could be termed "special" or "critical" instances of situations, usually requiring some type of immediate or near-term response; similar processing techniques to Level 2 are used to formulate these estimates. Finally, Level 4 is the functional process within which what could be called a "control law" for the fusion process is invoked, providing the adaptive feedback to the overall processing operation. In recent research and prototyping, Level 4 has involved a variety of adaptive strategies ranging from adaptive sensor management (called "collection management" in the intelligence community), to adaptive algorithm adaptation or sensor control (e.g., adaptive detection thresholding or waveform switching) to multiple-algorithm management to achieve robust operation across changing problem conditions. Table 1.1 shows a tabular notional summary of the different methodologies upon which each level primarily (but not exclusively) depends. Hall and Llinas also provide an overview of the primary processing paradigms by level in [7].

It will be argued in other chapters of this book that certain fusion functions are carried out at any of the JDL levels and at any node in a fusion process architecture. There are subtleties, however, that are peculiar to each level. For example, the nature of what is happening in regard to association processes is semantically different at each level. For example, at Level 1, it is typical that relatively raw data are being associated to an estimation hypothesis being developed algorithmically for a physical entity; a typical example is the association of multiple radar range and angle measurements to the estimated kinematic properties of multiple moving objects. The association process usually results in discrete assignments of detections, measurements, or features to the various algorithms that are estimating object properties. Strengths of association here exploit knowledge of statistical error properties of sensors and of the estimation processes (Kalman filters as typical exemplars) and are probabilistically couched. At Levels 2 and 3, the association operations are directed to more of an aggregation function, where complex relations among situational components are trying to be estimated. Here, association strength is measured via strength of semantic similarity or relatedness, accounting as best as possible for various uncertainties that may exist and that can be estimated. At Level 4, the association operations are trying to support a best control action choice and are thus framed as an action-utility association operation. Steinberg, in [5], also discusses these ideas in one of the first papers to begin a fusion community dialog on the nature of the JDL model.

Table 1.1 Algorithmic classes for each data fusion level

Level 0	Level 1	Level 2/Level 3	Level 4
Detection, detection fusion	Multisensor/multitarget tracking methods	Bayesian networks	Stochastic adaptive control
Track before detect	Classifiers and classifier combining methods	Knowledge representation and reasoning	Mathematical programming-based optimization
Non-commensurate data processing	Least squares, maximum likelihood	Agent based modeling	Information theoretic
Upstream data processing methods	Fuzzy logic	Evidential reasoning	Reinforcement learning

1.1.3 Remarks About the Data and Information in IF Architectures

As we have described the IF processes, we have noted that the inputs are from a "multisensor" front-end type capability. From a historical point of view, there is no doubt that IF system and IF technology concepts were framed around the notion that the input was sensor data. Such sensor systems were what have rather recently been called "physics-based" sensors, meaning the usual type of electromechanical devices that are designed around ideas that exploit sensory capability in some range of the electromagnetic spectrum. The idea here is to frame the observational capability of a problem space of interest around its naturally occurring "signals" that result either from passive emanations such as heat signals from any object or from active or responsive emanations that come from an object being illuminated by a radiating sensor such as a radar. Usually, the sensors are in either search mode or a directed mode, pointed to objects and spatiotemporal areas of interest. Using the terminology that we will introduce below, such data of this type are focused on some collective, multisensory-based spatiotemporal area of interest, an AOI, which can be conceptualized as bounded by the joint spatiotemporal boundaries of the multisensory system resolutional capabilities. Our point here is that such data are usually focused on items and activities of interest and do not take advantage of any "surrounding" data or information beyond the AOI. It is true of course that an IF system design could also take advantage of supportive data base and other information peculiar to the IF processing, such as a "Track File" that maintains files on all object kinematic tracks. But at least historically (roughly, pre-year 2000), the data and information in an IF system design have not typically included anything of a contextual type.

1.1.4 For Further Reading

Information fusion has been studied now since the 1980s, and numerous references are available for the interested reader to pursue further study of this topic. The earliest text is by Waltz and Llinas [8], and this has been followed by several edited works to include "Handbooks" on the topic (e.g., [9–12]). Many of these texts are directed to defense and security applications (a central topic for this book as well), but there are many other good texts on other than these applications:

- Robotics [13];
- Non-Destructive Testing [14];
- Remote Sensing [6];
- Information Retrieval [15];
- Data Mining [16];
- Image Fusion [17];
- Geographic Information Systems [18];

And there are yet other application-directed texts. This broad list gives evidence to the claim that IF is a truly multidisciplinary field of study as well as a truly cross-domain technological capability and process.

1.2 Context in Fusion

There has been active research on how to represent and exploit context in the fusion processes in the past 15 years. While recent works can be found in the special issue [19], and surveys on contextual tracking approaches in [20, 21], we here provide in Table 1.2 only a breakdown of the most significant works according to the fusion process enhanced by contextual information: sensor characterization, physical and procedural constraints, prediction models, data association methods, information management, and high-level fusion.

Regarding the type of information used as context, static physical context is the most usual, such as geographic data files as GIS with surface descriptions, bathymetry records, road maps, etc. The use of tactical or procedural information besides physical is also an option and predictions can be also refined by using tactical rules, and operational domain knowledge. This is usual in the examples at the highest fusion levels. Finally, dynamic context variables such as meteorological conditions, sea state, situation variables, or inputs coming from an inference engine have also been considered. In this sense, the decision process takes the form of a knowledge-based system (KBS) to infer the contextual state.

Table 1.2 shows how, save shows how, save for [82] which presents a framework for the inclusion of contextual information in high-level fusion processes (Levels 2, 3, 4), all the works focus on a specific fusion process and provide a solution which applies only to specific functions. Most examples are in fact tailored to the characteristic of the problems addressed instead of general processes to design context-integrated fusion systems. No initiative has been done towards exploiting context in the fusion process in a systematic way separating context knowledge as information to be modeled and processed in the appropriate way to the fusion functions. For instance, analysis of reliability, consistency, relevance to the fusion processes, induced uncertainties, etc., aspects which will be discussed in the coming sections of this chapter.

1.3 Perspectives on Information Fusion and Context

As difficult as it is to be very precise in defining "fusion" boundaries described above, we will see in this text that the definitions of context and "contextual information" are equally difficult to define. We suggest the reader to be flexible in this regard; terms and definitions in an edited book reflect the contributions of a number of well-qualified authors that, for such a slippery term, offer different

Table 1.2 Survey of some works exploiting context in typical fusion processes according to the JDL model [21]

High/low	JDL level	Function	Techniques
Low	Level 0	Sensor characterization	Geographic aspects [22–24]
			Weighting [24–26]
			Fuzzy systems [27–29]
		Signal fusion	Context enhancement [30–33]
	Level 1	Data association	Confidence-based association [34–36]
			JPDA [37, 38]
			PDAF [38]
			MHT [39, 40]
			Fuzzy association [41–43]
		Filtering	Physical and maps context [24, 28, 44]
			Road layout [38, 45–50]
			PHD [45, 51, 52]
			Multiple-model [53–57]
			Nonlinear filters [48, 58, 59]
			Tactical rules [23, 52, 60, 61]
		Track management	[40, 62]
		Classification	[63]
High	Level 2	Knowledge representation	Ontologies [64]
		Situation assessment	Activity monitoring [65–68]
			Situation understanding [69–71]
			Natural language understanding and linguistics [72, 73]
		Decision-making	[74–79]
	Level 3	Intent assessment	[80–82]
	Level 4	Process refinement	Context discovery [83]
			Context adaptation [79]
			Context learning [51, 84, 85]

explications and flavors and nuances. However, we believe that this lack of precision is not critical to the reading audience, considered to largely be comprised of researchers and technical developers, and may be helpful to stimulate readers to rethink the various definitions to the betterment of their own purposes.

One overarching assertion we will make, however, (as in Sect. 1.1) is that information fusion (IF) is at its heart an estimation process, more specifically an *automated* estimation process or at least largely so; our central focus in this book is on algorithmic or otherwise automated processes, although the insertion of human intelligence is not disallowed. These automated processes are enabled in software, and thus vulnerable to the "garbage-in/garbage-out" constraint. IF functional capabilities are developed to estimate some aspect of a real world that is of interest to some user. Those capabilities are bounded by a number of factors, such as the quality of the available data or information that can be used to form the estimates[2] as well as the complexity of the world being observed. Gauging the complexity of any world includes the degree to which that world is hospitable to or cooperative with the observational or other information-providing mechanisms upon which the IF estimation processes depend. In adversarial domains such as defense and security domains—although adversarial postures can certainly be taken in the business world as well—there can be purposeful actions to foil or corrupt any IF process; such environments lead to the endless exchange of actions that are intended to overcome each step of each adversary, in an endless game type framework. IF researchers and developers hope to enable an IF capability that aids in human "sensemaking" (see e.g., [88, 89]) a.k.a reasoning, so anything that can be done in IF process design toward moving the IF system to function in a way that mimics and/or supports human reasoning would be considered beneficial.

Well then, how do humans reason or make sense of things? This of course is a huge question and well beyond the intended core content of this book. However, the question is worth considering, if nothing else than for purposes of better understanding IF, and also the role and purpose of context in its formulation. Reasoning is generally seen as a means to improve knowledge and make better decisions, although there is a lot of empirical evidence that quantifies a number of error types, biases, and inefficiencies that occur in human reasoning. There is literature that distinguishes between reasoning and inferencing (e.g., [90]); one definition of inferencing [90] is "Inference (as the term is most commonly understood in psychology) is the production of new mental representations on the basis of previously held representations." Mercier and Sperber argue in [90] that "Reasoning, as commonly understood, refers to a very special form of inference at the conceptual level, where not only is a new mental representation (or conclusion) consciously produced, but the previously held representations (or premises) that warrant it are also consciously entertained." Continuing, they say that what characterizes reasoning is that it includes and is distinguished by the notion of a formed "argument," and has a purpose oriented to persuasion. In this approach, the premises that are reasoned over are seen as providing reasons to accept the conclusion. Thus, [90] argues that what characterizes reasoning is the awareness not just of a conclusion but of an argument that justifies accepting that conclusion. If we pursue this notion a bit, we can ask what a premise is; most definitions label a premise as "A statement that is assumed to be true and from which a conclusion can be drawn."[3] So, premises are those statements or assertions that support the forming of a conclusion.

---

[2]Quality is another difficult term to gain consensus on; data quality has been written about for general applications [86] as well as for IF-specific applications [87]; we will address the quality issue as part of the general content of this book in various ways and in various chapters.

[3]E.g., http://www.audioenglish.org/dictionary/premise.htm.

1.3.1 Contextual Premises as Distinct from Focal Premises

Intuitively, contextual information could be said to be that information that "surrounds" a situation of interest in the world. It is information that aids in understanding the (estimated) situation and also aids in reacting to the situation, if a reaction is required. Devlin [91] takes this view, defining context as follows: "a feature F is *contextual* for an action A if F constrains A, and may affect the outcome of A, but is not a constituent of A." Contextual premises can thus be seen as a set of constraints to a reasoning process about a situation; Kandefer and Shapiro also define it in a constraint-based sense [92]: "the structured set of variable, external constraints to some (natural or artificial) cognitive process that influences the behavior of that process in the agent(s) under consideration." There are of course other definitions of this somewhat slippery term, such as that offered by Dey and Abowd [93], who state that context is "any information (either implicit or explicit) that can be used to characterize the situation of an entity." These definitions imply that these contextual premises are constraints to other premises that could be called "focal" to the formation of our "argument" or conclusion. For example, Kent writes that "It is the context of the situation alone which gives point and meaning to the subsequent elements of the speculation," implying that there is a situational premise that is separate from the contextually augmented (or constrained) premises. Heuer, in the well-known work of [94] writes, "The significance of information is always a joint function of the nature of the information and the context in which it is interpreted," where he distinguishes "the (focal) information" and "the context" of it.

In this chapter, we will use these viewpoints to develop a perspective as follows: In many problems involving interpretation and the development of meaning, there is often some focal data that is purposely collected to help in developing such understanding—in a surveillance application these are the sensor data and possibly human-based observational data. Through analysis, these data can support the formation of what we will call "focal premises"—statements (propositions) about some aspect of the "condition or situation" of interest. To the extent that separate contextual data or information are available, they too can be analyzed to form additional premises—propositions that we will call "contextual premises"—that, together with the focal premises, can lead to the formation of an "argument"—a conclusion traceable to the foundations of the joint set of these premises.

1.3.2 Information Fusion Process Implications

If we consider a very basic depiction of an IF process in light of the preceding remarks, it would look something like that shown in Fig. 1.2. In Fig. 1.2 we depict an area under surveillance by a multisensory IF system. The multiple-sensor system is directed to the operational area of Interest but the situation in that AOI is

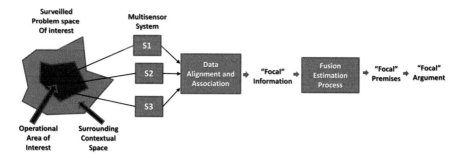

Fig. 1.2 Notional information fusion process with focal aspects

occurring within a surrounding contextual space. Data from the multisensory system is aligned and associated as in any IF process (see Sect. 1.1 above that provides an overview of basic IF processing), producing an associated body of evidence which we call here the "Focal Information." The estimation (inferencing) capability of the IF process produces "statements" or propositions about some situational component within the AOI, the "Focal Premise(s)." The automated IF system may as well, depending on its inherent knowledge and algorithmic features, produce what could be called the "Focal Argument," in the frame of the preceding discussion. The concept shown in Fig. 1.2 could be called "traditional" in that it exploits the sensor system data that is (at least ideally) directed to the AOI. This traditional system does not account for any premises that could be derived from the data/information in the surrounding contextual space. These contextually influenced interpretations have typically been left to the humans in the system. Heuer [94] notes for example that "The context is provided by the analyst in the form of a set of assumptions and expectations concerning human and organizational behavior."

1.3.3 Integrating Context into Information Fusion Processes

How then do we improve on IF process designs to automatically incorporate contextual information to enable the formation of premises and the formation of improved arguments or conclusions? Dealing with this question requires some diversion here to reexamine some of the pointed papers on the notion of context. For example, Kokinov [95] distinguishes between (citing many references) external context and internal context: "*External context* refers to the physical and social environment or the setting within which the subjects behavior is generated. *Internal context* refers to the subjects current mental state within which the subjects behavior is generated." So then we can agree with Heuer that a human specifies a context but Kokinov and others would say this is internal context, housed in a mental model. In our applications where there are human analysts using the IF system, we can agree that they bring a personal context to the final interpretation of the automated argument that the IF system offers—in this book we are rarely dealing with internal context, as we are focusing on automated system design. It also has to be appreciated that contextual information and implied premises can be dynamic and changing at perhaps a different rate than the AOI problem is changing. So with these considerations, we are concerned with external context—physical and social (and perhaps other) factors—but not a mentally housed internal context. Following Kokinov then, we are focused on physical and social and possibly other factors from which relevant contextual premises could be formed.

Another issue is *relevance*. The situation or problem of concern is that in the AOI. So how do we decide, even if we know the details of the data and information surrounding the AOI, what derived contextual premises influence the argument about the AOI that the IF system is trying to develop? In turn, this raises the question of when, in the lifecycle of the IF system of interest, is this relevance question being asked. If it is at design time, when the evolving design ideas for the system are being formed, then one has the advantage of knowing (a) what arguments or estimates the IF system is being designed to perform, and (b) what area of the world and what societal environment the system will be directed to. Knowing (a), one knows the goal-arguments that the system will be trying to develop; knowing (b), one knows the physical and social and perhaps other contextual information that could be available, and from which relevant premises could be formed. Integrating the focal, sensor-data-derived premises with the context-information-derived premises into a combined argument framework is a separate and possibly complex design challenge.

We choose to label this design case an "a priori" framework that is formed at design time for exploitation of contextual information that attempts to account for the effects of contextual premises on goal-argument formation (such as situational estimation). As just said, there is a question of the ease or difficulty involved in integrating contextual premises into a fusion system design or into any algorithm designs. This issue is influenced in part by the nature of the contextual information and the manner of its native representation, e.g., as numeric or symbolic, and the nature of the derived premise, and also the corresponding goal-argument algorithm typically designed to exploit focal information and premises. (We use, henceforth, CI/CP for contextual information and related premises, and FI/FP for focal information and premises.) Strategies for integrated exploitation of CI/CP and FI/FP may thus require the invention of new hybrid methods that incorporate CI/CP into whatever algorithm normally designed to employ FI/FP in estimation with an adjunct CI/CP exploitation process. (For example, integrating contextual information effects, usually involving linguistic/textual information, into a numerical/statistical FI/FP algorithm framework like a Kalman filter creates the need to invent a hybrid symbolic–numeric process.) Note also that CI/CP may, like observational FI/FP data, have errors and inconsistencies itself, and accommodation of such errors is a consideration for hybrid algorithm design. In this case then, we have a notional processing operation as shown in Fig. 1.3.

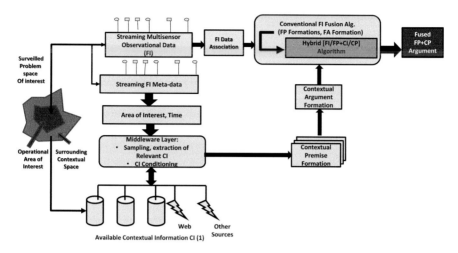

Fig. 1.3 "A Priori/Design-Time" fused focal/contextual argument formation

The data and operations flow through Fig. 1.3 are as follows:

- Multisensor FI data from the AOI stream into the system at the top, and are associated to form a correlated body of FI evidence
- The associated FI is sent to the conventional fusion process for formation of FPs and the focal argument FA
- The metadata related to the FI data signify the spatiotemporal coordinates of the collected AOI data; this provides the specifics of the area of interest and time interval related to the FI data collected
- Presuming (a nontrivial assumption) that this system has either direct or indirect ability to collect CI data from the region surrounding the AOI (these specifics not addressed here), a middleware layer shown conducts the functions of:

  - Determining the spatiotemporal extent of CI data to be collected
  - How to sample that data
  - How to condition it for use by a context-premise forming function

- The relevant CPs are formed and support the function that forms the contextual argument
- The CA is provided to the hybrid fusion algorithm that combines either the premises (FP, CP) and/or arguments (FA, CA) to form the combined (FI/FP + CI/CP) fused argument or conclusion.

This is all very notional and the hybrid process may work in different ways, as might some of the other operations. Middleware operations can impose a nontrivial challenge in design and also in functionality, especially in sampling and conditioning. There are yet other system engineering issues. The first is the question of *accessibility*; CI must of course be accessible in order to use it, but accessibility may not be a straightforward matter in all cases. One question is whether the most current CI is *available*; another may be that some CI is controlled or secure and may have limited availability. The other question is one of representational form. CI data can be expected to be of a type that has been created by "native" users for example weather data, important in many fusion applications as CI, is generated by meteorologists, for meteorologists (not for fusion system designers)—thus, even if these data are available, there is a need for conditioning the data for CP formulation. In even simpler cases, this middleware may be required to reformat the data from some native form to a useable form.

In this a priori framework, we can assume that the system designers know what CI type information is relevant to the intended goal-arguments of the fusion process. The concept of relevance is cited by Kandefer and Shapiro in [92] as, "The relevancy problem is defined by Ekbia and Maguitman as

> the problem of identifying and using properly [only] the information that should exert an influence on our beliefs, goals, or plans

[96]". Said otherwise, relevant CI is only that information that, through the formation of a CP, influences our interpretation or understanding of the formation of the goal-argument. Presuming that a relevancy filter can be crafted, the middleware function would explore the available or retrievable CI and make this CI available to the CP-forming function.

Similarly, we envision the need for an "a posteriori" CI exploitation framework, due to at least two factors:

1. That all relevant CI may not be able to be known at system/algorithm design time, and may have to be searched for and discovered at runtime, as a function of the current goal-argument/situation estimate and evolving mission objectives.
2. That such CI may not be of a type that was integrated into the system/algorithm designs at design time and so may not be able to be easily integrated into the goal-argument/situation estimation process.

In this case then we envision that at least part of the job of posteriori CI exploitation would be of a type that checks the consistency of a current (a priori-based) fused argument with the newly discovered (and relevant) CI, but also —if the argument hypothesis is in fact consistent—adds some explanatory aspects to the declared hypothesis. That is, if the current argument or hypothesis is also consistent with the new, additional CI/CP, that argument should be tagged as such, indicating that it is a "stronger" hypothesis. The notional view of this "a posteriori" CI exploitation framework—by this we mean "after the formation of a candidate argument by some process"—here the "a priori-based" fusion process (this could also be from some legacy system)—is shown in Fig. 1.4.

The flow here is as follows:

- The process starts with the availability of the "a priori-based" fused hypothesis Hf (upper left of figure), along with the metadata that points to the spatiotemporal region of the AOI, and also any updated mission-related information to aid in CI relevance determination. Note that Hf can include the effects of CI(1)—the

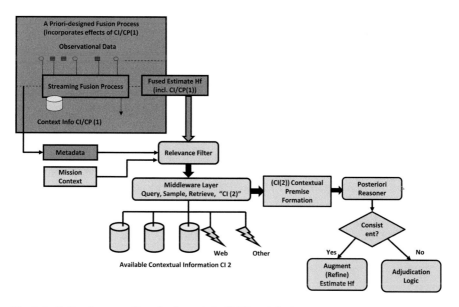

Fig. 1.4 Notional process flow for "a posteriori" CI exploitation

nature of CI(1) must also be communicated to the Relevance Filter to avoid double-counting aspects.

- That information goes into a Relevance Filter that is connected to the Middleware Layer (notionally as in Fig. 1.3) that takes this relevance guidance and again searches and samples the CI(2) database.
- Relevant CI(2) is provided to the CP(2) formation function that develops these new premises.
- The CP(2) premises are employed in an A Posteriori Reasoner function that checks if Hf (CI(1)) is consistent with the CP(2) premises.
- If they are, an augmented Hf argument is formed; if not, there is a CI(1)-CI(2)-based conflict that must be arbitrated by some type of adjudication logic.

There are other system engineering issues lurking in the effort to realize the goal of incorporating contextual information into fusion processes. One is that it can be argued that any FI/FP, AOI-based situation lies in possibly more than one relevant context. In the above, we have in a subtle way assumed that the logic and functions of these processes could account for multiple CP premise formation and that any fusion process would account for all CP effects. There is also the fact that everything is dynamic and we have assumed correct temporal reasoning being applied in all the functions described here.

But the first thing we feel is to develop a functional characterization of the ways that contextual information and associated premises could be exploited in any fusion operation; hopefully, the frameworks of Figs. 1.3 and 1.4 are helpful toward such understanding.

1.4 Conclusions

The JDL model of the fusion process, while having served as an extraordinarily helpful framework for thinking, researching, and even constructing (although its stated purpose was not as an architecture) automated Data and Information Fusion prototype processes, never really addressed the notion of exploitation of contextual information in process design. This has been a result, in part, of the fact that continued discussion and elaboration of the model has not been carried on since the JDL organization was terminated in the 1990s. The model remains helpful, however as a starting point for new expansions of the framework, and will be seen in other sections of this book. Our thoughts about the frameworks described in Figs. 1.3 and 1.4 should be taken, as was mentioned in the Abstract, as suggested starting points for expanding ideas in the community for how contextual information can be employed in functional and software system designs. While we have employed these ideas in some of our continuing work such as in context-aided target tracking applications, other applications may require modification of these frameworks for achieving the most efficient and effective system constructs.

Acknowledgments This work was partially supported by ONRG Grant N62909-14-1-N061.

References

1. F.E. White, Data fusion lexicon. Tech. rep., Joint Directors of Laboratories, Technical Panel for C3, Data Fusion Sub-Panel, Naval Ocean Systems Center, San Diego, CA (1987)
2. O. Kessler, K. Askin, N. Beck, D. Buede, D. Hall, J. Llinas, J. Lynch, F. White, Functional description of the data fusion process. Tech. rep., Office on Naval Research, Naval Air Development Center, Warminster, PA, USA (1992)
3. D.L. Hall, J. Llinas, An introduction to multisensor data fusion. Proc. IEEE **85**(1), 6–23 (1997)
4. J. Llinas, C.L. Bowman, G.L. Rogova, A.N. Steinberg, E.L. Waltz, F.E. White, Revisiting the JDL data fusion model II, in *Proceedings of the Seventh International Conference on Information Fusion*, vol. II (Stockholm, Sweden, 2004), pp. 1218–1230
5. A.N. Steinberg, C.L. Bowman, F.E. White, Revisions to the JDL data fusion model, in *Proceedings SPIE, Sensor Fusion: Architectures, Algorithms, and Applications III*, vol. 3719, pp. 430–441 (1999). doi:10.1117/12.341367
6. Q. Weng, *Advances in Environmental Remote Sensing: Sensors, Algorithms, and Applications* (CRC Press, Boca Raton, FL, 2011)
7. D.L. Hall, J. Llinas, *Multisensor Data Fusion*, 2nd edn., Chap. 1. Electrical Engineering and Applied Signal Processing (CRC Press, Boca Raton, FL, 2009), pp. 1–14
8. E. Waltz, J. Llinas, *Multisensor Data Fusion* (Artech House, Norwood, MA, 1990)
9. D.L. Hall, S.A. McMullen, *Mathematical Techniques in Multisensor Data Fusion* (Artech House, Norwood, MA, 2004)
10. L.A. Klein, *Sensor and Data Fusion: A Tool for Information Assessment and Decision Making*, 2nd edn. (SPIE Press, 2012)
11. M.E. Liggins, D.L. Hall, J. Llinas (eds.), Handbook of Multisensor Data Fusion: Theory and Practice, 2nd edn. The Electrical Engineering and Applied Signal Processing Series (CRC Press, Boca Raton, FL, 2008)

12. H.B. Mitchell, *Multi-Sensor Data Fusion: An Introduction* (Springer Publishing Company Incorporated, Heidelberg, 2007)
13. M. Abidi, R. Gonzalez, *Data Fusion in Robotics and Machine Intelligence* (Academic Press, San Diego, 1992)
14. X. Gros, *NDT Data Fusion* (Elsevier, Amsterdam, 1996)
15. S. Wu, *Data Fusion in Information Retrieval, Adaptation, Learning, and Optimization*, vol. 13 (Springer, 2012)
16. V. Torra (ed.), *Information Fusion in Data Mining* (Springer, Secaucus, NJ, 2003)
17. T. Stathaki, *Image Fusion: Algorithms and Applications* (Academic Press, Amsterdam, The Netherlands, 2011)
18. V. Popovich, C. Claramunt, T. Devogele, M. Schrenk, K. Korolenko (eds.), Information fusion and geographic information systems: towards the digital ocean. Lecture Notes in Geo Information and Cartography, vol. 5 (Springer, 2011)
19. L. Snidaro, J. García, J.M. Corchado, Context-based information fusion. Inf. Fusion **21**, 82–84 (2015). doi:10.1016/j.inffus.2014.02.001. (Guest Editorial)
20. E. Blasch, J. García Herrero, L. Snidaro, J. Llinas, G. Seetharaman, K. Palaniappan, *Overview of Contextual Tracking Approaches in Information Fusion*, pp. 87470B–87470B-11 (2013). doi: 10.1117/12.2016312
21. L. Snidaro, J. García, J. Llinas, Context-based information fusion: a survey and discussion. Inf. Fusion **25**, 16–31 (2015). doi:10.1016/j.inffus.2015.01.002
22. K. Benameur, B. Pannetier, V. Nimier, A comparative study on the use of road network information in gmti tracking, in *8th International Conference on Information Fusion, 2005*, vol. 1 (IEEE, Philadelphia, USA 2005), pp. 1–8
23. T.K. Bhattacharya, P. Scarlett, C. Gautier, Artificial intelligence techniques for enhanced tracking performance VTS radars, in *Proceedings of the 1996 IEEE National Radar Conference, 1996* (IEEE 1996), pp. 106–111
24. I. Visentini, L. Snidaro, Integration of contextual information for tracking refinement, in *Proceedings of the 14th International Conference on Information Fusion (FUSION), 2011* (IEEE, 2011), pp. 1–8
25. A. Bastiere, V. Chalmeton, V. Nimier, Contextual information and multisensor data fusion for battlefield applications, in *RTO SCI Symposium on Sensor Data Fusion and Integration of the Human Element*, Ottawa, Canada (1998)
26. L. Snidaro, R. Niu, G. Foresti, P. Varshney, Quality-based fusion of multiple video sensors for video surveillance. IEEE Trans. Syst. Man Cybern. Part B **37**(4), 1044–1051 (2007)
27. F. Caron, E. Duflos, D. Pomorski, P. Vanheeghe, GPS/IMU data fusion using multisensor kalman filtering: introduction of contextual aspects. Inf. Fusion **7**(2), 221–230 (2006)
28. V. Nimier, A. Bastiere, N. Colin, M. Moruzzis, MILORD, an application of multifeature fusion for radar NCTR, in *Proceedings of the Third International Conference on Information Fusion, 2000*, Paris, France (2000)
29. J. Wang, Y. Gao, The aiding of mems ins/gps integration using artificial intelligence for land vehicle navigation. IAENG Int. J. Comput. Sci. **33**(1), 61–67 (2007)
30. Y. Cai, K. Huang, T. Tan, Y. Wang, Context enhancement of nighttime surveillance by image fusion, in *18th International Conference on Pattern Recognition (ICPR 2006)*, vol. 1 (IEEE, 2006), pp. 980–983
31. Z. Liu, E. Blasch, Z. Xue, J. Zhao, R. Laganiere, W. Wu, Objective assessment of multiresolution image fusion algorithms for context enhancement in night vision: a comparative study. IEEE Trans. Pattern Anal. Mach. Intell. **34**(1), 94–109 (2012)
32. R. Raskar, A. Ilie, J. Yu, Image fusion for context enhancement and video surrealism, in *Proceedings of the 3rd International Symposium on Non-photorealistic Animation and Rendering*, Annecy, France, pp. 85–93 (2004)
33. T. Wan, G. Tzagkarakis, P. Tsakalides, N. Canagarajah, A. Achim, Context enhancement through image fusion: a multi resolution approach based on convolution of cauchy distributions, in *IEEE International Conference on Acoustics, Speech and Signal Processing, 2008 (ICASSP 2008)* (IEEE, 2008), pp. 1309–1312

34. S.S. Intille, J.W. Davis, A.F. Bobick, Real-time closed-world tracking, in *Proceedings of 1997 IEEE Computer Society Conference on Computer Vision and Pattern Recognition, 1997* (IEEE, 1997), pp. 697–703
35. M. Kristan, J. Perš, M. Perše, S. Kovačič, Closed-world tracking of multiple interacting targets for indoor-sports applications. Comput. Vis. Image Underst. **113**(5), 598–611 (2009)
36. M. Vespe, M. Sciotti, F. Burro, G. Battistello, S. Sorge, Maritime multi-sensor data association based on geographic and navigational knowledge, in *IEEE Radar Conference, 2008 (RADAR'08)* (IEEE, 2008), pp. 1–6
37. R. Lherbier, B. Jida, J.C. Noyer, M. Wahl, Use of contextual information by bayesian networks for multi-object tracking in scanning laser range data, in *9th International Conference on Intelligent Transport Systems Telecommunications (ITST), 2009* (IEEE, 2009), pp. 97–102
38. M. Mertens, M. Ulmke, Ground moving target tracking with context information and a refined sensor model, in *11th International Conference on Information Fusion, 2008* (IEEE, 2008), pp. 1–8
39. L. Cuiping, S. Jinping, M. Shiyi, L. Desheng, Tracking ground targets with road constraint using multiple hypotheses tracking, in *2nd International Conference on Signal Processing Systems (ICSPS), 2010*, vol. 2 (IEEE, 2010), pp. V2-265
40. H. Fargetton, J.G. Siedler, Control of multi sensor system based on anomaly mapping and expert system, in *Sensor Data Fusion: Trends, Solutions, Applications* (IEEE, 2011)
41. Y. Lemeret, E. Lefevre, D. Jolly, Improvement of an association algorithm for obstacle tracking. Inf. Fusion **9**(2), 234–245 (2008)
42. S.C. Stubberud, K.A. Kramer, Data association for multiple sensor types using fuzzy logic. Instrum. Measur. IEEE Trans. **55**(6), 2292–2303 (2006)
43. S.C. Stubberud, K.A. Kramer, Fuzzy logic based data association with target/sensor soft constraints, in *IEEE 22nd International Symposium on Intelligent Control, 2007 (ISIC 2007)* (IEEE, 2007), pp. 620–625
44. G. Jemin, J.L. Crassidis, T. Singh, Threat assessment using context-based tracking in a maritime environment, in *12th International Conference onInformation Fusion (FUSION'09)* (IEEE, Seattle, USA, 2009), pp. 187–194
45. S. Cong, L. Hong, J.R. Layne, Iterative robust filtering for ground target tracking. IET Control Theory Appl. **1**(1), 372–380 (2007)
46. A.M. Fosbury, J.L. Crassidis, T. Singh, C. Springen, Ground target tracking using terrain information, in *10th International Conference on Information Fusion, 2007* (IEEE, 2007), pp. 1–8
47. F. Gustafsson, U. Orguner, T.B. Schön, P. Skoglar, R. Karlsson, *Handbook of Intelligent Vehicles, chap. Navigation and Tracking of Road-bound Vehicles* (Springer, Berlin, 2012)
48. W. Li, H. Leung, Constrained unscented kalman filter based fusion of gps/ins/digital map for vehicle localization, in *Proceedings of the IEEE 2003 International Conference on Intelligent Transportation Systems* (IEEE, Shanghai, China, 2003)
49. G.W. Ng, C.H. Tan, T.P. Ng, Tracking ground targets using state vector fusion, in *8th International Conference on Information Fusion, 2005*, vol. 1 (IEEE, 2005), 6 pp
50. D. Streller, Road map assisted ground target tracking, in *11th International Conference on Information Fusion, 2008* (IEEE, Cologne, Germany, 2008), pp. 1–7
51. E. Maggio, A. Cavallaro, Learning scene context for multiple object tracking. Image Proc. IEEE Trans. **18**(8), 1873–1884 (2009)
52. E. Pollard, B. Pannetier, M. Rombaut, Convoy detection processing by using the hybrid algorithm (gmcphd/vs-immc-mht) and dynamic bayesian networks, in *12th International Conference on Information Fusion, 2009 (FUSION'09)* (IEEE, Seattle, USA, 2009), pp. 907–914
53. G. Battistello, M. Ulmke, F. Papi, M. Podt, Y. Boers, Assessment of vessel route information use in bayesian non-linear filtering, in *15th International Conference on Information Fusion (FUSION), 2012* (IEEE, Singapore, 2012), pp. 447–454
54. Y. Cheng, T. Singh, Efficient particle filtering for road-constrained target tracking. IEEE Trans. Aerosp. Electron. Syst. **43**(4), 1454–1469 (2007)

55. T. Kirubarajan, Y. Bar-Shalom, K.R. Pattipati, I. Kadar, Ground target tracking with variable structure IMM estimator. IEEE Trans. Aerosp. Electron. Syst. **36**(1), 26–46 (2000)
56. E. Semerdjiev, L. Mihaylova, Variable-and fixed-structure augmented interacting multiple model algorithms for manoeuvring ship tracking based on new ship models. Int. J. Appl. Matehmatics Comput. Sci. **10**(3), 591–604 (2000)
57. C. Yang, E. Blasch, J. Patrick, D. Qiu, Ground target track bias estimation using opportunistic road information, in *Proceedings of the IEEE 2010 National Aerospace and Electronics Conference (NAECON)* (IEEE, 2010), pp. 156–163
58. G. Battistello, M. Ulmke, Exploitation of a priori information for tracking maritime intermittent data sources, in *Proceedings of the 14th International Conference on Information Fusion (FUSION), 2011* (IEEE, Chicago, USA, 2011), pp. 1–8
59. M. Roth, F. Gustafsson, U. Orguner, On-road trajectory generation from gps data: a particle filtering/smoothing application, in *15th International Conference on Information Fusion (FUSION), 2012* (IEEE, Singapore, 2012), pp. 779–786
60. W. Koch, Information fusion aspects related to gmti convoy tracking, in *Proceedings of the Fifth International Conference on Information Fusion, 2002*, vol. 2 (IEEE, Annapolis, USA, 2002), pp. 1038–1045
61. W. Liu, J. Wei, M. Liang, Y. Cao, I. Hwang, Multi-sensor fusion and fault detection using hybrid estimation for air traffic surveillance. Aerosp. Electron. Syst. IEEE Trans. **49**(4), 2323–2339 (2013)
62. A. Benavoli, L. Chisci, A. Farina, L. Timmoneri, G. Zappa, Knowledge-based system for multi-target tracking in a littoral environment. IEEE Trans. Aerosp. Electron. Syst. **42**(3), 1100–1119 (2006)
63. X.B. Song, Y. Abu-Mostafa, J. Sill, H. Kasdan, M. Pavel, Robust image recognition by fusion of contextual information. Inf. Fusion **3**(4), 277–287 (2002)
64. P. Bouquet, F. Giunchiglia, F. van Harmelen, L. Serafini, H. Stuckenschmidt, Contextualizing ontologies. Web Semant. Sci. Serv. Agents World Wide Web **1**(4), 325–343 (2004)
65. M.P. Jenkins, G.A. Gross, A.M. Bisantz, R. Nagi, Towards context aware data fusion: modeling and integration of situationally qualified human observations to manage uncertainty in a hard + soft fusion process. Inf. Fusion **21**, 130–144 (2015). doi:10.1016/j.inffus.2013.04.011
66. A. Jouan, Y. Allard, Y. Marcoz, Coastal activity monitoring with evidential fusion of contextual attributes from multi-pass radarsat-1, in *7th International Command and Control Research and Technology Symposium* (2002)
67. L. Snidaro, I. Visentini, K. Bryan, Fusing uncertain knowledge and evidence for maritime situational awareness via markov logic networks. Inf. Fusion **21**, 159–172 (2015). doi:10.1016/j.inffus.2013.03.004
68. G. Suarez-Tangil, E. Palomar, A. Ribagorda, I. Sanz, Providing SIEM systems with self-adaptation. Inf. Fusion **21**, 145–158 (2015). doi:10.1016/j.inffus.2013.04.009
69. A. Padovitz, S.W. Loke, A. Zaslavsky, B. Burg, C. Bartolini, An approach to data fusion for context awareness, in *Proceedings of the 5th International Conference on Modeling and Using Context* (Springer, 2005), pp. 353–367
70. G.L. Rogova, Context-awareness in crisis management, in *Proceedings of the Military Communications Conference* (IEEE, 2009), pp. 1–7
71. A.N. Steinberg, Context-sensitive data fusion using structural equation modeling, in *Proceedings of the 12th International Conference on Information Fusion* (IEEE, 2009), pp. 725–731
72. G. Ferrin, L. Snidaro, G. Foresti, Contexts, co-texts and situations in fusion domain, in *14th International Conference on Information Fusion* (Chicago, Illinois, USA, 2011)
73. A. Steinberg, G. Rogova, Situation and context in data fusion and natural language understanding, in *Proceedings of the Eleventh International Conference on Information Fusion*, Cologne, Germany (2008)

74. E.P. Blasch, D.A. Lambert, P. Valin, M.M. Kokar, J. Llinas, S. Das, C. Chong, E. Shahbazian, High level information fusion (hlif): survey of models, issues, and grand challenges. IEEE Aerosp. Electron. Syst. Mag. **27**(9), 4–20 (2012)
75. P. Hilletofth, S. Ujvari, R. Johansson, Agent-based simulation fusion for improved decision making for service operations, in *Proceedings of the 12th International Conference on Information Fusion* (IEEE, 2009), pp. 998–1005
76. G. Rogova, M. Hadzagic, M.O. St-Hilaire, M.C. Florea, P. Valin, Context-based information quality for sequential decision making, in *Proceedings of the IEEE International Multi-Disciplinary Conference on Cognitive Methods in Situation Awareness and Decision Support*, San Diego, CA, US (2013)
77. A. Smirnov, T. Levashova, N. Shilov, Patterns for context-based knowledge fusion in decision support systems. Inf. Fusion **21**, 114–129 (2015). doi:10.1016/j.inffus.2013.10.010
78. B. Solaiman, É. Bossé, L. Pigeon, D. Gueriot, M. Florea, A conceptual definition of a holonic processing framework to support the design of information fusion systems. Inf. Fusion **21**, 85–99 (2015). doi:10.1016/j.inffus.2013.08.004
79. A.N. Steinberg, C.L. Bowman, G. Haith, E. Blasch, Adaptive context assessment and context management, in *Proceedings of the International conference on Information Fusion*, Salamanca, Spain (2014)
80. E.G. Little, G.L. Rogova, Designing ontologies for higher level fusion. Inf. Fusion **10**(1), 70–82 (2009)
81. G.M. Powell, M.M. Kokar, C.J. Matheus, D. Lorenz, Understanding the role of context in the interpretation of complex battle space intelligence, in *Proceedings of the 9th International Conference on Information Fusion* (IEEE, Florence, Italy, 2006)
82. K. Sycara, R. Glinton, B. Yu, J. Giampapa, S. Owens, M. Lewis, L. Grindle, An integrated approach to high-level information fusion. Inf. Fusion **10**(1), 25–50 (2009)
83. A.N. Steinberg, C.L. Bowman, Adaptive context discovery and exploitation, in *Proceedings of the 16th International Conference on Information Fusion* (IEEE, Istanbul, Turkey, 2013)
84. O. Brdiczka, P.C. Yuen, S. Zaidenberg, P. Reignier, J.L. Crowley, Automatic acquisition of context models and its application to video surveillance, in *18th International Conference on Pattern Recognition, 2006 (ICPR 2006)*, vol. 1 (IEEE, 2006), pp. 1175–1178
85. L. Snidaro, I. Visentini, J. Llinas, G.L. Foresti, Context in fusion: some considerations in a JDL perspective, in *Proceedings of the 16th International Conference on Information Fusion* (IEEE, Istanbul, Turkey, 2013)
86. Y.W. Lee, L.L. Pipino, J.D. Funk, R.Y. Wang, *Journey to Data Quality* (The MIT Press, 2009)
87. G. Rogova, E. Bossé, Information quality in information fusion, in *Proceedings of the 13th International Conference on Information Fusion*, Edinburgh, U.K. (2010)
88. G. Klein, B. Moon, R.R. Hoffman, Making sense of sensemaking 2: a macrocognitive model. IEEE Intell. Syst. **21**(5), 88–92 (2006)
89. P. Pirolli, S. Card, The sensemaking process and leverage points for analyst technology as identified through cognitive task analysis, in *Proceedings of International Conference on Intelligence Analysis*, vol. 5, Mitre McLean, VA, pp. 2–4 (2005)
90. H. Mercier, D. Sperber, Why do humans reason? Arguments for an argumentative theory. Behav. Brain Sci. **34**(02), 57–74 (2011)
91. K. Devlin, Confronting context effects in intelligence analysis: how can mathematics help? Center for the Study of Language and Information, Stanford University (2005, unpublished)
92. M. Kandefer, S.C. Shapiro, Evaluating spreading activation for soft information fusion, in *Proceedings of the 14th International Conference on Information Fusion* (IEEE, 2011)
93. A. Dey, G. Abowd, Towards a better understanding of context and context-awareness, in *Proceedings of the Workshop on the What, Who, Where, When and How of Context-Awareness*, The Hague, The Netherlands (2000)
94. R.J. Heuer, Psychology of intelligence analysis. Center for the Study of Intelligence, Central Intelligence Agency (Lulu.com, Washington, D.C., 1999)

95. B. Kokinov, A dynamic theory of implicit context, in *Proceedings of the 2nd European Conference on Cognitive Science*, Manchester, UK (1997)
96. H. Ekbia, A. Maguitman, Context and relevance: a pragmatic approach, in *Proceedings of the Third International and Interdisciplinary Conference on Modeling and Using Context*, Dundee, UK, (2001)

Part II
Concepts of Context for Fusion

Chapter 2
Formalization of "Context" for Information Fusion

Galina L. Rogova and Alan N. Steinberg

Abstract Context exploitation can provide benefits for information fusion by establishing expectations of world states, explaining received data, and resolving ambiguous interpretations; thereby improving process efficiency, reliability, and trustworthiness of the fusion product. While everybody recognizes the importance of considering context in inferencing, designers of information fusion processes only recently have begun to incorporate context explicitly into fusion processes. Effective context exploitation requires a clear understanding of what context is, how to represent it in a formal way, and how to use it for particular information fusion applications. Although these problems are similar to the ones discussed by researchers in many other fields, consideration of context in designing information fusion systems also poses additional challenges such as understanding the relationships between situations and context, utilizing context for understanding and fusion of natural language data, context dynamics, context recognition, and contextual reasoning under the uncertainty inherent in fusion problems. This chapter provides a brief discussion on possible ways of confronting these challenges while designing information fusion systems.

Keywords Context *of* and context *for* · Contextual and problem variables · Context quality · Abduction · Natural language understanding

2.1 Introduction

The problem of context has a long history in such diverse fields as artificial intelligence, philosophy, psychology, and linguistics, among others. Although the value of considering context in information fusion is obvious, system designers

---

G.L. Rogova (✉)
State University of New York at Buffalo, Buffalo, NY, USA
e-mail: rogova@buffalo.edu

A.N. Steinberg
Independent Consultant, Woodbridge, VA, USA
e-mail: alaneilsteinberg@gmail.com

© Springer International Publishing Switzerland (outside the USA) 2016
L. Snidaro et al. (eds.), *Context-Enhanced Information Fusion*,
Advances in Computer Vision and Pattern Recognition,
DOI 10.1007/978-3-319-28971-7_2

have only recently considered methods for systematically exploiting the rich contextual information that is often available in their system applications. In particular, there is an untapped potential to exploit the enormous quantity of available multimedia and multispectral data—together with information from diverse, geographically distributed sources—to provide context for information fusion to improve understanding of the entire domain of interest. Much of this information may be of low or of indeterminate quality. It may be uncertain, unreliable, redundant, or conflicting, and its relevance to a particular inference problem may not be self-evident.

Context can be used both to transform source data into information and knowledge [1, 2] and to acquire knowledge [3, 4]. Context may provide information about the conditions of data and information[1] acquisition, and it may constrain and influence the reasoning about objects and situations of interest. In addition, there is an enormous body of potentially valuable information in the form of natural language: across the Internet, in social media (Twitter, Facebook, Flicker, etc.) and traditional media sources (television, newspapers, etc.), as well as in various forms of intelligence reporting. Natural language sources may provide essential contextual information not available from structured sensor data alone. Natural language understanding is also vital in modeling interpersonal communications. However, natural language is itself fraught with ambiguities—phonetic, lexical, syntactic, semantic, pragmatic—that can only be resolved by contextual considerations.

Context is represented by contextual information that may be obtained from various sources and formalized in different ways. Various formal context definitions and formalization models will be discussed in Sect. 2.2. In general, context consideration can improve and simplify agent interactions in multi-agent-based fusion systems, which may be comprised of either automatic, human, or both human and automatic agents. Figure 2.1 shows some important relationships between context and a fusion-based human–machine system. The context engine here interacts with and supports fusion at all levels by

- representing an initial overall context under considerations;
- establishing relevance, thereby constraining ontology of the domain, observations, rules, and statistics;
- providing the fusion processes with constraints on relationships among objects, situations, hypotheses, arguments, beliefs, and preferences;
- supporting situation and threat discovery;
- constraining the feasible meanings of messages, thereby facilitating effective communications among actors.

Designing dynamic fusion processes requires clear understanding of what context is and the relation between context on the one hand, and data, information, and

---

[1]While we recognize the difference between data and information, we will generally use these terms interchangeably throughout this chapter.

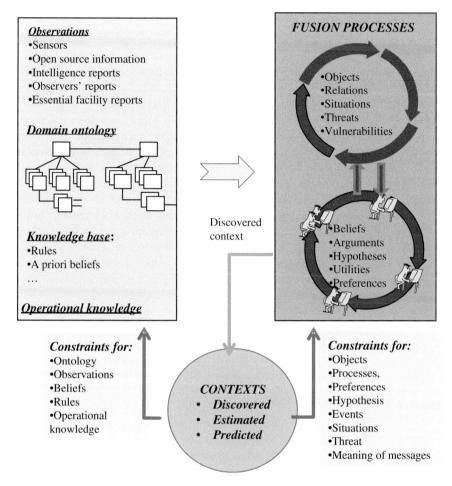

Fig. 2.1 Context and information fusion

knowledge on the other. It is also necessary to understand (a) how to represent context in a formal way to support contextual reasoning in fusion processing; (b) the role of context in inter-level information exchange; and (c) how to deal with context dynamics, context recognition and discovery, and contextual reasoning under uncertainty inherent in data fusion problems. The remaining sections of this chapter discuss potential solutions to these problems. Thus, Sect. 2.2 presents context definitions; Sect. 2.3 discusses relationship between context and knowledge; Sect. 2.4 describes various context models; Sect. 2.5 examines relationship between context and information quality while Sect. 2.6 discusses the problem of context in natural language understanding. Finally, the chapter concludes in Sect. 2.7.

2.2 What Is Context?

The notion of context has been used in diverse research areas for a long time but
"while most people tacitly understand what context is they find it hard to elucidate
[5]." Context has many facets that sometime leads to defining it based on certain
narrow characteristics of the particular problem being addressed. For example, in
[6] context is defined as objects, location, identities of nearby people, and objects.
In other works [7], it is considered as a computable description of the terrain
elements, the external resources and the possible inferences that is essential to
support the fusion process while in [8] context is represented by the operational
knowledge. Such definitions are too specific to the problem under consideration
making it difficult, even sometime impossible, to understand which characteristics
of all situations are important and should be taken into account in general. In [9]
context is defined as the subset of physical and conceptual states of interest to a
particular entity while in [10] it is defined as the whole set of secondary characteristics of a situation or secondary properties of a cognitive or motivational state of
an individual which may modify the effect of an effective stimulation (stimulus) or
an oriented activity.

Brezillon in [11] defines context as a collection of relevant conditions such as
space, time, environment, and surrounding influences that make a situation unique
and comprehensible. That author further categorizes context as primary or secondary to distinguish between relatively fixed characteristics of the situation and the
ones that are more dynamic. Such and other similar definitions (see, e.g. [12, 13])
are too general and equate context to the surrounding environment or situation.
They do not provide specifics for understanding the difference between context and
situation, a distinction that is very important to situation assessment, one of the
important components of information fusion.

A definition that does allow for better understanding of context—and therefore
one that is more appropriate for formalizing and utilizing context in building
information fusion processes—was proposed in [14]. This definition assumes two
different context paradigms introduced in [14] and further discussed in [13] and
[15]: "*Context of X*" (CO) and "*Context for X*" (CF), which correspond to two basic
meanings conveyed by dictionaries [14]:

> To knit or bind together; to unite closely (CO) and
> That which surrounds, and gives meaning to, something else (CF).

A reference item X is a topic of interest represented by any physical or conceptual entity, for example, a situation and event of interest such as a natural
phenomenon or terrorist threat.[2] Reference items are represented by a set of state
variables and their relationships that an agent wishes to evaluate (*problem*

---

[2]A topic might be a real entity, but it doesn't have to be. The atmospheric conditions on Mars are
used as a context for inferring a low probability that there are living beings there. Life on Mars that
is the reference item, not the Martians (who may not exist).

variables). A CO is a part of the environment representing a set of items and relationships of interest "grouped or contained by X." We have certain expectations about X based on a given CO, e.g., in the context of earthquake we can expect damaged roads and bridges or in the context of wildfire we can expect burn victims. Alternatively, a CF defines the contextual space of items externally related to and referenced by X: the weather provides a *context for* search and rescue after an earthquake (*context of*). In both examples *earthquake* represents a reference item.

A set of items and relationships defining context can be called *context variables*. Context variables characterizing CF represent auxiliary variables determined (by some process) to be relevant to a given problem. They affect knowledge about problem variables contained in a CO, reasoning about them and, therefore, affect decisions and actions based on the values and behaviors of problem variables. While COs can be declared, inferred, or discovered as the result of reasoning, CFs are either given, obtained as the result of direct observations, or extracted from the application-specific ontology. A CO is a background context, which provides a more general and stable environment while a CF offers secondary characteristics, which can be more dynamic.

Consideration of CO and CF provides for complex hierarchical relationships among characteristics of problem variables and context variables. It also offers a clear understanding of relations between context and situations. Reasoning about entities and relationships while considering them as problem variables within a certain context corresponds to reasoning about situations. Such reasoning produces an answer to the question "what is going on in the part of the environment corresponding to the reference item(s) within a specific context?" Context variables can serve as problem variables when they represent reference items for a different context. Thus we can define a *problem context* as a meta-situation (situation of higher level of granularity) comprising a set of relationships involving context variables. Various information needs may require assessment of different reference items and different context at various times and at different levels of granularity.

2.3   Context and Knowledge

The ultimate goal of context-sensitive information fusion is to support decision-making and actions by providing knowledge about problem variables to each decision maker, relevant to his goals and function. Thus it is important to consider the concept of *knowledge* along with the concept of *context*. The authors of [16] show strong relationships between these concepts. They consider context as "a shared knowledge space that is explored and exploited by participants." They introduce the notions of *external* and *contextual knowledge*: *External knowledge* is a part of context, which represents the general knowledge of the environment related to the problem but not directly relevant to a certain step of the decision-making or action. *Contextual knowledge* is a part of the context, which is relevant to a given problem at hand for a given agent (human or automatic).

It contains knowledge necessary for reasoning and decision-making applicable to all kinds of inferencing encountered in data fusion. Contextual knowledge is the part of knowledge that can have several realizations ("proceduralized contexts"), which instantiates contextual knowledge and transforms it into "functional knowledge" used for reasoning, decision-making, or action according to a specific focus of a specific agent. We can consider external, contextual, and proceduralized knowledge as CO and CF at different levels of granularity. Although the concepts of *knowledge* and *context* share multiple characteristics, they differ when it comes to decision-making and action: context is subjective and specific to goals and functions of the decision maker and represents a part of the knowledge used for decision-making and action. In contrast, knowledge is objective and not task oriented and is related to theoretical understanding of the phenomena ("knowing that") [16, 17].

2.4 Context Formalization

Several papers in the literature discuss context models (see, e.g. [15, 18–20]). Among the major types of context models considered, the *key-value*, *ontology-based*, and *logic-based* models appear to be the most applicable to information fusion. We shall survey these types of context representation and discuss their applicability to different context-aware information fusion problems.

The simplest of context models considered are *key-value models* [21], in which context is represented by values of context attributes (e.g., location) as environmental information. A key-value model utilizes exact matching algorithms on these attributes, in the same way that objects are usually represented and recognized in general. These models are easy to manage and may be used for CF representation. They may suffice for use in object assessment [22] but they lack capabilities for complex structuring required by situation and threat assessment.

As defined in the previous section, context is a meta-situation for a set of problem variables under consideration; therefore its formalization appropriate for higher level fusion processing requires more complex modeling to permit representation not only of context attributes but also of objects, their characteristics, and interrelationships. Models with these characteristics are similar to ones used for situation assessment and include *ontology-based* and *logic-based* models.

Ontology is an established framework for knowledge representation and for reasoning about situations [23, 24]. Since contexts can be considered as situations, ontology-based models offer an appropriate way of their modeling. These models can provide a high degree of rigor in specifying core concepts, sub-concepts, facts, and their inter-relationships to enable realistic representation of contextual knowledge for reasoning, information sharing, and reuse. Current approaches to ontology-based context modeling can be classified into three main areas: contextualization of ontologies, ontology design patterns, and context-aware systems [25].

Logic-based models define contexts in terms of facts, expressions, and rules. McCarthy [20] introduces a formalization of logic-based models built on a relation *ist(c,p)*, read as "proposition *p* holds in the context *c*." The *ist* concept can be interpreted as validity: *ist(c, p)* is true if and only if the proposition *p* is true in context *c*. McCarthy's context formalization includes two main forms of expression:

- *c'*: *ist(c,p)* means that *p* is true in context *c*, and *ist(c,p)* itself is asserted in an context of a higher level of granularity;
- *value(c,e)* defines the value of term *e* in the context *c*, which means that context *c* defines some values for *e*.

Information fusion systems generally deal with uncertain data and therefore we would like context representation in logic-based models to allow for uncertain statements, rules, and beliefs assigned to them. To use *ist(c,p)* concept for making assertions about uncertain situational items, it is necessary to expand McCarthy's definition of *ist(c, p)* by incorporating of an uncertainty measure—expressed as probability, possibility, or belief—in place of McCarthy's binary *belief*. For example, *bel(a,ist(c,p))* can be used to represent an agent *a*'s belief that proposition *p* is true in the context *c*. Since an agent's knowledge about context can be uncertain, *bel* may represent a combination of belief in the validity of proposition *p* and belief associated with context characteristics.

McCarthy introduces hierarchical relationships among contexts by defining partial ordering over contexts $(c_1 \preceq c_2)$, which means that context c_2 is no less general than context c_1; i.e., c_2 contains all the information of the context c_1 and possibly more. McCarthy also defines a "lifting" formula [20] that relates propositions in a context to more general propositions and terms in a broader context (an "outer context"). The partial ordering of context along with the notion of lifting allows for formalization of relations between problem variables and CF and CO at a selected level of granularity.

A similar logic-based context formalization is presented in [26], in which context is related to knowledge and defined in terms of a set of facts from the knowledge base along with the reasoning method allowing to compute with it. Under this formulation, a context c_i is a triple $(\lambda_i, \alpha_i, \delta_i)$, where λ_i is the formal language used to describe what is true in that context, e.g., propositional language; α_i is a set of axioms; and δ_i is an inference mechanism. In this formalization, McCarthy's formula *c'*: *ist(c,p)*,—with context *c* and an outer context *c'*—becomes $\frac{\langle A,c\rangle}{\langle ist(c,A),c'\rangle}$; i.e., "if *A* can be proven in context *c*, then we can prove in context *c'* that we can prove *A* in *c*."

Another representation of this type is the *extended situation theory* [27], which modifies situation theory [28, 29] to allow for uncertain information, as commonly encountered in data fusion. Situation theory represents units of information as *infons,* which are denoted as $\sigma = (R, a1, \ldots, a_n, i)$, where *R* is an *n*-place relation and $a1, \ldots, a_n$ are state variables that range over entities of types appropriate for a given relation *R*. In "classical" situation theory, *i* is a binary variable, which is equal to 1 if a relationship $R(a1, ..., a_n)$ holds, 0 otherwise. An operator ' $\models$ ' expresses the notion of contextual applicability, so that 's $\models \sigma$ ' can be read as "situation s supports σ" or "σ is true in situation s." This operator allows consistent representation of factual, conditional, hypothetical, and estimated information [29].

In extended situation theory [27], context is modeled by situation types corresponding to objects of a situation theory that supports two kinds of infons: (i) factual infons to state facts, and (ii) constraints, which correspond to parametric conditionals capturing the if-then relations holding within the context. To capture uncertain if-then relations holding within the context representing a part of the uncertain environment, it is necessary to consider *uncertain* infons. Extended situation theory incorporates uncertain infons simply by redefining the binary variable i of classical situation theory as a continuous variable $i \in [0, 1]$ to represent the belief that R holds. An equivalent probabilistic extension of situation theory was derived independently in [30].

2.5   Context and Information Quality

Quality of Context is defined in [31] as "any information describing the quality of information that is used as context information." Another definition is given in [32], where *Quality of Context* is defined as "any inherent information that describes context information and can be used to determine the worth of information for a specific application." These definitions specify different types of information quality with the former referring to objective measures of quality such as the accuracy, certainty, or reliability of measurements or estimations; while the latter characterizes both objective and subjective quality, which uses values of objective quality to measure the "fitness of use," i.e. the degree to which context satisfies the needs of a particular application.

Having this in mind we propose to define the quality of a context as the degree to which it satisfies the needs of an application, expressed as a function of quality of the data defining the context. Such an application could be, for example, refining uncertainty in sensors' output, in communications, in situation, and threat assessment, or in the utility of actions. The degree to which context satisfies the needs of a particular application can be represented either by a single quality characteristic (e.g., the credibility of object recognition) or by a combination of characteristics (e.g., the result of combination of credibility and reliability of a hypothesis about the state of the environment). Selection of a particular quality characteristic or combination depends on the application.

The information defining a context can be obtained from available databases, observations, the result of sensor fusion, received reports, mining of available information sources (e.g., traditional and social media), or from various levels of information fusion. Of course, the quality of any such information as well as the inference process for obtaining it could be insufficient for a particular use: it might be uncertain, unreliable, irrelevant, or conflicting. Knowledge of the quality of this information and its effect on the quality of context characterization can improve contextual knowledge. At the same time, knowledge about a current context ("CO") can improve the quality of observation and fusion results.

There are two interrelated problems concerning both information and context quality: imperfect information used in context estimation and discovery negatively impacts context quality while imperfect context characterization adversely affects the characterization of quality of information used in fusion as well as the fusion results. This interrelationship represents one of the challenges of modeling and evaluating context quality and of using context in defining the quality of information used in fusion and the quality of fusion process results.

Information quality is a type of meta-information (information about information). As such, it is best characterized and measured in terms of its attributes. Certain attributes can be considered as "the higher-level quality," which measures how well the quality of information is assessed.

The need for considering information quality stems from the fact that there are limitations to fusion processes as well as to processes of assessing the value of the attributes of information quality. These limitations are often due to lack of context consideration or to insufficient quality of context and contextual attributes. The lack of proper consideration of context may result in using inadequate or erroneous domain knowledge or inappropriate models and parameters for quality assessment.

Several attributes of information quality have been cited including quality of information, quality of information source, and quality of information presentation [33]. Furthermore, each of these attributes can be characterized in terms of various interdependent factors such as credibility, accuracy, timeliness, relevance, etc. There are several important quality characteristics affecting quality of context estimation and discovery and thereby affecting the quality of information fusion results. Figure 2.2 shows interrelationships among the quality observations and reports, fusion processes, quality of context, and important quality characteristics influencing them. As shown, fusion designed to estimate problem variables can be over direct estimations and contextual information selected or weighted for accuracy, reliability, consistency, and relevance. Indices are shown for contexts, both CO and CF, to stress that relevant contexts are often dynamic. Fusion outputs can be state estimates at any fusion level (of objects, situations, impacts, etc.). Context consideration can improve the results of fusion products by taking into account the quality of input information (e.g., reliability of observations and reports) as well as quality of interim results of the processes involved in fusion. For instance, a CO can serve for selecting relevant observations and provide expectations for sensor and process management. A *CF* can, for example, be used to improve fusion results by incorporating context-based reliability into sources' predictive uncertainty models such as probability or belief [34].

A very important quality characteristic is *relevance*. Relevance in context-sensitive information fusion processes is used for estimation and selection of contextual variables, and for evaluation and dynamic selection of input information. The problem here is to decide which piece of information should be considered relevant and how the level of relevance should be measured. According

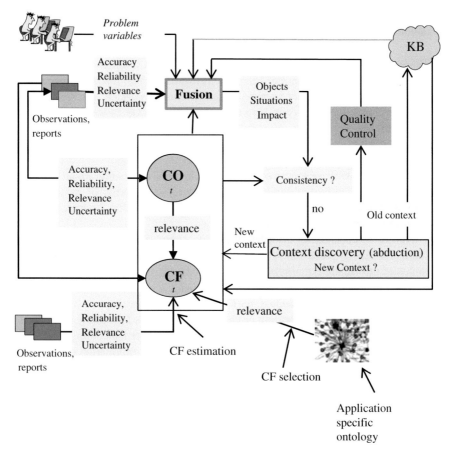

Fig. 2.2 Interrelationships among the quality observations and reports, fusion processes, quality of context, CO and CF, and important quality characteristics influencing them

to the Webster dictionary (http://www.merriam-webster.com/), information is relevant if it has "significant and demonstrable bearing on the matter at hand." Relevant information can improve knowledge whereas considering irrelevant information as relevant can degrade knowledge. Consideration of relevance is especially important for selection of CF, which has to be relevant to both CO and problem variables. Selection of CF can be performed based on constraints imposed by a domain-specific ontology. Contextual variables can be considered relevant if incorporation of them into fusion processes can:

- reduce uncertainty and increase accuracy of fusion results;
- improve utility of information (e.g., of refining the value of a problem variable) and ultimately of decisions and actions based on fusion results utilizing this information; or
- decrease information conflict [15].

Relevance is often time-dependent and its evaluation can involve a dynamic process. This, of course, can increase computation cost of selection of context variables and fusion processes.

Selection of contextual variable assumes that we can determine the ambient "context of" a given reference item or inference problem. In some cases this context is defined (declared or estimated). However, in some cases context can be unknown or different from what was expected. This often happens in highly dynamic environments, in which observations, situational items, and relationships constantly change. In such cases, relevant context needs to be discovered. Discovery of underlying new context can be initiated based on another important characteristic of context quality: *consistency*. New context can be manifested by new observations or estimated reference items that are inconsistent with the currently assumed context characteristics, for example, contained in the knowledge base. The major problems here are how and when to decide whether inconsistency exits, what is the source of this inconsistency, and whether the currently assumed context is no longer relevant.

Context consistency is evaluated based on comparison of the characteristics and behavior of problem variables based on the observed or estimated data and information with the ones that are defined by contextual knowledge, which includes both CO and CF. Inconsistency can be the result of such factors as (1) poorly characterized observations and reports; (2) insufficient quality of estimated characteristics and behavior of situational items based on these observations and evaluated within current context; (3) incomplete or inadequate domain knowledge about current context; (4) poor quality of context characteristics, e.g. consideration of irrelevant contextual variables or the fact that the defined earlier context has changed. Discovery of the source of this inconsistency can be performed by abductive reasoning (so-called "reasoning for best explanations") [35]. The result of abductive reasoning can improve inferencing in different ways. It can lead to discovery of new, hidden context, which in turn can improve the estimation of problem variables. It can also lead to discovery of the fact that the inconsistency was the result of poor quality of observations, reports, their processing or insufficient quality of estimated or containing in the knowledge base certain context characteristics, which can lead to their better estimation.

2.6 Context and Natural Language Understanding

The importance of natural language understanding in the information fusion domain has grown significantly due to increased role of "raw" natural language in information fusion processes. The Internet has expanded the body of readily accessed natural language information from traditional media sources (television, books, newspapers, etc.). Additional important information may be buried within the enormous amount of dynamic information contained in social media (Facebook, Instagram, Twitter, etc.). However, natural language is itself fraught with ambiguities—phonetic, lexical, syntactic, semantic, pragmatic—that can only be resolved by contextual considerations.

Exploitation of natural language sources requires that semantic, referential, and pragmatic information content be extracted, aligned in quality and relevance and fused with other available information. Therefore, the types and issues of context exploitation that apply to these basic fusion functions apply to natural language understanding.

Polysemy—a word having multiple different but related meanings—is so pervasive that it is often unnoticed by native speakers. All the common verbs and prepositions in English—*have, give, take, up, in* and their ilk—are massively ambiguous and can only be understood in context: a person can have brown eyes, have pneumonia, have an idea, have a fight, have it out, take a coin, take a drink, take a taxi, take a nap, take it easy, look up, show up, throw up, finish up, run up (a bill, a flight of stairs),... Much polysemy is due to the pervasiveness of metaphorical meanings. As Pinker notes, "Metaphor is so widespread in language that it's hard to find expressions for abstract ideas that are *not* metaphors" [36].[3] A dispute between the White House and the Kremlin is not really a dispute between two buildings. We have not really traveled anywhere when we follow a train of thought, pursue a dream, or reach a conclusion.

So natural language expressions are often wildly ambiguous when viewed out of context. "*When I use a word,*" *Humpty Dumpty said, in a rather scornful tone, "it means just what I choose it to mean—neither more nor less.*" [39]. Nonetheless, pace Mr. Dumpty, the conventions of language and of discourse do impose constraints on the range and distribution of possible meanings. Many cases of polysemy follow regular and predictable patterns.

Furthermore, a most general constraint on meanings is a pragmatic one: as means for conveying information (expressive as well as literal declarative information), the meanings a speaker assigns to utterances should be readily inferable by hearers.[4] This is Grice's cooperative principle [40]. A speaker is expected to choose his expressions such that their understanding is evident, given their range of conventional meanings and the discourse, situational and participant contexts. Context can guide expectations for meanings in amusing ways, e.g. in hearing "a forest full of toiletries." Here, the discourse context (CO) can provide false lexicologic and semantic clues (the syllable /trēs/ in the context of 'forest').

Indeed, many linguistic expressions are intrinsically undetermined in the absence of context. Beside polysemy, context exploitation is usually essential to resolve

---

[3]Indeed, George Lakoff and other developers of Generative Semantics and Cognitive Linguistics have argued that "Our ordinary conceptual system, in terms of which we both think and act, is fundamentally metaphorical in nature" [37, 38]. They argue that our minds begin with a small number of basic experiential concepts involving substance, space, time and causation. From these we generate ever more abstract concepts by metaphor: time is conceived as moving object, goals are destinations, knowing is seeing, society is a family, etc. [36].

[4]Our discussion throughout this chapter is independent of the communication means; therefore, 'speaker' and 'hearer' will do equal service for 'writer' and 'reader'.

referential ambiguity and relativity of scale [41]. As an example of the latter, in interpreting a statement, "Malacoda is near Calcabrina," it would help if we know whether Malacoda and Calcabrina are mitochondrial structures, towns, or galaxies; or whether the statement occurs within a conversation concerning microbiology, geography, or astronomy, etc.[5]

Natural language understanding can be posed as a hearer's (or reader's) problem of inferring a speaker's (or writer's) intended phonetic, syntactic, semantic, and referential interpretation of an utterance. The hearer uses contextual clues to hypothesize the speaker's intended meaning. Specifically, the hearer is required to estimate a three-place relationship, involving a text string, its speaker, and the latter's intended meaning. Note that we treat *meaning* as a random variable, with various possible instantiated values. As Humpty Dumpty demonstrates, it is a relational variable involving symbols and their users.

As such inference problems almost always rely on fusion of the utterance or text segment with contextual information in the discourse or discourse setting, they involve the basic data fusion functions: data alignment, data association, and state estimation.

Data alignment issues occur in phonetic, syntactic, and semantic registration problems. These processes establish the assumed language conventions between speakers and hearers: what language is being spoken, what systematic biases are present in a speaker's dialect, etc.

Data association issues occur in conversational syntactic problems: subject–verb–object associations and referential associations among noun phrases (e.g., anaphora). As in the general cases described in previous sections, determining relevant contexts for syntactic semantic and referential understanding is a data association problem.

Estimation and recognition issues occur in conversational semantics problems: estimating the meanings that speakers intend for their product and of the pragmatic effects of the production; i.e., the speech acts and their impacts [40–42].

Data used in these inference processes can include the received acoustic or visual signal data from the specific utterance or text segment. They can also use contextual information, to include

- *Discourse context*: Information in the surrounding spoken or written discourse;
- *Discourse situation context*: Information concerning the physical and social environment in which the discourse occurs, including assumed linguistic conventions;
- *Discourse participant context*: Information about the backgrounds and interests of the speakers and intended hearers.[6]

---

[5]They are demons in the eighth circle, fifth bolge, of Dante's Inferno.
[6]These follow the applicable types of evidence that we have employed in source characterization; i.e. in inferring and predicting the fidelity of information received from an information source [43].

What counts as a relevant segment of discourse regarding a given utterance will be determined by Grice's cooperative principle, noted above [40]. The cooperative principle as it applies to speakers is that one should contribute to a conversation only such utterances as further the aims and direction of the conversation. The cooperative principle as it applies to hearers may be read as one of tolerance: to assume that each speaker is himself honoring that principle, unless there are good grounds for thinking otherwise [40, 44].

As in the general data fusion problem, determining the relevance of candidate discourse, situation or participant contexts can be formulated in terms of the estimation of contextual variables (e.g., in estimating the value of the variable *scale* in interpreting the use of the word 'near').

If the estimation of semantic meaning is a problem akin to the classic *estimation* problems of data fusion: target location, classification, etc. Similarly, the estimation of data associations in natural language—including association of candidate contexts—is akin to the classical *data association* problems of data fusion: report-to-track, track-to-track association, etc.

Consider the problem of understanding anaphoric reference (or cross reference) in the discourse fragment

1. *A man met a woman with nine children. She told them to introduce themselves to him.*

Without knowing anything of the textual or discourse context, we can use gender and number to associate the pronouns and noun phrases with some confidence.

If, however, the fragment is

2. *A woman met another woman with a child. She told her to introduce herself to her;*

then the anaphoric-referential ambiguity is such that we are pressed to grasp for contextual clues, perhaps social expectations as who would be more likely to make such a request of a child given the vaguely defined relationships among the characters [43].

As in physical target tracking, referential association is based on the hypothesis of common referents. Just as in tracking, three types of evidence are used to associate pronouns and noun phrases: (a) expected spatio–temporal proximity; i.e., distance within a discourse, based on a discourse dynamic model, analogous to a kinematic dynamic model; (b) feature similarity, to include syntactic features: gender and number as well as semantic features (e.g., descriptive information in a noun phrase); and (c) situationally derived expectations as to relevant topics and attitudes of the interlocutors [44].

Correspondence measures may be used as well: in feature-aided target tracking this is correspondence with the observable features of an assumed referenced target; in anaphoric analysis this is correspondence with the characteristics of an assumed referent. For example, if in Washington, DC., in May 2008 (a "CO") we overheard someone saying "… his support in the Afro-American community is holding, but she's losing support among woman," a reasonable hypothesis is that Senators

Obama and Clinton are being discussed in the context of the 2008 U.S. presidential election. An utterance of this expression either five years before or after 2008 would likely be massively ambiguous.

2.7 Conclusions

This chapter has discussed the problems of context definitions, formalization, quality, and exploitation in information fusion, including understanding and fusion of natural language data.

Contexts can be characterized as meta-situations at various levels of granularity. As such contexts can be used to:

- support reasoning at each fusion level;
- eliminate or reduce ambiguity;
- detect inconsistencies;
- explain observations; and
- constrain fusion processing.

One of the significant problems of context exploitation is the interrelationship among context quality, the quality of observations, and the results of fusion processes. Solution of this problem is necessary for improved fusion performance. This and the problem of context discovery in uncertain dynamic environments pose a significant challenge in linguistic pragmatics, as in data fusion in general.

References

1. B. Wilson, *Systems: Concepts, Methodologies and Applications* (Wiley, Chichester, 1984)
2. M.H. Zack, Managing codified knowledge. Sloan Manag. Rev. **40**(4), 45–58 (1999)
3. J.R. Anderson, J.R. Language, *Memory and Thought* (Hillsdale, Erlbaum NJ, 1976)
4. P. Brézillon, J.-Ch. Pomerol, Misuse and nonuse of knowledge-based systems: the past experiences revisited, in *Implementing Systems for Supporting Management Decisions*, ed. by P. Humphreys, L. Bannon, A. McCosh, P. Migliarese, and J.-Ch. Pomerol (Chapman and Hall, London, 1996), pp. 44–60
5. A. Dey, Understanding and using context, *Personal and Ubiquitous Computing,* vol. 5(1) (Springer, London, 2001 Feb)
6. B. Schilit, M. Theimer, Disseminating active map information to mobile hosts. IEEE Netw. **8** (5), 22–32 (1994)
7. K. Sycara, R. Glinton, B. Yu, J. Giampapa, S. Owens, M. Lewis, C. Grindle, An integrated approach to high-level information fusion. Inf. Fusion **10**, 25–50 (2009)
8. J. Gómez-Romero, M.A. Serrano, J. García, J.M. Molina, G. Rogova, Context-based multi-level information fusion for harbor surveillance. Inf. Fusion **21**, 173–186 (2015)
9. J. Pascoe, Adding generic contextual capabilities to wearable computers, in *Proceedings of 2nd International Symposium on Wearable Computers* (1998), pp. 92–99
10. G. Tiberghien, Context and cognition: introduction. Cahier de Psychologie Cognitive **6**(2), 105–119 (1998)

11. P. Brezzilon, Context in problem solving: a survey. Knowl. Eng. Rev. **14**(1), 47–80 (1999)
12. B. Schilit, M. Theimer, Disseminating active map information to mobile hosts. IEEE Netw. **8** (5), 22–32 (1994)
13. D. Salber, A.K. Dey, C.D. Abowd, The context toolkit: aiding the development of context-enabled applications, *in The Proceedings of CHI'99* (1999), pp. 434–441
14. L. Gong, Contextual modeling and applications, V1, in *Proceedings of IEEE International Conference on SMC* (2005)
15. A.N. Steinberg, G.L. Rogova, Situation and context in data fusion and natural language understanding, in *Proceedings of Eleventh International Conference on Information Fusion* (Cologne, 2008)
16. J.-Ch. Pomerol, P. Brézillon, About some relationships between knowledge and context, in *CONTEXT '01 Proceedings of the Third International and Interdisciplinary Conference on Modeling and Using Context* (Springer, London, 2001), pp. 461–464
17. G. Ryle, *The Concept of Mind* (Barnes and Noble, New York, 1949)
18. T. Stang, C. Linnhoff-Popien, A context modeling survey, in *First International Workshop on Advanced Context Modelling, Reasoning and Management* (2004)
19. C. Bettini, O. Brdiczka, K. Henricksen, J. Indulska, D. Nicklas, A. Ranganathan, D. Riboni, A survey of context modelling and reasoning techniques. Pervasive Mob. Comput. **6**(2), 161–180 (2010)
20. J. McCarthy, Notes on formalizing context, in *Proceedings of the Thirteenth International Joint Conference in Artificial Intelligence* (Chambery, France, 1993), pp. 555–560
21. B. Schilit, N. Adams, R. Want, Context-aware computing applications, in *IEEE Workshop on Mobile Computing Systems and Applications* (Santa Cruz, CA, US, 1994)
22. J. George, J.L. Crassidis, T. Singh, Threat assessment using context-based tracking in a maritime environment, in *Proceedings of the 12th International Conference on Information Fusion (Fusion 2009)*, Seattle, USA, 2009, pp. 187–194
23. M. Kokar, C.J. Matheus, K. Baclawski, Ontology-based situation awareness. Inf. Fusion **10**, 83–98 (2009)
24. E.G. Little, G. Rogova, Designing ontologies for higher level fusion. Inf. Fusion **10**, 70–82 (2009)
25. J. Gómez-Romero, F. Bobillo, M. Delgado, Context representation and reasoning with formal ontologies, in *Proceedings of the Activity Context Representation Workshop in the 25th AAAI Conference (AAAI 2011)*, San Francisco, USA, 2011
26. F. Giunchiglia, Contextual reasoning, in *Proceedings IJ CAI'93 Workshop on Using Knowledge in its Context*, Chambery, France, 1993, pp. 39–49
27. M. Akman, M. Surav, The use of situation theory in context modeling. Comput. Intell. (1997)
28. J. Barwise, J. Perry, The situation underground, in *Working Papers in Semantics*, vol. 1 (Stanford University Press, 1980)
29. K. Devlin, *Logic and Information* (Press Syndicate of the University of Cambridge, 1991)
30. A.N. Steinberg, Foundations of situation and threat assessment, in *Handbook of Multisensor Data Fusion*, ed. by M. Liggins, D. Hall, J. Llinas, Chapter 26 (CRC Press, 2008)
31. T. Buchholz, A. Kupper, M. Schiffers, Quality of context information: what it is and why we need it, vol. 200, in *Proceedings of the 10th International Workshop of the HP OpenView University Association (HPOVUA)* (Hewlett-Packard OpenView University Association, Geneva, Switzerland, 2003)
32. M. Krause, I. Hochstatter, Challenges in modelling and using quality of context (QoC), in *Mobility Aware Technologies and Applications*. Lecture Notes in Computer Science, vol. 3744 (2005), pp. 324–333
33. G. Rogova, E. Bosse, Information quality in information fusion, in *Proceedings of FUSION'2010-13th Conference on Multisource Information Fusion* (Edinburgh, Scotland, 2010)
34. G. Rogova, V. Nimier, Reliability in information fusion: literature survey, in *Proceedings of the FUSION'2004-7th Conference on Multisource-Information Fusion* (2004)

35. J. Josephson, On the logical form of abduction, in *AAAI Spring Symposium Series: Automated Abduction* (1990), pp. 140–144
36. S. Pinker, *The Stuff of Thought: Language as a Window into Human Nature* (Penguin Books, New York, 2007)
37. George Lakoff, *Women, Fire and Dangerous Things: What Categories Reveal about the Mind* (University of Chicago Press, Chicago, 1987)
38. G. Lakoff, M. Johnson, *Philosophy in the Flesh* (MIT Press, Cambridge, MA, 2000)
39. L. Carroll, *Through the Looking Glass and What Alice Found There* (Digital Scanning, Inc., 2007)
40. H.P. Grice, Presupposition and conversational implicature, in *Radical Pragmatics*, ed. by P. Cole (Academic Press, 1981),`14
41. J.R. Searle, *Speech Acts* (Cambridge University Press, 1969)
42. J.L. Austin, *How to do Things with Words* (Oxford University Press, 1965), 12
43. A. Steinberg, J. Llinas, A. Bisantz, C. Stoneking, N. Morizio, Error characterization in human-generated reporting, in *Proceedings of MSS National Symposium on Sensor and Data Fusion* (McLean, VA, USA, 2007)
44. A.N. Steinberg, Reference and description in natural language, in *SPIE Proceedings of Applications of Artificial Intelligence*, vol. 937 (1988)

Chapter 3
Context as an Uncertain Source

James Llinas, Anne-Laure Jousselme and Geoff Gross

Abstract Source characterization is a fundamental function in fusion process design; this chapter addresses the issues involved when the characteristics of contextual information include uncertain and imprecise qualities and examines the associated impacts on computational operations. An overview regarding the general issue of uncertainty in fusion processes is provided, along with a survey of literature that addresses uncertainty in contextual information and the related issues of the ontology of and quality factors for contextual information. An extended use case discussion is also provided related to the role of and specific exploitation strategies for contextual information to support threat assessment for harbor protection; this use case derives from in-depth research at the NATO Center for Maritime Research and Experimentation (CMRE; La Spezia, Italy).

Keywords Context · Uncertainty · Ontology · Probabilistic · Quality · Harbor protection

3.1 Uncertainty in Information Fusion Processes

Most experienced researchers in the field of Information Fusion (IF) would agree that a major goal to be achieved or strived for in a well-designed IF process is to control or manage the degree of uncertainty in the final estimate or inference that the process produces. Historically, at least, the main inputs to an IF process were observational data as produced by electromechanical/solid state type sensors and the subsequent

J. Llinas (✉)
Center for Multisource Information Fusion and Department of Industrial and Systems
Engineering, University at Buffalo, Buffalo, NY, USA
e-mail: llinas@buffalo.edu

A.-L. Jousselme
NATO STO Centre for Maritime Research and Experimentation (CMRE), Viale San
Bartolomeo 400, 19126 La Spezia, Italy, USA

G. Gross
Osthus Inc., Melbourne, FL, USA

© Springer International Publishing Switzerland (outside the USA) 2016
L. Snidaro et al. (eds.), *Context-Enhanced Information Fusion*,
Advances in Computer Vision and Pattern Recognition,
DOI 10.1007/978-3-319-28971-7_3

45

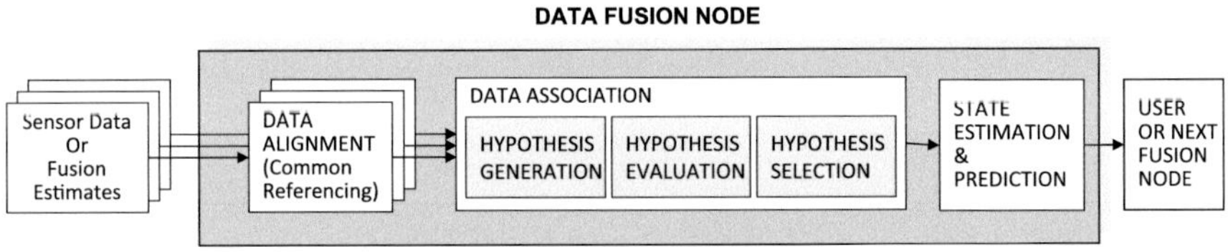

DATA FUSION NODE

Fig. 3.1 Nominal fusion node [1]

measurement–creation logics that followed. In a multisensor system supporting IF processes, the following functions involve the traditional "Fusion Node" operations of common referencing, association, and state estimation [1], as shown in Fig. 3.1.

Here, the data association function is expanded to show the generation, evaluation, and selection processes for each of the possibly several candidate association hypotheses. Then, in regard to the notion of managing and minimizing uncertainty through this process, an audit trail of sequential changes in uncertainty as the data flow through these processes toward developing the final state estimate has to be developed and analyzed. There are various difficulties in conducting this analysis of uncertainty propagation. One main factor is that these processes are not interconnected by closed-form mathematics; so, the interdependencies cannot be developed through a clean series of connected equations; this is clearly a main impediment. Instead, some type of empirically based assessment of interfunction uncertainty sensitivities needs to be developed. Further, if we cast these ideas in a larger context of a high-level fusion process architecture that would be realized through an integrated set of fusion nodes as above, the complexities of following the evolution of uncertainty dependencies becomes even more difficult.

Let us now consider an IF process that has access to and intends to exploit contextual information in the design of an IF process. We take the case of "a priori" exploitation of contextual information as discussed in Chap. 1, and present a modified form of that architecture here for discussion; we repeat Fig. 3.1 as an insert here to show the locations where the alignment, association, and state estimation processes occur.

In the version of Fig. 3.2, we have added the red boxes along the contextual data path on the lower right, to further elaborate where the conditioning, common referencing, and data association functions occur as applied to the contextual data. (Conditioning was originally within the "Middleware" function in the Chap. 1 version but we excerpt it here for highlighting purposes.) Recall that conditioning is inserted based on the assertion that meaningful amounts of contextual data will be in some external, native format created by the originators of that data; the example we often cite is weather data—always a contextual factor but the data are created by meteorologists and exist in some native "weather data" format, such as the sea state expressed on Douglas scale as discussed in Sect. 3.6. Similar assertions can be made for many other types of contextual data such as sociocultural, political, demographic, etc. Conditioning involves those operations such as sampling of the data and possibly mathematical or other operations that alter the data for intended

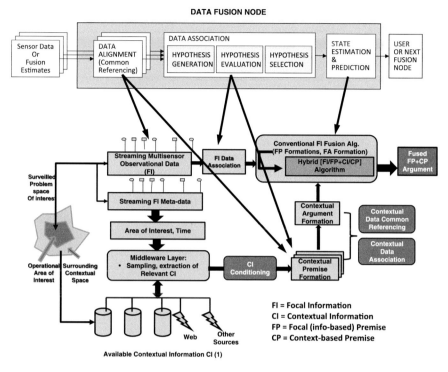

Fig. 3.2 "A Priori/Design-Time" fused focal/contextual argument formation (modified)

use in the fusion process. In our thinking (using the "argument" paradigm as in Chap. 1), we envision that different types of contextual data are used to form premises that then form context-based arguments that need to be combined/fused with the focal-data-based arguments or estimates. (These are notional characterizations, not reflective of any detailed architecture). Subsequent to conditioning, the contextual data are subject to operations of alignment/common referencing, these guided by the meta-data provided by the focal data stream or possibly other sources, to enable normalization of all contextual data minimally in a space-time framework, although other factors may be considered. Notice that the focal/multisensory data also need to be aligned as well. As regards uncertainty in the contextual sources, and again asserting the "native-source" point, it is very likely that any characterizations of uncertainty in the contextual data will be in disparate formats as drawn from the original source of that contextual information. This implies that common referencing operations for uncertainties in varied contextual information could likely require uncertainty normalization techniques; this topic is addressed in Sect. 3.5.1 and some additional perspectives are sketched in Sect. 3.6.4.4. Notice that there are various options here based on the general assertion that across a typical range of contextual data types there will be disparateness in uncertainty representations—we see of course probabilistic forms used but also possibilistic/fuzzy forms especially since some contextual data will be in linguistic form, and even belief-based versions as well. This in turn creates a potential trade-off issue and interdependencies between common referencing methodological choices and data association strategy choices; these will also be discussed in Sect. 3.5.1. Both the focal data and contextual information need to be associated, as pointed out in Fig. 3.2; these associations are based on metadata space-time values but also on relevance levels that need to be asserted for the contextual data. In a final step, the integration of either associated focal and contextual data could be possible or an integration of data-specific state estimates (focal and contextually-based) would need to be designed and developed. That is, the composite focal plus contextually-based state estimate needs to be formed in consideration of both the focal and contextually-based premises and arguments, as was described in Chap. 1. We point out (not shown in Fig. 3.2) that another aspect of the context of the above process is that the context from a superordinate (i.e., "higher-level" in the JDL sense) fusion process could also add a contextual aspect to the operations of Fig. 3.2; as our focus here is on the probabilistic aspects of context we do not elaborate on this idea. Thus, as noted for sensor data in the opening paragraphs, here too for contextual data we have similar issues and complexities in the evolution of uncertainty as the various design choices for these functional operations are decided.

We offer some further remarks here about contextual uncertainty and IF processes by considering a higher level view of IF from the perspective of the JDL fusion process model [2–7]. Depending on which version of the model is chosen, the model has 3–5 levels (Levels of abstraction in estimation); we choose to use the 5-level version to make some points. To recount that model's structure (see [7] for further details), we use Fig. 3.3, drawn and modified from [7].

This model is very traditional in showing just sensor data as input but it serves our purpose in showing the five Levels. Definitions for the first four Levels are offered by Steinberg and Bowman [7] as follows:

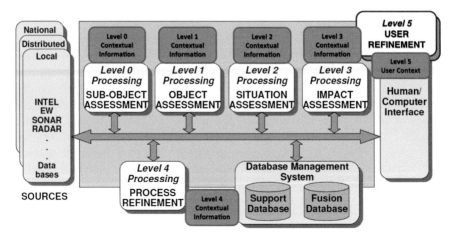

Fig. 3.3 A 5-level JDL fusion process model depiction (from [7], modified)

- Level 0: Signal/Feature Assessment—estimation and prediction of signal or feature states;
- Level 1: Entity Assessment—estimation and prediction of entity parametric and attributive states (i.e., of entities considered as individuals/singletons);
- Level 2: Situation Assessment—estimation and prediction of the structures of parts of reality (i.e., of relations among entities and their implications for the states of the related entities); relation estimation is key at this Level
- Level 3: Impact Assessment—estimation and prediction of the utility/cost of signal, entity, or situation states—including predicted impacts given a system's alternative courses of action;
- Level 4: Performance Assessment—estimation and prediction of a system's performance as compared to given desired states and measures of effectiveness.

Blasch and Plano, who are generally credited with nominating Level 5 [6], offer the following characterization for Level 5:

- Level 5: User refinement (an element of Knowledge Management): adaptive determination of who queries information and who has access to information. (e.g., information operations) and adaptive data retrieved and displayed to support cognitive decision making and actions (e.g., altering the sensor display).

As noted, these levels depict different (but importantly interrelated) estimation processes directed to forming estimates at different levels of abstraction, and it can thus be expected that there are different types and levels of abstraction as well in any contextual information that could aid the formation of each of these estimates; this notion of level-specific contextual information is shown notionally in Fig. 3.3 along the top of the figure. And as well, it can be assumed that these bodies of contextual information have varying degrees of uncertainty and uncertainty representations. In the course of dynamically evolving estimates at any level, then (see [4] for a discussion about interlevel dependencies and estimation operations) the evolving estimates are dependent on the particular qualities of the level-specific contextual information; it is feasible to think that conflicts could arise in these operations if the influences of one body of contextual information are different than those at another level. Adjudication techniques may be required in fact across the entire IF process to harmonize the potentially conflicting influences of possibly disparate contextual data sets.

The heterogeneity of contextual information across levels of abstraction is discussed in [8] and Chap. 16.

Various additional issues involved with the topic of heterogeneity and multilevel problems are also discussed in [8]. In [9], Glinton et al. develop an approach for contextual exploitation that reminds us that the higher level state estimates in fusion themselves represent an estimated context and that contextual information should not be thought of as bounded solely to external information. They develop a Markov Random Field-based approach that combines estimated contextual information with such a priori context as terrain information in developing threat-state estimates. Steinberg and Bowman [10], along with Llinas et al. [4] also remind of this perspective that there is interplay across the levels in fusion. In dynamic, streaming environments, these dynamics impute a need for managing the coherence of multilevel estimation/inferencing processes in a temporal sense. Such works, however, seem to be rather rare, and robust multilevel incorporation of layered uncertain contextual information in IF processes or systems has not yet been seriously addressed, and the study and assessment of these issues are ripe areas for novel research opportunities. It could be argued that what is needed is a kind of overarching context-monitoring and "common referencing" process that is assuring that evolving multilevel estimates are coherent in the sense of the composite influences of the contextual information across the levels.

3.2   Reviewing Literature Addressing Uncertainty in Contextual Information

In carrying out a literature search on this topic, we find that the research communities involved with "pervasive systems", and "context-aware systems (CAS)" have by far addressed the issue of contextual uncertainty more than other application areas. It is important therefore to understand this field and the general application areas of these works and possible extensions to broader IF systems applications. Context-aware systems are, according to [11], a subdomain of the field of "pervasive systems", that are those wide-ranging types of systems that can exploit the ubiquitous availability of mobile computing devices. Various works argue that the term 'pervasive' was introduced first by Weiser in 1991 [12], and refers to the seamless integration of mobile computing and other devices into the everyday life of people. Thus, much of the work has to do with understanding "activities of daily life," and how such understanding impacts the control of the environments that people are in, usually being so-called "smart spaces" such as intelligent meeting rooms, smart homes, and smart vehicles. In maritime security (see Sect. 3.6), the detection and characterization of patterns of life as represented by maritime routes are used as a basis for anomaly detection (off-route vessels, rendezvous, high-speed vessels, etc.). (Notice that, in the broader sense of non-CAS applications, the actual focus of fusion-based estimation could be the "activities of daily life," i.e., as what can be called a "problem variable" versus data that provides context; this is a subtle but important distinction for non-CAS-type problem domains). Context-aware systems are able to modify their operations for providing some type of service to the current context without explicit user intervention and thus aim at increasing usability and effectiveness by taking context into account. According to [11], the history of context-aware systems started when Want et al. [13] introduced their Active Badge Location System in 1992 which is considered to be one of the first context-aware applications. Using these dates as reference then, pervasive and context-aware systems would seem to date from the early 1990s and are thus in the range of 25 years old as areas of research and development.

Baldauf et al. [11] discuss the means by which contextual information is gathered in these systems, enumerating three types: (1) Direct sensor access, where contextual information is constructed from the sensor data—from the uncertainty point of view then, this approach propagates the uncertainty in the sensor data directly; (2) Middleware infrastructure, a concept as we have argued for in Chap. 1, that hides the low-level sensing details, but may also gather already-processed contextual information—here the uncertainty is layered across the data and has to be considered from a source-specific point of view; and (3) Context server which is a larger middleware notion that accesses remote data sources—uncertainty here is also layered and related to source pedigree etc.

Chen et al. [14] provide a rather broad architectural view of a generalized CAS application and make clear distinctions between the contextual information derived from the "intelligent spaces" of typical CAS applications as just mentioned, and contextual information derived from external sources, all operating in a multiagent-type framework. This work does not mention issues of uncertainty but introduces an argument for improved quality of contextually-based reasoning grounded on the need for CAS's to employ ontologies in relation to deriving contextual understanding; we discuss the role of ontologies in contextual under-standing in Sect. 3.4.

3.3 Classification of Context

To get a sense of the nature of uncertainty in regard to contextual information, it is considered helpful if a classification scheme for contextual information was available. The CAS community has carried out studies of different classification schemes, as for instance in [15] where the authors identify the six following context categories [15]:

- "User context (Who?)—e.g., User's profile: identifications, relation with others, to do lists, etc.
- Physical context (Where?)—e.g., Physical Environment: humidity, temperature, noise level, etc.
- Network context (Where?)—e.g., Network environment: connectivity, band-width, protocol, etc.
- Activity context (What occurs, when?)—e.g., What occurs, at what time: enter, go out, etc.
- Device context (What can be used?)—e.g., Profile and activities of devices: identifications, location, battery lifetime, etc.
- Service context (What can be obtained?)—e.g., Information on functions which system can provide: file format, display, etc."

What is helpful from such a classification scheme is that it motivates the corresponding types of uncertainties that could exist within each class-type. For example, activity recognition (a level 2-type inference from the JDL Fusion Model

Table 3.1 Examples of contextual information for the six categories of [15] along three JDL levels

Context category from [15]	Examples		
	JDL Level 1	JDL Level 2	JDL Level 3
User	*User*: Tracking analyst *Task*: Detect, track, recognize new objects	*User*: VTS operator *Task*: Detect anomalies	*User*: Watch Officer *Task*: Threat assessment
Physical	E.g., coast lines, sea state	E.g., Anchorage areas, channels	E.g., country, region
Network	E.g., network of radars	E.g., AIS communication network	E.g., hierarchical chain of command, other command entities
Activity	E.g., usual tracks or routes	E.g., season, routes, patterns of communication with port authorities	E.g., social media activity, Harbor Protection Level
Device	E.g., radar and camera locations and associated performances	E.g., AIS coverage	E.g., availability and accessibility of sources
Service	E.g., location (lat, long), heading (degrees)	E.g., limitation of routes display	E.g., identification format such as STANAG 1241

point of view) is a semantically-based concept for which the CAS and IF communities have applied various methods for gauging uncertainty, to include evidential and possibilistic schemes. In turn, the means to represent uncertainty in physical context typically derives from sensor data and thus would usually be probabilistically based. By introducing a classification scheme for contextual information, one implicitly derives an uncertainty classification for these categories, which again raises the issue of an uncertainty transformation scheme in relation to the "Common Referencing" or alignment function for basic IF operations (as in Fig. 3.1). Table 3.1 (in Sect. 3.6) is derived to classify the various contextual levels shown in the JDL model of Fig. 3.3.

In [16] Kaenampornpan et al. provide a survey of works addressing context classification largely for CAS-type applications; some 9 papers are reviewed, that show a broad range of approaches for developing classification schemes. They conclude that most of these works are incomplete in failing to develop an adequately-broad classification scheme that reveals the interrelationships among the different class types. As all of these CAS-based schemes are largely related to reasoning about "activities of daily life," they provide a very first attempt to use Activity Theory as a basis for a new classification approach. For the broader applications of interest to the IF community, there is a clear need to develop a well-grounded and complete context classification scheme. One possible framework could be developed around the JDL Level notions and the different levels of abstraction of interest, and consideration of the types of contextual information that would have influence on the development of the corresponding inferences and estimates.

3.4 The Role of Ontology and Probabilistic Ontology

According to [17–23], ontologies have been part of the knowledge and software engineering landscape since about the 1990s. Development and exploitation of ontologies in software has been driven by the need to address semantics and semantic complexities in modern applications. As mentioned in Sect. 3.2 [14], arguments for the use of ontological structures in CAS can be made as one basis for improving the understanding of contextual conditions and/or influences on what is being estimated. Ontologies can also provide a basis for interoperability across systems that share common ontologies. In [18–24], a good overview of issues and tradeoffs in the use of ontologies for CAS applications is provided. Boury-Brisset provides an equally good overview of the use of ontologies in IF systems and applications in [19]. To give an IF-based example of the need for ontologies, one can consider the goal of JDL Level 2 inferencing toward composing situational estimates. From an abstract point of view, a situation could be considered as a "set of elements (in the broad sense) in a set of relations." Boury-Brisset [19] shows Fig. 3.4 as a more detailed construct of situational elements for a notional military/defense application:

Notice that the relationships among these elements are not shown but it should be clear that clarification and normalization (supportive of Common Referencing and Data Association) of these complex semantic structures is needed for efficiency and interoperability. The why and how of employing ontologies in both CAS and IF

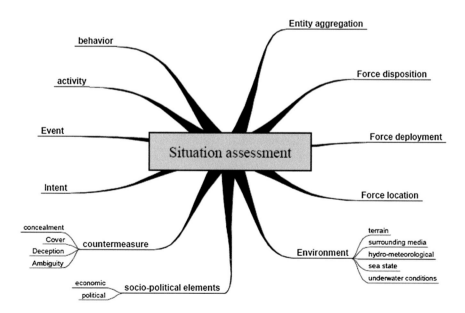

Fig. 3.4 Elements of situational assessment (Level 2 processing; from [19])

applications is a complex issue and one that we do not enter into here in any depth, as there are many good references to study for these details.

From a philosophical point of view, ontologies are supposed to be a "specification of the (true) world"; there is some controversy about the issue of uncertainty and ontology. It would seem that a plausible argument can be made that the accuracy of an ontological specification is bounded by bounds of knowledge. A good example [20] is in the medical domain where causal relations between diseases and causes or treatments, etc. are simply not known, but could be approximated from empirical studies, and probabilities or other measures of associability assigned to the relationships, as derived from such studies. As for some of the other issues surrounding ontologies, we will not enter into the details of this discussion, but present some looks at the use of probabilistic ontologies in IF applications.

We follow here some of the works of Laskey et al. at George Mason University in the USA who have developed the overall methodologies and software prototypes involving the use of probabilistic ontologies for IF applications. Laskey, Costa, and Janssen say, in [21], that "... attempts to represent uncertainty in ontology languages tend to begin with constructs for attaching probabilities as attributes of entities. This approach is clearly inadequate, in that it fails to account for structural features such as conditional dependence (or independence), double counting of influence on multiply connected graphs, and context-specific independence." These assertions are followed by the definition, design, and development of an overarching approach to higher level fusion inferencing that is based on a probabilistic ontology web language (PR-OWL; see [22]) and a Bayesian approach to uncertainty representation and management (Multientity Bayesian Networks (MEBN); see [23]). In this approach, the ontology includes context nodes that can have uncertainty aspects as well. The overall reasoning in this process is driven by the MEBN; details are provided in [22–24]. The PR-OWL/MEBN framework considers uncertainty under the form of probabilities, representing only the type "discord" to be discussed in the following.

3.5 Contextual Information Quality

Defining and measuring the quality of contextual information is a relatively new research topic in both the CAS domain and in the IF domain. In [25], a characterization of the Quality of Context (QoC) is split into QoC Parameters and QoC Sources [25]:

"**QoC Parameters**:

- **Generic**

  - Up-to-dateness
  - Trust-worthiness
  - Completeness

- Representation Consistency
- Precision

- **Domain-Specific**

  - Significance
  - AccessSecurity

  QoC Sources

- **Sensed**

  - SourceLocation
  - InformationEntityLocation
  - MeasurementTime
  - SensorDataAccuracy

- **User Profiled**

  - SourceState
  - SourceCategory
  - LifeTime
  - CriticalValue
  - MeasurementUnit"

In Fig. 3.5, it can be noted that while accuracy and precision are mentioned, there is no mention of uncertainty. The notion of quality here is also partitioned into those factors dependent on the parameters of the information but also, in a kind of "pedigree" sense, the sources of the information are weighed as to gauging the overall quality. Rogova and Bossé, in [26], address the topic of quality of information in the overall (not context-specific) sense for IF systems, and show the following ontological characterizations:

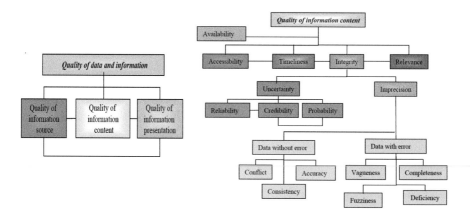

Fig. 3.5 Quality of information and information content for IF Systems (from [26])

Clearly, the characterization regarding quality of information content shows a considerable influence of uncertainty on quality, where uncertainty is broken into three factors: reliability, credibility, and probability. There are a few overlaps in Fig. 3.5 and the quality of context characterization of [25] introduced above; note that both show a quality dependence on source (pedigree is the term most often used in the IF community). It could perhaps be argued that Fig. 3.5, in including trustworthiness, does have some uncertainty aspect in its definition. Trust in heterogeneous and disparate sources, even in a coalition environment, can be a complex issue to understand and manage as part of any scheme for quality control. In [49], Smets distinguishes between three types of imperfect information, uncertainty, imprecision and inconsistency, while the common referred kinds of uncertainty in the field of Generalized Information Theory are nonspecificity, fuzziness and discord [31]. These kinds will be used as a basis for discussion in the following and exemplified in Sect. 3.6. In [27], Arunkumar et al. develop an approach to trust using subjective logic triples (i.e., belief, disbelief, and uncertainty) for representing trust and a Bayesian inference network that exploits a priori domain knowledge. The system extracts trust metadata from streaming raw data that formulates the basis for a query into the domain knowledge system and the trust-scoring mechanics.

3.5.1   Uncertainty Transformations

We have said that a complete scheme of contextual exploitation toward developing fusion-based estimates will involve a broad range of contextual information classes; the literature as discussed here shows this to be true even for the bounded applications of CAS systems. Since choices of uncertainty representations are typically dependent on the underlying nature of the core information type, it can be expected that in an IF system with "complete" contextual information classes that there will be disparate forms of uncertainty representation across these classes. If these classes are JDL-level-specific, then any interlevel inferencing or estimation operation, in addressing the need for common referencing, will need to normalize or transform one representation into another.

There is a large literature on the comparisons, equivalences, and transformations among and between different schemes for representing uncertainty. Even within given classes of uncertainty schemes such as probabilistic, there are many papers addressing subtle and not so subtle issues between different schemes; the Bayesian–Dempster–Shafer comparisons are extensive in the literature as one example. The notion of transforming one representational scheme to another is however an even more complex issue. These are the cases where the underlying frameworks are fundamentally different, such as probabilistic and possibilistic as one example. Here, probabilistic forms are used to represent ambiguous data whereas possibilistic forms are used to represent vague data (e.g., the frequent examples of representing "tall-ness" etc.). In these cases, one has to be careful in defining what is meant by "transforming" one to the other.

What can be seen in the literature for such cases are approaches that impose some type of constraint on the transformation, as a kind of condition under which the transform is "valid." In the case of the probabilistic to possibilistic transformations, a review of the literature indicates that over a dozen transformation models exist for information exchange between possibilistic and probabilistic domains. Seminal papers reviewing a range of possibility–probability transformation models are described in [28–30]. In one exemplar approach, Geer and Klir [29] proposed the "information preserving transformation" (IPT) concept in transforming possibility and probability [31]. The IPT requires that the amount of "total" uncertainty and information be preserved under the transformation. According to [31], total uncertainty in the possibility theory is composed of two kinds of uncertainties: nonspecificity and discord, (corresponding to imprecision and uncertainty respectively, as distinguished by Smets [49]—see Sect. 3.6.4.2). On the other hand, the Shannon entropy, is typically used as a measure of uncertainty and information formulated in terms of probability theory, quantifying the discord only. The IPT approach then forms a transform strategy that equates these two forms, allowing the derivation of the transform scheme.

It should also be noted that the presence of different uncertainty representation schemes also generates questions about how to perform data association as well. There have also been a number of studies comparing probabilistic and possibilistic methods for data association, such as in [32, 33].

3.5.2 Conflicting, Suspicious, and Inconsistent Information

As contextual information can come from a variety of sources that are often external to the focal application under study, it is likely that the overall information quality of these varied sources will also be quite varied. In addition to the notions of quality discussed above, there are additional quality-related factors that may need to be considered. While Fig. 3.5 and the QoC characterization mention, respectively, "Representational Consistency" and "Integrity," these taxonomies do not address other attributes that we believe affect the quality of information. These are the features of conflicting information, information that would be considered suspicious, and information that is inconsistent, or "CSI" features of information. This is addressed by Smets' structured thesaurus, under the term inconsistency [49]. The same notion is covered partially by the concept of credibility of the STANAG 2511 [50]. (These three categories are clearly not an exhaustive list; one can think of other features such as illogical or unnatural, etc.; the degree to which to invest in detecting and addressing such types of information toward improved quality control is a case-by-case design and payoff choice.) The types of errors or defects comprising CSI-Info include errors in reporting, transmission errors, statements of opinion, new information resolving a previous uncertainty, errors in automated processing, etc. In addition to these unintentional-type factors, in many environments (not only defense/military environments) one cannot discount intentional attempts to deceive that may result in CSI features as well. In adversarial, nonco-operative environments, there are other thoughts that need to be considered in addressing quality control, since in such cases there can be the case where totally coherent, technically correct information is nevertheless being employed for deceitful purposes. Addressing this class of problems requires proactive under-standing of the adversary and imputes an overarching situation of countermeasure versus countermeasure in some type of iterative approach to information quality control. This latter type of problem will not be addressed here; we are just pointing out the potential for such cases.

In developing an approach to detect and possibly mitigate the ramifications of CSI data in contextual sources, there is a need to think about "within-source" and "cross-source" processes. While many CSI-info elements are identified within a single data source (e.g., formatting inconsistencies), others require a cross-source cumulative (associated) data view for their identification. Data association (with data fusion) [34] is an enabling technology for the formation of a cumulative (cross-source) knowledge base that can be necessary to address this class of CSI issues. Through the recognition of common entities, events, and relationships across data sources, fused knowledge about these entities, events, and relationships enables conclusions regarding validity, etc. which could not be drawn from within a single data source.

There are at least two goals of any process that is addressing the CSI issue: the first is to detect the presence of any such data, and the second is to reconcile or "fix" the data if at all possible.

In such an approach, the major system components would operate on the fol-lowing data levels:

- **Within-source**—format inconsistency resolution, uncertainty alignment, sta-tistical CSI-info identification, and rule-based CSI-info identification
- **Cross-source**—data association, contradiction identification, statistical CSI-info identification, rule-based CSI-info identification, suspicion, and deception indicator identification

Note the statistical and rule-based CSI-info identification and resolution pro-cesses operate both within and across data sources. The within-source identification and resolution operations serve to resolve CSI-info before data association, enabling an improved association result.

3.6 Use Case Discussion

In this section, we illustrate some of the elements put forward in the previous sections on a maritime scenario use case. The use case sketched below has been used and validated during the table top exercise (TTX) held at the NATO Centre for Maritime Research and Experimentation (CMRE; La Spezia, Italy) on November 24–27, 2014, to which 32 operational staff from 9 NATO nations participated. The map has been designed for the exercise's purposes [40] and the scenario has been designed for one of the three games in the overall exercise plan, called the *risk game* [41]. It describes a problem of harbor threat assessment where two events of interest must be considered and comparatively analyzed.

3.6.1 Threat Assessment for Harbor Protection

Harbor protection is a complex problem in which the state and nonstate organizations should unify their strengths and synchronize together as well as with local authorities for efficient coordinated surveillance and intervention. It is frequent that coalition forces are deployed during or right after a period of harbor crisis and must ensure that daily life and economic activities return to normality. In a phase of security assistance, the secure transit of cargos and tankers, but also peaceful fishing, ferry connections, and recreational activities are of primary concerns for the coalition forces. The benefit of using data and information fusion technologies for harbor protection has been widely covered by the NATO workshop on data fusion technologies for harbor protection held in 2005 in Estonia [38] and followed other works such as [39].

3.6.2 Contextual Factors and Categories of Contextual Information

Details of this use case can be found in [41] and we detail below the aspect related to contextual information, along the context categories introduced in Sect. 3.3. Table 3.1 exemplifies context categories for three levels of the JDL.

Site The concern is a possible terrorist attack toward the port of "CentreLand" from "RightLand" (artificial locations and countries).[1] The story takes place in CentreLand, a country marked out by LeftLand on the left and RightLand on the right. Figure 3.6 displays CentreLand and RightLand only. Harbor zones characteristics are represented in Fig. 3.6: Water depths, channels, restricted areas, fishing areas, borders, harbors (fishing, recreational, etc.), shipping lanes, ferry lane, military and liquefied natural gas (LNG) anchorage areas, etc... The channel lies on the border between RightLand and CentreLand. The fishing area is located between RightLand and CentreLand (see coordinates F1-F3 X L1-L3).

Geopolitical LeftLand (LL), CentreLand (CL), and RightLand (RL) are three non-NATO countries. A conflict between LL and CL lasted for 2 years. The situation in CL was desperate, lawless, and volatile. LL incursion into CL has brought

---

[1]The Use Case sketched here has been inspired by the Vehicle-Borne IED scenario for the Uncertainty forum at the 2012 Fusion conference in Edinburgh (UK) [42].

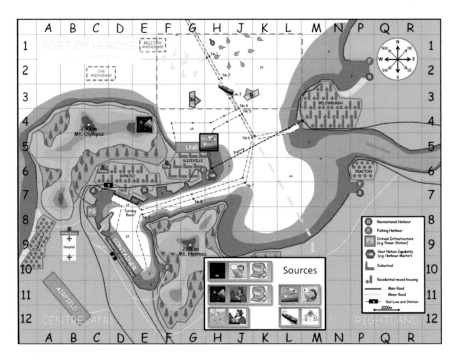

Fig. 3.6 Port of Herosé in CentreLand - Map developed for the table top exercise (TTX) held at CMRE, November 2014 [40]

about UN Security Resolution to restore national boundaries. NATO forces have been tasked to drive LL forces back over the border. CL government has given NATO forces permission to use the harbor of Herosé, but cannot guarantee harbor security. RL is neutral and mostly sympathetic to the CL struggle; however, an element within RL shares ethnicity with the majority in LL. The risk of asymmetric attack from RightLand cannot be discounted. After this period of tension between LeftLand and CentreLand, the NATO forces in CentreLand are now operating in a phase of security assistance [40].

Global threat level The Harbor Protection Level (HPL) is set to TWO, which corresponds to a security alert state DELTA. This security state applies in the immediate area where a terrorist attack has taken place or when intelligence has been received that terrorist action against a specific location or person is likely. Normally this alert state is issued as a localized warning. Due to the HPL, the security assistance force will consider as hostile, any vessel from RightLand approaching CentreLand facilities with no specific preagreement. The HPL summarizes the recent terrorist activities, tensions, manifests, or other fear feelings observed possibly through social media monitoring.

Rules and Patterns of Life Fishing vessels usually go back to their respective fishing port at the end of the day. They are not allowed to cross the border; however, it is quite usual that they do, still remaining in the vicinity of the border.

Although it is mandatory for any fishing vessel of length higher than 25 meters to report its AIS information (location, heading, type, unique ID, etc.), some do not for instance to protect their fishing zones. Fishing vessels from CentreLand are subject to a more strict control than RightLand vessels and thus better respect the rule than RL vessels, although some may not.

Meteorological conditions Although no fog is present, the sea state is quite rough (level 4 on Douglas scale[2]). This creates a lot of clutter on synthetic aperture radar images.

Time and period of the year Time t is 16h45 in Spring so there is daylight.

Traffic density At that time of the day, fishing vessels go back to the port and the traffic density is quite heavy including among others recreational boats and service ships.

Decision making The watch officer (WO) is monitoring the area with the aim of detecting and mitigating any suspicious event. By means of the different sensing devices together with analyst support teams (e.g., tracking analyst, SAR analyst, camera analyst, Vessel Traffic System (VTS) operator), he needs to reach a sufficient level of situation awareness for an informed decision. As countermeasures to mitigate the risk, he has the options to decide to send a patrol (being either an aircraft (costly) or a boat (less fast)) for further checking, or to place the patrol under an alert state, etc. He needs to consider also the impact of his decision on the population, the resources left, etc. Excessive control on fishermen, in particular, will disturb their activities and increase their feelings of hostility and anger against the coalition forces. The watch officer is in charge of mitigating the risk of a terrorist attack against the port of CL while preserving daily activities of citizens from CL. The decision of the WO is directly linked to his identification decision according to the NATO standard identity classes of various entities [43]:

$$ID = \{Unknown, Assumed\ Friend, Friend, Neutral, Suspect, Hostile\}$$

If the vessel is identified as suspect or hostile, an intervention will be decided.

Prior information One hour ago, a group of fishing vessels from RightLand is fishing in RL fishing area (purple symbols in Fig. 3.6). A group of fishing vessels from CentreLand is fishing in CL fishing area (Yellow symbols in Fig. 3.6). At that time, the situation was quiet and no abnormal event was reported.

Sources and devices A coastal radar (range 25 km) located in CentreLand, a SAR (Synthetic Aperture Radar) image taken 30 min ago and a visible surveillance camera (range of 4 km) located on the LNG terminal are available to cover LeftLand area. To compensate for the low range of the camera, additional visual sighting to RightLand is provided by a cargo captain heading to the port through the channel on the border between CL and RL. The VTS operator has established radio contact with the cargo captain, who does not want to deceive him and provides the best information he can.

---

[2]http://en.wikipedia.org/wiki/Douglas_Sea_Scale.

As enumerated here, it can be seen that there are a number of contextual factors and a large set of types of contextual information classes that have influence on the reasoning processes that support decision making. It can be appreciated that much of the information is dynamic and also uncertain and perhaps only partially available. It can also be noticed the diversity and heterogeneity of the contextual sources and associated information regarding the attributes provided, their scale of values (binary, real, integer, nominal, etc.), the associated type of uncertainty, etc. As a consequence and as pointed out earlier in the chapter, it can also be seen that the Contextual Information bears on different types of uncertainty representation and reasoning in the categories of the JDL Fusion Levels.

3.6.3   Event of Interest

At time *t*, the vessel traffic service (VTS) operator reports the loss of the AIS track of a fishing vessel, a trawler with RightLand flag, 1 h ago. All the information provided by its last AIS emission is available together with the associated information from the vessels database (length, width, type, maximum speed, picture, etc.). Before reporting the event to the watch officer, the VTS operator tried to establish a radio contact with the lost vessel without success. He analyzed the maritime picture and identified two unknown tracks originating from each group of fishing vessels and possibly being the lost vessel, not emitting AIS information and not answering the radio calls from the VTS operator (see Fig. 3.6): One track in RightLand area and another one in LeftLand heading south, being thus possibly a threat.

3.6.4   Uncertainty Dimensions of Context

Among the different dimensions of information and source quality, we consider in the following some **ontological** elements about the description of the situation allowed but also constrained by sources limitations in terms of expertise and language, some **epistemic** elements about the ways sources can express uncertainty, and some **semantic** elements covering the intentional meaning of numerical values output, the way they have been obtained, etc.

3.6.4.1   Ontological Dimension

As introduced in Sect. 3.4, ontology includes both problem and contextual variables, their relationships as well as their associated uncertainty, further characterized as range (the set of possible values it can take) and granularity (a partition of an underlying finest-grained set of values).For a given variable, the range together with the associated granularity defines either (1) the user's needs (user context) or (2) sources' limitations in terms of both perception and language (device context).

The user's goal is represented (partially) by his targeted decision as represented by the decision variables including the range and the granularity required. Let us denote by V, one of the two vessels of interest, VA or VB. Considering the identification decision, a series of relevant variables (or attributes) describing the problem are identified such as the distance of V from the LNG terminal, the speed of V, the position of V, the size of V, the pattern followed by V, the meteorological conditions (e.g., sea state), the traffic density of the area, etc. We split the set of relevant variables related to the decision and distinguish between:

1. *Problem variables* among which we have

   (a) The *decision variables* such as

   (i) $ID(V,t) \in \{$Unknown; Assumed Friend; Friend;

   Neutral; Suspect; Hostile$\} = $ Identification of V

   (ii) $A = \{$Send a patrol; Do not send a patrol$\} = $ Patrol sending

   (b) The *observational variables* (possibly for several instants in time, i.e., current, past and predicted states) such as

   (i) $S(V,t) \in [0; 250]$km/h = speed of V
   (ii) $H(V,t) \in [0; 360]^\circ$= heading of V
   (iii) $L(V) \in [2; 100]$m = length of V
   (iv) $T(V) \in \{$Trawler; Seiner; ...$\}$ = type of V
   (v) $R(V,t) \in \{R_1; R_2; ...; No\}$ = route followed by S
   (vi) $AD(V) \in \{$Normal; Suspect$\}$ = anomaly detector of S

2. *Contextual variables* such as

   (i) $TD(P,t) \in \{$Light; Normal; Medium; Heavy$\}$

   = Maritime traffic density

   (ii) $Th(P,t) \in \{1; 2; 3; 4; 5\}$ = Harbor Protection Level;
   (iii) $t = $ Time, Day, Month, Season, Year;
   (iv) $R \in \{R1; R2; R3; ...\}$ = Set of possible routes (patterns of life);
   (v) $SS \in \{0; 2; ...; 9\}$ = Sea State (Douglas scale);
   (vi) $NE \in [1; 2; 3; ...]$ = Number of recent events similar to the concern

Figure 3.7 depicts possible links between the set of variables split into problem variables (blue circles) and contextual variables (green squares). The elements of situational assessment ontology identified in Fig. 3.4 are represented: Contextual elements, including *Environment* (Sea State SS, Routes R, Traffic Density TD, time t), *Socio-political* (Harbor Protection Level Th), but also other elements such as *Behavior* (Anomaly Detection AD), *Intent* (Identification ID). Some elements of *Level 1* fusion about individual entities are also represented (Length L, Type T, Speed S, and Heading H).

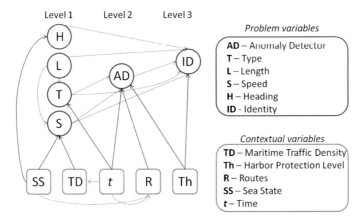

Fig. 3.7 Problem and contextual variables and possible dependencies (Color figure online)

Table 3.2 Relevant expertise of context as represented by the set of contextual variables

Source	Relevant expertise
Harbor Protection Coordinator (HPC)	Th—Harbor Protection Level
Meteorological center	SS—sea state
Radar (automated processing or analyst)	SS—sea state (wave length), TD—traffic density
SAR (automated processing or analyst)	SS—sea state (wave length), TD—traffic density
AIS + route extractor	R—routes, TD—traffic density
SAR analyst	TD—traffic density
Clock, calendar	t—time
Context	**Th, SS, TD, R, t**

Such knowledge about the attributes and their relationships reasonably describes the relevant description of the world as required by the user's needs (*User context*, according to the Quality of Context classification scheme presented in Sect. 3.5). This representation could further be used as a basis for reasoning for example within the PR-OWL/MEBN framework [25] introduced in Sect. 3.4.

As a source of information, the (field of) *expertise* of the context can be described by the set of attributes about which the context is able to provide information. Because by definition, context variables are the ones relevant to the user's goal, the relevant expertise of the context is captured by the set of contextual variables as summarized in Table 3.2.

The relevant expertise of the context (as a source of information) is thus the union of the expertise of each of its individual sources and summarized as the corresponding list of variables in the last row of the table. Each variable (problem or contextual) can be further described along its domain (range and granularity), as defined by either the user's needs (column 4) or sources' limitations (columns 5–10), as exemplified in Table 3.3.

Table 3.3 Contextual variables and associated domains of definition including range and granularity

Attribute name	Variable	Domain (finest-grained)	User needs	Sources domain definition (range and granularity)					
				Habor Protection Coordinator (HPC)	MARCOM (NATO)	Meteorological center	Radar + automated processing	SAR imagery + ATR	AIS data + route extractor
Global security level	Th	{1; 2; 3; 4; 5}	{3; 2; 1} (ISPScode)	{1; 2; 3; 4; 5}	{Delta; Charlie; Bravo; Alpha}	–	–	–	–
Sea state	SS	{0; ...; 9} (Douglas)	{Calm; Slight; Rough; High}	–	–	{0; ...; 9}	Wave length	Wave length	–
Traffic density	TD	Nb of vessels/km^2	{Low; Medium; High}	–	–	–	Nb of vessels/km^2	Nb of vessels/km^2	Nb of vessels/km^2
Route	R	{R1; R2; ...., Rn} for any type of ship	Fishing vessels routes only	–	–	–	–	–	{R1; R2; ...; Rn}
Time	t	Hour, Day, Month, Season, Year	Hour, Special day	*Provided by any clock and calendar*					

For instance, about the global security level, the decision maker may expect an International Ship and Port Facility Security (ISPS) code between 1 and 3, 1 being the highest level of threat, while the harbor protection coordinator provides a 5-level code, 1 being the lowest level of threat. However, the NATO Maritime Command Center (MARCOM) provide security alert states over a scale of four values: DELTA, CHARLIE, BRAVO, ALPHA. This set of values defines a basic limitation of the source in its ability to further express information. In relation to the user's need, this may or may not be an issue: In the example above, it is not since the granularity required by the user is lower than that of the source, and because a one-to-one correspondence between the NATO scale and the ISPS code exists.

3.6.4.2 Epistemic Dimension

The **epistemic** elements of uncertainty representations concern the expression of uncertainty itself by the source and can be of different types [45], corresponding to some Information Quality Dimensions introduced in Sect. 3.5. We discuss here the three uncertainty types as defined by Klir and Yuan (Nonspecificity, Discord and Fuzziness) and the close connection to the mathematical expressions possibly used to represent them. Table 3.4 summarizes some examples of these different quality dimensions for the contextual variables introduced previously, further detailed below.

Nonspecificity
Nonspecificity (or imprecision) is expressed by providing several values, represented by intervals or subsets of the domain Xa of a given contextual variable a. Any subset A of Xa expresses the inability of the source to discriminate between its elements by listing all the values it "believes" as possibly true. This can be considered as the first level of uncertainty expression.

For instance, rather than a single number of vessels per unit area, the SAR image processing may output an interval of integer values, e.g., [20, 30] meaning that it is

Table 3.4 Example of contextual information quality

Contextual variables	Contextual information uncertainty		
	Imprecision		Discord
	Nonspecificity	Fuzziness	
Th—Harbor Protection Level	–	–	Bel(Th = 2) = 80 %
SS—Sea state	3 or 4	*High* waves	Bel(SS = 3) = 70 %
TD—Traffic density	[20, 30] vessels per unit area	*Medium* density	Density map turned into a probability distribution
R—Routes	Shipping versus non-shipping routes	Routes for large vessels	80 % cargo route, 20 % tanker route
t—time	Afternoon	Daylight time	N(14h00,30 min)

certain that the real number of vessels is somewhere between 20 and 30, but is not able to tell more. As another example, the AIS route extractor may label the routes according to more or less fine-grained partitions of the type of vessels, e.g., shipping routes vs nonshipping routes, or fishing vessels, cargos, ferries, etc., routes [44].

For nominal attributes, nonspecificity is commonly measured by Hartley measure which relies on the cardinality of the subset A of Xa: The lower the cardinality, the more informative the subset and the lower the uncertainty.

Discord

Discord[3] (internal) is expressed by numerical degrees (generally over the [0;1] interval) assigned to some subset A of the domain Xa and represents some belief or confidence of the source in the corresponding event A being true. This can be considered as the second level of uncertainty expression and is done by means of monotone measures [46],[4] which depending on the set of properties they satisfy are named as probabilities, possibilities, λ-measures, belief measures, upper and lower probabilities, etc. Monotone measures are built upon a binary logic, meaning that the underlying event is either true or false.

Nonadditive measures (e.g., belief, possibility) define an uncertainty interval which can be interpreted as some second-order uncertainty: the exact belief or probability degree is known only to belong to some interval. For instance, the belief and plausibility measures of a given event A, $\mathrm{Bel}(A)$, and $\mathrm{Pl}(A)$ can be interpreted as lower and upper bounds of the partially known probability of A, $\mathrm{P}(A)$.

Based on AIS contacts, a map of vessel traffic density may be estimated for a given area of interest. Being normalized, this function can be turned into a probability distribution and interpreted as a confidence one has in detecting a vessel at a specific position: The higher the value (i.e., the density), the higher the chance of finding a vessel (or making a collision, etc.). The human SAR analyst may express some degree of belief about the sea state which could be represented by a probability function or a belief function.

The informational content (or equivalently the uncertainty) is usually quantified using extended Shannon entropy measures: The more focused the monotone measure, the lower the uncertainty. Both possibilities and belief functions are able to jointly express nonspecificity and discord as reflected in the associated measures of uncertainty.

Fuzziness

The human source is also able to express uncertainty using natural language and vague concepts, such as *Low, Medium, High*. As nonspecificity, fuzziness expresses the limited ability of the source to distinguish between several values, either due to the limitation of natural language (linguistic) or to perception (epistemic). However,

---

[3]This notion of discord is an internal one, as represented for instance by a probability distribution, and is distinct to the notion of conflict between two sources discussed in Sect. 3.5.2.

[4]Monotone measures are called fuzzy measures in [46], but we prefer the term "monotone" to avoid confusion with fuzzy sets.

rather than a precise interval expressing nonspecificity only, expressing uncertainty by means of natural language terms induces a fuzzy interval: Some values belong more or less to the interval.

Fuzziness is usually expressed by fuzzy membership functions, defining then fuzzy events which may be more or less true or false. For instance, the SAR analyst rather than providing a numerical value (or even an interval of values) for the waves' height can declare that the waves are *high*. Due to that linguistic vagueness, the event "the waves are high" is neither true nor false but can be assigned some degree of truth as represented by a fuzzy membership function.

Fuzziness measures exist as well, some of them extending the Hartley measure.

Combined Uncertainty Types

The above types can be combined to express further complex uncertainty statements such as "I don't believe that the waves are high" (fuzziness and discord), "I believe that the object is either a Trawler or a Seiner" (nonspecificity and discord), etc. Some mathematical frameworks are better dedicated to represent these different types of uncertainty which often requires transformation between frameworks as discussed in Sect. 3.5.1.

3.6.4.3   Semantic Dimension

The **semantic** elements of uncertainty representations concern the meaning of the uncertainty expressions. Uncertain contextual information can also be characterized according to its semantic content for both ontological and epistemic elements.

About the ontological elements, the truth assignment defines the values of reference considered as the "truth" by the source, and define the semantic of the underlying logic. For instance, the meaning of linguistic terms (such as *high*) may differ from one source to another, which would lead to different fuzzy membership functions, in the case this model is used for the representation of linguistic terms.

The interpretation of the monotone function numerical values refer to how these values have been obtained, and commonly distinguish between objective (through statistics leading to a frequentist interpretation or classically by enumerating all the possible states) and subjective (through a mental process). Most of human statements are subjective expressing a degree of belief the analyst is not necessary able to explain the underlying reasoning. For instance, the cargo captain saying "the probability that the vessel is a fishing vessel is 0.8" is a subjective assessment compared to an objective assessment based on an AIS vessels enumeration such as "80 % of vessels of the area are fishing vessels".

Regardless of the way the values have been obtained, several meanings can further be assigned either as a confidence degree, belief degree, likelihood degree, betting degree, fuzzy membership degree, possibility degree, etc.

3.6.4.4 Perspectives for Uncertainty Alignment of Contextual Information

Any of the elements described above should have its associated uncertainty alignment task. Indeed, in order to reach a common referencing framework, one should take care how two different descriptions of the world can be conciliated. This includes not only the sets of concepts and links (commonly referred as ontology alignment) but also the domain of associated variables which further constrain the epistemic expression of uncertainty. Indeed, how to aggregate information about the wave length (real number scale) with that about the sea state (integers) with that about the wind speed? How to aggregate information expressed on different types of scales?

Epistemic uncertainty transformations address the problem of transforming possibilities in probabilities, belief functions in possibilities, etc., which is sometimes done at the price of a loss of information, as discussed in Sect. 3.5.1.

Although barely addressed, the problem of semantic alignment of uncertainty representation is also of interest: What is the meaning of the resulting aggregation of a frequentist probability distribution with a subjective probability? Although the tools exist to provide an updated or aggregated measure, its resulting meaning is not clear.

3.7 Summary

This chapter has introduced the issues involved with both the representation and propagation of uncertainties within and across varying categories of contextual information. It was asserted both theoretically and in the use case example that there are challenges involved in defining a coherent architectural approach and design to the handling of contextual information and its uncertainties when there are disparate types of contextual information present in an IF process. Further, these issues become even more complex when there is the combination of disparate types of contextual information coupled across a multilevel (in the JDL sense) IF Inferencing and estimation process. As was mentioned early in the chapter, the more that these issues are examined, the stronger it is that what seems to be needed is a kind of overarching context-monitoring and "common referencing" process that is assuring that evolving multilevel estimates are coherent in the sense of the composite influences of the contextual information across the levels. Whether the best way to architect this scheme as a Middleware element of an architecture or to keep the operations within any given JDL-level of operation is the type of architectural tradeoff that needs to be carried out. Further, the issue of uncertainty normalization and transformation as a fundamental requirement in any nontrivial case for dealing with contextual exploitation is one that remains fairly new to the IF community and both the methods for such transformations and their placement in an architecture will also have to be assessed for future robust applications.

References

1. K. Sambhoos, J. Llinas, Research in Evaluation Methods for Data Fusion-Capable Tactical Platforms and Distributed Multi-platform Systems in Electronic Warfare and Information-Warfare Related Missions, Final Technical Report, Center for Multisource Information Fusion, University at Buffalo, Feb 2009
2. F.E. White, A model for data fusion, in *Proceedings of 1st National Symposium on Sensor Fusion*, Johns Hopkins Applied Physics Lab., Laurel, MD, July 1988
3. A.N. Steinberg, C.L. Bowman, F.E. White, Revisions to the JDL model, sensor fusion: architectures, algorithms, and applications, in *Proceedings of the SPIE*, vol. 3719 (1999)
4. J. Llinas, C. Bowman, G. Rogova, A. Steinberg, Revisiting the JDL Data Fusion Model II, in *Proceedings of the International Conference on Information Fusion*, Stockholm, Sweden, July 2004
5. O. Kessler, Functional description of the data fusion process, in *Technical Report for the Office of Naval Technology Data Fusion Development Strategy*, Naval Air Development Center, Warminster, PA, Nov 1991
6. E. Blasch, S. Plano, JDL Level 5 fusion model: user refinement issues and applications in group tracking, in *Aerosense Conference, Proceedings of the SPIE*, vol. 4729 (2002)
7. A.N. Steinberg, C.L. Bowman, Rethinking the JDL data fusion levels, in *Proceedings of the Military Sensing Symposia (MSS) National Symposium on Sensor and Data Fusion (NSSDF)*, Columbia, MD, July 2004
8. L. Snidaro, I. Visentini, J. Llinas, G.L. Foresti, Context in fusion: some considerations in a JDL perspective, in *Proceedings of the International Conference on Information Fusion, Istanbul*, Turkey, July 2013
9. R. Glinton, J. Giampapa, K. Sycara, A Markov random field model of context for high-level information fusion, in *Proceedings of the 9th International Conference on Information Fusion*, Florence, Italy, July 2006
10. A.N. Steinberg, C.L. Bowman, Adaptive context discovery and exploitation, in *Proceedings of the 16th International Conference on Information Fusion*, Istanbul, Turkey, 9–12 July 2013
11. M. Baldauf, S. Dustdar, F. Rosenberg, A survey on context-aware systems. Int. J. Ad Hoc Ubiquit. Comput. **2**(4) (2007)
12. M. Weiser, The computer for the 21st century. Sci. Am. 94–104 (1991)
13. R. Want, A. Hopper, V. Falcao, J. Gibbons, The active badge location system. ACM Trans. Inf. Syst. **10**(1), 91–102
14. H. Chen, T. Finin, A. Joshi, An ontology for context-aware pervasive computing environments. Knowl. Eng. Rev. **18**(3) (2003)
15. M.A. Razzaque, S. Dobson, P. Nixon, Classification and modeling of the quality of contextual information. J. Auton. Trusted Comput. (2006)
16. M. Kaenampornpan, E. O'Neill, V. Kostakos, A. Warr, Classifying context classifications: an activity theory perspective, in *Proceedings of 2nd UK-UbiNet Workshop*, University of Cambridge, UK, 5–7 May 2004
17. Wikipedia; Ontology: http://en.wikipedia.org/wiki/Ontology_%28information_science%29
18. R. Krummenacher, T. Strang, Ontology-based context modeling, in *Workshop on Context-Aware Proactive Systems*, 2007
19. A.-C., Boury-Brisset, Ontology-based approach for information fusion, in *Proceedings of 6th International Conference on Information Fusion*, Cairns, Australia, July 2003
20. M. Kayaalp, Why do we need probabilistic approaches to ontologies and the associated data, in *Proceedings of the AMIA Annual Symposium*, 2005
21. K.B. Laskey, P.C.G. Costa, T. Janssen, Probabilistic ontologies for knowledge fusion, in *Proceedings of 11th International Conference on Information Fusion*, Cologne, Germany, July 2008

22. P.C.G. Costa, Bayesian semantics for the Semantic Web, Doctoral Dissertation, Volgenau School of Information Technology and Engineering, George Mason University, Fairfax, VA, 2005

23. K.B. Laskey, MEBN: a language for first-order bayesian knowledge bases. Artif. Intell. **172**(2–3) (2007)

24. R.N. Carvalho, P.C.G. Costa, K.B. Laskey, K.C. Chang, PROGNOS: predictive situational awareness with probabilistic ontologies, in *Proceedings of 13th International Conference on Information Fusion*, Edinburgh, Scotland, July 2010

25. A. Manzoor, H. Truong, S. Dustdar, On the evaluation of quality of context. Smart Sens. Context Lect. Notes Comput. Sci. **5279**, 140–153 (2008)

26. G. Rogova, E. Bossé, Information quality in information fusion, in *Proceedings of 13th International Conference on Information Fusion*, Edinburgh, Scotland, July 2010

27. S. Arunkumar, Trust assessment when observing and orienting with uncertain, multi-source streaming information, in *Proceedings of the 2013 Pervasive Computing and Communications Workshops (PERCOM Workshops)*, San Diego, CA, March 2013

28. M. Oussalah, On the probability/possibility transformations: a comparative analysis. Int. J. Gen. Syst. **29**(5), 671–718 (2000)

29. J.F. Geer, G.J. Klir, A mathematical analysis of information-preserving transformations between probabilistic and possibilistic formulations of uncertainty. Int. J. Gen. Syst. **20**, 143–176 (1992)

30. G.J. Klir, B. Parviz, Probability-possibility transformations: a comparison. Int. J. Gen. Syst. **21** (1), 291–310 (1992)

31. G.J. Klir, T. Folger, *Fuzzy Sets, Uncertainty, and Information* (Prentice Hall, Englewood Cliffs, 1988)

32. C.L. Bowman, Possibilistic versus Probabilistic Tradeoff for Data Association, in *Proceedings of SPIE Conference on Signal and Data Processing of Small Targets*, vol. 1954, Orlando, FL, 1993

33. A. Ayoun, P. Smets, Data association in multi-target detection using the transferable belief model. Int. J. Intell. Syst. Spec. Issue Data Knowl. Fusion **16**(10), 1167–1182 (2001)

34. G. Tauer, R. Nagi, M. Sudit, The Graph Association Problem: Mathematical Models and a Lagrangian Heuristic, in *Naval Research Logistics*, vol. 60(3) (Feb 2013), pp. 251–268

35. G. Tauer, R. Nagi, A map-reduce lagrangian heuristic for multidimensional assignment problems with decomposable costs. Parallel Comput. **39**(11), 653–668 (2013)

36. K. Date, G.A. Gross, S. Khopkar, R. Nagi, K. Sambhoos, Data association and graph analytical processing of hard and soft intelligence data, in *Proceedings of 2013 16th International Conference on Information Fusion (FUSION)*, Istanbul, pp. 404–411

37. G. Gross, R. Nagi, K. Sambhoos, D. Schlegel, S. Shapiro, G. Tauer, Towards hard+soft data fusion: processing architecture and implementation for the joint fusion and analysis of hard and soft intelligence data, in *15th International Conference on Information Fusion*, Singapore, 9–12 July 2012

38. E. Shahbazian, G. Rogova, M.J. DeWeert (eds.) *Harbour Protection Through Data Fusion Technologies*. NATO Science for Peace and Security Series—C: Environmental Security, Tallinn, Estonia, 27 June–1 July 2005. Proceedings of the NATO Advanced Research Workshop on Data Fusion Technologies for Harbour Protection (Springer, Dordrecht, 2009)

39. J. Garcia, J. Gomez-Romero, M.A. Patricio, J.M. Molina, G. Rogova, On the representation and exploitation of context knowledge in a harbor surveillance scenario, in *Proceedings of the 14th International Conference on Information Fusion*, Chicago, Illinois, USA, 5–8 July 2011

40. J. Locke, C. Strode, K. Bryan, A matrix game to support the development of NATO harbour protection capability, Technical Report CMRE-MR-2015–006, NATO STO Centre for Maritime Research and Experimentation, 2015

41. A.-L. Jousselme, G. Pallotta, J. Locke, A risk game to measure the impact of information quality on human threat assessment and decision making, Technical Report. CMRE-FR-2015-009, NATO STO Centre for Maritime Research and Experimentation, 2015

42. J. Dezert, P. Gill, S. Godsill, J. Lavery, A. Martin, S. Maskell, D. Mercier, The uncertainty forum, plenary session presentation, in *International Conference on Information Fusion*, Edinburgh, UK, July 2010
43. STANAG 1241, NATO standard identity description structure for tactical use—MAROPS, 5th edn, April 2005. NATO unclassified
44. G. Pallotta, M. Vespe, K. Bryan, Vessel pattern knowledge discovery from AIS data—a framework for anomaly detection and route prediction, Entropy (2013)
45. G.J. Klir, B. Yuan, *Fuzzy Sets and Fuzzy Logic: Theory and Applications* (Prentice Hall International, Upper Saddle River, 1995)
46. G. Choquet, Theory of capacities. Annales de l'Institut Fourier **5**, 131–295 (1953)
47. M. Sugeno, Fuzzy measures and fuzzy integrals—A survey, in *Fuzzy Automata and Decision Process*, eds. by M.M. Gupta, G.N. Saridis, B.R. Gaines, chap. 6 (North-Holland, Amsterdam, 1977), pp. 89–102
48. G.J. Klir, Generalized information theory: aims, results, and open problems. Reliab. Eng. Syst. Safety **85**, 21–38 (2004)
49. P. Smets, Imperfect information: imprecision—Uncertainty, in *Uncertainty Management in Information Systems. From Needs to Solutions,* eds. by A. Motro, P. Smets (Kluwer Academic Publishers, Dordrecht, 1997), pp. 225–254
50. STANAG 2511, Intelligence reports (edition 1), Jan 2003 (NATO unclassified)

Chapter 4
Contextual Tracking Approaches in Information Fusion

Erik Blasch, Chun Yang, Jesús García, Lauro Snidaro
and James Llinas

Abstract Many information fusion solutions work well in the intended scenarios; but the applications, supporting data, and capabilities change over varying contexts. One example is weather data for electro-optical target trackers of which standards have evolved over decades. The operating conditions of technology changes, sensor/target variations, and the contextual environment can inhibit performance if not included in the initial systems design. In this chapter, we seek to define and categorize different types of contextual information. We describe five contextual information categories that support target tracking: (1) domain knowledge from a user to aid the information fusion process through selection, cueing, and analysis, (2) environment-to-hardware processing for sensor management, (3) known distribution of entities for situation/threat assessment, (4) historical traffic behavior for situation awareness patterns of life (POL), and (5) road information for target tracking and identification. Appropriate characterization and representation of contextual information is needed for future high-level information fusion designs to take advantage of the large data content available for a priori knowledge target tracking algorithm construction, implementation, and application.

E. Blasch (✉)
Air Force Research Lab, Rome, NY, USA
e-mail: erik.blasch@gmail.com

C. Yang
Sigtem Technology Inc., San Mateo, CA, USA
e-mail: chunyang@sigtem.com

J. García
Universidad Carlos III de Madrid, Madrid, Spain
e-mail: jgherrer@inf.uc3m.es

L. Snidaro
University of Udine, Udine, Italy
e-mail: lauro.snidaro@uniud.it

J. Llinas
Center for Multisource Information Fusion and Department of Industrial and Systems
Engineering, University at Buffalo, Buffalo, NY, USA
e-mail: llinas@buffalo.edu

© Springer International Publishing Switzerland (outside the USA) 2016   73
L. Snidaro et al. (eds.), *Context-Enhanced Information Fusion*,
Advances in Computer Vision and Pattern Recognition,
DOI 10.1007/978-3-319-28971-7_4

Keywords Context-aware tracking · Sensor management · Patterns of life · Traffic behavior · Road information · Situation awareness · Group tracking · Wide-area motion imagery

4.1 Introduction

Target tracking has matured to include non-Gaussian nonlinear tracking methods to detect numerous targets over varying terrain. However, there are needed external sources for robust target tracking solutions such as map updates, roads and road conflation, detection of patterns of life, trafficability maps, and other products that relate to context information. Figure 4.1 highlights some issues where (1) *cues* relate to standard situation assessment of target tracking and classification, (2) *context* supports situation awareness over physical, computational, and environment issues, and (3) *channels* for situation understanding over ambient intelligence, language, and networks.

Target tracking is a subset of information fusion which supports many applications [2]. One commonly accepted information fusion model is the Data Fusion Information Group (DFIG) model [3] (shown in Fig. 4.2) originally developed for military systems, but used by many in the International Society of Information Fusion (www.isif.org) as a common processing framework.

The levels (L) determine the processing in the system such as L0 data registration, L1 object tracking and ATR assessment [4] (shown in Fig. 4.3), L2 situation awareness [5, 6] and L3 impact assessment [7]. The complementary control levels are: L4 sensor management, L5 user refinement [8], and L6 mission management. Figure 4.3 highlights that target tracking composes many aspects of which all the

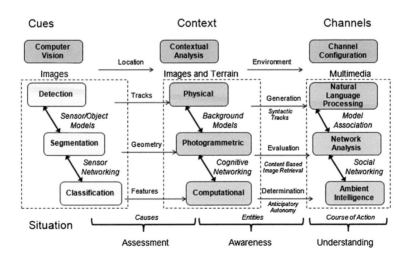

Fig. 4.1 Contextual awareness and understanding [1]

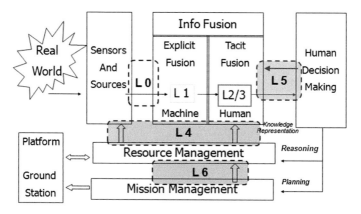

Fig. 4.2 Data fusion information group model (L = Level)

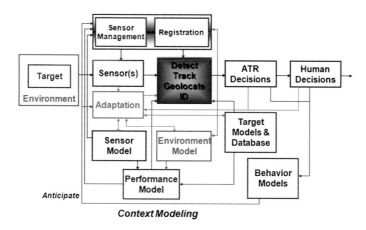

Fig. 4.3 Context modeling to support target tracking

models (e.g., sensor, target, environment, behavior, and performance) inherently provide context to improve target tracking performance.

Context has well been explored in the last decade for target tracking and information fusion issues especially for group tracking [9]. Using a group tracking example [10], as adapted from Steinberg [11], context supports all levels of information fusion and management, shown in Fig. 4.4. For example, context has been reported for user refinement (L5) [12], situation assessment (L2) [13], resource management (L4) [14], and threat/scenario assessment (L3) [15, 16] of targets. Current needs of information fusion and target tracking models include information exploitation and management to take advantage of all the contextual information [17]. Context can therefore be exploited as binding element for the synergic interaction of techniques residing at different DFIG levels [18, 19].

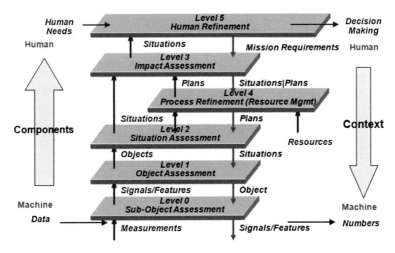

Fig. 4.4 Context in support of information fusion [8]

Context is a widely used term by philosophers and scientists with many different definitions and connotations [20–22], also discussed in Chap. 1. Nevertheless, there are very general definitions where context is a subset of a physical or conceptual state, which is related to a specific entity, as in Dey and Abowd [23] where an application-driven definition is reported. Context can be framed as "*any information that can be used to characterize the situation of entities that are considered relevant to the interaction between a user and an application*", or more general, "between the operator and the system" [24]. It is generally an addition to sensing devices data, and "surrounds" a situation of interest, aiding comprehension and interaction [18].

4.2 Background on Contextual Tracking Methods

Context in support of tracking has well been explored to support or enhance target state estimation and display the results of simultaneous tracking and classification/identification to aid user contextual analysis [25]. Of the many examples explored over the years, context can be based on three aspects: sensor information, target capabilities, and environmental constraints [26]. It is the environmental constraints that affords **context-enhanced target tracking** (DFIG Level 1), wherein improved performance is reported. While the advent of big data machine analytics (Sect. 4.4), due to high-performance computers and cloud computing, is new, one of the first context tracking papers uses video results to index context [27].

For target tracking, other mediums such as radar-based ***group tracking*** sought methods combined the use of group target associations as well as these groups of targets ***constrained on roads*** [28, 29]. In this sense, context was used in the form of both the targets themselves as well as the environment. Then, researchers applied methods for convoy tracking [30], improvement of track association [31], use of speed for kinematic target selection [32], and map information to improve target location accuracy [33]. Other examples included feature selection based on context [34] and learning spatial relations for moving target assessment [35]. Recent results include using road networks to correct for track bias [36].

As contextual information from roads added to tracking algorithms, new non-linear tracking methods were demonstrated to show improvement not only to capture **non-linear motion estimation**, but also how contextual information from roads support the motion estimation [37]. In specific domains such as airport traffic monitoring, the knowledge of taxiway layout and motion rules at surface allowed significant improvement in tracking results [38]. Movement of vehicles expanded to include developments in people tracking [39], and methods to improve driver's ability to stay on roads [40, 41]. Similarly, methods of mathematical performance analysis were developed for maneuvering target pose [42], maneuvering target state estimation [43] and tracking robustness for spatial-temporal context [44].

In a related approach, improvements in **audio tracking** utilized context. For audio tracks, methods were developed for phonemics [45] and use of semantic context for modeling audio tracking [46]. Other methods included context to constrain Hidden Markov Models [47] and beat tracking [48]. These methods could be useful for determining the tracks associated with targets on roads with GPS capabilities and cell phones [49].

In 2007, there were multiple applications of using context to support **video tracking**. Sanchez et al. [50], demonstrated tracking for video by using both a general tracking layer and a context layer. Specifically, the context layer supports track initiation, maintenance, and updates of the tracks. Other methods included appearance context to re-acquire lost targets [51] which can be used to restart lost tracks or initiate new tracks. Other prominent methods included pedestrian systems [52] and methods to improve target search for video-based simultaneous tracking and classification [53] (as an extension by Nguyen to [44]).

Further refinements of the use of contextual information supported the estimation algorithms for **sensor management** (DFIG, Level 4 Fusion) such as matrix refinement [54] and sensor models [55]. Contextual estimation constraints included road networks [56] and track states [57]. Likewise, "**context-aware visual tracking**," [58] was coined to demonstrate that tracking multiple objects in the scene provides context for the designated target. New developments also supported the use of tracking to update other contexts such as ontologies for situation assessment (DFIG Level 2) video tracking [59] (as an extension by Sanchez et al. to [50]), surveillance [60] and threat assessment (DFIG Level 3) [61]. Finally, using context supports route planning [62], scene context [63], and multimodal fusion [64]. As an example, context tracking issues were summarized in a Bayesian Tracking tutorial by Koch [65].

The representation of contextual domain knowledge with **ontologies** allowed the integration of data from available hard/soft sources (surveillance sensors, human reports, databases, etc.) in the context of a situation [66]. Gomez-Romero et al. [67]

utilized ontology-based models to specify concepts and relationships of contextual knowledge by separation of context reasoning and feedback to support track management. Contextual information is represented with ontologies, which are used to model the heterogeneous entities present in the domain (the abstract scene model) and the normal situations (the normalcy model). The normalcy model contains axioms and rules to classify vessel behavior as compliant to the operational rules or not in a maritime domain awareness scenario. The harbor domain brings challenges to advanced fusion systems [68]. Also, the representation of context with ontologies has been used to classify harbor objects and basic situations by deductive reasoning according to the harbor regulations (e.g. navigation rules) [69].

In 2011, there were many tracking solutions using tracking as method of ***dealing with environment context*** for such aspects of occlusions [70, 71] and feature adaptation for target signature variation [72, 73]. A novel method by Rice and Vasquez [74] demonstrated the use of context for hyperspectral sensor-based target tracking. Other developments included methods for effective computing [75], hybridized methods for group tracking [76], multimodal fusion from electro-optical and infrared sensing [77], anomaly detection from known path of travels [78], and track-segment association [79]. Finally, another application versus ground target tracking, was for underwater tracking [80, 81].

Contextual tracking, aided by situational awareness, has been explored through ***logical methods***. Visentini and Snidaro [24] explored context of natural language expression of physical entities in environments to reduce the ambiguity and uncertainty of measurements through likelihood maps to constrain the location estimate of a target in a building. They followed up [82] by introducing domain expert knowledge as context through Markov Logical Networks (MLN) which are a form of Statistical Relational Learning (SRL) with advanced results in [83]. MLNs combine first-order logic and graphical models (e.g. Markov). First-order logic, in contrast to propositional logic, represents complex environments in a concise way. Contextual information was developed for a maritime domain tracking example by using the "isA" formulation over locations, tracks, situations, and threats. An operator supplied given evidence which provided contextual information to refine the sensor observed evidence (DFIG Level 5). As related to ontological methods [60] for insertion of contextual information into tracking systems, logical methods support situation awareness for high-level information fusion.

Continuations of ground target tracking methods included methods for mobile tracking [84], ***context-aided tracking*** [85], and occlusions [86]. Other methods included learning target labeling [87], vehicle detection [88], and background context [89]. Currently methods include using context for sensor management and placement [90, 91], anomaly detection from stochastic free grammars [92], color [93], and finally towards the growth of machine analytics in dictionary learning to support target identification context [94].

One final area of discussion of context is in moving target classification assessment. This has been coined as "***context enhancement***" [95] as improvements on tracking and classification/recognition/identification [96, 97]. Context awareness including: environments, sensors, and targets, improved multi-source robustness

[98] and clutter suppression [99]. Currently, context-enhancement is being mapped to common qualitative and quantitative results for user assessment (DFIG Level 5) and refinement of context moving and stationary target data (DFIG Level 1) [100]. Next we present an overview of the categories of contextual analysis for target tracking based on the literature review.

4.3   Contextual Tracking

From the review of the many methods in contextual tracking, we sought to organize the previous methods as well as consider future needs. Our preliminary categorization includes:

1. Road information for target tracking and identification, group detection, and *context-aided tracking*;
2. Environment-to-hardware processing for sensor modeling/management, and *context enhancement*;
3. Historical traffic behavior for situation awareness patterns of life (POL) for *context awareness*;
4. Known distribution of entities for situation/threat/scenario assessment for *context inference*; and
5. Domain knowledge from a user to aid tracking through selection and analysis for *context cognition*.

Categories (1) and (2) have well been vetted in the literature. Category (3) relates to the use of tracking as well as the constraints available to provide context awareness. For example, in video tracking, many examples track the scene to infer behavior. Over the many issues for contextual target tracking, we looked at the variations in the themes and while there is discussion on *context awareness* (as situation awareness using ontologies and logical networks), there was limited analysis of connections to threat assessment [101] for *context inference*. Ideas exist for game-theoretic modeling of multiple affiliation entities being tracked [102]; however, there is a need for context-based human, social, cultural, and behavior (HSCB) modeling and assessment [103]. For example, HSCB can be used can be used with road information to isolate which pedestrians, how fast cars are moving on roads, and clutter mitigation that does not conform to social, cultural and behavioral norms which leads to human, animal, vehicle and clutter (HVAC) target categorization. As detailed in [18], García, Snidaro, and Visentini advocate the need for *context cognition* by the user (DFIG L5 fusion).

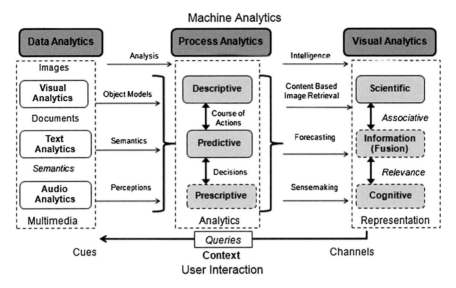

Fig. 4.5 Big data analysis

4.4 Machine Analytics for Contextual Tracking

With the enormous amount of data types, distributed locations, and various connections to different applications (e.g. finance to surveillance) resulting from the
expansion of the World-Wide Web, new techniques are needed to exploit context.
Related concepts recently emerging are context awareness (Fig. 4.1) and machine,
descriptive, prescriptive, predictive, visual, and other analytics, shown in Fig. 4.5.
There are three issues of importance *hardware* (e.g., Apache Hadoop data intensive
distributed architecture), *software* (e.g., machine analytics), and *user/domain*
applications [104] (e.g. visual analytics, text analytics). Data, process, and visual
analytics pave the wave for big-data processing to utilize more contextual information in target tracking [17].

4.5 Contextual Tracking Sensors, Targets,
and Environments

Using a multimodal cooperative sensing example, we are interested in simultaneous
target tracking and identification (STID) [105]. Multi-modal measurements could
be from infrared, visual, and/or wide-area motion imagery (WAMI). Together,
contextual environmental modeling of the weather for the aerial sensors and the
terrain information for the ground sensors would aid in the analysis of the complete
system for accurate automatic target recognition (ATR) (i.e., high probability of
detection with low false alarms [106]). One recent complex challenge that requires

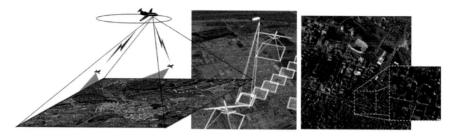

Fig. 4.6 Wide area motion imagery (WAMI) data

Table 4.1 Contextual analysis over the levels of information fusion

Info fusion	Measurement	Model	Algorithm
Level 0—data registration	Pixels	Terrain	Road-assisted
Level 1—object assessment	Kinematic/features	Kinematic/target	Context aware (assisted) tracking
Level 2—situation assessment	Object groups	Behavioral	Group tracking
Level 3—impact assessment	Threat (FFN)	Intent/allegiance	Anomaly detection
Level 4—sensor management	Sensor type	Camera	Sensor, appearance, models
Level 5—user refinement	POL	Cognitive	Activity, behavioral analysis
Level 6—mission management	Objectives	Goal-driven	Social, cultural modeling

contextual information is WAMI target tracking [107] with information management that supports moving intelligence [108]. Complications of real-time WAMI sensor processing include a low frame rates [109] and mappings to geospatial intelligence systems [110] such as environmental (e.g., terrain modeling). Together, machine analytics and contextual tracking support enhanced situation awareness [111] for cooperative control of multimodal sensors as depicted in Fig. 4.6.

Accurate contextual statistical modeling is needed of the environment, sensor, and target data (i.e., operating conditions) to support the mathematical algorithms as shown in Table 4.1. Note that identification includes composing ATR and kinematic data for threat assessment of friend, foe, and neutral (FFN) affiliation [112].

Managed layers of sensors offer capabilities to robustly track targets over various operating conditions of differing targets, sensors, and environments. Numerous advances in algorithms, database methods, and sensors offer opportunities for future capabilities. Inherent in the analysis are three techniques: (1) feature extraction, processing, and tracking for targeting [113], (2) common data sets for analysis and algorithm comparison over environmental conditions, and (3) persistent wide-area motion imagery for long-term consistent sensing.

4.5.1   Feature Tracking and Identification (Targets)

For tracking targets, various features are important to determine the automatic target recognition/classification/identification, behavior, and location [114]. These features (such as group dynamics) would aid in tracking through occlusions, illumination changes, and links to common data bases [115, 116]. The behavioral features are those related to the global movement, relation of vehicles to the center motion for local movements, and common attributes that aid in affiliation/association of members in group movement. Features can also be elements of graphical methods, Markov Logic Networks, ontologies, and situation attributes that can be continuous or discrete to constrain target state estimates (e.g., recognition/classification/ identification, behavior, and location).

4.5.2   Wide Area Motion Imagery (Sensors)

Wide Area Motion Imagery (WAMI) is an emerging capability that affords large spatial coverage, constant monitoring over time, and potential for diverse frequency sensing (e.g., electro-optical, radar) for tracking and identification wide area surveillance [117]. Since the WAMI data covers a city (see Fig. 4.7), the ability to maintain track (after initiation) is increased as the objects are within the sensed region of interest for potentially an extended duration [118], activity analysis [119, 120], and occlusion detection [121]. Likewise, with constant staring, there is the increased advantage of extending track lifetime by linking associated tracks, projecting tracks onto road networks, recovering from lost tracks, and coordinating hand-off to ground sensors. Finally, with the advent of WAMI, there are other modalities emerging for electro-optical visual cameras, moving synthetic aperture radar (SAR), and hyperspectral imaging (HSI) methods. Together, these sensors provide a rich new set of contextual data that needs to be exploited using novel fusion (e.g. ATR) methods over small pixel resolutions in addition to the traditional vehicle tracking.

Fig. 4.7 Wide area motion imagery (WAMI) examples, context, and patterns of life [124]

4.5.3   Situations and Scenarios (Environment)

WAMI data provides new opportunities that relate to targets [122] and environments [123], increasingly so when combined with other sensors such as ground-based detectors. WAMI data sets cover a broad range of environmental conditions and various target behaviors. Using contextual information for target tracking algorithm development, the basic techniques such as tracking and behavioral semantic labels can be applied over a larger spatial distances and temporal intervals. As an example, using in the Columbus Large Image Format (CLIF) data set, identified contextual conditions include sensor system performance (camera motion and frame rate, contrast, and camera model fidelity), targets (turning, type, and speed), and environments (shade, occlusion, on and off roads), as shown in Fig. 4.7. The environment can be used to constrain target motion (e.g., roads), but also the tracking measurements can be used as history of normalcy and abnormal behavior. For example, the normalcy models, shown in Fig. 4.7, of tracking behavior demonstrate vehicle data that are used to extract the roads including direction, speed, and turns.

4.6   Road Constrained Tracking and Identification Example

4.6.1   Road Network (Environment)

In this section, we introduce the idea of representing the road network with one-dimensional (1D) models for target tracking. The 1D model simplifies the target kinematics considerably but renders the observation equations highly non-linear. A key merit of this 1D modeling is it relates a tracking filter more closely to the physical reality since a ground vehicle has one degree of freedom (1DOF) when traveling along roads. In addition, this modeling also provides a means to explicitly incorporate road information into the tracking filters.

From the point of view of target tracking, the ground target trajectory when in traverse of a road network can be modeled as straight or curved segments connected with arcs of different curvature. A ground target spends most of time on the straight or curved segments with speed-up and slow-down near both ends and then makes quick and sharp turns along the connecting arcs. Three pieces of information can uniquely locate a mobile target: time, street name (a road segment), and street number (distance relative to a reference point on the street).

For simplicity, we consider a 2D map of roads without topographic features. It can then be generalized to 3D with height. Similarly, we consider a width-less road at this point of time, which may represent the centerline of either left or right lane of

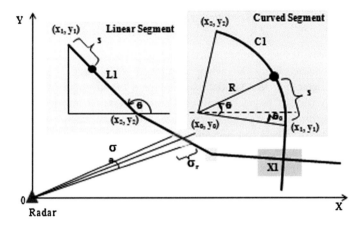

Fig. 4.8 1D representation of road segments

a road. The road width is meaningless for a point target if the width is comparable to the measurement error. It is always possible to add the road width and even surface orientation either deterministically or probabilistically when extended targets are considered with high-resolution sensors.

Figure 4.8 shows an area map, which has four linear segments, one curved segment, and one intersection. As shown, only large arcs are parameterized while short brief curves are replaced with direct connection of linear segments. Such a simplification depends on the length of a curve and the sampling rate of radar.

For linear segments, there can be several parameterizations, one of which is presented below. Each linear segment is characterized by two pairs of points: the starting pair (x_1, y_1) and the ending pair (x_2, y_1), from which the length of the segment as well as its orientation can be calculated as:

$$\theta = \tan^{-1}\left(\frac{y_1 = y_2}{x_2 - x_1}\right) \tag{4.1a}$$

$$S = \sqrt{(x_2 - x_1)^2 + (y_2 - y_1)^2} \tag{4.1b}$$

In the model, the location of a target along a road segment is determined by its distance from a reference point, typically the starting point of the segment. As a mileage count, this parameter has a physical meaning and provides the same reading as the odometer in the ground vehicle. As such, this mileage count has its first and second time-derivatives being the speed and acceleration, respectively. Kinematic modeling of this variable depends on how a driver negotiates the road and will be addressed in the next section.

Denote the mileage count by s. Then an arbitrary point within the linear segment is given by:

$$\begin{cases} x(s) = x_1 + s \cos \theta \\ y(s) = y_1 + s \sin \theta \end{cases}; \quad 0 \le s \le S \tag{4.2}$$

where θ and S are given by Eqs. (4.1a) and (4.1b), respectively.

For a *circular arc* as shown in Fig. 4.8, it can be characterized by three pairs of points: the starting pair (x_1, y_1), the ending pair (x_2, y_2), and the circle center (x_0, y_0), It is then easy to determine the initial angle, the radius and the angle extended by the arc (the cosine theorem) as:

$$\theta_0 = \tan^{-1}\left(\frac{y_1 - y_0}{x_1 - x_0}\right) \tag{4.3a}$$

$$\begin{aligned} R &= \sqrt{(x_0 - x_1)^2 + (y_0 - y_1)^2} \\ &= \sqrt{(x_0 - x_2)^2 + (y_0 - y_2)^2} \end{aligned} \tag{4.3b}$$

$$\Theta = \cos^{-1}\left[1 - \frac{(x_2 - x_1)^2 + (y_2 - y_1)^2}{2R^2}\right] \tag{4.3c}$$

Using the mileage count s as the parameter, any point along the curved segment is given by:

$$\begin{aligned} x(s) &= x_0 + R \cos(\theta_0 + \theta) \\ &= x_0 + R \cos\left(\theta_0 + \frac{s}{R}\right) \end{aligned} \tag{4.4a}$$

$$\begin{aligned} y(s) &= y_0 + R \sin(\theta_0 + \theta) \\ &= y_0 + R \sin\left(\theta_0 + \frac{s}{R}\right) \end{aligned} \tag{4.4b}$$

where $0 \le \theta \le \Theta$, θ_0, R and Θ are given in Eqs. (4.3a)–(4.3c).

For a road segment of *arbitrary shape*, it can be locally curve-fitted into linear and circular segments as in Fig. 4.8. Alternatively, it can be characterized with a nonlinear model after polynomial fitting. It can even be represented numerically with a look-up table. In any rate, the 1D representation of a road segment can be written as:

$$\begin{cases} x(s) \mid g_x(s) \\ y(s) + g_y(s) \end{cases}; \quad 0 \le s \le S \tag{4.5}$$

where $g_x(\cdot)$ and $g_y(\cdot)$ are continuous functions of s.

For a local area map, when the roads are characterized as y-functions of x (a Cartesian coordinate system), there are many y values for each given x, unless each road is named separately. In this sense, it is still a two-dimensional representation not in x and y but in street name and street number.

4.6.2   Models for Target Measurements (Sensors)

Shown in Fig. 4.8 is a tracking radar located at the origin of the X-Y coordinate system. The radar provides the measurements of range and bearing to target, denoted by r and θ, respectively. The measurements are related to the target position (x, y) in a nonlinear manner:

$$\begin{bmatrix} r \\ \theta \end{bmatrix} = \begin{bmatrix} \sqrt{x^2 + y^2} \\ \tan^{-1}(y/x) \end{bmatrix} + \begin{bmatrix} n_r \\ n_\theta \end{bmatrix} \tag{4.6}$$

where n_r and n_θ are the measurements noise with variances σ_r^2 and σ_θ^2, respectively.

Both r and θ are implicit functions of s through the intermediates of the target position (x, y), which can be written in a more general form as:

$$\begin{cases} r(s) = h_r(x(s), y(s)) = h_r(g_x(s), g_y(s)) \\ r(s) = h_\theta(y(s), y(s)) = h_\theta(g_x(s), g_y(s)) \end{cases} \tag{4.7}$$

where $0 \le s \le S$.

4.6.3   Models for a Target at a Road Intersection (Targets)

We now consider a ground vehicle running down to an intersection and about to choose its road after the junction. If the traffic light is green for its direction or there is no stop sign at the intersection, the vehicle may slow down slightly and proceed to cross the intersection if the traffic is clear. We leave the issues related to interaction with other vehicles at the intersections to the next subsection and concentrate on a single target.

With a stop sign at an intersection, a target initially running at a constant velocity will follow the stopping model described above. From the point of view of a target tracker, it can foresee several possibilities: the target remains at the intersection or it turns onto one of the roads out of the intersection if a U-turn is ruled out and no other irregular move will occur.

The more a target stays at the stop, the greater is the probability that it will move at the next observation time. The mean time for a single target to move across a clear intersection can be used to set up the transition probability as a function of sojourn time at the stop.

Once on the new road out of the intersection, the target will speed up and then stay at a newly established constant velocity for that road segment. With the 1D representation of roads, the formulation of exit hypotheses is quite easy, each being one of the possible roads extending out from the intersection. Each road model will be used to propagate the target's mileage count along that road and to generate the measurement prediction for update. Once a road is confirmed as being true, all other hypotheses will be deleted.

The change from one road segment to another requires activation of a new road (and simultaneous deactivation of the old) and initialization of a new mileage count. If the arc connecting two road segments is short and smoothing, some of target state components, namely, velocity s and acceleration s, can be transferred directly. If the connecting arc is short but their orientations differ greatly, the process noise in the filter may be raised a little bit to account for speed change.

The ease at which the transition from one road segment to another is one of the advantages the ID modeling technique offers in tracking ground targets on road. These are error-prone junctions for conventional tracking algorithms.

4.6.4 Contextual Tracking Example—Results

The 1D representation of road segments makes it possible to incorporate target interactions into tracking algorithms, thus helping the management of target kinematic models efficiently. Most of target tracking algorithms are developed for a single target. Even in cases where multiple crossing targets are concerned, individual targets are still considered to behave independently.

Group tracking deals with multiple targets and models their relationship. This is an aspect of interaction but it only treats multiple targets that have some similarity in their movement. And it is typically done in the target track level.

For ground targets traveling along roads, their interactions are limited and more regular, thus making its use possible. One example is one target passing over another. Another example is when multiple vehicles come to an intersection, where the right of way governs their moving across the junction.

The act of one target passing over another can be detected by a tracking algorithm when the distance of separation between the two vehicles rapidly decreases. The first vehicle may or may not reduce its speed to facilitate the taking over by the second. The second certainly speeds up particularly when it is ready to shift the lane to by-pass the first.

Without explicitly taking this into account, the tracking algorithm may run into trouble in such situations where two vehicles fall into the same resolution cell of the radar (in range and bearing); one target is obscured by the other; and two returns (or more from clutter) come close together. Knowing the passing process, on the other hand, the obscured target can be tracked as same as the visible one (an instantaneous grouping). It can further help reject false returns in a clutter environment.

(a)   **(b)**

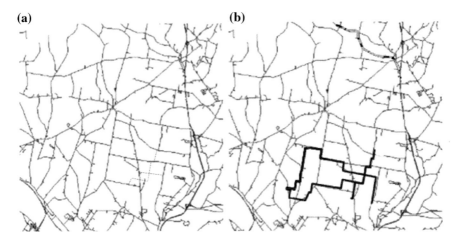

Fig. 4.9 a Road network and **b** road network with measurements for analysis

Fig. 4.10 PDAF/EKF with
and without the road network

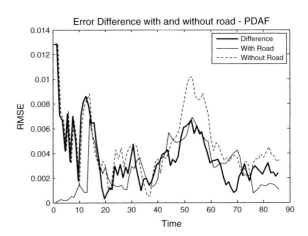

Closely spaced returns can be assigned with a better rate of correctness to the
appropriate vehicles.

Using the scenario in upper part of Fig. 4.9b, we did a comparison of tracking
with and without road networks using three contemporary methods (1) the extended
Kalman Filter (EKF) in the Probability Data Association Filter (PDAF), (2) the
Unscented Kalman Filter (UKF), and (3) the Particle Filter (PF). Figure 4.10 shows
the case of the linear Gaussian approach of the PDAF; while Fig. 4.11 shows the
case of the nonlinear-non-Gaussian approach of the UKF and PF.

What is interesting is the combined evaluation in which all methods benefit from
the road network (as added information). The surprise is that for the semi-linear

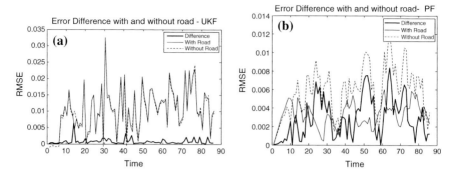

Fig. 4.11 **a** UKF and **b** PF with and without the road network

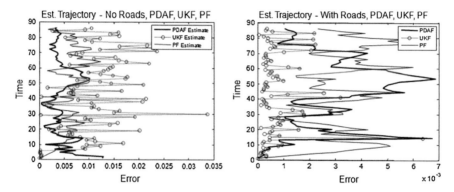

Fig. 4.12 Comparison of PDAF, UKF, and PF with and without the road network

road segment, the PDAF does better than the UKF at a lower computational cost. However, with the road information, the UKF does better as the covariance is aligned with the road segment to improve tracking as shown in Fig. 4.12.

Using the scenario at the bottom of Fig. 4.9, there are many intersections that will enhance the track accuracy. The table of results of a larger simulation (with Monte Carlo runs), is shown below to advocate the use of the road networks.

4.7 Discussion

In Table 4.2, we list the issues associated with contextual information over the sensors, targets, and the environment.

Table 4.2 Issues for contextual tracking

Concept	Advantage	Limitation
Sensors		
WAMI	Wide area scene understanding	Increased computations from environment (roads) for ***context-aided tracking*** with limited bandwidth
Multimodal	Can combine HSI, radar, and EO	Inconsistent geo-registration of multiple mixed resolution sensors hinders real-time ***context analysis***
Ground sensors	Ability to get high-resolution pixels for classification/ recognition/identification	Accuracy of reported and project information of change appearance for ***context enhancement***
Targets		
Pedestrians/vehicles	Can track through various dynamic changes (e.g. on-off roads)	Prediction of movement through occlusions requires predicted (versus estimated) ***context awareness***
Tracking	Increased track lifetime from extended spatial coverage	Increased number of confuser objects that require rudimentary ***context scene analysis***
Group association	Maintain database of associations of common movements, affiliations, and reduced state estimates	Separating activities of interest for group association versus that of routine and independent activities for verifiable ***context awareness***
Patterns of life	Can determine normalcy modeling of behaviors and activities	Determining the unknown actions resulting from sparse activities for ***context inference/cognition***
Intent	Can link person to a priori known places of activity to help in tracking, and/or build up notion of behavioral intent	Determining the social/cultural norms of various groups that have yet to be identified or actions which are routine but require ***context cognition***
Environment		
Roads	***Context aiding*** through realizable vehicle/pedestrian paths of travel	Requires machine analytics *t* maintain known road networks and travel for ***context awareness***
Weather	With different modalities, have the opportunity for distance and weather invariant observations.	Some sensors need to detect the variations in features due to changes in weather (e.g. illumination) requiring ***context enhancement***
Terrain	Can observe through varying conditions (e.g. occlusions, obscuration)	Need to detect change in conditions linking HCSB with routes for ***context awareness***

(continued)

Table 4.2 (continued)

Concept	Advantage	Limitation
Use		
Analysts	Provide context information to operators	Cueing of information to many users who all have different roles and functions of *context cognition*
Social networks	Link to available machines analytics databases for social networks	Requires context based indexing for efficient retrieval to support *context cognition/awareness*
Cultural networks	Determine activities of activities (e.g. credit card transactions, police records, vehicle registration records, etc.)	Delay of information to support context tracking needs, including time latency and low confidence correlations impeding *context cognition*
Sensor management	Increased correlation of features for tracking and performance models	Real-time model updates for changing targets; high demand for limited assets requiring *context assessment*

4.8 Conclusions

This chapter overviewed the many discussions of context in the domain of target tracking. Through explorations of the subject and multiple discussions, we presented various themes on the subject and provided an example for road-assisted tracking where context aids wide-area surveillance, group tracking, maritime-domain awareness, and patterns-of-life estimation. Our current categories include:

1. *Context-aided tracking*: road information for target tracking and identification, group detection, and targeting;
2. *Context enhancement*: environment-to-hardware processing for sensor modeling/management;
3. *Context awareness*: historical traffic behavior for situation awareness patterns of life (POL) and scene analysis;
4. *Context inference*: known distribution of entities for situation/threat/scenario assessment; and
5. *Context cognition*: domain knowledge from a user to aid tracking through selection and analysis of objectives.

To further target tracking techniques, we envision that machine analytics and human social, cultural, and behavioral modeling will be incorporated into future context aided-tracking, enhancement, awareness, inferencing, and cognition. Current work focuses on utilizing human knowledge as context to enhance tracking methods [125].

Acknowledgments This work is partly supported by the Air Force Office of Scientific Research (AFOSR) under the Dynamic Data Driven Application Systems program and the Air Force Research Lab.

References

1. E. Blasch, Book review: 3C vision: cues, context, and channels. IEEE Aerosp. Electron. Syst. Mag. **28**(2) (2013)
2. E. Blasch, E. Bosse, D.A. Lambert, *High-Level Information Fusion Management and Systems Design* (Artech House, Norwood, 2012)
3. E. Blasch, S. Plano, DFIG level 5 (user refinement) issues supporting Situational assessment reasoning. Int. Conf. Info Fusion (2005)
4. E. Blasch, L. Hong, Simultaneous identification and track fusion. IEEE Conf. Decision Control (1998)
5. J. Salerno, E. Blasch, M. Hinman, D. Boulware, Evaluating algorithmic techniques in supporting situation awareness, in *Proceedings of SPIE,* vol. 5813 (2005)
6. E. Blasch, Situation, impact, and user refinement, in *Proceedings of SPIE,* vol. 5096 (2003)
7. D. Shen, G. Chen, E. Blasch, G. Tadda, Adaptive Markov game theoretic data fusion approach for cyber network defense. IEEE Mil. Commun. Conf. (MILCOM) (2007)
8. E. Blasch, S Plano, JDL level 5 fusion model 'user refinement' issues and applications in group Tracking, in *Proceedings of SPIE,* vol. 4729 (2002)
9. E. Blasch, Sensor, user, mission (SUM) resource management and their interaction with level 2/3 fusion, in *International Conference Information Fusion* (2006)
10. E. Blasch, T. Connare, Group information feedback for objects under trees. *National Symposium on Sensor and Data Fusion* (2001)
11. A.N. Steinberg, C.L. Bowman, Revisions to the JDL data fusion model Ch 2, in *Handbook of MultiSensor Data Fusion*, eds. by D.L. Hall, J. Llinas (CRC Press, Boca Raton, LA, 2001)
12. E. Blasch, S. Plano, Cognitive fusion analysis based on context, in *Proceedings of SPIE,* vol. 5434 (2004)
13. E. Blasch, I. Kadar, J.J. Salerno, M.M. Kokar, S. Das, G.M. Powell, D.D. Corkill, et al. Issues and challenges in situation assessment (level 2 fusion). J. Adv. Inf. Fusion **1**(2), 122–139 (2006)
14. E. Blasch, I. Kadar, K. Hintz, J. Biermann, C-Y. Chong, J. Salerno, S. Das, Resource management coordination with level 2/3 fusion issues and challenges. IEEE Aerosp. Electron. Syst. Mag. **23**(3), 32–46 (2008)
15. E. Blasch, J. Llinas, D. Lambert, P. Valin, S. Das, C-Y. Chong, M.M. Kokar, E. Shahbazian, High level information fusion developments, issues, and grand challenges—fusion10 panel discussion, in *International Conference Information Fusion* (2010)
16. E. Blasch, D.A. Lambert, P. Valin, M.M. Kokar, J. Llinas, S. Das, C-Y. Chong, et al., High level information fusion (HLIF) survey of models, issues, and grand challenges. IEEE Aerosp. Electron. Syst. Mag. **27**(9) (2012)
17. E. Blasch, A.N. Steinberg, S. Das, J. Llinas, C-Y. Chong, O. Kessler, E. Waltz, F. White, Revisiting the JDL model for information exploitation, in *International Conference Information Fusion* (2013)
18. J. García, L. Snidaro, I. Visentini, Exploiting context as binding element for multi-level fusion. Panel Discussion Paper, International Conference on Information Fusion (2012)
19. L. Snidaro, I. Visentini, J. Llinas, G.L. Foresti, Context in fusion: some considerations in a JDL perspective, in *Proceedings of the 16th International Conference on Information Fusion* (2013)
20. A.N. Steinberg, G.L. Rogova, Situation and context in data fusion and natural language understanding, in *International Conference on Information Fusion* (2008)

21. G. Ferrin, L. Snidaro, G.L. Foresti, Contexts, co-texts and situations in fusion domain, in *International Conference on Information Fusion* (2011)
22. L. Snidaro, J. Garcia, J. Llinas, Context-based information fusion: a survey and discussion. Inf. Fusion **25**, 16–31 (2015). doi:10.1016/j.inffus.2015.01.002
23. A. Dey, G. Abowd, Towards a better understanding of context and context-awareness. *Workshop on the What, Who, Where, When and How of Context-Awareness* (2000)
24. I. Visentini, L. Snidaro, Integration of contextual information for tracking refinement, in *International Conference on Information Fusion* (2011)
25. E. Blasch, Assembling a distributed fused Information-based human-computer cognitive decision making tool. IEEE Aerosp. Electron. Syst. Mag. **15**(5), 11–17 (2000)
26. B. Kahler, E. Blasch, Sensor management fusion using operating conditions, in *IEEE National Aerospace Electronics Conference* (2008)
27. M. Maziere, F. Chassaing, L. Garrido, P. Salembier, Segmentation and tracking of video objects for a content-based video indexing context, in *IEEE International Conference on Multimedia and Expo* (2000)
28. E. Blasch, T. Connare, Group tracking of occluded targets, in *Proceedings of SPIE,* vol. **4365** (2001)
29. E. Blasch, T. Connare, Improving track accuracy through Group Information Feedback, in *International Conference on Information Fusion* (2001)
30. W. Koch, Information fusion aspects related to GMTI convoy tracking, in *International Conference on Information Fusion* (2002)
31. C.M. Power, D.E. Brown, Context-based methods for track association, in *International Conference on Information Fusion* (2002)
32. S.M. Arulampalam, N. Gordon, M. Orton, B. Ristic, A variable structure multiple model particle filter for GMTI tracking, in *International Conference on Information Fusion* (2002)
33. J. García, J.A. Besada, J.R. Casar, Use of map information for tracking targets on airport surface. IEEE Trans. Aerosp. Electron. Syst. **39**(2), 675–694 (2003)
34. J. Wang, P. Neskovic, L.N. Cooper, context-based tracking of object features, in *IEEE International Joint Conference on Neural Networks* (2004)
35. S.J. McKenna, H. Nait-Charif, Learning spatial context from tracking using penalised likelihoods, in *International Conference on Pattern Recognition* (2004)
36. L. Chen, R. Ravichandran, Automated track projection bias removal using Frechet distance and road networks, in *International Conference on Information Fusion* (2014)
37. C. Yang, E. Blasch, M. Bakich, Nonlinear constrained tracking of targets on roads, in *International Conference on Information Fusion* (2005)
38. J. García, J.M. Molina, G. de Miguel, A. Soto, Design of an A-SMGCS prototype at Barajas airport: data fusion algorithms, in *International Conference on Info Fusion* (2005)
39. A. Chella, H. Dindo, I. Infantino, A system for simultaneous people tracking and posture recognition in the context of human-computer interaction, in *International Conference on Computer as a Tool*, EUROCON (2005)
40. J.C. McCall, M.M. Trivedi, Performance evaluation of a vision based lane tracker designed for driver assistance systems, in *IEEE Intelligent Vehicles Symposium* (2005)
41. S.Y. Cheng, S. Park, M.M. Trivedi, Multiperspective thermal IR and video arrays for 3D body tracking and driver activity analysis, in *IEEE Computer Vision and Pattern Recognition —Workshops* (2005)
42. C. Yang, E. Blasch, Pose angular-aiding for maneuvering target tracking, in *International Conference on Information Fusion* (2005)
43. T. Brehard, J.P. Le Cadre, Closed-form posterior cramaer-rao bound for a maneuvering target in the bearings-only tracking context using best-fitting gaussian distribution, in *International Conference on Information Fusion* (2006)
44. H.T. Nguyen, Q. Ji, A.W.M. Smeulders, Robust multi-target tracking using spatio-temporal context, *IEEE Computer Society Conference on Computer Vision and Pattern Recognition* (2006)

45. M. Lee, J. van Santen, B. Mobius, J. Olive, Formant tracking using context-dependent phonemic information. IEEE Trans. Speech Audio Process. Part: 2, **13**(5), 741–750 (2005)
46. W-T. Chu, W-H. Cheng, J-L. Wu, Generative and discriminative modeling toward semantic context detection in audio tracks, in *International Multimedia Modeling Conference* (2005)
47. D.T. Toledano, J.G. Villardebo, L.H. Gomez, Initialization, training, and context-dependency in HMM-based formant tracking. IEEE Trans. Audio Speech Lang. Process. **14**(2), 511–523 (2006)
48. M.E.P. Davies, M.D. Plumbley, Context-dependent beat tracking of musical audio. IEEE Trans. Audio Speech Lang. Process. **15**(3), 1009–1020 (2007)
49. E. Blasch, C. Banas, M. Paul, B. Bussjager, G. Seetharaman, Pattern activity clustering and evaluation (PACE), in *Proceedings of SPIE*, vol. 8402 (2012)
50. A.M. Sanchez, M.A. Patricio, J. Garcia, M.A. Molina, Video tracking improvement using context-based information, in *International Conference on Information Fusion* (2007)
51. S. Ali, V. Reilly, M. Shah, Motion and appearance contexts for tracking and re-acquiring targets in aerial videos, *IEEE Conference on Computer Vision and Pattern Recognition* (2007)
52. T. Gandhi, M.M. Trivedi, Pedestrian protection systems: issues, survey, and challenges. IEEE Trans. Intell. Transp. Syst. **8**(3), 413–430 (2007)
53. H.T. Nguyen, J. Qiang, A.W. M. Smeulders, Spatio-temporal context for Robust multitarget tracking. IEEE Trans. Pattern Anal. Mach. Intell. **29**(1), 52–64 (2007)
54. M. Feldmann, W. Koch, Road-map assisted convoy track maintenance using random matrices, in *International Conference on Information Fusion* (2008)
55. M. Mertens, M. Ulmke, Ground moving target tracking with context information and a refined sensor model, in *International Conference on Information Fusion* (2008)
56. C. Yang, E. Blasch, Fusion of tracks with road constraints. J. Adv. Inf. Fusion **3**(1), 14–32 (2008)
57. C. Yang, E. Blasch, Kalman filtering with nonlinear state constraints. IEEE Trans. Aerosp. Electron. Syst. **45**(1), 70–84 (2009)
58. M. Yang, Y. Wu, G. Hua, Context-aware visual tracking. IEEE Trans. Pattern Anal Mach. Intell. **31**(7), 1195–1209 (2009)
59. A.M. Sanchez, M.A. Patricio, J. Garcia, J.M. Molina, A context model and reasoning system to improve object tracking in complex scenarios. Expert Syst. Appl. **36**(8), 10995–11005 (2009)
60. J. Gomez-Romero, M.A. Patricio, J. Garcia, J.M. Molina, Context-based reasoning using ontologies to adapt visual tracking in surveillance, *IEEE International Conference on Advanced Video and Signal Based Surveillance* (2009)
61. J. George, J.L. Crassidis, T. Singh, Threat assessment using context-based tracking in a maritime environment, in *International Conference on Information Fusion* (2009)
62. D. Balakrishnan, A. Nayak, P. Dhar, Adaptive and intelligent route learning for mobile assets using geo-tracking and context profiles, in *International Conference on Computational Science and Engineering* (2009)
63. E. Maggio, A. Cavallaro, Learning scene context for multiple object tracking. IEEE Trans. Image Process. **18**(8), 1873–1884 (2009)
64. H. Ling, L. Bai, E. Blasch, X. Mei, Robust infrared vehicle tracking across target change using L_1 regularization, in *International Conference on Information Fusion* (2010)
65. W. Koch, On Bayesian tracking and data fusion: a tutorial introduction with examples. IEEE Aerosp. Electron. Syst. Mag. Part: 2, **25**(7), 29–52 (2010)
66. J. Gómez-Romero, J. García, M. Kandefer, J. Llinas, J. M. Molina, M.A. Patricio et al., Strategies and techniques for use and exploitation of contextual information in high-level fusion architectures, in *International Conference on Information Fusion* (2010)
67. J. Gomez-Romero, M.A. Patricio, J. Garcia, J.M. Molina, Ontology-based context representation and reasoning for object tracking and scene interpretation in video. Expert Syst. Appl. **38**(6), 7494–7510 (2011)

68. J. Garcia, J.M. Molina, T. Singh, J. Crassidis, J. Llinas, Research opportunities in contextualized fusion systems. The harbor surveillance case, in *International Conference on Artificial Neural Networks* (2011)
69. J. Garcia, J. Gomez-Romero, M.A. Patricio, J.M. Molina, G. Rogova, On the representation and exploitation of context knowledge in a harbor surveillance scenario, in *International Conference on Information Fusion* (2011)
70. P. Guha, A. Mukerjee, V.K. Subramanian, Formulation, detection and application of occlusion states (Oc-7) in the context of multiple object tracking. *IEEE International Advanced Video and Signal-Based Surveillance* (AVSS) (2011)
71. X. Mei, H. Ling, Y. Wu, E. Blasch, L. Bai, Minimum error bounded efficient L1 tracker with occlusion detection, in *IEEE Computer Vision and Pattern Recognition* (2011)
72. D.P. Chau, F. Bremond, M. Thonnat, A multi-feature tracking algorithm enabling adaptation to context variations, in *International Conference on Imaging for Crime Detection and Prevention* (2011)
73. X. Peng, Z. Xing, X. Tan, Y. Yu, W. Zhao, Iterative context-aware feature location: (NIER track), in *International Conference on Software Engineering* (ICSE) (2011)
74. A. Rice, J. Vasquez, Context-aided tracking with an adaptive hyperspectral sensor, in *International Conference on Information Fusion* (2011)
75. Z. Sun, H. Yao, S. Zhang, X. Sun, Robust visual tracking via context objects computing, in *IEEE International Conference on Image Processing* (ICIP) (2011)
76. B. Pannetier, J. Dezert, Extended and multiple target tracking: evaluation of an hybridized solution, in *International Conference on Informational Fusion* (2011)
77. Y. Wu, E. Blasch, G. Chen, L. Bai, H. Ling, Multiple source data fusion via sparse representation for Robust visual tracking, in *International Conference on Information Fusion* (2011)
78. J. George, J.L. Crassidis, T. Singh, A.M. Fosbury, Anomaly detection using context-aided target tracking. J. Adv. Inf. Fusion **6**(1) (2011)
79. S. Zhang, Y. Bar-Shalom, Track segment association for GMTI tracks of evasive move-stop-move maneuvering targets. IEEE Trans. Aerosp. Electron. Syst. **47**(3), 1899–1914 (2011)
80. K.M. Han, H.T. Choi, Shape context based object recognition and tracking in structured underwater environment, in *IEEE International Geoscience and Remote Sensing Symposium* (IGARSS) (2011)
81. D. Qiu, R. Lynch, E. Blasch, C. Yang, Underwater navigation using location-dependent signatures, in *IEEE-AIAA Aerospace Conference* (2012)
82. L. Snidaro, I. Visentini, K. Bryan, G.L. Foresti, Markov logic networks for context integration and situation assessment in maritime domain, in *International Conference on Information Fusion* (2012)
83. L. Snidaro, I. Visentini, K. Bryan, Fusing uncertain knowledge and evidence for maritime situational awareness via Markov logic networks. Inf. Fusion **21**, 159–172 (2015). doi:10.1016/j.inffus.2013.03.004
84. D. Balakrishnan, A. Nayak, An efficient approach for mobile asset tracking using contexts. IEEE Trans. Parallel Distrib. Syst. **23**(2), 211–218 (2012)
85. E.D. Marti, J. Garcia, J.L. Crassidis, Improving multiple-model context-aided tracking through an autocorrelation approach, in *International Conference on Information Fusion* (2012)
86. L. Lamard, R. Chapuis, J-P. Boyer, Dealing with occlusions with multi targets tracking algorithms for the real road context, in *IEEE Intelligent Vehicles Symposium* (IV) (2012)
87. L. Cerman, V. Hlavac, Tracking with context as a semi-supervised learning and labeling problem, in *International Conference on Pattern Recognition* (ICPR) (2012)
88. X. Shi, H. Ling, E. Blasch, W. Hu, Context-driven moving vehicle detection in wide area motion imagery, in *International Conference on Pattern Recognition (ICPR)* (2012)

89. A. Borji, S. Frintrop, D.N. Sihite, L. Itti, Adaptive object tracking by learning background context, in *IEEE Conference on Computer Vision and Pattern Recognition Workshops (CVPRW)* (2012)
90. C. Yang, L. Kaplan, E. Blasch, Performance measures of covariance and information matrices in resource management for target state estimation. IEEE Trans. Aerosp. Electron. Syst. **48**(3), 2594–2613 (2012)
91. C. Yang, L.M. Kaplan, E. Blasch, M. Bakich, Optimal placement of heterogeneous sensors for targets with Gaussian priors. IEEE Trans. Aerosp. Electron. Syst. **49**(3), 1637–1653 (2013)
92. M. Fanaswala, V. Krishnamurthy, Detection of anomalous trajectory patterns in target tracking via stochastic context-free grammars and reciprocal process models. IEEE J. Sel. Topics Signal Process. **7**(1), 76–90 (2013)
93. P. Liang, H. Ling, E. Blasch, Encoding color information for visual tracking: algorithms and benchmark, in Submitted to IEEE Transaction on Pattern Analysis and Machine Intelligence, Aug 2014
94. Y. Yang, M. Li, F. Nian, H. Zhao, Y. He, Vision target tracker based on incremental dictionary learning and global and local classification, Abstr. Appl. Anal. (2013)
95. Z. Liu, E. Blasch, Z. Xue, R. Langaniere, W. Wu, Objective assessment of multiresolution image fusion algorithms for context enhancement in night vision: a comparative survey. IEEE Trans. Pattern Anal. Mach. Intell. **34**(1), 94–109 (2012)
96. C. Yang, E. Blasch, Mutual aided target tracking and identification. *Proceedings of SPIE,* vol. 5099 (2003)
97. E. Blasch, B. Kahler, Multi-resolution EO/IR Tracking and Identification, *International Conference on Information Fusion* (2005)
98. Y. Wu, E. Blasch, G. Chen, L. Bai, H. Ling, Multiple source data fusion via sparse representation for Robust visual tracking, in *International Conference on Information Fusion* (2011)
99. B. Kahler, E. Blasch, Decision-Level Fusion Performance Improvement from Enhanced HRR Radar Clutter Suppression, J. Adv. Inf. Fusion **6**(2) (2011)
100. Y. Zheng, W. Dong, E. Blasch, Qualitative and quantitative comparisons of multispectral night vision colorization techniques. Opt. Eng. **51**(8) (2012)
101. E. Blasch, Level 5 (User Refinement) issues supporting information fusion management, in *International Conference on Information Fusion* (2006)
102. E. Blasch, Modeling intent for a target tracking and identification scenario, *Proceedings of SPIE,* vol. 5428 (2004)
103. M. Wei, G. Chen, J.B. Cruz, L.S. Haynes et al., Multi-Pursuer multi-evader pursuit-evasion games with jamming confrontation. AIAA J. Aerosp. Comput. Inf. Commun. **4**(3), 693–706 (2007)
104. E. Blasch, J. Salerno, I. Kadar, S.J. Yang, L. Fenstermacher, M. Endsley, L. Grewe, Summary of human, social, cultural, behavioral (HCSB) modeling for information fusion, in *Proceedings of SPIE*, vol. 8745 (2013)
105. E. Blasch, L. Hong, Data association through fusion of target track and identification sets, in *International Conference on Information Fusion* (2000)
106. S. Alsing, E. Blasch, R. Bauer, Three-dimensional receiver operating characteristic (ROC) trajectory concepts for the evaluation of target recognition algorithms faced with the Unknown target detection problem, in *Proceedings of SPIE,* vol. 3718 (1999)
107. O. Mendoza-Schrock, J.A. Patrick, E. Blasch, Video image registration evaluation for a layered sensing environment, in *Proceedings of IEEE National Aerospace Electronics Conference (NAECON)* (2009)
108. E. Blasch, S. Russell, G. Seetharaman, Joint data management for MOVINT data-to-decision making, in *International Conference on Information Fusion* (2011)
109. H. Ling, Y. Wu, E. Blasch, G. Chen, L. Bai, Evaluation of visual tracking in extremely low frame rate wide area motion imagery, in *International Conference on Information Fusion* (2011)

110. E. Blasch, P.B. Deignan Jr, S. L. Dockstader et al., Contemporary concerns in geographical/geospatial information systems (GIS) processing, in *Proceedings of IEEE National Aerospace Electronics Conference (NAECON)* (2011)
111. E. Blasch, G. Seetharaman, K. Palaniappan, H. Ling, G. Chen, Wide-area motion imagery (WAMI) exploitation tools for enhanced situation awareness, in *IEEE Applied Imagery Pattern Recognition Workshop* (2012)
112. E. Blasch, T. Connare, Feature-aided JBPDAF group tracking and classification using an IFFN sensor, in *Proceedings of SPIE,* vol. 4728 (2002)
113. Y. Wu, J. Wang, L. Cheng, H. Lu et al., Real-time probabilistic covariance tracking with efficient model update. IEEE Trans. Image Process. **21**(5), 2824–2837 (2012)
114. E. Blasch, J.J. Westerkamp et al., Identifying moving HRR signatures with an ATR belief filter, in *Proceedings of SPIE,* vol. 4053 (2000)
115. E. Blasch, T. Connare, Improving track maintenance through group tracking, in *Proceedings Workshop on Estimation, Tracking, and Fusion; A Tribute to Yaakov Bar Shalom* (2001), pp. 360–371
116. T. Connare, E. Blasch, J. Schmitz et al., Group IMM tracking utilizing track and identification fusion, in *Proceedings of Workshop on Estimation, Tracking, and Fusion; A Tribute to Yaakov Bar Shalom,* pp. 205–220, May 2001
117. E. Blasch, *Derivation of a belief filter for simultaneous high range resolution radar tracking and identification*, Ph.D. Thesis, Wright State University, 1999
118. P. Hanselman, C. Lawrence, E. Fortunano, B. Tenney et al., Dynamic tactical targeting, in *Proceedings of SPIE,* vol. 5441 (2004)
119. K. Palaniappan, F. Bunyak, P. Kumar et al., Efficient feature extraction and likelihood fusion for vehicle tracking in low frame rate airborne video, in *International Conference on Information Fusion* (2010)
120. E. Blasch, C. Banas, M. Paul et al., Pattern activity clustering and evaluation (PACE), in *Proceedings of SPIE,* vol. 8402 (2012)
121. X. Mei, H. Ling, Y. Wu, E. Blasch, L Bai, Efficient minimum error bounded particle resampling L1 tracker with occlusion detection. IEEE Trans. Image Process (T-IP) **22**(7), 2661–2675 (2013)
122. P. Liang, G. Teodoro, H. Ling et al., Multiple Kernel learning for vehicle detection in wide area motion imagery, in *International Conference on Information Fusion* (2012)
123. X. Shi, P. Li, W. Hu, E. Blasch, H. Ling, Using maximum consistency context for multiple target association in wide area traffic scenes, in *International Conference on Acoustics, Speech and Signal Processing (ICASSP)* (2013)
124. J. Gao, H. Ling, E. Blasch, K. Pham, Z. Wang, G. Chen, Patterns of life from WAMI objects tracking. SPIE Newsroom (2013)
125. R.I. Hammoud, C.S. Sahin, E.P. Blasch, B.J. Rhodes, T. Wang, Automatic association of chats and video tracks for activity learning and recognition in aerial video surveillance. Sensors **14**, 19843–19860 (2014)

Chapter 5
Context Assumptions for Threat Assessment Systems

Steven A. Israel and Erik Blasch

Abstract Decision support systems enable users to quickly assess data, but they require significant resources to develop and are often relevant to limited domains. This chapter identifies the implicit assumptions that require contextual analysis for decision support systems to be effective for providing a relevant threat assessment. The impacts of the design and user assumptions are related to intelligence errors and intelligence failures that come from a misrepresentation of context. The intent of this chapter is twofold. The first is to enable system users to characterize trust using the decision support system by establishing the context of the decision. The second is to show technology designers how their design decisions impact system integration and usability. We organize the contextual information for threat analysis by categorizing six assumptions: (1) specific problem, (2) acquirable data, (3) use of context, (4) reproducible analysis, (5) actionable intelligence, and (6) quantifiable decision making. The chapter concludes with a quantitative example of context assessment for threat analysis.

Keywords High-level information fusion · Situation assessment · Threat assessment · Context · Timeliness · Uncertainty · Unknowns

5.1 Introduction

A threat is an assessment that an individual or group has the potential to cause harm to specific entity or entities. Threat assessment has three parameters: intent, capacity, and knowledge or intent, capability, or opportunity [1]. During the Cold War, sovereign nations engaged other sovereign nations using military-specific vehicles operating in collaborative groups. The battle groups were centrally

S.A. Israel
Raytheon, Chantilly, VA, USA
e-mail: Steven.a.Israel@Raytheon.com

E. Blasch (✉)
Air Force Research Lab, Rome, NY, USA
e-mail: erik.blasch@gmail.com

© Springer International Publishing Switzerland (outside the USA) 2016
L. Snidaro et al. (eds.), *Context-Enhanced Information Fusion*,
Advances in Computer Vision and Pattern Recognition,
DOI 10.1007/978-3-319-28971-7_5

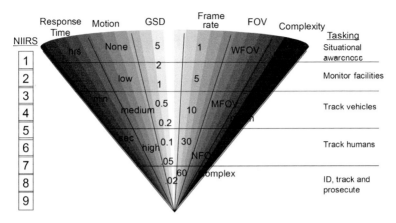

Fig. 5.1 Image quality parameters versus tasks: courtesy of David Cannon [5]

coordinated and positioned away from civilian activities to maximize their maneuverability [2].

The Cold War military performed directed data collection, which means that they maintained custody of the information throughout the stovepiped exploitation chain. Enemy intent and capacity were based upon knowledge of the leaders, military strength and readiness, and doctrine. For example, the Cold War threats were so well understood that the required information and analyst tasks determined the design for imaging sensors [3, 4]. Figure 5.1 identifies that design relationship including ground sampling distance (GSD) and field of view (FOV) for the National Imagery Interpretability Rating Scale (NIIRS).

In addition to the traditional Cold War threats, threats to sovereign nations also include: organized crime, narcotics trafficking, terrorism, information warfare, and weapons of mass destructions (WMD) [6]. Non-national actors pose different threats in the following manner: (1) there is no identifiable battlefront; (2) non-national actors keep and garrison few if any pieces of heavy military hardware, rocket launchers, tanks, etc., which both reduces their physical signature and minimizes their liabilities; (3) they maintain no persistent doctrine; (4) their numbers and actions form only a small fraction of a percentage of the resident population; and (5) they dictate attacks in the political, financial, cyber, and cultural domains in addition to the geospatial, when their opportunity for success is greatest [7–9].

One example of a terrorist event is the bombing during the 2013 Boston Marathon. The bomber's intent was to destabilize the public trust. The bomber's capacity was a small amount of funds and two individuals. The bomber's technical knowledge was in home-made explosives and the operational knowledge of the crowd movement during the marathon to maximize their impact.

The remainder of this chapter is laid in the following manner. Threats to sovereign nations are defined. The common elements of those threats and their impacts on decision supports systems are identified. The assumption used by decision support system developers are made explicit. Finally, an example of how the developer assumptions can be quantified using evidence theory is performed.

5.2 Defining Threats

5.2.1 Threat Assessment

To identify the threat's intent, capacity, and knowledge, analysts seek information from four basic knowledge types (Table 5.1): entity knowledge provides the static *who* or *what, where,* and *when* information; the activity or transaction knowledge provides dynamic components for *how*; association knowledge provides *with whom* and *link method* information; and finally context knowledge provides *why* information. Using these information types, the analyst seeks to answer the following:

- Is the threat credible?
- Who are the individuals or groups composing the threat?
- What is the impact and likelihood of threat against individuals, entities, and locations?
- How has the threat evolved since the previous assessment?

Table 5.1 Diversity of knowledge types

Information level	Description	Example questions	Metadata
Entity	Static target, noun: person, car, building, website, idea	Determine type of target, location, and time: where, what, and when?	Name, work, ownership, membership, address, area extent, topic, and content
Activity/Event	Entity performing action	Tracking entity, routes, estimating traffic patterns, transactions, volume, changes: where's it going, is it moving with the rest of traffic, how many file downloads?	Traffic volume, direction, diversity, mode, domain type (financial, physical, social media), coordinated activities, criminal acts, and daily commute
Association	Functional relationship among entities	Network, membership, purpose: who are the friends of the entity, what is the purpose for their association?	Interpersonal (family, friends, employer), social interactions (people, places), topic, purpose, accessibility, cost, and transaction type
Context	Conditions under which entity interacts within its environment	Determine activity/event/transaction purpose along with tactics, techniques, and procedures: why?	Culture, geography, cost, politics, subject, history, religion, social interaction, availability, and access

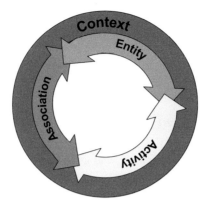

Fig. 5.2 Knowledge types for evidence in the human environment

Information from one knowledge type can be used to cue another (Fig. 5.2). Evidence is data or rules about individuals or other entities, activities/transactions, associations, and context used to characterize a threat. Evidence accumulation is conceptualized as building a legal case rather than the Cold War target prosecution [10]. Evidence can take the form of direct or circumstantial. Direct evidence links a signature (entity, activity, association) to known actor(s) or entities; i.e., labeled data. Circumstantial evidence requires an inference to link information to an entity.

Activity and entity information can be nested to describe transactions and events. Transactions are linked activities, where information or materials are passed. Events are related activities occurring over a given domain and time [11].

Information from the four knowledge types is now being exploited by corporations and private citizens. Intelligence can be sold to advertisers; used for bootstrapping on other types of attacks, business espionage, and generation of high-quality predictions of future activities [12]. The majority of these data are provided willingly and unconsciously by the public [13].

5.2.2 Threat Assessments Should Have Unique System Requirements

Intelligence questions can be broken into three basic categories: assessment, discovery, and prediction [14]. Though the focus of this chapter is threat assessment, many of the concepts are applicable to discovery and prediction. To perform threat assessment, evidence accumulation must be structured to track activities of individuals independent of collection mechanism [15]. Individuals may be cooperative, such as member of online social networks that provide a wide range of personal information; noncooperative individuals limit their public footprint; and uncooperative individuals actively seek to defeat attempts of their signature being collected.

Jonas [16] suggested the following traits that a decision support system should possess.

- *Sequence neutral processing*: knowledge is extracted as it becomes available and assessed as evidence immediately. Note: the system must be cognizant that data may arrive out of order from when it was collected.

  - The decision and confidence may change with time as additional confirming and rejecting evidence are reported.

- *Raw data must be processed only once* [17], because access, collection-evaluation, and transmission of data generate a tremendous computational, storage and network burden due to the 5V (volume, velocity, veracity, variety, and value) issues.
- *Relationship aware*: links among individuals to either known or discovered individuals become part of the entity meta-data.
- *Extensible*: system must be able to accept new data sources and attributes
- *Knowledge-based thesaurus*: support functions exist to handle noise when comparing queries to databases.

  - Cultural issues such as transliteration of names or moving from the formal to the informal.
  - Imprecision such as a georeference being a relative position rather than an absolute location; i.e., *over there* versus a specific latitude and longitude [18].
  - Text, rhetoric, and grammar change often and the change rate is even faster in social media than more formal communications such as broadcast news.

- *Real-time*: changes must be processed on the fly with decisions happening in an actionable timeline; i.e., online learning.

  - Perpetual analytics: no latency in alert generation.

- *Scalable*: able to expand based upon number of records, users, or sources.

5.3 Assumptions for Decision Support Systems

The remainder of this chapter describes the assumptions for threat assessment decision support system. Figure 5.3 is an engineering functional block diagram for a generic information exploitation system. For a given *problem statement*, there are assumptions included in the threat assessment. These assumptions are organized into the Data Fusion Information Group (DFIG) model levels (L1 … L5) of information fusion. Together, the assumptions along the processing chain are included in the *generated information* that accompanies a threat decision. However,

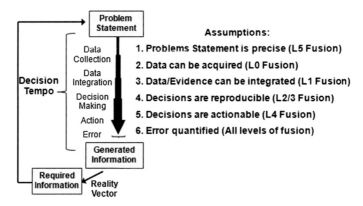

Fig. 5.3 Assumptions within the human environment

there must be a *reality vector* that translates the decision into the required information. The ops tempo determines the amount of context that can be accurately relayed in the assumptions that accompany a decision. At each functional block, the common assumptions made by users or technology developers are made explicit [19]. Within each section, the assumption is further resolved.

Each assumption in Fig. 5.3 contributes to intelligence errors and intelligence failures [20]. Intelligence failure is the systemic organizational surprise resulting from incorrect, missing, discarded, or inadequate hypotheses. Intelligence errors are factual inaccuracies in analysis resulting from poor or missing data. Though this chapter focuses on threats to governments [21], the concepts are applicable for understanding threats within social networks [22], by criminals [23], and to financial systems [24].

Assumption 1 The Problem is Specific

Assumption 1: The Problem Statement is Specific
The problem statement in specific assumes that the decision support system's output relates to the problem statement [25], which is noted in Fig. 5.3 as the reality vector. The problem statement assumption asks fundamental questions: Can the threat be described as a question or hypothesis? Is the decision relevant the question?

Assumption 1.1 Can the Threat be described as a Question or a Hypothesis?
The first part is to understand the type of question being asked. Asking the right question relates directly to context. For current insurgent warfare [2], nations face

threats from a number of groups each with different outcome intent, capacity, and knowledge as shown in Fig. 5.4. This uncertainty in the enemy probably led Donald Rumsfeld [26] to state the following:

- There are known knowns; there are things we know that we know.
- There are known unknowns; that is to say there are things that, we now know we don't know.
- But there are also unknown unknowns—there are things we do not know we don't know.

Treverton [27] described this taxonomy as puzzles, mysteries, and complexities. Figure 5.4 highlights the ability to translate unknowns into knows. The first case, and obvious to information fusion is a *data-driven* approach in which the perceived unknowns are mapped to perceived knowns (whether reality has been satisfied). For example, collections can verify that the perceived unknown is still unknown. The second case is a *knowledge-driven* in which the unknown reality is moved to a known reality. To make things known, *context-driven* approaches match the unknown perceived unknowns into reality through evidence analysis.

The next part of the question is to understand blindspots. Originally, analysts assumed that threat networks consisted of a central hierarchical authority. Analysts would then look for evidence of a kingpin and assess their capacity to do harm, which is similar to the Federal Bureau of Investigation (FBI) combating organized crime in the 1950s and 1960s [23, 28]. Although this paradigm might have been prevalent prior to the 9/11 attacks [29], Al Qaeda and its confederates moved away from that model shortly afterward [2]. Current threat networks are transient based upon opportunity and mutual interests [30].

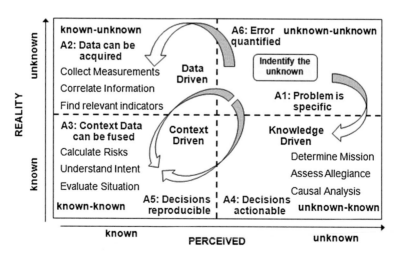

Fig. 5.4 Context-driven threat assessment

Fig. 5.5 Strategy for
attacking loose confederation
networks

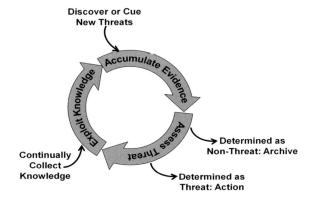

There is no clear solution for how to ask the right question or even that having the right information guarantees success. For example, given a chess board arranged in the normal starting position, no single opening move exists for the white player that guarantees a win even though (s)he has perfect situational awareness. The strategy to chess is to play the game until a small number of alternatives exist before taking finishing action. The same strategy is essential for assessing and countering threats (Fig. 5.5) [31].

Assumption 1.2 Is the Decision a Relevant Question?

Analytical workflows commonly focus on specific data modalities, exploitation techniques. The reliance on existing processing chains has a number of causes. The first cause is *mechanical*; sensor data have known workflows. Their output products have known and quantifiable performance metrics. The second cause is *organizational inertia*; adopting new business processes takes strong leadership for change and involves risk. The third cause is the *lack of resources* [32]: the number and skill set for analysts are very focused among a relatively small cadre [33]. The fourth cause is changing any element in the exploitation chain requires training and a *learning timeline* which is a large investment of time, money, and most likely a near-term reduction in performance. The fifth cause is that though a new or different knowledge source may contain *sufficient information content*, its technological readiness could be insufficient for operational usage.

To test the problem statement, all evidence must be structured to either confirm it or reject it. Therefore, individuals who generate problem statements must also understand the structure of the output. The downstream cost is the burden of transforming the data prior to analysis.

Currently, evidence accumulation is a manual, cognitive process. However, analysts spend much of their time locating data sources than assessing information. Government and industry have problems federating disparate data repositories and resolving entities across those systems. Other issues facing the analysts are that their customer bases and product diversity are increasing. Another unfortunate circumstance for the current generation of analysts is that the timelines have shortened and they rarely have the time to perform their after action reviews (AARs) to assess system performance and usability.

Johnston [20] produced a series of tools and techniques to address the issues stated by Rumsfeld, which include questioning the foundation assumptions, looking for precursor actions, alternative analysis, etc. For example, black-hatting friendly capabilities which includes a hacker who violates computer security for little reason beyond mischievous or satisfaction behavior. Other researchers are rediscovering that the critical actors that enhance threat capacity are those individuals and entities with unique skills and capabilities that arrives *just-in-time*, i.e., the strength of weak ties [34].

Assumption 2 Context Data can be Acquired

Assumption 2: Context Data can be Acquired to Fill Knowledge Gaps
The assumption that data can be acquired to fill knowledge gaps is a holdover from the directed collections of the Cold War. The purpose for data collection is to improve decision confidence above some threshold. Many data streams are continually generating information, so the context is dynamic. So, data collection is less important than continually trolling known databases for new content or determining the location of relevant data sources. Data acquisition assumes a number of issues: data collection is unbiased, target signatures are constant, data quality can be determined, and all the information is collected [35].

Assumption 2.1 Data Collection is Unbiased
Nondirected data sources have diverse origins and their chain of custody is incomplete. The provenance links may also contain a level of uncertainty, which reduces the trustworthiness of the source [36, 37]. Although the total amount of data is large, the amount of data available as evidence may be sparse for a specific problem set, location, or entity.

Assumption 2.2 Target Signatures are Constant
Target signatures are the information types (entity, activity, association, or context) that describe an individual within a domain (geospatial, financial, cyber, etc.). The assumption has two basic components. First, an individual's or entity's interactions with their environment are invariant over time and space. Second, observed activity has a known and constant meaning. Interpreting activities is difficult because they vary with:

- **External stressors**: such as the arrest of a threat network member, will cause a change in the Tactics, Techniques, and Procedures (TTPs) of the group, ala Maslow's hierarchy. Yet, the network itself may remain intact [38].
- Not all threat activities are anomalies; and not all anomalies are threats.

- **Cultural difference within a population**: Eagle [39] showed that the individual's use of communication is a function of their anthropological attributes as well as network strength and stability.
- **Type and size of network**: Members of a threat network are also members of the general population [40]. The majority of the threat individual's actions are benign. Therefore, even knowing that an individual is part of a threat network, determining which of their actions contributes to a threat is difficult.
- **Anonymity**: Threat actors in the cyber domain may usurp authorized user's identity [41]. Identity theft is commonplace in financial transactions even with tokens and passwords, i.e., credit cards and online banking [42].

Sakharova [24] documented the change in Al Qaeda's financial transactions since 9/11. Originally, the group was highly centralized using commercial banking institutions, money laundering techniques, and countries with lax laws and poor banking oversight. As western countries cracked down on their legitimate banking operations, the group changed tactics to holding and transferring money in fixed commodities such as gold. Alternatively, these groups used the more traditional Islamic money transfer method of Hawala, which is comparable to Western Union transfers using trusted, usually unaffiliated, individuals without formal record-keeping.

To mitigate the effect of changing target signatures, analysts attempt identify individuals across all domains in which they operate. The tracking process is called certainty of presence. Certainty of presence has the added benefit to discover when a signature for a particular entity is no longer valid in a given domain. Though membership within modern threat networks are based on mutual gains, individuals generally interact among those who they trust and have deep ties [43, 44].

Assumption 2.3 Data Quality is Measureable

Data quality deals with the accuracy and precision of each data source [45]. For many directed sensors, the inherent data quality can be computed by convolving target, sensor, and environmental parameters [46] (Fig. 5.6). However, nondirected and nonsensor data have aspects of human interactions that include missing attributes, incorrect or vague inputs, and even ill-defined attribute classes. Incorrect or incomplete data could be due to human input errors, such as day/month/year variations or even leading zeros. Depending upon the context, incorrect information could be an indicator of hostile activity; i.e., deliberate malfeasance.

Human interactions make digital data, cyber in particular, suspect as evidence because: (1) Altering digital records is easy and the chain of custody is difficult to confirm; (2) Forensic data review may not yield information about file manipulation; (3) Lack of standards for the collection, verification, exploitation, and preserving digital evidence; (4) The 5Vs make the organization, scanning, and sifting functions by investigators difficult for determining the responsible party for the digital attack; and (5) Assigning the information to a unique individual is difficult to prove [21].

Fig. 5.6 Operating quality conditions affecting data quality

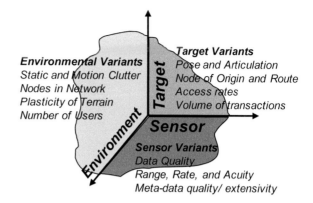

Target Variants
Pose and Articulation
Node of Origin and Route
Access rates
Volume of transactions

Environmental Variants
Static and Motion Clutter
Nodes in Network
Plasticity of Terrain
Number of Users

Sensor

Sensor Variants
Data Quality
Range, Rate, and Acuity
Meta-data quality/ extensivity

Assumption 2.4 All Knowledge is Collected

This assumption assumes that analysts have access to all the directed and nondirectional data collection and that those data contain all threat information. In reality, however, users only know the volume of data they can access and are most likely unable to estimate the amount of missing information. The assumption is that the available information can fully describe the threat. The cost of false alarms can be computed and related to intelligence errors. However, the cost of missing evidence cannot be computed and most likely to lead to surprise—intelligence failures.

Assumption 3 Context Data can be Fused

Assumption 3: Data can be Fused

The fundamental goal for data fusion is to develop discrete decision on a threat assessment. Fusing disparate data can add error as to whether the observations relate to a common entity, activity, or association [47]. As the amount of evidence increases, these uncertainties are expected to resolve. Two fundamental assumptions associated with data fusion are: the data fusion strategy is fixed and knowledge can be abstracted to different resolutions, which require context (or for that matter the right context) to change fusion strategies to produce the correct fidelity.

Assumption 3.1 The Data Fusion Strategy is Fixed

This discussion parallels the relevance of the decision process from Assumption 1. Since the combination of intent, capacity, and knowledge is unique for each threat, there is no expectation that that a specific data type can be collected [48–50]. Information Fusion is the interaction of sensor, user, and mission [51] for situation and threat assessment [52]. Challenges for information fusion [53] include the design of systems to identify and semantically classify threats as information

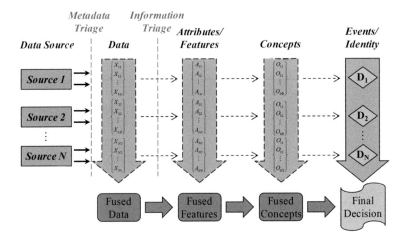

Fig. 5.7 Data structures for knowledge types

exploitation as information management [54]. The integration should be based upon the constraints of the data streams (Fig. 5.7). Many constraints exist for data level integration that require the individual sources to be aligned in space and time, classically called data fusion. Usually, only image data are layered in this fashion. More commonly, attribute/feature integration is performed where the data are only constrained by time or space. However, for threat information there must be relevant features that come from threat concepts for a given threat event identification.

Data fusion errors include the duplication of information across fields, fields incorrectly populated, and extensive use of unstructured data. Time stamps contribute to misregistration by either poor definition of the clock or incorrect values. To mitigate these issues, background processes are required to test for duplication and trustworthiness, which is often described as metadata triage. Information triage assesses the individual data streams for information content.

Assumption 3.2 Knowledge can be abstracted from Other Resolutions
This assumption states that data of differing resolutions can be combined without a loss of information content. Anomaly detection is often performed by observing deviations from the norm [55]. If data are generalized to coarser resolution, then the observed differences between an anomaly and the normal will be smoothed: possibly below a detection threshold. If the data are assigned to higher than collected rates, uncertainty creeps into the relationship among entities, activities, or events.

Assumption 4 Context Decisions are Reproducible

Assumption 4: Context Decisions are Reproducible
Decisions are reproducible assumes that the decision making process is robust and auditable [56]. The assumptions built into the earlier functional blocks

are expressed during decision making. Each piece of evidence's impact on the decision is assessed as it arrives. At decision time, the decision confidence is quantified. The assumptions made about the decision process are: threat assessment is pattern recognition, the operational context is understood, and human decision making is a good model for a computational engine.

Assumption 4.1 Threat Assessment is Pattern Recognition
The conventional pattern recognition paradigm contains assumptions that are violated by evidence accumulation [57].

- Threats fall within specific classes, are known a priori, exclusive, and exhaustive
- Data are not perishable
- Knowledge classes are generated offline
- Target signature variation is fully understood
- Performance degrades predictably with signal aberrations

The reality is that evidence accumulation for threat assessment does not adhere to any of the above assumptions, because no two threats are the same. Human activities are not independent, but interactive. Therefore, supervised classifiers that map input attributes to output classes are not relevant.

The current threat assessment philosophy is to use anomaly detection. Anomaly detection requires a mechanism to continually sample the environment and measure normal conditions. Currently researchers use graph theory to map individuals within threat networks, and then infer the impact and likelihood [58]. The cost is that graph analysis is not computationally scalable.

Machine decisions require the system to determine both an upper and lower evidence threshold, which can be conceptualized as a hypothesis test. The upper threshold is to accept the threat hypothesis and alert the user to take action. The lower threshold is to reject the hypothesis and alert telling the user that no threat exists. Irvine and Israel [59] used Wald [60] sequential evidence to provide evidence bases using this strategy.

Assumption 4.2 Operational Context is Understood
Context is fundamental to decision making [61]. Context is the environment for interpreting activities [62]. Prior to the Boston Marathon Bombing, the bomber's activities were consistent with those of the crowd. Even if the authorities were able to review the imagery and social media available of the bombers, they had no basis to interpret the bomber's activities as anomalies or threats. After the explosions, the context changed as the suspects began to flee Boston when their identities were discovered.

Assumption 4.3 Human Decision Making is a model for Computational Decision Engine

Humans perform evidence accumulation similar to the model in Fig. 5.5 [63] and have specific thresholds for recognition and understanding from which decisions are rendered, i.e., the *Eureka moment* [9, 32, 64–66]. Other uniquely human issues also contribute to failure are:

- Stereotyping based upon consistency, experience, training, or cultural and organizational norms
- Not rejecting hypotheses that do no longer fit the situation; not questioning data completeness
- Evidence evaluation

  - Greater faith placed in evidence that the analyst collected or experienced
  - Absence of evidence = Evidence of absence
  - Inability to incorporate levels of confidence into decision making

Several research studies have refuted this assumption by relating decision performance to include reduced timelines, criticality of decision, visibility of decision maker, experience, etc. [20, 67–69]. This class of problems are often called time-critical decision making. Time-critical decisions in humans are often characterized by the following:

- Decreased emphasis on identifying and tracking alternatives
- Exaggerated influence on negative data
- Pieces of available evidence are often missed or not accounted for during the decision process
- Tendency toward automated decisions; faster than actually required
- Mistakes tend to grow dramatically even for low-complexity situations
- Increased time allocated to the wrong step in the decision process

Analysts operating in a time-critical decision making environment will be affected by their personality towards risk; i.e., being risk-averse, risk-neutral, or risk prone. Also, the decision maker's presence in the environment is a factor along with their ability to evaluate the situation. However, the research shows that decision making within a stressed environment can be improved through training. The training should contain four elements: increasing the individual's knowledge base, develop policies and procedure so the individual has a cognitive look up table, perform tasks in simulated stressful environments, and provide cognitive tools for handling stress. The goal is to change the decision maker's process from cognitive to automatic [70].

Assumption 5 Context Decisions are Actionable

> **Assumption 5: Decisions are Actionable**
> Actionable decisions require trust in the decision process, unambiguous interpretation of the decision, and time to act. Actionable decision is no guarantee of a correct or optimal decision.

Assumption 5.1 Decision Engines are Trusted

Trust is a uniquely human concept. Cyber and financial systems have been using trust to describe authentication. Measures exist for data quality [71]. However, trust for computational decision engines, trust relates to human confidence in the results. Trust can be developed by providing decision lineage, where lineage is the audit trail for the decision's entire processing chain. Threat assessment also looks for agreement across disparate points of view (political, business, civil, secular, etc.). No automated measure has been discovered for this chapter.

User trust issues then are confidence (correct detection), security (impacts), integrity (what you know), dependability (timely), reliable (accurate), controllability, familiar (practice and training), and consistent (reliable).

Assumption 5.2 Decisions are Rendered Unambiguously

This assumption is the relationship between the rendered evidence and decision confidence. Cognitive interpretation of graphical information is a function of contrast among elements, graphical complexity, and human experience [72, 73]. Graph representations require simplifications to demonstrate relationships [74], which may mask other interactions [75, 76]. Ideally rendered decisions will also characterize the decision to the closest alternative, relationship to the evidence threshold, and that the context is correctly classified.

Assumption 5.3 Decisions are Timely

Under ideal conditions, computational decisions are rendered instantly. However, computational decisions have the same issues as humans with respect to finite timelines [77]. The concept is called time-sensitive computing (Fig. 5.8). Many computational applications fall into this realm of *conditional performance profiles* that allow meta-data to control processing time based upon time allocation or input quality [78]. So, the algorithms operate until either the performance threshold or the available time has been met.

Assumption 6 Context Errors can be fully Quantified

> **Assumption 6: Error can be fully quantified**
> Identifying error sources assumes that the system can be decomposed into its functions and their components. Then, the combination of the component

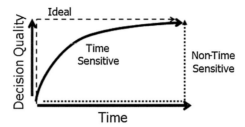

Fig. 5.8 Data structures for knowledge types time versus decision quality for computational strategies (adapted from [78])

metrics can be combined to match the system level performance measures (Fig. 5.4—Error arrow). Error analysis does not provide any information for decision relevance [79].

The problems with this assumption are that: (1) Components are often tested using their local or domain specific metrics and translation to a global measures are either impractical or have no cognitive basis; (2) Metrics often relate to the performance of an algorithm, called producer's performance rather than the amount of evidence a user must review to make a decision, called users performance; and (3) Component-level errors are incorrectly assumed to be uncorrelated.

While the error analysis leads to incorrect threat analysis, we can assume that the threat analysis is pessimistic (e.g., lower bound). It is not that threat should not be determined, but rather that the results (with the many assumptions) should error on the side of caution. Measures of effectiveness [80] require that the many sources of uncertainty be account for in the process. Currently, the International Society of Information Evaluation and Testing of Uncertainty Reasoning Working Group (ETURWG) [81] is investigating these issues for both context analysis and future interoperable standards [82].

5.4 Context-Based Threat Example

The following example shows how the earlier assumptions are accounted for quantitatively. In the example, Bayes Rule is used for data fusion and Dempster's Rule is used for evidence accumulation. We seek to address the assumptions: (6) quantifiable, (5) actionable, (4) reproducible, (3) use of context data, (2) acquirable, and (1) specific for which we use evidence theory through Proportional Conflict Redistribution (PCR).

Recently, [83] has shown that Dempster's rule is consistent with probability calculus and Bayesian reasoning if and only if the prior $P(X)$ is uniform. However, when the $P(X)$ is not uniform, then Dempster's rule gives a different result. Yen

[84] developed methods to account for nonuniform priors. Others have also tried to compare Bayes and evidential reasoning (ER) methods [85]. Assuming that we have multiple measurements $Z = \{Z_1, Z_2, ..., Z_N\}$ for cyber detection D being monitored, Bayesian and ER methods are developed next.

5.4.1 Relating Bayes to Evidential Reasoning

Using the derivation by Dezert [83], assuming conditional independence, one has the Bayes method:

$$P(X|Z_1 \cap Z_2) = \frac{P(X|Z_1)P(X|Z_2)/P(X)}{\sum_{i=1}^{N} P(X_i|Z_1)P(X_i|Z_2)/P(X_i)} \tag{5.1}$$

With no information from Z_1 or Z_2, then $P(X | Z_1, Z_2) = P(X)$. Without Z_2, then $P(X | Z_1, Z_2) = P(X | Z_1)$ and without Z_1, then $P(X | Z_1, Z_2) = P(X | Z_2)$. Using Dezert's formulation, then the denominator can be expressed as a normalization coefficient:

$$m_{12}(\varnothing) = 1 - \sum_{X_i;X_j|X_i \cap X_j} P(X_i|Z_1)P(X_i|Z_2) \tag{5.2}$$

Using this relation, then the total probability mass of the conflicting information is

$$P(X|Z_1 \cap Z_2) = \frac{1}{1 - m_{12}(\varnothing)} \cdot P(X|Z_1)P(X|Z_2) \tag{5.3}$$

which corresponds to Dempster's rule of combination using Bayesian belief masses with uniform priors. When the prior's are not uniform, then Dempster's rule is not consistent with Bayes' Rule. For example, let $m_0(X) = P(X)$, $m_1(X) = P(X | Z_1)$, and $m_2(X) = P(X | Z_2)$, then

$$m(X) = \frac{m_0(X)\, m_1(X)\, m_2(X)}{1 - m_{012}(\varnothing)} = \frac{P(X)\, P(X|Z_1)\, P(X|Z_2)}{\sum_{i=1}^{N} P(X_i)P(X_i|Z_1)\, P(X_i|Z_2)} \tag{5.4}$$

Thus, methods are needed to deal with nonuniform priors and appropriately redistribute the conflicting masses.

5.4.2 *Proportional Conflict Redistribution*

Recent advances in DS methods include *Dezert-Smarandache Theory* (DSmT). DSmT is an extension to the Dempster–Shafer method of ER which has been detailed in numerous papers and texts [86]. In [87] are introduced the methods for reasoning and presented the hyper power-set notation for DSmT [88]. Recent applications include the DSmT Proportional Conflict Redistribution rule 5 (PCR5) applied to target tracking [89].

The key contributions of DSmT are the redistributions of masses such that no refinement of the frame Θ is possible unless a series of constraints are known. For example, Shafer's model [90] is the most constrained DSm hybrid model in DSmT. Since Shafer's model, authors have continued to refine the method to more precisely address the combination of conflicting beliefs [91] and generalization of the combination rules [92, 93]. An adaptive combination rule [94] and rules for quantitative and qualitative combinations [95] have been proposed. Recent examples for sensor applications include electronic support measures, [96], physiological monitoring sensors [97], and seismic-acoustic sensing [98].

Here we use the *Proportional Conflict Redistribution* rule no. 5 (PCR5). We replace Smets' rule [99] by the more effective PCR5 to cyber detection probabilities. All details, justifications with examples on PCRn fusion rules and DSm transformations can be found in the DSmT compiled texts [86]. A comparison of the methods is shown in Fig. 5.9.

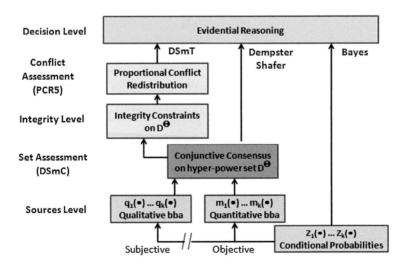

Fig. 5.9 Comparison of Bayesian, Dempster–Shafer, and PCR5 fusion theories

In the DSmT framework, the PCR5 is used generally to combine the basic belief assignment (BBAs). PCR5 transfers the conflicting mass only to the elements involved in the conflict and proportionally to their individual masses, so that the specificity of the information is entirely preserved in this fusion process. Let $m_1(.)$ and $m_2(.)$ be two independent BBAs, then the PCR5 rule is defined as follows (see [86] for full justification and examples): $m_{PCR5}(\varnothing) = 0$ and $\forall X \in 2^\Theta \backslash \{\varnothing\}$, where $\varnothing$ is the null set and 2^Θ is the power set:

$$
\begin{aligned}
m_{PCR5}(X) = &\sum_{\substack{X_1; X_2 \in 2^\Theta \\ X_1 \cap X_2 = X}} m_1(X_1) + m_2(X_2) \\
&+ \sum_{\substack{X_2 \in 2^\Theta \\ X_2 \cap X = \varnothing}} \left[\frac{m_1(X_1)^2 m_2(X_2)}{m_1(X_1) + m_2(X_2)} + \frac{m_1(X_1) m_2(X_2)^2}{m_1(X_1) + m_2(X_2)} \right]
\end{aligned}
\tag{5.5}
$$

where $\cap$ is the interesting and all denominators in the equation above are different from zero. If a denominator is zero, that fraction is discarded. Additional properties and extensions of PCR5 for combining qualitative BBAs can be found in [86] with examples and results. All propositions/sets are in a canonical form.

5.4.3 Threat Assessment from Context

In this example, we assume that policies of threat analysis are accepted and that the trust assessment of must determine whether the dynamic data is trustworthy, threatening, or under attack (Assumption 6—quantifiable). The application system collects raw measurements on the data situation, such as Boston Bomber activities as an attack, (Assumption 2—acquirable). Situation awareness is needed to determine the importance of the information for societal safety (Assumption 1—specific). With a prior knowledge, data exploitation can be used to determine the situation (Assumption 3—use of context data). The collection and processing should be consistent for decision making (Assumption 4—reproducible) over the data acquisition timeline. Finally, the focus of the example is to increase the timeliness of the machine fusion result for human decision making (Assumption 5—actionable).

Conventional information fusion processing would include Bayesian analysis to determine the state of the attack. However, here we use the PCR5 rule which distributes the conflicting information over the partial states. Figure 5.10 shows the results for a societal status undergoing changes in the social order such as events indicating an attack and the different methods (Bayes, DS, and PCR5) to access the threat. An important result is the timeliness of the change in situation state as depicted. In the example, there is an initial shock of information that lasts for a brief time (time 20–27 s) while the situation is being assessed (threat or no threat);

Fig. 5.10 Results of
Bayesian, Dempster–Shafer,
and PCR5 fusion theories for
trust as a measure of a threat
attack

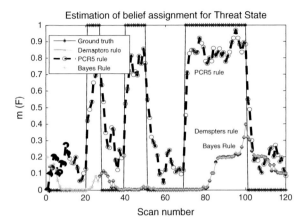

followed by another repeated event (time 40–50 s). As shown the change in state is
not recorded by Bayes, but the PCR5 denotes the change. After the initial attacks,
the threat state is revealed (time 70–100 s) from which a Bayesian method starts to
indicate a change in the threat state.

Here it is important to note that context is used in the PCR5 as the knowledge of
the first event leads to a contextual change (that is not detected by using Bayes
Rule). Likewise, the possibility for a state change (unknown unknown) is determined from the conflicting data. The conflict used in the example is 20 % which is
an example where some intelligence agencies are reporting the facts (threat event),
while others are reporting differently since they cannot confirm the evidence. The
notional example is only shown to highlight the importance of context. Two cases
arise: (1) whether the data is directly accessible, hence conflict in reporting, and
(2) exhaustively modeling all contextual data to be precise is limited—leading to
some failures.

Trust is then determined with percent improvement in analysis for the state
change. Since the classification of attack versus no attack is not consistent, there is
some conflict in the processing of the measurement data going from an measurements of attack and vice versa. The constant changing of measurements requires
acknowledgment of the change. The initial conflict in the reported evidence requires
the data conflict as measured from which the PCR5 method better characterizes the
information—leading to improved trust in the fusion result.

The improvement of PCR5 over Bayes is shown in Fig. 5.11 and compared with
the modest improvement from DS. The average performance improvement of PCR5
is 50 % and DS is 1 %, which is data, context, and application dependent. When
comparing the results, it can be seen that when a system goes from a normal to an
attack state, PCR5 responds quicker in analyzing the attack, resulting in maintaining trust in the decision. Such issues of data reliability, statistical credibility, and
application survivability all contribute to the presentation of information to an
application-based user. While the analysis is based on behavioral situation

Fig. 5.11 Results of Bayesian, Dempster–Shafer, and PCR5 fusion theories for threat detection improvement

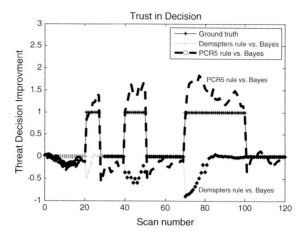

awareness, it is important to leverage context, but also be aware when the contextual factors are not complete, hence conflict.

5.5 Discussion

The chapter explicitly identified the common assumptions incorporated into computational decision engines. The assumptions at each functional block propagate through the system and dramatically affect the utility of their output. In the case of threat assessment, these assumptions could lead to intelligence failures. Context is important, but not completely measureable in a timely method. By understanding these assumptions, system users can mitigate these pitfalls by employing skepticism and confirmation in the results. The notional example provided a method of a change in the threat state that would aid in emergency response.

5.6 Conclusions

We outlined the analysis of threat assessment given the context of the situation. Threat analysis needs were juxtaposed against the assumptions developers use to make the computational decision support system tractable. We showed that the long-term system goals have some very real near-term realities. We organized the contextual information for threat analysis by categorizing six assumptions: (1) specific problem, (2) acquirable data, (3) use of context, (4) reproducible analysis, (5) actionable intelligence, and (6) quantifiable decision making. Together, a notional example was presented to highlight the need for evidence theory (e.g., PCR) to deal with conflicting information in building a context assessment.

We hope that we enlighten users of tools to question the accuracy and relevance of the computer generated analysis. Likewise, we hope that developers better understand the user's needs of these tools in an operational environment. Context for threat assessment must be discernible by both the machine and the user.

Acknowledgments This work is partly supported by the Air Force Office of Scientific Research (AFOSR) under the Dynamic Data Driven Application Systems program and the Air Force Research Lab.

References

1. A.N. Steinberg, Foundations of situation and threat assessment, Chap. 18, in *Handbook of Multisensor Data Fusion*, ed. by M.E. Liggins et al. (CRC Press, London, 2009)
2. T.X. Hammes, *The Sling and the Stone: On War in the 21st Century* (Zenith Press, 2006)
3. J. Leachtenauer, National Imagery Interpretability Ratings Scales: Overview and Product Description. *American Society of Photogrammetry and Remote Sensing Annual Meetings*, pp. 262–271, 1996
4. J.M. Irvine, National imagery interpretability rating scales (NIIRS): overview and methodology, in *Proceedings of SPIE*, vol. 3128 (1997)
5. J.M. Irvine, D. Cannon, J. Miller, J. Bartolucci, G. O'Brien, L. Gibson, C. Fenimore, J. Roberts, I. Aviles, M. Brennan, A. Bozell, L. Simon, S.A. Israel, Methodology study for development of a motion imagery quality metric, in *Proceedings of SPIE*, vol. 6209 (2006)
6. J.T. Picarelli, Transnational threat indications and warning: the utility of network analysis, in *AAAI Fall Symposium on Artificial Intelligence and Link Analysis Technical Report* (1998)
7. D. Galula, *Counterinsurgency Warfare: Theory and Practice* (Praeger Security International, Westport, 1964)
8. R. Trinquier, *Modern Warfare: A Frenchy View of Counterinsurgency* (Praeger Security International, Westport, 1964)
9. R.K. Betts, Analysis, war, and decision: why intelligence failures are inevitable. World Polit. **31**, 61–89 (1978)
10. D.L. Thomas, Proving constructive possession in Virginia: a change in the tradewinds. Colonial Lawyer **18**, 137–166 (1989)
11. S.A. Israel, Toward a common lexicon for exploiting activity data, in *IEEE Applied Imagery and Pattern Recognition Workshop: Computer Vision: Time for Change*, pp. 6 pages (2012)
12. Y. Altshuler, N. Aharony, A. Pentland, Y. Elovici, M. Cebrian, Stealing reality: when criminals become data scientists (or vice versa). IEEE Intell. Syst. 2–10 (2011)
13. C.R. Vincente, D. Freni, C. Bettini, C.S. Jensen, Location-related privacy in geo-social networks. IEEE Internet Comput. 20–27 (2011)
14. R. Colbaugh, K. Glass, J. Gosler, Some intelligence analysis problems and their graph formulations. Intell. Community Res. Dev. **315**, 27 (2010)
15. A. Vinciarelli, Capturing order in social interactions. IEEE Signal Process. Mag. 133–152 (2009)
16. J. Jonas, Threat and fraud intelligence, Las Vegas style. IEEE Secur. Priv. 28–34 (2006)
17. A.E. Gattiker, F.H. Gebara, A. Gheith, H.P. Hofstee, D.A. Jamsek, J. Li, E. Speight, J.W. Shi, G.C. Chen, P.W. Wong, Understanding system and architecture for big data. IBM, pp. 4 pages (2012)
18. C.Y. Lin, L. Wu, Z. Wen, H. Tong, V. Griffiths-Fisher, L. Shi, Social network analysis in enterprise. Proc. IEEE **100**(9), 2759–2776 (2012)
19. M.J. Duggin, C.J. Robinove, Assumptions implicit in remote sensing data acquisition and analysis. Int. J. Remote Sens. **11**, 1669–1694 (1990)

20. R. Johnston, *Analytic Culture in the US Intelligence Community: An Ethnographic Study* (Center for Study of Intelligence, Central Intelligence Agency, Washington, 2005), pp. 173 pages
21. D. Chaikin, Network investigations of cyber attacks: the limits of digital evidence. Crime Law Social Change **46**, 239–256 (2006)
22. S.A. Macskassy, F. Provost. A brief survey of machine learning methods for classification in networked data and an application to suspicion scoring, in *Workshop on Statistical Network Analysis at the 23rd International Conference on Machine Learning* (2006)
23. J.H. Ratcliffe, *Intelligence-Led Policing* (Willan Publishing, Cullompton, Devon, 2008)
24. I. Sakharova, Al Qaeda terrorist financing and technologies to track the finance network, in *IEEE Intelligence and Security Informatics* (2011)
25. J. Nagl, *Learning to Eat Soup with a Knife: Counterinsurgency Lessons from Malaya and Vietnam* (Praeger Publishers, Westport, 2002)
26. D. Rumsfeld, Known-knowns, in *Defense.gov News Transcript: DoD News Briefing—Secretary Rumsfeld and Gen. Myers* (United States Department of Defense (defense.gov), 2002)
27. G.F. Treverton, *Intelligence for an Age of Terror* (Cambridge University Press, New York, 2009)
28. S. Ressler, Social network analysis as an approach to combat terrorism: past, present, and future research. Homel. Secur. Affairs **2**, 10 (2006)
29. V.E. Krebs, Mapping networks in terrorist cells. Connections **24**, 43–52 (2002)
30. P. Klerks, The network paradigm applied to criminal organizations: theoretical nitpicking or a relevant doctrine for investigators? Recent developments in the Netherlands. Connections **24**, 53–65 (2001)
31. B. Bringmann, M. Berlingerio, F. Bonchi, A. Gionis, Learning and predicting the evolution of social networks. IEEE Intell. Syst. 26–24 (2010)
32. R. Travers, The coming intelligence failure. Studies in Intelligence (CIA) **40**, 35–43 (1997)
33. T.J. Burger, Inside the Nerve Center of America's counterterrorist operations, in *Time Magazine* (2004)
34. M.S. Granovetter, The strength of weak ties. Am. J. Sociol. **78**, 1360–1380 (1973)
35. M.K. Sparrow, The application of network analysis to criminal intelligence: an assessment of the prospects. Soc. Networks **13**, 251–274 (1991)
36. P. Buneman, S. Khanna, W.C. Tan, Data provenance: some basic issues. Found. Softw. Technol. Theor. Comput. Sci. 87–93 (2000) Springer
37. E. Blasch, A. Jøsang, J. Dezert, P.C.G. Costa, K.B. Laskey, A.-L. Jousselme, URREF self-confidence in information fusion trust, in *International Conference on Information Fusion* (2014)
38. E.H. Powley, Reclaiming resilience and safety: resilience activation in the critical period of crisis. Hum. Relat. **62**, 1289–1326 (2009)
39. N. Eagle, Behavioral inference across cultures: using telephones as a cultural lens. IEEE Intell. Syst. 62–64 (2008)
40. S. Milgram, The small-world problem. Psychol. Today **1**, 61–67 (1967)
41. G. Lawton, Invasive software, who's inside your computer. IEEE Comput. **35**, 15–18 (2002)
42. S. Graham, The urban battlespace. Theor. Cult. Soc. **26**, 278–288 (2009)
43. S. Saavedra, F. Reed-Tsochas, B. Uzzi, Asymmetric disassembly and robustness in declining networks. Proc. Natl. Acad. Sci. **105**, 16466–16471 (2008)
44. H. Sundaram, Y.R. Lin, M. DeChoudhruy, A. Kelliher, Understanding community dynamics in online social networks. IEEE Sign. Proc. Mag. 33–40 (2012)
45. B. Kahler, E. Blasch, L. Goodwon, Operating condition modeling for ATR fusion assessment, in *Proceedings of SPIE*, vol. 6571 (2007)
46. B. Kahler, E. Blasch, Sensor management fusion using operating conditions, in *Proceedings of IEEE National Aerospace Electronics Conference (NAECON)* (2008)
47. S. Rassler, Data fusion: identification problems, validity, and multiple imputation. Austrian J. Stat. **33**, 153–171 (2004)

48. I. Bloch, A. Hunter, Fusion: general concepts and characteristics. Int. J. Intell. Syst. **16**, 1107–1134 (2001)
49. D.L. Hall, *Mathematical Techniques in Multisensor Data Fusion* (Artech House) (1992)
50. J. Llinas, C. Bowman, G. Rogova, A. Steinberg, E. Waltz, F. White, Revisiting the JDL data fusion model II, in *International Conference on Information Fusion* (2004)
51. E. Blasch, Sensor, User, mission (SUM) resource management and their interaction with level 2/3 fusion, in *International Conference on Info Fusion* (2006)
52. E. Blasch, E. Bosse, E. Lambert, *High-Level Information Fusion Management and Systems Design* (Artech House, Norwood, MA, 2012)
53. E. Blasch, D.A. Lambert, P. Valin, M.M. Kokar, J. Llinas, S. Das, C.-Y. Chong, E. Shahbazian, High level information fusion (HLIF) survey of models, issues, and grand challenges. IEEE Aerosp. Electron. Syst. Mag. **27**(9) (2012)
54. E. Blasch, A. Steinberg, S. Das, J. Llinas, C.-Y. Chong, O. Kessler, E. Waltz, F. White, Revisiting the JDL model for information exploitation, in *International Conference on Info Fusion* (2013)
55. C. Drummond, Replicability is not reproducibility: nor is it good science, in *26th ICML Evaluating Methods for Machine Learning*, pp. 4 pages (2009)
56. E. Blasch, C. Banas, M. Paul, B. Bussjager, G. Seetharaman, Pattern activity clustering and evaluation (PACE), in *Proceedings of SPIE*, vol. 8402 (2012)
57. R.O. Duda, P.E. Hart, D.G. Stork, *Patten Classification*, 2nd edn. (Wiley, New York, 2001)
58. T.E. Senator, H.G. Goldberg, A. Memory, Distinguishing the unexplainable from the merely unusual: adding explanations to outliers to discover and detect significant complex rare events, in *ODD '13 Proceedings of the ACM SIGKDD Workshop on Outlier Detection and Description*, pp. 40–45 (2013)
59. J.M. Irvine, S.A. Israel, A sequential procedure for individual identity verification using ECG. EURASIP J. Adv. Signal Process. Recent Adv. Biometric Syst. A Signal Process. Perspect. **243215**, 13 (2009)
60. A. Wald, *Sequential Analysis* (Dover, New York, 1994)
61. C.E. Callwell, *Small Wars: Their Principles and Practice* (University of Nebraska Press, 1906)
62. J.R. Hipp, A. Perrin, Nested loyalties: local networks' effects on neighbourhood and community cohesion. Urban Stud. **43**, 2503–2523 (2006)
63. J.D. Lee, K.A. See, Trust in automation: designing for appropriate reliance. Hum. Factors **46**, 50–80 (2004)
64. R. Parasuraman, V. Riley, Performance consequences of automation induced complancey. Int. J. Aviat. Psychol. **3**, 1–23 (1993)
65. E.J. Ploran, S.M.M. Nelson, K. Velanova, D.I. Donaldson, S.E. Petersen, M.E. Wheeler, Evidence accumulation and the moment of recognition: dissociating decision processes using fMRI. J. Neurosci. **27**, 11912–11924 (2007)
66. D.M. Trujillo, Are intelligence failures inevitable? *e-International Relations* (2012)
67. S. Brown, M. Steyvers, E.J. Wagenmakers, Observing evidence accumulation during multi-alternative decisions. J. Math. Psychol. **53**, 453–462 (2009)
68. A. Neal, P.J. Kwantes, An evidence accumulation model for conflict detection performance in a simulated air traffic control task. Hum. Factors **51**, 164–180 (2009)
69. C.F. Chabris, D.I. Laibson, C.L. Morris, J.P. Schuldt, D. Taubinsky, The allocation of time in decision-making. J. Eur. Econ. Assoc. **7**, 628–637 (2009)
70. I. Cohen, Improving time-critical decision making in life threatening situations: observations and insights. Decis. Anal. **5**, 100–110 (2008)
71. E. Agichtein, C. Castillo, D. Donato, A. Gionis, G. Mishne, Finding high-quality content in social media, in *Web Search and Web Data Mining* (ACM, Palo Alto, 2008)
72. A.M. MacEachren, *Some Truth with Maps: A Primer on Symbolization and Design* (American Association of Geographer, 1994)
73. M. Monmonier, *How to Lie with Maps*, 2nd edn. (University of Chicago Press, 1996)

74. R. Amar, J. Eagan, J. Stasko, Low-level components of analytic activity in information visualization, in *IEEE Symposium on Information Visualization*, Minneapolis, pp. 111–117 (2005)
75. A. Perer, B. Shneiderman, Balancing systematic and flexible exploration of social networks. IEEE Trans. Vis. Comput. Graphics **12**, 693–700 (2006)
76. Z. Shen, K.L. Ma, T. Eliassi-Rad, Visual analysis of large heterogeneous social networks by semantic and structural abstraction. IEEE Trans. Vis. Comput. Graphics **12**, 1427–2439 (2006)
77. E. Blasch, Introduction to level 5 fusion: the role of the user, Chap. 19, in *Handbook of Multisensor Data Fusion,* 2nd edn., ed by M.E. Liggins, D. Hall, J. Llinas (CRC Press, 2008)
78. S. Zilberstein, An anytime computation approach to information gathering, in *AAAI Spring Symposium Series on Information Gathering from Distributed, Heterogeneous Environments* (1995)
79. S.A. Israel, Performance metrics: how and when. Geocarto Int. **21**, 23–32 (2006)
80. E. Blasch, P. Valin, E. Bossé, Measures of effectiveness for high-level fusion, in *International Conference on Info Fusion* (2010)
81. P.C.G. Costa, K.B. Laskey, E. Blasch, A.-L. Jousselme, Towards unbiased evaluation of uncertainty reasoning: the URREF ontology, in *International Conference on Information Fusion* (2012)
82. E. Blasch, K.B. Laskey, A.-L. Joussselme, V. Dragos, P.C.G. Costa, J. Dezert, URREF reliability versus credibility in information fusion (STANAG 2511), in *International Conference on Information Fusion* (2013)
83. J. Dezert, Non-bayesian reasoning for information fusion—a Tribute to Lofti Zadeh. submitted to J. Adv. Inf. Fusion (2012)
84. J. Yen, A reasoning model based on the extended Dempster Shafer theory, in *National Conference on Artificial Intelligence* (1986)
85. E. Blasch, J. Dezert, B. Pannetier, Overview of Dempster-Shafer and belief function tracking methods, in *Proceedings of SPIE*, vol. 8745 (2013)
86. J. Dezert, F. Smarandache, Advances and applications of DSmT for information fusion (collected works), vols. 1–3 (American Research Press, 2009) http://www.gallup.unm.edu/~smarandache/DSmT.htm
87. J. Dezert, Foundations for a new theory of plausible and paradoxical reasoning. Inf. Secur. Int. J. **9** (ed. by Prof. Tzv. Semerdjiev)
88. J. Dezert, F. Smarandache, On the generation of hyper-powersets for the DSmT, in *International Conference on Info Fusion* (2003)
89. E. Blasch, J. Dezert, B. Pannetier, Overview of dempster-shafer and belief function tracking methods, in *Proceedings SPIE*, vol. 8745 (2013)
90. G. Shafer, *A Mathematical Theory of Evidence* (Princeton University Press, Princeton, NJ, 1976)
91. A. Josang, M. Daniel, Strategies for combining conflict dogmatic beliefs, in *International Conference on Information Fusion* (2006)
92. F. Smaradache, J. Dezert, Information fusion based on new proportional conflict redistribution rules, in *International Conference on Information Fusion* (2005)
93. M. Daniel, Generalization of the classic combination rules to DSm hyper-power sets. Inf. Secur. Int. J. **20**, 4–9 (2006)
94. M.C. Florea, J. Dezert, P. Valin, F. Smarandache, A.-L. Jousselme, Adaptive combination rule and proportional conflict redistribution rule for information fusion, in *COGIS '06 Conference* (2006)
95. A. Martin, C. Osswald, J. Dezert, F. Smarandache, General combination rules for qualitative and quantitative beliefs. J. Adv. Inf. Fusion **3**(2) (2008)
96. P. Djiknavorian, D. Grenier, P. Valin, Approximation in DSm theory for fusing ESM reports, in *International Workshop on Belief functions* (2010)
97. Z.H. Lee, J.S. Choir, R. Elmasri, A static evidential network for context reasoning in home-based care. IEEE Trans. Sys. Man Cyber-Part A Syst. Hum. **40**(6), 1232–1243 (2010)

98. E. Blasch, J. Dezert, P. Valin, DSMT applied to seismic and acoustic sensor fusion, in *Proceedings of IEEE National Aerospace Electronics Conference (NAECON)* (2011)
99. P. Smets, Analyzing the combination of conflicting belief functions, in *International Conference on Information Fusion* (2005)

Chapter 6
Context-Aware Knowledge Fusion for Decision Support

Alexander Smirnov, Tatiana Levashova and Nikolay Shilov

Abstract The purpose of this chapter is to investigate knowledge fusion processes with reference to context-aware decision support. Various knowledge fusion processes and their possible outcomes are analyzed. A context-aware decision support system for emergency management serves as a possible application in which knowledge fusion processes go on. This system provides fused outputs from different knowledge sources. It relies upon context model, which is the key to fuse information/knowledge and to generate useful decisions. The discussion is complemented by examples from a fire response scenario.

Keywords Context-aware decision support · Constraint-based ontology · Information fusion model · Knowledge fusion · Emergency management · Fire response

6.1 Introduction

Information fusion deals with various forms of information integration (aggregation, union, merging, etc.) from multiple sources. Some time ago, sources of data and information (databases, sensors, etc.) provided an input for information fusion. The JDL model for data fusion was proposed in 1985 by the US Joint Directors of Laboratories Data Fusion Group (DFG) and revised over the years

A. Smirnov · T. Levashova · N. Shilov (✉)
St. Petersburg Institute for Informatics and Automation of the Russian
Academy of Sciences, 39, 14th Line, St. Petersburg 199178, Russian Federation
e-mail: nick@iias.spb.su

T. Levashova
e-mail: tatiana.levashova@iias.spb.su

A. Smirnov
ITMO University, 49, Kronverkskiy pr., St. Petersburg 197101, Russian Federation
e-mail: smir@iias.spb.su

© Springer International Publishing Switzerland (outside the USA) 2016   125
L. Snidaro et al. (eds.), *Context-Enhanced Information Fusion*,
Advances in Computer Vision and Pattern Recognition,
DOI 10.1007/978-3-319-28971-7_6

[1] due to observed shortcomings. Currently, this model is the most popular among other information fusion models. Initially proposed for the military applications, now it is widely used in civil domains as well, such as business or medicine. The levels with the JDL/DFG model are: source pre-processing/subject assessment (level 0), object assessment (level 1), situation assessment (level 2), impact assessment/threat refinement (level 3), process refinement (level 4), and user refinement/cognitive refinement (level 5). Through its different levels, the model divides the fusion processes according to the different levels of abstraction of the data fused and the different problems the data fusion is applicable to (e.g., characteristic estimation vs. situation recognition and analysis). The model does not prescribe a strict ordering of the processes and the fusion levels, and the levels are not always discrete and may overlap. The JDL/DFG model is useful for visualizing the data fusion process, facilitating discussion and common understanding, and important for system-level information fusion design [2].

Recently, research on information fusion extended the set of input sources with ontologies, text documents, the web, etc. That is, the focus of data and information fusion has changed to knowledge fusion.

Information fusion and knowledge fusion are tightly related [3]. Referring to various perspectives on information fusion (e.g., [2, 4–8]), this technology is aimed at facilitation of situation awareness and improvement of decision making. The main result of information fusion is a new meaningful piece of information that is beneficial to decision making in less uncertainty, more preciseness, and/or more comprehensibility then the contributing parts [9–11].

The objective of knowledge fusion is to integrate information and knowledge from multiple sources into some common knowledge that may be used for decision making and problem solving or may provide a better insight and understanding of the situation under consideration [12–15]. Knowledge fusion is defined as a process that merges heterogeneous information from multiple sources to create knowledge that is more complete, less uncertain, and less conflicting than the input [16]. Therefore, knowledge fusion is viewed as a process that creates new knowledge.

It can be seen that information fusion and knowledge fusion pursue similar goals —creation of knowledge that makes systems and humans situation aware and can be used for decision making. The main difference between these processes lies in input sources. In case of information fusion, the input is a set of information sources representing data organized (interconnected) to produce meaning [17]. The input for knowledge fusion is a set of knowledge sources, i.e., information that can be used to make decisions [18].

New knowledge is the outcome of both the information fusion process and the knowledge fusion process. In the present research, this outcome is considered as the distinguishing feature of the both processes. It is supposed that information is represented in an ontology-based way, that is, sources of information can be considered as knowledge sources. No differences between the information fusion and knowledge fusion problems are made; the both problems are referred to as knowledge fusion problem.

In this chapter, knowledge fusion problem is defined as intelligent integration of data, information and knowledge from multiple sources in result of which new knowledge is created. The new knowledge may be used for problem solving and decision making to yield actionable knowledge. At that, any kind of integration (aggregation, union, alignment, merging, etc.) is possible. The knowledge fusion problem is considered applying to decision support systems intended for usage in dynamic environments. Such systems heavily rely upon large volumes of information and knowledge available in different sources, which independently provide information and knowledge to enable a variety of problem-solving and decision-making activities. Context serves to integrate information and knowledge from the independent sources for the current purposes in the current situation. Knowledge fusion issue arises here.

Semantics is the key to intelligent knowledge integration. Semantics ensures that several knowledge sources come to the same meaning of the context. This is one of the reasons for contexts formalized by means of ontologies support most efforts on knowledge fusion and situational awareness (e.g., [19–22]). Ontology-based context specifies information needed to describe the current situation, makes this information sharable and interpretable by the knowledge sources and the decision support system, and supports ontological reasoning over the fused information and knowledge.

Emergencies are a good example of dynamic environments. The very nature of an emergency is unpredictable and can change in scope and impact. Success in emergency management strongly depends on availability of guidance during the emergency. This chapter demonstrates advantages of context for knowledge fusion and enabling dynamic decision support as applied to the problem of emergency response. Generally, knowledge sources can provide tacit and explicit knowledge. Tacit knowledge integration is embedded in societal activities and interactions. This kind of integration goes beyond the present research, which focuses on the fusion of explicit knowledge.

The rest of the chapter is structured as follows. The following section presents different results that knowledge fusion can produce. Section 6.3 proposes overview of the context-aware decision support system for emergency management, introduces the decision support model, describes knowledge fusion processes by an example of decision support in a fire situation, and provides a summarizing discussion. The conclusion generalizes the roles of context and knowledge fusion in decision support and decision making.

6.2 Knowledge Fusion: State of the Art

Currently, many research efforts are focusing on knowledge fusion. The general purpose of these efforts is to integrate information and knowledge from multiple sources to provide uniform access to them enabling querying the sources in a uniform way. In the application domains, the purpose of knowledge fusion becomes more specific. Knowledge fusion technology supports intelligent query–answering systems aiming at providing the users with nonrecurring, consistent, and unambiguous answers to their query under redundancy/lack of information (e.g., [23–27]. Some research efforts deal with knowledge fusion of multiple knowledge sources to build a new knowledge base [28–31]. Several knowledge fusion efforts are devoted to knowledge integration with the problem-solving purposes [27, 32–35]. A number of knowledge fusion applications deal with fusing information to obtain a model of the situation [36–40]. Knowledge fusion is supported by various techniques. They include logic-based reasoning, fusion rules, belief functions, Bayesian networks, neural networks, etc.

As it was mentioned in the introduction, knowledge fusion is characterized by creation of new knowledge. The analysis of a number of knowledge fusion studies [14, 35, 41–46]; as well as those mentioned above) has revealed the following kind of new knowledge produced as the knowledge fusion outcomes:

- *new knowledge created from data/information*. This outcome is a result of intelligent fusion of huge amounts of heterogeneous data/information from a wide range of sources into a new form which represents information having been processed, organized, or structured in a way that may be used by systems and humans as the basis for problem solving and decision making;
- *a new type of knowledge*. This outcome means integration of knowledge from various knowledge sources resulting in a completely different type of knowledge or integration of different types of knowledge (domain, procedural, derived, presentation, etc.) eventuating in a new knowledge type (service, process, technology, etc.);
- *a new problem-solving method* or *a new idea how to solve the problem*. This is the result of combining existing knowledge in new circumstances. For example, successfully applying an existing method or a sequence of existing methods to solve a problem different from the problem these methods usually solve means appearance of the new problem method. As well, a comprehensive discussion about how to solve an ad hoc problem may bring a completely new idea of how to do this comparing to the existing approaches;
- *new knowledge about the conceptual scheme*. This result concerns changes in schemes formally representing knowledge. For instance, changes may appear as a result of inference of explicit knowledge from information/knowledge hidden in knowledge sources being integrated, or as a result of combining knowledge from different sources in different ways in different scenarios, which implies discovery of new relations between the knowledge from different sources or/and between the entities this knowledge represents. New relations, concepts, properties, etc., appearing in existing schemes are examples of new knowledge;
- *new capabilities/competencies of an object* (an actor, a knowledge source, a knowledge source network, etc.). The new capabilities/competencies may appear as the result of knowledge reuse in new scenarios. It is, for instance, the case when an existing knowledge source network is reconfigured so that it

achieves a new configuration with new capabilities or competencies, or when an actor takes a new practice;

- *a solution for the problem.* This is the case of involvement of knowledge from various sources (perhaps, knowledge of different types) in problem solving that results in a problem solution;
- *a new knowledge source* created from multiple sources. This result is a generalization of different knowledge fusion results. It implies origination of a new source to represent the new knowledge. For instance, the process of creating new knowledge from data/information presupposes existence of a source to represent this knowledge. As well, a new knowledge source may be needed to represent a problem solution.

Below, a context-aware decision support system (CADSS) Context-aware decision support for emergency management is discussed. The system provides fused outputs from different knowledge sources at various stages of its exploitation. The purposes of the discussion are introducing the decision support model used in the system, familiarization with the conceptual framework the system is built upon, and presenting the knowledge fusion results found at the system's stages.

6.3 Context-Aware Decision Support System for Emergency Management

6.3.1 Decision Support Model

Search for a "satisfactory" decision is the main principle of the decision-making model proposed by Simon [47]. The main conclusions from the Simon's investigation can be formulated as follows: the efforts of decision makers to evaluate consequences of the possible alternatives and the dependence of the decision makers on the multiple factors influencing their choice should be minimized. Simon proposed a "satisfactory" decision as a result of decision making. That is a decision that is neither efficient nor optimal, but the decision that satisfies all parties interested in it.

In part of emergency management, the CADSS focuses on response actions planning. In the CADSS, the planning problem including the multiple influencing factors (e.g., the preferences of the stakeholders interested in the decision, intervals of the knowledge sources' availabilities, the knowledge sources' costs, etc.) are formalized by means of constraints. The planning problem formalized as it is described can be solved as a constraint satisfaction problem [48]. Consequently, a set of "satisfactory" alternative emergency response plans each corresponding to a decision that can be made in the current situation is received. An emergency response plan is a set of emergency responders with required helping services, schedules for the responders' activities, and transportation routes for the mobile responders. Since any influencing factors are embedded into the planning problem formalization, the plans do not depend on decision makers' attentions, information they have, or stress.

The decision maker chooses one plan from the set of alternative ones by selecting any plan from the set or taking advantage of some predefined efficiency criteria (e.g., minimal time of the response actions or minimal cost of these actions, minimal time of transportation of the injured people to hospitals, etc.). The chosen plan is considered to be the decision.

In the CADSS, decision support follows preliminary and execution phases; the phases cover seven main steps. Below these steps are introduced shortly.

1. *Application ontology building.* Domain experts build the application ontology for the emergency management domain. A special internal tool supports the experts to import pieces of existing ontologies and integrate them into one ontology.
2. *Matching the application ontology and knowledge sources.* The experts match the application ontology against semantic models of knowledge sources. The knowledge sources are sensors, databases, computational devices, and other kinds of sources forming the environment of the CADSS. The purpose of matching is to specify what information from knowledge sources can be used to instantiate ontology classes. The matching procedure is supported by another internal tool implementing the ontology matching model [49].
3. *Creation of a model of the current emergency situation.* The application ontology is the source for obtaining a model of the current emergency situation. This model is an ontology-based representation of the situation at the non-instantiated level and a GIS-based representation of the situation at the instantiated level. The model incorporates knowledge representing the planning problem. This model is created automatically. An inference mechanism is used to extract knowledge relevant to the situation from the application ontology, and thereby to produce a non-instantiated situation model. Reasoning proposed by the mechanism of object-oriented constraint networks is used to instantiate the situation model.
4. *Knowledge source network configuration.* Knowledge source network is con-figured to instantiate the non-instantiated level of the situation model and to solve the planning problem. The network is configured based on the references to the knowledge sources that have matching with the knowledge included in the situation model. A self-organization mechanism is used for network configuration.
5. *Solving the planning problem.* Problem-solving knowledge sources forming the network solve the planning problem incorporated in the situation model. Different mechanisms can be used for this. In this research, it is supposed that the knowledge source network includes a constraint solver.
6. *Decision making.* The set of solutions generated by the network for the planning problem is the basis for decision making. Decision making is choice of an emergency response plan from the set of alternative ones by the decision maker,

approval of the plan by the emergency responders, and in some cases a plan revision.

7. *Archiving.* After the implementation of the emergency response plan, information about the emergency situation, the situation participants, alternative plans, and the decision made in this situation is saved in a system archive. The archive can be used for several purposes (e.g., user profiling, ontology assessment, models verification, etc.). In this paper, the archive is a source of situation models. A comparative analysis of these models enables finding hidden relationships (if any) between the models' components.

The following section provides a detailed description of the introduced steps.

6.3.2 Conceptual Framework

The phases of the system scenario (Fig. 6.1) comprise several stages; at some of them knowledge fusion processes occur.[1]

6.3.2.1 Preliminary Phase

The preliminary phase covers steps 1 and 2 of the decision support model introduced above. At this phase, the application ontology is built and matched against knowledge sources.

The application ontology describes knowledge of the emergency management domain. This ontology represents non-instantiated knowledge like domain knowledge and problem solving one. The domain knowledge represents various types of emergency events and knowledge that can be used to describe situations caused by such events; the problem-solving knowledge represents knowledge that may be required to solve the problem of emergency response actions planning. The application ontology is the result of the integration of multiple pieces of different ontologies provided by various ontology libraries and is semi-automatically created by domain experts. A description of the procedure of application ontology building and the ontology operations that this procedure uses can be found in [52, 53].

For the ontology representation, the formalism of object-oriented constraint networks [54] is used. The formalism supports object-oriented knowledge specification. An ontology (*A*) is described as: $A = \langle O, Q, D, C \rangle$ where *O*—a set of classes ("*classes*"); *Q*—a set of attributes ("*attributes*") for each class in *O*; *D*—a set of domains ("*domains*") for each attribute in *Q*, and *C*—a set of *constraints* on classes in *O* and attributes in *Q*. The set of constraints *C* comprises six types of constraints. Namely, constraints used to specify pairs <class, attribute> (C^1); constraints on

---

[1]The detailed description of the framework underlying the CADSS can be found in [50, 51].

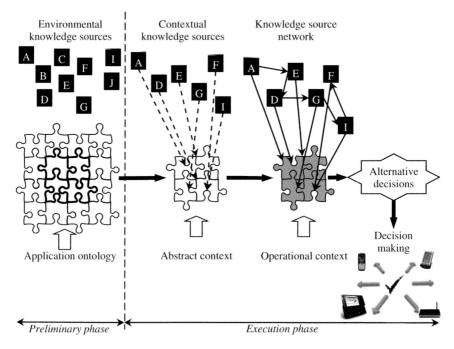

Fig. 6.1 Context-aware decision support

domains of the attribute values (C^2); class compatibility constraints (C^3); constraints used to represent taxonomical (C^4, type 1), hierarchical (C^4, type 2), and associative relationships (C^5) between classes; and functional constraints for class attributes (C^6). The application ontology specified as it is referred here corresponds to a (non-instantiated) object-oriented constraint network.

After the application ontology is built, correspondence relations between the knowledge sources and the application ontology are searched for. An ontology matching model [49] is used for the purpose of seeking the correspondences. The tool implementing the model provides hypotheses about possible correspondences and then domain experts relate the representations for knowledge sources and the ontology. The relations indicate what knowledge source can instantiate a certain class' attribute. An attribute can receive its value from a knowledge source such as a sensor or database, etc., or as a result of problem solving.

The main result of the preliminary phase is the application ontology related to a set of knowledge sources. From the knowledge fusion perspective, this ontology fuses two types of knowledge: "domain knowledge" and "problem solving knowledge." The result of this is a new knowledge source representing a new knowledge type: "application knowledge." The application ontology is used unchanged during the execution phase, which follows the preliminary one.

6.3.2.2 Execution Phase

The execution phase concerns context-aware support of the decision maker with alternative decisions, decision making, decision implementation, and archiving. This phase covers steps 3–7 of the decision support model. It is the very phase where the context-aware knowledge fusion takes place.

In the framework being discussed, ontology-based context serves to model the knowledge about the current emergency situation. A two-level representation of the emergency situation is used (Fig. 6.1).

Abstract context is responsible for the representation of the situation at the *first level*. This context captures the knowledge specific to the current emergency situation from the application ontology. It significantly reduces the amount of knowledge represented in the ontology and correspondingly the number of knowledge sources to be used in the current situation. The abstract context is a non-instantiated object-oriented constraint network just like the application ontology. Both components (domain and problem-solving knowledge) making up the application ontology are presented in the abstract context.

The procedure of the abstract context construction is performed automatically. In short it can be described as follows. The input of the procedure is the type of the emergency situation, and optionally a set of problems to be solved and a set of any other specializing terms. Here we assume that the ontology vocabulary is used for the input terms representation. The input terms are marked in the application ontology. Based on the constraints relating the marked terms, a set of ontology slices is formed. These slices are integrated into an abstract context. The ontology slicing algorithms are described in [55].

At the *second level,* the situation is represented by an *operational context*. The operational context is an instantiation of the abstract context with the actual information.

A subset of all available environmental knowledge sources is organized to instantiate the abstract context. This subset is referred to as contextual knowledge sources. The subset comprises knowledge sources that can provide data values to create instances of the classes represented in the abstract context or solve the problems specified in it. The contextual knowledge sources with the specified sequence of their execution organize a knowledge source network. Nodes of this network are knowledge sources providing data values and/or solving the problems; network arcs signify the order of the nodes execution.

Initially, the operational context is a copy of the abstract context where the variables of the constraint network representing this context are empty or take default values. The instantiation is carried out using constraint satisfaction technology. When an argument in the object-oriented constraint network is satisfied, it is mapped on the corresponding argument value in the operational context.

The operational context is the basis for solving the planning problem. As it is said above, the result of its solution is a set of alternative emergency response plans. Based on this set a decision is made.

The instantiation and the problem solving are carried out using a constraint solver (see, e.g., [35]).

The decision is delivered to the emergency responders included in the plan, i.e., to the actors responsible for the plan implementation. They have to approve the decision confirming their readiness to participate in the response actions (the decision implementation). The emergency responders are enabled to participate in the approval procedure using any Internet-accessible devices. The approval of the decision by the actors allows to avoid hierarchical decision making, which is time-consuming and therefore is not good for emergencies.

The approved decision, the abstract context, and the corresponding operational context along with the knowledge source network are saved in an archive. The operational context and the knowledge source network are saved in their states at the instant of the alternatives' generation.

The following section illustrates context-aware support of decisions on fire response actions planning.

6.3.3   Fire Response

The context-aware functions of the CADSS manifest themselves at the executive phase of the CADSS. The fire response scenario offered here, focuses on exactly this phase. Steps 3, 5–7 of the decision support model are discussed below. Step 4 dealing with the knowledge source network configuration is left out since this problem goes beyond the issues discussed in the present paper. The principles of such configuration are described, e.g., in [56]. Some ideas how knowledge sources configure the network can be found in Sect. 6.3.3.3 devoted to abstract context reuse.

6.3.3.1   Abstract Context Construction

The procedure of the abstract context construction refers to step 3 of the decision support model in part of obtaining a non-instantiated model of the fire situation. The procedure consists in selection of knowledge relevant to the current emergency situation in the application ontology, its capturing, and integration into a new consistent knowledge fragment. The relevant knowledge is defined based on the type of the current emergency situation (fire in the considered scenario). A system user enters this type to the CADSS or it is recognized based on the data from sensors. Practically, the procedure of the integration consists in the integration of multiple ontology slices representing pieces of the relevant knowledge into one knowledge fragment. This knowledge fragment corresponds to the abstract context.

Let us address the example in Fig. 6.2 that gives a fragment of the abstract context created for a fire situation. The created context, along with other issues, specifies that in the fire situation the services provided by acting resources are

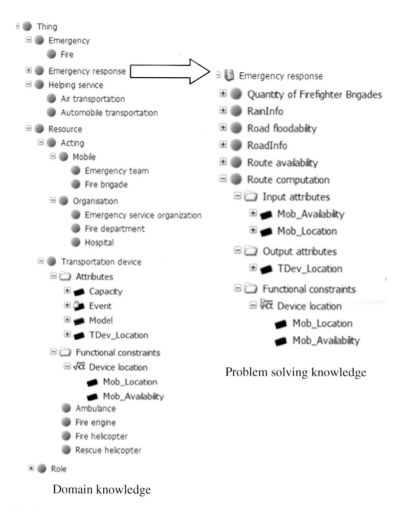

Domain knowledge

Problem solving knowledge

Fig. 6.2 Abstract context (a fragment)

required. These resources are represented by class "Acting resources" generalizing mobile and static resources. The class of mobile resources is divided into subclasses used to represent emergency teams and fire brigades. Class "Organization" represents the static resources. This class includes emergency service organizations, fire departments, and hospitals. The mobile resources use different transportation devices for movements. Class "Transportation device" represents such devices. They are ambulances, fire engines, and special purpose helicopters.

For instance, referring to the notation introduced above, emergency teams in the abstract context are represented using the constraints below.

$$c_1^4 = \langle \text{Mobile}, \text{Emergency team}, 1 \rangle$$

an emergency team is a kind of a mobile resource (class "Emergency team" is a subclass of class "Mobile");

$$c_1^1 = (\text{Emergency team}, \text{ID}), \quad c_2^1 = (\text{Emergency team}, \text{Name}),$$

class "Emergency team" is characterized by a set of attributes, e.g., identifier (attribute "ID"), name (attribute "Name"), etc.;

$$c_1^2 = (\text{Emergency team}, \text{ID}, \text{Long Integer}),$$
$$c_2^2 = (\text{Emergency team}, \text{Name}, \text{String})$$

data type of the attribute "ID" is long integer, the attribute "Name" can take values of string data type;

$$c_2^4 = \langle \text{Emergency team}, \text{Emergency service organization}, 2 \rangle \qquad (6.1)$$

an emergency team is a part of an emergency service organization (class "Emergency team" is a part of class "Emergency service organization");

$$c_1^5 = (\{\text{Emergency team}, \text{Ambulance}\}),$$
$$c_2^5 = (\{\text{Emergency team}, \text{Rescue helicopter}\})$$

emergency teams can use ambulances and rescue helicopters for transportation (class "Emergency team" is associated with the classes "Ambulance" and "Rescue helicopter");

$$c_3^5 = (\{\text{Emergency team}, \text{First aid services}\})$$

emergency teams provide first aid services (not presented in the fragment of the abstract context in Fig. 6.2).

In the expressions above, $c_i^n \subset C^n$, where n $(1 \leq n \leq 6)$ is type of the constraint, i is sequence number of the constraint c in the set C^n.

In Fig. 6.2, the problem-solving knowledge specified in the abstract context is collapsed in the "Emergency response" class. Partly, this class is shown expanded in the figure on the right. The domain and problem-solving knowledge here are related as follows. Any problem is represented by a hierarchy of methods that can be used to solve this problem. The methods are treated the same way as classes; their input and output arguments are represented as attributes. Functional constraints relate the input and output method arguments to class attributes contained in the representation of the domain knowledge. These constraints indicate which attribute values serve as values of methods' input arguments or what attribute values are instantiated as a result of methods' execution.

Equations (6.2) give an example of the specification of relationships between domain and problem-solving knowledge for the method "Resource selection" (not represented in Fig. 6.2). This method selects feasible emergence teams for response actions planning. In (6.2), values of the attributes representing identifiers (f_1), availabilities (f_2), current locations (f_3), and facilities (f_4) of emergence teams serve as input arguments. Some outputs of the method "Resource selection" serve as inputs for the routing method (this method is represented by the class "Route computation"). In the abstract context, this is specified through a set of corresponding functional constraints (e.g., $c_k^6 = f(\langle \text{Resource selection, Res\_ID} \rangle) = \langle \text{Route computation, Mob\_ID} \rangle$, where Res_ID – identifier of the resource selected by the method "Resource selection," Mob_ID – identifier of the resource as an input argument for the routing method).

$$c_1^6 = \begin{cases} f_1(\langle \text{Emergency team, ID} \rangle) = \langle \text{Resource selection, Team\_ID} \rangle \\ f_2(\langle \text{Emergency team, Availability} \rangle) = \langle \text{Resource selection, Available} \rangle \\ f_3(\langle \text{Emergency team, Location} \rangle) = \langle \text{Resource selection, Resource location} \rangle \\ f_4(\langle \text{Emergency team, Facility} \rangle) = \langle \text{Resource selection, Resource facility} \rangle \end{cases}$$

$$(6.2)$$

At the stage of the abstract context construction, the result of knowledge fusion is a new knowledge source (the abstract context) fusing multiple pieces of the application knowledge. Referring to decision support purposes, the abstract context provides the CADSS and its users with an ontology-based representation of the current emergency situation supplemented with the ontology-based specification of the problems requiring solutions in this situation.

6.3.3.2 Abstract Context Refinement

Abstract context refinement is not considered as an autonomous step. It is an integral part of abstract context construction procedure.

For instance, in the course of construction of the abstract context for the fire situation a new relationship between the knowledge unspecified in the application ontology is inferred (Fig. 6.3). Namely, the application ontology specifies the routing problem as a hierarchy of methods one of which ("GetLocation") (6.3) returns the current locations of objects in the format of point coordinates on the map. A value for the variables representing the current location of a transportation device serves as an input variable of this method (6.4).

The class "mobile" representing a mobile resource and the class "transportation device" are linked by functional relationships (6.5) stating that the location of a mobile resource is the same as the location of the transportation device this resource goes by. In the abstract context, a new functional relationship (6.6) is inferred. This relationship means that a value of the attribute representing the current location of a

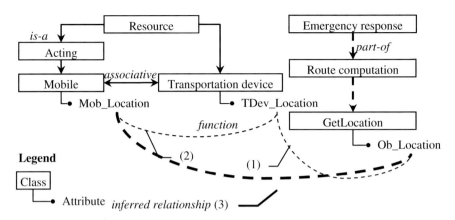

Fig. 6.3 Inferred relationship

mobile resource serves as an input argument of the method "GetLocation." In other words, values for the both attributes representing the current location of a transportation device or the current location of a mobile resource can be used as one of the input arguments by this method.

$$c_3^4 = \langle \text{Route computation}, \text{GetLocation}, 2 \rangle \tag{6.3}$$

$$c_2^6 = f(\langle \text{Transportation device}, \text{TDev\_Location}\rangle) = \langle \text{GetLocation}, \text{Ob\_Location}\rangle \tag{6.4}$$

where "TDev_Location" is an attribute of the class "Transportation device" representing values of the locations of transportation devices, "Ob_Location" is an input argument of the method "GetLocation."

$$c_3^6 = \begin{cases} f_1(\langle \text{Transportation device}, \text{TDev\_Location}\rangle) = \langle \text{Mobile}, \text{Mob\_Location}\rangle \\ f_2(\langle \text{Mobile}, \text{Mob\_Location}\rangle) = \langle \text{Transportation device}, \text{TDev\_Location}\rangle \end{cases} \tag{6.5}$$

$$c_4^6 = f(\langle \text{Mobile}, \text{Mob\_Location}\rangle) = \langle \text{GetLocation}, \text{Ob\_Location}\rangle \tag{6.6}$$

In the illustrative example, the knowledge fusion at the stage of the abstract context refinement results in a new relationship, that is a new knowledge about the conceptual scheme. Referring to the knowledge fusion processes presented in Sect. 6.2, this outcome is a result of inference of explicit knowledge from knowledge hidden in the knowledge sources being integrated. The multiple pieces of the application knowledge integrated into the abstract context play the role of the knowledge sources mentioned.

Generally, any kind of element of the conceptual scheme can be inferred. Perhaps, the new inferred knowledge might be considered as a consequence of the knowledge fusion process taking place at the stage of the abstract context construction rather than an independent result. In the CADSS, the refined abstract context creates more complete representation of the current situation.

6.3.3.3 Abstract Context Reuse

The abstract contexts are reusable components of the CADSS. Reuse of an existing abstract context is one more way to obtain a non-instantiated model of the situation. When there are reusable contexts in the archive, the step of abstract context reuse substitutes the step of abstract context construction. The step of abstract context reuse corresponds to step 3 of the decision support model in part of obtaining a non-instantiated situation model.

Reuse of an abstract context when available knowledge sources are not intended to solve problems specified in this context, makes it possible to find alternative problem-solving methods. A basic condition for finding alternatives is availability of knowledge sources that provide methods that can be used to solve the specified problems.

Figure 6.4 illustrates the case when it is required to determine the locations of hospitals. As it is said in the previous section, the method "GetLocation" serves for the purpose of object locations determination. This method uses data from sensors for the static objects, like hospitals (6.7).

$$c_5^6 = f(\langle \text{Sensor\_ID}, \text{Loc} \rangle) = \langle \text{GetLocation}, \text{Ob\_Location} \rangle \qquad (6.7)$$

where "Loc" is the attribute representing values that sensors read.

In the settings where the abstract context (Fig. 6.2) is reused, the set of environmental knowledge sources comprises no sensors dealing with static objects, but this set comprises some other sources. One of them (A) implements a method ("MedicalCareSuggestions") intended to make recommendations what medical care organizations can be used to access some specific medical service. This source contains a database with information about the hospitals. The source A returns the hospitals' addresses in an address format.

The class "Hospital" and the method "MedicalCareSuggestions" are linked by the functional constraint (6.8). This constraint specifies that the value of the output argument "Sug_Address" of the method "MedicalCareSuggestions" instantiates the attribute "Address" of the class "Hospital."

$$c_6^6 = f(\langle \text{MedicalCareSuggestion}, \text{SugAddress} \rangle) = \langle \text{Hospital}, \text{Address} \rangle \qquad (6.8)$$

The other source (B) implements the method ("Conversion") that converts the address formats into the format of coordinates. Applying this method to hospitals,

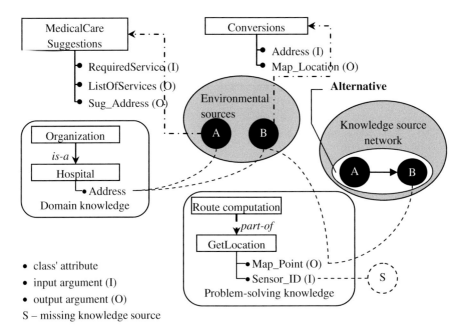

Fig. 6.4 Discovery of alternative problem-solving methods

we get the constraint (6.9). The output of this method is represented by the attribute "Map_Location."

$$c_7^6 = f(\langle \text{Hospital, Address} \rangle) = \langle \text{Conversion, Post\_Address} \rangle, \qquad (6.9)$$

the input argument "Post_Address" of the method "Conversion" takes its values from the attribute "Address" of class "Hospital."

As well, the methods "GetLocation" and "Conversions" are linked by the constraint (6.10) specifying that the output argument "Map_Location" of the method "Conversion" and the output argument "Map_Point" of the method "GetLocation" have the same meaning.

$$c_8^6 = \begin{cases} f_1(\langle \text{GetLocation, Map\_Point} \rangle) = \langle \text{Conversion, Map\_Location} \rangle \\ f_2(\langle \text{GetLocation, Map\_Point} \rangle) = \langle \text{GetLocation, Map\_Point} \rangle \end{cases} \qquad (6.10)$$

The successive execution of the methods "MedicalCareSuggestions" and "Conversions" is an alternative way to calculate the hospitals' locations in the format of coordinates.

In the abstract context, the methods "MedicalCareSuggestions" and "Conversion" are not specified as an alternative to the method "GetLocation." A set of constraints (6.9, 6.11, 6.12) have to be introduced to get this alternative explicitly specified.

$$c_4^4 = \langle \text{Route computation, Conversion}, 1 \rangle \qquad (6.11)$$

the method "Conversion" is one of the (alternative) methods that can be used to determine the objects' locations.

$$c_5^4 = \langle \text{Conversion, MedicalCareSuggestions}, 2 \rangle \qquad (6.12)$$

the method "MedicalCareSuggestions" is a part of the method "Conversion."

The constraint (6.3) should be replaced with the constraint $c_3^4 = \langle \text{Route computation, GetLocation}, 1 \rangle$ (the method "GetLocation" is one of the (alternative) methods that can be used to determine the objects' locations).

As the constraint (6.9) relates the class "Hospital" and the method "Conversion," the alternative (6.11) is applicable to hospitals only.

The domain experts introduce the constraints (6.9, 6.11, 6.12) into the abstract context. This leads to the extension of this context with new knowledge representation items, in other words to abstract context refinement.

At the stage of the abstract context reuse knowledge fusion results appear in two ways: as a new (alternative) problem-solving method and as a new configuration of the knowledge source network.

6.3.3.4 Operational Context Producing

The procedure of the operational context producing refers to the step 3 of the decision support model in part of obtaining an instantiated model of the fire situation.

An operational context is produced through the semantic fusion of data/information from multiple sources within the abstract context structure. Figure 6.5 depicts a GIS-based view of the operational context produced based on the abstract context (Fig. 6.2) at some time instant. The CADSS produces such views to make the operational context readable by humans (decision makers). The way of operational context representation reflects all changes in information incoming from the knowledge source network (e.g., the decision maker observes that mobile resources are changing their locations). In Fig. 6.5, the bold dot indicates the fire location. Emergency teams, fire brigades, and hospitals shown in the figure are the autonomous entities whose efforts to be joined in the fire response operation. The operational context also characterizes the fire situation as the situation with nine victims (not shown in the figure) to be transported to hospital.

Producing the operational context gives rise to two knowledge fusion results: (1) the operational context represents a new knowledge created from data/ information; and (2) this context is a knowledge source of a new (dynamic) type. For the CADSS's users, the operational context is a schematic picture of the emergency situation.

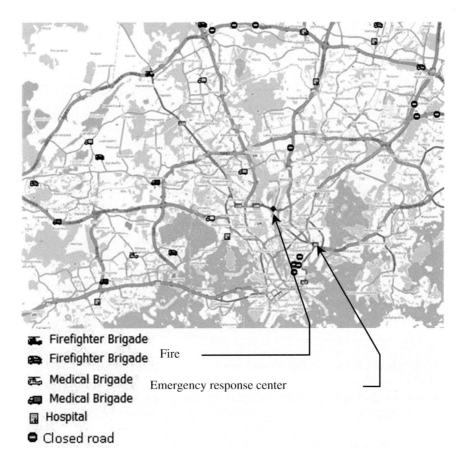

Firefighter Brigade
Firefighter Brigade   Fire
Medical Brigade   Emergency response center
Medical Brigade
Hospital
Closed road

Fig. 6.5 Operational context [50]

6.3.3.5 Problem Solving

Problem solving is the fifth step of the decision support model. The problem of planning fire response actions is considered referring to the main purpose of decision support. Due to the formalism used, this problem can be processed as constraint satisfaction problem. The knowledge source network generates a set of feasible problem solutions. This set comprises alternative feasible plans for the joint activities of the emergency teams, fire brigades, and hospitals.

Choice of a plan for the set of alternatives is the sixth step of the decision support model. Figure 6.6 shows an example of such a plan selected as the decision. This plan is represented in the schematic picture of the operational context. The dotted lines indicate the routes to be used for the transportations. The plan relates earlier independent entities (emergency teams, fire brigades, and hospitals), i.e., new relationships between these entities have arisen. These relationships are the result of knowledge fusion. Particularly, fusion of the ontology-based representations for

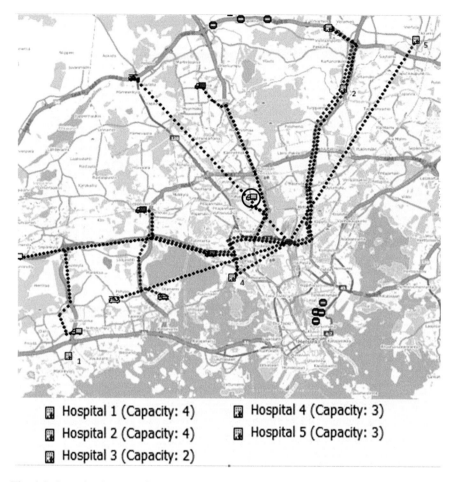

▦ Hospital 1 (Capacity: 4)	▦ Hospital 4 (Capacity: 3)
▦ Hospital 2 (Capacity: 4)	▦ Hospital 5 (Capacity: 3)
▦ Hospital 3 (Capacity: 2)	

Fig. 6.6 Operational context fused with decision [50]

independent entities and the non-ontological result of problem solving produce new contextual knowledge about the entities.

Therefore, at the problem-solving step, a new knowledge source of a new type that is the operational context fused with the decision, new relations between entities, and a set of problem solutions are outcomes of knowledge fusion. It should mention that all kinds of new knowledge produced here are temporal, they are true for the context only.

6.3.3.6 Decision Implementation

Previously to putting the emergency response plan into action, the emergency responders included in this plan approve it. The procedures of plan approval as well

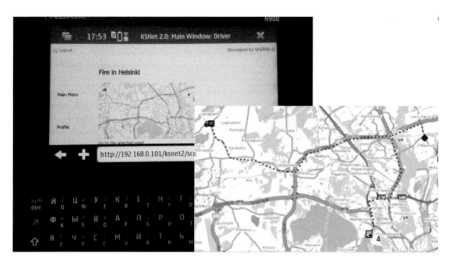

Fig. 6.7 Plan for actions for an emergency team

as choice of the plan take place at the sixth step of the decision support model. The emergency responders can access the knowledge source representing the operational context fused with the plan using any Internet-accessible devices (notebooks, PDAs, mobile phones, etc.). Figure 6.7 shows part of the plan displayed on the Tablet PC of the leader of an emergency team going by ambulance. He/she can accept or reject this plan (a special option is provided for this). The option of rejection is provided for due to the rapidly changing emergency situations—something may happen between the moment when the plan is selected and the time when the emergency responders receive this plan.

In some cases, the plan can be adjusted. An example of such case is when an emergency responder failed, and its functions can be delegated to another emergency responder or redistributed between other responders. For instance, an emergency team trained to rescue operations has failed in the course of actions because of road destruction, ambulance blockage, etc. If some of available teams agree to take such operations, the plan is adjusted accordingly.

In the CADSS, emergency responders are represented by their profiles. If a team agrees to participate in some activity that its profile does not provide for, then this profile is extended with a new capability. This is the case of fusion of implicit (unspecified capabilities) knowledge and explicit (profile) knowledge. The knowledge fusion result is gaining new capabilities/competencies by a knowledge object.

6.3.3.7 Archival Knowledge Management

After the implementation of the fire response plan, at the seventh step of the decision support model, the implemented plan, the abstract context for the fire situation, and the corresponding operational context along with the knowledge source network are saved in the archive. Archival knowledge management deals with management of knowledge contained in the archived components. The main intention of such management is inference of new knowledge based on the accumulated knowledge. For instance, new relations between the knowledge represented in the operational contexts can be discovered based on a comparative analysis of these contexts accumulated in the archive. Finding the same instance in different operational contexts may lead to revealing new relations for this instance.

For example, the emergency team encircled in Fig. 6.6 participated in different emergency response actions. Different operational contexts for the actions planning were produced based on the same abstract context. Besides the constraints used to represent emergency teams, which are given in Sect. 6.3.3.1, this abstract context comprises constraints to represent emergency service organizations and hospitals:

$$c_6^4 = \langle \text{Organisation}, \text{Emergency service organization}, 1 \rangle \qquad (6.13)$$

an emergency service organization is a kind of organization;

$$c_7^4 = \langle \text{Organisation}, \text{Hospital}, 1 \rangle$$

a hospital is a kind of organization.

In the operational context (Fig. 6.6), the relationship (6.1) (*Part of*) for the emergency team named "Ambulance 2" is found to be not instantiated. Based on the constraints (6.1 and 6.13), the assumption (6.14) is generated.

$$c_{a_1}^4 = \langle \text{Ambulance 2}, \text{Organisation}, 2 \rangle \qquad (6.14)$$

the emergency team "Ambulance 2" is a part of an organization (any instance of an organization represented in the operational context).

Given a set of operational contexts representing "Ambulance 2," the assumptions generated for this team are tested (Fig. 6.8). Testing consists in checking if assumptions generated for one context retain meaningful in other contexts. The procedure stops when the set of assumptions includes only one meaningful assumption. Referring to the example with "Ambulance 2," if this emergency team is found in the context, which represents an organization not represented in the context (Fig. 6.6), the assumption about belonging of "Ambulance 2" to this organization becomes pointless. The meaningless assumptions are removed from the set of assumptions.

Figure 6.9 illustrates the simplest case when the operational context represents "Ambulance 2" (6.15) and only one organization that the operational context (Fig. 6.6) represents; this organization is a hospital named "Hospital 5" (6.16).

input: instance *inst*
for c = 1 to OC   'OC number of operational contexts representing *inst*
    for i = 1 to $|As_c|$ ' As_c – the set of assumptions for *inst* in the context *c*
        if $as_i \in As_c$ is wrong **then** $As_c = As_c \setminus as_i$
    endfor
    if $|As_c| = 1$ **then**
        output: assumption $as \in As_c$ 'referral to experts
    else $As_c = As_c \bigcup As_{c+1}$
    endif
endfor
output: message "no assumptions have been proven"

Fig. 6.8 Assumptions testing

Fig. 6.9 History for an emergency team

The assumption (6.17) about belonging of the emergency team "Ambulance 2" to the hospital "Hospital 5" is a subject of expert judgment. If the experts decide that this is really so then *Part-of* relationship between the "Hospital 5" and the emergency team "Ambulance 2" is the new revealed relation.

$$c_1^2 = (\text{Emergency team}, \text{ID}, 00000003), \quad c_2^2 = (00000003, \text{Name}, \text{Ambulance 2})$$
$$(6.15)$$

$$c_3^2 = (\text{Hospital}, \text{ID}, 20000000), \quad c_4^2 = (20000000, \text{Name}, \text{Hospital 5}) \quad (6.16)$$

$$c_{a_1}^4 = \langle 00000003, 20000000, 2 \rangle \tag{6.17}$$

The revealed relation cannot be interpreted unambiguously without expert assistance. On the one hand, this relation can be generalized in the application ontology so, that the classes "Emergency response organization" and "Hospital" can be related with *Part-of* relationship ("Emergency response organization" is a part of "Hospital"). This conclusion does not seem to be a general case. On the other hand, the knowledge concept with the new relation can be considered as a new concept non-classified in the ontology.

The archival knowledge management enables to manifest two knowledge fusion results. First, explicit knowledge can be revealed from the hidden ones. Second, the revealed knowledge may appear as new relations between originally unrelated knowledge or as new knowledge concepts refining the existing representations.

6.3.4 Knowledge Fusion in the CADSS

Table 6.1 shows the correspondences between the steps of the constraint-based framework and the phases of the Simon's model as well as the correspondences of the framework steps with the JDL/DFG model accepted in the information fusion community. The Simon's model specifies decision making consisting of "intelligence," "design," and "choice" phases. The decision-making model offered in the framework exceeds the bounds of the Simon's model proposing two more steps:

Table 6.1 Three-phase model with reference to information fusion model

Phase	Phase content	Steps of Simon's model	Steps of constraint-based approach	Levels of JDL/DFG model
Intelligence	Finding, identifying, and formulating the problem or situation that calls for a decision	Fixing goals	Abstract context construction	1
		Setting goals	Operational context producing	1, 2
Design	Search for possible decisions	Designing possible alternatives	Constraint-based generation of feasible alternative satisfactory solutions	3
Choice	Evaluation of alternatives and choosing one of them	Choice of a satisfactory decision	Choice of an efficient satisfactory decision	4
Implementation	Putting the decision into action	–	Communications of the actors with the CADSS for their actions	5

search for an efficient satisfactory decision and communications on the implementation of this decision.

The steps of the constrained-based framework can be mapped in the JDL/DFG model as follows. The preprocessing/subject assessment level (level 0) of the JDL/DFG model dealing with hypothesizing the presence of a signal and estimating its state goes beyond the framework. Levels 1 (object assessment) and 2 (situation assessment) are covered by the steps of abstract context construction and operational context producing. Types of entities involved in the current situation, their characteristics, and classes of relationships between the entities are defined at the step of abstract context construction. At the step of operational context producing, the above abstractions gain the concrete embodiments which enables to get a view of the current situation and assess it. The step of feasible solutions (decisions) generation corresponds to the impact assessment level (level 3). At this step, the possible action plans are designed and plan outcomes can be estimated. The estimation can include costs of the plans, times taken for their implementations, etc. The step of decision choice supports mission objectives; it is a planning step and here the actors are assigned the task. With reference to the JDL/DFG model, this step corresponds to level 4 of process refinement. The step of actor communications accords with level 5 of user refinement. At this step, the actors are supported with information displayed on the actors' devices about their actions.

Table 6.2 summarizes the results of the context-based knowledge fusion with reference to the CADSS. The table lists the results as they are presented in the Sect. 6.2, indicates the system's stages where these results appear and the processes leading to them, and introduces the benefits that the context gives for decision support.

In the CADSS, a new knowledge source created from multiple knowledge sources appears at the stage of the abstract context construction. Although the abstract context integrates multiple prices of the single knowledge source (application ontology), this context is believed a result of knowledge fusion since these pieces can be considered as multiple homogeneous knowledge sources.

A new type of knowledge appears at the stage of the operational context producing, which concerns knowledge instantiation. At this stage, the abstract static non-instantiated knowledge becomes instantiated knowledge with time-varying parameters. This is considered as the appearance of a new knowledge source of a new type and that is dynamic type. This dynamic knowledge includes one more knowledge fusion result that is a new knowledge created from data/information, i.e., the stage of operational context producing gives rise to two different sorts of new knowledge.

A new knowledge about the conceptual scheme appears as the results of various inferences and problem solving. Generally, the inferences may imply any knowledge representation items (concepts, relationships, properties, etc.). These newly inferred items organize the new knowledge about the conceptual schemes. In this research, the stages involving the inferences are "Abstract context refinement," "Abstract context reuse," "Problem solving," and "Archival knowledge management."

Table 6.2 Context-based knowledge fusion results in the CADSS

Knowledge fusion result	Stage	Process leading to the result	Context contribution
New knowledge source created from multiple sources	Abstract context creation	Integration of multiple knowledge pieces into new fragment	An ontology-based representation of the emergency situation
New knowledge created from data/information	Operational context producing	Knowledge instantiation	A schematic picture of the emergency situation
New type of knowledge	Operational context producing	Knowledge instantiation	A schematic picture of the emergency situation
	Problem solving	Problem solving	A schematic picture of the emergency situation fused with a set of problem solutions or the decision
New problem-solving method	Abstract context reuse	Inference-Reconfiguration of the knowledge source network	An ontology-based representation of the reusable emergency situation
New knowledge about the conceptual scheme	Abstract context refinement	Inference	More complete ontology-based representation of the emergency situation or a better representation for the application knowledge
	Abstract context reuse	Inference	
	Problem solving	Problem solving	
	Archival knowledge management	Discovery of new knowledge based on the accumulated one	
New capabilities/competencies of a knowledge object	Decision implementation	Decision adjustment	Demand in capabilities/competencies in the current situation
Problem solution	Problem solving	Problem solving	Context-based solutions for the problem(s)

The knowledge objects gain new capabilities/competencies as a result of making agreement on taking unplanned activities at the decision implementation stage. To be more general, a knowledge object gains new capabilities/competencies as a result of some interactions. The processes leading to such result are supposed to be oriented on agent technologies, web communities, or other technologies dealing with behavioral objects.

A new problem-solving method or idea how the problem can be solved may come when existing knowledge is used in new settings or situations. This issue is treated at the abstract context reuse stage. The abstract context specifies existing knowledge about what the environmental knowledge sources are expected to do in the emergency situations of a given type. When this context is put in a situation with a new set of sources, these new sources try to adapt to the context. As a result, a new configuration of the knowledge source network appears. This configuration may suggest alternative methods to solve the problems specified in the context, whereas it can be suggested that the resource management technologies provide techniques to discover new problem-solving methods. A new idea of how to solve the problem may come as a result of conscious interactions, discussions, and practices. This last issue is not considered in the current research.

The CADSS generates a set of the problem solutions as a result of knowledge fusion at the problem-solving stage. These solutions are the result of solving the problem of planning emergency response actions as a constraint satisfaction problem.

6.4 Conclusion

The knowledge fusion processes in the context-aware decision support system for emergency management were investigated and their outcomes were analyzed. The investigation has shown several aspects, in which context is beneficial for decision support and decision making:

- context specifies information relevant to describe the current situation and knowledge needed to solve the problems requiring solutions in this situation;
- context makes the information sharable and interpretable by the various environmental sources and the decision support system;
- ontology-based context supports ontological reasoning over the information and knowledge being integrated or fused;
- context model that includes specifications of the problems requiring solutions in the current situation, enable to provide decision makers with a set of alternative decisions;
- a set of contexts representing similar situations enable inference of explicit knowledge from the hidden one;
- context allows various entities involved in the current situation to be interoperable (this includes the interoperability of the environmental knowledge sources and the interoperability of the executives of the decision).

Summing up the items above, context introduces intelligence into the decision support systems. In the context-aware decision support system discussed in this work, a number of knowledge fusion results have been revealed. Based on these results, it can be concluded that knowledge fusion enables to refine context, to make it more complete and less uncertain, and therefore to make decision support more efficient.

An important issue of information fusion is treatment of incomplete and uncertain information. At the moment, the present research does not address this issue. The future work is planned in this direction. Namely, it is planned to develop the formalism of fuzzy constraint network, which is an extension to the used formalism of object-oriented constraint networks, and to develop models, methods, and architectures supporting management of fuzzy and incomplete knowledge.

Acknowledgements The present research was partly supported by the projects funded through grants 14-07-00345, 14-07-00378, 14-07-00427, 15-07-08092 (the Russian Foundation for Basic Research), the Project 213 of the Program 8 "Intelligent information technologies and systems" (the Russian Academy of Sciences (RAS)), the Project 2.2 of the basic research program "Intelligent information technologies, system analysis and automation" (the Nanotechnology and Information Technology Department of the RAS), and grant 074-U01 (the Government of the Russian Federation).

References

1. D. Hall, J. Llinas, *Handbook of Multisensor Data Fusion* (CRC Press, Boca Raton, 2001)
2. E. Blasch, É. Bossé, D.A. Lambert (eds.), *High-level information fusion management and systems design* (Artech House, Boston, 2012)
3. C. Laudy, H. Petersson, K. Sandkuhl, Architecture of knowledge fusion within an integrated mobile security kit, in *Proceedings of the 13th International Conference on Information Fusion*, Edinburgh, UK, 26–29 July 2010. http://ieeexplore.ieee.org/stamp/stamp.jsp?tp=&arnumber=5711868. Accessed 25 Apr 2015
4. M.A. Abidi, R.C. Gonzalez, *Data Fusion in Robotics and Machine Intelligence* (Academic Press, San Diego, 1992)
5. A. Appriou, A. Ayoun, S. Benferhat et al., Fusion: general concepts and characteristics. Int. J. Intell. Syst. **16**, 1107–1134 (2001)
6. J.A. Kennewell, B.-N. Vo, An overview of space situational awareness, in *Proceedings of the 16th International Conference on Information Fusion*, Istanbul, Turkey, 9–12 July 2013, pp. 1029–1036
7. S. Paradis, B.A. Chalmers, R. Carling, P. Bergeron, Towards a generic model for situation and threat assessment, in *Digitalization of the Batterfield II. SPIE Aerosense Conference*, vol. 3080, Orlando, April 1997, pp. 171–182
8. A.N. Steinberg, C.L. Bowman, Adaptive context discovery and exploitation, in *Proceedings of the 16th International Conference on Information Fusion*, Istanbul, Turkey, 9–12 July 2013, pp. 2004–2011
9. B.V. Dasarathy, Information fusion—what, where, why, when, and how? Inf. Fusion **2**(2), 75–76 (2001)
10. M.B.A. Haghighat, A. Aghagolzadeh, H. Seyedarabi, Multi-focus image fusion for visual sensor networks in DCT domain. Comput. Electr. Eng. **37**(5), 789–797 (2011)
11. E.L. Waltz, J. Llinas, *Multisensor Data Fusion* (Artech House, Norwood, MA, 1990)
12. C.W. Holsapple, A.B. Whinston, Building blocks for decision support systems, in *New Directions for Database Systems*, ed. by G. Ariav, J. Clifford (Ablex Publishing Corp, Norwood, 1986), pp. 66–86
13. V. Phan-Luong, A framework for integrating information sources under lattice structure. Inf. Fusion **9**(2), 278–292 (2008)
14. A. Preece et al., Kraft: an agent architecture for knowledge fusion. Int. J. Coop. Inf. Syst. **10**(1–2), 171–195 (2001)
15. R. Scherl, D.L. Ulery, Technologies for army knowledge fusion (2004). Monmouth University, Computer Science Department, West Long Branch, Monmouth. Final report ARL-TR-3279

16. A. Hunter, R. Summerton, *Fusion rule technology* (2002–2005). http://www0.cs.ucl.ac.uk/staff/a.hunter/frt/. Accessed 20 Apr 2015
17. B.C. Landry, B.A. Mathis, N.M. Meara, J.E. Rush, C.E. Young, Definition of some basic terms in computer and information science. J Am Soc Inf Sci **24**(5), 328–342 (1970)
18. C. Zins, Conceptual approaches for defining data, information, and knowledge. J Am Soc Inf Sci Technol **58**(4), 479–493 (2007)
19. N. Baumgartner et al., BeAware!—Situation awareness, the ontology-driven way. Data Knowl. Eng. **69**, 1181–1193 (2010)
20. J. Garcia, et al., Context-based multi-level information fusion for harbor surveillance. Inf. Fusion (2014). http://dx.doi.org/10.1016/j.inffus.2014.01.011
21. J. Gomez-Romero, M.A. Patricio, J. Garcia, J.M. Molina, Ontology-based context representation and reasoning for object tracking and scene interpretation in video. Expert Syst. Appl. **38**(6), 7494–7510 (2011). doi:10.1016/j.eswa.2010.12.118
22. M.M. Kokar, C.J. Matheus, K. Baclawski, Ontology-based situation awareness. Inf. Fusion **10**(1), 83–98 (2009). doi:10.1016/j.inffus.2007.01.004
23. S. Dumais, M. Banko, E. Brill, J. Lin, A. Ng, Web question answering: is more always better?, in *Proceedings of the 25th Annual International ACM SIGIR Conference on Research and Development in Information Retrieval*, Tampere, Finland, 11–15 Aug 2002, pp. 291–298
24. O. Etzioni, D. Weld, A softbot-based interface to the internet. Commun. ACM **37**(7), 72–76 (1994)
25. A. Levy, The information manifold approach to data integration. IEEE Intell. Syst. **13**(5), 12–16 (1998)
26. X. Nengfu, W. Wensheng, Y. Xiaorong, J. Lihua, Rule-based agricultural knowledge fusion in web information integration. Sensor Lett. **10**(8), 635–638 (2012)
27. A. Preece, K. Hui, A. Gray, P. Marti, T. Bench-Capon, D. Jones, Z. Cui, The KRAFT architecture for knowledge fusion and transformation. Knowl. Based Syst. **13**(2–3), 113–120 (1999)
28. M. Craven, D. DiPasquo, D. Freitag, A. McCallum, T. Mitchell, K. Nigam, S. Slattery, Learning to construct knowledge bases from the World Wide Web. Artif. Intell. **118**, 69–113 (2000)
29. J. Gou, J. Yang, Q. Chen, Evolution and evaluation in knowledge fusion system, in IWINAC 2005, *International Work-Conference on the Interplay Between Natural and Artificial Computation*, J. Mira, J.R. Alvarez, vol 3562, Las Palmas de Gran Canaria, Canary Islands, Spain, 15–18 June 2005. Lecture Notes in Computer Science (Springer, Heidelberg, 2005), pp. 192–201
30. T.-T. Kuo, S.-S. Tseng, Y.-T. Lin, Ontology-based knowledge fusion framework using graph partitioning, in *IEA/AIE 2003, 16th International Conference on Industrial and Engineering Applications of Artificial Intelligence and Expert Systems*, ed. by P.W.H. Chung, C.J. Hinde, M. Ali, vol. 2718, Laughborough, UK, 23–26 June 2003. Lecture Notes in Artificial Intelligence (Springer, Berlin, 2003), pp. 11–20
31. J. Masters, Structured knowledge source integration and its applications to information fusion, in *Proceedings of the Fifth International Conference on Information Fusion*, vol. 2, Annapolis, Maryland, USA, 8–11 July 2002, pp. 1340–1346
32. S. Amin, C. Byington, M. Watson, Fuzzy inference and fusion for health state diagnosis of hydraulic pumps and motors, in *NAFIPS 2005, Annual Meeting of the North American*, Detroit, MI, USA, 26–28 June 2005 (Fuzzy Information Processing Society, 2005) doi:10.1109/NAFIPS.2005.1548499
33. D. Ash, B. Hayes-Roth, Using action-based hierarchies for real-time diagnosis. Artif. Intell. **88**, 317–348 (1996)
34. R.N. Carvalho, K.B. Laskey, P.C.G. Costa, M. Ladeira, L.L. Santos, S. Matsumoto, Probabilistic ontology and knowledge fusion for procurement fraud detection in Brazil, in *Uncertainty Reasoning for the Semantic Web II, International Workshops URSW 2008–2010 held at ISWC and UniDL 2010 held at Floc*, vol. 7123, ed. by F. Bobillo, et al. Lecture Notes in Computer Science (Springer, Heidelberg, 2013), pp. 19–40

35. A. Smirnov, M. Pashkin, T. Levashova, N. Chilov, Fusion-based knowledge logistics for intelligent decision support in network-centric environment. Int. J. Gen. Syst. **34**(6), 673–690 (2005)
36. A.C. Boury-Brisset, Towards a knowledge server to support the situation analysis process, in *Proceedings of the 4th International Conference on Information Fusion*, Montréal, Canada, 7–10 August 2001. url:http://isif.org/fusion/proceedings/fusion01CD/fusion/searchengine/pdf/ThC23.pdf. Accessed 20 Apr 2015
37. T. Erlandsson, T. Helldin, G. Falkman, L. Niklasson, Information fusion supporting team situation awareness for future fighting aircraft, in *Proceedings of the 13th International Conference on Information Fusion*, Edinburgh, UK, 26–29 July 2010 (IEEE). url:http://ieeexplore.ieee.org/stamp/stamp.jsp?tp=&arnumber=5712064. Accessed 20 Apr 2015
38. K.B. Laskey, P.C.G. Costa, T. Janssen, Probabilistic ontologies for knowledge fusion, in *Proceedings of the 11th International Conference on Information Fusion*, Cologne, Germany, 30 June 2008–3 July 2008 (IEEE, 2008). url:http://ieeexplore.ieee.org/stamp/stamp.jsp?tp=&arnumber=4632375. Accessed 20 Apr 2015
39. O.M. Mevassvik, K. Bråthen, B.J. Hansen, A simulation tool to assess recognized maritime picture production in C2 systems, in *Proceedings of the 6th International Command and Control Research and Technology Symposium*, Annapolis, Maryland, USA, June 2001. url: http://www.dodccrp.org/events/6th_ICCRTS/Tracks/Papers/Track6/065_tr6.pdf. Accessed 20 Apr 2015
40. X. Pan, L.N. Teow, K.H. Tan, J.H.B. Ang, G.W. Ng, A cognitive system for adaptive decision making, in *Proceedings of the 15th International Conference on Information Fusion*, Singapore, 9–12 July 2012, pp. 1323–1329
41. P. Besnard, E. Gregoire, S. Ramon, Logic-based fusion of legal knowledge, in *Proceedings of the 15th International Conference on Information Fusion*, Singapore, 9–12 July 2012, pp. 587–592
42. H.A. Grebla, C.O. Cenan, L. Stanca, Knowledge fusion in academic networks. Broad Res. Artif. Intell. Neurosci. (BRAIN) **1**(2) (2010). url:http://www.edusoft.ro/brain/index.php/brain/article/download/60/145. Accessed 14 Apr 2015
43. C. Jonquet et al., NCBO resource index: ontology-based search and mining of biomedical resources. J. Web Semant. **9**(3), 316–324 (2011)
44. K.R. Lee, Patterns and processes of contemporary technology fusion: the case of intelligent robots. Asian J. Technol. Innov. **15**(2), 45–65 (2007)
45. L.Y. Lin, Y.J. Lo, Knowledge creation and cooperation between cross-nation R&D institutes. Int. J. Electron. Bus. Manag. **8**(1), 9–19 (2010)
46. M.J. Roemer, G.J. Kacprzynski, R.F. Orsagh, Assessment of data and knowledge fusion strategies for prognostics and health management, in *2001 IEEE Aerospace conference*, vol. 6, Big Sky, Montana, USA, 10–17 Mar 2001, pp. 2979–2988
47. H.A. Simon, Making management decisions: the role of intuition and emotion. Acad. Manag. Exec. **1**, 57–64 (1987)
48. E. Tsang, *Foundations of Constraint Satisfaction* (Academic Press, London, 1995)
49. A. Smirnov, A. Kashevnik, N. Shilov, S. Balandin, I. Oliver, S. Boldyrev, On-the-fly ontology matching in smart spaces: a multi-model approach, in *Smart Spaces and Next Generation Wired/Wireless Networking. Proceedings of the Third Conference on Smart Spaces, ruSMART 2010, and the 10th International Conference NEW2AN 2010*, vol. 6294, St. Petersburg, Russia, 23–25 Aug 2010. Lecture Notes in Computer Science (Springer, Heidelberg, 2010), pp. 72–83
50. A. Smirnov, T. Levashova, N. Shilov, Patterns for context-based knowledge fusion in decision support. Inf. Fusion **21**, 114–129 (2015). doi:10.1016/j.inffus.2013.10.010
51. A. Smirnov, M. Pashkin, N. Chilov, T. Levashova, Constraint-driven methodology for context-based decision support. J. Decis. Syst. **14**(3), 279–301 (2005)
52. A. Smirnov, M. Pashkin, N. Chilov, T. Levashova, Agent-based support of mass customization for corporate knowledge management. Eng. Appl. Artif. Intell. **16**(4), 349–364 (2003)

53. A. Smirnov, N. Shilov, T. Levashova, L. Sheremetov, M. Contreras, Ontology-driven intelligent service for configuration support in networked organizations. Knowl. Inf. Syst. **12**(2), 229–253 (2007)
54. A. Smirnov, M. Pashkin, N. Chilov, T. Levashova, F. Haritatos, Knowledge source network configuration approach to knowledge logistics. Int. J. Gen. Syst. **32**(3), 251–269 (2003)
55. A. Smirnov, T. Levashova, M. Pashkin, N. Shilov, Semantic interoperability in self-configuring service networks for context-driven decision making. Syst. Inf. Sci. Notes **2**(1), 27–32 (2007)
56. A. Smirnov, T. Levashova, N. Shilov, A. Kashevnik, Hybrid technology for self-organization of resources of pervasive environment for operational decision support. Int. J. Artif. Intell. Tools **19**(2), 211–229 (2010). doi:10.1142/S0218213010000121

Part III
Systems Philosophy of Contextual Fusion

Chapter 7
System-Level Use of Contextual Information

Alan N. Steinberg and Galina L. Rogova

Abstract A system that exploits information—e.g. to support decision making—can use contextual information both in providing expectations and in resolving uncertain inferences. In the latter case, contextual reasoning involves inferring desired information (values of "problem variables") on the basis of other available information ("context variables"). Relevant contexts are often not self-evident, but must be discovered or selected as a means to problem-solving. Therefore, context exploitation involves (a) predicting the value of contextual information to meet information needs; (b) selecting information types and sources expected to provide information useful in meeting those needs; (c) determining the relevance and quality of acquired information; and (d) applying selected information to a problem at hand. Fusion of contextual information can improve the quality of inferences, but involves concerns about the quality of the contextual information. The availability and quality of predictive models dictate the ways in which contextual information can be used. Many applications are benefitted by inference systems that adaptively discover and exploit context and refine such models to meet evolving information states and information needs.

Keywords Context-sensitivity · Relevance · Abduction · Problem modeling · Problem-solving · Decision support · Adaptive inferencing · Context discovery · Context exploitation

The original version of this chapter was revised: Order of the names of authors was changed to Alan N. Steinberg and Galina L. Rogova. The erratum to this chapter is available at DOI 10.1007/978-3-319-28971-7_26

A.N. Steinberg (✉)
2568 Fox Ridge Ct, Woodbridge, VA 22192, USA
e-mail: alaneilsteinberg@gmail.com

G.L. Rogova
State University New York at Buffalo, Buffalo, USA
e-mail: rogova@buffalo.edu

© Springer International Publishing Switzerland (outside the USA) 2016
L. Snidaro et al. (eds.), *Context-Enhanced Information Fusion*,
Advances in Computer Vision and Pattern Recognition,
DOI 10.1007/978-3-319-28971-7_7

7.1   Chapter Scope and Organization

This chapter examines issues and methods for using contextual information in inferencing and decision support. Section 7.2 provides a working definition of "context" and describes the uses of contextual information. Section 7.3 discusses the role of contextual information in inference and its use in specific data fusion functions. Methods to determine context relevance and accuracy are treated in Sect. 7.4. Section 7.5 discusses the value of adaptive discovery and exploitation of context to meet evolving situations and evolving information needs; categorizing inference problems and methods in terms of the availability and use of prior, posterior, and contextual information. Two architectures for such adaptive context exploitation are presented in Sects. 7.6 and 7.7. Section 7.8 considers the relationship between predictive modeling and context exploitation: (a) using contextual information to develop and refine models of targets and of information sources and (b) using predictive models in assessing and using contextual information.

7.2   Context in Information Exploitation

Let us use "information exploitation system" as a very broad term to describe any entity that uses information to improve its estimate of states of the world and/or to improve its response to world states to meet explicit or implicit objectives. Examples of information exploitation systems range from automated or partially automated data fusion systems used in decision support; to most any sort of biological organism that responds to its environment; to entire intelligence organizations that task, collect, prepare, exploit, and disseminate information.

The importance of context-sensitivity is becoming increasingly recognized in diverse fields. It can be argued that attempts at automation in natural language understanding, robotics, machine vision and other domains of Artificial Intelligence have foundered largely because of insensitivity to context: to a deficient understanding of the ways of the world and how they apply to specific situations of concern.

System-level issues in using context in all these applications include (a) how to determine contexts that are relevant for particular applications; (b) how to assess the fidelity of such information; and (c) how to incorporate contextual information into inference processes. These three issues clearly relate to the three basic functions of data fusion: to data association, data alignment and state estimation, respectively (Fig. 7.1). Corresponding to these data fusion functions are the three management functions of planning, response alignment and control. In context exploitation, these become (a) planning how to acquire and use relevant information; (b) managing models of information sources and of dependencies between contexts and operational concerns; and (c) acquiring desired contextual information [1].

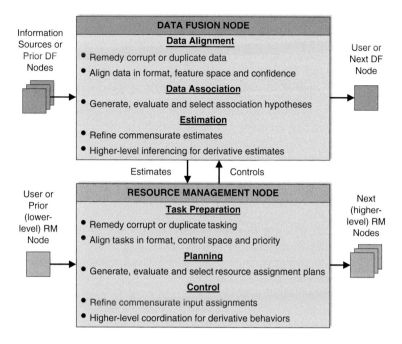

Fig. 7.1 Representation of DF and RM processing nodes

The relevance of context to system objectives can be stated in term of the effect on the appropriateness of the system's response to the given situation. Context can include factors which (if known) would elicit different responses, given the system's planning and control strategy. Your car's navigation system may have a rule "If a given route is jammed with traffic, seek faster alternate routes." If the system were provided with contextual knowledge that the month is September and that a baseball game is being played at National Stadium, together with a situation model to the effect that "South Capitol Street is usually jammed when a game is on at National Stadium, particularly late in the season," then such a context-sensitive system should endeavor to avoid South Capitol Street.

In general, a planning and control problem such as this depends on solving an inference problem: that is to say, "What to do?" requires an answer to "What's happening?"

As the example illustrates, a sophisticated context-sensitive inference system may use context recursively: the relevance of a baseball game will trigger acquisition of pieces on information that were not necessarily considered as part of the navigation problem: is a game being played and (with relevance perhaps only determined by the answer to the first question) what month is it?

Such context-sensitivity requires an ability to predict the relevance of situation elements (ballgames) to inference and management problems (getting home). Therefore, situation modeling is an essential part of context-sensitive operation.

7.2.1 *"Context-of" and "Context-for"*

In Chapter 2, we discuss numerous candidate definitions and models of "context" found in the technical literature. As with many widely used abstract terms, "context" is commonly applied to several related, but ontologically different things

- in some uses, a context is considered to be a *situation* of some type or in some particular use (as "the bombing can be understood in the context of the Middle East Crisis");
- in others, it is an *element* of such situations (as in "the enhanced security measures make sense in the context of the recent bombing"); and
- in yet others, a context is *information* about a situation or even a *source* of such information.

Often, these very different uses are blurred such that it is difficult to discern whether they are literal, elliptical, or metonymic.

In this chapter, we adopt what we hope to be a useful working definition that is applicable in a wide variety of problem domains. We define a context as a *relevant situation*, by which we mean a situation that can be used to provide information either (a) to condition expectations or (b) to improve the understanding of a given inference or management problem. These two ways in which context can be used relate to a formulation by Gong [2] as elaborated in [3, 4], contrasting the notions of "context-of" (C-O) and "context-for" (C-F)

(a) C-O: We can have certain expectations based on situations; e.g., "in the *context of* the present economic and political situation, we would expect an increase in property crime;"
(b) C-F: Alternatively, we can assess reference items—whether individual entities or situations—in context: "the economic and political situation provides a *context for* understanding this crime."

We prefer to dispense with Gong's term "reference item" as it presupposes the existence of a referent. In many inference problems encountered in data fusion, entity existence is itself treated as a random variable, such that state estimation is of the states of *perceived* or *postulated* entities. Accordingly, rather than a "reference item," we may speak of a set of variables of concern in the given problem (i.e., endogenous or, equivalently, "problem variables"). Therefore, a problem context is a situation that is relevant for evaluating problem variables.

A given situation can be a "Context-Of" or a "Context-For," depending on how it is used in reasoning.

C-O reasoning is data-driven: it starts with a perceived situation to derive expectations about constituent entities, relationships and activities: a ballgame increases the probability of a traffic jam (Fig. 7.2). C-O may be thought of as a framework for asserting prior probabilities; indeed, any information that establishes a rationale for asserting priors information defines a C-O.

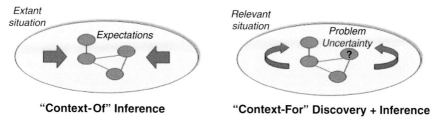

Fig. 7.2 Two uses of context [3]

In contrast, C-F reasoning is goal-driven: as seen in Fig. 7.2, C-F reasoning starts with a particular problem—which might be an inferencing problem (what's happening?) or a management problem (what's to be done?)—and seeks additional information that can resolve uncertainties in the problem solution: how soon can I get home via South Capitol Street?

The C-O/C-F distinction also relates to that made by cognitive psychologist Kahneman [5] in describing two "systems" of mind.

It is System 1 that does the pattern recognition by which we quickly and spontaneously recognize familiar people and situations. In the terms we have been using, System 1 identifies situations that serve as contexts (C-O) that condition expectations.

System 2 performs systematic reasoning, as in "deliberate memory search, complex computations, comparisons, planning, and choice." [5]. System 2 is triggered when System 1 detects elements that are anomalous with regard to assumed patterns. This defines a "problem"—a topic of interest—which System 2 addresses not by pattern recognition, but by reasoning. Among techniques System 2 can use is searching for contextual information (C-F) that will facilitate the estimation of the presented situation.[1]

A combination of System 1 and System 2 processes is employed in the Case-Based Reasoning methods used in Artificial Intelligence: System 1-like processes match the patterns observed in received data with stored "cases" (situation models). A described situation serves as a context (C-O) that conditions expectations for constituent activities. Mismatches between the observed situation and stored cases trigger a System 2-like process that diagnoses the discrepancies, perhaps searching for pertinent contextual information (C-F). If the diagnosis suggests a significant systematic cause for the differences, a new C-O is generated. The reasoning process might interpret this as a sub-case of an existing case, with inheritance of pertinent attributes.

---

[1]In Sect. 7.5.2 we distinguish four categories of reasoning. Anomaly-based detection is Category 1.

7.2.2   Problem Variables and Context Variables

As defined, a Context-Of can generate expectations or concerns for the states of constituent entities, thereby defining problems to be solved. In contrast, a Context-For is a notion that is relative to an identified problem to be solved.

We can call these larger situations *problem contexts*. We can define a topic of interest as a set of state variables that an agent wishes to evaluate, calling these *problem variables* or, equivalently, *endogenous variables*.

An inference problem can be stated in terms of a utility function on the resolution of a set of problem variables. In some cases, problem-variable resolution is equivalent to estimation accuracy, as in target location and tracking problems. However, resolution is not necessarily the same thing as estimation accuracy. In decision-support applications, inference problem variables map into management decision variables. If the information exploitation system would respond differently if a given target were of class A versus B, or in activity state C versus D, the resolution is equivalent to discrimination between these states or classes of states. In some cases, decision boundaries are conditional: the system may respond differently to near versus distant targets. Decision boundaries and, therefore, resolution utility may be imprecise. Utility is typically non-linear relative to resolution, but depends on the utility of consequent responses. More is not necessarily better: if the response to any target of class A would be identical, there is no added utility to resolution to a subclass.

One's assessment of topics of interest (or "targets") can be conditioned on larger situations in which these occur.[2] A problem context (C-F) is a relevant situation for evaluating problem variables.

Just what counts as relevant is not always easy to determine. Relevance is not binary or unique for any given problem. Indeed, some contexts can be more relevant than others. In general, a person or other reasoning system chooses or assumes a situation as relevant to his/her/its information needs. Let us consider how contexts can be used in evaluating problem variables to meet information needs.

An important distinction can be drawn between *refinement* and *inference* of values of variables. In many data fusion problems, multiple measurements of a given variable are averaged or (with model-based or data-driven weighting) filtered to refine the estimate of that variable; exploiting independence in the measurement-to-measurement noise. Bayesian and Dempster-Shafer classifiers are examples of refinement processes.

Often, however, the problem variables to be estimated are not themselves measured, or are not measured with sufficient accuracy or confidence to meet users' needs. In such cases, the values of problem variables would need to be inferred totally or partially on the basis of other variables. Such inference assumes a model

---

[2]We will use the term 'target' throughout this chapter to refer to any real, perceived or postulated entity of interest at any level of abstraction: a feature, signal, individual, attribute, event, relationship, aggregation, process, concept, etc.

of the dependencies between measurement variables and problem variables. Inference methods include, for example, structural equations, Bayesian belief networks, and neural networks.

We may distinguish, then, between explicit problem variables and ancillary variables used in inference. We call the latter *context variables*.

A context variable is a variable that the information exploitation system selects to predict, evaluate or refine an estimate of one or more problem variables. As such, a context can be defined in terms of context variables. When a situation is used as a Context-Of, these are simply situational variables ranging over relationships and relational complexes.

When used as a Context-For, a problem context is a situation, comprising a set of entities and their relationships involving defined problem variables and selected context variables. An information exploitation system selects a situation as a problem context for its presumed usefulness in solving the particular problem; i.e., in resolving problem variables (given our definition of *resolution*). Two different systems may select different contexts (i.e., different sets of context variables) in resolving a particular inference problem. The utility of resolving a set of context variables can be defined in terms of the degree to which such resolution correlates with resolution of one or more problem variables and the utility of the latter resolution.

The relevance of a value y of candidate context variable Y in determining a specific value x of problem variable X can be stated in terms of statistical relevance, as introduced by Salomon [6]

$$\text{Rel}(y, x) = \frac{p(x|y)}{p(x|-y)}.$$

Relevance in a context s is, of course, given as

$$\text{Rel}(y, x|s) = \frac{p(x|s, y)}{p(x|s-y)}.$$

The utility to a given inference problem q of evaluating a variable Y for the purpose of evaluating a (problem) variable X in the context of a situation s is

$$\omega_q(Y; X|s) = \omega_q(x|s) \int_X \int_Y \text{Rel}(y, x|s) \mathrm{d}y\mathrm{d}x.$$

For discrete-valued variables, integration can be replaced by summation.

X or Y in this formulation can be an individual variable or a vector of variables. For example, the set of variables $Y = \{$ballgame, month, location$\}$ can provide useful context for resolving joint states of interest in the set of problem variables $X = \{$traffic conditions, location$\}$. By definition, one problem variable can serve as a context variable for resolving another problem variable. For example, an aircraft's observed speed may be used as a context for resolving its type and, conversely, its estimated type can be used for resolving its feasible speed [7].

Context variables and problem variables may be either static or dynamic: a ground target tracking process may make use of the local terrain (context variables that are assumed to be static over the timescale of concern) and weather (context variables that are assumed to be dynamic over the timescale of concern).

A Context-Of provides expectations or concerns for the states of constituent entities. For example the context of a certain military situation might motivate an inference problem such as "determine the types, locations, equipment, activity states and C3 network of adversary air defenses in sector G."

Imagine that a fighter aircraft's radar warning receiver detects modulated RF energy. The known military situation and the aircraft's location over adversary territory provides a context (C-O) from which certain expectations can be generated concerning the presence and activity states of various types of entities (at diverse fusion levels), to include emitter types and RF allocations. These expectations are used to determine prior probabilities.

Let us assume that, on the basis of a stored model of radars and their emissions and these prior probabilities, the aircraft systems recognize that this is an emission from a certain type of radar. If recognition were not unambiguous, an adaptive information exploitation system might resort to identifying and resolving context variables that are modeled as being relevant to resolving one or more of the problem variables. In our example, such context variables might relate to the disposition and coordinated activities of forces.

The identified radar now provides a context (C-O) in which further expectations can be made. Let us suppose that the recognition model indicates that a radar of the identified type typically has the role of air target tracking as an element of a particular type of surface-to-air missile (SAM) battery, which generally includes four missile launchers of a specific type. On this basis, the presence, type, activity state, and composition of a SAM battery and associated missile launchers are inferred (Fig. 7.3). Additionally, given some estimate of the operational context, our context-sensitive system should be able to infer the presence of a larger integrated air defense system of which this battery is an element, as well as the ownership, general composition and mission objectives (viz., to defend such-and-such a region

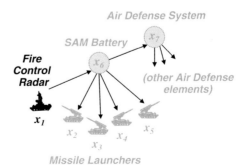

Fig. 7.3 Illustration of situation assessment inferencing

of Sector G from air attacks). In short, the estimated fire control radar provides a context (C-O) in which the presence of the SAM battery and its remaining elements can inferred.

All this information is inferable, with various degrees of certainty, from the single piece of data: the detection of the radar signal. Such inference is performed by using a predictive model of entities, their relationships, the observable indicators of entity states and relationships and of expectations for related entities and of additional relationships.

7.3 Context in Data Fusion

Data fusion is often an integral component of information exploitation. We have defined data fusion as the process of combining multiple units of data for the purposes of estimating the state of aspects of the universe [8, 9].

State estimation functions differ broadly according to the types of state variables to be estimated; target states being distinguished in terms of "levels" corresponding to the levels described in various versions of the JDL model (Table 7.1).

We argue in [10] that it is preferable to distinguish inference problems on the basis of type of entity state variables rather than by type of entity: a given entity can be addressed at more than one level. For example, a vehicle can be the "target" of a level 1 data fusion (DF) process if level 1 states (e.g., its location, velocity, size, weight, type, identity or activity) are being estimated. The same vehicle can be the target of a level 2 DF process if it is considered as a complex or a structure, such that level 2 states (e.g., the relationships among its components or its subassemblies) are being estimated. It could also be the target of a level 3 DF process if it is considered as a dynamic process, such that level 3 states (e.g., its course of action and outcome) are being estimated [11]. It could even be the target of a level 4 DF process if it is considered as the system performing the estimation and level 4 states (e.g., operating conditions and performance) are being estimated.

Often there is a natural flow from "higher" to "lower" fusion levels, whereby estimated scenarios provide expectations for situation states, which in turn provide expectations for constituent object states, which provide expectations for the signal/feature environment and, therefore, for expected measurements.

In this way, information flowing downward across the data fusion levels can often be used as a C-O; estimates of higher-level states being used to condition entity states; for example, by determining prior probabilities:

- L4 → L3: estimates of the state of the system's resources, goals and utility valuation provide expectations for utility of potential courses of action, or scenarios;
- L3 → L2: estimates of a course of action or scenario provide expectations for the states of constituent situations (stages or outcomes of the evolving course of action or scenario);

Table 7.1 Entity state, data fusion, and management "levels" [10]

Level	Entity class	Example Continuous state variables	Example Discrete state variables	Data fusion (inference) level	Management level
0	Patterns; e.g., features or signals	Temporal/spatial/spectral extent, amplitude and shape/modulations	Signal/feature class, type, attributes	Signal/feature assessment	Signal/feature management
1	Individuals; e.g., physical objects or events	Location, velocity, size, weight, event time	Object class, type, identity, activity or attributes	Individual entity assessment	Individual resource management
2	Structures; e.g., relationships and situations	Distance, force/energy/information transfer	Type, identity or attributes of relations, their arguments, or situations	Situation assessment	Resource relationship management (coordination)
3	Processes; e.g., courses of action, scenarios and outcomes	State utility, duration, transition conditions	State transitions; type, identity, attributes of processes or scenarios	Scenario/outcome assessment	Mission objective management
4	System resources	(All of the above, applied to system resources)	(All of the above, applied to system resources)	System assessment	System management

- L2 → L1: estimates of a relationship or situation provide expectations for the states of constituent entities;
- L1 → L0: estimates of the state of an individual provide expectations for the states of signals or features [10].[3]

Considering a situation as a C-O is useful to condition expectations in the predictions used in level 1 target tracking or in level 3 scenario/outcome assessments in which unobserved states (e.g., future or past states) are estimated. Similarly, reasoning from a C-O is often useful in level 2 fusion to infer unobserved (latent) situation variables.

Context variables in C-F inferencing are chosen on the basis of their perceived utility in solving a given problem. Such utility, of course, depends on the type of problem as well as on the agent whose problem it is. As shown in Fig. 7.1, data fusion includes problems of data alignment, data association, and estimation.

Context-Sensitive State Estimation. In solving an estimation problem, context variables are selected on the basis of the degree to which the predicted resolution of these variables is expected to improve the resolution of problem variables. This assumes an explicitly or implicitly defined utility function on problem variable resolution and on the costs of acquiring and processing the contextual information. As noted above, variable resolution is not always the same as estimation accuracy.

Both C-O and C-F can play essential roles in state estimation at any fusion level, but they are especially important in higher-level fusion, in which variables of interest include relation-, relationship- and situation-variables that are not directly observable, but must be inferred.

While a C-F is selected for its use in evaluating specific attributive and relational states, a C-O provides a means for understanding expectations for and implications of such states. Generally, the larger context in which a problem is considered, the more fully will be problem understanding, being conditioned on a larger number of mutually independent context variables.

Context-Sensitive Data Association. Many data fusion approaches require data association as a precondition for state estimation. Context variables may be selected on the basis of the information their evaluation provides in associating data to perceived entities (e.g., to "tracks"). For example, information on road and weather conditions can be used to infer a reduced likelihood that a given vehicle could have traveled fast enough to be associated with particular observations.

If contexts are (as per our definition) situations that are used or useable in certain ways, context assessment is a species of situation assessment. Accordingly, determining the relevance of a situation as a context for (C-F) a given inference

---

[3]In [10] we examine these traditional fusion levels derived from the JDL Data Fusion Model, suggesting that the partitionings are not clear-cut. In particular, the dissimilarity of the L4 → L3 flow relative to other inter-level flows indicates that L4 does not obey the same partitioning criteria as the other levels. Additionally, the example state variables listed in Table 7.1 suggest that "level 4" fusion issues are the same as those for the other levels, but applied reflexively to the particular system doing the fusing.

problem is a data association problem at fusion level 2. As with level 1, level 2 association is performed on the basis of data consistency, conditioned on a density function on state estimates.

Context-Sensitive Data Alignment. Data alignment directly affects, and is often taken as a precondition for, data association and estimation. Data alignment functions can include format normalization, spatial registration, measurement calibration, and quality management (e.g., confidence normalization). Alignment itself involves both data fusion processes for estimating system biases (an aspect of level 4 fusion) and management processes for bias compensation and confidence assignment.

Context variables may be employed to improve the accuracy of alignment terms. For example, fiducial objects or tie-points are used to register images beyond that achievable via the navigation estimate derived, e.g., from GPS and inertial sensors.

Data alignment is closely related to information source characterization: determining the factors that affect the performance of an information source. These can include statistics of systematic and random measurement/reporting errors, as well as probabilities of detection and false alarm. Evaluation of such variables must be inferred from the ensemble of measurements and prior sensor and target models that serve as context variables in the standard statistical data association processes. We examine modeling issues concerning source characterization in Sect. 7.8.

7.4 Quality Control in Context Exploitation

The problem of building context-aware information exploitation systems is complicated by the fact that information obtained from sensors, data repositories or other sources can vary in quality: information may be of low fidelity, contradictory, or redundant. Furthermore, the quality in any of these terms might be unknown or misevaluated. Thus, it is necessary to implement quality control at each step of the fusion process: when information enters the system, when information is transferred within and between fusion modes, and when fusion results are presented to a system user.

Quality control requires methods for representing and measuring the quality of information and criteria to determine when information quality is inadequate for intended uses. Contextual information can be used to assess data quality and to determine the quality required for system operation in a given environment. However, such contextual information is also generally obtained from observations and/or estimations; presenting the same issues of quality control. These problems interact:

- imperfect context characterization adversely affects the characterization of the quality of information used in fusion as well as the fusion results;
- imperfect information used in context estimation and discovery degrades the quality and utility of contextual information.

Information quality is meta-information; i.e., information about information. As such, information quality is best represented and measured through its attributes; which may include credibility, accuracy, timeliness, and relevance. Quality attributes often must be evaluated in relation to contexts: an optical sensor can be very reliable during a sunny day but unreliable at night.

Depending on the context, the overall information quality may relate to one or several attributes. Methods of quality control that have been discussed [12, 13] include:

- eliminating from consideration any problem and/or context variables of insufficient quality;
- explicitly incorporating estimation of context-dependent information quality into models and fusion processes; and
- delaying a decision concerning poor quality information, hoping that quality will improve with additional observations and/or computations.

Selection of a particular quality control measure depends on context and quality characteristic pertinent to a particular fusion process. For example, elimination of input information into the fusion process can be based on its relevance to the problem variables or to the fusion method under consideration in a specific context.

Eliminating information from consideration may apply not only to incoming information and inter-nodal fusion results but also to the selection of context variables.

Selection of context variables can be based on a constraining domain-specific ontology of context variables and their relationships with problem variables. As discussed in Sects. 2.2 and 7.2.2, candidate context variables can be determined to be relevant to a set of problem variables if the values of interest of these problem variables are correlated with the values of the candidate context variable. This relevance can be defined in terms of utility-weighted mutual information between problem and candidate context variables.

Determining relevance in practice is complicated by the fact that inference problems, problem contexts and available information are often dynamic such that information can change in credibility or relevance over time. At a certain time available information may be of low fidelity and unreliable, or simply irrelevant; but quality may be improved with arrival of new information or change of circumstances.

To deal with such a possibility, it might be beneficial to invoke an additional quality control measure: delay of information elimination; i.e., waiting for additional information that might improve the quality [14–16]. However, waiting can create additional problems: information can become obsolete, and the cost of the course of action can change. The latter may involve costs of data collection, communications and processing, as well as lost opportunity costs. Thus, waiting cannot be indefinite and a context-dependent time horizon may be considered. A decision to wait can be based on the Maximum Expected Utility Principle.

Similarly, information needs are often dynamic; making the utility of information (e.g., the utility of refining a problem variable to a certain degree) time-variable. Situations of interest are often dynamic, so that the availability of any sought data may also be time-variable. Furthermore, the cost of data acquisition and processing varies with situation and resource state.

Modeling these utility, likelihood and cost factors is one of the challenges of contextual reasoning. One criterion that has been suggested is the comparison of the quality characteristic under consideration with a context-dependent threshold, taking into account a context-dependent time horizon [14–16].

Inference ultimately includes determining a degree of belief in hypotheses under consideration; perhaps expressible quantitatively in terms of confidence, probability, likelihood, etc. It is therefore important to consider the quality of these beliefs, for example by comparison with a problem and context-dependent threshold. Quality of belief has alternatively been expressed as a second-order quality factor that can be represented by reliability coefficients $\alpha \epsilon [0, 1]$ [13, 17]. Utilization of reliability factors allows for quality control by explicitly incorporating information quality into models (e.g., α is close to zero if estimation is unreliable).

Once again, reliability must be considered not only on the basis of a selected model but also on characteristics of the particular contextual situation. Reliability evaluated as a function of context has been reported in several fusion-related publications; e.g., [14, 17, 18]. In [14], context-based reliability is modeled as a function of situation characteristics; specifically, in terms of a time-dependent distance relationship between a sensor and an observed target and environment characteristics.

In [17], context is modeled by a set of parameters influencing the reliability of each information source and expert knowledge is used to represent the validity of the source domain as a fuzzy membership function of the context. Reliability coefficients are modeled thereby as the probability of fuzzy events.

Two other methods of defining sensor reliability based on contextual information are introduced in [19]. Both methods utilize expert knowledge to represent contextual information within the framework of the theory of fuzzy events. Such knowledge is used in connection with probability theory to compute the fuzzy probability of validity of each sensor or set of sensors.

In one such method, Local Contextual Combination, probability derived in this way is used to evaluate the reliability for each sensor/source, each hypothesis and context. The derived reliability values are used before fusion in a discounting rule introduced in [20].

In the second of these methods, Global Contextual Processing—which is inspired by the method suggested in [17]—the reliability of one or a combination of several sensors is computed as the probability mass of validity of conjunction of the fuzzy subsets corresponding to each source for each contextual variable. This reliability factors is incorporated in the fusion process. All these publications report benefits of utilizing context-based information quality control.

Selecting contextual variables, building context-aware inference processes, selecting quality attributes for consideration, and quality control all assume some knowledge of the ambient C-O. In some cases this context can be determined with a high level of certainty; e.g., in an observed highly disruptive situation such as an earthquakes or terrorist attack. Sometimes, however, this context is unknown or poorly characterized, or an assumed context might no longer be extant. For example, reasoning about situations in a post-disaster environment would be conducted in the context of the dominant event that caused this environment (e.g., an earthquake) [21]. However, during this initial disaster, additional events—say, a torrential rain storm—can occur that drastically change the ambient context.

A mistaken assumption about context can produce inconsistency between expected and actual values of observed or latent problem variables; leading to poor characterization of information, selection of wrong models or parameters of inference processes, and ultimately to wrong decisions and actions.

In highly dynamic environments, such inconsistency can also be the result of insufficient quality of ephemeral information or inappropriate inference processes; e.g., bad choice of models used or poor quality of model parameters, or poorly selected or characterized context variables. Therefore, consistency control is required for determining the causes and for correcting false inferences.

Consistency control can be carried out by abduction: "reasoning for best explanations" [22]. The result of abduction may reveal unexpected contextual elements. It may also indicate the poor quality of the estimated values of problem variables under consideration, or of the prior models used in characterizing problem or contextual elements.[4]

Consistency control may be coupled with delaying decisions: inconsistent information may become consistent with time, or the abducted explanation may change. Use of such techniques for context discovery under uncertainty has been reported, for example, in [21, 23].

7.5 Adaptive Context Exploitation

In this section we consider concepts for information exploitation that adapt to evolving information needs, evolving information states and evolving opportunities for information acquisition. Specific system implementation concepts are discussed in Sects. 7.6 and 7.7.

7.5.1 The Value of Adaptivity in Information Exploitation

Adaptive exploitation of information can be an important method for improving on the closed-world, forward-fed and model-dependent limitations of most current data fusion systems. Let us examine these limitations in turn:

---

[4]We discuss abduction in Sect. 7.5.2 as Category 2 reasoning.

Closed World. Current data fusion systems are generally designed to process only pre-defined types of data from predetermined data sources (e.g., sensors or data repositories). Restricted system ontologies, data formats and predictive models often allow no opportunity to use data in novel ways or to deal with additional data types or sources. This limits the ability to use the wealth of "big data" as available across the Internet and from other sources of stored data, as well as from the proliferation of novel electronic sensors.

Accordingly, there is a desire for systems that automatically learn to characterize the potential relevance of data sources and data items for use both as C-O and C-F: providing expectations for targets and activities of interest and to resolve inference or management problems.

Forward-Fed. As quipped in [24], "we've started at the wrong end and continue to focus on the wrong end." By this we meant that data fusion has traditionally been construed as an open-loop process driven by available data, rather than by goals: "do the best you can with whatever information happens to be presented by sensors or other sources."

What is needed are systems that adapt information needs as knowledge states and goals change, exploiting context opportunistically in-mission as dictated by current information needs and perceived opportunities for satisfying these needs. The process should be recursive: using evaluated context variables to evaluate yet other context variables.

Model-Dependent. Classical target recognition is performed by matching observations against representations of candidate targets, whether in the form of prior exemplars, generalized templates or causal models. Similarly, classical target tracking relies on target motion models. The dependence on stored reference data is a severe limitation in applying recognition and prediction methods to problems that are poorly modeled; whether due to sparse sampling, heavy-tail distributions or unpredictable dynamics. These difficulties are exacerbated under conditions of intentional countermeasures, concealment or deception. With increased concern for less well-modeled problems—to include ones dominated by human behavior as in many higher-level inference problems—classical model-dependent recognition methods become increasingly inadequate.

Consequently, there would be value in systems that use acquired information to evaluate and refine predictive models of targets, contexts and of system resources. Also, in cases in which acquired data are too sparse for statistical modeling, the system should make use of alternative methods for understanding. Categories of such cases and methods are discussed in the following subsection.

7.5.2 Categories of Inference Problems and Methods

It is fruitful to consider differences in problem characteristics and corresponding differences in appropriate inference techniques. An adaptive inference system

Table 7.2 Categories of inference problems and methods

Cat	Approach	Assumed prior models	Observational data	Inference method
0	Model-based recognition	Targets	Yes	Deduction and induction
1	Anomaly-based detection	Backgrounds	Yes	Deduction and induction
2	Hypothesis-based explanation	Situation context and components	Yes	Abduction
3	Context-based feasibility	Targets and backgrounds	No	Deduction and induction

should apply techniques as appropriate to given problems as they arise, reasoning across such methods in complex or dynamic situations.

Waltz [25] has proposed a categorization of inference problems. We adapt this scheme in [10, 26, 27] to distinguish inference methods by the way they use observational data and predictive models, as summarized in Table 7.2:

Category 0 (Model-Based Recognition). This category encompasses methods used in traditional target recognition systems, assuming high-confidence models of target characteristics and behaviors. Prediction can involve deductive and inductive methods, whereby target entities and activities are recognized by matching observations to those predicted by models, possibly conditioned by the context of such factors as information source characteristics, viewing geometry, observation media, and background.

Category 1 (Anomaly-Based Detection). It can happen that background (or "normal") activities are better characterized than uncooperative target activity can be. By matching observations with prior models of background activities, anomalous phenomena are detected as indication of possible activities of interest.

Both categories 0 and 1 assume the availability of observational data and of prior models that have been validated in one way or another: in category 0 these are models of target entities or activities; in category 1 these are models of normal or background activities. Recognition and prediction (deductive and inductive) methods can be used in processing model data to derive expected observations for use in the matching process.

In contrast, category 2 and 3 methods are used to overcome deficiencies in prior models or in observable data, respectively. In category 2 new models are composed adaptively to explain observed data. In category 3, activities of interest might not be observable; rather their prior feasibility is determined on the basis of contextual information.

Category 2 (Hypothesis-based Explanation). The process in this category is one of abductive reasoning: building and testing models to best explain available data. Such a process is applicable to situations in which there is insufficient prior analytic understanding or training data to develop predictive models. An analyst or an automated process constructs a situation or scenario hypothesis in an attempt to account for observed data. As in the classical scientific method, the hypothesis is evaluated to predict further observables that could either confirm or refute the hypothesis. By acquiring such data as available, explanatory, predictive models of the observed situation or scenario are refined, selected or rejected.

Category 3 (Context-based Feasibility). These methods do not rely on direct observational data. Rather, contextual cues are used to determine the feasibility of broad classes of activities: domain constraints on adversary capability developments, strategic planning, etc. Such methods are the only ones available when activities of interest are unlikely to be detectable or discriminable at all.[5]

7.6　Adaptive Compositional Modeling

An alternative method to forward-fed, model-based target recognition was developed in the 1990s in a series of programs sponsored by the U.S. Defense Advanced Research Projects Agency (DARPA). The processing paradigm developed under these programs was called the "Model-Based Classifier (MBC)" [28]. This design addressed the inadequacy of traditional model-matching methods for target recognition to cope with the variability of target characteristics, observation geometry, and—*a propos* our present topic—the effects of such contextual factors as scene background, occlusion, illumination angle and shadowing.

The MBC uses knowledge bases of physical models of possible constituents of target scenes as might be observed in imagery. The model set includes computer-aided design models of available sensors, of targets of interest and of pertinent ambiguity sets in the sensors' feature spaces, and—for ground-based scenes—of various types of ground cover. This allows data-driven models of an observed scene to be composed, from which expected measurements can be predicted and compared against the actual measurements.

A combination of Category 0, 1, and 2 techniques can be employed to

(a) recognize well-modeled targets in simple observation conditions: not occluded, obscured or camouflaged;
(b) find hidden targets by detecting anomalies relative to the background; and
(c) adaptively compose scene "models" that explain the observable data, in the form of hypothesized scene elements and their interrelationships.

Notionally depicted in Fig. 7.4, an adaptive compositional modeling process can involve the following steps:

---

[5]It might be useful to add yet another category (perhaps Category-1) to encompass estimation refinement via filtering or smoothing in the absence of a model; e.g., without model-driven filter gains.

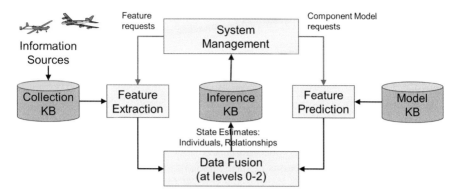

Fig. 7.4 Adaptive compositional modeling for scene understanding

0. Accept user-supplied specification of prior probabilities, initial information needs and an initial information acquisition plan;
1. Process collected sensor data sets (e.g., an image) by extracting features (PV and CV values) in accordance with the information acquisition plan;
2. Match features found in the collected data with features predicted by candidate target, sensor and context models:

   (a) Use model-based detection and recognition methods (Category 1 and 0 reasoning, respectively) to evaluate PVs (and CVs) to estimate the presence and state of targets of interest;
   (b) Use these ambiguities to select models of possible scene elements from the Model Knowledge Base; manipulate and combine these models to hypothesize different possible scenes to account for the acquired data (Category 2 processing): target variability, observed target aspect, occlusions, shadowing, etc., conditioned on the known or assumed sensor state and observing conditions;
   (c) If match is sufficient or if all possible acquired data and plausible model compositions have been tested go to 5;

3 Use the ambiguities in the state estimates to refine information needs in terms of a utility function on PV resolution (specifically target states of interest);
4. Generate, evaluate, and select information acquisition plans:

   (a) Map PVs into feasible "observable" PVs and CVs;
   (b) Go to 1;

5. Post selected hypotheses and unresolved scenes, flag targets/activities of interest and await additional data acquisition or tasking (changed information needs).

7.7 Opportunistic Adaptability

The Model-Based Classifier design was developed for target recognition applications in which target scenes are adequately understood in terms of the feasible constituent physical objects and underlying physical processes. Context exploitation in this system is largely in the form of understanding the contribution of background elements and observing conditions on target observations. It helps that it is rather straightforward to manipulate and combine physics-based models of targets, backgrounds, viewing conditions and contributing electronic sensors to derive high-confidence predictions of measurements from postulated target scenes.

However, such a system is only a step toward full adaptive, context-sensitive information exploitation, which would add the following functions:

- *Adaptive data acquisition*: collection, retrieval, and extraction of data based on emerging assessment of net utility;
- *Adaptive data batching*: selection of sets of data to be processed together in a particular data fusion network node (aligning and associating data for use in state estimation);
- *Adaptive technique selection and control*: selection of algorithms to implement functions in each data fusion node, setting factor weights, data conditioning, bias compensation, and decision thresholding, etc.
- *Adaptive modeling:* refining the characterization of target entities (with our very broad definition of "target") and of system resources; and
- *Adaptive information quality control:* selection of data sets and processing techniques to improve the estimation of information quality; i.e., to reduce second-order uncertainty.

Figure 7.5 shows a notional architecture for such an enhanced system.

In addition to level 0–3 data fusion functions that estimate states of entities external to the information exploitation system, this conceptual system would incorporate level 4 functions that estimate the state of various aspects of the system itself, involving some or all of the following functions:

- *Source Assessment*: estimating the operating states and performance characteristics of available information sources (sensors, knowledge bases, web sites, etc.);
- *Process Assessment*: estimating usage, operating states and performance of processing resources;
- *Model Assessment*: estimating error characteristics (i.e., fidelity) of available predictive models of entities, generally to include level 4 models of system resources and level 0–3 models of external entities of pertinent types (signals, features, individuals, relationships, situations, scenarios, concepts of various sorts, etc.); and
- *Performance Assessment*: characterizing the system's performance in terms of estimated values of defined performance metrics; e.g., of information needs satisfaction.

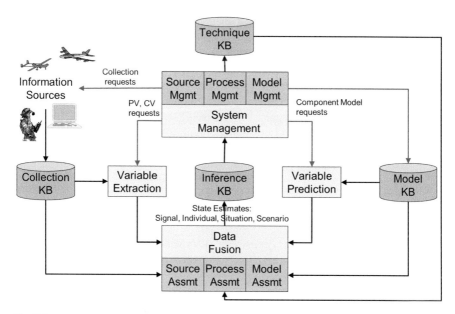

Fig. 7.5 Architecture for opportunistic context-sensitive information exploitation

Analogous management functions include:

- *Source Management*: Managing data acquisition both by tasking available physical sensors and by mining data repositories;
- *Enhanced Process Management:* Allocation/tasking of processing resources, data batching and routing, managing data alignment (e.g., bias compensation and data quality control), technique selection and control;
- *Model Management*: Refining models of level 0–4 entities (discussed in Sect. 7.8); and
- *Performance Management*: Orchestrating the above assessment and management processes to improve system performance relative to objectives; e.g., tuning of system parameters to an estimated context (C-F).

Such an opportunistically adaptable process might operate as follows (with steps aligned with those listed for the MBC):

0. Estimate the operating environment to determine prior probabilities of PV value (Category 3 processing of a C-O), given an initial specification of information needs and an information acquisition plan;
1. Implement the information acquisition plan to obtain data via sensor data collection or data mining and extract features (PV and CV values) in accordance with information needs;
2. Match features found in acquired data with features predicted by candidate target, information source and context models:

(a) Use model-based detection and recognition methods (Category 1 and 0 reasoning, respectively) to evaluate PVs (and CVs as required) to meet information needs;

(b) Use these ambiguities to select models of possible situation/scenario elements from the model knowledge base; manipulate and combine these models to hypothesize different possible situations/scenarios to account for the acquired data (Category 2 processing), conditioned on the known or assumed source state and observing conditions;

(c) If match is sufficient or if all possible acquired data and plausible model compositions have been tested go to 5;

3. Use the ambiguities in the state estimates to refine information needs in terms of a utility function on PV resolution;

4. Generate, evaluate, and select information acquisition plans:

(a) Map PVs into feasible "observable" PVs and CVs;

(b) Generate candidate information acquisition and processing plans; which may involve new collection, data mining, data selection/batching and management of processing techniques to infer values of PVs and associated CVs;

(c) Evaluate plan net utility in terms of sought information utility, probability of acquiring such information and acquisition cost;

(d) Select an information acquisition plan;

(e) Go to 1;

5. Post selected hypotheses and unresolved situations/scenarios, flag targets/activities of interest and await additional data acquisition or tasking (changed information needs);

6. As a background task, evaluate the sources, techniques and models used in the inference and refine associated models accordingly.

The system architecture depicted in Fig. 7.5 incorporates knowledge bases for system inputs and outputs. System inputs are maintained in stores of collection data, processing techniques and predictive models.

Collection KB. The system may receive data via electronic or biological sensors, or via mining of text or other symbolic data. Resources may be capable of acquiring direct measurements or estimates of one or another problem variable. On the other hand, an input may be a measurement or a report of a set of variables that may be correlated in some way with one or more problem variables. Such variables can be used as context variables used in resolving problem variables.

Technique KB. The system maintains a library of available information acquisition, fusion, management and other available processing techniques, with associated usage and control criteria. Process management functions draw from this library to compose processes predicted to best meet current mission requirements (e.g., current information needs);

Inference KB. The system maintains products of system inference processes, including data association hypotheses and state estimates at any level; e.g., estimates of patterns, individuals, situations, scenarios and outcomes, and of system resources.

Model KB. An information exploitation system will generally require predictive models for entities at some or all levels. In the following section we discuss the relationship between predictive models and the states that they are used to recognize or predict. This leads to concepts whereby models used in inferencing can be assessed and refined jointly with such inferencing.

7.8   Use of Context in Predictive Modeling

Information exploitation relies in one way or another on predictive models of information sources and of entities of interest ("targets" at all appropriate state estimation levels). For example, a simple level 1 data fusion system will use models of sensors and of target objects to recognize, locate and track such objects. A system that incorporates sensor registration or calibration is one that permits modification of these sensor models. More sophisticated information exploitation systems may incorporate models of observation media and backgrounds, terrain and road networks, etc. Systems performing level 2–3 data fusion will likely include models of patterns of target interactions/relationships and courses of action.

Systems capable of adaptive management—e.g., adaptive collection management or adaptive fusion—will employ process and performance models of various selectable or controllable system resources, such as sensor systems, processing hardware and software, and of any reactive physical resources.

As discussed, it should be feasible to develop an information exploitation system that assesses and modifies the target and source models it uses at all fusion and management levels. In a sophisticated information exploitation system, Model Management processes can control the predictive models used in inferencing and planning:

- *Source model management* can involve selection of compensation parameters in response to estimated sensor biases (sensor registration and calibration) and adjustments to sensor accuracy models in response to estimated error statistics;
- *Target model management* can involve modifications to predictive models of target, situation and situation types in response to new estimates of the characteristics and behaviors of such entities based on system observation and inference.

A predictive model can be considered to be a state estimate; one that is usually a product of a data fusion process. However, there is an important distinction to be made between such estimates and the state estimates that are the products of other, more familiar data fusion processes. The latter are estimates of *instantiated states* of particular entities (which may be entities of any type: signals, features, individuals, relationships, situations, scenarios, concepts, etc.). In contrast, a predictive model is an estimate of *possible states* of such entities; e.g., an estimate of the probability distribution of states of a particular entity or of a class of entities.

As model management in such a system performs all the classical management functions shown in Fig. 7.1, so model assessment performs all the classical functions of data fusion:

- *Data alignment*: assuring consistency in format, in spatio-temporal and measurement frameworks and in quality assignment;
- *Data association*: generating, evaluating and selecting hypotheses of a model's scope; i.e., of the range of phenomena to be explained by the model; and
- *State estimation*: estimating and predicting the distribution and dependencies of characteristics and behavior of entities or entity classes within the model's scope.

Model state estimation can take the form of induction from observed states to the distribution of possible states. It also can involve explanation of observed phenomena. Explanation—abduction as employed in Category 2 reasoning—involves model integration or subsumption to higher-level models [22]. As examples, many biological phenomena are "explained" by integration of Biology with Chemistry. Chemistry, in turn, is fully "explained" by subsumption to Physics.

In this way Physics becomes a context for (C-F) understanding Chemistry; providing means for evaluating such problem variables as elemental valences, electron energy states, bonding energies, phase transition conditions, etc.

Postulating a "reason" for some pattern—e.g., quantum theory to explain chemical valence—is not terribly different than the level 2/3 fusion processes that infer relationships with contextual entities that help explain or predict the evolution of a situation (for example, inferring that an adversary is expected to be influenced by loyalty to a political faction).

Adaptive exploitation of diverse bodies of data provides wider and wider contexts for validating and refining specific models, by subsuming them to more general models of the world. In effect, this contextual knowledge—which, ultimately, is the product of inference and estimation—serves in lieu of any direct knowledge of "ground truth."

Given the relationship between predictive models and the states that they are used to recognize or predict, estimating the states (e.g., the fidelity) of models and of model instantiations can be attacked as a joint estimation problem.

7.9 Summary

We find the definition *context* as *relevant situation* to be useful in developing context-sensitive information system.

Context-sensitive reasoning can begin either with an assumed context or with an inference problem. In the former case ("context-of"), the given situation provide expectation for states of constituent elements. In contrast, "context-for" reasoning attempts to use selected situations as contexts for resolving given inference or management problems. Such a problem can be defined as a utility function on the resolution of a set of "problem" variables. In decision-support applications, "resolution" is defined in terms of decision discrimination requirements. A "context for" such a problem can be stated in terms of sets of additional variables, "context variables," that are selected because of their assumed usefulness in making desired discriminations in values of problem variables.

Challenges in developing systems that perform "context-for" reasoning include

(a) predicting the value of contextual information to meet information needs;
(b) selecting information types and sources expected to provide information useful in meeting those needs;
(c) determining the relevance and quality of acquired information; and
(d) applying selected information to a problem at hand.

A categorization of inference problems and methods is suggested, based on the way that acquired data and predictive models are used:

0. in model-based recognition, context conditions expectations for target states and observables;
1. in anomaly-based detection, well-modeled background activity is used as context for detecting anomalous activities;
2. in hypothesis-based explanation, models are composed that explain observed activities and their context;
3. in context-based feasibility assessment, expectations are derived in the context of an ambient situation.

Two system architectures are discussed that perform context-for reasoning adaptively to meet evolving information needs. The first—exemplified by the DARPA Model-Based Classifier—infers values of problem variables by constructing scene hypotheses to serve a context for resolving uncertainty in the characterization of an individual target.

The second system architecture—a conceptual augmentation of the first—adds functions for assessing and managing sensors/sources, processes and models; thereby enhancing the responsiveness of the information exploitation process to relevant situations. Predictive models are estimates of distributions of possible instantiated states. Therefore, an adaptive context-sensitive inference process could evaluate the states (i.e., the fidelity) of models and of model instantiations as a joint estimation problem.

References

1. C.L. Bowman, Process assessment and process management for intelligent data fusion & resource management systems, in *Proceedings of AIAA Space 2012*, Pasadena, CA, Sept 2012
2. L. Gong, Contextual modeling and applications, in *Proceedings of IEEE International Conference on SMC*, V1, 2005

3. A.N. Steinberg, G.L. Rogova, Situation and context in data fusion and natural language understanding, in *Proceedings of Eleventh International Conference on Information Fusion* (2008)

4. A.N. Steinberg, Context-sensitive data fusion using Structural Equation Modeling, in *Proceedings, Twelfth International Conference on Information Fusion*, Seattle (2009)

5. D. Kahneman, *Thinking, Fast and Slow* (Farrar, Straus and Giroux, New York, 2011)

6. W.C. Salmon, *Statistical Explanation and Statistical Relevance* (University of Pittsburgh Press, Pittsburgh, 1971)

7. D. Angelova, L. Mihaylova, Sequential Monte Carlo algorithms for joint target tracking and classification using kinematic radar information, in *Proceedings of 7th International Conference on Information Fusion* (2004)

8. A.N. Steinberg, Foundations of situation and threat assessment, Chap. 18, in *Handbook of Multisensor Data Fusion*, eds. by M.E. Liggins, D.L. Hall, J. Llinas (CRC Press, London, 2009)

9. A.N. Steinberg, C.L. Bowman, Revisions to the JDL data fusion model, Chap. 3, in *Handbook of Multisensor Data Fusion*, eds. by M.E. Liggins, D.L. Hall, J. Llinas (CRC Press, London, 2009)

10. A. Steinberg, L. Snidaro, Levels?, in *Proceedings, Eighteenth International Conference on Information Fusion*, Washington, D.C., USA, pp. 1985–1992 (2015)

11. D.A. Lambert, A unification of sensor and higher-level fusion, in *Proceedings of 9th International Conference on Information Fusion* (2006)

12. G. Rogova, E. Bosse, Information quality in information fusion, in *Proceedings of 13th International Conference on Information Fusion* (2010)

13. G. Rogova, V. Nimier, Reliability in information fusion: literature survey, in *Proceedings of the FUSION'2004-7th Conference on Multisource-Information Fusion* (2004)

14. G. Rogova, M. Hadrazagic, M-O. St-Hilaire, M. Florea, P. Valin, Context-based information quality for sequential decision making, in *Proceedings of the 2013 IEEE International Multi-disciplinary Conference on Cognitive Methods in Situation Awareness and Decision Support (CogSIMA)* (2013)

15. G. Rogova, P. Scott, C. Lollett, Distributed reinforcement learning for sequential decision making, in *Proceedings of 5th International Conference on Information Fusion* (2002)

16. G. Rogova, Adaptive real-time threat assessment under uncertainty and conflict, in *Proceedings of 2014 IEEE International Multi-disciplinary Conference on Cognitive Methods in Situation Awareness and Decision Support (CogSIMA)* (2014)

17. V. Nimier, Supervised multisensor tracking algorithm by context analysis, in *Proceedings of the International Conference on Information Fusion* (1998), pp. 149–156

18. F. Delmotte, P. Borne, Context-dependent trust in data fusion within the possibility theory, in *Proceedings of IEEE International Conference on Systems, Man and Cybernetics* (1998), pp. 78–88

19. S. Fabre, A. Appriou, X. Briottet, Presentation and description of two classification methods using data fusion based on sensor management. ELSEVIER J. Inf. Fusion **2**, 47–71 (2001)

20. A. Appriou, Situation assessment based on spatially ambiguous multisensory measurements. Intl. J. Intell. Syst. **16**(10), 1135–1166 (2001)

21. G. Rogova, P. Scott, C. Lollett, R. Mudiyanur, Reasoning about situations in the early post-disaster response environment, in *Proceedings of 9th International Conference on Information Fusion* (2006)

22. J. Josephson, On the logical form of abduction, in *AAAI Spring Symposium Series: Automated Abduction* (1990), pp 140–144

23. J. Juan Gómez-Romero, M.A. Serrano, J. García, J.M. Molina, G. Rogova, Context-based multi-level information fusion for harbor surveillance. Inf. Fusion **21**, 173–186 (2015)

24. D.L. Hall, A.N. Steinberg, Dirty secrets in multisensor data fusion, Chap. 21, in *Handbook of Multisensor Data Fusion*, eds. by D.L. Hall, J. Llinas (CRC Press, London, 2001)

25. E. Waltz, *Knowledge Management in the Intelligence Enterprise* (Artech House, 2003)

26. A.N. Steinberg, A model for threat assessment, Chap. 15, in *Fusion Methodologies in Crisis Management: Higher Level Fusion and Decision Making*, ed. by G. Rogova, P. Scott (Springer, 2016)
27. A.N. Steinberg, Situations and contexts, in *Perspectives on Information Fusion* 1(1), International Society on Information Fusion, 16–24 (2016)
28. R. Hummel, MSTAR: next generation ATR technologies, in *IDGA Image Fusion Conference* (2005)

Chapter 8
Architectural Aspects for Context Exploitation in Information Fusion

Jesús García, Lauro Snidaro and James Llinas

Abstract This chapter describes a proposed architecture to integrate context sources in fusion processes in a general way, so that any fusion system in which contextual knowledge is available can be developed following this architecture. We introduce some architectural concepts to be considered in the development of fusion systems including contextual knowledge. The two basic concepts in the chapter are context access through middleware, and a multilevel adaptation mechanism following the JDL data fusion model reference. The chapter is written at a general level, so that context input is abstracted as a service and the "middleware" concept is exploited.

Keywords Context-aware computing · Information fusion architecture · Middleware · Process management · JDL level 4

8.1 Introduction

In order to take advantage of the available context sources in information fusion processes, it is needed an analysis of architecture alternatives and requirements for context formalization and exploitation. Research on appropriate architectures and algorithms for multi-sensor fusion needs taking a fresh look at architectural

J. García (✉)
Applied Artificial Intelligence Group, Universidad Carlos III de Madrid,
c/Avenida Gregorio Peces-Barba Martínez, 22, 28270, Colmenarejo, Spain
e-mail: jgherrer@inf.uc3m.es

L. Snidaro
Department of Mathematics and Computer Science, University of Udine, Udine, Italy
e-mail: lauro.snidaro@uniud.it

J. Llinas
Center for Multisource Information Fusion and Department of Industrial and Systems
Engineering, University at Buffalo, Buffalo, NY, USA
e-mail: llinas@buffalo.edu

© Springer International Publishing Switzerland (outside the USA) 2016
L. Snidaro et al. (eds.), *Context-Enhanced Information Fusion*,
Advances in Computer Vision and Pattern Recognition,
DOI 10.1007/978-3-319-28971-7_8

design [1]. Both the architectural and functional issues to represent and exploit contextual information (CI) to improve the fusion process need to be explored. The main challenge is the definition of fusion architectures for general-purpose, it will serve as a core to be adapted to the different applications considered. It should define the main processing blocks and interrelations, so specific modules could be developed with the specific characteristics of different scenarios, contextual knowledge, sensor and dynamic models, algorithm libraries, etc.

The approach is intended to be applicable in the most general way, and so does not make assumptions or puts restrictions about specific fusion processes or information and context sources, but it will be defined at an abstract level so that specific algorithms and applications can be developed based on the proposed architecture. In the first place, the types of context sources are commented upon, and a general mechanism to access context from fusion processes is proposed, following a middleware paradigm. Then, the adaptive information fusion framework is explained. The key idea is the exploitation of context knowledge to adapt the information fusion processes in order to optimize its performance. First, a general fusion node is used as basic element, composed of basic functions needed to carry out any information fusion process. The adaptation will be detailed for different types of information fusion processes, following the familiar JDL data fusion model,[1] including the possibility of multilevel adaptive strategies [3]. The impact of CI for any information fusion system will be analyzed by defining the impact over the basic information fusion functions, with an analysis for each level and for the inter-level processes.

The key concept of middleware is considered here as a separate component running in parallel to the fusion node and allowing global interaction between context and information fusion algorithms. This middleware would be responsible for making the available information usable and useful in the fusion process, providing relevant and up-to-date information. With a predefined interface, context knowledge of very different nature needs to be integrated: access to available databases, maps, constraints, human observers, results inference procedures, etc. These interfaces include access to both the static and dynamic context, which is continuously updated as the situation evolves.

Finally, the architecture is presented as self-adaptive because it takes into account contextual input and implements adjustment approaches typical of "Level-4" JDL processes. The novelty is including the middleware element as general access to all CI, which can be exploited in the most appropriate way by the fusion functions.

The rest of the chapter is organized as follows: Sect. 8.2 analyzes the sources of context knowledge according to their nature and meaning, Sect. 8.3 introduces the basic architectural aspects, Sect. 8.4 discusses the middleware concept as element providing IF processes with the relevant CI, and Sect. 8.5 presents the architecture

---

[1]For a recent discussion on other possible partitioning schemes of data fusion problems the reader is referred to [2].

to exploit this information both within the fusion processes and in the inter-level logic. Section 8.6 draws some final conclusions.

8.2 Types of Context Knowledge and Available Sources

As discussed in Chap. 1, in the scope of this book, context is understood as information that surrounds the situation of interest, whose knowledge may aid in understanding the (estimated) situation and also in reacting to that situation. An equivalent definition was also pointed out in a constraint-based sense [4]: "the structured set of variable, external constraints to some (natural or artificial) cognitive process that influences the behavior of that process in the agent(s) under consideration." Therefore, context may play a vital role at any level of a modern fusion system: from object recognition through physical context exploitation, to intent estimation through linguistic communication analysis. It can be the key element to gain adaptability and improved performance of information fusion processes. As pointed out by Steinberg and Rogova [5], context can be used in data fusion to

- refine ambiguous estimates
- explain observations and
- constrain processing, whether in cueing or tipping-off or in managing fusion or management processes.

A fusion system may have access to a number of different sources of information, depending on the specific domain, providing information that can be expressed as context variables, that is, random variables that can influence the value of problem variables (the latter typically being estimated through observations) [1]. As depicted in Fig. 8.1, CI can be available by different means, such as static data files, access to data services, human observers, inference processes, etc.

Contextual sources can be categorized by several criteria in terms of the nature of the available information; we consider here three dimensions to develop the classification and highlight the multifaceted characteristics of CI:

- Static versus dynamic information
- Physical versus logical information
- Observed versus inferred information

In many applications, CI may be available in static repositories such as maps, GIS databases, representations of roads, channels, bridges, etc.; in other cases, context may be available as dynamic data, such as meteorological conditions changing in space and time. In the latter case, context variables need to be continuously updated, implying that context access and update processes are running in parallel with the core fusion processes.

In both static and dynamic cases, we can distinguish physical and logical context. In the first case, we will have descriptions (like GIS files) or variables (like

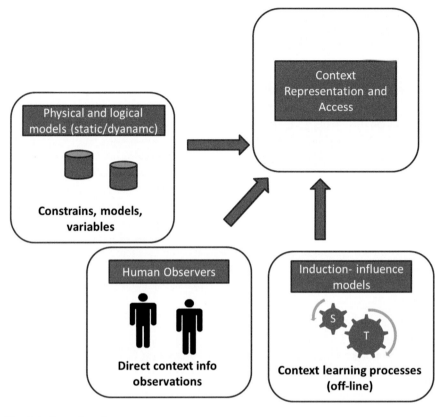

Fig. 8.1 Examples of context source types

meteorological phenomena) regarding physical quantities of the world which are measurable objectively. Logical knowledge takes instead typically the form of constraints, rules, or influence models such as entities engaged in a coordinated trajectory, traffic regulations, protocols, mission goals, etc.

Finally, sometimes CI cannot be observed directly, but indirectly deduced from other sources (inferred context). CI (or, more specifically, instantiated values for context variables) can be available directly, both from hard sources (humidity or wind sensors, for instance) or soft sources (such as human messages about environmental conditions). In other cases, these variables are not directly observable, but can be inferred from a relation or "influence model."

This taxonomy of the main types of context sources is summarized in Tables 8.1 and 8.2 (illustrating the eight cases along the three dimensions indicated above), with examples for each type.

Table 8.1 contains examples of static physical and logical context, such as the configuration files containing man-made structures (roads, bridges, channels, etc.) or geographic information. Examples of inferred physical context could be the

Table 8.1 Taxonomy of context sources, examples of static context

Static context		
	Physical context	Logical context
Observed context	Maps, GIS	Traffic regulations, hierarchical relations
Inferred context	Map refinements (e.g., reported evidence of obstacles, occlusions, road/terrain state)	Patterns of life, social norms, use of buildings

Table 8.2 Taxonomy of context sources, examples of dynamic context

Dynamic context		
	Physical context	Logical context
Observed context	Weather conditions	Traffic information, user agenda
Inferred context	Inferred weather state	Loyalty, user emotion, threat level

result of a learning process applied to recorded data, for instance to detect modifications in the maps through other observations (e.g., inferring closed roads from traffic conditions or inferring sea state from wind speed), or in the logical dimensions the presence of patterns of life driving the behaviors of individuals (such as common trajectories, or use of buildings by workers during their workday).

Analogous distinctions can be done over dynamic context in Table 8.2. Weather reports are a direct source of physical observed context, but weather state could be indirectly obtained in some cases, such as the presence of heavy clutter in certain areas of a maritime scenario, an indirect indication of sea waves produced by strong wind. Again, inferences can be made both by human or automatic inference process, the latter leading to the idea of a parallel representation of a context process with its own operations and sources available, separate from the fusion processes working with problem variables.

8.3 Architectures-Related Works

The word "Framework" is not a precise term, a typical definition mentions "a conceptual structure intended to serve as a support or guide for the building of something that expands the structure into something useful" [6]. Here, we take this definition in the sense that a framework is an abstraction, free of domain-specific components, so that inclusion of domain-specific elements converts the framework into a particular structure.

In [6], a survey of papers drawn from the literature addresses IF framework concepts and issues. Some works just discuss issues but do not offer a framework proposal, others offer constructs in the sense of a process flow and control architecture, but usually the concept is often domain-specific, although many good ideas are offered. Some of these ideas are integrated into the framework we offer below.

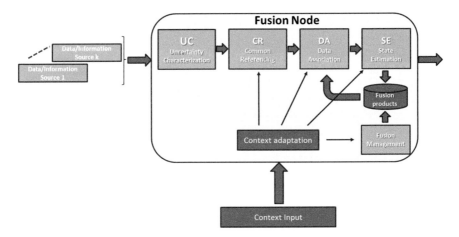

Fig. 8.2 Fusion node comprising the four basic functions of uncertainty characterization, common referencing, data association, and state estimation

One aspect typically overlooked in these papers is the critically important adaptive feedback and dynamic process control.

This is the main aspect considered here, the use of context for adaptation. The architecture taken as reference uses the "fusion node" [7] consisting in four basic functions, complemented with a management process representing any IF process (Fig. 8.2):

- **Uncertainty Characterization**: assessment of the uncertainty associated to the information provided by the source.
- **Common Referencing**: normalization operations are performed, such as coordinate or units transformations, to align data from information sources to be fused.
- **Data association**: input estimates or measurements are examined in order to determine which (hypothetical) entity that the system believes to exist they are associated to or come from.
- **State estimation**: e.g., kinematic properties, classification attributes such as color, identity, etc., exploiting prediction models and estimation/inference processes.
- **Fusion management**: actions to control the fusion processes, such as creation, deletion, merging, etc.

The architecture presented later is based on this fusion node, which can be generalized for any fusion process at any level of the JDL hierarchy.

8.4   Middleware Approach

The idea of middleware is basically an abstraction to interconnect processes operating at different levels and working with diverse types of information. It is associated to the concept of service-oriented computing: the information workflows are split into elementary building blocks as independent reusable services components with a homogenous interface. Middleware is a common term in several domains to facilitate distributed processing, connecting different applications over a network.

8.4.1   Middleware in IF Literature

In the IF literature, there exist approaches to employ middleware architectures, such as the network-enabled capability (NEC) [8]. Each information fusion process involves two fundamental elements: (1) information to be fused, and (2) operations applied to the information to produce the output information. Here, the access to context knowledge can be implemented as available services:

- Information source services are the sources of primary data to be fused.
- Information fusion services perform the actual fusion on the data obtained from previous information source services or other fusion services working at a lower level.

With this perspective, fusion processes can be viewed as workflows composed of different types of services, which are composed either manually by a human expert, or automatically by appropriate service composition tools. DFuse [9] is a data fusion framework that facilitates transfer of different areas of application-level information fusion into the network to save power. DFuse does this transfer dynamically by determining the cost of using the network using cost functions. More examples of adaptive middleware are Adaptive Middleware [10] and MidFusion [11]. MidFusion is an architecture to facilitate information fusion in sensor network applications. It discovers and selects the best set of sensors or sensor agents on behalf of applications (transparently), depending on the quality of service (QoS) guarantees and the cost of information acquisition, with some theoretical analysis to do selections. Nexus [12] is another middleware for service-oriented information fusion developed in BTs Pervasive ICT research center. It implements three key concepts, i.e., service-oriented computing, automated service workflow composition and peer-to-peer architecture.

Here, we propose following an analogous approach to interconnect data fusion processes with contextual resources. The access to context is done through the context middleware, defining this component responsible to access and provide the context knowledge to the fusion processes in the appropriate way. The operations to be done by the context middleware services are indicated in the following subsections.

8.4.2 Middleware Approach: Query Service from IF to CI

As indicated above, the proposed architecture needs a context inference module, in charge of inferring useful information about the focal elements of the fusion processes (at any abstraction level, accordingly to application) and their surrounding *context*.

Taking this architectural perspective, a way to systematically address advanced and generic context-based IF design deals with a context access and management system, in charge of providing useful CI about the entities as a transversal independent module. Context services supporting fusion processes could include, as examples, access to reference databases, meteorological information, image repositories, GIS systems, texts, Internet, etc.

The basic mechanism would be a query process (Fig. 8.3): the middleware returns the selected relevant CI from the available sources, accordingly to

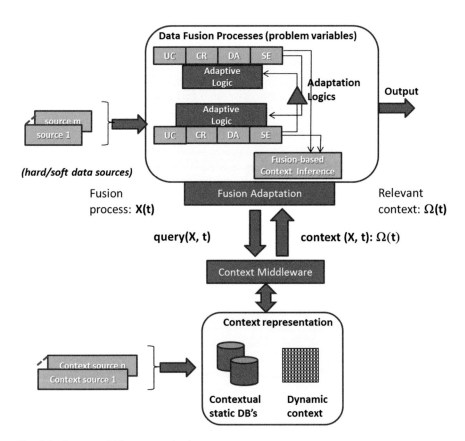

Fig. 8.3 Context middleware mechanism

hypotheses raised by fusion processes. Following the figure, two basic elements can be identified at both sides:

- At the context side (bottom), the middleware manager is responsible for collecting, updating, and making context knowledge usable by fusion processes. Static and dynamic sources are conveniently preprocessed to keep an updated and consistent repository of contextual information (with the necessary adaptations mentioned in next subsection), so it is ready to be delivered accordingly to the Fusion Adaptation queries.
- At the fusion side (top), the adaptation logic takes the contextual inputs and directs them to relevant fusion processes, generically represented as nodes composed by the four general functions described above. As shown in the figure, the adaptation can take place both within fusion processes or in the interaction logic among several processes, as will be detailed in the next section.

To this end, all processes need to be designed as context-aware in order to properly exploit contextual inputs. It is mainly a "pull" mechanism from the IF node requiring the pertinent and applicable context knowledge, although the middleware could also detect relevant context changes and report, complementing the query/response basic mechanism.

There are some system engineering issues [13]. An important question is related with representational form. CI data can be expected to be of a type that has been created by domain users—for example weather data, important in many fusion applications as CI, is generated by meteorologists for meteorologists (not for fusion system designers). For instance, in Fig. 8.4, a possible example with a meteorological service map is depicted; the wind strength is sampled in a certain grid, which may be useful, for instance, to predict maritime traffic conditions. The data provided is discretized as shown in Table 8.3, for instance the heading is provided

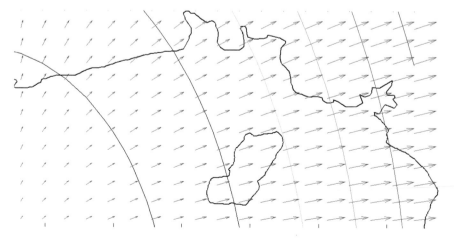

Fig. 8.4 Meteorological example of wind strength and direction as a vector field

Table 8.3 Example of
reported meteorological data
in tabular form

	Wind	Average to gust (mph)	Temperature (° C)
01:00	SW	8–17	10
04:00	WSW	8–23	10
07:00	WSW	8–18	9
10:00	W	13–20	14
13:00	WNW	13–18	16
16:00	WNW	14–18	16
19:00	WNW	9–18	12
22:00	WNW	8–24	8

in steps of 11.25° (between South, S, and West, W, there are five levels: S, SSW, SW, WSW, W).

Therefore, even if contextual data is available, there is likely to be a need for a middleware layer to incorporate the necessary logic and algorithms to sample these data and shape them into a form suitable for use in fusion processes of various types. Even in simple cases, the middleware may be required to reformat the data from some native form to a useable one.

8.4.3 Middleware Functions. Requirements for Use in IF Processes

CI should be usable by the whole set of fusion processes and, thus, it must be accessible to every other component in the system. The global design requirements for the system providing CI can be summarized as:

- It must provide up-to-date online information (this is especially important when dynamic context is available).
- The results must be readily available for any component requesting them. The result of such request will be a self-contained data element, such as a tuple of values with an associated timestamp.

Therefore, CI of course needs to be accessible in order to use it, but accessibility may not be a straightforward matter in all cases. For instance, CI could be available but controlled or secured at the same time, so that the most-current CI would not be available when needed.

These requirements imply the need to develop some functions that are detailed next. The key elements are the selection of relevant context sources according to the current hypotheses raised by the fusion processes, spatial and temporal alignment of context with the fusion data, adaptation of the granularity of the information, and characterization of uncertainty in context input.

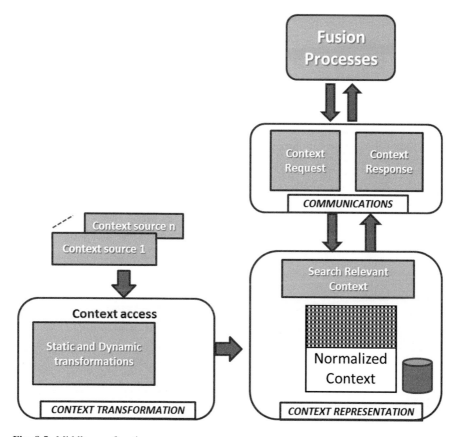

Fig. 8.5 Middleware functions

The transformation operations to be done by the context middleware are sketched in Fig. 8.5. In order to be useful, context needs to be spatially and temporally aligned with the fusion data, adapted to the granularity of the information, and the associated uncertainty should be available or needs to be estimated.

The main operations required are listed next. First, regarding the search of applicable context to the fusion query ("Search Relevant Context" in the figure):

- Search of context relevant to the situation: both physical (close roads, bridges, channels, etc.) and logical (such as applicable operational rules).
- Compatibility: the retrieved information must be validated as appropriate for the query and check its compatibility (e.g., map, number of objects, etc.). In some cases, context may be not applicable (e.g., off-road, operational rules not followed, etc.)

Regarding the transformations to get the "Normalized Context" in the figure:

- Context correlation and alignment with the fusion process (this is especially relevant for the use of real-time "dynamic" contextual sources such as meteorological services):
  - Spatial alignment (fundamental for efficiency): search with appropriate representation and algorithms (maps, GIS, roads, etc.)
  - Time alignment (necessary when context is dynamic): simple temporal indexing, extrapolation models, etc.

- It must provide up-to-date context: it must integrate on-line information appropriate and potentially useful for the fusion processes.
- Granularity: it implies adaptation to the needs of the fusion algorithm. Some aggregation or interpolation may be required to adapt the scales at both sides.
- Characterization of the uncertainty in the source of CI.

At the fusion process side, the development of functions supporting the adaptation mechanisms is needed, thus comprising:

- Library of alternative models that can be selected according to context (such as on/off road motion models).
- Impact on applicable models, sets of parameters, algorithms, etc.
- Applicable rules to drive the fusion processes, such as constrains, hypotheses applicable, etc.
- Closed-world models depending on the situation (number of objects, appearance/disappearance assumptions, convoy motion, etc.)

Of the middleware functions described above, two of them deserve special attention: uncertainty and relevance of CI. With respect to uncertainty, it is important considering not only the intrinsic uncertainty in CI but also the propagation through the query (for instance uncertainty in the location to index spatial context). As an example, in the domain of air traffic control, the authors in [14] model aircraft motion following the air routes and standard maneuvers that usually take place at waypoints (navaids). The recorded trajectories show spatial variability, but also variability in the time instants where maneuvers start, the flight mode transitions occur close but not exactly at the expected waypoints. This uncertainty in context (the route followed by aircraft, will be also increased by the uncertainty on the own location where the position is read before accessing the trajectories). There are many other examples in which the CI uncertainty is very important and thus cannot be directly taken as error-free information.

With respect to context relevance, as commented in Chap. 1, a big challenge is determining the selection of context variables. In general, such selection should be based on previous knowledge of relations among context variables and problem variables. A possibility could be the development of an ontology based on relevancy of contextual variables to problem variables and their consistency. A context variable can be called relevant to a set of problem variables defining the reference items and relations between them if the values of these problem variables change with the value of the context variable under consideration. Another criterion for determining a particular context as relevant may be the increase in information as the result of utilizing that context variable for estimation and/or inference. Finally, the problem of selecting context variables is more complex since relevance is often time-variable. Situations of interest are often dynamic, such that the availability of any sought data may also be time-variable. Even mission-driven information needs and fusion processes can be also dynamic, making the utility of information given by context pieces also time-variable.

A middleware approach is therefore proposed to generalize context access and exploitation by fusion processes, organized as a set of operations done over the information available from different sources. The context middleware manager is responsible for searching and providing the relevant and updated information in the expected format and scale, considering the needs and requirements of the fusion node, so that fusion operations can take into account the context and its associated uncertainty, independently of the specific strategy adopted. The service-oriented architecture is the key to develop a general perspective in the design and avoid particular solutions depending on the specific types and nature of the contextual sources available.

8.5 Multi-level Adaptive Architecture Based on Context Input

The adaptive fusion architecture presented in this section is depicted in Fig. 8.6, as an extension of [6] and further discussed with respect to [15]. Raw input data, covering both hard (electronic, physics-based) sensors and soft (human observers) sources enter into a detection, semantic labeling, and flow control composite functions. Semantic labeling can also involve complex automated processes, such as automatically labeling detected image entities with correct semantic labels. Once the best-qualified detections have been achieved, there is the question of assigning them to the various fusion nodes. The figure depicts a general situation in which several fusion processes at different abstraction levels (with JDL notation) can be running in parallel so the data is delivered to the appropriate processes.

The key to keep interaction with the contextual sources, through the middleware interface presented in the previous section, is a function module called **Problem-Space Characterization** below the detection operations in Fig. 8.6. To adaptively manage a system with a library of alternative algorithms that address a generically common problem space (e.g., object tracking problems), knowledge of the performance bounds of any library algorithm in terms of an observable set of parameters needs to be known. With such knowledge, an intelligent algorithm manager—we see this as part of the Internodal Adaptive Logic—can terminate and invoke the best algorithm for the current problem-space condition. Besides, we may distinguish a static configuration logic, describing all problem-space variables and

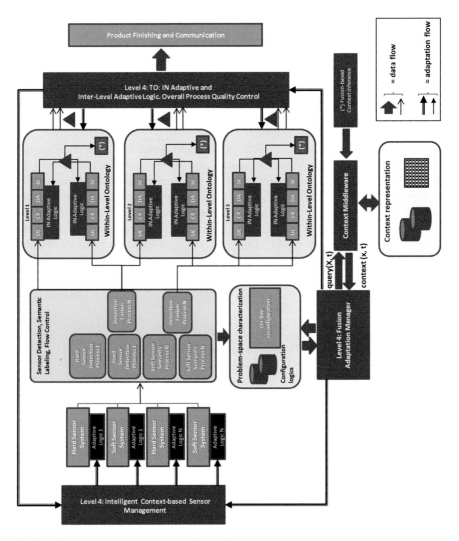

Fig. 8.6 Proposed adaptive information fusion framework

interrelations, and the possibility of dynamic adaptation. A typical example is the set of categories in a classification problem, which may change dynamically accordingly to the operative conditions or available context. The adaptation strategy can be related with the type of interactions existing between context sources and state variables in the estimation inference processes, two main alternatives can be identified [16]:

- *Context as constraints.* In many cases context implies constraints, such as roads, channels, obstacles, routes, traffic regulations, etc., for vehicle/vessel movement. As mentioned, constraints can be physical constraints or procedural (such as forbidden operations), and can be applied through the adaptation logic in different ways depending on the fusion algorithm (projection, inference rules, probabilistic conditioning such as Bayesian or Markov networks, etc.).

- *Context as additional features, semantics, or situation elements.* In some applications context is not directly a constraint over the estimation space (in the sense of reduction in the uncertainty in the search space), but brings new problem dimensions. In this case, context adds dimensionality, opening hypothetical or more detailed ways to interpret the data. An example can be the knowledge of semantic features, such as presence of high-value locations, which open hypotheses to explain maneuvers. The problem-space reconfiguration can be triggered as a response to this type of contextual inputs.

So, the context middleware presented in the previous section will be feeding the knowledge base and control logic. It is in charge of providing the appropriate context pieces according to the state of the fusion variables. This context is delivered by the adaptation manager to the different adaptive processes defined along the architecture, including the specific processes at the sources, the functions composing each individual fusion process (IN Adaptive logic boxes) and the inter-level processes, depending on the type of solution developed.

All the adaptation processes in Fig. 8.6 (darker red boxes) can be considered process refinement approaches (JDL level 4), which are the basic goals of the architecture, exploiting the context in order to refine and adapt the different fusion processes (including data sources). These adaptation elements can be described as follows:

- **Intelligent Context-based Sensor Management (ICSM)**: This module has a global view of the sensor set, geographical disposition, and the data needed by the fusion process. It manages sensors and DBs for a composite, system-level, quality control policy. Sensor control can be either in the sense of space–time schedules for sensors (cueing) or by controlling various sensor operating parameters such as waveform or power level (or yet other parameters, as modern sensors are very agile).
- **Overall Process Quality Control (OPQC) and Internodal Adaptive Logic (IAL)**: The overall process quality control is in charge of evaluating the combined fusion products, with appropriate quality metrics, in order to identify performance incidences and opportunities. Then, the IN adaptive logic can drive the data processing functions within the node, with facilities such as parameters adaptation or multi-algorithm management based on contextual input.
- **Inter-Level Adaptive Logic (ILAL)**: This module drives the interaction among different fusion processes, controlling the interchanged fusion products or coordinated adaptations to context. We assert that the framework should show adaptive internodal feedback to allow (or perhaps require) the nodes sharing and exploiting information if possible. One can see this in traditional level 1 fusion for tracking and identification usually done in two separate fusion nodes; kinematics are of course helpful for identification, and identification can be exploited for example to know an object's feasible dynamic motion. In turn, an

adaptive inter-level feedback process is also shown, allowing situational estimates to feedback their estimates to other levels; an example of this would be a
situational estimate that would suggest that maneuvering behaviors could be
expected, informing the level 1 object tracking logic that would enlarge the
tracking gates to capture the diverging measurements occurring upon the
maneuver, i.e., as a maneuver-anticipation strategy instead of the (generally
too-late) post-maneuver detection strategies often employed in tracking systems.
- **Fusion Adaptation Manager (FAM)** is the access point to the available CI, and
  can access a description of the problem space, in order to orchestrate the different adaptation processes of the data fusion system, as described below.

Therefore, feedback is a fundamental aspect in the adaptation mechanism. Note
that all control loops need to define stopping criteria that terminate the otherwise
endless loop; that requirement is shown by the triangles in Fig. 8.6. Another loop is
shown coincident with the output layers of levels 1–3, which incorporates a value or
quality-driven strategy for the output or final estimates and employs that logic to
adaptively control the hard and soft sensor system through the module for intelligent context-based sensor management.

The adaptation process, triggered by the FAM, basically follows the scheme
shown in Fig. 8.7. It starts with the OPQC module detecting events in the fusion
process (e.g. sudden decreases in quality indicators, unexpected events, etc.) and
opportunities to improve the quality of the products. Combining this information
with the problem-space characterization, the FAM identifies other elements in the
fusion system that can have an influence through transitive property. Then, the
context middleware is queried for contextual data relevant to the identified elements
according to spatial, time, and other context metadata criteria. The relevant context
serves two purposes. In the first place, it is used by the FAM to identify needs or
desired changes in the flow control and in sensor scheduling. These needs/changes
are disseminated together with relevant context data to the ICSM and the ILAL.

Once it has relevant context data, the ILAL can define the actions to be taken to
improve the process, which are classified in inter-level and intra-level. The second
set of actions is forwarded to the IAL. The ICSM receives CI, and requests/needs
from both the FAM and the OPQC. This information is used to decide which is the
best sensor spatial–temporal scheduling, and also forwards requests/needs to individual sensor adaptive logics to change the individual sensor parameterization. As
mentioned, the proposed adaptation flow combines both context-based and other
regular adaptation processes (such as those based on quality control) in a single
process.

Therefore, this architecture proposes a multilevel fusion adaptation mechanism.
Each fusion node can have defined its own specific adaptation methods for its functions and abstraction level. The architecture has a tight control over the internal
organization of fusion processes, with a global inter-level mechanism outside the
fusion nodes which combines information from all levels to determine the required
adaptive actions, and supervises how the Fusion Nodes interact with themselves. The

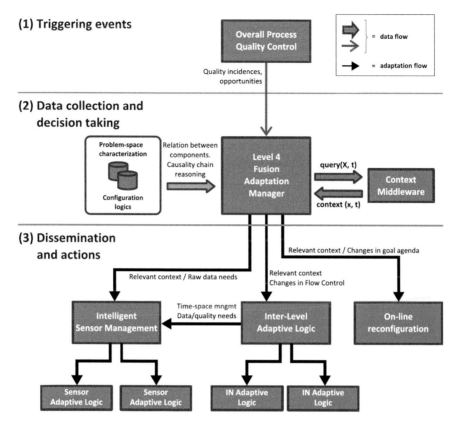

Fig. 8.7 Data flow view of the context-based adaptation process

adaptation mechanisms described (sensors, internode and inter-level) are assimilated to level 4 (process refinement) in the JDL model, a meta-process transversal to levels 0–3, in charge of supervising the performance of the system and taking corrective actions. In particular, the main function of ILAL is to adapt the fusion logic between levels to maintain or improve fusion quality. It can submit instructions or recommendations to intra-level adaptation mechanisms and modify how IF nodes are connected. Thanks to its capacity to see the "big picture," it can also interact with the context middleware to indicate if some IF node requires additional CI.

8.6   Conclusions

This chapter introduces an analysis of CI as determinant element to adapt IF processes. This discussion motivates also the architectural proposal to develop context-based fusion systems with a more general approach. Middleware is the structural element here discussed to unify context access from fusion processes, taking care of its correctness and relevance according to the needs of the fusion tasks requiring it.

The applicability of CI to a certain IF process depends on certain factors such as relevance, granularity, uncertainty, etc. The context middleware is responsible for determining this applicability, and of adapting CI when possible to maximize its utility.

Research in this architectural line, from the authors' point of view, can be an aspect to fertilize the development of a new generation of fusion systems able to integrate context in a general way beyond stove-piped solutions.

Acknowledgments This work was supported by ONRG Grant N62909-14-1-N061 and in part by project MINECO TEC2014-57022-C2-2-R.

References

1. L. Snidaro, J. Garcia, J. Llinas, Context-based information fusion: a survey and discussion. Inf. Fusion **25**, 16–31 (2015). doi:10.1016/j.inffus.2015.01.002
2. A. Steinberg, L. Snidaro, Levels?, in *Proceedings of the 18th International Conference on Information Fusion*, Washington, DC, 6–9 July 2015, pp. 1985–1992
3. L. Snidaro, I. Visentini, J. Llinas, G.L. Foresti, Context in fusion: some considerations in a JDL perspective, in *Proceedings of the 16th International Conference on Information Fusion*, Istanbul, Turkey, 9–12 July 2013
4. M. Kandefer, S.C. Shapiro, Evaluating spreading activation for soft information fusion, in *Proceedings of the 14th International Conference on Information Fusion* (IEEE, 2011)
5. A. Steinberg, G. Rogova, Situation and context in data fusion and natural language understanding, in *Proceedings of the Eleventh International Conference on Information Fusion*, Cologne, Germany, 2008
6. J. Llinas, A survey and analysis of frameworks and framework issues for information fusion applications. Hybrid Artif. Intell. Syst. 14–23 (2010)
7. J. Llinas, C.L. Bowman, G.L. Rogova, A.N. Steinberg, E.L. Waltz, F.E. White, Revisiting the JDL data fusion model II, in *Proceedings of the Seventh International Conference on Information Fusion*, vol. II (Stockholm, Sweden, 2004) pp. 1218–1230
8. A. Alston, Network enabled capability—the concept. J. Defence Sci. **8**(3), 108–116 (2003)
9. R. Kumar, M. Wolenetz, B. Agarwalla, J. Shin, P. Hutto, A. Paul, U. Ramachandran, DFuse: a framework for distributed data fusion, in *1st international conference on Embedded networked sensor systems* (2003), pp. 114–125
10. M.C. Huebscher, J.A. McCann, Adaptive middleware for context-aware applications in smart-homes, in *Proceedings of the 2nd Workshop on Middleware for Pervasive and Ad-hoc Computing* (ACM, 2004), pp. 111–116
11. H. Alex, M. Kumar, B. Shirazi, Midfusion: an adaptive middleware for information fusion in sensor network applications. Inf. Fusion **9**(3), 332–343 (2008)
12. M. Jakob, N. Kaveh, R. Ghanea-Hercock, Nexus-middleware for decentralized service-oriented information fusion. Technical report, DTIC Document (2006)
13. J. Gómez-Romero, J. García, M. Kandefer, J. Llinas, M.A. Molina, Patricio, M. Prentice, S.C. Shapiro, Strategies and techniques for use and exploitation of contextual information in high-level fusion architectures, in *Proceedings of the 13th International Conference on Information Fusion* (Fusion 2010), Edinburgh, UK: 28–30 July 2010

14. W. Liu, J. Wei, M. Liang, Y. Cao, Multi-sensor fusion and fault detection using hybrid estimation for air traffic surveillance. IEEE Trans. Aerosp. Electron. Syst. **49**(4), 2323–2339 (2013)
15. L. Snidaro, L. Vaci, J. García, E. Marti, A.-L. Jousselme, K. Bryan, D.D. Bloisi, D. Nardi, A framework for dynamic context exploitation, in *Proceedings of the 17th International Conference on Information Fusion*, Washington, DC, USA, 6–9 July 2015, pp 1160–1167
16. R.T. Antony, J.A. Karakowski, Towards greater consciousness in data fusion systems, in *Proceedings of the MSS National Symposium on Sensor and Data Fusion* (2007), pp. 11–14

Chapter 9
Middleware for Exchange and Validation of Context Data and Information

Jurgo-Soren Preden, James Llinas and Leo Motus

Abstract In Chap. 1 of this book, the notion of some type of middleware was put forward as a likely component of an architecture for Context-Enhanced Information Fusion process designs. In this chapter, the details of a proposed middleware component are elaborated, based on the consideration of the Open System of Systems (SoS) concept and the critical concerns in such an SoS framework for maintaining data integrity and quality. The approach is developed in part by examining interdependencies among Information Fusion, Sensemaking and Decision Support processes as part of the Data-to-Decisions (D2D) paradigm described herein. In this framework, we describe the details of Middleware that facilitate the development of distributed systems by accommodating heterogeneity, hiding distribution details and providing a set of common and domain specific services. We specifically describe a middleware design called ProWare that delivers the data needed by individual fusion nodes based on their current information needs. A central concept of ProWare is the subscription-based data exchange model, which delivers data to a computing node only if the data has been requested by that node. In order to ensure correctness of the fusion algorithm output, the correctness of the input data is validated from the data consumer perspective.

Keywords Middleware · System · ProWare · Validation · Decision-making · Network

J.-S. Preden (✉) · L. Motus
Research Laboratory for Proactive Technologies, Tallinn University
of Technology, Tallin, Estonia
e-mail: jurgo.preden@ttu.ee

J. Llinas
Center for Multisource Information Fusion and Department of Industrial and Systems
Engineering, University at Buffalo, Buffalo, NY, USA

© Springer International Publishing Switzerland (outside the USA) 2016   205
L. Snidaro et al. (eds.), *Context-Enhanced Information Fusion*,
Advances in Computer Vision and Pattern Recognition,
DOI 10.1007/978-3-319-28971-7_9

9.1 Middleware for Exchange and Validation of Context Data and Information

9.1.1 Relevance of Context in Dynamic Fusion Systems

It can be argued that information fusion processes are always operating within a well-defined context. Historically, the contexts for systems are assumed to be fixed (at least for a reasonable period of time), being implicitly defined by the application the system has been designed for; such systems therefore need not be very adaptive. However, the expectations for modern systems are much higher—they must be able to operate reliably even while the environment, the system's composition and the tasks that the system is used for are changing dynamically. This requires efficient monitoring of the context, putting additional importance on validation of the consistency of variables expressing context information and reliable operation of such a system depends heavily on well-tuned communication system.

Many modern systems, including fusion systems (e.g. Intelligence, Surveillance and Reconnaissance (ISR) systems) are Systems of Systems (SoS) as they are made up from many individual systems, which exhibit a greater or lower level of autonomy [1]. The composition of such a SoS may change dynamically and the individual systems that make up the SoS must work in unison while maintaining a level of autonomy. In order to achieve the unified operation of the individual systems and to ensure a correct output of the fusion process, up to date contextual information must be acquired and exchanged between the systems.

The complexities that arise in acquisition, forming and exchange of context information for a SoS are not realistically manageable at the application level (e.g. fusion process) or end-user level, so an intermediate communication layer has to be added, which handles part of the complexity (such as information request and delivery, validation, etc.), while at the same time hiding it from the application layer. By application layer, we mean in the real-time fusion algorithms that exploit context, while producing their information products based on sensor or other types of source data.

As the SoS composition may vary in time and space, each individual system must be able to cater to its own performance, such as timing, types of data needed and provided, assessment of the quality of data, accuracy, metadata tags, trustworthiness, etc., which means that every system must be able to cope with all the features of other systems with which it interacts or depends upon.

Another aspect, which complicates the design of such systems, is that one cannot assume that the systems making up an ISR SoS are developed and deployed in an integrated, holistic fashion as a complete system; instead, the individual systems may originate from different vendors, they may be deployed at different times, and they may not be owned by the same actor, e.g. in case of a coalition operation there may be a desire to cross-use sensor assets between coalition partners. The coordination between the individual systems must be realized at the individual system level as involving central coordinating authorities presents additional challenges, since one cannot expect that a central coordinating entity would have global detailed knowledge of individual assets and their capabilities. This means that the individual systems must be able to use data services from other systems without expecting support from the others (i.e. without manual reconfiguration of the individual systems).

9.1.2 Interactive Computation Processes in Open System of Systems Design

Fusion Processes are a special type of Open System of Systems and the design paradigms applicable for the Open SoS are also applicable for Fusion Processes. The Open SoS are typically composed of non-synchronized, heterogeneous and autonomous but nevertheless collaborating components. Those systems are composed of interacting mixtures of algorithms (i.e. mathematical abstractions), real-world physical processes, and social processes—and may be simultaneously governed by a set of metric and/or topological times, that can only approximately be reduced to Coordinated Universal Time (UTC) or some other time standard. Different components have different susceptibility to the system's attempts to control their behaviour; in addition, each component may have different (varying in time, and/or depending on location) characteristics (such as jitter and delays in timing and/or response, etc.). Due to incomplete information about the system, autonomy of components, varying properties of environment and potentially varying composition of the system; the designers of these systems need to be prepared to tackle the significant impact of possible emergent behaviour [2].

Conventional computer science studies computational processes that evaluate (a subset of) mathematical functions—an algorithm maps initial input values into output values ignoring the external world while it is executing. The respective feature is imposed by the noninterference axiom; such calculations have been called "ballistic" calculations by Sloman [3]. "Ballistic" calculations have caused difficulties since the early days of embedded control and monitoring systems as well as in many applications of artificial intelligence. A necessity to more precisely analyze the behaviour of networked cyber-physical systems, autonomous computing, proactive computing, and other systems has been noted, and is one of the many factors that have activated the study of non-classical models of computation, an area which is still gaining momentum.

Non-classical models of computation attempt to better match laws of physics and those of abstract computation. Stepney [4] stresses that laws of physics cannot be ignored in practical computation. At the same time, in classical models of computation (e.g. Turing machine) all the limitations imposed by available time resources, realistic synchronization, required computational power and available memory space have been abstracted away. Classical models of computation are inherently sequential, parallel processing (i.e. processing separate threads of a program

in parallel) is considered exceptional in these models. At the same time, in Nature
we observe truly parallel (a.k.a. forced parallel) interacting processes which cannot
be described within classical model of computation, i.e. as parallel processing of
program threads. Truly parallel processes in Nature can be more precisely modelled
as simultaneous/parallel processing of agents in a multi-agent system.

Some researchers in non-classical models of computation have posed many
ambitious questions invoked by a trend to match laws of physics with laws of
computation, which lead to the ultimate question—are laws of computation more
fundamental than laws of physics (see [4]). Others attempt to maintain smooth
collaboration between classical and non-classical models of computation [5] by
removing unnatural limitations (e.g. the noninterference axiom that is the cause of
"ballistic" computations). Some aspects of sample research projects [2, 6] on
interactive models of computation are discussed in the following. These projects
focused on two challenges

- to enable, or foster, dynamic validation and verification of system's behaviour
  (e.g. after any changes in system's composition, or in properties of the environment, or in the system's goals)
- to detect the emergent behaviour in a temporally responsive way, assess its
  effect on the system, and provide appropriate response.

Capabilities of situation-aware, interactive models of computation are relevant in
a generic computing system that

- is distributed on a dynamically reconfigurable heterogeneous computer network
- interacts immediately with the non-computer components of the artificial and/or
  natural environment
- contains (smart) components with environmental perceptivity, that are capable
  for autonomous and proactive behaviour
- provides persistently ongoing service that supports algorithmic concurrency, as
  well as forced, a.k.a. true concurrency
- has a logical structure that can be described as a collection of loosely coupled,
  context-aware, interacting autonomous components that satisfy all the behavioural requirements and constraints imposed by the environment and by its
  interacting elements.

Each interacting autonomous component may have its own time counting system
and each of those time counting systems may apply its own metrics. Strictly
speaking, the time instants and intervals defined in different time counting systems
(time models) can only be compared within known uncertainty limits. Hence, one
time dimension for the whole computing system—that so far has been the conventional approach in computer science and software engineering—cannot solve
the time awareness problem in asynchronous systems with autonomy. Time in
computing systems has usually been considered in concordance with the traditions
of computer science, i.e. time is an additional dimension of the state space—
meaning that a single time variable is introduced for the whole system.

Some pragmatists interpret systems comprising interacting autonomous components as a success story of the "divide and rule" paradigm since the system's maintenance has become simpler. At the same time, they completely neglect potential benefits and dangers of increased behavioural complexity caused by emergent behaviour and fostered by autonomy of components. In artificial systems, the act of giving a component capabilities of and privilege to apply (although restricted) self-control is a major step forward in engineering systems that triggers changes in many related disciplines, including theory of computation, and challenges the applicability of some widely accepted software engineering concepts and toolsets. Autonomy of a component in artificial systems is always restricted—i.e. an autonomous component can usually make its own decisions and perform required actions, but certain decisions and actions can be prohibited, coerced, or forced by the system as required by its goal function(s). In other words, the systems' overall behaviour should, independent of autonomous decisions, remain within a defined safety envelope.

One of the ongoing research challenges is to improve the observability and controllability of the overall system by using specifically implanted mediated interactions whose major task is to support detection and suppression of unwanted emergent behaviour and encouragement of beneficial emergent behaviour. The concept and formal description of mediated interactions follows from the properties of an interaction-centric, situation-aware model of computations [6]. The same underlying formalism serves as the basis for implementation of smart features in the proactive middleware.

9.1.3   Interdependencies in Information Fusion Architectures

When designing Information Fusion (IF) processes, there is almost always the question of defining the boundaries of the process. While system boundaries are always a systems-engineering question, this is particularly true for IF processes since they are, most of the time, a supportive process within a larger systemic framework; said otherwise, they are often sub-systems and part of a larger system concept, making the Fusion systems an element of a System of Systems (SoS). This view can be seen in much of the literature on IF process design, such as in [7–9] where, in [7] for example, the first design question is to decide the "role" of the IF process, meaning its role in a contributory or sub-system nature to the "parent" system.

The IF processes are one element in a larger SoS, consuming data from sensors and feeding information to the decision-making processes. Careful design of IF processes from this point of view can be successful, as long as the requirements for the IF process have been developed with equal care and perspective. Here, we reexamine the perspective from which such requirements should evolve. We take two views in this regard: (1) a decision-making or analysis perspective, where the IF process is supporting humans doing either or both of these functions, and (2) the network perspective, in which there are multiple IF processing nodes that are interacting in some way. In both cases, the IF process can communicate with other entities, such as data sources.

9.1.3.1 The Analysis and Decision-Making Perspective

Broadly speaking, the function of IF processes is to provide a multisource-based estimate of a situation of interest. That product is typically presented to a human analyst involved in a "Sensemaking (SM)" process (see [10, 11] in regard to SM) that is a dynamic, iterative process in which the fused situation estimate (algorithmically computed) is considered and combined with human judgment and contextual factors to develop, from a mixed-initiative operation, a "final" situation estimate (at this point, the human has achieved a best-estimate of "situational awareness (SA)", a state that only humans can achieve). In turn, that SM process and its product of best SA is usually the basis for considerations regarding decision-making (DM). However, there are variables and constraints in any DM process that can interact with the SM operation and thus, in turn, the IF processing operations; it is these three-way interdependencies that must be considered in developing IF requirements that are often overlooked in IF process design. The middleware that is described in the current chapter can cater for these interactions, enabling dynamic communication of variables and constraints stemming from the DM processes to the IF processes.

So how do these processes interact, as we are asserting here? Figure 9.1 shows a functional characterization of how these functions might be designed. To appreciate the implications regarding interdependencies, let us review the general functions of each process:

- IF, a largely automated inferencing/estimation-providing process that offers:
  - Algorithmically developed situational estimates
  - Organized raw observational data—note these are hard (sensor) and soft (linguistic)
  - Controllable collection/sensor management of observational data

- Sensemaking, a semi-automated, human-in-the-loop process that
  - Considers the IF-provided estimates
  - Forages over these hypotheses as well as the data (e.g. drill-down, etc.)

    Assesses the nature of the problem complexity at hand (see below on this point)

  - Considers possible Contextual, Policy, Authority and Mission factors
  - Culminates in a "Final Adjudicated Situation Hypothesis" (i.e. Situation Awareness) that is also judged as to acceptability; if not acceptable, this

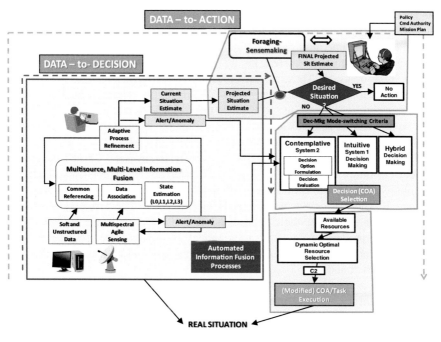

Fig. 9.1 Interconnected/dependent IF-sensemaking-DM-resource management processes

hypothesis is the starting point for decision-making and action-taking to "manage the situation"

- Decision-making, also a semi-automated, human-on-the-loop process that

  - Operates in a System 1, 2 or "hybrid/mixed" DM mode as will be discussed below
  - Yields a selected Course of Action
  - That triggers a Resource Optimization process to define specific resources that physically enable the selected COA onto the real-world situation

Interdependencies

Let us consider some of the interdependencies among these processes; for additional detail on these issues see [12, 13]. One critical issue is temporal coherence across the IF-SM-DM functional operations. The Real-Situation in the world is generally constantly evolving, and the observational data are constantly streaming and changing. IF algorithms that form situational estimates usually process the data to develop a situational estimate at some usually current time (the "now" situation). However, both SM and DM will take time to form the best situational estimate and the best decision and course of action. Thus, if decisions are taken on the "now" situation from SM, they will be out of synchronization with the real world that has moved to a later time during the SM and DM delays. That is, DM is acting on the "old" or "now" situation whereas the world has moved to a time of [Now + Sum (SM + DM delays)]. Thus, as one example, IF requirements should include requirements to forward-propagate "now" estimates to estimates at these future times; this requires a capability to estimate these delays in real-time. The IF system must be also able to adapt its behaviour (adjusting the depth of the future estimates) according to the dynamic assessment of the SM and DM delays. This notion of what some call "plausible futures" or the ability to project IF-based situational estimates to future decision times, has been a relatively recent challenge for the IF community. In addition, another example would be the need for a flexible interface between IF and SM, since most models of SM show that part of this process involves "foraging" over the data and the IF-generated estimates as part of the human-based process of developing situational awareness. This means that there should be requirements to enable back-and-forth querying and response between the IF and SM functions.

Figure 9.1 shows a characterization of the DM process that involves what are called "System 1" and "System 2" processes. These terms are used in the DM literature to designate: (a) a contemplative-type DM (System 2) where the DM process allows for option development, comparison and selection toward a Course of Action (COA), and (b) an Intuitive DM, where the operational tempo is very high and decisions need to be made quickly and thus are based partly on intuition, prior experience, and available automated support from IF. Thus, there is another important IF-SM-DM interdependency since the manner in which IF needs to perform will be (ideally) different when the DM process is in System 2 mode versus System 1 mode, which can be determined by considering the relevant context. Regarding IF requirements then, these requirements should drive the IF process to be adaptive to these DM styles, and the DM process needs to communicate its current mode to the IF process to enable these mode changes in the IF process. These considerations are, in large part, contextually based; for example the operational tempo is an external contextual factor that could be either estimated in real-time or provided as an external input.

9.1.3.2 The Network Perspective

The Value Chain in the Network-Centric Warfare (NCW) case is descriptive of the interdependencies among, and value contributions of, the links from network-centric organizations and improved (value-adding) information processes —and information products—to more effective mission outcomes (see [14] for various details). As will be discussed later, there are two core assertions that underlie this concept: (1) that the collaborative framework provided by the net infrastructure will improve the quality of *organic (individual-node)* information, and (2) that the same net infrastructure will provide for *improved share-ability* of

Fig. 9.2 Information fusion
value chain in NCW

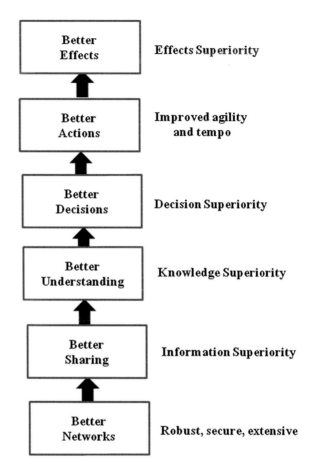

information, in turn leading to more creative, agile and timely situation assessments
and decision-making.

The NCW literature has various diagrammatic representations of the Value
Chain; here, we use a simple construct in Fig. 9.2 depicting the process and its
important components and functions, showing how value is built up in the course of
"good" network operations. The figure shows that the first requirement to enable
NCW is connectivity via some type of network infrastructure. Shared observational
data, Data Fusion, and Information Management, done well, lead to significantly
improved situational awareness, which when properly shared and integrated into a
command and control (C2) and decision-making environment, have the potential to
yield measurable improvements in mission effectiveness. Closely related to the
concept of the Value Chain is the "Conceptual Framework" of NCW, depicted here
using the diagram from the Network Centric Operations Conceptual Framework
[15] as Fig. 9.3.

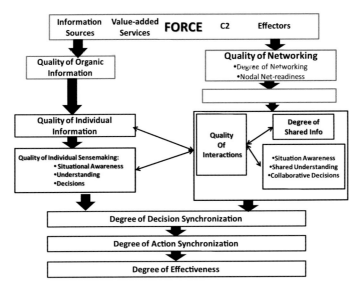

Fig. 9.3 Information fusion process components and functions [15]

Most of Fig. 9.3 is, first of all, about information and its flow in the network but it is (toward the bottom) also about the use of the information in decision-making and action-taking. Important themes in this framework revolve around a few special words and the implied functions: quality—sharing—degree—synchronization.

It is important here to make a "fusion" remark in light of the implications of Fig. 9.3. Any fusion node can only fuse two things: that information which is available to it organically—i.e. information over which it has control, such as locally managed sensor devices—and that information which comes to it *somehow* from the network. Notice the emphasis on "somehow"; it is only through well-designed Information-Sharing Strategies (ISS) that some type of information flows to a node from the network. Such flows can be the result of a multiplicity of interwoven ISS's such as broadcasts from some nodes, responses to service requests from other nodes, and flows from nodes that the receiving node subscribes to, or yet other flow patterns driven by specified protocols. The middleware described in the current chapter can cater for these information exchange needs, discovering and delivering data that is currently needed to a specific fusion node based on the requirements of the SM and DM processes. But it is emphasized that the nature of "non-organic" fusion that can happen at a node is only the result of the synthesis of any such directed or requested (and responsive) information flows, which in turn are the result of defined protocols and policies. It could be also argued that the "Level 4: Process Refinement" function of the fusion process could contribute to the nature of the information sharing and other inter-nodal interactions in a positive way, depending on the control authority aspects of how the network is managed.

Further, fusion process design is often spoken of as impacted by "push" requirements—those requirements driven by the input-side, and "pull" requirements,
driven by the user-side. The network environment influences both of these
requirements-sets in possibly many ways. It can be said that the information flow in
the network can be characterized as both delayed and out-of-observation-time-
order, and probably Poisson in arrival-rate distribution, all of which could potentially affect fusion algorithm and process operations.

9.1.3.3   Implications for Information Exchange (Middleware)

The interdependencies among IF-SM-DM processes and intermodal IF processes
described here represent only a top-level perspective of these issues; there are many
details involved in both of the general descriptions provided here that space limits
prevent from being discussed. Broadly, all of these interdependencies could be
considered as setting an overarching processing and operational context for the
functioning of the overall SoS. Clearly, these interdependencies are complex and
dynamic, and combinatorial. One approach to process designs for these functions
would embed the needed control and communication and data exchange operations
within the functional designs. Such an approach would yield rather brittle designs
that have inter-functional impacts whenever some interdependency factor (such as
the configuration of the SoS or the functional or non-functional properties of
individual systems) changes. Utilizing middleware as the facilitator of
inter-functional timing, control and communication operations yields a more robust
system architecture, which can dynamically adjust to changes in system configuration. Encapsulating the timing, control and communication aspects in middleware
simplifies the design of the IF process, as one can assume that data satisfying the
constraints and requirements of the IF process is being delivered to the process, so
the IF process design must not cater for checking and adjustment of these aspects.

9.1.4   Utilizing Middleware for Applying Data to Decision
(D2D) Concept to Fusion

The concept of Data to Decision (D2D) is used in decision-making scenarios, where
actionable data must be identified and delivered to decision makers based on their
current data needs, which stem from the specific decisions that must be made at the
specific time. Data-to-Decision (D2D) concepts have evolved as a framework for a
more holistic approach toward achieving effective integration of fusion, sensemaking and decision-making processes as described in Sect. 9.1.3.1. In such
environments, the behaviour of individual systems is changed depending on the
estimation of current contextual information. So taking a very broad view, one can
argue that the D2D process is part of the context for a fusion system, which must be

considered by the fusion processes. The context information is needed for the entire system to be cued to the information needs of the consumer.

Modern sensing and data acquisition technologies (for example in the context of ISR systems the high availability of ground and airborne sensor assets and communication technologies) present the opportunity to use the sensor assets for very high granularity sensing. This approach, sometimes also called the Big Data approach allows to achieve high information quality via fusion not only by using high quality sensor assets but also by combining data from a large number of sensing nodes with relatively mediocre capabilities, enabling effective use of legacy systems and cheaper sensing and processing assets. However, pursuing this approach presents many theoretical and practical challenges, such as bandwidth allocation, asset management and coordination of data flows, including delivery of specific data items to individual IF and other algorithms and assessing the quality and correctness of the outputs of these algorithms. One must also note that just collecting and generating the maximum amount of data and information may lead to information superiority but not to decision superiority—the IF processes must be adapted based on the actual information needs of the information consumers (decision makers). One viable approach for tackling this type of Big Data is to push a substantial part of the computation to the edge of the network, thereby reducing bandwidth requirements and computational capabilities needed at central locations and also reducing the challenges on communication as only abstracted information must be exchanged. In order to manage the computation occurring at the edge of the network the Data to Decision approach can be applied, cueing and tuning the algorithms executed there, which also helps to ensure relevance of the derived information for the decision maker, (hopefully) resulting in decision superiority.

Data to Decision (D2D) characterizes decision-making scenarios, where the data sources are potentially able to provide an abundant amount of information and where it is difficult to assemble the appropriate collection of data for rapid decision-making [16]. D2D highlights the collection and fusion of actionable information to provide adequate contextual information for assessing options, threats and consequences of decisions [17]. Although D2D concepts can be applied at all levels of the decision-making hierarchy, these concepts are in particular applicable to individuals on the edge, who, with the aid of modern mobile information and communication platforms, could potentially have access to real-time actionable information. In addition to military applications, providing actionable information to operators in the field is also very critical in emergency response and law enforcement, where adequate situation awareness (based on real-time and consistent information) to aid rapid decision-making is critical. Optimizing the information flows using the D2D approach and delivering only information currently needed for the fusion processes reduces not only the bandwidth requirements but also potentially the overload for the operator, which is a serious challenge with the flood of data provided by modern ISR systems [18].

Applying the D2D approach for managing the behaviour of fusion systems facilitates optimal use of sensor assets while providing the required level of situational information to the decision maker. Combining the D2D approach with the

Fog Computing paradigm proposed by Cisco [19], where the computation is pushed to the edge of the network, would offer many advantages when compared to classical approaches. However, the *Fog Computing* paradigm suggests that computation is pushed to gateway type of devices in the network, thus burdening these devices with an additional load, concentrating data flows around these devices and also creating individual points of failures. A more promising approach would be to push the *Fog Computing* paradigm even further to *Mist Computing* [20] where the computation really occurs in end devices, such as sensor nodes. This allows taking advantage of Big Data potentially generated by the sensor systems while keeping the resource requirements manageable in terms of bandwidth. Combining the D2D approach with the *Mist Computing* paradigm makes it possible to utilize optimally a large number of sensing nodes while overcoming technical bandwidth challenges and providing the consumers the required situational information with optimal use of resources.

Applying the D2D approach in the *Mist Computing* paradigm means that a request for information made by the information consumer must be directed to the sensor assets in the field, closest to the area of interest. The routing of information requests to a specific information provider may be done using many alternative methods, e.g. geo-routing, using a central service directory or some other service discovery mechanism. The requests may be passed through a server, if an architecture requires that, but conceptually there is no need for a central server or coordinator. In such a scenario the optimal method for information exchange is to apply a proactive middleware, which handles the information requests and cues the individual sensing nodes to provide the requested information; this approach yields improved effectiveness and robustness as well as context-based responsiveness. The proactive middleware is executed on every sensing and computing node, the individual instances being aware of the capabilities and data requirements of the local node. Based on the information requests, the algorithms are assigned and primed in the computing device providing the information service (e.g. sensor or fusion node). Service requests for information are made to the data sources (sensor nodes) from which data is needed by the IF processes for computing the requested situational information.

In order to better facilitate understanding of the system concept and the role of middleware, an operational scenario developed in the context of the European Defence Agency research project IN4STARS2.0 is described below; the concept of the scenario is depicted on Fig. 9.4.

In the scenario, the human user requests context-sensitive situational information, for example information on tracked vehicle movement in a specific area. This information can be inferred by fusing sensor data from specific sensors in the area. The fusion nodes in the network subscribe to source data from sensor nodes using a proactive middleware. The data and information flows set up based on situational information requests may involve several sensor modalities and sensor nodes. The initial detection of a vehicle can be performed by a movement sensor using PIR (Pyroelectric InfraRed) technology, which has extremely low power consumption requirements. Once an object has been detected by the movement sensor, it can

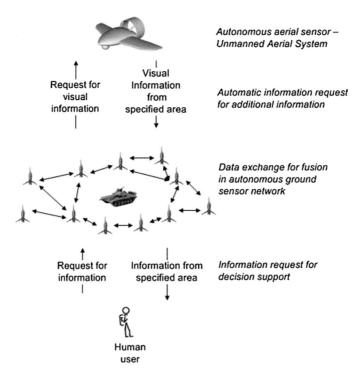

Autonomous aerial sensor –
Unmanned Aerial System

Request for visual information | Visual Information from specified area

Automatic information request
for additional information

Data exchange for fusion
in autonomous ground
sensor network

Request for information | Information from specified area

Information request for
decision support

Human
user

Fig. 9.4 Data and information exchange in the IN4STARS ISR application

trigger the operation of one or more acoustic arrays. An acoustic array is much more capable in terms of object type and location identification, since information from several autonomous acoustic array elements can be fused to identify the type of object, its speed and approximate location. If an object was detected, which is of type that is of interest to the information consumer, the fusion node can notify a UAS (Unmanned Aerial System) to provide visual information on the detected object. If the UAS resource is available, it can re-plan its trajectory and fly to the indicated area, acquire images from the area and provide them to the fusion node on the ground, which can provide it then to the original information consumer but also to other consumers that have requested information from the specific area. The exchange of data and information in the network in this scenario is facilitated by the proactive middleware, which ensures validity of data for the fusion and other operations, described in more detail in the next sections. The fusion process involving many autonomous sensing and computing entities can be viewed as an interactive computation process, which concept was introduced in the beginning of the chapter.

9.1.5 Middleware

Before we can dive into a discussion on the specifics of the proactive middleware suitable for the fusion processes, we offer a general overview of the middleware concept and the types of middleware. Middleware is usually understood as a specific software layer in a computing system that connects applications, or software components and consists of a set of services that allow multiple processes that run on one or more machines to interact across a network [21]. Middleware facilitates the development of distributed systems by accommodating heterogeneity, hiding distribution details and providing a set of common and domain-specific services [22]. Management of complexity translates directly to significant savings in systems development effort—a decrease of up to 50 % has been reported in software development time and costs [22] for distributed systems where a middleware has been employed. While utilization of middleware promises significant savings in development time and cost it also introduces caveats as applying general-purpose middleware for development of real-time systems (which fusion systems typically are) is not always possible due to the specific requirements of these systems. Therefore, specialized middleware designs are developed and applied in these types of systems.

Middleware can be classified into four different categories according to the communication models that are adopted into middleware: (1) procedural middleware, (2) message-oriented middleware, (3) transactional middleware and (4) object middleware [23]. Procedural middleware offers remote procedure calls for obtaining remote data while message-oriented middleware relies on straightforward message exchange, which can be realized with a publish-subscribe model. Transactional middleware as the name implies relies on a two phase transaction protocol for ensuring correctness of transactions. Object middleware applies the object-oriented programming paradigm in a distributed setting. While every middleware type has its benefits, one has to carefully consider the requirements of the specific applications before choosing a middleware category. The proactive middleware used for exchange of context information described in the current chapter combines features or procedural middleware (as certain functionality in individual computing nodes is only invoked when a procedure call has been received) with message-oriented middleware (as it implements a publish-subscribe model, where data is delivered to computing nodes that have subscribed to it).

The proactive middleware is an active "mediator" of context information, providing services for sharing context information in a SoS. Conceptually, it can be said that the middleware is a smart communication environment that provides services for filtering, partial validation, and distribution of information according to personal access rights of computing nodes. The middleware features and design is described in more detail in the sections below.

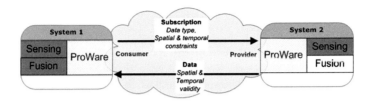

Fig. 9.5 Concept of middleware operation

9.1.6   Proactive Middleware—ProWare

In order to successfully implement a fusion process, which involves data from several remote network nodes and which supports the D2D paradigm, the proactive middleware is applied. In order to ensure the implementation of the IF processes produce usable results they must rely on a theoretically sound design, which takes into account the implications of the interactive model of computation inherent to such systems. The proactive middleware described in detail in the current section enables exchange of relevant context data, while considering properties (such as validity in various domains) of the exchanged data.

A fixed network architecture and fixed interaction partnerships between system components are not applicable when *Mist Computing* approaches are used in combination with the D2D paradigm as the information needs change dynamically over time. For every data item needed the (temporal, spatial) validity constraints must be specified by the data consumer and the data must be delivered to the nodes consuming the data from the source nodes with the validity constraints satisfied. Data validity in a distributed setting is discussed in greater detail in Sect. 9.1.7.

In order to facilitate the dynamic nature of interactions in an information processing network, a proactive middleware concept called ProWare[1] has been developed; the concept diagram of ProWare operation is presented on Fig. 9.5. ProWare delivers the data needed by individual fusion nodes based on their current information needs. A central concept of ProWare is the subscription-based data exchange model, which delivers data to a computing node only if the data has been requested by that node. In order to ensure correctness of the fusion algorithm output the correctness of the input data is validated from the data consumer perspective.

The information exchange in ProWare is controlled by mediators that are located at every computing node (the box with the label "ProWare" on Fig. 9.5), the mediator implementing locally the functionality of ProWare. The ProWare mediator concept has been previously introduced in [24] and elaborated upon in [25]. The mediator interacts locally with the fusion algorithms, receiving requests for data from the algorithms and delivering requested data to the algorithms.

---

[1]ProWare is a proactive middleware, which has been developed at the Research Laboratory for Proactive Technologies at Tallinn University of Technology, Estonia.

ProWare relies on a situation parameter concept to facilitate data exchange among autonomous computing entities. Exchange of data occurs in the form of situation parameter values, which are requested and delivered by mediators, which are software components attached to every computing node in the network. When a computing node requires data from another node, it notifies the local mediator, which upon locating a data provider from the network subscribes to the data from the provider. The role of the mediator is to keep track of the data required by the local computing node and deliver the data to the node while also delivering the data generated locally to other computing nodes on the network that have requested the data.

In order to deliver the data that satisfies the specified constraints to the situation parameter computation algorithm, the concept of mediated interaction [26] is applied. At an abstract level the mediator can be compared to the channel function in the Q model [27], as it transmits only data that satisfies the constraints set by the consumer (i.e. the situation evaluation algorithm). The Q model is a formalism for modelling communicating processes, which was originally introduced by Quirk and Gilbert [28] and was later modified by Motus and Rodd [27].

9.1.6.1 Situation Parameter Concept

Situation management [29] has been mostly viewed from the perspective of human requirements and processing capabilities. Traditionally computers have been used to aid humans in achieving situation awareness. However, the concepts of situational information and situational hierarchies can be also applied when building up situation hierarchies computed and managed by a distributed artificial system. At an abstract level we can also view the data items exchanged in a fusion system as situation parameters, as every data item characterizes an aspect of a specific situation.

A hierarchical buildup of situations (by using the situation parameter concept) inspired by Endsley [30] can be quite well applied where the lower level parameter values are more or less directly derived from sensor data. The information is abstracted from these lower level concepts to more abstract concepts. A hierarchical buildup of situation parameters is depicted in Fig. 9.6; note also the horizontal arrows from the individual situation abstraction levels, characterizing the possibility to exchange situation parameters at various levels. A situation parameter reflects a property of a parameter of interest, and composing them allows the computation of the values of higher-level parameters of interest by using the values of lower level parameters and all the other relevant information, including contextual factors.

In the case of a distributed fusion system, the evaluation of situation parameters can be performed if the algorithms have been designed to accept situation parameter values as input. The algorithms use source data to compute the required outputs and for every type of source data the constraints (in the form of validity intervals in the relevant validity domains, such as temporal, spatial or confidence) must be specified

Fig. 9.6 Hierarchical buildup of situation parameters

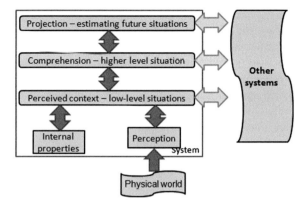

in order to guarantee the validity of the situation assessment. Note that such constraints could in fact be a result of contextual considerations.

9.1.6.2 Subscription-Based Information Exchange

Data exchange between a provider and consumer is set up based on the data types required by the consumer and the constraints set by the consumer for these data types. There are two general approaches that could be used to establish the data exchange partnerships.

The first, a more classical approach, would be for the providers to publish their capabilities and then let the consumers contact the providers that are able to provide the situation parameter values of interest. This makes the entire network and its capabilities visible to the potential information consumers, but hides the consumers and their needs. Setting up an aggregation task in this scenario would be centralized, up to the final consumer.

The alternative, which is an approach that ProWare facilitates is to have the consumers publish their data requirements and have the providers decide if their data is suitable and create a data exchange partnership. The main benefits of this approach is that the consumer needs to know very little about how the network is set up and can actually start by stating a request for aggregated high level situation parameters (the rules and algorithms for computing these parameter values are located in the computing nodes themselves), leaving the organization of various parts of the needed aggregation to the providers in the network. This lets the providers optimize the data flows near the source. With this approach, the requirements for data are public in the context of the system, that is, all providers can see what the consumer is looking for. The message exchange for the subscription-based data exchange mechanism is depicted on Fig. 9.7. The *Consumer* in the context of the diagram is the fusion algorithm that needs data from the network and the provider is the algorithm or sensor source that is able to provide the required data.

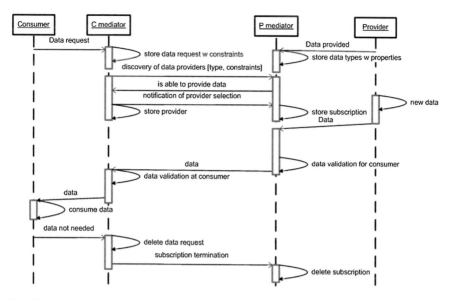

Fig. 9.7 Message exchange in the subscription-based model

In this approach, the consumer mediator sends out a subscription request that contains the data types and the constraints on the data. The temporal constraints for data specify in the temporal domain the maximum age of data and what is the maximum interval between individual data items. This automatically sets up data production tasks for data providers that need sampling and serves as a filter for spontaneous data sources. The extended option is to specify rules that control when data is sampled or actions taken. The actions that a specific node takes based on the received data may be set by the communicated rules or they may be part of the inherent behaviour description of the node. The rules can use other data sources as input, for example an image from a UAV may be requested if an object of interest has been detected in the area or the operation of an acoustic array when movement is detected in the vicinity. Any provider mediator receiving the request that is able to provide the requested data from its local provider responds to the subscription.

The mechanisms for generating data by the provider may be fixed, for example the rate at which the data is produced, which may be limited by power, sensor or local processing capabilities. This means that the consumer has to make do with the data that the specific provider is able to provide. Alternatively the provider may tune its operation to suit the needs of the consumer. This may entail the execution of certain data processing algorithms, producing data at a certain rate at certain moments in time or also changing the location of the provider to generate data from the area where the consumer needs it from.

9.1.6.3 Data Mediator

A data mediator in the form of a ProWare component is associated with each computing node, the mediator being responsible for delivering data to the individual algorithms and delivering data generated by the algorithms to the other nodes. It can be said that the mediator represents a computing node in interactions as depicted on Fig. 9.8.

The mediator is responsible for handling the interactions, including subscription establishment, fulfilment as well as data validity checking.

Every mediator stores at least the following knowledge for the local computing node:

- Data requirements for the node (data types and constraints for the subscriptions for these data)
- Data types (including properties) provided by the node
- Data providers to the node (will be discovered at run time) with properties of the provider (e.g. clock offset)
- Data consumers for data generated by the agent with requirements (constraints) for data to be delivered (will emerge at run time)

Mediator checks incoming data for validity and ensures that only data is sent out that is valid for the consumer when it reaches the consumer. Mediator is responsible for (1) finding the appropriate data providers, which are able to deliver data satisfying the specified requirements and (2) delivering data to consumers.

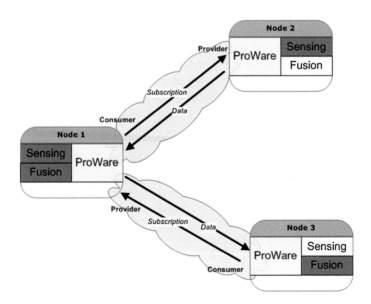

Fig. 9.8 Mediators responsible for interactions for computing nodes

9.1.7 Data Validation

A critical issue in the distributed IF processes is the validity of the data—when a situation parameter value is computed, it must be possible to estimate where and when that situation parameter is valid and the validity information must complement the individual data items as they are communicated over the network. So, in order for it to be possible to use an individual data item (a situation parameter value) in computation, the data must be accompanied with metadata that describes the validity properties of data (e.g. temporal and spatial validity).

The validity estimation of data must be performed based on the validity of the source data—starting from the raw sensor data a situation parameter value inferred from this sensor data is only valid in the region where the sensor data is valid and also for the period of time when the sensor data is valid, which depends on the dynamic properties of the process being monitored. So, the properties of the situational parameters that are monitored determine the validity of the situations inferred based on these parameter values.

The mediator of the consumer of the situation parameter values verifies that the validity values of the parameters do match the constraints set on the incoming data. The output of the situation assessment algorithm is the situation parameter value accompanied with the metadata.

9.1.7.1 Data Quality Aspects

The usability of information resulting from the fusion processes is defined by the quality of the estimates or inferences (hypotheses) produced by fusion processes, which in turn depend on how well the data sources are modelled, the appropriateness of the data processes used, and the accuracy and applicability of the prior knowledge. The majority of fusion operators are based on optimistic assumptions about the quality of data sources and information they produce, while in reality this information may be unreliable, of low fidelity, with insufficient resolution, contradictory and/or redundant. Thus, designing dynamic multi-level fusion processes requires incorporation of quality control to be aware of and compensating for the possible insufficient information quality at each step of information exchange. This can be achieved by [31]:

- Eliminating information of low quality from consideration
- Explicitly incorporating information quality into models and processing
- Utilizing process refinement by sensor management and process management
- Delaying communication of information until it has matured as a result of additional observations and/or computations by improving their associated quality
- Combination of several strategies listed above

The implementation of quality control measures requires methods of representing and measuring quality values and criteria for defining whether the quality of information is sufficient, e.g. deciding that the information is usable. Such criteria can also be based on context and problem specific thresholds or value of information. Specific quality attributes and their combination have to be considered in relation to specific source types and fusion functions in a specific situational context.

The mediator associated with each computing entity is responsible for enforcing the quality requirements of the consumer it is associated with. The quality characteristics have to be measured and used by the quality control function (implemented in the mediator), which should be selected depending on the quality characteristics or their combination, at every step of information exchange. Thus, for example, irrelevant and redundant information, and information obtained from the sources of poor reputation should be eliminated from consideration. UAV reliability and HUMINT (human intelligence) reputation can be, respectively, incorporated into fusion by discounting the probability of detection of an object on the ground and probability of certain events; timeliness and credibility of the result of fusion of information obtained from UAV, UGS and HUMINT used by patrol vehicles can be controlled by delaying the fusion results until they mature as a result of additional observations and/or computations by improving their credibility.

One of the challenges of quality control is the problem of measuring the value of quality characteristics and methods of their combination. An important source here can be a priori domain knowledge about them or a level of agreement between sources to be fused, outputs of models and processes producing this information subjective judgment of human users and experts based on their perception.

9.1.7.2   Data Validation Operations

Validation of data is based on the constraints set by the information consumer. To convey the general principles only temporal validity examples are considered below. The same mechanisms can be also applied for other validity dimensions.

The operators for expressing temporal validity constraints are loosely based on Linear Temporal Logic (LTL) [32], which has been extended with some operators. To convey the general principle a detailed example with the G (global) operator is brought. The logic used in the example can be easily extended to other operators, such as *until*, *weak until*, *existence* and *finally*. In case of the G operator, the temporal validity intervals of two situation parameters must be fully overlapping as illustrated on Fig. 9.9.

We start the example by looking at the validity of data produced by the producer process. In order to perform a formal evaluation of the data validity one must define the process execution timeset. We assume periodic execution of IF algorithms, thus we must look at cyclic process execution. For every cyclic process (e.g. acquisition

Fig. 9.9 Global temporal
validity evaluation, valid data

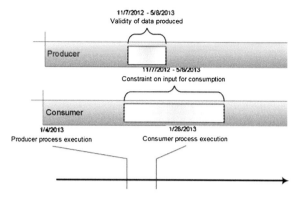

of a sensor reading) executed (the execution can occur at the consumer or the
provider) the process timeset can be expressed as follows:

$$T(f) = \{t : t_n = t_0 + nt_a\}, \tag{9.1}$$

where t_a is the regular interval between two successive elements and n is the index
of the nth execution.

The temporal validity interval of a data item of the process can be expressed as
follows:

$$\left[t_n + T(E_f), t_n + T(E_f) + T(v_f)\right], \tag{9.2}$$

where $T(v_f)$ is the validity interval of function output and $T(E_f)$ is the execution
time of the function.

For a data item (a situation parameter value) requested by the consumer, the
temporal validity parameters are specified by the consumer. In case of a periodic
request for the data (as we stated above that we assume periodic execution of IF
algorithms, thus cyclic process execution can be expected) first the timeset of the
consumer process must be specified:

$$T(p) = \{t : t_n = t_0 + nt_a\}, \tag{9.3}$$

where t_a is the regular interval between two successive elements and n is the index
of the nth element. In addition to the timeset, the required validity, $T(v_r)$ must be
specified.

The suitability of data items for the consumer process originating from the
provider process must be evaluated by checking the overlap of the validity interval
of the incoming data items at the consumer with the validity interval specified by
the consumer for the incoming data items. The validity interval of an incoming data
item can be expressed as

$$\left[t_{n\_\text{producer}} + T(D_{\text{channel}}), t_{n\_\text{producer}} + T(v_p) \right] \tag{9.4}$$

The temporal variable $T(D_{\text{channel}})$ expresses the communication channel delay, $T(v_p)$ is the validity interval for the data item computed at the producer. The channel delay must be added to the start of the interval because the data item cannot be consumed before it has arrived at the consumer, which happens after the channel delay has expired.

When the data item is received by the consumer mediator its validity must be evaluated. The acceptable temporal validity intervals for the data item can be expressed as follows:

$$\left[t_{n\_\text{consumer}}, t_{n\_\text{consumer}} + T(v_r) \right], \tag{9.5}$$

where t_{n_consumer} is the nth consumption event of the input data item. In case of the G operator the validity interval of the data item used as an input to the consuming process must overlap with this consumption interval.

Following from this the expression for evaluating the validity of a data item for consumption can be evaluated by checking the truth value of the following expression:

$$\left(t_{n\_\text{consumer}} + T(v_r) \geq t_{n\_\text{producer}} \right) \& \left(t_{n\_\text{consumer}} \leq t_{n\_\text{producer}} + T(v_p) \right) \tag{9.6}$$

The same evaluation methods are used for evaluating the validity of a situation parameter in other validity domains, so validity intervals for any property defined in any n-dimensional space can be checked.

9.1.8 Summary

The chapter gave an overview of the challenges and possible approaches involved in designing a distributed fusion system, which may have a dynamically changing configuration. Such applications are reflective of the direction of modern applications and designs, and the chapter also addressed how contextual factors play into these design methods. The chapter also gave an overview of the interactive computation model, which is one of the theoretical challenges involved in the design of such a computing system, introduced by the distributed nature of the computation. An overview of interdependencies of information fusion architectures, considering also the contextual and networking aspects, was presented. The requirements and design aspect of a middleware, which is able to facilitate this type of data and information exchange in a distributed fusion system were introduced. The concept of situation parameters inclusive of contextual parameters as a method for organizing hierarchical situational information was presented and an overview of the proactive middleware ProWare was given, which facilitates exchange of situation parameters, enabling the creation of a dynamic distributed fusion system while ensuring correctness of the involved computations. The chapter concluded by looking at some issues related to specific data validation methods.

References

1. A. Riid, J. Preden, S. Astapov, Detection, identification and tracking of mobile objects with distributed system of systems, in *9th International Conference on System of Systems Engineering* (SOSE), 2014 (IEEE, Adelaide, Australia, 2014)
2. L. Motus, et al., Self-aware architecture to support partial control of emergent behavior, in *Proceedings IEEE 7th International Conference on Systems of Systems Engineering* (IEEE, 2012), pp. 422–427
3. A. Sloman, The irrelevance of turing machines to AI. Comput. New Dir. 87–127 (2002) (MIT Press)
4. S. Stepney, Non-classical hyper-computation. Int. J. Unconv. Comput. **5**(3–4), 267–276 (2009)
5. P. Wegner, Why interaction is more powerful than algorithms. Comm. ACM **40**(5), 81–91 (1997)
6. L. Motus, M. Meriste, W. Dosch, Time-awareness and proactivity in models of interactive computation. Electronic Notes in Theoretical Computer Science **141**, 69–95 (2005)
7. C. Bowman, A. Steinberg, A systems engineering approach for implementing data fusion system, in *Handbook of Multisensor Data Fusion*, ed. by DL Hall, James (CRC Press, Boca Raton, 2001)
8. A. Steinberg, Data fusion system engineering, in *Proceedings of Third Internationl Symposium on Information Fusion* (Paris, France, 2000)
9. E. Waltz, J. Llinas, *Multisensor Data Fusion* (Artech House Inc., Boston, 1990)
10. G. Klein, B. Moon, R. Hoffman, Making sense of sensemaking 2: a macrocognitive model. IEEE Intell. Syst. **21** (5) (2006)
11. P. Pirolli, S. Card, The sensemaking process and leverage points for analyst technology as identified through cognitive task analysis, in *Proceedings of International Conference on Intelligence Analysis* (McLean, VA, 2005)
12. J. Llinas, A survey of automated methods for sensemaking support, in *Proceedings of SPIE Defense and Security Conference* (*Next-Generation-Analyst Conference*) (SPIE, Baltimore, MD, 2014)
13. J. Llinas, Reexamining information fusion–decision making inter-dependencies, in *Proceedings of IEEE Conference on Cognitive Situation Management* (CogSIMA). (IEEE, San Antonio, TX, 2014a)
14. J. Llinas, Chapter 3 in *Distributed data fusion for network-centric operations*, in *Network Centric Concepts: Impacts to Distributed Fusion System Design*, ed. by D. Hall, C. Chee-Yee, L. James, M. Liggins II (CRC Press, Boca Raton, 2012)
15. J. Gartska, Network centric operations conceptual framework. Report prepared by Evidence Based Research Inc for the Office of Force Transformation (2003)
16. A. Preece, et al., Integrating hard and soft information sources for D2D using controlled natural language, in *Proceedings of 15th International Conference on Information Fusion* (FUSION) (2012)
17. B. Broome, Data-to-decisions: a transdisciplinary approach to decision support efforts at ARL, in Proceedings of Ground/Air Multisensor Interoperability, Integration, and Networking for Persistent ISR III, vol. 8389 (SPIE, Baltimore, 2012)
18. A. David, Keynote Address, GEOINT 2009

19. F. Bonomi, et al., Fog computing and its role in the internet of things, in *Proceedings of the MCC Workshop on Mobile Cloud Computing* (MCC '12) (ACM, New York, USA, 2012)
20. J. Preden, et al., The Benefits of Self-Awareness and Attention in Fog and Mist Computing. IEEE Computer Magazine, July, 2015
21. L. Motus, M. Meriste, J. Preden J, Towards middleware based situation awareness, in *5th IEEE Workshop on Situation Management, Military Communications Conference* (IEEE Operations Center, Boston, 2009)
22. L. JingYong, et al., Middleware-based distributed systems software process. Int. J. Adv. Sci. Technol. **13**, 27–48 (2009)
23. P. Jiyong, S. Kim, W. Yoo, Designing real-time and fault-tolerant middleware for automotive software, in *SICE-ICASE 2006 International Joint Conference* (IEEE Computer Society, 2006), pp. 4409–4413
24. J. Preden, et al., Situation awareness for networked systems, in *Proceedings of IEEE International Multidisciplinary Conference on Cognitive Methods in Situation Awareness and Desicion Support—IEEE COGSIMA 2011* (IEEE, Miami, USA, 2011)
25. J. Preden, et al., On-line data validation in distributed data fusion, in *Ground/Air Multisensor Interoperability, Integration, and Networking for Persistent ISR IV: SPIE Defense, Security and Sensing* (SPIE, Baltimore, USA, 2013)
26. J. Ramage, et al., Design considerations and technologies for air defence systems, SCI-181 (NATO RTO Publications, Paris, 2010), pp. 149–174
27. L. Motus, M.G. Rodd, *Timing Analysis of Real-Time Software* (Elsevier, Oxford, 1994)
28. W.J. Quirk, R.P. Gilbert, The formal specification of the requirements of complex realtime of complex realtime systems. At. Energy Res. Establ. Comp. Sci. Syst. Div. (1977) (United Kingdom, Harwell)
29. G. Jakobson, J. Buford, L. Lewis, Situation management: basic concepts and approaches, in *Information Fusion and Geographic Information Systems* (2007), pp. 18–33
30. M.R. Endsley, D.J. Garland, *Situation Awareness Analysis and Measurement* (Lawrence Erlbum Associates, London, 2000)
31. E. Rogova G.ö Bossé, Information quality in information fusion, in *Proceedings of the 13th International Conference on Information Fusion* (2010), pp. 1–8
32. A. Pnueli, The temporal logic of programs, in *Proceedings of the 18th Annual Symposium on Foundations of Computer Science* (FOCS) (1977), pp. 46–57

Chapter 10
Modeling User Behaviors to Enable Context-Aware Proactive Decision Support

Benjamin Newsom, Ranjeev Mittu, Mark A. Livingston, Stephen Russell, Jonathan W. Decker, Eric Leadbetter, Ira S. Moskowitz, Antonio Gilliam, Ciara Sibley, Joseph Coyne and Myriam Abramson

Abstract The problem of automatically recognizing a user's operational context, the implications of its shifting properties, and reacting in a dynamic manner are at the core of mission intelligence and decision making. Environments such as the OZONE Widget Framework (http://www.owfgoss.org) (OWF) provide the foundation for capturing the objectives, actions, and activities of both the mission analyst and the decision maker. By utilizing a "context container" that envelops an OZONE Application, we hypothesize that both user *action* and *intent* can be used to characterize user context with respect to operational modality (strategic, tactical, opportunistic, or random). As the analyst moves from one operational modality to another, we propose that information visualization techniques should adapt and present data and analysis pertinent to the new modality and to the trend of the shift. As a system captures the analyst's actions and decisions in response to the new visualizations, the context container has the opportunity to assess the analyst's perception of the information value, risk, uncertainty, prioritization, projection, and insight with respect to the current context stage. This paper will describe a conceptual architecture for an adaptive work environment for inferring user behavior and interaction within the OZONE framework, in order to provide the decision

B. Newsom (✉)
Next Century Corporation, 7075 Samuel Morse Drive, Columbia, MD 21046, USA
e-mail: ben.newsom@nextcentury.com

R. Mittu · M.A. Livingston · J.W. Decker · E. Leadbetter · I.S. Moskowitz · A. Gilliam · C. Sibley · J. Coyne · M. Abramson
Naval Research Laboratory, 4555 Overlook Avenue, Washington, DC 20375, USA

S. Russell
Army Research Laboratory, 2800 Powder Mill Road, Adelphi, MD 20783, USA

© Springer International Publishing Switzerland (outside the USA) 2016
L. Snidaro et al. (eds.), *Context-Enhanced Information Fusion*,
Advances in Computer Vision and Pattern Recognition,
DOI 10.1007/978-3-319-28971-7_10

maker with context relevant information. We then bridge from our more conceptual OWF discussion to specific examples describing the role of context in decision making. Our first concrete example demonstrates how the Web analytics of a user's browsing behavior can be used to authenticate users. The second example briefly examines the role of context in cyber security. Our third example illustrates how to capture the behavior of expert analysts in exploratory data analysis, which coupled with a recommender system, advises domain experts of "standard" analytical operations in order to suggest operations novel to the domain, but consistent with analytical goals. Finally, our fourth example discusses the role of context in a supervisory control problem when managing multiple autonomous systems.

Keywords Context-driven · Decision making · Dynamic modeling · Operational modality · Temporal reasoning

10.1 Introduction

Today's warfighters operate in a highly dynamic world with a high degree of uncertainty, compounded by competing demands. Timely and effective decision making in this environment is increasingly challenging. The phrase "*too much data —not enough information*" is a common complaint in most naval operational domains, and in the world in general. Finding and integrating decision-relevant information (vice simply data) is difficult. Mission and task context is often absent (at least in computable and accessible forms), or sparsely/poorly represented in many information systems. This limitation requires decision makers to mentally reconstruct, or infer, contextually relevant information through laborious and error-prone internal processes as they attempt to comprehend and act upon data. Furthermore, decision makers may need to multitask amongst competing and often conflicting mission objectives, further complicating the management of information and decision making. Clearly, there is a need for advanced mechanisms for the timely extraction and presentation of data that has value and relevance to decisions for a given *context*.

To put the issue of context in perspective, consider the fact that nearly all national defense missions involve Decision Support Systems (DSS)—that is, systems that attempt to decrease the time from the gathering of data to an operational decision. The proliferation of sensors and large data sets are overwhelming DSSs, since they lack the tools to efficiently process, store, analyze, and retrieve vast amounts of data. Additionally, these systems are relatively immature in helping users recognize and understand important context (i.e., cues). The next generation systems must leverage predictive models to enable *Proactive* Decision Support (PDS). These systems will need to understand and adapt to user context (missions, goals, tasks). By aligning the data with the user in the appropriate context, more relevant information can be provided to the user, i.e., information likely to be of higher value for decision making. The key challenges, therefore, are not only

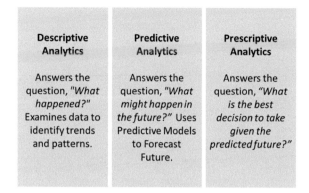

Descriptive Analytics	Predictive Analytics	Prescriptive Analytics
Answers the question, *"What happened?"* Examines data to identify trends and patterns.	Answers the question, *"What might happen in the future?"* Uses Predictive Models to Forecast Future.	Answers the question, *"What is the best decision to take given the predicted future?"*

Fig. 10.1 Comparison of different forms of analytics

to model the user's decision-making context, but to recognize when such context has shifted! With regard to Fig. 10.1, we hypothesize that concepts associated with PDS closely align with Prescriptive Analytics (i.e., understanding and modeling decision trajectories and the relevant information necessary for those decisions).

The problem of automatically recognizing/inferring user context, understanding the implications of its shifting properties, and reacting in a dynamic manner is at the core of mission intelligence and decision making. An environment such as the OZONE Widget Framework provides the foundation for capturing the objectives, actions, and activities of the mission analyst/decision maker. By utilizing a "context container" that envelops an OZONE Application, we can capture both action and intent, which allows us to characterize this context with respect to its operational modality (strategic, tactical, opportunistic, or random)—Fig. 10.2 (*Visual Analytics* representation).

Note that context is fluid over time, and the relative mix of strategic versus tactical versus opportunistic actions/activities is also dynamic. Therefore, knowing both the time frame and the distribution of activities gives us insight into the analyst's changing operational modality. A temporal storage approach, such as a context-aware memory structure (CAMS), provides the basis for comparison of the "current" decision stage against prior stages and is used to predict phase shift.

Methods for understanding user context can be found in logic-based or probabilistic artificial intelligence (AI) approaches under predictive analytic methods, or through more traditional methods based on descriptive analytics. Using a descriptive analytics approach, models may be developed that map missions, goals, and tasks to information requirements in order to represent "decision context." With regard to deriving context within the predictive and visual analytics models, the *challenging questions become*: Can a user's decision context be modeled, based upon information seeking, interaction, or analysis patterns [1]? What research can be leveraged from the AI community (plan recognition) to infer which decision context (model) is active? Can we reason about which decision context (model) should be active? What similarity metrics enable the selection of the appropriate

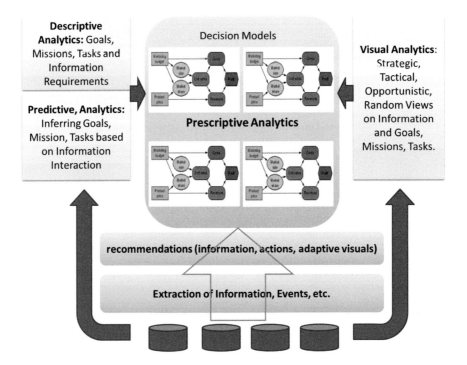

Descriptive Analytics: Goals, Missions, Tasks and Information Requirements

Predictive, Analytics: Inferring Goals, Mission, Tasks based on Information Interaction

Decision Models

Prescriptive Analytics

Visual Analytics: Strategic, Tactical, Opportunistic, Random Views on Information and Goals, Missions, Tasks.

recommendations (information, actions, adaptive visuals)

Extraction of Information, Events, etc.

Fig. 10.2 Context understanding in relation to analytics

model for a given context? Can we recognize context shift based on work that has been done in the machine learning community with "concept drift," and how well does this approach adapt to noisy data? The emphasis for this paper will be on the *Visual Analytics* representation for understanding context, but the questions span across the *Predictive Analytics* representation as well.

In Sect. 10.2, we provide a notional operational example to guide the framework discussion. In Sect. 10.3, we describe APTO (Latin for adapt) as our conceptual system architecture. In Sect. 10.4, we briefly describe the idea of Context Container for the APTO framework. In Sects. 10.5, 10.6 and 10.10 we describe the Context-Aware Memory Manager and context shift recognition. In Sects. 10.7–10.10 we discuss the adaptive visualization informed through the APTO architecture, event, activity, and workflow manager, respectively.

10.2 Notional Operational Example

Consider the scenario of the intelligence analyst on a 24 × 7 watch floor (Fig. 10.3). As the analyst moves from one operational modality to another, the information visualization techniques should adapt and present data and analysis pertinent to the

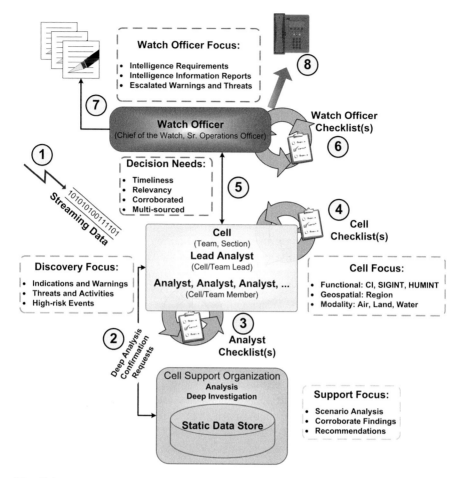

Fig. 10.3 Example watch floor scenario

new modality and to the trend of the shift. If we can capture the analyst's actions and decisions in response to the new visualizations, *the **context** container may be able to infer the analyst's perception of the information value, risk, uncertainty, prioritization, projection and insight.* This information, in combination with the ability to infer the user's current context stage, would provide the ability for DSS's to pre-stage information that is tailored to the user's current needs and preferences along a decision trajectory.

Each watch floor is configured and organized to address their unique and specialty mission and intelligence requirements. As such, any solution proposed must be able to adapt and conform to the specific needs of the watch. In Fig. 10.3, we show an example set of watch floor responsibilities with the proposed solution focusing on analyst activities (3), Cell activities (4), and Watch Officer activities (6).

In general, a watch floor is organized around cells of responsibility. A cell (also known as a *Team* or *Section*) may have only one analyst with a singular focus, or it may have multiple analysts with a lead analyst (also known as the cell or team lead). A cell is monitoring and accumulating streaming data (1) to discover indications and warnings about threats and high-risk events in their scope of consideration. Timeliness of analysis and interpretation is critical. The cell may have a support organization that can perform deep analysis (2) and confirm an analyst's or cell's findings. For often-detected indications, the analyst will have a set of standard operating procedures or checklist (3) of activities they need to perform to reach the decision to escalate the detected event to the next level. In a multi-person cell, the next level may be the Cell Officer who has his or her own set of standard operating procedures or checklist (4) of activities that need to be performed to escalate out of the cell (5).

An event (threat or warning) escalated out of the cell (5) goes to the Watch Officer who is accumulating information and comparing escalated events to their intelligence requirements. Similar to the analyst and the cell, the Watch Officer has a set of standard operating procedures or checklist (6) of activities to perform in response to the combination of escalated events that they are receiving from all of the cells on the watch floor. The Watch Officer makes the trade-off decisions to only track and log (7) the events (threats) or escalate identified, confirmed, credible threats (8) to the next level.

The watch floor situation has intense analytical problems requiring timely analyses and/or responses. Analytical problems are often sensitive and associated with high stakes for success or failure. In many analytical subdomains, the objectives of the analysis can be open and shifting, and analysts must sometimes determine for themselves the goals and priorities of their data collection or research. The proposed framework identifies the context in which the events and activities are occurring and provides situational awareness and accuracy up and through the chain of decision makers.

The proposed system architecture should extend and enhance existing mission solutions to include PDS focusing on context shift recognition and staging of the information (or combinations of information) the analyst requires in making the "next" decision. Along with determining the information to be staged, the adaptive work environment needs to react to the context shift and determine the appropriate stage-related information visualization techniques.

To accomplish the objective of inferring a user's context and recognizing context shifts, there are three broad areas of required innovation:

- Capturing context actions and events through normal analyst interaction with OZONE Framework applications.
- Characterizing the user's actions and events along their operational modality (i.e., strategic, tactical, random discovery, and opportunistic discovery), their temporal relationship, and situational objectives.
- Recognizing the change or shift in context through the development of context shift models and predictive analysis.

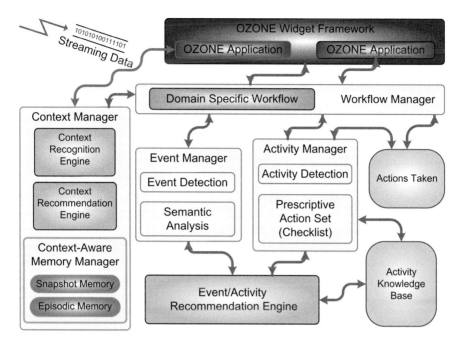

Fig. 10.4 Conceptual APTO architecture

10.3   APTO System

10.3.1   Long-Term Goal

*In order to create a **context**-aware adaptive work environment*, specific elements such as the memory components, the context manager, and the activity manager are necessary for recognizing context and context shift. APTO is a conceptual architecture, shown in Fig. 10.4, that depicts a context-aware environment within the OZONE Widget Framework.

10.3.2   Technical Approach

The premise of our approach is that the combination of an intelligence analyst's OZONE Application (sometimes referred to as widgets) usage pattern and the information being visualized (and how it is visualized) can be used as an indicator of the analyst's context mode. The analyst is viewing all of the situational characteristics through a particular lens searching for strategic insights, tactical clues, opportunistic indicators, or the random-scramble searching for the information nugget that connects decision streams together. Through adaptation and innovative extensions to the OZONE Widget Framework, it will be possible to capture traces of user interactions with the widgets, as well as interactions between widgets. We believe this situational capture of the decision making process will form distinctive, predictable patterns of behavior corresponding to the analyst's intent, information value, and prioritization.

The next four sections form the basis for the "Context Elements."

10.4   Context Container for OZONE Apps

*The concept of a "**context** container"* for OZONE Apps does not exist in the current OZONE Widget Framework. In the overall architecture it is part of the interaction between the user experience, or presentation layer, and the context manager. We believe that we can define and create a container or software envelope that would "wrap" an OZONE application (a collection of one or more widgets and data sources) and automatically capture both what the decision was and an indication of why (operational modality) the decision or choice was made. This collection of activity, interaction, and/or decisions represents a context vector that would be stored in the context-aware memory manager.

10.5   Context-Aware Memory Manager

To model the analyst's context, a *learning **context** memory model* (a context-aware memory manager—CAMS) [2] could be constructed. This model would capture the OWF widget interactions and process them to construct a context memory reflecting the user's regular activity. The concept of a context-aware memory manager that interacts with the OZONE Widget Framework does not currently exist.

Context memory is a mechanism for retaining and recalling interesting and relevant past experiences or actions [3]. We believe that an analyst's context consists of a striation, or mix, of strategic, tactical, opportunistic, and random actions. In each layer there are a collection of short-term or "snapshot" memories and long-term or "episodic" memories.

10.5.1   Snapshot Memory

The snapshot memory (context working memory) processes and stores context attributes from context input vectors. Attributes are stored in Artificial Recognition Balls (ARBs) [4], which describe a certain region around the context attribute—in the case of OZONE Apps it would be the context container—and enables CAMS to perform data compression by eliminating the need for repetition. ARBs come from work in artificial immune theory which describes a cluster of cells with similar attributes via a single cell which acts as the representative of that cluster. This is similar to the idea of a congruence class representative in mathematics [4]. For example, a particular type of action can be represented by a single ARB instead of all individual actions that occur within the container; every ARB has a resource level R associated with it, being an indicator for how frequently it recognizes context attributes. The algorithm used in CAMS is based on the principles of unsupervised and reinforcement learning. Unsupervised learning allows us to construct a system that can cluster input data without any prior knowledge about the structure of every class. Reinforcement learning requires feedback from a trainer. However, an explicit trainer is not desirable in most context-aware systems, therefore an ARB receives positive feedback (stimulation) when context attributes fall within a certain distance from the center, resulting in an increase in its resource level. Negative feedback is introduced by the notion of "forgetting," which gradually decays all resource levels. For example, actions a user performs less often have their resource level reduced by a decay factor, but every re-occurrence stimulates it again, which enables these actions to remain in memory.

10.5.2 Episodic Memory

To capture a significant part of human activity, the connections between consecutive events or actions are essential. The snapshot memory is able to capture every individual action, but not the set of actions that comprise a specific decision. As the user is most likely to login/logout, startup an application, etc., these actions have a higher resource level R. Once R reaches a predefined level, the oft-repeated actions are passed from the snapshot memory to the episodic memory, which captures all individual attribute values between them. The context memory manager component regulates the division of the memory mechanism into snapshot and episodic memory. This division is essential for keeping the complexity of the search space at a manageable level. Without this division all attributes and connections between them would have to be stored in a directed graph in order to detect and capture meaningful consecutive events—which would result in an NP complete search problem. Instead, only the attribute vectors between ARBs with a high resource level need to be stored; after the validation of an episode, this is reduced to storing only references to ARBs recognizing the attributes in these vectors. The ARBs with a high resource level R passed on from the snapshot memory are stored in a cache structure.

Initially, the user will be asked to name and validate a new or preliminary episode, bridging the gap between the data representation within CAMS and the real-world meaning. An episode is an ordered 3-tuple containing a start ARB, an end ARB, and an ordered list of all context vectors encountered. Ideally, in order for the proposed system to diffuse into everyday environments, APTO could learn from the human-assisted validation and move toward automatic recommendations for naming and validation. Only frequently occurring episodes would be presented.

10.6 Context Shift Model and Shift Recognition

We believe that we can create a network model of the ordered 3-tuple activities that represent each of a context mode's three stages: entering a mode, *"in-the-flow"* of a mode, and exiting a mode based on user interaction patterns. *These **context** mode stage models can be compared to a dynamic modeling of the analyst's real-time activities for detecting shifts and flows of focus.* Each mode stage (entering, inflow, leaving) is a combination or mix of the operational modalities (strategic, tactical, opportunistic, or random) within a particular time frame.

This mix is constantly changing as new information is being presented to the analyst. This combination of actions (e.g., 80 % strategic, 12 % tactical, 6 % opportunistic and 2 % random) collected from the analyst's interaction with APTO, will provide the context profile for that analyst at that given time. As they interact with APTO, their profile trend changes, thus their context and items of interest change.

In particular, the user experience activity of "zooming in" on the temporal aspect of streaming data typically characterizes a tactical desire to narrow the focus for an immediate decision. Typically, a "zooming out" follows this behavior to take a more strategic view of the information, looking for particular clusters of relevant events or activities. Although this is typical, not all analysts operate in the same manner. Our proposed approach is to accommodate an individualized recognition of pattern and transition indicators [5]. By capturing usage patterns and successful episodes on an individualized basis, the system will be able to adapt its shift recognition to the specific analyst. Over time, the patterns accumulated could become the basis for identification of a best practice approach for often-repeated situations.

10.7 Context Shift-Aware Staging and Visualization

Our "context shift" goal is to deliver an individual-focused, context-aware component that can feed its analysis and *recognition of transition stages to our **context**-aware components so that they can anticipate and pre-stage data and recommendations.* The analyst's *"view of the world"* should adapt to the individual's operational modality (strategic, tactical, opportunistic, or random). This includes recognizing the data sources, widgets, and visualization techniques that are applicable to the particular mode. This identification process will rely heavily upon the context container that encompasses and defines the operational characteristics of the OZONE App.

The next three sections focus on operator roles.

10.8 Event Manager

The basis for the event manager comes from the Event Representation and Structuring of Text (EVEREST) project, sponsored by the Office of Naval Research. It is a Small Business Research Initiative (SBIR) that has developed text analytic technology that crosses the semantic gap into the area of event recognition and representation. The EVEREST system searches for mappings to a semantic event model, interactively suggesting evidence for the occurrence of whole or partial events for human analysis and reporting. The semantic targeting approach extends the ideas of Open Information Extraction [6], Event Web [7], Semantic Web [8], and the OZONE Widget Framework. EVEREST's event-centric approach is critical for generating narratives that confer meaning upon large, complex, uncertain, and incomplete data sets.

10.8.1 Event Detection

The event detection component is based on an Open Information Extraction (Open IE) [9] approach. Open IE systems distill huge volumes of text into a long list of tuples (two entities and one relation that binds them) without asking a human for examples of those relations first. We consider each entity→relationship→entity tuple to be an event assertion. The extractions of assertions from the text are entirely lexical in nature. The assertion extraction utilizes Stanford's core Natural Language Processing (NLP) libraries and makes use of a *part-of-speech* tagger (annotator) and noun phrase "chunker." To locate the word in the vicinity of the two nouns (or noun phrases) that mostly likely intended to express their relationship, the detection algorithm employs conditional random fields. In essence, this is a statistical model that is sensitive to its lexical **context**.

10.8.2 Prescriptive Event Recognition

The Prescriptive Event Recognition component comprises an event semantic model (metadata and list of assertions) and event inference engine that compares predetermined Target Event models with Reports (detected metadata and list of assertions) in the input stream. The event semantic model is based on Westerman and Jain [10].

The event inference engine is a mixed-initiative application, i.e., one with a human in the loop, which compares extracted assertions against a prescribed model using a rules-over-graphs approach. The key idea is that many inferencing algorithms used by logic-based AI systems can be heuristically approximated by a much simpler and more efficient system based on graph-matching algorithms. The assertions associated with a target event are modeled as a graph of nodes and edges. The nodes are the entities of the tuple. The edges are the relationships between the entities. Similarly, the event assertions detected in the incoming data stream are modeled as a graph of nodes and edges. The graphs are compared for shape, structure, directionality of the edges, content (metadata) of the nodes, and content (metadata) of the edges. Each comparison is scored, or ranked, to determine how closely the detected event assertion matches the target event.

The Prescriptive Event Recognition component offers a list of assertions that are candidate matches for a target event. The initial list of candidate assertions are ranked by the inference engine based on its searches for class, instance, and relation isomorphisms between all of the assertions and its semantic event models; an assertion with a closer resemblance will find itself higher on the list. The informational value of the assertion—whether it would fill a central node or an outlier in the graph—will influence the rank as well. The user can decide to accept (or reject) the assertion after consulting his or her own knowledge, source documents, or other materials. This process could be utilized to fill in missing parts of a graph, which in turn could be utilized by the system to uncover new pieces of information, and this cycle would continue until a target concept has been proven.

10.9 Activity Manager

The activity manager is focused on activities that are occurring inside the APTO architecture. It interacts with OZONE applications via the context container, with the context manager module, and the actions taken repository.

10.9.1 Action Detection

The action detection component interacts with OZONE applications via the context container and the actions taken repository. It monitors all of the activities occurring within APTO and identifies actions of interest to the domain-specific workflow and routes these actions to the prescriptive action component.

10.9.2 Prescriptive Action Set

The prescriptive action component comprises an action semantic model (metadata and a list of assertions) and an activity inference engine that matches predetermined action sets (checklists) with events (detected metadata and a list of assertions) and actions taken. Similar to the common event model proposed by Westerman and Jain [10], the action semantic model contains temporal elements (the time horizon over which the action should occur), spatial elements (the geographic location where the action should occur), structural elements (the set of action assertions, process steps, or checklist items that need to occur), informational elements (the actor that should perform the action), and causal elements (the set of event assertions that caused this particular action model to be selected).

10.9.3 Suadeo Recommendation Engine

Suadeo [11] (Latin for recommend/advise) is a prototype context-aware, model-driven, recommender system that utilizes "static" persistent data and streaming data as the basis for deriving its recommendations. The intent of the Suadeo prototype is to be a hybrid recommender system that is context-aware, with the context model being defined along multiple dimensions such as person, place, time, and incident. The recommendation engine is driven from a graph-based analysis of the actions taken metadata and tuples. Although the description of the recommendation engine in the context of Fig. 10.4 is to provide a predefined set of actions in the form of recommended checklists, in the more general setting the recommendations could be new information sources that might be relevant for a given decision.

One of the challenges with regard to the development of a recommendation engine is to how the system should "understand" and adapt to the various biases inherent in the way humans explore their information environment. For example, information bias (the tendency to seek information even when it cannot affect action), confirmation bias (the tendency to search for or interpret information or memories in a way that confirms one's preconceptions), and anchoring (the tendency to rely too heavily, or anchor, on one trait or piece of information when making decisions) may be guiding the human information seeking patterns. Any *recommender system, through its ability to better manage and understand user-context and the decision making environment*, should help overcome these limitations.

10.10 Workflow Manager

Although the specific example of a 24 × 7 watch floor is used to describe the concepts of APTO, the intent of the architecture is to accommodate a broader class of problems. The general characteristics of these problems are that they have a high volume of streaming and static data that is composed of structured components and unstructured data (predominately text data). The unstructured data can be given structure in the form of an event assertion (a semantic tuple). From the combination of the original structured components and the discovered event assertions, events can be determined. Once an event (or set of events) is determined, a set of actions needed to respond to the event can be determined. In many, but not all, situations, it is desired that the system identify, track, and remember the actions taken.

Depending on the specific domain or scenario being addressed by APTO, only some of the process steps are required in order to reach the end state of having actionable information for decision making. To accommodate different workflows (or process steps), the APTO architecture is comprised of independent, reusable modules whose interactions represent a workflow. Every module in the architecture reports what it has done to the workflow manager. For example, when a new event assertion is created, the workflow manager is notified. Based upon the notification received and the specific workflow that is being executed, the next process step is determined and executed. It is envisioned that there may be multiple concurrent workflows executing within APTO.

10.10.1 Domain-Specific Workflow

A domain-specific workflow component defines how data (objects) flow through the APTO architecture, determines which action taken items are important, and which action taken items trigger new activities (or action sets).

10.10.2 Actions Taken

The actions taken component contains all of the actions that have occurred within the APTO architecture. Similar to our target events and reports, the action taken domain object is a collection of metadata and a list of assertions (tuples). Essentially, an action taken item is a realized instance of an action semantic model. Where the model in the prescriptive action set identifies what "should" occur, the action taken object identifies what actually happened answering the "Who," "What," "When," "Where," and "Why" questions related to **context**.

10.11   HABIT: An Authentication Decision Framework

HABIT (Habitual Activity Behavior Identification Toolkit) is a framework for behavioral authentication from Web browsing behavior within or across websites. Web browsing has become a ubiquitous activity and the negligible lag in response time has made it possible to capture accurate individual profiles based upon spontaneous usage. Browsing habits are developed to accomplish goals with minimum effort through the mediation of a browser. Once a habit is formed to achieve a goal (e.g., communicate, search, etc.), the activation of the goal triggers an automatic response [12]. While passwords can be broken and IP addresses spoofed [13], habits such as behavioral patterns are hard to duplicate because they encapsulate a unique individual strategy and are resistant to change. Goals arise from context. *The time of day is a **context** for many habitual activities. HABIT takes temporal information into account in the authentication decision.* Exogenous events, such as holidays, can shift the context and thereby change goals and associated habits.

10.11.1 Related Work

Behavioral authentication within a browser is distinguished from the authentication of Web clients through browser characteristics. In [14], several detection methods such as HTTP cookies, Etags, and IP geolocation are described. These methods assume interaction with a specific website and can be counteracted (or spoofed). For example, the NoScript[1] Firefox browser extension selectively disables executables.

Authentication from human–computer interaction with a browser has been addressed from several viewpoints. In the context of mobile phone user authentication, IP requests from Web browsing clicks provide "implicit identifiers" indicating user preferences [15]. Unlike phone numbers, the commonality of certain websites was found to be an issue in distinguishing between users [16].

User-generated content enables authorship based on stylometry. In [17], keyboard dynamics are combined with linguistic and stylistic data for authentication. The particular choice of words or n-grams gives additional features from which to identify users. Additionally, this work has also been applied to detect the personality of a user.

10.11.2 Methodology

The data of Web browsing behavior is in the form of clickstream data which can be captured on the client side within a browser or on the server side. Clicks consist of the timestamp, url visited, and user-agent. Figure 10.5 illustrates HABIT's general framework on the client side. A browser extension, WebTracker, captures clicks as they appear in the address bar of the browser. Sessions, which are sequences of clicks delimited by pauses of 30 min or longer, are the data points in our study.

Encoding is necessary to obtain reusable patterns of behavior. We encode the semantic and stylistic content of webpages into genres. Genres are functional categories of information presentation. In other words, genres are a mixture of style, form, and content. For example, books have many genres such as mystery, science fiction, literature, etc. Similarly, webpages have evolved their own genres (e.g., blog, homepage, article). Basically, the genre of a document is tied to its purpose

---

[1]https://noscript.net/.

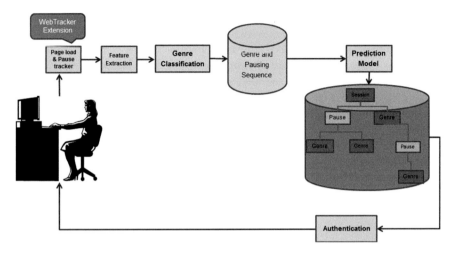

Fig. 10.5 HABIT conceptual architecture

and reflects social conventions for disseminating and searching information. We claim that genres are more indicative than topics for distinguishing Web browsing behavior. For example, some people are more frequent visitors of discussion forums (e.g., reddit) than blogs (e.g., wordpress) regardless of content. However, genres and topics do combine in important ways (e.g., spam is a combination of content and style). Previous work leveraged from a web-based genre classifier.[2] The future work will be based on a customizable genre classifier from URLs [18].

A model is then learned from the genre-pause sequences from which to base the authentication decision. We describe below two types of models: the bag-of-words (BoW) model and the temporal model.

10.11.2.1 Bag-of-Words (BoW) Model

In this approach, a prediction model is built from the aggregation of features extracted from clickstream data [19]. Three types of features were identified: global session features (e.g., time-of-day, day-of-week, session duration); time-variant features (e.g., pauses or elapsed time between clicks, revisits, bursts); semantic features such as webpage genre. One-class classification methods are relevant in the context of authentication where only positive examples are provided. The goal of one-class classification is to detect all classes that differ from the target class without knowing them in advance. One-class classification is similar to unsupervised learning, but tries to solve a discriminative problem (i.e., self or not self) rather than a generative problem as in clustering algorithms or density estimation.

---

[2]http://www.diffbot.com.

Several algorithms have been modified to perform one-class classification including one-class support vector machines (OCSVMs) available with LibSVM.[3] SVMs are large-margin classifiers that map feature vectors to a higher dimensional space using kernels. In addition, a stochastic gradient descent approach is possible for incremental learning. Independently though, each feature set is not sufficient to authenticate a user. Moreover, all time-variant features exhibit a common distribution between users and it is only at a high resolution that users can be distinguished (e.g., pauses below 5 min). What has been shown to work is the combination of those features using ensemble models of OCSVMs based on the random subspace method [19]. Authentication accuracy differences among users and average authentication was within 80 %, based upon one month of data from 14 volunteers in an uncontrolled environment.

10.11.2.2 Temporal Model

A BoW model ignores the temporal navigational aspect of Web browsing behavior. In addition, our experiments have shown that pauses or genre n-grams frequent patterns taken independently are not sufficient to authenticate a user. Hidden Markov models (HMMs) [20] have long been the preferred method to model behavior, but they are limited in their capability to represent constraints between any two states because of their Markov assumption and the independence assumption of the observations [20]. In addition, the statistical approach of HMMs requires considerable training data to produce accurate models. Our approach [21] is based on conditional random fields (CRFs), a probabilistic approach predicated on the interaction of neighboring label sequences that relaxes the Markov assumption of hidden Markov models [22] and discriminative learning (such as logistic regression). CRFs, through the powerful exploitation of feature functions (Fig. 10.6), fuse diverse information to relate a set of inputs to a set of outputs such as a sequence or a graph with correlations or constraints between the parts. In this approach, time-of-day (hour), day-of-week, and URL n-grams are combined as observations to predict a label given by the genre of the webpage in a linear-chain CRF. Several discriminative learning methods can be used to learn the parameters (i.e., the weight of the feature functions). Here, stochastic gradient descent coupled with the Viterbi algorithm as the label prediction method updates the weight of the feature functions. A threshold determined by the equal error rate between false positives and false negatives authenticates users. In subsequent experiments [21], the first five clicks of a Web browsing session were found sufficient to authenticate users with the same accuracy obtained in the BoW approach. The uncertainty of a sequence of clicks is compounded in longer sessions.

---

[3]https://www.csie.ntu.edu.tw/~cjlin/libsvm/.

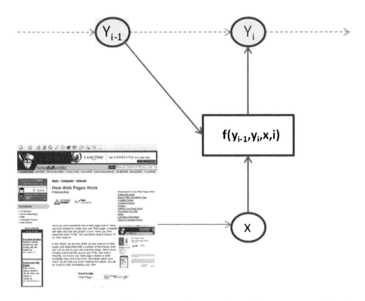

Fig. 10.6 CRF feature function relating observations and labels in a sequence. The figure shows how inputs at time $i - 1$ affect values at time i

10.11.2.3   Authentication Decision

In the approaches described above, the authentication decision is made on a session-by-session basis. Each authentication decision is independent of past decisions (Fig. 10.7 illustrates the cumulative success frequencies). However, the decision to re-authenticate is a sequential decision-making problem that must be made based on accumulated decisions and preferences for user flexibility versus security. A persistent failure rate should prompt re-authentication while intermittent successes should sustain the current authentication despite occasional failures. We examine here if taking into account the decision context itself can improve on the overall authentication accuracy based on successes and failures.

10.11.3   Summary Discussion

The proliferation of sensors monitoring human activities and the availability of large amount of spontaneous usage behavior due to the popularity of social media has made possible the capture of unconscious patterns of behavior to characterize cognitive fingerprints and personalize information presentation. HABIT is a predictive analytics framework for behavioral data from digital traces. Although our attention has been focused primarily on Web browsing behavior, a passive type of

Fig. 10.7 Profile comparison
between pairs of users from
independent assessments

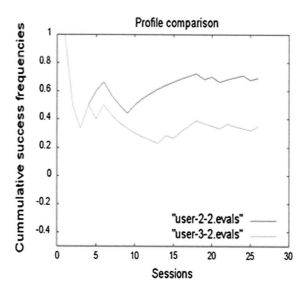

digital trace, this framework could extend to other types of digital traces such as social media activities or GPS records.

Our experiments have shown that although individual features of Web browsing behavior are not individually strong enough to authenticate users, methods that fuse diverse sources of information such as the random subspace projection in an ensemble of SVMs or CRFs' feature functions can address difficult learning tasks characterized by high-dimensionality and noisy data. Further work includes addressing temporal drift and using frequent overlapping activity patterns to model dependencies between non-contiguous clicks.

10.12   Context Awareness Motivation from Cyber Security

Security issues cannot be looked at solely in terms of a metric. Any such metric must be used in a **context**-*aware manner*. Then, and only then, can any decision be made in a pragmatic manner.

As an example of this we will first discuss the capacity of a covert channel, and then we will discuss stego channels.

A *covert channel* is an unintended means of communication in a secure computer system. Since the only truly secure computing device seems to a brick, a clever bad guy always has some way of transmitting information that is not allowed. The security world is well aware of this weakness, and allows certain violations to a security policy of a minimal nature with a *context* sensitive basis being an additional gauge of the leakage. Historically, in the world of multi-level security (MLS), there were two classes of users/files/etc., High and Low. The

Bell–LaPadula (BLP) model principles [23, 24] of secure computing are that Low may not read High files, and that High may not write to Low. In terms of the BLP model a covert channel is a violation of the BLP principles.

The standard metric, ever since the famous Orange book of the Rainbow series [25], for measurement of a covert channel is its Shannon channel *capacity*. The original bound for a dangerous versus safe covert channel was the now ludicrous capacity of 100 (bits per second) bps. Of course over time the capacity (or bandwidth, as it was unfortunately originally referred to as) has greatly increased. However, whatever bound we have on transmission speed we must keep the *context* of the covert channel in mind. If one has a cryptographic key of N bits, and the cryptographic key is changed every hour, we need not be overly concerned with a covert channel that has a capacity much less than N bits per day. Keep in mind that capacity is the upper bound for essentially error free communication, as shown by Shannon in his famous noisy coding theorem [26]. This bound by Shannon is existential though. How to build a coding system that comes close to information transfer at a rate near (but never over) the capacity is another story, and a field of great interest!

Let us discuss the context sensitive nature of this now. For Paul Revere, the important fact was that the British were coming. That is, one bit of information started the birth of the USA. It was not important that he yelled five words a minute or seven: the words he yelled amount to one bit of information, thus the *context* of this channel (albeit not a covert one, unless we count the church light that signaled him) is what is important.

Now we return to covert channel capacity. One would certainly think that a covert channel with zero capacity is no threat at all, but, in *context*, this is not true at all. Consider the following example from [27]: a noiseless channel where distinct symbols are received at different times. We let Sn be the set of all messages that take time up to time n, and we let |Sn| be the size of this set. Shannon's definition of capacity (we use the limit superior to be more precise) is

$$C_t = \limsup_{n \to \infty} \left(\frac{\log |S_n|}{n} \right)$$

in units of bpt. In our channel a 0 or 1 is noiselessly sent in 1 time tick t, then it is sent in 2t, then 4t, then 8t, etc. Thus, the nth noiseless transmission of a bit takes 2^{n-1} t units of time to send. Thus, the nth transmission takes $1 + 2 + \cdots + 2^{n-1}$ time units t, and there are 2^n different possible symbol patterns. This gives us a capacity of

$$C_t = \lim_{n \to \infty} \frac{\log 2^n}{\sum_{i=0}^{n-1} 2^i} = \lim_{n \to \infty} \frac{n}{2^n - 1} = 0$$

But, to say that this covert is benign is ludicrous. We must ask ourselves in what *contexts* are we concerned with this covert channel? If our *context* is the leakage of a small message, then this covert channel is quite damaging. If our concern is a slightly larger message in a moderate amount of time then this channel may also be of concern.

Now let us look at steganography [28]. Steganography is the art and science of sending a message so that the existence of that stego message is unknown to all but the sender and the receiver. Steganography is not cryptography. In cryptography we do not try to hide the existence of the hidden message, only the meaning of the hidden message. A common form of exercising a stego channel is to hide information in an image. There is no perfect stego detection mechanism in existence. However, if a stego message is large enough it can be detected. This brings us back to the above analysis of covert channels. If we can hide 10 bits steganographically in an image and our message requires 100 bits, one image will not suffice. However, if the *context* in which we are dealing allows multiple image transmission without raising alarm, then we must be concerned about the stego channel.

The importance of these examples from cyber security is that only once the context of the threat is understood, and analyzed, can we then make proactive decisions.

10.13   CEDARS: Combined Exploratory Data Analysis Recommender System

We present a framework for recommender systems (RS) to support exploratory data analysis (EDA) in analytical decision making. EDA helps the domain expert, often not a statistical expert, to discover interesting relationships between variables and thus be motivated to explain the behavior. Capturing the behavior of expert analysts in EDA could then use RS to advise domain experts of "standard" analytical operations and suggest operations novel to the domain but consistent in analytical goals with requested operations. We enhance our framework with rules that encapsulate standard analytical practice and by incorporating user preferences. We present a scalable framework architecture, which we implemented in a prototype system, and discuss a use case where the prototype was exercised to analyze experimental data of visualization techniques.

10.13.1   Introduction and Related Work

In a modern age of large data, "data analyst" is a role many fill from time to time. Recommender systems (RS) can benefit users who have data analysis decisions to make. Given a decision making context, often the first question after gaining an understanding of the available data is: What data should be explored? followed by, What analytics might be appropriate in that exploration? Usually the user has some hypothesis for what data to use and might investigate one or more appropriate analytics. Similar to searching through many products, this process can be cumbersome and require significant effort. Even when the analysis is being conducted by a person familiar with the data and appropriate analytics, interesting patterns or other data characteristics can be overlooked as a result of familiarity-bias [29].

When posed as "What items are relevant and what services might complement those items?" answering the question of what data and what analytic operations to use are questions that RS can support [30]. This support is particularly relevant under ambiguity and uncertainty in the process or goal, often the case with exploratory data analysis (EDA) [31].

EDA [32] provides insight into how data visualization might help analysts generate hypotheses to test. Tukey believed EDA would lead to new data collection and experiments—that is, confirmatory data analysis using traditional statistical tools (such as hypothesis testing). Arguing for both, he noted that EDA requires human judgment whereas confirmatory analysis (e.g., statistical hypothesis testing) is "a routine easy to computerize."

Our work began with the observation that many people who find themselves in the role of data analyst are not sufficiently familiar with the tools of EDA or data analysis in general, and that we can and should find ways to automate the exploratory process. Our goal may be succinctly stated as capturing an expert's approaches for analysis, so that these approaches may be intelligently recommended or automatically applied to future analyses by the expert or by others. Such a tool could automate analyses of complex data sets, help novice analysts develop expertise, assist domain experts in creative analysis, and perhaps unify architectures for analysis with other EDA factors, such as layout and visual representation.

In this section, we present the Combined Exploratory Data Analysis Recommender System (CEDARS), an analytically scalable architecture that seeks to address the challenge of EDA by providing cued and learned recommendations, coupled with augmented analysis, to deliver proactive decision support. Herlocker et al. [33] list eleven common tasks where RS provide direct benefit. In the context of CEDARS, applicable tasks include (1) find some good items; (2) annotation in context: given an existing context, e.g., a list of items, emphasize some items depending on the user's preferences; (3) recommend a sequence; (4) recommend a bundle; (5) help with browsing; and (6) improve the profile by integrating user preference into the decision making task. Cast in the context of EDA, RS are complementary, particularly in the intelligence phase of decision making [34]. Data analysis is a critical part of the intelligence phase of decision making, and EDA is an approach to data analysis that emphasizes the use of graphical methods as a way to reach insights about the data. Graphics should start with simple plots, and the initial statistical methods should focus on simple summary statistics alongside raw data [32]. The goal is to enable the analyst to keep an open mind, rather than enforce a pre-conceived notion of the data. The latter approach might direct an analyst away from appropriate methods or insight.

ForceSPIRE [35] is an EDA system that adjusts the layout of information on the screen to bring related pieces of information together. By changing the weights of entities, the system captures the semantics implied by user interactions. This enables the system to adapt to different entities of interest and hypotheses during each user's analytical process. In a rule-based system for EDA, Petasis et al. [36] use the C4.5 decision tree machine learning algorithm to discover the need to update rules in a rule-based recognition and classification system for named entities in text corpora. Such semi-supervised systems can extend disambiguation rules using entities that were automatically identified.

One significant contribution of RS to suggestive decision aiding is incorporation of user feedback in a discovery activity. Since hyperparameters control how regular parameters of a predictive model are selected, their optimization improved prediction accuracy of RS in retail applications [37]. The use of hyperparameters is a model selection paradigm for a learning algorithm to obtain a good generalization [38]. This approach improved recommendations by combining machine learning techniques with rules in a structured workflow. This combination of statistical inference, bounded by domain logic to guide user decision-making is a foundational characteristic of RS, particularly contextually aware RS [39]. Despite the richness of research on RS, research on RS for data exploration and analytical applications is sparse. Our research attempts to bridge this gap between adaptive EDA and RS in workflows.

10.13.2 System Architecture

The metaphor we apply to the EDA user, data, and statistical operations is a movie RS. EDA users may be viewed as customers who wish to purchase a movie, but do not know which movie they would like. They have some preference and perhaps a general sense of the subject area. Preferences and subject area understanding translate to knowledge of the data domain. Data variables are items (movies) that can be classified into data types and relevant analytical operations that aggregate them (genres). Through this metaphor, rule-based approaches can be combined with collaborative filtering (CF) recommendation methods.

CEDARS employs a content-based recommendation approach augmented by preference CF gathered from users to address cold-start (a lack of user feedback) challenges and enrich exploratory creativity. Further, categorical classifications (e.g., genres) of the data can address issue of ambiguity in the CF recommender algorithm (i.e., sparseness, cold start, and expert proxy) [40]. For example, a movie has genre information provided by movie experts. Following the metaphor, data variables have types that can be inferred from the data values, and CEDARS has expert-prescribed analytical operations that are appropriate for those data types. The categorical information is reliable and can be used to both augment and derive user interest. Moreover, data newly ingested in CEDARS will always be able to infer or have built-in categorical information, thus minimizing cold-start problems.

CEDARS implements rules that define appropriate operations for the system to execute based on user selections or elicited through automated processing. The rules provide a framework in which CF mechanisms operate. An example rule when analyzing user study data (Sect. 10.3): apply a post hoc t-test after an F-test finds a significant difference for an independent variable with more than two levels. This is the standard practice in analysis of hypothesis testing. For our applications, scalability is a significant consideration, both from the perspective of data analysis and recommendation methodology.

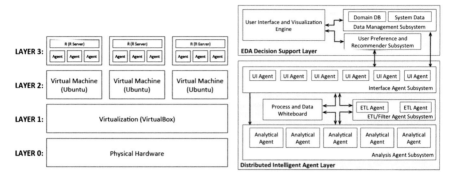

Fig. 10.8 *Left* Prototype implementation enables multiple users, using one or multiple virtual machines, which in turn may be realized on one or more physical devices. *Right* System architecture. The EDA layer has a user interface and RS. The agent layer assigns operations to one of the agents that sit on (distributed) virtual machines. The EDA layer initiates operations (via user request or by the RS), and the agent layer returns results to the database

CEDARS approaches scalability by implementing a tiered distributed architecture through virtualization and agent technology; this reduces the need for fine-grain parallelism of analytical operations (i.e., for custom code), incorporating coarse-grain parallelism. While CEDARS could be implemented using popular NoSQL and map-reduce based technologies (e.g., Hadoop, Accumulo, Spark, etc.), the CEDARS system processing architecture generalizes the approaches implemented on these platforms and provides a lower implementation overhead for new features. Additionally, the CEDARS system processing system architecture does not preclude the use of these technologies and can actually enhance them with reasoning agents. Figure 10.8 (left) illustrates each processing layer on a single physical hardware device; these layers can be replicated across multiple hardware systems or distributed across a network. Additionally, the number of layer elements in layers 2 and 3 can be increased or reduced to suit application processing demands and hardware capacity. Figure 10.8 (right) presents a generalized component architecture for CEDARS. The user interface provides interaction between user and system, creating and digesting requests and tasks for the agents to complete.

10.13.2.1   Data Organization

For rapid development, our agents use the Django web framework[4] with Python[5] scripts to ingest data in comma-separated value (CSV) files. The Django data organization module stores data in a MongoDB[6] database and passes interest-values

---

[4]https://www.djangoprojct.com.

[5]https://www.python.org.

[6]http://www.mongodb.org.

to the agents. The number and distribution of agents are abstracted from user specificity and allow for dynamic scaling of processing functionality depending on the deployment architecture; our prototype uses one agent on each node of an 18-node cluster. Each agent uses R[7] for statistical computations. By being layered on top of R, agents' statistical behaviors can be easily expanded beyond initial capabilities. When the EDA agent collects data from the analytical/processing agents, it passes the data back to the user interface as plain text tables, which are parsed and loaded into the Django database. The database has tables of all variables and potential operations, as well as results (of operations) and user ratings for interest. Interest is distributed from user feedback on analytical results to variables and operations and accumulated from statistical significance. Undiscovered analytical operations are recommended through discovery of "interesting" operations and "interesting" variables; if a combination of these has no result in the database, the EDA layer requests it from the agent system. To simplify user interaction and maintain the scheme of a loosely coupled scalable architecture, users interact with the system by accessing the Django-based Web server using a common Web browser client.

10.13.2.2 User Interface

The interface (Fig. 10.9) lists available results (sorted by interest value); an AJAX[8] request is made to the Django Web server for the sorted list. Once the user selects a result from the list, it is displayed in a draggable window within a Firefox[9] tab. This window has a close button, and an up arrow (positive for interest) and down arrow (negative for interest). Interest points (positive or negative) create an AJAX request to Django, which updates the database accordingly and sends back a new sorted list of analytical results. Operations are associated with an output graph type: correlations in scatterplots with regression lines, F-tests and t-tests in bar graphs, etc. Charts are drawn using Google Charts[10] and defined with Javascript. An automatic rule determines variable type as string, integer, or floating-point. Summaries (e.g., histograms, computed through Google Charts; pie charts for a small number of repeated strings or integers) are shown, with interest indicators. This interest is applied only to a variable, and outweighs statistical significance. Operational results have their interest distributed mostly to variables, but also to the operation itself. Interest in operations may be triggered directly by user action or indirectly via rules for interesting operations. In the example above, (dis-)interest in an F-test would propagate to the post hoc t-test. Thus interest propagates through all variables and operations.

---

[7]http://www.r-project.org.

[8]https://code.djangoproject.com/wiki/AJAX.

[9]http://www.mozilla.org/en-US/firefox/.

[10]https://developers.google.com/chart/.

10.13.3   Use Case

Our first use case is using EDA for metrics on images in user studies of multivariate visualization techniques [41]: whether objective measures of image properties offer insight into user performance (error and response time). Objective properties included target/distraction differences in color or intensity distribution, edge strength or orientation, texture frequency, etc. Measures are computed via various operators, multiplying the number of individual statistics and introducing the need for an intelligent agent to help search for relationships to present to the analyst. As noted above, the user first sees summaries of variables (Fig. 10.9, top left), in this case, selected from the list of "results" of computing summary statistics. Interest in the variables of error and response time leads the system to conduct F-tests (Fig. 10.9, top right) and show significant results in bar graphs. This illustrates that our framework can rapidly provide the most commonly used results for a user study, in this case showing that one technique known as Data-Driven Spots (DDSpots) exhibited significantly lower error and faster response time than other techniques. This result was known before we began analysis with this framework; CEDARS replicated the findings of the standard approach. After an F-test, correlation may be recommended (Fig. 10.9, bottom left); it provides an

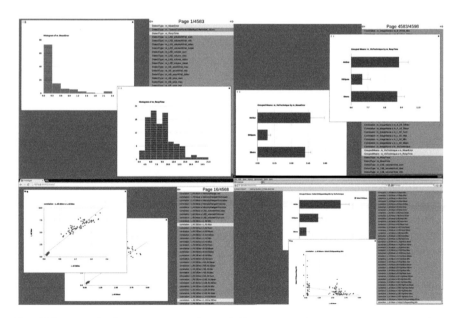

Fig. 10.9 *Top left* Histograms summarize variables the user found in the list of potentially interesting results. *Top right Bar graphs* show significant F-tests for the main effects of visual technique on error and response time. *Bottom left Scatterplots* show correlations and help identify redundant variables. *Bottom right* Novel use of variables recommended as operands gives technical insight into user performance

opportunity to see if independent variables predict dependent variables (a similar purpose to an F-test, but using a continuous, rather than categorical, independent variable.) CEDARS has no knowledge of whether such tests make sense or will be of interest, and (we argue) it should not try to anticipate such knowledge without guidance from the domain expert. A data analyst might also be unable to determine this; we do not require the data scientist to become a domain expert to provide analysis services. As this propagates to other variables, the user may trim variables that correlate in a way that implies redundancy. This is all in addition to the t-test following an F-test. The most interesting possibility introduced by the CEDARS framework is discovery of results that have potential to yield insight but might not have been requested by a domain expert. In our use case, the user identified two interesting variables (error and response time). Then an F-test was also deemed interesting, indicating another variable (visual technique) of possible interest (at least for its effect on the first two variables). The recommended F-tests and group means found a significant main effect (visual technique on mean luminance of all targets). This result gets pushed up the list of recommended results to explore. Visual technique and mean luminance are both independent variables, so it is not an analytical operation that even a domain expert would have been likely to request. But the interest the analyst has shown thus far, along with the statistical significance, makes this a recommended result.

It is up to the user to determine whether this difference in luminance is a result worthy of further investigation or not. This indicates a difference in strategy of the visualization techniques. CEDARS makes no such judgments, but leaves this to the domain expert. The domain expert would reason about the error and thus the strength of the intensity cue to provide insight in one visual technique versus other perceptual cues (such as hue, in other techniques). Similarly, CEDARS recommends a significant F-test for one of the edge operators as a function of visualization technique (Fig. 10.9, bottom right). This is another analysis on two independent variables an expert analyst would not have run when selecting candidate operations and operands. It is unclear whether the domain expert would have thought to analyze this. It becomes recommended because visualization technique is interesting, the F-test showed significance, and some F-tests were selected as interesting. A domain expert would look at this result and consider the perceptual interpretation: "Targets and distractions had similar edge strength in the Slivers technique; users could not see which data layers were present. Layers had different edge strengths in Attribute Blocks, but it did not help users; perhaps the sampling grid and background confused the measure and users. I could test this hypothesis."

10.13.4   Discussion and Future Work

The goal in EDA is to uncover relationships that promote understanding of the data. CEDARS uses analytical results and user recommendations (interest) to recommend analytical operations. We showed that our prototype CEDARS can both replicate standard analytical practice through simple rules and provide deep analysis by recommending operations on variables that the domain expert had not thought to test. The ultimate goal in EDA, and thus CEDARS, must be to help the user tell a story that explains the data. CEDARS separates developing analytical operations from interpreting results; it may help the domain expert user learn analysis methods from recommendations; it may remind the domain expert of the standard practice. CEDARS may lead to undesired computation; we accept this in the exploratory phase, when the analyst may not be able to direct resources. By applying the framework of RS to operations to be performed during analysis, we can capture the expertise of both the data scientist and the domain expert, use that expertise to lend expert guidance to nonexperts, remind experts of potentially forgotten operations, and promote the adoption of analysis methods that are novel to a domain. Thus CEDARS potentially improves usability of analytical tools. The future work will recommend factors important to EDA (e.g., layout [7] or visual representation), widen variety of data sets and operations, and evaluate recommendations across data sets.

10.14   A-TASC: Adaptive Task Assignment in Supervisory Control

We present A-TASC (Adaptive Task Assignment in Supervisory Control), a framework for proactively scheduling and allocating tasking among a team of unmanned system operators. For the purposes of A-TASC, context is considered on two dimensions: user context and mission context. *Within the A-TASC framework a combination of user and mission **context** variables are analyzed to dynamically and proactively alert operators to tasks that need to be performed while maximizing the likelihood of mission success.*

10.14.1   A-TASC Motivations

Advances in technology are changing the way humans interact with the world and with one another. Roles and tasks that used to be filled by people are slowly being supplanted by automation as computers become faster and smaller, and algorithms become more "intelligent" and reliable. These advances in technology, however, also have human performance consequences, since automation rarely operates in complete isolation or can conduct cognitive functions reliably (e.g. decision making), and therefore requires human interaction, oversight, and management [42]. One high impact area of automation is the use of drones, or unmanned aerial vehicles (UAVs). These systems have made significant press coverage over the past decade as their use in military operations has become increasingly prevalent [43].

As the automation continues to increase in these systems, the tasking of the human operator is transforming from direct control to a more supervisory role. Despite this paradigm shift, most current UAV operations still require multiple human operators (typically three) to conduct a mission with one UAV. In this current state, each operator maintains one of three specialized and distinct roles: Mission commander (MC), air vehicle operator (AVO), and payload operator (PO), each of whom is responsible solely for the tasks associated with that role. This specialized role structure is applied regardless of the particular mission context or objective, often resulting in significant fluctuations in workload among team members (or fusion cell). A large number of UAV mishap reports implicate extremes in operator workload (i.e., very low or very high workloads) as causing suboptimal operator states, such as channelized attention and/or lapses in situation awareness (SA) [43, 44].

The Department of Defense (DoD) recognizes that this current team structure is inefficient and problematic, given task demands are highly variable and unbalanced across team members during a mission; in part due to increased automation causing significant operator downtime. This inefficiency has led the DoD's desire to invert the ratio of operators to UAVs and move towards a supervisory control paradigm [45]. The Naval S&T Plan contends that this will require improvements in "task allocation/assignment, planning, coordination and control for heterogeneous systems" [46]. Despite this push for less manning and greater efficiency, however, questions remain as to the best way to allocate operator tasking and structure teams of operators to ensure high levels of performance (i.e., high SA, moderate mental workload, high engagement) and safety (i.e., preventing errors) under a varied assortment of possible mission contexts. The Adaptive Task Assignment in Supervisory Control (A-TASC) system presented here suggests a user-centric approach for allocating and balancing operator tasking across team members, to ensure operators are attending to the right task at the right time, and do not get caught in situations where they are at either extreme of workload.

10.14.2 A-TASC Predictive Model

Context within A-TASC is considered along two dimensions: mission context and user context. First we discuss mission context. In order to develop an initial task schedule/plan, information about the upcoming mission and its component tasks must be considered. First, a mission must be deconstructed into its constituent tasks, at which point each individual task's complexity and average time to complete needs to be computed. One complexity measure that may be considered is the R-TACOM metric [47], which computes an aggregate complexity value based upon the three dimensions: task scope, structurability, and uncertainty. Validating those measures with subject matter experts is also critical. Complexity measurements for each task, in addition to time completion estimates should provide the means to construct initial plans that balance tasking among operators, given constraints such as priorities, deadlines, etc. When and if new tasking is provided and replanning needs to occur, information about the new task and current user tasking should provide a partial solution for determining who is best suited to perform the new task, which is how traditional schedulers work.

The second contextual dimension that is often ignored is the user (i.e., operator). Physiological sensor data can provide information about a user's state in near-real time. For example, previous research has shown that an individual's mental effort correlates with pupil size [48, 49] and heart rate variability [50]. Furthermore, eye gaze analysis can be used to assess where an individual is allocating attention (or failing to attend to), and therefore be employed to provide alerts and prevent errors in real time [51, 52]. Lastly, key-logging can be used as a secondary measure of workload and means of measuring operator "percent busy time," when the operator is actively engaged in a task, which impacts user performance on a task (i.e., when utilization exceeds 70 %, operator performance decreases) [53]. When considered together, pupil size, heart rate variability, gaze analysis, and key-logging can be used to predict an operator's level of mental effort and where he/she is allocating attention.

Furthermore, predictive models can be generated by considering both mission and user contextual data together, such that success on a task can be predicted, given a user's current state. A predictive model can be used to drive future tasking, as seen in Fig. 10.10, and proactively allocate tasking to operators based not just on complexity of current tasks, but also on the operator's state. Additionally, this information can be used to predict when a user may be particularly susceptible to error (e.g., if the operator has not fixated on an important piece of information for several minutes and his/her blink durations have increased, indicating fatigue). This could then be used to provide more effective alerting.

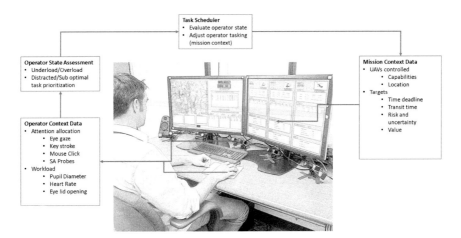

Fig. 10.10 Conceptual data model for A-TASC

10.14.3 Methodology

NRL developed a simulation environment, named the Supervisory Control Operational User Testbed (SCOUT™), to collect human performance data as users interact with and control various simulated unmanned systems. SCOUT was developed primarily for purposes of exploring unmanned aerial vehicle (UAV) operator performance in a futuristic supervisory control context, given various team structures and within different mission contexts (e.g., low to high operational tempo, uncertainty, priority, and task type). This futuristic control paradigm assumes advances in automation and technologies, but also maintains the functionality and high-level tasking (e.g. decision making such as prioritization, communication with customers, controlled airspace management) that is representative of current UAV operations. The flexibility of SCOUT makes it an ideal environment for testing the A-TASC framework.

The SCOUT 1.0 version, to date, is a single user platform that allows an operator to control multiple simulated unmanned assets. A future networked version of SCOUT is currently under development to allow shared control of vehicles among multiple operators. SCOUT 1.0 features the core elements of unmanned vehicle control (e.g., airspace management, route planning, target risk assessment), and also enables the investigation of higher order cognitive processes, such as decision making under uncertain conditions. The ability to manipulate uncertainty and frequency of tasking allows investigation of the impact of different mission contexts and task allocation strategies on operator performance.

SCOUT enables investigation of how varying levels of tasking impacts elements of supervisory control such as communication performance, decision making, and mission awareness. A key element of the testbed, however, is the ability to capture and synchronize data streams from eye tracking, heart, and respiration sensor systems via both network and Bluetooth packets. Mouse and keystroke logging are also captured along with the other data streams, all of which are synchronized with mission events transpiring in SCOUT. This data integration is a key step in providing real-time analysis and understanding of the user's context, via performance, eye tracking, physiological, mouse, and keystroke data. This functionality enables examination of human performance metrics within the context of the current mission as it is unfolding. For example, an experimenter can compute in real time how long it takes a user to look at and detect a new high priority target opportunity, or not detect it, in which case an alert can be provided. Additionally, a combination of performance data and eye tracking data can be used to inform tasking, such that if a user is performing poorly and his/her eye fixations have been constrained to small area of the display, tasks may be shed and reallocated to other available operators/teammates.

The physiological information serves as a continuous measure of an operator's state (i.e., context), which is especially useful in UAV mission contexts where very limited performance measures are available. These situations are becoming increasingly prevalent as autopilot systems have all but replaced the piloting duties, and once waypoints have been determined and set, there are extended periods while a UAV is en-route to an objective and no operator tasking or system interaction is required. During periods such as these, eye tracking data provides the ability to assess where an operator is allocating attention (i.e., assessing gaze patterns), how much mental effort he/she is expending (i.e., pupil diameter), and whether the operator is fatigued/engaged (i.e., eye lid closure). Furthermore, SCOUT features situation awareness probes which provide additional performance measures to assess the user's awareness of the current situation, by requiring the user to recreate the most current mission objectives, including the location of assets and targets, as well as the points various objectives are worth.

Figure 10.11 depicts left and right screens of SCOUT and Table 10.1 lists the tasks associated with the different functional areas of the screens. Within SCOUT an operator's mission tasking comprises two phases: a mission planning phase,

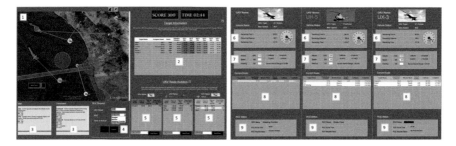

Fig. 10.11 *SCOUT* supervisory control operations user testbed left and right screens. Numerically labelled items in the testbed correspond with the following tasks: (*1*) route planning/replanning and airspace management; (*2*) *route planning/replanning*; (*3*) *information requests/communication and information updates*; (*4*) airspace management; (*5*) route planning/replanning; (*6*) fuel management; (*7*) information updates; (*8*) information updates; (*9*) airspace management

Table 10.1 SCOUT functional areas

Area	Task	User action	Behavioral measure
1, 2, 5	Route planning/replanning	Operator drags objective from target box to vehicle box	Decision performance, plan time
1, 4, 9	Airspace management	Operator identifies potential conflicts on the map and works with airspace manager to gain access or navigates around	Airspace violations, response time after alert, response time after approval/denial
3	Information requests	Operator provides requested information	Response time, accuracy
3, 7, 8	Information updates	Operator updates information on objectives or assets, and responds to requestor	Response time, accuracy
6	Fuel management	Operator monitors vehicle fuel and returns asset to refueling location when necessary	Fuel violations (time below reserve)

where the user must determine the best plan for assigning objectives to different vehicles; and a mission execution mode where the user monitors vehicle statuses, responds to communication requests, and makes updates to the overall plan as new or updated objectives arise. Various tasks have different priority levels, which are manipulated via a point system, where the operator's overall goal is to maximize points. Points can also be deducted for making errors, such as sending a UAV into a restricted area without requesting access. Various SCOUT scenarios and tasking are currently being employed as use-cases for assessing the A-TASC framework.

10.14.4   Future Work

We presented A-TASC, a framework for adaptive task allocation based upon operator and mission context. This framework is currently being tested within the single-user SCOUT 1.0 simulation environment, with the overall objective of reducing operator errors and maximizing overall mission performance and efficiency. In the next series of experiments, we will assess A-TASC within a team environment, using SCOUT-N, the future networked version of SCOUT.

10.15   Conclusion

This paper has discussed a context-aware Proactive Decision Support framework concentrating on the OZONE environment. Furthermore, several longer term challenges have been briefly described with regard to modeling decision context, metrics for recognizing operational context, and techniques for recognizing context shift. We have also described four specific examples in which user context has been modeled or how it could be modeled in order to move toward an improved implementation of a context-aware proactive decision support system. We also recommend the interested reader to see the work by Blasch and Plano [54].

Additional research areas include:

- Adequately capturing users' information interaction (seeking) patterns (and subsequently user information biases).
- Reasoning about information seeking behaviors in order to infer decision making context; for example, the work being done by researchers within the Contextualized Attention Metadata community [55] and the Universal Interaction Context Ontology [56] might serve as a foundation.
- Instantiating formal models of decision making based on information seeking behaviors.
- Leveraging research from the AI community in plan recognition to infer which decision context (model) is active, and which decision model should be active.

- Recognizing decision shift based on work that has been done in the Machine Learning community with "concept drift," and assessing how well this approach adapts to noisy data and learns over time.
- Incorporating uncertainty and confidence metrics when fusing information and estimating information value in relation to decision utility.

Elaborating further on the ideas presented in the paper, longer term research should be focused on the following:

Decision Models for goal-directed behavior: Instantiation of prescriptive models of decision making, which integrate information recommendation engines that are context-aware. Furthermore, techniques that can broker across, generalize, or aggregate, individual decision models would enable application in broader contexts such as group behavior. Supporting areas of research may include similarity metrics that enable the selection of the appropriate decision model for a given situation, and intuitive decision model visualizations.

Information Extraction and Valuation: Locating, assessing, and enabling, through utility-based exploitation, the integration of high-value information within the decision models, particularly in the big data realm is a research challenge due to the heterogeneous data environment. In addition, techniques that can effectively stage relevant information along the decision trajectory (while representing, reducing and/or conveying information uncertainty) would enable the wealth of unstructured data to be maximally harnessed.

Decision Assessment: Modeling decision "normalcy," in order to identify decision trajectories that might be considered outliers and detrimental to achieving successful outcomes in a given mission context would be areas for additional research. Furthermore, techniques that proactively induce the correct decision trajectory to achieve mission success are also necessary. Lastly, metrics for quantifying decision normalcy in a given context can be used to propose alternate sequences of decisions or induce the exact sequence of decisions. This would require the pre-staging of the appropriate information needed to support the evaluation of those decisions and would potentially improve the speed and accuracy of decision making.

Operator/Human Issues: Understanding, modeling, and integrating the human decision making component as an integral part of the aforementioned areas is a novel area of research. The challenges are to represent human decision-making behavior computationally, to mathematically capture the human assessment of information value, risk, uncertainty, prioritization, projection and insight; and computationally representing human foresight and intent.

Acknowledgment We appreciate the efforts of Ms. Linda McGibbon in the preparation of this chapter. Her efforts are always beyond the call of duty.

References

1. F. Radlinski, M. Szummer, N. Craswell, Inferring query intent from reformulations and clicks, in *Proceedings of the 19th International Conference on World Wide Web* (ACM Press, 2010), pp. 1171–1172
2. P.H. Mohr, N. Ryan, J. Timmis, Capturing regular human activity through a learning context memory, in *Proceedings of the 3rd International Workshop of Modelling and Retrieval of Context (MRC 2006) in Conjunction with AAAI-06* (2006), p. 6
3. P.H. Mohr, J. Timmis, N. Ryan, Immune inspired context memory, in *Proceedings of the 1st International Workshop on Exploiting Context Histories in Smart Environments* (2005), p. 4
4. M. Neal, Meta-stable memory in an artificial immune network, in *Proceedings of the 2nd International e-Conference on Artificial Immune Systems* (2003), pp. 229–241
5. V. Agrawal, G. Heredero, H. Penmetsa, A. Laha, L. Shastri, Activity context aware digital workspaces and consumer playspaces: manifesto and architecture, in *AAAI Workshops* (2013)
6. M. Banko, M.J. Cafarella, S. Soderland, M. Broadhead, O. Etzioni, Open information extraction from the web, in *IJCAI* (2007), pp. 2670–2676
7. R. Jain, EventWeb: developing a human-centered computing system. IEEE Comput. **41**(2), 42–50 (2008)
8. J. Hendler, Web 3.0 emerging. IEEE Comput. **42**(1), 111–113 (2009)
9. A. Fader, S. Soderland, O. Etzioni, Identifying relations for open information extraction. EMNLP **2011**, 1535–1545 (2011)
10. U. Westermann, R. Jain, Toward a common event model for multimedia applications. IEEE Multimed. **14**(1), 19–29 (2007)
11. J. Hoxha, Cross-domain recommendations based on semantically-enhanced User Web Behavior. Ph.D. Dissertation, Karlsruher Institute (KIT), (2014)
12. H. Aarts, A. Dijksterhuis, Habits as knowledge structures: automaticity in goal-directed behavior. J. Pers. Soc. Psychol. **78**(1), 53 (2000)
13. S.M. Bellovin, Security problems in the tcp/ip protocol suite. ACM SIGCOMM Comput. Commun. Rev. **19**(2), 32–48 (1989)
14. W. Huba, B. Yuan, Y. Pan, S. Mishra, Towards a web tacking profiling algorithm, in *Proceedings of IEEE International Conference on Technologies for Homeland Security (HST)* (IEEE, 2013), pp. 12–17
15. J. Pang, B. Greenstein, R. Gummadi, S. Seshan, D. Wetherall, 802.11 user fingerprinting, in *Proceedings of the 13th Annual ACM international Conference on Mobile Computing and Networking* (ACM Press, 2007), pp. 99–110
16. E. Shi, Y. Niu, M. Jakobsson, R. Chow, Implicit authentication through learning user behavior. Inf. Secur. 99–113 (2011) (Springer)
17. P. Juola, M. Ryan, P. Brennan, J. Noecker Jr., A. Stolerman, R. Greenstadt, Keyboard behavior based authentication for security, IT Professional (2013), p. 1
18. M. Abramson, D. Aha, What's in a URL? Genre classification from URLs, in *AAAI Workshop on Intelligent Techniques for Web Personalization and Recommendation (ITWP)* (2013)
19. M. Abramson, D. Aha, User authentication from web browsing behavior. Florida Artif. Intell. Soc. (FLAIRS-26), 268–273 (2013)
20. L. Rabiner, A tutorial on hidden Markov models and selected applications in speech recognition, in *Proceedings of the IEEE* (1989), pp. 257–286
21. M. Abramson, Learning temporal user profiles of web browsing behavior, in *6th ASE International Conference on Social Computing* (SocialCom '14), (2014)
22. J.A.P. Lafferty, A. McCallum, F. Pereira, Conditional random fields: probabilistic models for segmenting and labeling sequence data, in *International Conference on Machine Learning (ICML)* (2001)
23. D. Bell, L. LaPadula, *Secure Computer Systems: Mathematical Foundations* (MITRE Corporation, 1973)

24. D. Bell, Looking back at the Bell-LaPadula model, in *Proceedings of the 21st Annual Computer Security Applications Conference* (1976), pp. 337–351
25. DoD Trusted Computer System Evaluation Critieria, 5200.28-STD (1983/1985)
26. C. Shannon, A mathematical theory of communication. Bell Syst. Tech. J. **27**(3), 379–423 (1948)
27. I. Moskowitz, M. Kang, Covert channels here to stay?, in *Proceedings of the Ninth Annual Conference on Computer Assurance, COMPASS'94* (1994), pp. 235–243
28. I. Moskowitz, G. Longdon, L. Chang, A new paradign hidden in steganography, in *Proceedings of 2000 Workshop of New Security Paradigns* (ACM Press, 2000), pp. 41–50
29. D. Kahneman, A. Tversky, On the psychology of prediction. Psychol. Rev. **80**(4), 237–251 (1973)
30. T. Mahmood, F. Ricci, Improving recommender systems with adaptive conversational strategies, in *Hypertext* (ACM Press, 2000), pp. 73–82
31. M. Goebel, L. Gruenwald, A survey of data mining and knowledge discovery software tools. SIGKDD Explor. Newsl. **1**(1), 20–33 (1999)
32. J.W. Tukey, Exploratory data analysis (Addison-Wesley, Boston, 1977)
33. J. Herlocker, J. Konstan, L. Terveen, J. Riedl, Evaluating collaborative filtering recommender systems. ACM Trans. Inf. Syst. **22**(1), 5–53 (2004)
34. H. Simon, The new science of management decision (Prentice Hall PTR, 1977)
35. A. Endert, P. Fiaux, C. North, Semantic interaction for sensemaking: inferring analytical reasoning for model steering. IEEE Trans. Visual Comput. Graphics **18**(12), 2879–2888 (2012)
36. G. Petasis, F. Vichot, F. Wolinski, G. Paliouras, V. Karkaletsis, C. Spyropoulos, Using machine learning to maintain rule-based named-entity recognition and classification systems, in *39th Conference of Association for Computational Linguistics*, pp. 418–425
37. S. Chan, P. Treleaven, L. Capra, Continuous hyperparameter optimization for large-scale recommender systems, in *IEEE International Conference on Big Data* (2013), 350–358
38. J. Bergstra, Y. Bengio, Random search for hyperparameter optimization. J. Mach. Learn. Res. **13**(1), 281–305 (2012)
39. G. Adomavicius, D. Jannach, Special issue on context-aware recommender systems. User Model User-Adap. Inter, vol. 24, no. 1–2, pp. 1–5 (2014)
40. S.-M. Choi, S.-K. Ko, Y.-S. Han, A movie recommendation algorithm based on genre correlations. Expert Syst. Appl. **39**(9), 8079–8085 (2012)
41. M. Livingston, J. Decker, Z. Ai, Evaluation of multivariate visualization on a multivariate task. IEEE Trans. Visual. Comput. Graph. **18**(12) (2012, Dec)
42. R. Parasuraman, V. Riley, Humans and automation: use, misuse, disuse, abuse. Hum. Factors **39**, 230–253 (1997) doi:10.1518/001872097778543886
43. J. Gertler, US unmanned aerial systems (Library Of Congress Washington DC Congressional Research Service, 2012, Jan)
44. K. Williams, A summary of unmanned aircraft accident/incident data: human factors implications (No. DOT/FAA/AM-04/24). Federal Aviation Administration Oklahoma City, OK (2004)
45. Department of Defense, FY2009–2034 unmanned systems integrated roadmap (2009)
46. Office of Naval Research, Naval S&T strategic plan (Arlington, 2011)
47. J. Park, W. Jung, A study on the revision of the TACOM measure. IEEE Trans. Nucl. Sci. **54**(6), 2666–2676 (2007)
48. J. Beatty, B. Lucero-Wagoner, The pupillary system, in *Handbook of Psychophysiology*, ed. by J.T. Cacioppo, L.G. Tassinary, G.G. Berntson. 2 ed. (Cambridge University Press, 2000), pp. 142–162
49. C. Sibley, J. Coyne, C. Baldwin, Pupil dilation as an index of learning, in *Proceedings of the Human Factors and Ergonomics Society Annual Meeting* (Human Factors and Ergonomics Society, Las Vegas, 2011), pp. 237–241

50. N. Hjortskov, D. Rissén, A. Blangsted, N. Fallentin, U. Lundberg, K. Søgaard, The effect of mental stress on heart rate variability and blood pressure during computer work. Eur. J. Appl. Physiol. **92**, 84–89 (2004) doi:10.1007/s00421-004-1055-z
51. R. Ratwani, J. Mccurry, J. Trafton, Single operator, multiple robots: an eye movement based theoretic model of operator situation awareness, in *Proceedings of the 5th ACM/IEEE International Conference on Human-Robot Interaction* (IEEE, Osaka, Japan, 2010), pp. 235–242
52. R. Ratwani, J. McCurry, J. Trafton, Predicting postcompletion errors using eye movements, in *Proceedings of the SIGCHI Conference on Human Factors in Computing Systems*, pp. 539–542 (ACM Press, 2008)
53. M.L. Cummings, C.E. Nehme, Modeling the impact of workload in network centric supervisory control settings, in Neurocognitive and Physiological Factors During High-Tempo Operations (Ashgate Publishing Ltd, 2010), pp. 23–39
54. E. Blasch, S. Plano, Proactive decision fusion for site security, in *International Conference on Information Fusion* (2005)
55. http://www.dlib.org/dlib/september07/wolpers/09wolpers.html. Retrieved on 1 Nov 2013
56. A. Rath, D. Devaurs, S. Lindstaedt, UICO: an ontology-based user interaction context model for automatic task detection on the computer desktop, in *CIAO '09, Proceedings of the 1st Workshop on Context, Information and Ontologies* (ACM Press, 2009), p. 10

Part IV
Mathematical Characterization
of Context

Chapter 11
Supervising the Fusion Process by Context Analysis for Target Tracking

Vincent Nimier

Abstract We propose in this paper, a methodology for combining contextual information and sensors derived information to improve the process of data fusion. Even if this methodology can be used in different types of fusion processes (detection, classification, etc.), we focus here on a multisensor tracking one. The objective of this combination is to supervise the classical fusion process by context analysis so that this fusion process can adapt itself to the variations of the context.

Keywords Multisensor · Data fusion · Supervision · Tracking · Context analysis

11.1 Introduction

The latest developments in perception systems enhance the need for the joint use of multiple sensors. Indeed, the expected benefits are promising: a greater ability to analyze complex situations, and an increased robustness to the environment aliases. Applications for perception systems range from the industrial environment with assembly tasks, mobile robotics, to military domain and mainly in the field of C4ISR. The integration and fusion of heterogeneous information remains a process under investigation and can be considered as a very active research field. While conventional estimation and classification techniques, based on probability theory, have seen their scope expanded to subsume data fusion, the emergence of new and specific problems for multisensor systems has led research for new models to multiple source information processing. Among these alternatives, fuzzy logic [1] and the theory of Dempster–Shafer [2] have emerged as alternatives to Bayesian probability theory without replacing it. They allow to manipulating and processing information from heterogeneous and uncertain origins. Generically, if the probability theory is mainly used for modeling random phenomena, fuzzy logic is tuned

V. Nimier (✉)
Department of Information Processing and Modelling, ONERA,
BP 80100 Chemin de la Hunière et des Joncherettes, Châtillon FR-91123, France
e-mail: Vincent.Nimier@onera.fr

© Springer International Publishing Switzerland (outside the USA) 2016   271
L. Snidaro et al. (eds.), *Context-Enhanced Information Fusion*,
Advances in Computer Vision and Pattern Recognition,
DOI 10.1007/978-3-319-28971-7_11

toward the representation of human knowledge. Duality between these two theories can be used, including for a multisensor system. Indeed, the processed information obeys this same duality: random measurements from each sensor, and symbolic knowledge provided mainly by operators, are useful for the system from the conception to the use.

In the fields of detection and estimation, the proposed algorithms lay almost exclusively on a probabilistic modeling. In many of these algorithms, the probability density is assumed to be known and invariable. Moreover, the considered probability density is assumed to be context independent. However, this density is often dependent on the probability density of external conditions and varies according to these conditions. This is particularly true for multisensor systems. Indeed, if we consider, for example, a system composed of a camera operating in the visible domain and a radar, then the lack of information on the use time of the system, day or night, or on the expected altitude of the target, high or low, can affect directly the performance of the system. In the following, we will introduce a formal definition of context. We will then present the use of the contextual concept in the estimation process followed by the integration of the proposed concept in a multisensor fusion methodology for air target tracking.

In the last few years, the use of contextual information in data fusion knows a renewed interest. For example in [3], the authors list a wide variety of contextual information and develop their use at the different levels of JDL model. In [4], five different categories of contextual information are defined. These categories are the following: domain knowledge, environment to hardware processing, known distribution of entity, traffic behavior history, road information for traffic tracking. The contextual information used in this paper belongs to the first category of domain knowledge.

The ideas developed in this paper were first published by the author [5] in a French journal and a resumé was published in [6] in ISIF conference on data fusion. Some of the presented ideas were later used in [7, 8]. In these papers, the authors have shown that taking account of the context give better results for data fusion.

11.2   Definition of Contextual Information

We consider that a particular context can be identified by so-called "contextual" variables. The nature and origin of these variables are very diverse. One can consider measurements made by annexes sensors such as those measuring rainfall, pressure, or outdoor temperature, etc. Similarly an operator, through a man/machine interface, can give valuable information on operational conditions. Additional information measuring, for example SNR, the width of correlation peak, and other parameters or indicators that, in some cases, can assess the signal quality or indicate the operating status of each sensor, can be considered. Knowledge representation that describes the operating status of each sensor, and therefore the quality of the measurements it is capable of providing, is based on a description in terms of fuzzy logic [1]. This knowledge is established by the expert to assess the performance and limitations of each sensor by means of membership functions defined on contextual variables. Therefore, in a real situation, and knowing values for each contextual variable, the membership functions establish valid measurements from a selected set of sensors. Thus, it is possible to define the association of sensors measurements that are the best suited to a particular context, and to take only, into account in the estimation process, the measures resulting from this association.

11.3 Contextual Space

Taking into account the context appears as a fairly natural idea for a person in charge of the realization of a system. However, its effective implementation is not straightforward and often leads to the development of some system-related heuristics providing satisfactory results in spite of their dependence on the concerned application. There is, to our knowledge, no general methodology to formalize the problem. The formalism, we provide in this paper, allows to define a contextual space and to establish, on this space, logic to operate with the system. This logic is then used to oversee the estimation process.

11.3.1 Contextual Variable

Let S be a system composed by n sensors and Let z define a contextual variable, on a contextual space $Z \subseteq R^{n \times p}$ with $i \in \{1, \ldots, n\}$ and $j \in \{1, \ldots, p\}$ where p is the maximal number of contextual variables used by a sensor. For a sensor s_i his subset of contextual variable is a vector of the form $z_i = \{z_i^1, \ldots, z_i^q\}$ with $q \leq p$. As presented previously, z_i^j can be a measurement of the fog density, of the rainfall, of the SNR, etc. The unit of the contextual variable depends on the contextual environment, the mm/m^2, for the example, environment: rain. The contextual variable can be without unit if this variable is provided by some image or signal processing. This variable is associated with a sensor s_j. The "validity" of a sensor defines the fact that the sensor provides measurements in accordance to the model used in the estimation process. We define a membership function $\mu_i^j(z_i^j)$ on the value of z_i^j like Fig. 11.1.

In Fig. 11.1 we can see a membership function which defines the validity of the sensor s_i. In fact, for $z_i^j \in [0, s_1]$ the membership function is equal to 1. It follows that sensor s_i is valid, i.e., the measurements it provides correspond to the model being used in the estimation process. For $z_i^j \in [s_2, \infty]$ the sensor is not valid and the provided measurements do not correspond to the used model. For $z_i^j \in [s_1, s_2]$, we use a linear interpolation. If the sensor, as for example 2, has more than one contextual variable then its validity can be defined by a domain as shown in Fig. 11.2.

Fig. 11.1. Membership function of Fuzzy Set

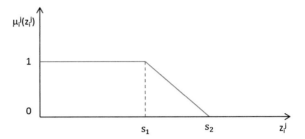

Fig. 11.2. Validity domain of sensor s_i in the space formed by two contextual variables

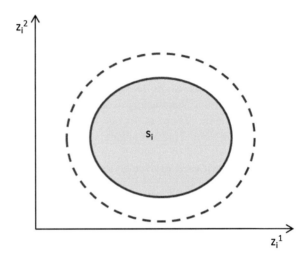

This domain is generally defined by human in accordance with his own expertise. It can also be defined through a learning base or experimental tests. The objective is to specify, once the contextual variable is found, the range of this variable corresponding to optimal sensor performances.

In Fig. 11.2, the blue zone defines the validity domain of the sensor s_i. It is the domain where the membership function $\mu_i(z_i^1, z_i^2) = 1$. The dotted line represents the border where the membership function $\mu_i(z_i^1, z_i^2) = 1$ changes from positive value to zero.

We can now extend the previous definition to the system S with n sensors $s_i, i \in \{1, \ldots, n\}$. Let define p the maximum number of contextual variables. For a system S, a context is defined by the values taken by the contextual matrix

$$z = \begin{bmatrix} z_1^1 & \cdots & z_1^r & 0 & \cdots & 0 \\ \cdots & & \cdots & & & \\ z_m^1 & & \cdots & & 0 & z_m^p \\ \cdots & & & & & \\ z_n^1 & & & z_n^q & 0 & 0 \end{bmatrix}$$

Fig. 11.3. Validity domains
of three sensors

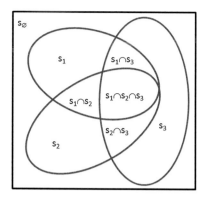

q and $r \leq p$. The validity of the context is given by the value taken by the membership function.

Let us consider a system with three sensors $S = \{s_1, s_2, s_3\}$.

Figure 11.3 shows the validity domains of $s_1, s_2,$ and s_3. For simplicity, and unlike in Fig. 11.2, we limited our drawing to the domain where the membership function is equal to 1. We can note that a new domain appears in the figure. This new domain, defined by $s_\varnothing$, is the domain where no sensor is valid.

For a classical multisensor fusion algorithm which does not take into account the context, the implicit assumption is that the context is favorable to all sensors.

In Fig. 11.4, the common domain of validity between sensors is presented in green.

From the given example, we can see that the domain of validity of a suite of sensors is smaller than the potential domain that we can have by considering the union of all sensors validity domains as given in Fig. 11.5.

Fig 11.4. Validity domains
for all three sensors

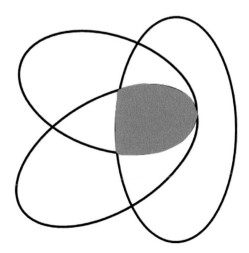

Fig. 11.5. The union of the three validity domains

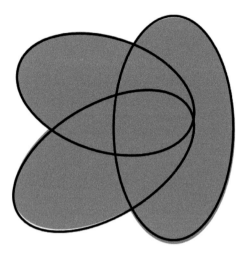

To build a multisensor system that has a domain of validity as given in Fig. 11.5, we have to identify precisely the context and to select well-performing sensor or subset of sensors in this context.

Let us define two types of validity domains: The first one is the inclusive validity domain that we note s_i (here, we take the same notation to name the sensor and its validity domain). It corresponds to the area shown in Fig. 11.2 where the sensor is valid without taking into account the properties of the other sensors of the system. The second definition is the exclusive validity domain s^i. It corresponds to the only domain where a sensor or a subset of sensors is valid while ascertaining the exclusion of all other domains. For example, the inclusive validity domain s_1 is given in Fig. 11.6a and the exclusive validity domain s^1 is given in Fig. 11.6b.

The logical relation between the exclusive and inclusive domains, for sensor 1 in a system with three sensors, is the following:

$$s^1 = s_1 \cap \overline{s_2} \cap \overline{s_3} \tag{11.1}$$

Furthermore, for the association of sensors $\{1,3\}$, the inclusive domain is given by the formula:

$$s^{\{1,3\}} = s_1 \cap \overline{s_2} \cap s_3 \tag{11.2}$$

For a system S with n sensors, let us define $2^S = \left\{ s^\varnothing, s^1, s^2, \ldots, s^{\{1,2\}}, \ldots, s^{\{1,2,\ldots,n\}} \right\}$ the set of exclusive validity domains of all possible combination of sensors. The general formula between inclusive and exclusive domains is given by:

$$s^J = \bigcap_{j \in J} s_j \bigcap_{i \in \overline{J}} \overline{s_i} \tag{11.3}$$

With $J \subseteq \{1, \ldots, n\}$.

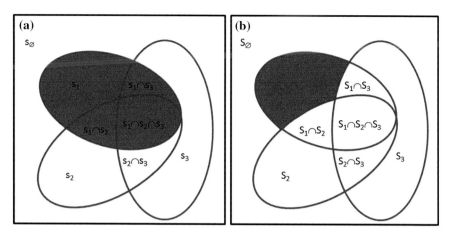

Fig 11.6. Definitions of validity domains. **a** Inclusive validity domain s_1. **b** Exclusive validity domain s^1

We can note that $s^{\varnothing} = \bar{s}_1 \cap \bar{s}_2 \cap \cdots \cap \bar{s}_n$ represents the absence of any valid sensor.

11.3.2 Probability of a Sensor or a Subset of Sensors Validity

In the following, we explain how to calculate the probability of a sensor association given the context analysis. This probability will then be used to represent the sensor adaptation to the situation. For this, we define the probability of the event "the sensor s_i is valid" when the membership function is specified with a binary logic and we define the probability of a fuzzy event "the sensor s_i is valid" when the sensor validity domain is defined by the membership function of a fuzzy set. In the case of many sensors, we define the probability of a group of sensors. Two cases with two types of probability can be defined therefore: The first one is the inclusive probability of the group in reference to the inclusive domain of validity. The second one is the exclusive probability of the group in reference to the exclusive validity domain.

11.3.2.1 Binary Logic

In binary logic, the validity domain s_i on Z, where Z is the contextual space, can be represented by a binary function $I_i(z)$ where the variable z is composed of p elementary contextual variables z_i^j. This binary function can take the value 1 for the values of z where the sensor i is valid and 0 elsewhere. We consider that the global binary function $I_i(z)$ is given by the relation:

$$I_i(z) = I_i^1(z) \wedge \cdots \wedge I_i^p(z) \tag{11.4}$$

with binary function $I_i^j(z)$ defining the validity of sensor i for the contextual variable z_i^j. We take the hypothesis that $I_i^j(z) = 1$ if z_i^j does not carry information on the validity of the sensor. Most of the contextual variables are in fact measurements from other sensors like humidity, temperature, etc., or estimates following the processing of the signal of interest (SNR, correlation pick width, etc.). It follows that z can be considered as a stochastic vector with a probability density given by: $p(z|z_m)$. Where z_m is the measured vector of the contextual variables. To take into account this uncertainty in the evaluation of the validity of a sensor, we can calculate the probability for a sensor to be valid. This probability is given by the relation:

$$P(s_i|z_m) = \int I_i(z)p(z|z_m)\mathrm{d}z \tag{11.5}$$

If we know the value of the contextual vector z_m, we can evaluate the probability $P(s_i|z_m)$ of the sensor validity.

11.3.2.2 Fuzzy Logic

The fuzzy logic provides an additional shade in the representation of the validity domains of a sensor. Indeed, in binary logic the limits used to define the range of the validity domain are often arbitrary. This arbitrary nature can be relaxed by replacing the binary function $I_i(z)$ by a membership function $\mu_i(z)$ which takes its values in the interval [0 1].

Figure 11.7 shows the difference between a binary function and a membership function. As above if we have p contextual variables then the membership function of the sensor i can be written as

$$\mu_i(z) = \mu_i^1(z) \wedge \cdots \wedge \mu_i^p(z) \tag{11.6}$$

Knowing this membership function and the probability density of the measurement vector, we can define the probability of a fuzzy event "the sensor is valid" by:

$$P(s_i|z_m) = \int \mu_i(z)p(z|z_m)\mathrm{d}z \tag{11.7}$$

where z_m is the measured contextual variable. The definition of the probability of a fuzzy event is given by Zadeh [9]. When the uncertainty relating to the measurement of a contextual variable is insignificant we can replace probability density $p(z|z_m)$ by a Dirac $\delta(z - z_m)$ such that the validity probability of the sensor is given by the value of the membership function at the measured contextual variable

Fig. 11.7. Membership function

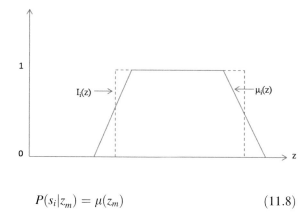

$$P(s_i|z_m) = \mu(z_m) \tag{11.8}$$

When the contextual variables are independent, and taking the operator min as a conjunctive operator, the previous equation can be written as follows:

$$P(s_i|z_m) = \int \min(\mu_i^1(z_1), \ldots, \mu_i^p(z_p))p(z|z_m)dz_1\ldots dz_p \tag{11.9}$$

11.3.3   Inclusive Validity Probability of a Group of Sensors

Several sensors can be associated. The inclusive validity probability of this group of sensors is equal to the probability of the associated fuzzy event.

For $J \subseteq \{1,\ldots,n\}$, the inclusive probability is given by

$$P\left(\bigcap_{i\in J} s_i|z_m\right) = \int \min(\mu_i^1(z_1), \ldots, \mu_i^p(z_p))p(z|z_m)dz_1\ldots dz_p \tag{11.10}$$

11.3.4   Exclusive Validity Probability of a Group of Sensors

Once the inclusive validity probability is defined we can define the exclusive validity probability. It is given by the formula

$$\beta_J = P(s^J) = \sum_{\{I \subseteq N / J \subseteq I\}} (-1)^{|I-J|} P\left(\bigcap_{i\in I} s_i\right) \tag{11.11}$$

where $\beta_\varnothing = P(s^\varnothing) = P(\bigcap_{i\in N} \bar{s}_i)$ with $N = \{1,\ldots,n\}$.

The symbols I and J are subsets of the set N. The notation $|I - J|$ defines the cardinality of the subset $I - J$. For the sake of simplicity, we have omitted to write the conditional by measured variable z_m in the probability term. $P(s^J)$ must be read as $P(s^J|z_m)$. There is as many probability expressions as there are elements in N that means 2^n. The probability β_J verifies the following condition:

$$\sum_{J \subseteq N \cup \emptyset} \beta_J = 1 \tag{11.12}$$

11.4 Estimation Taking Account of the Context

The probabilities, we have defined above, are used to evaluate the validity of all possible grouping of sensors. In this way, they are used to validate the measurements provided by a group of sensors forming the association of sensors being evaluated. When several associations are valid at the same time, the fusion result is the weighted mean of the estimates provided by the different associations with weightings equal to the probabilities of associations.

In the following, we distinguish two situations for the estimation: a static one where the estimates depend on the present time and a dynamic one, where the present estimates depend on previous ones.

11.4.1 Static Estimation

11.4.1.1 Problem Formulation

We will study a system with n sensors, each of them providing a measurement y_i with $i \in N$. The observation equation, for each sensor i, is defined by

$$\mathbf{y}_i = H_i(\mathbf{x}, \mathbf{b}_i) \tag{11.13}$$

where $H_i, i \in N = \{1 \ldots n\}$ defines the observation function and $\mathbf{b}_i$ is the noise of the sensor.

In the following we consider that the noise is white Gaussian, with mean equals to zero and with variance $E(\mathbf{b}_i \mathbf{b}_j^T) = \mathbf{R}_i \delta_{ij}$, where δ is the Kronecker symbol. Vector $\mathbf{Y}^T = \{\mathbf{y}_1, \ldots, \mathbf{y}_n\}$, where T is the transpose operator that defines the set of all measurements.

11.4.1.2   Estimation Equation

The optimal mean square estimate of the state $\mathbf{x}$ is given by the relation:

$$\hat{\mathbf{x}} = E(\hat{\mathbf{x}}|\mathbf{Y}) = \int \mathbf{x}p(\mathbf{x}|\mathbf{Y})d\mathbf{x} \qquad (11.14)$$

We can expand the probability $p(x|Y)$ in the following form:

$$p(\mathbf{x}|\mathbf{Y}) = \sum_{J \subseteq N \cup \varnothing} p(\mathbf{x}, s^J)P(s^J) \qquad (11.15)$$

There is 2^n probabilities $p(\mathbf{x}|\mathbf{Y}, s^J)$ taking account of all possible sensors associations. The estimate of x which takes account of the context is obtained by substituting the probability $p(\mathbf{x}|\mathbf{Y})$ in (11.14) by its value given in (11.15).

$$\hat{\mathbf{x}} = P(s^\varnothing) \int \mathbf{x}p(\mathbf{x}|\mathbf{Y}, s^\varnothing)d\mathbf{x} + \sum_{J \subseteq N} P(s^J)E(\mathbf{x}|\mathbf{Y}, s^J) \qquad (11.16)$$

The conditioning by s^J in the probability expression means that only sensors that have theirs suffixes in J are valid. Therefore, only the measurements corresponding to these sensors must be taken into account. We note $\mathbf{Y}_J = \{\mathbf{y}_i\}$ for $i \in J$ the subset of measurements provided by sensors which have suffix in J. The relation (11.16) can be written as

$$\hat{\mathbf{x}} = \hat{\mathbf{x}}_\varnothing \beta_\varnothing + \sum_{J \subseteq N} \beta_J E(\mathbf{x}|\mathbf{Y}_J, s^J) \qquad (11.17)$$

The coefficients β^J are given in the relation (11.11). The variable $\hat{\mathbf{x}}_\varnothing$ that appears in the relation (11.17) is given by the relation:

$$\hat{\mathbf{x}}_\varnothing = \int \mathbf{x}p(\mathbf{x}|\mathbf{Y}, s^\varnothing)d\mathbf{x} \qquad (11.18)$$

Because $s^\varnothing$ means that no sensor is valid, so $\mathbf{Y}_\varnothing$ is empty. The state $\hat{\mathbf{x}}_\varnothing$ represents the a priori value when no measurement is available. In case of the lack of a priori value, the relation (11.17) takes the following form:

$$\hat{\mathbf{x}} = \frac{\sum_{J \subseteq N} \beta_J E(\mathbf{x}|\mathbf{Y}_J, s^J)}{1 - \beta_\varnothing} \qquad (11.19)$$

Each probability β_J is divided by $1 - \beta_\varnothing$ so that the normalization condition is maintained.

11.4.1.3 Remark

In force operations, operational intelligence staff uses two coefficients to evaluate the trueness of information. The first coefficient is the credibility of the information and the second one is the reliability of the source that gives the information. The fusion approach that is presented in this paper can be viewed in the same manner. The credibility of the information is represented by the probability a posteriori of the state $p(\mathbf{x}|\mathbf{Y}, s^J)$ and the reliability of the source, in our case it is a subset of sources, by the probability $P(s^J)$. Equations (11.15) or (11.16) give a rule to combine credibility of information and reliability of a source. In [10] a literature survey of the use of reliability in data fusion can be found.

11.4.1.4 Example

The following example illustrates the proposed formulation. We consider a system with two sensors: a radar noted s_1 and a visible light camera noted s_2. Two parameters are used to identify the context: z_1 is an internal parameter of the radar and z_1 is a parameter which measures the luminosity. The two membership functions defining the validity domains of both sensors are noted $\mu_1^1(z_1)$ and $\mu_2^2(z_2)$

For this system the formula (11.11) gives the following probability:

$$
\begin{aligned}
\beta_{\{\varnothing\}} &= P(\overline{s_1} \cap \overline{s_2}) = P(s^{\varnothing}) \\
\beta_{\{1\}} &= P(s_1) - P(s_1 \cap s_2) \\
\beta_{\{2\}} &= P(s_2) - P(s_1 \cap s_2) \\
\beta_{\{1,2\}} &= P(s_1 \cap s_2)
\end{aligned}
\tag{11.20}
$$

If we suppose that observation equations of the two sensors are linear:

$$
\begin{aligned}
y_1 &= x + b_1 \\
y_2 &= x + b_2
\end{aligned}
\tag{11.21}
$$

where b_1 and b_2 are additive, independent Gaussian noises, with means equal to zero and with variances σ_1^2 and σ_2^2, respectively. Under the assumption that the a priori probability density is uniform, the different estimates are:

$$
\begin{aligned}
E(x|y_1) &= y_1 \\
E(x|y_1) &= y_1
\end{aligned}
\tag{11.22}
$$

$$
E(x|\{y_1, y_2\}) = y_1 \frac{\sigma_2^2}{\sigma_1^2 + \sigma_2^2} + y_2 \frac{\sigma_1^2}{\sigma_1^2 + \sigma_2^2}
\tag{11.23}
$$

Moreover, we consider that

$$E(x|\varnothing) = x_\varnothing \qquad (11.24)$$

$x_\varnothing$ defines the default value of x when none of the sensors is valid.

The global estimator is given by the formula (11.17). We have replaced the probability terms β^J by their values given by the relation (11.20) and the estimates by their values given by (11.22), (11.23), (11.24). The result is given by the following relation:

$$\hat{x} = P(s) + y_1\left[P(s_1) - \frac{\sigma_1^2}{\sigma_1^2 + \sigma_2^2}P(s_1 \cap s_2)\right] + y_2\left[P(s_2) - \frac{\sigma_2^2}{\sigma_1^2 + \sigma_2^2}P(s_1 \cap s_2)\right]$$

$$(11.25)$$

If we consider that measurement errors are negligible, it follows that the probability densities of contextual variable can be replaced by Dirac functions. The inclusive probability is therefore, for each association of sensors, given by

$$\begin{aligned}
P(s_\varnothing) &= \mathrm{Min}(1 - \mu_1^1(z_1); 1 - \mu_2^2(z_2)) \\
P(s_1) &= \mu_1^1(z_1) \\
P(s_2) &= \mu_2^2(z_2) \\
P(s_1 \cap s_2) &= \mathrm{Min}(\mu_1^1(z_1); \mu_2^2(z_2))
\end{aligned} \qquad (11.26)$$

In the following, we consider the study of four special cases:

Case 1: For $\mu_1^1(z_1) = \mu_2^2(z_2) = 1$ the context is in favor of the use of all sensors. Replacing $\mu_1^1(z_1)$ and $\mu_2^2(z_2)$ in formula (11.26), and using the derived probability value (11.25), we obtain:

$$\hat{x} = E(x|\{y_1, y_2\}) = y_1\frac{\sigma_2^2}{\sigma_1^2 + \sigma_2^2} + y_2\frac{\sigma_1^2}{\sigma_1^2 + \sigma_2^2} \qquad (11.27)$$

This result is in accordance with the classical result we obtain in data fusion when the context is not considered.

Case 2: For these conditions $\mu_1^1(z_1) = 0$ and $\mu_2^2(z_2) = 1$, sensor 1 is not valid while sensor 2 is a valid one. Using the conditions values in Eqs. (11.25) and (11.26), we obtain the following result:

$$\hat{x} = y_2 \qquad (11.28)$$

The only information considered is the one provided by sensor 2. This result is in accordance with the concept of an adaptive system: The measurement provided by a nonvalid sensor, sensor 1, is rejected.

Case 3: An intermediate situation is given by $\mu_1^1(z_1) = 0.5$ and $\mu_2^2(z_2) = 1$. Sensor 1 is partially invalid. The estimate of x is given by

$$\hat{x} = y_1 \frac{0.5\sigma_2^2}{\sigma_1^2 + \sigma_2^2} + y_2 \frac{\sigma_1^2 + 0.5\sigma_2^2}{\sigma_1^2 + \sigma_2^2} \tag{11.29}$$

We can see a more important weight given to the measurement from sensor 2 than to the one from sensor 1.

Case 4: For $\mu_1^1(z_1) = 0$ and $\mu_2^2(z_2) = 0$. This limit case is reached when none of the sensors is valid. The only possible estimate is given by the a priori value we have $x_\varnothing$. In this static estimation the a priori value is arbitrary (we can choose a possible value). In a dynamic estimation, a judicious value to be taken is the prediction of the state as we will see in the next paragraph.

Remark The estimate $E(x|\{y_1, y_2\})$ given in case 1 is the classical and optimal formula for data fusion. This is no more than a weighted mean that favors the measurement of the more accurate sensor and not of the more reliable one. Furthermore, the variance of the estimate is the following:

$$\sigma_{\hat{x}}^2 = \frac{\sigma_1^2 \sigma_2^2}{\sigma_1^2 + \sigma_2^2} \tag{11.30}$$

This variance is always smaller than the variance associated with each sensor. By fusing data we have a gain in accuracy. This gain is maximum when the two sensors have the same variance σ^2.

Moreover, a multisensor system is often composed of sensors that have very different resolutions (camera, radar, etc.) which leads also to very different variances. The estimate variance, in this case, is very close to the variance of the sensor with the best resolution. The most important gain with a multisensor system, which is not attainable by a unique sensor, is a gain in reliability. This gain is obtained based on the fact that the system is composed of sensors using different physical phenomena (IR, electromagnetics, acoustics, etc.). These phenomena are rarely disrupted at the same time. But as we have shown previously, a supervision process must be implemented to ensure a best potential use of all sensors.

The algorithm outline is presented in Fig. 11.8. There are two levels of processing. The high level is the context analysis. Based on membership function defined by human experts, the parameters z_j obtained, for example, from an external sensor (humidity, temperature, etc.) and z_j obtained from an internal sensor parameter or from signal processing (SNR, pic correlation width, etc.) are analyzed to define the context. As a result of this analysis, the coefficients β^k are transmitted to the low-level processing to weight different associations of sensors.

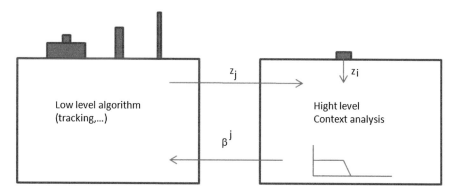

Fig. 11.8. Algorithm outline

11.4.2 Dynamic Estimation

11.4.2.1 Problem Formulation

In this part we will address the problem of tracking a target with a system composed of n sensors.

We note $\mathbf{x}_k$ the state vector at the time k. The dynamic model is supposed to be linear and invariant with equation:

$$\mathbf{x}_k = \mathbf{F}\mathbf{x}_{k-1} + \mathbf{v}_k \tag{11.31}$$

F is the state transition matrix. The noise $\mathbf{v}_k$ is a Gaussian stochastic process, with zero mean and covariance matrix $E\left(\mathbf{v}_i \mathbf{v}_j^T\right) = \mathbf{Q}\delta_{ij}$, where δ is the Kronecker symbol. We have n observation equations:

$$\mathbf{y}_k^i = \mathbf{H}_i \mathbf{x}_k + \mathbf{b}_k^i \tag{11.32}$$

with $i \in N = \{1, \ldots, n\}$ as the number of the sensor. The matrices $\mathbf{H}_1 \ldots \mathbf{H}_n$ are the n observation matrices, one for each sensor. The observation noise, $\mathbf{b}_k^i$ is Gaussian with zero mean and with covariance matrix $E\left(\mathbf{b}_k^i \mathbf{b}_l^j\right) = \mathbf{R}\delta_{kl}\delta_{ij}$. The set of measurements provided by the sensor i up to the time k is denoted as $\mathbf{Y}_k^i = \left\{\mathbf{y}_l^i\right\}_{l=1}^{l=k}$ and the set of all measurements from all the sensors is denoted as $\mathbf{Y}_k = \left\{\mathbf{Y}_l^i\right\}_{l=1}^{l=k}$. Moreover for all subsets $J \subseteq N$, we define $\mathbf{Y}_k^J = \left\{\mathbf{Y}_k^i\right\}_{i \in J}$ the set of measurements up to k provided by the association of sensor identified by J.

11.4.2.2   Equation of the Filter

Update Equation for an Association of Sensors Without Taking Account of the Context

For an association of sensors whose suffix are elements of J, the estimate is given by

$$\hat{\mathbf{x}}^J_{k/k} = E(\mathbf{x}_k|\mathbf{Y}^J_k) \qquad (11.33)$$

The resulting update equation of this estimate is the update equation for data fusion [4, 11]. The optimal estimate at time k is provided by the relation:

$$\hat{\mathbf{x}}^J_{k/k} = \hat{\mathbf{x}}^J_{k/k-1} + \sum_{i \in J} \mathbf{K}^i_J(k)(\mathbf{y}^i_k - \mathbf{H}_i \hat{\mathbf{x}}^J_{k/k-1}) \qquad (11.34)$$

where $\mathbf{K}^i_J$ is the Kalman gain associated with sensor i belonging to the set of sensors J. Given that Kalman equations for a multisensor system are easier and expressed in the information form, in the following, we consider the information presentation. However, when implementing the filter, the preferable form is the sequential one that we will present in the simulation section of the paper. The Kalman gain is defined by

$$\mathbf{K}^i_J(k) = \mathbf{P}_J(k/k)\mathbf{H}^{\mathrm{T}}_i\mathbf{R}^{-1}_i \qquad (11.35)$$

The covariance matrix $\mathbf{P}_J(k|k)$ is given by the formula:

$$\mathbf{P}^{-1}_J(k/k) = \mathbf{P}^{-1}_J(k/k-1) + \sum_{i \in J} \mathbf{H}^{\mathrm{T}}_i\mathbf{R}^{-1}_i\mathbf{H}_i \qquad (11.36)$$

For a system composed with n sensors the Kalman equations are the same as above, we have just to substitute J by N.

Update Equation for an Association of Sensors with Context Information

Now, considering all possible associations of sensors J with $J \subseteq N \cup \{\varnothing\}$, we derive the expression for a global estimate. The estimate is given by

$$\hat{\mathbf{x}}_{k/k} = E(\mathbf{x}_k|\mathbf{Y}_k) \qquad (11.37)$$

To take into account the context we develop the following formula:

$$\hat{\mathbf{x}}_{k/k} = \mathbf{x}^{\varnothing}_k\beta_{\varnothing}(k) + \sum_{J \subseteq N} \beta_J(k)E(x_k|Y^J_k) \qquad (11.38)$$

The global estimate is composed of elementary estimates provided by the association of sensors. When none of the sensors is valid, we consider the prediction $\hat{\mathbf{x}}_{k/k-1}$ as the a priori knowledge. In (11.38) the elementary estimates $E(\mathbf{x}_k|\mathbf{Y}_k^J)$ can be substituted by their values given in (11.34) where each elementary prediction $\hat{\mathbf{x}}_{k/k-1}^J$ of the association of sensor J is replaced by the global prediction $\hat{\mathbf{x}}_{k/k-1}$. The relation (11.38) can then be written as follows:

$$\hat{\mathbf{x}}_{k/k} = \hat{\mathbf{x}}_{k/k-1} + \sum_{J \subseteq N} \sum_{i \in J} \beta_J(k)\mathbf{K}_J^i(k)(\mathbf{y}_k^i - \mathbf{H}_i\hat{\mathbf{x}}_{k/k-1}) \qquad (11.39)$$

This last relation can be simplified by considering the following notation:

$$\mathbf{K}_i(k) = \sum_{\{J/i \in J\}} \beta_J(k)\mathbf{K}_J^i(k) \qquad (11.40)$$

$\{J/i \in J\}$ defines the set of all associations of sensors containing sensor i. Equation (11.40) can then be formulated as follows:

$$\hat{\mathbf{x}}_{k/k} = \hat{\mathbf{x}}_{k/k-1} + \sum_{i \in N} \mathbf{K}_i(k)(\mathbf{y}_k^i - \mathbf{H}_i\hat{\mathbf{x}}_{k/k-1}) \qquad (11.41)$$

The covariance matrix is given by the relation:

$$\mathbf{P}(k/k) = \sum_{J \subseteq N \cup \{\varnothing\}} \beta_J(k)[\mathbf{P}_J(k/k) + \left(\hat{\mathbf{x}}_{k/k} - \hat{\mathbf{x}}_{k/k}^J\right)\left(\hat{\mathbf{x}}_{k/k} - \hat{\mathbf{x}}_{k/k}^J\right)^{\mathrm{T}}] \qquad (11.42)$$

which is similar to the covariance matrix expression of a Gaussian mixture. The matrix $\mathbf{P}_J(k/k)$ is the covariance matrix of the elementary estimate $\hat{\mathbf{x}}_{k/k}^J$ obtained following the association of sensors J.

Finally with the updated state and covariance, the prediction equations are classically given by

$$\hat{\mathbf{x}}_{k+1/k} = F\hat{\mathbf{x}}_{k/k} \quad \text{and} \quad \mathbf{P}(k+1/k) = F\mathbf{P}(k/k)F^{\mathrm{T}} + \mathbf{Q} \qquad (11.43)$$

11.4.2.3 Algorithm

Although the previous equations can be directly implemented with any programming language, in data fusion, we often prefer the sequential form of the filter. First, this form is easier to implement and second it is well appropriate for asynchronous sensors. In the sequel, the sequential version of the algorithm is presented following two forms: with and without taking into account the context.

For simplicity, we consider a system composed of three sensors. The generalization of the algorithm to a system composed of n sensors is straightforward.

Fusion Algorithm Without the Context Information

We consider here the sequential form of the Kalman filter for a synchronous system. The state equations for a system S composed of three sensors are the following:

$$S \begin{cases} \mathbf{x}_k = \mathbf{F}\mathbf{x}_{k-1} + \mathbf{v}_k & \text{Dynamics} \\ \mathbf{y}_k^1 = \mathbf{H}_1\mathbf{x}_k + \mathbf{b}_k^1 & \text{Sensor 1} \\ \mathbf{y}_k^2 = \mathbf{H}_2\mathbf{x}_k + \mathbf{b}_k^2 & \text{Sensor 2} \\ \mathbf{y}_k^3 = \mathbf{H}_3 x_k + \mathbf{b}_k^3 & \text{Sensor 3} \end{cases}$$

An equivalent form of this system of equations is given by

$$S_1 \begin{cases} \mathbf{x}_k^1 = \mathbf{F}\mathbf{x}_{k-1}^1 + \mathbf{v}_k & \text{Dynamics} \\ \mathbf{y}_k^1 = \mathbf{H}_1\mathbf{x}_k + \mathbf{b}_k^1 & \text{Sensor 1} \end{cases}$$

$$S_2 \begin{cases} \mathbf{x}_k^2 = \mathbf{F}\mathbf{x}_{k-1}^1 & \text{Dynamics} \\ \mathbf{y}_k^2 = \mathbf{H}_2\mathbf{x}_k + \mathbf{b}_k^2 & \text{Sensor 2} \end{cases}$$

$$S_3 \begin{cases} \mathbf{x}_k^3 = \mathbf{F}\mathbf{x}_{k-1}^2 & \text{Dynamics} \\ \mathbf{y}_k^3 = \mathbf{H}_3\mathbf{x}_k + \mathbf{b}_k^3 & \text{Sensor 3} \end{cases}$$

This decomposition allows the processing in four consecutive steps. The first one, corresponding to s_1, is the prediction step. The second one is the estimation of an intermediate state $\mathbf{x}_k^1$. The third step, corresponding to s_2, allows the estimation of a second intermediate state $\mathbf{x}_k^2$. The last step, corresponding to s_3, allows the estimation of the global state $\mathbf{x}_k$.

Step 1
From the estimated state given by the $k - 1$ iteration, the prediction is given by the classical Eq. (11.43) above.

Step 2
The prediction is updated based on the formula

$$\hat{\mathbf{x}}_{k/k}^1 = \hat{\mathbf{x}}_{k/k-1} + \mathbf{K}_1(k)(\mathbf{y}_k^1 - \mathbf{H}_1\hat{\mathbf{x}}_{k/k-1})$$

and

$$\mathbf{P}_1(k/k) = (\mathbf{I} - \mathbf{K}_1(k)\mathbf{H}_1)\mathbf{P}(k/k-1)$$

with

$$\mathbf{K}_1(k) = \mathbf{P}(k/k-1)\mathbf{H}_1^{\mathsf{T}}(\mathbf{H}_1\mathbf{P}(k/k-1)\mathbf{H}_1^{\mathsf{T}} + \mathbf{R}_1)^{-1}$$

Step 3

$$\mathbf{P}_1(k/k)$$

Considering s_2, the prediction is simply obtained by substituting the predicted state $\hat{\boldsymbol{x}}_{k/k}$ by $\hat{\boldsymbol{x}}_{k/k}^1$ and $\mathbf{P}(k/k)$ by $\mathbf{P}_1(k/k)$ and updating the state and the covariance matrix. The Kalman gain is now

$$\boldsymbol{K}_2(k) = \boldsymbol{P}_1(k/k)\boldsymbol{H}_2^{\mathsf{T}}(\boldsymbol{H}_2\boldsymbol{P}_1(k/k)\boldsymbol{H}_2^{\mathsf{T}} + \boldsymbol{R}_2)^{-1}$$

Step 4
This step is the same as the previous one but now we substitute $\hat{\boldsymbol{x}}_{k/k}^1$ by $\hat{\boldsymbol{x}}_{k/k}^2$ and $\mathbf{P}_1(k/k)$ by $\mathbf{P}_2(k/k)$. The Kalman gain is now

$$\boldsymbol{K}_3(k) = \boldsymbol{P}_2(k/k)\boldsymbol{H}_3^{\mathsf{T}}(\boldsymbol{H}_3\boldsymbol{P}_2(k/k)\boldsymbol{H}_3^{\mathsf{T}} + \boldsymbol{R}_3)^{-1}$$

Remark In each update step (2, 3, 4), the noise covariance matrix $\mathbf{R}_i$ of the associate sensor is taken into account in the Kalman gain. It is this covariance matrix that weights more or less the measurement of the sensors. More the covariance of a sensor is important (the trace of the matrix is big) less the measurement of this sensor will be taken into account in the fusion process. It is a first approach to adapt the fusion algorithm to the deterioration in the sensor performances. The principle is to calculate the covariance matrix of the noise regularly for each sensor and to take into account the new covariance matrix in computing the Kalman gain. However, this method is not sufficient because it is possible to calculate a good covariance matrix with a sensor that is providing false information.

Fusion Algorithm Taking Account of the Context

The proposed algorithm is based on the previously presented algorithm with the main difference that we must calculate $2^n - 1$ estimates for a system with n sensors instead of n as it was the case in the previous algorithm. Each estimate corresponds to an association of sensors. The combinatorial should not be an obstacle because in general a multisensor system is composed of a limited number of sensors (two to three sensors).

We will describe here five steps for the processing. The first step is still dedicated to the prediction. The following three steps are for computing estimate for different association of sensors. The fifth step is the step that allows to take into account the context ion assigning to the different associations of sensor 1 probability and by computing a weighted mean of the estimates.

Step 1

Like the preceding algorithm, this step is used to predict the estimate and the covariance matrix. From the estimate computed at the preceding iteration $\hat{x}_{k-1/k-1}$ and $\mathbf{P}(k-1/k-1)$ this step compute the prediction $\hat{x}_{k/k-1}$ and $\mathbf{P}(k/k-1)$ thanks to the formula (11.44).

Step 2

In this step the predicted state and covariance matrix are updated by the three measurements $\mathbf{y}_k^i$ provided by the three sensors in order to obtain three estimated states $\hat{\mathbf{x}}_{k/k}^i$ and $\mathbf{P}_i(k/k)$ with $i \in \{1, 2, 3\}$. Each state and covariance matrix will be used in Step 3 for the second phase of the estimation.

Step 3

The fusion of all couples of sensors is computed. In the case treated in this article there are three couples: $\{1, 2\}$, $\{1, 3\}$, $\{2, 3\}$. For the couple $\{1, 2\}$, for example, we note the estimate $\hat{\mathbf{x}}_{k/k}^{12}$ and its covariance matrix $\mathbf{P}_{12}(k/k)$. To compute this estimate and this covariance matrix we simply take the estimate $\hat{\mathbf{x}}_{k/k}^1$ and the $\mathbf{P}_1(k/k)$ and update them with the measurement $\mathbf{y}_k^2$ and the noise covariance $\mathbf{R}^2$ provided by sensor 2. For the couple $\{1, 3\}$ we take the estimate $\hat{\mathbf{x}}_{k/k}^1$ and the covariance matrix $\mathbf{P}_1(k/k)$ and we update them by considering the measurement and covariance matrix of sensor 3. For the couple $\{2, 3\}$ it is the same approach as previous: the state $\hat{\mathbf{x}}_{k/k}^2$ and the covariance matrix $\mathbf{P}_2(k/k)$ are updated by the measurement and its noise $\mathbf{R}^3$ provided by sensor 3.

Step 4

At this level, the global fusion of the three sensors corresponding to the subset $\{1, 2, 3\}$ is made. We can take one of the three states computed in the preceding step and update it by the measurement from the sensor that is not already contributing to the update of the selected state. For example, if we take the state $\hat{\mathbf{x}}_{k/k}^{12}$ and its covariance matrix $\mathbf{P}_{12}(k/k)$, we update them by the measurement $\mathbf{y}_k^3$ and the covariance matrix $\mathbf{R}^3$ in order to obtain $\hat{\mathbf{x}}_{k/k}^{123}$ and $\mathbf{P}_{123}(k/k)$. The order of the indices does not matter. In fact $\hat{\mathbf{x}}_{k/k}^{123} = \hat{\mathbf{x}}_{k/k}^{231} = \hat{\mathbf{x}}_{k/k}^{312}$.

Step 5

This fifth step introduces the context in the computation of the estimate. At the time of the estimation each contextual variable has a value which allows to compute, thanks to the membership function of the fuzzy set, the coefficients $\beta_J(k)$. These coefficients are used to compute the global estimate $\hat{\mathbf{x}}_{k/k}$ and the global covariance $\mathbf{P}(k/k)$ based on the formulae (11.41), (11.42), (11.43).

11.5 Simulation

11.5.1 Simulation Conditions

The purpose of the following simulation is to fuse the measurements provided by a system consisting of three sensors. The first sensor which provides measurement y1 is a search radar with poor resolution but this sensor is never jammed or deceived. The second sensor which provides measurement y2 is a tracking radar which is jammed in the time interval [75, 125]. The third sensor is an IR camera providing measurement y3 which is an IR camera. In Fig. 11.9, we can see some decoys between time 20 and time 120.

The measurement y1 has a Gaussian noise with standard deviation $\sigma_1 = 6$. The measurements y2 and y3 have equal Gaussian noises with standard deviation $\sigma_2 = \sigma_3 = 2$. Between time 75 and time 125 we add a noise with a standard deviation $\sigma_2 = 10$ to the measurement y2. To simulate a jamming between time 20 and time 120 we add randomly, in time, a peak with a Gaussian amplitude and a standard deviation $\sigma_2 = 20$ to simulate a decoy.

On the tracking radar, a parameter z_2 can indicate the instant when the radar is jammed. For example, z_2 can be the SNR ratio and when this ratio is under a certain value z_m then $\mu_2(z_m) = 0$. The membership function of the fuzzy set on this parameter takes the values given in Fig. 11.10.

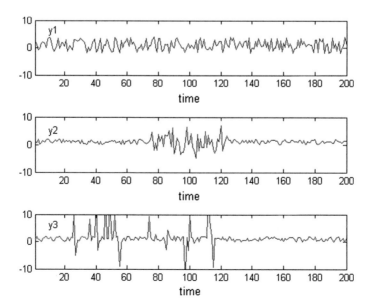

Fig. 11.9. Measurements of the sensors, the Y-axis is given in radians and the X-axis is the time in seconds

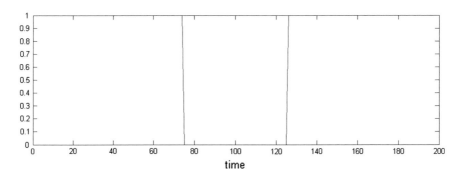

Fig. 11.10. Time evolution of $\mu_2(z_2)$, the X-axis is the time in seconds and the Y-axis is a logical value without dimension

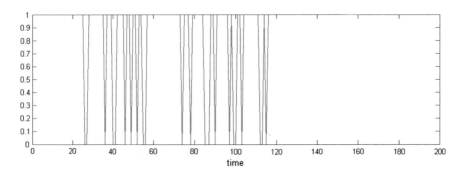

Fig. 11.11. Time evolution of $\mu_3(z_3)$, the X-axis is the time in seconds and the Y-axis is a logical value without dimension

For the detection of the decoy, the parameter z_3 is used and the fuzzy set function on this parameter takes the values given in Fig. 11.11. The parameter z_3 can be a parameter score given by image processing and when the score is under a limit z_1 then $\mu_3(z_1) = 0$. We do not describe what the contextual variables are nor does their membership function because it is very application dependent.

11.5.2 *Results*

The results of the simulation are given in the following figures:

In Fig. 11.12 the upper plot shows the result xf of the tracking without taking account of the context while the lower plot shows the result xfc of the tracking when the context is taken into account.

We can see that xfc is less noisy than xf. This difference can be seen in another way in Fig. 11.13.

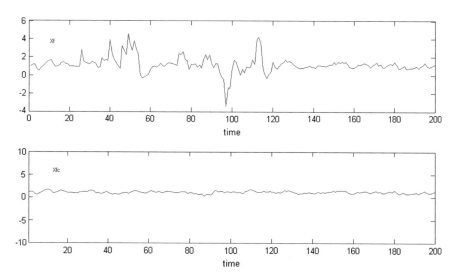

Fig. 11.12. Results, the Y-axis is given in radians and the X-axis is the time in seconds

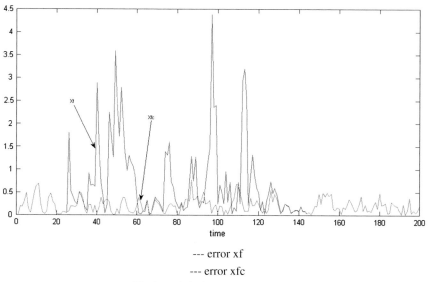

--- error xf

--- error xfc

The X-axis is the time in seconds

Fig. 11.13. Error

In this figure, we can see that before time $t = 20$ the errors of xf and xfc are the same. It is normal because only the probability of the association of three sensors is equal to 1, the other probabilities of association are reduced to zero, so the two algorithms are equivalent. In the time interval [75, 125] the error of xfc is almost always inferior to that of xf showing the benefit of taking account of the context. After $t = 125$ the error in the two algorithms converge toward the same value and we can see that the errors are the same a small time after $t = 140$.

11.5.3 Remarks

The two algorithms used in the simulation do not use the same information and the comparison is thereby biased. The objective of the simulation is to illustrate that if the contextual information is available, its use can seriously improve the results of the fusion process. An alternative to the proposed algorithm exists. It is the one based on adapting the covariance matrix in real time: we calculate signal noise variance on the output signal of each of the different sensors in real time and we update the state and the covariance matrix in real time given the time-varying noises. This way of doing has two drawbacks. The first one is calculating the variance of the noise based on several signal samples takes time and the reaction to exclude data obtained from the noisy sensor can be too late. The second drawback is that the noise variance of the signal is not the only parameter that explains the quality of the sensor signal. It is quite possible to have a signal with a good variance but worthless in information as it is the case when a sensor is lured.

11.6 Conclusion

We have proposed a fusion algorithm which takes into account the context. This is essential for a multisensory system because it allows the selection of relevant measurements and the importance reduction or simply the elimination of measurements that can disturb the useful information. The context is analyzed by a symbolic level of processing that is the outcome of an expert preliminary analysis of the system employment conditions and of the favored sensor associations.

This level of processing treatment allows supervising classical numerical fusion algorithms. This approach shows the synergy we can develop between two levels of processing. The obtained results in this paper as well as the simulation example are based on simple linear observation models. The extension to the nonlinear case is straightforward. The approach developed here for a tracking algorithm can also be adopted for numerous other applications.

References

1. L.A. Zadeh, *Fuzzy Set Information and Control*, vol. 8 (1965)
2. G. Shafer, *A Mathematical Theory of Evidence* (Princeton University Press, Princeton, 1976)

3. L. Snidaro, I. Visentini, J. Llinas, G.L. Foresti, Context in fusion: some considerations in a JDL perspective, in International Conférence in Information Fusion (Istanbul 9–12 July 2013)
4. E. Blasch, J.G. Herrero, L. Snidaro, J. Linas, G. Steetharrama, K. Palaniappan, Overview of contextual tracking approaches in information fusion, SPIE Digital Library, 2013, http://proceedings.spiedigitallibrary.org
5. V. Nimier, Introduction d'informations contextuelles dans des algorithmes de fusion multicapteur Revue du Traitement du Signal. **14**, 110–119 (1997)
6. V. Nimier, Supervised multisensor tracking algorithm, in International Conference on Information Fusion, Las Vegas, 6–9 july 1998, pp. 149–156
7. F. Caron, E. Duflos, D. Pomorski, P. Vanheeghe, GPS/IMU data fusion using multisensor Kalman filtering: introduction of contextual aspects. Inf. Fusion **7**(2), 221–230 (2006)
8. I. Visentini, L. Snidaro, Integration of contextual information for tracking refinement, in *14th Conference on Information Fusion* (Chicago, 28 June 28–1 July 2011)
9. L.A. Zadeh, *Probability of a Fuzzy event JMAA*, vol. 63 (1968)
10. G.L. Rogova, V. Nimier, Reliability in information fusion: literature survey, in *7th International Conference on Information Fusion Stockolm* (Sweden, 2004)
11. C.Y. Chong, Hierarchical estimation 2nd MIT/ONR workshop on distributed communication and decision problems. Monterey (1979)

Chapter 12
Context Exploitation for Target Tracking

**Giulia Battistello, Michael Mertens, Martin Ulmke
and Wolfgang Koch**

Abstract Target tracking is the estimation of the state of one or multiple, usually moving, objects (*targets*) based on a time series of measurements. Widely addressed within the Bayesian statistical framework, it requires the modeling of the target state evolution and the measurement process. Information on the constraints posed by the context in which the target evolves and the measurement geometry is often available. This knowledge can be modeled, often in a statistical way, and integrated in the tracking filters to enhance their performance. This chapter presents several approaches to exploit different types of context knowledge and demonstrates context-enhanced tracking based on real and simulated data. Numerical results are given for the inclusion of sea-lanes in ship tracking and route propagation, and for road-map assisted air-to-ground radar tracking.

Keywords Bayesian tracking · Constrained tracking · Context base · Navigation field · Sea-lanes · Road maps · GMTI

12.1 Introduction

Target tracking is the estimation of the state of one or multiple (generally an unknown number) of evolving objects (*targets*) based on a time series of measurements coming from one or several sources (*sensors*). The goals of target tracking are (i) to establish a one-to-one correspondence between the estimated

G. Battistello (✉) · M. Mertens · M. Ulmke · W. Koch
Dept. Sensor Data and Information Fusion, Fraunhofer FKIE, Wachtberg, Germany
e-mail: giulia.battistello@fkie.fraunhofer.de

M. Mertens
e-mail: michael.mertens@fkie.fraunhofer.de

M. Ulmke
e-mail: martin.ulmke@fkie.fraunhofer.de

W. Koch
e-mail: wolfgang.koch@fkie.fraunhofer.de

© Springer International Publishing Switzerland (outside the USA) 2016
L. Snidaro et al. (eds.), *Context-Enhanced Information Fusion*,
Advances in Computer Vision and Pattern Recognition,
DOI 10.1007/978-3-319-28971-7_12

objects (*tracks*) and the true targets in the scene, and (ii) to generate precise estimates of the kinematic state of the targets (potentially augmented by further attributes), including measures of the accuracy and reliability of the estimates.

Generally, target tracking comprises the tasks of data alignment, association, filtering, and track management [1], which are repeated at each iteration or update of the estimated tracks. Data alignment supports indeed the association step by preprocessing (e.g., interpolating or extrapolating) the collected sensor data, if required by the selected processing scheme. Then, input data (e.g., measurements) are assigned to the existing tracks or used to initiate new tracks through a given plot-to-track association strategy. This step is particularly challenging in the case of dense target scenarios and high false alarm rate, i.e. high rate of input measurements that are not originated by true targets (e.g., due to measurement noise, clutter or interferences). For each successful data association, the state estimate of that track is updated in the filtering step, using the actual measurement. Finally, track management consists of several functions to establish a clear and unique track picture, like track extraction (initialization), track split, track merging, track numbering and track-to-track fusion.

There exists a vast literature on the topic of target tracking [2–4], which is today addressed in the frame of sensor data and information fusion [1]. We hereafter resort to the Bayesian estimation theory [5], which is shortly recalled in Sect. 12.2. Specifically, we focus on the aspects of Bayesian tracking that are relevant for the integration of context information, also denoted as *background information* or *knowledge base*, into widely known target tracking filters. Context is considered as any external factor, which affects or constrains the evolution of the targets of interest or the measurement process we rely on. These factors might be partially or completely known a priori or discovered during the estimation; hence, they can be made available to the tracking filter in order to improve its performance. Specifically, this knowledge base is hereinafter modeled as constraints to the target state vector, and how to exploit them by the tracking filter is the main topic of this chapter.

Examples of constrained tracking filters are present in literature (e.g., [6–8]). Constraining the evolution of the target usually leads to modification of its motion model. As the true target motion is usually unknown and/or not deterministic, the model includes parameters describing the typical behavior of the class of the object under consideration and a stochastic modeling of the unknown and indeterministic behavior. Additionally, the modeling of the target motion may include constraints on the feasible kinematic parameters (e.g., velocity and acceleration) as well as on accessible geographic areas such as roads, maximum inclination, waterways, air corridors, and many more. In the track extraction process also the information on possible object path origins, like airports or harbors, can be exploited. Examples of this class of constrained tracking filters are discussed in Sect. 12.4. Specifically, two different approaches to the exploitation of context data for the modeling of maritime objects' motion are presented in Sects. 12.4.2.1 and 12.4.2.2, while the road-map assisted tracking is reported in Sect. 12.4.3.1.

Alternatively the measurement process itself can be constrained, since realistic, quantitative modeling of the sensor behavior allows a higher tracking performance.

Sensor modeling includes the choice of the measured quantities, distribution of measurement errors, sensor resolution, detection performance, and false alarm rate. While a detailed quantitative sensor model may lead to precise tracks, the model uncertainties have to be taken into account too, in order to obtain a robust tracking performance. The modeling of a possible *blindness* of the sensor, i.e., certain target states or target-to-sensor geometries for which the target cannot be observed, is particularly interesting. Using this kind of knowledge, a missing detection may serve as useful sensor information (sometimes denoted as "negative information", [9]). An example on the exploitation of this type of context information is given in Sect. 12.4.3.2.

This chapter is organized as follows. The general Bayesian formalism for linear and nonlinear tracking filters is summarized in Sect. 12.2, while the theoretical formulation of constrained Bayesian tracking is derived in Sect. 12.3. Some examples for constrained tracking filters are described in Sect. 12.4. Finally, Sect. 12.5 reports some results of the application of the constrained filters to simulated and real data. As the range of possible constraints and filters is enormous, the chapter is not aimed at an exhaustive overview of constrained filtering, but is intended to provide the reader with tools for deriving his own filter.

12.2 Bayesian Target Tracking

The estimation process attempts to calculate the statistics of the state of a static or dynamically evolving system based on noisy measurements provided by a single or multiple sensors in an optimal manner, i.e., by maximizing a reasonable optimality criterion. Figure 12.1 gives an overview of the relevant components of the general estimation problem.

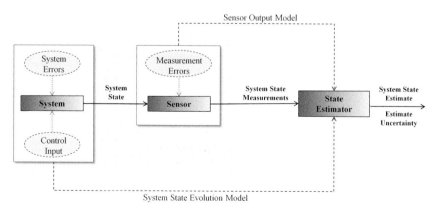

Fig. 12.1 Components of the general estimation problem

The system is affected by disturbances, i.e., the system noise, and possibly by some kind of control input. The system state is observed by a sensor that is influenced by measurement errors. A state estimator processes the noisy sensor measurements and utilizes the knowledge about the system state evolution and an ad hoc sensor output model to obtain the estimate of the system state.

In the following, the basic principle of estimation in the context of discrete-time linear systems is presented and briefly explained. Based on the Bayesian formalism, the system state is sequentially calculated through a two-step estimation scheme, as discussed in Sect. 12.2.2. Linear system and measurements equations lead to the Kalman filter-type update schema, as shown in Sect. 12.2.3, while the more general nonlinear case is discussed in Sect. 12.2.4.

12.2.1 System Equations

The general state-space representation of a discrete-time system evolving from time step t_k to t_{k+1} can be written as [2, 4]

$$\mathbf{x}_{k+1} = \mathbf{f}_k(\mathbf{x}_k) + \mathbf{v}_k, \tag{12.1}$$

where $\mathbf{f}_k$ is a possibly nonlinear function of the target state vector $\mathbf{x}_k$ and $\mathbf{v_k}$ is the input disturbance or process noise. The state vector and the process noise vector have dimensions of n_x and n_v, respectively. Equation (12.1) assumes that the system state at time step t_{k+1} depends on the state at time step t_k. If a nonlinear relationship between sensor measurements $\mathbf{z}_k$ and system state and an additive stochastic disturbance affecting the measurements are assumed, then the sensor output can generally be written as [2, 4]

$$\mathbf{z}_k = \mathbf{h}_k(\mathbf{x}_k) + \mathbf{w}_k, \tag{12.2}$$

where $\mathbf{h}_k$ is a nonlinear function of the target state vector $\mathbf{x}_k$, and $\mathbf{w}_k$ is the measurement noise vector with dimension n_z. The random process and measurement noises in (12.1) and (12.2) introduce nondeterministic components into the system state equations. Thus, in order to handle the stochastic behavior adequately, it is necessary to formulate the estimation problem within a probabilistic framework.

12.2.2 Bayesian Prediction and Filter Update

The general objective of the stochastic problem is to infer the system state $\mathbf{x}_k$ from the available information of noisy sensor measurements $\mathscr{Z}^k = \{Z_1, Z_2, \ldots, Z_k\}$, with $Z_k = \{\mathbf{z}_k^m\}_{m=1}^{m_k}$ the sensor data at each time step t_k consisting of m_k measurement vectors $\mathbf{z}_k^m$. If we consider $\mathbf{x}_k$, $\mathbf{v}_k$, $\mathbf{z}_k$ and $\mathbf{w}_k$ as random variables, from a

Bayesian point of view this estimation problem is solved by the recursive evalu-
ation of the probability density function (pdf) $p(\mathbf{x}_k|\mathscr{Z}^k)$. Such recursion comprises
two steps, the prediction and the update of the state vector descriptors. Let us
assume that at time step t_{k-1} the *posterior pdf* $p(\mathbf{x}_{k-1}|\mathscr{Z}^{k-1})$ is available. The *prior
pdf* $p(\mathbf{x}_k|\mathscr{Z}^{k-1})$, i.e., the prediction density function of $\mathbf{x}_k$, is given by the
Chapman-Kolmogorov equation:

$$p(\mathbf{x}_k|\mathscr{Z}^{k-1}) = \int p(\mathbf{x}_k|\mathbf{x}_{k-1})\, p(\mathbf{x}_{k-1}|\mathscr{Z}^{k-1})\, d\mathbf{x}_{k-1}, \qquad (12.3)$$

where $p(\mathbf{x}_k|\mathbf{x}_{k-1})$ is the *transitional pdf*, which describes the evolution of the
system on the basis of the evolution model in (12.1). Here, the Markov property
[2, 10] is assumed for the stochastic process, i.e., the state $\mathbf{x}_k$ at t_k only depends on
the state at the previous time step t_{k-1} and all system states $\mathbf{x}_l$ with $l < k - 1$ are
irrelevant for the calculation of $p(\mathbf{x}_k|\mathscr{Z}^{k-1})$. Once the measurements Z_k at t_k are
available, the prior pdf is updated with the new information as a consequence of
Bayes rule, [5]:

$$p(\mathbf{x}_k|\mathscr{Z}^k) = \frac{p(Z_k|\mathbf{x}_k)\, p(\mathbf{x}_k|\mathscr{Z}^{k-1})}{\int p(Z_k|\xi_k)\, p(\xi_k|\mathscr{Z}^{k-1}) d\xi_k}. \qquad (12.4)$$

The pdf $p(Z_k|\mathbf{x}_k)$ is the *likelihood function*. It contains the sensor output model in
(12.2) and reflects all possibilities to interpret the given sensor output. The
denominator in (12.4) serves as normalization factor. The conditional pdf $p(\mathbf{x}_k|\mathscr{Z}^k)$
is the *posterior density* as it is obtained after computing the normalized product of
likelihood and prior density.

Once the pdf in (12.4) is available, different criteria can be defined to obtain the
optimal estimate of the system state. For example, the *minimum mean square error*
(MMSE) and the *maximum* a posteriori (MAP) estimators are commonly used.
The MMSE estimate is defined as the value of $\mathbf{x}_k$ which minimizes the *mean square
error* (MSE) [2], i.e.,

$$\hat{\mathbf{x}}^{\mathrm{MMSE}}(\mathscr{Z}^k) = \underset{\hat{\mathbf{x}}}{\arg\min}\; E\left[(\hat{\mathbf{x}} - \mathbf{x}_k)^\top (\hat{\mathbf{x}} - \mathbf{x}_k)\,|\,\mathscr{Z}^k\right]. \qquad (12.5)$$

On the other hand, the MAP criterion searches the argument that maximizes the
posterior density $p(\mathbf{x}_k|\mathscr{Z}^k)$:

$$\hat{\mathbf{x}}^{\mathrm{MAP}}(\mathscr{Z}^k) = \underset{\mathbf{x}_k}{\arg\max}\; p(\mathbf{x}_k|\mathscr{Z}^k). \qquad (12.6)$$

A close analysis of (12.3) and (12.4) reveals the fundamental structure of a
Bayesian tracking filter: based on the posterior density at the previous time step t_{k-1}
and the transitional density, the prior pdf in (12.3) can be computed. After that, the
posterior density for the current time step n (12.4) is calculated as the normalized

product of the prior density and the likelihood function, which is determined by the current sensor data and the sensor model. Thus, a Bayesian tracking filter results in a sequential update scheme for the recursive calculation of the conditional target state pdf[1] $p(\mathbf{x}_k | \mathscr{Z}^k)$, consisting of a prediction step and a subsequent filter update step at each iteration:

$$p(\mathbf{x}_{k-1} | \mathscr{Z}^{k-1}) \xrightarrow[\text{Motion Model}]{\textbf{Prediction}} p(\mathbf{x}_k | \mathscr{Z}^{k-1}) \xrightarrow[\substack{\text{Sensor Model} \\ \text{New Sensor Data}}]{\textbf{Filter Update}} p(\mathbf{x}_k | \mathscr{Z}^k). \qquad (12.7)$$

A key step towards a Bayesian target state estimation algorithm (*tracking*) is the possibility to handle realistic conditions, where sensor measurements are generally incomplete, imprecise, ambiguous and uncertain. If the sensor is characterized by a probability of detection $P_d < 1$ and spatial false alarm density $\rho_f > 0$, the likelihood function $p(Z_k | \mathbf{x}_k)$ in (12.4) is generalized in order to comprise all the possible sensor data interpretations. Due to $P_d < 1$, the target might be detected or missed and because of $\rho_f > 0$ also several false alarms are potentially included in the current data set Z_k. Under the assumption that only one detection per target is possible, the expression of the *generalized likelihood function* is given by [2, 3]:

$$p(Z_k, m_k | \mathbf{x}_k) = \Lambda \left[(1 - P_d) + \frac{P_d}{\rho_F} \sum_{m=1}^{m_k} p(\mathbf{z}_k^m | \mathbf{x}_k) \right], \qquad (12.8)$$

where Λ is independent from $\mathbf{x}_k$ and, for Poisson-distributed clutter, given by $\Lambda = \rho_f^{m_k} / (m_k!) \, e^{-\rho_f |\text{FoV}|}$, with FoV as the field of view of the sensor. Based on this likelihood function, a Bayesian tracking filter is able to handle the more realistic sensor outputs. The first addend, $(1 - P_d)$, describes the missed detection hypothesis whereas the sum of pdfs denotes the m_k hypotheses that the detection with index m is the correct target measurement and all others are false alarms.

12.2.3 Linear Gaussian Systems

Under the restrictive assumptions of linear system equations and Gaussian noise, the optimal solution for the recursive scheme in (12.3) and (12.4) is available in closed form and given by the **Kalman filter** (KF) [2, 4, 10, 11]. Under these conditions, the Gaussian structure of the recursively calculated target state pdf $p(\mathbf{x}_k | \mathscr{Z}^k)$ is conserved at each time step. The system equations in (12.1) and (12.2) become:

---

[1]It will be shown later that the Bayesian update scheme is not restricted to the propagation of conditional target state pdf's.

$$\mathbf{x}_{k+1} = \mathbf{F}_k \mathbf{x}_k + \mathbf{v}_k \tag{12.9}$$

$$\mathbf{z}_k = \mathbf{H}_k \mathbf{x}_k + \mathbf{w}_k, \tag{12.10}$$

where $\mathbf{F}_k$ and $\mathbf{H}_k$ are the evolution and the measurement matrices of dimension $(n_x \times n_x)$ and $(n_z \times n_x)$, respectively. Random sequences $\mathbf{v}_k$ and $\mathbf{w}_k$ are zero-mean white Gaussian with covariances $\mathbf{Q}_k$ and $\mathbf{R}_k$.

A Gaussian distribution exhibits the particular feature that it is fully determined by its first two moments, i.e., its mean and the associated variance (or covariance in the context of multivariate random variables). Therefore, the recursive update scheme of the Kalman filter consists of update equations for the estimated mean target state and the associated estimated covariance. In the following, the recursive Kalman filter prediction-update equations are reported.

The **prediction step**, which can be illustrated by

$$p\left(\mathbf{x}_{k-1} | \mathscr{Z}^{k-1}\right) \xrightarrow[\mathbf{F}_{k-1}, \mathbf{Q}_{k-1}]{\text{Motion Model}} p\left(\mathbf{x}_k | \mathscr{Z}^{k-1}\right) \tag{12.11}$$

$$\mathscr{N}\left(\mathbf{x}_{k-1}; \mathbf{x}_{k-1|k-1}, \mathbf{P}_{k-1|k-1}\right) \xrightarrow[\mathbf{F}_{k-1}, \mathbf{Q}_{k-1}]{\text{Motion Model}} \mathscr{N}\left(\mathbf{x}_k; \mathbf{x}_{k|k-1}, \mathbf{P}_{k|k-1}\right), \tag{12.12}$$

utilizes the target dynamics model to compute a first estimate of the target state $\mathbf{x}_{k|k-1}$ and its covariance $\mathbf{P}_{k|k-1}$. Due to the linearity of the target motion model and the white Gaussian process noise with covariance $\mathbf{Q}_{k-1}$, the motion model is introduced into the algorithm by the normal density $\mathscr{N}(\mathbf{x}_k; \mathbf{F}_{k-1} \mathbf{x}_{k-1}, \mathbf{Q}_{k-1})$. The Eq. (12.3) can be written as

$$p(\mathbf{x}_k | \mathscr{Z}^{k-1}) = \int \underbrace{\mathscr{N}(\mathbf{x}_k; \mathbf{F}_{k-1} \mathbf{x}_{k-1}, \mathbf{Q}_{k-1})}_{\text{Motion model}} \underbrace{\mathscr{N}(\mathbf{x}_{k-1}; \mathbf{x}_{k-1|k-1}, \mathbf{P}_{k-1|k-1})}_{\text{Posterior pdf at } t_{k-1}} d\mathbf{x}_{k-1}. \tag{12.13}$$

The integrand can be transformed into a product of two Gaussians in which one pdf does no longer depend on the integration variable $\mathbf{x}_{k-1}$ by making use of the identity [4, 12]

$$\mathscr{N}(\mathbf{a}; \mathbf{b}, \mathbf{A}) \, \mathscr{N}(\mathbf{c}; \mathbf{B}\mathbf{a}, \mathbf{C}) = \mathscr{N}(\mathbf{c}; \mathbf{B}\mathbf{b}, \mathbf{D}) \, \mathcal{N}(\mathbf{a}; \mathbf{b} + \mathbf{E}\mathbf{d}, \mathbf{A} - \mathbf{E}\mathbf{D}\mathbf{E}^{\top}), \tag{12.14}$$

with $\mathbf{d} = \mathbf{c} - \mathbf{B}\mathbf{b}$, $\mathbf{D} = \mathbf{B}\mathbf{A}\mathbf{B}^{\top} + \mathbf{C}$ and $\mathbf{E} = \mathbf{A}\mathbf{B}^{\top}\mathbf{D}^{-1}$. This yields the following Kalman filter prediction equations for the mean and covariance of the prior density $p(\mathbf{x}_k | \mathscr{Z}^{k-1})$:

$$\mathbf{x}_{k|k-1} = \mathbf{F}_{k-1} \mathbf{x}_{k-1|k-1} \tag{12.15}$$

$$\mathbf{P}_{k|k-1} = \mathbf{F}_{k-1}\,\mathbf{P}_{k-1|k-1}\,\mathbf{F}_{k-1}^{\top} + \mathbf{Q}_{k-1}. \qquad (12.16)$$

In the **filter update step** illustrated by

$$\mathcal{N}(\mathbf{x}_k;\mathbf{x}_{k|k-1},\mathbf{P}_{k|k-1}) \xrightarrow[\substack{\text{Sensor Model}\\\text{New Sensor Data}\\ \mathbf{H}_k,\,\mathbf{R}_k,\,\mathbf{z}_k}]{} \mathcal{N}(\mathbf{x}_k;\mathbf{x}_{k|k},\mathbf{P}_{k|k}), \qquad (12.17)$$

the Kalman filter equations are obtained as follows: as the measurement Eq. (12.10) is a linear function of the target state, it is reasonable to write the likelihood pdf as $p(\mathbf{z}_k|\mathbf{x}_k) = \mathcal{N}(\mathbf{z}_k;\mathbf{H}_k\mathbf{x}_k,\mathbf{R}_k)$. Then, the Bayes theorem (12.4) is given by

$$p(\mathbf{x}_k|\mathscr{Z}^k) = \frac{\mathcal{N}(\mathbf{z}_k;\mathbf{H}_k\mathbf{x}_k,\mathbf{R}_k)\,\mathcal{N}(\mathbf{x}_k;\mathbf{x}_{k|k-1},\mathbf{P}_{k|k-1})}{\int \underbrace{\mathcal{N}(\mathbf{z}_k;\mathbf{H}_k\boldsymbol{\xi}_k,\mathbf{R}_k)}_{\text{likelihood function}}\,\underbrace{\mathcal{N}(\boldsymbol{\xi}_k;\mathbf{x}_{k|k-1},\mathbf{P}_{k|k-1})}_{\text{prior density}}\,d\boldsymbol{\xi}_k}. \qquad (12.18)$$

The integrand in the denominator can be again transformed into a product of two Gaussians in which one pdf no longer depends on the integration variable $\boldsymbol{\xi}_k$ by exploiting (12.14). In addition, also the Gaussian product in the numerator can be rewritten based on (12.14). This leads to the following Kalman filter update equations for the mean and covariance of the posterior density $p(\mathbf{x}_k|\mathscr{Z}^k)$:

$$\mathbf{x}_{k|k} = \mathbf{x}_{k|k-1} + \mathbf{K}_k(\mathbf{z}_k - \mathbf{H}_k\mathbf{x}_{k|k-1}) \qquad (12.19)$$

$$\mathbf{P}_{k|k} = \mathbf{P}_{k|k-1} - \mathbf{K}_k\mathbf{S}_k\mathbf{K}_k^{\top} \qquad (12.20)$$

$$\mathbf{S}_k = \mathbf{H}_k\mathbf{P}_{k|k-1}\mathbf{H}_k^{\top} + \mathbf{R}_k \qquad (12.21)$$

$$\mathbf{K}_k = \mathbf{P}_{k|k-1}\mathbf{H}_k^{\top}\mathbf{S}_k^{-1}, \qquad (12.22)$$

where $\mathbf{S}_k$ is the innovation covariance and $\mathbf{K}_k$ is the Kalman gain matrix. Due to its mathematical structure, the Kalman gain introduces a high degree of adaptivity into the filter equations: depending on the possibly time-varying motion and measurement model error covariances, the gain matrix $\mathbf{K}_k$ determines how much information of the currently processed sensor data needs to be added to the predicted state estimate to deliver an optimal estimation result. The update equations of the Kalman filter have a predictor-corrector structure, because the first estimate of the target state at time step t_k, which is based on the target motion model and the input from t_{k-1}, is corrected or improved by the current sensor measurements, yielding the optimal estimate of the target state at time step t_k.

12.2.4   Nonlinear Systems

The problem of estimating the target state on the basis of the sensor measurements might become highly nonlinear. Nonlinearity comes from several sources. For example, the target range, range-rate and bearing measurements from a conventional radar system undergo the nonlinear coordinate transformation to the Cartesian state space. Also the target dynamics could be nonlinear especially when the target is subject to significant angular speed and acceleration (e.g., turning maneuver). Similar estimation problems are often handled by decomposing the maneuver into phases [13, 14], hence switching among different target dynamic models. Nevertheless, for some phases the assumption of linear system equations and Gaussian noise do not hold, and the optimal Bayes solution to the filtering problem needs to be approximated. The **extended Kalman filter** (EKF) falls into the local linearization class of approximate solutions. So, when nonlinear and non-Gaussian conditions hold, the EKF offers an approximation of the posterior pdf in (12.4). Other approaches are based on the *unscented transformation* [15, 16], grid-based numerical integration, and sequential Monte Carlo estimation, [17, 14, 18]. The closeness to the optimum depends on the tracking conditions. For instance, the EKF approximation presented in [19] diverges from the optimal solution in highly nonlinear/non-Gaussian conditions. Conversely, the **particle filter** (PF) allows solving optimally the Bayesian filtering problem, independently from the severity of the nonlinearity, if a large number of particles is considered. Particles are indeed a numerical approximations of the probability density function of the target state, which is sought in the Bayes approach. These two nonlinear filtering techniques are briefly recalled in the following.

The **extended Kalman filter** is based on the first-order local approximation of the functions $\mathbf{f}(.)$ and $\mathbf{h}(.)$ in (12.1) and (12.2). The mean value and the covariance matrix of the pdfs in (12.3) and (12.4) result:

$$\mathbf{x}_{k|k-1} = \mathbf{f}_{k-1}(\mathbf{x}_{k-1|k-1}) \tag{12.23}$$

$$\mathbf{P}_{k|k-1} = \mathbf{F}_{k-1}\mathbf{P}_{k-1|k-1}\mathbf{F}_{k-1}^{T} + \mathbf{Q}_{k-1}, \tag{12.24}$$

and

$$\mathbf{x}_{k|k} = \mathbf{x}_{k|k-1}\mathbf{K}_{k}[(\mathbf{z}_{k} - \mathbf{h}_{k}(\mathbf{x}_{k|k-1}))] \tag{12.25}$$

$$\mathbf{P}_{k|k} = \mathbf{P}_{k|k-1} - \mathbf{K}_{k}\mathbf{S}_{k}\mathbf{K}_{k}^{T}, \tag{12.26}$$

where

$$\mathbf{S}_{k} = \mathbf{H}_{k}\mathbf{P}_{k|k-1}\mathbf{H}_{k}^{T} + \mathbf{R}_{k} \tag{12.27}$$

$$\mathbf{K}_{k} = \mathbf{P}_{k|k-1}\mathbf{H}_{k}^{T}\mathbf{S}_{k}^{-1}. \tag{12.28}$$

Matrices $\mathbf{F}_{k-1}$ and $\mathbf{H}_k$ result from the linearization of functions $\mathbf{f}_{k-1}$ and $\mathbf{h}_k$: they coincide with the Jacobian of the two equations, evaluated in $\mathbf{x}_{k-1|k-1}$ and $\mathbf{x}_{k|k-1}$, respectively.

Particle filters are Sequential Monte Carlo (SMC) techniques, which use a discrete representation of probability density functions. The pdf $p(\mathbf{x}_k|\mathscr{Z}^k)$ in (12.4) is approximated by a weighted sum over N_p *particles*, $\{\mathbf{x}_k^i, \pi_k^i\}_{i=1}^{N_p}$, as:

$$p(\mathbf{x}_k|\mathscr{Z}^k) \approx \sum_{i=1}^{N_p} \pi_k^i \delta(\mathbf{x}_k - \mathbf{x}_k^i), \qquad (12.29)$$

where $\mathbf{x}_k^i$ is the state vector and π_k^i the weight of the ith particle. In the following section, we resort to the sequential importance resampling (SIR) particle filter algorithm, [17, 14]. This algorithm implements the following steps: (i) it draws the $\mathbf{x}_k^i$ particle from the proposal distribution, i.e., the transitional prior pdf, $\mathbf{x}_k^i \sim p(\mathbf{x}_k^i|\mathbf{x}_{k-1}^i)$, (ii) it evaluates the corresponding weight π_k^i from the likelihood function $\tilde{\pi}_k^i = p(Z_k|\mathbf{x}_k^i)$, (iii) it normalizes the weights of the N_p particles, and (iv) performs resampling (i.e., particles with low weights are discarded and replaced with samples with high importance weights).

As there are, in principle, no restrictions on the functional form of the transitional pdf nor on the likelihood function, it is easy to include even strongly nonlinear constraints in a particle filter. Typical implementations are the *rejection sampling* and the *pseudo measurement* approaches, discussed in Sects. 12.4.1.1 and 12.4.1.2, respectively. In spite of the, usually, simple implementation, the efficiency of the particle filter strongly depends on the actual system equations and constraints, in particular on the overlap of the prior pdf with the likelihood function [17].

12.3 Context-Enhanced Target Tracking

12.3.1 Introduction

The Bayesian recursion, illustrated in Sect. 12.2, allows incorporating different kinds of external factors, such as equality and inequality constraints, which can be modeled as linear or nonlinear functions of the target state vector. Context information for target tracking can be indeed considered as a constraining factor, since it affects the possible evolution of some of the positional/kinematic components of the state vector either bounding them or limiting a given nonlinear combination of them. Such constraining effect generally varies over time (i.e., at each time instant in the considered discrete-time system model), and depends from the state vector itself. This is due for example to the spatial (geographic) layout of the context in the area where the target evolves. In addition, the context-driven constraint might be fulfilled by the system in all cases (i.e., hard constraint), such as for instance the boundary between land and sea for a ground moving target, or mostly (i.e., soft constraint), such as the adherence to a traffic separation scheme.

In literature several algorithms are reported, which take into account constraints in the estimation process, depending on the addressed application and the nature of the constraint itself. A quite exhaustive overview is reported by Simon in [20]. In this survey, a preliminary distinction between the available techniques for linear and nonlinear dynamic systems and linear and nonlinear constraints is provided.

Specifically, when the system evolution is described by *linear* equations, techniques like estimate projection [21], gain projection [22], probability density function truncation [23] and interior point likelihood maximization [24] can be adopted for incorporating *hard inequality and linear* constraints. Other techniques, like model reduction [25], perfect measurements [26], and system projection [27], are used for dealing with equality constraints. In case of linear systems, the Kalman filter represents the solution for the recursive constrained state estimation. If the constraints result as *nonlinear*, a linearization step is required before adopting the above-mentioned techniques in the Kalman filter. If the constraints maintain their nonlinearities, solutions like the extended Kalman filter (EKF), unscented Kalman filter (UKF), and particle filter (PF) are considered for the target estimation process. Moreover, others methods to include the inequality constraints are taken into account. Among them we mention the second-order expansion of nonlinear constraints [28] and the moving horizon estimation (MHE, [29]).

As *nonlinear* systems are concerned, EKF, UKF, MHE, and PF-based algorithms combined with various techniques to handle constraints have been proposed in the literature. The MHE approaches result attractive but require excessive computational effort [30]. Techniques based on sequential Monte Carlo (SMC) methods are prone to the inclusion of additional information since they present no restriction on the type of models (e.g., target dynamics, noise distributions, etc.). Considering different motion models or filter parameters allows as well using KF extensions as constrained tracking filters.

Generally speaking an underlying aspect when comparing constrained Bayesian filters is the *entry point* of the constraint in the recursive formulation of Bayes. As recalled in the previous section, each estimation iteration is split into prediction and update steps, which lead to the calculation of the posterior density of the state vector $p(\mathbf{x}_k | \mathscr{Z}^k)$ through the evaluation of the prior pdf $p(\mathbf{x}_k | \mathscr{Z}^{k-1})$ and the likelihood function $p(Z_k | \mathbf{x}_k)$. The prior pdf is then calculated on the basis of the posterior pdf $p(\mathbf{x}_{k-1} | \mathscr{Z}^{k-1})$ at the previous time instant and the transitional probability $p(\mathbf{x}_k | \mathbf{x}_{k-1})$. The algorithms derived within the general Bayes formulation generally constrain either the prior pdf (or better the transitional density) or the likelihood function. The mathematical modification of the unconstrained pdf into the constrained pdf then varies from filter to filter, largely depending on the application sought for the estimator.

The general formulation of the constrained Bayesian filtering is reported in the following section, where we demonstrate the equivalence between the introduction of the constraint in the prediction step and the update step from a Bayes point of view.

12.3.2 Constrained Bayesian Filtering

In this section, the Bayesian recursion for the inclusion of constraints in the tracking process is presented. Let us consider, the most generic case, i.e., the context information is available in terms of *nonlinear inequality* constraints on the target state:

$$\mathbf{a}_k \leq \mathbf{C}_k(\mathbf{x}_k) \leq \mathbf{b}_k, \tag{12.30}$$

where $\mathbf{C}_k : \mathbb{R}^{n_x} \to \mathbb{R}^{n_c}$. The constraint as defined in (12.30) can be exactly satisfied (*hard* constraint) or it can present uncertainties. This could be due to the uncertainty of the boundaries, i.e., the vectors $\mathbf{a}_k$ and $\mathbf{b}_k$, or to the uncertainty of the constraint $\mathbf{C}_k$, which is allowed to exceed the boundaries with a certain probability (*soft* constraint). In the following, we focus on the perfect knowledge of *hard* constraints and the constraints space. The soft constraint case, briefly recalled in Sect. 12.4.1, is out of the scope of this chapter.

Given these considerations, let C_k be the set of states satisfying the (12.30) and C^k the sequence of C_k up to the time k:

$$C_k = \{\mathbf{x}_k : \mathbf{x}_k \in \mathbb{R}^{n_x}, \mathbf{a}_k \leq \mathbf{C}_k(\mathbf{x}_k) \leq \mathbf{b}_k\} \tag{12.31}$$

$$C^k = \{C_0, C_1, \ldots, C_k\}. \tag{12.32}$$

The inclusion of the sequence of constraints (12.32) in the Bayesian formalism requires the evaluation of the *constrained posterior pdf* $p(\mathbf{x}_k|\mathscr{Z}^k, C^k)$, where the conditioning is with respect to C^k, too.

The two-step recursion (prediction and update) for the evaluation of the constrained posterior pdf is modified in accordance to the new conditioning, and the expression in (12.7) becomes:

$$p(\mathbf{x}_{k-1}|\mathscr{Z}^{k-1},C^{k-1}) \xrightarrow[\text{Motion Model}]{\text{Constrained Prediction}} p(\mathbf{x}_k|\mathscr{Z}^{k-1},C^k) \xrightarrow[\substack{\text{Sensor Model} \\ \text{New Sensor Data }z_k}]{\text{Filter Update}} p(\mathbf{x}_k|\mathscr{Z}^k,C^k) \text{ (a)}$$

$$p(\mathbf{x}_{k-1}|\mathscr{Z}^{k-1},C^{k-1}) \xrightarrow[\text{Motion Model}]{\text{Prediction}} p(\mathbf{x}_k|\mathscr{Z}^{k-1},C^{k-1}) \xrightarrow[\substack{\text{Sensor Model} \\ \text{New Sensor Data }z_k}]{\text{Constrained Filter Update}} p(\mathbf{x}_k|\mathscr{Z}^k,C^k) \text{ (b)}$$

$$\tag{12.33}$$

Specifically, the information about the constraint can be either exploited in the prediction or in the update step [31], as stated in (12.33a) and (12.33b) respectively, leading to the same result from the Bayesian point of view as demonstrated in the following.

Inclusion of constraints in the Prediction Step

In this case, the *prior pdf* is defined as follows:

$$
\begin{aligned}
p(\mathbf{x}_k|\mathscr{L}^{k-1},C^k) &= \int p(\mathbf{x}_k,\mathbf{x}_{k-1}|\mathscr{L}^{k-1},C_k,C^{k-1})\,\mathrm{d}\mathbf{x}_{k-1}\\
&= \int \frac{p(\mathbf{x}_k,\mathbf{x}_{k-1},\mathscr{L}^{k-1},C_k,C^{k-1})}{p(\mathscr{L}^{k-1},C_k,C^{k-1})}\,\mathrm{d}\mathbf{x}_{k-1}\\
&= \int \frac{p(\mathbf{x}_k|\mathbf{x}_{k-1},\mathscr{L}^{k-1},C_k,C^{k-1})p(\mathbf{x}_{k-1},\mathscr{L}^{k-1},C_k,C^{k-1})}{p(\mathscr{L}^{k-1},C_k,C^{k-1})}\,\mathrm{d}\mathbf{x}_{k-1}\\
&= \int \frac{p(\mathbf{x}_k|\mathbf{x}_{k-1},\mathscr{L}^{k-1},C_k,C^{k-1})p(\mathbf{x}_{k-1}|\mathscr{L}^{k-1},C_k,C^{k-1})p(\mathscr{L}^{k-1},C_k,C^{k-1})}{p(\mathscr{L}^{k-1},C_k,C^{k-1})}\,\mathrm{d}\mathbf{x}_{k-1}\\
&= \int p(\mathbf{x}_k|\mathbf{x}_{k-1},\mathscr{L}^{k-1},C_k,C^{k-1})p(\mathbf{x}_{k-1}|\mathscr{L}^{k-1},C_k,C^{k-1})\,\mathrm{d}\mathbf{x}_{k-1}\\
&= \int p(\mathbf{x}_k|\mathbf{x}_{k-1},C_k)p(\mathbf{x}_{k-1}|\mathscr{L}^{k-1},C^{k-1})\,\mathrm{d}\mathbf{x}_{k-1}.
\end{aligned}
\tag{12.34}
$$

The *posterior pdf* definition is given by:

$$
\begin{aligned}
p(\mathbf{x}_k|\mathscr{L}^{k},C^k) &= \frac{p(\mathbf{x}_k,\mathbf{z}_k,\mathscr{L}^{k-1},C^k)}{p(\mathbf{z}_k,\mathscr{L}^{k-1},C^k)}\\
&= \frac{p(\mathbf{z}_k|\mathbf{x}_k,\mathscr{L}^{k-1},C^k)p(\mathbf{x}_k,\mathscr{L}^{k-1},C^k)}{p(\mathbf{z}_k,\mathscr{L}^{k-1},C^k)}\\
&= \frac{p(\mathbf{z}_k|\mathbf{x}_k,\mathscr{L}^{k-1},C^k)p(\mathbf{x}_k|\mathscr{L}^{k-1},C^k)p(\mathscr{L}^{k-1},C^k)}{p(\mathbf{z}_k|\mathscr{L}^{k-1},C^k)p(\mathscr{L}^{k-1},C^k)}\\
&= \frac{p(\mathbf{z}_k|\mathbf{x}_k)p(\mathbf{x}_k|\mathscr{L}^{k-1},C^k)}{p(\mathbf{z}_k|\mathscr{L}^{k-1},C^k)}.
\end{aligned}
\tag{12.35}
$$

The inclusion of constraints in the prediction step requires the evaluation of the *constrained transitional density* in (12.34), $p(\mathbf{x}_k|\mathbf{x}_{k-1},C_k)$.

Inclusion of constraints in the Update Step

The *prior pdf* is defined as follows:

$$
\begin{aligned}
p(\mathbf{x}_k|\mathscr{L}^{k-1},C^{k-1}) &= \int p(\mathbf{x}_k,\mathbf{x}_{k-1}|\mathscr{L}^{k-1},C^{k-1})\,\mathrm{d}\mathbf{x}_{k-1}\\
&= \int p(\mathbf{x}_k|\mathbf{x}_{k-1},\mathscr{L}^{k-1},C^{k-1})p(\mathbf{x}_{k-1}|\mathscr{L}^{k-1},C^{k-1})\,\mathrm{d}\mathbf{x}_{k-1}\\
&= \int p(\mathbf{x}_k|\mathbf{x}_{k-1})p(\mathbf{x}_{k-1}|\mathscr{L}^{k-1},C^{k-1})\,\mathrm{d}\mathbf{x}_{k-1}.
\end{aligned}
\tag{12.36}
$$

The *posterior pdf* definition is given by:

$$p(\mathbf{x}_k|\mathscr{L}^k, C^k) = \frac{p(\mathbf{x}_k, \mathbf{z}_k, \mathscr{L}^{k-1}, C_k, C^{k-1})}{p(\mathbf{z}_k, \mathscr{L}^{k-1}, C_k, C^{k-1})}$$

$$= \frac{p(\mathbf{z}_k|\mathbf{x}_k, \mathscr{L}^{k-1}, C^k)p(\mathbf{x}_k, \mathscr{L}^{k-1}, C^k)}{p(\mathbf{z}_k, \mathscr{L}^{k-1}, C^k)}$$

$$= \frac{p(\mathbf{z}_k|\mathbf{x}_k)p(C_k|\mathbf{x}_k)p(\mathbf{x}_k|\mathscr{L}^{k-1}, C^{k-1})}{p(\mathbf{z}_k|\mathscr{L}^{k-1}, C^k)p(C_k|C^{k-1})}. \qquad (12.37)$$

In this case, the existence of constraints brings to the definition of the *constrained likelihood function* in (12.37), $p(C_k|\mathbf{x}_k)$.

By comparing the Eqs. (12.35) and (12.37) it is easy to demonstrate that they coincide from the Bayesian point of view if the following equivalence holds:

$$p(\mathbf{x}_k|\mathscr{L}^{k-1}, C^k) = \frac{p(C_k|\mathbf{x}_k)p(\mathbf{x}_k|\mathscr{L}^{k-1}, C^{k-1})}{p(C_k|C^{k-1})}. \qquad (12.38)$$

The inclusion of equality constraints in the Bayesian recursion can be handled similarly.

12.4 Algorithms and Applications for Constrained Target Tracking

This section presents some algorithms for recursive target state estimation that exploits the context information. The constrained tracking filters are derived on the basis of the Bayesian recursion presented in Sect. 12.3.2 and the context is properly modeled in order to be included in the formalism depending on the application. Specifically, in Sect. 12.4.1 two general methods for constraint exploitation in target tracking are recalled, the *rejection sampling* and the *pseudo measurement* approach, both used for several target tracking applications. Section 12.4.2 presents some examples of filters designed for tracking maritime targets (i.e., vessels evolving with typical maneuvers at open sea and coastal areas). Finally, Sect. 12.4.3 focuses on algorithms for tracking ground targets (e.g., vehicles), presenting the models for the context and the filter implementation. It has to be stressed that some algorithms include the context information in the prediction phase of the tracking process; others are characterized by a constrained target state update. In all the cases we focus on *nonlinear* dynamic or measurement models that are subject to *hard* constraints.

12.4.1 General Purpose Filters

12.4.1.1 Rejection Sampling

The **rejection sampling** method imposes the constraints on the prior pdf, specifically on the transitional density in the Eq. (12.34), which is modified as follows (see [31]):

$$p(\mathbf{x}_k|\mathbf{x}_{k-1}, C_k) \propto \begin{cases} p(\mathbf{x}_k|\mathbf{x}_{k-1}), & \text{if } \mathbf{x}_k \in C_k \\ \alpha p(\mathbf{x}_k|\mathbf{x}_{k-1}), & \text{otherwise.} \end{cases} \qquad (12.39)$$

The parameter α is generally chosen in the interval $[0, 1[$. Since we are dealing with *hard* constraints, we set $\alpha = 0$.

This approach can be straightforward applied to a particle filter tackling the nonlinear estimation problem: only the particles that satisfy the constraints are accepted, the others are rejected. The solution is extremely simple, but is computationally expensive. In particular, the time required to perform rejection sampling, i.e., to generate a given number of particles is not known a priori. The smaller the fraction of the state space that fulfills the constraint, the more inefficient the rejection sampling approach becomes. For *equality* constraints this method cannot be applied at all, since the probability that a randomly drawn particle fulfills the constraint vanishes.

12.4.1.2 Pseudo Measurements

The **pseudo measurements** approach deals with constraining the instantaneous measurement. Specifically, the constraint is considered as an additional measurement. This impacts the posterior pdf and requires the evaluation of the constraint-based likelihood function $p(C_k|\mathbf{x}_k)$ in (12.37):

$$p(C_k|\mathbf{x}_k) = \begin{cases} 1 - \alpha, & \text{if } \mathbf{x}_k \in C_k \\ \alpha, & \text{otherwise,} \end{cases} \qquad (12.40)$$

where $\alpha \in [0, 1[$, which is multiplied to the measurement-induced likelihood function. Specifically, we set $\alpha = 0$ to deal with the *hard* constraint case.

In a particle filter application (see [31]) $p(C_k|\mathbf{x}_k)$ affects the weight of particles or even reduces them to zero if the (hard) constraint is not fulfilled. While in the rejection sampling approach (Sect. 12.4.1.1) the computation time is a priori unknown, in the pseudo measurement approach, there can be a large number of particles with small or vanishing weight leading to an inefficient filter, too. Like in the rejection sampling approach, the filter becomes more and more inefficient the smaller the constraint state space is. For this reason, in the limit of *equality* constraints, both variants cannot be applied.

12.4.2 Tracking Filters for Maritime Traffic Monitoring

The section presents potential strategies for context-based tracking filters in the area of maritime situational awareness (MSA). MSA is based on the exploitation of data from heterogeneous sources, which concur in providing the *maritime traffic picture* in the observed region. The involved systems include coastal active radars, navigation aids, air- and space-based monitoring services, and recently conceived passive sensors. It is clear that one of the major achievements to be sought for future MSA systems is the effective integration of all data sources.

The extraction of the global maritime picture has to cope with the limited performance of each sensor and the complexity of the operational scenario. Target signal fading, anomalous propagation conditions, clutter returns or interferences, transmission channel loss, sensor blockage or malfunctioning, intentional spoofing, etc., make the accurate and reliable extraction of tracks harder. In this perspective, context elements are expected to have an influence on the maritime traffic evolution, since they represent sources of a priori information that can be used in target inference. Geographical information on coastline, ports, maritime highways, and corridors, such as information on kinematics and route of each vessel, are elements that can be properly modeled and exploited in the target track filtering (i.e., the process of target state vector prediction and measurement update), as demonstrated in the following examples.

12.4.2.1 Navigation Field Assisted Target Tracking

According to the **Navigation Field Assisted EKF** [19] the transitional density can be expressed as a Gaussian pdf—due to the Gaussian assumptions and the local linearization—whose parameters vary according to the constraint. Specifically, we can write:

$$p(\mathbf{x}_k|\mathbf{x}_{k-1}, C_k) \cong \begin{cases} \mathcal{N}(\mathbf{x}_k; \mathbf{g}_{k-1}(\mathbf{x}_{k-1}); \mathbf{Q}^{\mathbf{g}}_{k-1}), & \text{if } \mathbf{x}_k \in C_k \text{ AND } \mathbf{x}_{k-1} \in D_{k-1} \\ \mathcal{N}(\mathbf{x}_k; \mathbf{f}_{k-1}(\mathbf{x}_{k-1}); \mathbf{Q}^{\mathbf{f}}_{k-1}), & \text{if } \mathbf{x}_{k-1} \notin D_{k-1} \\ 0, & \text{otherwise,} \end{cases}$$

$$(12.41)$$

where C_k is the state vector (equality constraint) that can be reached from $\mathbf{x}_{k-1}$, D_{k-1} is the ensemble of state vectors that are subject to the influence of the context at time instant $(k-1)$, $\mathbf{f}(.)$ and $\mathbf{g}(.)$ are transition functions of the state, which allows transiting from $\mathbf{x}_{k-1}$ to C_k and $\mathbf{Q}^{\mathbf{g}}_{k-1}$ and $\mathbf{Q}^{\mathbf{f}}_{k-1}$ are the covariance matrix of the process noise. It is evident that on the basis of the reported pdf, the transitional functions $\mathbf{f}(.)$ and $\mathbf{g}(.)$ to be used by the filter vary and generally their parameters depend on the actual context influence on the state vector $\mathbf{x}_{k-1}$. The influence might be negligible or actual on the basis of the value of some of the components of the state vector at a given time instant. In order to evaluate the expressions in (12.41), context elements generating the constraint are modeled as hereafter reported.

Fig. 12.2 Intensity KC map for a reference maritime scenario. Repulsive and attractive sources for transiting vessels are represented by the highest and the lowest values in the map, respectively

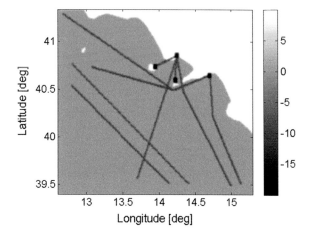

Context Modeling

In the **navigation field** model [19] context elements are considered as originators of attractive or repulsive sources for targets evolving in their proximity. They are described in a geographic map, whose pixels or cells indicate the *intensity KC* (refer to (12.42)) of their effect on targets. Specifically, for the maritime environment, ports, coastline, sea highways and corridors, interdicted areas are elements that can be easily represented on the map, providing a better understanding of the scenario (see Fig. 12.2).

If we consider that the context acts like a force on target, we can resort to the *navigation force field* (NFF) definition in [32], which describes the resulting effect as superposition of forces. Let $\vec{F}_{G_i}$ the force of the ith context source point acting on a given target. Its strength $|F_i|$ and direction $\angle F_i$ depend on (i) distance r_i between the target and the ith element, and (ii) the attractive or repulsive nature of this source.

If we choose a force model according to the law of gravity, for the superposition principle the total force exerted on target from N sources is given by:

$$\vec{F}_G = \sum_{i=1}^{N} \vec{F}_{G_i} = K_i C_i \frac{\vec{r}_i}{r_i^3}, \tag{12.42}$$

where K_i is the gravitation coefficient describing the strength of the interaction with the ith source, and $C_i \pm 1$ denotes the attractive or repulsive nature of the force.

Alternatively, instead of a radial force, the context element can induce a rotational momentum on the target around a pole O:

$$\vec{M}_G = \vec{F}_G \times \vec{l}, \tag{12.43}$$

where $\vec{l}$ is the rotation axis through O.

For a target evolving in a two-dimensional scenario, the total force $\vec{F}_G$ is dynamically evaluated for each discrete-time instant k as:

$$F_{Gx}(x_k, y_k) = \sum_{i=1}^{N} K_i C_i \frac{x_k - x_i}{R_{Di}^3} \qquad (12.44)$$

$$F_{Gy}(x_k, y_k) = \sum_{i=1}^{N} K_i C_i \frac{y_k - y_i}{R_{Di}^3}, \qquad (12.45)$$

where the F_{Gx} and F_{Gy} represent the force components in both X and Y direction, x_k and y_k the coordinates at time k and R_{Di} the distance between the target position and the ith cell. For the sake of simplicity, we assume that the track state is described with a finite set of motion models (MM), e.g., MM $= \{S, N, A, R\}$ and the force $\vec{F}_G$ dictates the actuation of the specific MM. In the S (still) state, the target is steady while in the N (navigation) state, we assume that it moves along a rectilinear path and is not subject to significant acceleration/deceleration. It can be considered as a point-like mass m, not subject to external forces (constant velocity model, CV, [3]). In the A (approaching) state, the target approaches a destination: its motion comprises deceleration and quick variation of the heading, which can be described by friction forces. Finally, in the R (rotating) state the target moves along a circular trajectory with constant speed, in accordance to the coordinated turn model, CT [3]. The navigation force $\vec{F}_G$ could affect the target by modifying its velocity module and/or its velocity vector orientation. In this case, the force is modeled as an additional acceleration which has a direct impact on the target motion (Model I). Alternatively, as stated in the Eq. (12.43), $\vec{F}_G$ is represented by means of rotational momentum $\vec{M}_G$ applied to the target seen as a dipole of length l, with inertial momentum I_T. Under this assumption, the combination of the exerted force, the target speed and the moment of inertia, leads to the angular acceleration $\dot{\omega}$ evaluation, since $\dot{\omega} = M_G / I_T$, (Model II). For both the models, the context information brings non-linearities into the system, independently from the measurement equation applicable to the problem. Thus, each model would require an EKF. It is to be stressed that the effect of the force $\vec{F}_G$ affects only the target state vector and the state covariance matrix predictions; the state vector and the state covariance measurement update equations are not subject to any modification with respect to the well-known EKF formulation recalled in Sect. 12.2.4.

Filter Implementation: Model I—Force as Acceleration
Let the state vector at discrete time k consist of position, velocity, and acceleration components of the target in Cartesian coordinates, i.e., $\mathbf{x}_k^0 = [x_k, y_k, \dot{x}_k, \dot{y}_k, \ddot{x}_k, \ddot{y}_k]$. For the considered target motion model, the accelerations components $\ddot{x}_k$ and $\ddot{y}_k$ are constant in $[k-1, k]$ and given by

$$\ddot{x}_k = F_{Gx}(x_k, y_k), \qquad \ddot{y}_k = F_{Gy}(x_k, y_k). \tag{12.46}$$

Thus, the problem of estimating the target kinematic state is reduced to the evaluation of the following state vector, $\mathbf{x}_k = [x_k, y_k, \dot{x}_k, \dot{y}_k]$.

By resorting to the EKF formulation and tacking into account the Eq. (12.41), the prediction of the target state and covariance are recursively defined as follows:

$$\hat{\mathbf{x}}_{k|k-1} = \mathbf{g}_{k-1}(\hat{\mathbf{x}}_{k-1|k-1}) = \mathbf{G}_{k-1}\hat{\mathbf{x}}_{k-1|k-1} + \mathbf{A}_{k-1} \tag{12.47}$$

$$\mathbf{P}_{k|k-1} = \hat{\mathbf{G}}_{k-1}\mathbf{P}_{k-1|k-1}\hat{\mathbf{G}}'_{k-1} + \mathbf{Q}^g_{k-1}, \tag{12.48}$$

with

$$\mathbf{G}_{k-1} = \begin{bmatrix} 1 & 0 & T & 0 \\ 0 & 1 & 0 & T \\ 0 & 0 & 1 & 0 \\ 0 & 0 & 0 & 1 \end{bmatrix}, \qquad \mathbf{A}_{k-1} = \begin{bmatrix} \frac{T^2}{2}\ddot{x}_{k-1} \\ \frac{T^2}{2}\ddot{y}_{k-1} \\ T\ddot{x}_{k-1} \\ T\ddot{y}_{k-1} \end{bmatrix}, \tag{12.49}$$

where T is the sampling interval and $\mathbf{A}_{k-1}$ is a vector of deterministic inputs that accounts for the observed acceleration (e.g., the constraint). The matrix $\mathbf{Q}^g_{k-1}$ in (12.48) represents the covariance of the process noise, while the local linearization $\hat{\mathbf{G}}_{k-1}$ of the nonlinear function $\mathbf{g}_{k-1}$ is given by its Jacobian:

$$\begin{aligned}
\hat{\mathbf{G}}_{k-1} &= \left[\nabla_{\mathbf{x}_{k-1}} \mathbf{g}^T_{k-1}(\mathbf{x}_{k-1}) \right]^T \Big|_{\mathbf{x}_{k-1}=\hat{\mathbf{x}}_{k-1|k-1}} \\
&= \begin{bmatrix} 1 + \frac{T^2}{2}\frac{\partial \ddot{x}}{\partial x} & \frac{T^2}{2}\frac{\partial \ddot{x}}{\partial y} & T & 0 \\ \frac{T^2}{2}\frac{\partial \ddot{y}}{\partial x} & 1 + \frac{T^2}{2}\frac{\partial \ddot{y}}{\partial y} & 0 & T \\ T\frac{\partial \ddot{x}}{\partial x} & T\frac{\partial \ddot{x}}{\partial y} & 1 & 0 \\ T\frac{\partial \ddot{y}}{\partial x} & T\frac{\partial \ddot{y}}{\partial y} & 0 & 1 \end{bmatrix}_{|x=\hat{x}_{k-1|k-1}, y=\hat{y}_{k-1|k-1}} .
\end{aligned} \tag{12.50}$$

If the navigation field does not impact the target motion (i.e., acceleration components in (12.46) are zero and $\mathbf{x}_{k-1} \notin D_{k-1}$), the target state vector and the covariance matrix prediction equations are:

$$\hat{\mathbf{x}}_{k|k-1} = \mathbf{f}_{k-1}(\hat{\mathbf{x}}_{k-1|k-1}) = \mathbf{F}_{k-1}\hat{\mathbf{x}}_{k-1|k-1} \tag{12.51}$$

$$\mathbf{P}_{k|k-1} = \hat{\mathbf{F}}_{k-1}\mathbf{P}_{k-1|k-1}\hat{\mathbf{F}}'_{k-1} + \mathbf{Q}^f_{k-1}. \tag{12.52}$$

Specifically, we have that $\mathbf{F}_{k-1} = \mathbf{G}_{k-1}$ in accordance to a CV target motion model. The matrix $\hat{\mathbf{F}}_{k-1}$ in (12.52) is computed as usual as:

$$\hat{\mathbf{F}}_{k-1} = \left[\nabla_{\mathbf{x}_{k-1}} \mathbf{f}_{k-1}^T (\mathbf{x}_{k-1})\right]^T \Big|_{\mathbf{x}_{k-1}=\hat{\mathbf{x}}_{k-1|k-1}}. \qquad (12.53)$$

Filter Implementation: Model II—Force as Angular Acceleration

For this model, the target state vector at discrete time k consists of position, velocity, and angular velocity, i.e., $\mathbf{x}_k^0 = [x_k, y_k, \dot{x}_k, \dot{y}_k, \omega_k]$.

The force allows the evaluation of the target angular acceleration $\dot{\omega}_k$ from which the target angular velocity ω_k is extracted:

$$\dot{\omega}_k = f\{F_{Gx}(x_k, y_k), F_{Gy}(x_k, y_k), \dot{x}_k, \dot{y}_k\} \qquad (12.54)$$

$$\omega_k = f\{x_k, y_k, \dot{x}_k, \dot{y}_k\} = \dot{\omega}_{k-1}T + \dot{\omega}_{k-1}. \qquad (12.55)$$

Also in this case, we deal with a reduced dimension target state vector, i.e., $\mathbf{x}_k = [x_k, y_k, \dot{x}_k, \dot{y}_k]$. The prediction of the target state and the covariance matrix are defined as follows:

$$\hat{\mathbf{x}}_{k|k-1} = \mathbf{g}_{k-1}(\hat{\mathbf{x}}_{k-1|k-1}) = \mathbf{G}_{k-1}\hat{\mathbf{x}}_{k-1|k-1} \qquad (12.56)$$

$$\mathbf{P}_{k|k-1} = \hat{\mathbf{G}}_{k-1}\mathbf{P}_{k-1|k-1}\hat{\mathbf{G}}_{k-1}' + \mathbf{Q}_{k-1}^g. \qquad (12.57)$$

It has to be stressed that the state-dependent angular velocity ω_{k-1} derived by the force as in (12.55) is used for the computation of $\mathbf{G}_{k-1}$. Specifically, on the basis of the CT motion model we have:

$$\mathbf{G}_{k-1} = \begin{bmatrix} 1 & 0 & \frac{\sin(\omega_{k-1}T)}{\omega_{k-1}} & -\frac{1-\cos(\omega_{k-1}T)}{\omega_{k-1}} \\ 0 & 1 & \frac{1-\cos(\omega_{k-1}T)}{\omega_{k-1}} & \frac{\sin(\omega_{k-1}T)}{\omega_{k-1}} \\ 0 & 0 & \cos(\omega_{k-1}T) & -\sin(\omega_{k-1}T) \\ 0 & 0 & \sin(\omega_{k-1}T) & \cos(\omega_{k-1}T) \end{bmatrix}, \qquad (12.58)$$

where the sign of the variable ω determines the clockwise and anticlockwise coordinated motion dynamics. Given, the (12.55), the $\hat{\mathbf{G}}_{k-1}$ is obtained via the Jacobian:

$$\hat{\mathbf{G}}_{k-1} = \left[\nabla_{\mathbf{x}_{k-1}} \mathbf{g}_{k-1}^T (\mathbf{x}_{k-1})\right]^T \Big|_{\mathbf{x}_{k-1}=\hat{\mathbf{x}}_{k-1|k-1}}. \qquad (12.59)$$

If the force does not influence the target motion, the angular velocity ω_{k-1} is not evaluated. Thus, the target prediction is made in accordance to another motion model (i.e., the CV), and the Eqs. (12.56) and (12.57) becomes:

$$\hat{\mathbf{x}}_{k|k-1} = \mathbf{f}_{k-1}(\hat{\mathbf{x}}_{k-1|k-1}) = \mathbf{F}_{k-1}\hat{\mathbf{x}}_{k-1|k-1} \tag{12.60}$$

$$\mathbf{P}_{k|k-1} = \hat{\mathbf{F}}_{k-1}\mathbf{P}_{k-1|k-1}\hat{\mathbf{F}}'_{k-1} + \mathbf{Q}^{\mathrm{f}}_{k-1}, \tag{12.61}$$

where

$$\mathbf{F}_{k-1} = \begin{bmatrix} 1 & 0 & T & 0 \\ 0 & 1 & 0 & T \\ 0 & 0 & 1 & 0 \\ 0 & 0 & 0 & 1 \end{bmatrix}, \qquad \hat{\mathbf{F}}_{k-1} = \left[\nabla_{\mathbf{x}_{k-1}}\mathbf{f}^T_{k-1}(\mathbf{x}_{k-1})\right]^T\Big|_{\mathbf{x}_{k-1}=\hat{\mathbf{x}}_{k-1|k-1}}. \tag{12.62}$$

12.4.2.2   Sea-Lane Assisted Target Tracking

As the **Sea-lane Assisted Tracking** approach [33] is concerned, the general assumption is that the context information drives the selection of the target dynamic motion model (DM$_k$) in the tracking filter at each time step. The constrained transitional density in (12.34) can be expressed as follows:

$$p(\mathbf{x}_k|\mathbf{x}_{k-1}, C_k) \cong \begin{cases} \mathcal{N}(\mathbf{x}_k; \mathbf{f}^{\mathrm{DM}}_{k-1}(\mathbf{x}_{k-1}); \mathbf{Q}^{\mathrm{DM}}_{k-1}), & \text{if } \mathbf{x}_k \in C_k \\ 0, & \text{otherwise,} \end{cases} \tag{12.63}$$

where $\mathbf{f}^{\mathrm{DM}}(.)$ is the context-driven transition function, which allows transiting from $\mathbf{x}_{k-1}$ to one of the possible states in C_k (inequality constraint) and $\mathbf{Q}^{\mathrm{DM}}_{k-1}$ is the covariance matrix of the process noise, which differs depending on the target dynamic motion model. Whereas a particle filter formulation is required, the constrained transitional density in (12.63) can be written for each ith particle $(i = 1, \ldots, N_p)$ of the cloud approximating the pdf as follows:

$$p(\mathbf{x}_k|\mathbf{x}^i_{k-1}, C_k) \cong \begin{cases} \mathcal{N}(\mathbf{x}_k; \mathbf{f}^{\mathrm{DM}i}_{k-1}(\mathbf{x}^i_{k-1}); \mathbf{Q}^{\mathrm{DM}i}_{k-1}), & \text{if } \mathbf{x}_k \in C_k \\ 0, & \text{otherwise.} \end{cases} \tag{12.64}$$

The choice of $\mathbf{f}^{\mathrm{DM}}$ and $\mathbf{Q}^{\mathrm{DM}}$ in (12.63) and for the particles in (12.64) depends on the models adopted to describe the target behavior and the context information. In the following these models are presented as well as the derived target tracking filters.

Target and Context Modeling

The concept of sea-lane (including port approaches, shipping lanes, sea highways and traffic separation schemes) has been addressed since it identifies the recommended or most likely route followed by the vessel (see for instance [34]). The general assumption is that the target is navigating with the aim of reaching a destination or following a predefined path. Therefore, each change of its trajectory (e.g., maneuver) is dictated by the influence of context elements. These

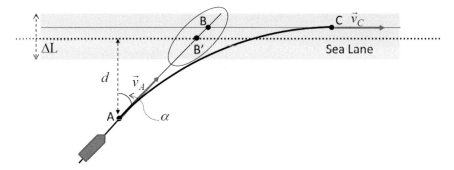

Fig. 12.3 Geometrical model for vessel maneuver

considerations allow adopting simple geometrical models describing the target behavior. Specifically, the trajectory is decomposed into linear segments connecting adjacent waypoints. Misaligned segments indicate a maneuver for the target, which is characterized by the time of maneuver, the angular speed and the limiting points. The position of future waypoints and the values of the maneuvering parameters are directly inferred from the context information. We assume that the target proceeds with *constant velocity* along a linear path and then follows a circular trajectory with a *constant angular speed* ω to perform the maneuver. Once completed, the target resumes the linear trajectory. It follows that the trajectory is split in a sequence of constant velocity and coordinated turn segments. The simplified geometrical model for the target maneuver is reported in the following picture:

In Fig. 12.3, A and C are the start and the end points of the maneuver, respectively. We assume the ship to maintain the same velocity magnitude, i.e., $|v_A| = |v_C|$. The problem is the evaluation of the sea lane entry point C, with $\mathbf{x}_C = [x_C, y_C, \dot{x}_C, \dot{y}_C]$, and the value of ω on the basis of geometric considerations and initial target state vector $\mathbf{x}_A = [x_A, y_A, \dot{x}_A, \dot{y}_A]$. We proceed as follows: (i) point A is chosen with a distance d from the lane axial direction; (ii) point B' is the intersection between the direction of the ship velocity vector in A and the lane axis; (iii) point B lies in $\overline{AB'}$ direction and has a displacement from B due to the uncertainty of the entry point within the lane. The distance $\overline{AB}$ is given by $\overline{AB} = \overline{AB'} + \xi$, where ξ is a random variable extracted form a truncated Gaussian random process with zero-mean value and standard deviation σ_ξ, i.e., $\xi \sim \mathcal{N}(0, \sigma_\xi)$, with

$$\sigma_\xi = \frac{\Delta L}{4 \cos \alpha}, \quad \xi \in \left[-\frac{\Delta L}{2 \cos \alpha}, \frac{\Delta L}{2 \cos \alpha} \right], \tag{12.65}$$

where ΔL is the lane width. Finally, (iv), point C is given by the intersection of the circle tangent to $\overline{AB}$ in A and the transverse axis passing in B. The value of ω is derived from the Coordinated Turn model as follows:

$$\omega = \begin{cases} \frac{\dot{y}_C - \dot{y}_A}{x_C - x_A}, & \text{if } x_A \neq x_C \\[2mm] \frac{\dot{x}_A - \dot{x}_C}{y_C - y_A}, & \text{if } y_A \neq y_C \end{cases} . \tag{12.66}$$

Filter Implementation: Context-driven Target Model Switching

The context information drives the selection of the target dynamic model (DM) in (1) for each time instant k. It has to be stressed that this selection follows a rule-based approach (i.e., target position sea-lane geometry as depicted in Fig. 12.3), so the dynamic motion model switching probability is not evaluated. Let the state vector at the discrete time k consist of position and velocity components of the target in Cartesian coordinates, i.e., $\mathbf{x}_k = [x_k, y_k, \dot{x}_k, \dot{y}_k]$.

With respect to the *EKF formulation* and the expression in (12.63), the prediction of the target state and covariance are recursively obtained as:

$$\hat{\mathbf{x}}_{k|k-1} = \mathbf{f}_{k-1}^{DM}(\hat{\mathbf{x}}_{k-1|k-1}) = \mathbf{F}_{k-1}^{DM}\hat{\mathbf{x}}_{k-1|k-1} \tag{12.67}$$

$$\mathbf{P}_{k|k-1} = \hat{\mathbf{F}}_{k-1}^{DM}\mathbf{P}_{k-1|k-1}\hat{\mathbf{F}}_{k-1}^{\prime DM} + \mathbf{Q}_{k-1}^{DM}. \tag{12.68}$$

Values of $\mathbf{F}_k^{DM}$ and $\mathbf{Q}_k^{DM}$ depend on the selected dynamic model. As the target trajectory is decomposed in linear and curvilinear segments covered at constant velocity, the $\mathbf{F}_k^{DM}$ assumes the form of:

$$\mathbf{F}_{CV} = \begin{bmatrix} 1 & 0 & T & 0 \\ 0 & 1 & 0 & T \\ 0 & 0 & 1 & 0 \\ 0 & 0 & 0 & 1 \end{bmatrix}, \quad \mathbf{F}_{CT} = \begin{bmatrix} 1 & 0 & \frac{\sin(\omega T)}{\omega} & -\frac{1-\cos(\omega T)}{\omega} \\ 0 & 1 & \frac{1-\cos(\omega T)}{\omega} & \frac{\sin(\omega T)}{\omega} \\ 0 & 0 & \cos(\omega T) & -\sin(\omega T) \\ 0 & 0 & \sin(\omega T) & \cos(\omega T) \end{bmatrix}, \tag{12.69}$$

under the CV and CT assumptions, respectively. T is the sampling interval and ω is the angular velocity for the CT, evaluated as in (12.66). Specifically, we have:

$$\begin{cases} \mathbf{F}_k^{DM} = \mathbf{F}_{CT}, & \hat{\mathbf{F}}_k^{DM} = \hat{\mathbf{F}}_{CT_k}, & \mathbf{Q}_k^{DM} = \mathbf{Q}_k^{CT} & \text{if}(\mathbf{x}_k \in C_k \text{ and } \mathbf{x}_{k-1} \in D_{k-1}) \\ \mathbf{F}_k^{DM} = \mathbf{F}_{CV}, & \hat{\mathbf{F}}_k^{DM} = \hat{\mathbf{F}}_{CV_k}, & \mathbf{Q}_k^{DM} = \mathbf{Q}_k^{CV} & \text{if}(\mathbf{x}_{k-1} \notin D_{k-1}) \end{cases} . \tag{12.70}$$

where D_{k-1} is the ensemble of state vectors that are subject to the influence of the context at time instant $(k-1)$. We refer to this filter as **SL-CV-CT-EKF**.

When a *PF technique* is adopted, $\mathbf{F}_k^{DM}$ value differs for each particle of the cloud, as the value of ω depends on the maneuver associated to each particle. Thus, the influence of the context information on the tracking filter is twofold. It drives the switching among different target dynamic models, and it tunes the parameters of the current model (e.g., ω, time for the entire maneuver). We refer to this filter as **SL-CV-CT-PF**.

12.4.3   Tracking Filters for Ground Target Tracking

Ground situation awareness of highly dynamic scenarios with many ground moving targets requires computer-aided extraction and maintenance of target tracks in the surveillance area. Although the use of airborne ground moving target indication (GMTI) radar promises high radar coverage of the surveillance region (regardless of daytime or weather conditions), several issues make automatic target tracking difficult, e.g., the clutter notch of the sensor, terrain obscuration, missed detections, false alarms, or data assignment ambiguities in the case of closely spaced targets.

   In the following section, we describe two different types of constraints relevant for ground target tracking: (i) constraints on the motion of road targets and (ii) constraints on the target state and sensor-target geometry implied by the (negative) outcome of a GMTI sensor measurement. The aim is to model the constraints in an appropriate way to enhance the tracking performance in terms of track precision and track continuity.

12.4.3.1   Roadmap Assisted Target Tracking

The use of roadmaps to enhance the tracking performance is a typical example of *map matching*, a frequently applied approach, e.g., for navigation systems. Roadmaps can, in principle, be exploited in different steps of the tracking filter (see, for example, [35–40]), e.g., by projecting the measurements or the state vectors to the road. In a road network or in the case of winding roads, however, the projections of the state estimate and in particular of the covariance onto the road are ambiguous. A different approach is to model the target dynamics in road coordinates. In the simplest case, this leads to a description of the target state in reduced dimensions, using the mileage and speed as target state parameters. As real roads are not strictly one-dimensional, their width, i.e., the motion transversal to the road direction, has to be modeled, too. In the following, we describe such an approach that models the target motion in road coordinates and performs the data processing in Cartesian coordinates [41, 42]. The nonlinear mapping between the two coordinate systems is done using a *Gaussian mixture* approach.

Context Modeling

A road can mathematically be described by a continuous 3-D curve $\mathscr{R}^*$ in Cartesian coordinates and is parametrized by the corresponding arc length l with $\mathscr{R}^*$: $l \mapsto \mathscr{R}^*(l)$. $\mathscr{R}^*$ can be approximated by a polygonal curve $\mathscr{R}$ consisting of n_r piecewise linear segments. The $n_r + 1$ nodes of this polygonal curve are given by the 3-D node vectors

$$\mathbf{r}_s = \mathscr{R}^*(l_s), \quad s = 1, \ldots, n_r + 1 \tag{12.71}$$

and for each road segment a normalized tangential vector

$$\mathbf{t}_s = \frac{\mathbf{r}_{s+1} - \mathbf{r}_s}{|\mathbf{r}_{s+1} - \mathbf{r}_s|}, \quad s = 1, \ldots, n_r \tag{12.72}$$

can be derived. With the segment length $\lambda_s = l_{s+1} - l_s$ and the indicator function defined by

$$\chi_s(l) = \begin{cases} 1 & \text{for } l \in [l_s, l_{s+1}) \\ 0 & \text{otherwise} \end{cases} \quad s = 1, \ldots, n_r \tag{12.73}$$

the polygonal curve $\mathscr{R}$ is then given by

$$\mathscr{R} : l \in [l_1, l_{n_r+1}) \mapsto \mathscr{R}(l) = \sum_{s=1}^{n_r} [\mathbf{r}_s + (l - l_s)\mathbf{t}_s] \chi_s(l) \tag{12.74}$$

with $\mathscr{R}^*(l_s) = \mathscr{R}(l_s) = \mathbf{r}_s$ and $s = 1, \ldots, n_r + 1$. Thus, each segment s of the polygonal road $\mathscr{R}$ is determined by the node vector $\mathbf{r}_s$, the arc length λ_s, and the normalized tangential vector $\mathbf{t}_s$. In addition, both the width and the accuracy of the road are described by a covariance matrix $\mathbf{R}_s^r$ which also accounts for the discretization error introduced by $\lambda_s - |\mathbf{r}_{s+1} - \mathbf{r}_s|$, i.e., the difference between the length of a segment and the actual distance traveled along this segment. Such a description makes sense when an estimate of the target position transversal to the road direction is not required, i.e., in particular when the measurement uncertainty is significantly larger than the width of the road or lane.

Filter Implementation: Tracking with Road Networks
Road network data generally contains several road sections, each consisting of a certain number of linear segments connected at specific nodes. This yields a complex structure exhibiting crossings and junctions. The basic idea of a tracking scheme utilizing complex roadmap data is, first of all, to introduce a local road for each target which consists of only a limited number of segments. Depending on the specific motion of a target along the road network, this local road then needs to be continuously adapted: as the target approaches the head of the road, new segments are added, and segments with vanishing probability at the tail of the road are pruned. In addition, the orientation of the local road is reversed if a target moves backwards along the associated road segments.

The trajectory of a realistic road target will include junctions and crossings. In such a case, the arising ambiguity can easily be resolved over time by utilizing a multiple model [43] approach with respect to the generated local roads. The possible paths of the moving object at the junction or crossing lead to different road hypotheses h with $h = 1, \ldots, N_h$, where each has a different continuation of the previous local road after the junction. An example for this is shown in Fig. 12.4. If a target approaches a junction or crossing, a road hypothesis for every possible continuation after the junction is generated. In the subsequent time steps, the probability of a particular road hypothesis, conditioned on the accumulated measurement sequence, is then calculated at the end of the filter update based on the

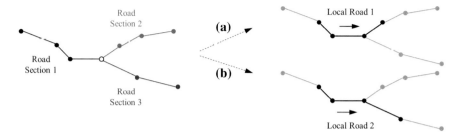

Fig. 12.4 *Left* Exemplary road network consisting of three road sections. *Right* Local roads generated for a target which moves from left to right and approaches the junction

computed component weights. In that way, the tracking algorithm is able to handle the arising ambiguity due to the different possible trajectories of the target. This ambiguity is then resolved over time as the target passes the junction or crossing and moves further away. The obtained target measurements then facilitate the discrimination among the different road hypotheses.

Following the approaches in [41, 42], the state vector of a road target at time step t_k is described in the road coordinate system, i.e., by its arc length l_k along the road and by the associated speed $\dot{l}_k$ as $\mathbf{x}_k^r = [l_k, \dot{l}_k]^\top$. In the following, a single iterative loop of the road tracking scheme is summarized: First of all, it is assumed that the target state pdf in continuous road coordinates at time step t_{k-1} is available and given by the expression

$$p(\mathbf{x}_{k-1}^r | \mathscr{Z}^{k-1}) = \sum_{h=1}^{N_h} P_{k-1}(h | \mathscr{Z}^{k-1}) \, p(\mathbf{x}_{k-1}^r | h, \mathscr{Z}^{k-1}). \qquad (12.75)$$

When the pdf for each road hypothesis h is determined by a single Gaussian, the pdf take the form of a Gaussian mixture.

Applying the Chapman-Kolmogorov Eq. (12.3), the predicted pdf, too, is given by a Gaussian mixture in continuous road coordinates.

This prior then has to be transformed into the ground coordinate system, so that the sensor data can be processed, i.e.,

$$\underbrace{p(\mathbf{x}_k^r | \mathscr{Z}^{k-1})}_{\text{in road coordinates}} \xrightarrow[\text{roadmap error}]{\text{roadmap}} \underbrace{p(\mathbf{x}_k^g | \mathscr{Z}^{k-1})}_{\text{in ground coordinates}} . \qquad (12.76)$$

By utilizing the linear segmentation of the constructed local road for each road hypothesis h with $n_r(h)$ segments (as discussed in the previous section), the prior density in ground coordinates is computed as [42]:

$$p(\mathbf{x}_k^g|\mathscr{Z}^{k-1}) = \sum_{h=1}^{N_h} P_{k-1}(h|\mathscr{Z}^{k-1}) \left[\sum_{s=1}^{n_r(h)} P_k^h(s|\mathscr{Z}^{k-1}) p(\mathbf{x}_k^g|s, \mathscr{Z}^{k-1}) \right]. \tag{12.77}$$

The expression $P_k^h(s|\mathscr{Z}^{k-1})$ denotes the probability that the target moves on segment s of local road h, based on the accumulated sensor data $\mathscr{Z}^{k-1}$.

The segment-dependent pdf in ground coordinates in (12.77) is calculated from the pdf in road coordinates as:

$$p(\mathbf{x}_k^g|s, \mathscr{Z}^{k-1}) = \int p(\mathbf{x}_k^g|\mathbf{x}_k^r, s)\, p(\mathbf{x}_k^r|s, \mathscr{Z}^{k-1})\, d\mathbf{x}_k^r. \tag{12.78}$$

Assuming Gaussian error on the road segments of the map, the transition density (12.78) is Gaussian, too, and the integration provides a pdf in ground coordinates, constrained to the segment s:

$$p(\mathbf{x}_k^g|s, \mathscr{Z}^{k-1}) = \mathcal{N}(\mathbf{x}_k^g; \mathbf{x}_{k|k-1}^g(s), \mathbf{P}_{k|k-1}^g(s)) \tag{12.79}$$

and the segment-dependent pdf (12.78), then, can be calculated as a Gaussian distribution. Explicit formulas for the arguments in (12.77) are given in [42].

In this approach, the pdf in road coordinates is unconstrained, but it is mapped by (12.76) to a pdf in ground coordinates that is constrained by the road geometry. As the mapping is based on Gaussian distributions, the constraints are, exactly speaking, only statistical and, therefore, soft.

In the filter update step, each component on the r.h.s. of (12.77) is updated with m measurements. After the generation of all hypotheses, each segment-dependent density $p(\mathbf{x}_k^g|m, s, \mathscr{Z}^k)$ is individually transformed back from Cartesian to road coordinates by a simple projection onto the corresponding road segment:

$$\underbrace{p(\mathbf{x}_k^g|m, s, \mathscr{Z}^k)}_{\text{in ground coordinates}} \xrightarrow{\text{roadmap}} \underbrace{p(\mathbf{x}_k^r|m, s, \mathscr{Z}^k)}_{\text{in road coordinates}}. \tag{12.80}$$

The pdf in continuous road coordinates for every road hypothesis h yields, for each of the generated hypotheses, a Gaussian mixture of segment-dependent probability densities with mean and covariance as given in [42]. For simplicity, this is then approximated by second-order moment-matching [2], resulting in a single density

$$p(\mathbf{x}_k^r|h, m, \mathscr{Z}^k) \approx w_k^m(h)\, \mathcal{N}(\mathbf{x}_k^r; \mathbf{x}_{k|k}^{r,m}(h), \mathbf{P}_{k|k}^{r,m}(h)), \tag{12.81}$$

with the component weights $w_k^m(h) = \sum_{s=1}^{n_r(h)} P_k^h(s|\mathscr{Z}^{k-1}) w_k^m(s)$. The posterior density of the target state in continuous road coordinates can finally be written as

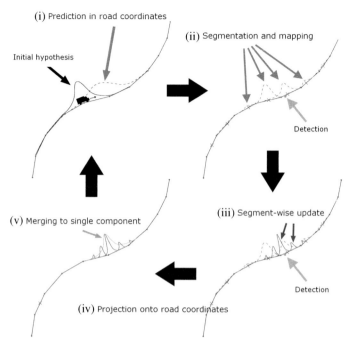

Fig. 12.5 Scheme of one iteration of the roadmap assisted tracking filter: (*i*) prediction in continuous road coordinates, (*ii*) segmentation into road segments and mapping to Cartesian coordinates, (*iii*) data processing in Cartesian coordinates, (*iv*) projection onto road coordinates, (*v*) merging (moment matching) to a single component. We thank Jost Koller for providing the graphic

$$p(\mathbf{x}_k^r | \mathscr{L}^k) = \sum_{h=1}^{N_h} P_k(h|\mathscr{L}^k) p(\mathbf{x}_k^r | h, \mathscr{L}^k), \tag{12.82}$$

with the posterior for each road hypothesis *h* determined by

$$p(\mathbf{x}_k^r | h, \mathscr{L}^k) = \sum_{m=0}^{m_k} w_k^m(h) \, \mathscr{N}(\mathbf{x}_k^r; \mathbf{x}_{k|k}^{r,m}(h), \mathbf{P}_{k|k}^{r,m}(h)). \tag{12.83}$$

As the new updated pdf in road coordinates (12.82) has the same structure as the one at time t_{k-1}, (12.75), this closes one iteration of the tracking filter, depicted in Fig. 12.5.

Particle Filter Approach

Alternatively to the Gaussian mixture approach described above, particle filter techniques can be applied (see, e.g., [35, 36, 38, 42]). Here, the particle states are given by two-dimensional vectors, describing position (mileage) and speed along the road. The low dimensionality of the state vectors has the advantage to enhance the efficiency of particle filter sampling. A corresponding *sampling importance resampling* (SIR) particle filter is described and evaluated in [42]. The nonlinear mapping to ground coordinates can be done exactly within the errors of the underlying roadmap. In this mapping, a noise term, proportional to the road segment width, is added which shifts the particle position across the road direction. The noise terms describes both the road width and the road mapping error. The particle positions in Cartesian coordinates are used to calculate the likelihood function, and hence, the updated particle weights. The SIR particle filter has been used as a benchmark for the above described Gaussian mixture approach and it has been shown that, for realistic scenarios and system parameters, the performance of the latter almost always is optimal [42].

12.4.3.2   Blind Zone Assisted Target Tracking

For the tracking of ground moving targets, measurements of airborne *ground moving target indication* (GMTI) radar [44] are well-suited due to its favorable wide-area illumination, all-weather, day and night availability as well as real-time capabilities. In general, moving objects are detected based on the Doppler shift in the reflected signal, induced by the radial motion of the targets. However, a large amount of the back-scattered radiation originates from the ground, but due to the motion of the sensor platform, these clutter measurements are also colored in Doppler, i.e., exhibit a nonzero Doppler shift. Therefore, a sophisticated clutter suppression technique has to be applied first in order to cancel out the general clutter background, before true detections from moving objects can be obtained and passed along to the tracking unit. The state-of-the-art technique for this clutter cancelation is *space-time adaptive processing* (STAP) [45, 46], which performs an optimal two-dimensional suppression of the clutter distribution.

A major challenge for a tracking algorithm using detections from airborne GMTI radar arises from the fact that reflections from moving targets can be suppressed by the STAP clutter filter. This is mostly the case if the radial speed of the target is below the *minimum detectable velocity* (MDV) threshold which indicates the width of the clutter distribution in the Doppler domain. Such *low-Doppler targets* may arise due to an unfavorable target-sensor geometry, slow targets, or due to a stopping maneuver. These targets will not be detected by the sensor, yielding possibly long sequences of missed detections. This blind spot of the GMTI sensor is called *Doppler blind zone* and its width is given by MDV.

If a target is masked by the Doppler blind zone, this introduces a constraint which confines the target motion to a certain region. In [41, 9, 47], the Doppler blind zone information is accounted for in a Bayesian tracking filter by utilizing a state-dependent detection probability, which takes low values whenever an object's range-rate is inside the suppressed Doppler interval. The impact of this blind zone on the detection probability is modeled by an inverse Gaussian, yielding a soft blind zone constraint. In the following, this technique is discussed.

Context Modeling

The distance from the blind zone center depends on the target state $\mathbf{x}_k$ and sensor position $\mathbf{r}_k^S$ and is defined by the *Doppler notch function*, $n_D(\mathbf{x}_k, \mathbf{r}_k^S) = \dot{r}_k - \dot{r}_k^c$, i.e., the difference in range-rate between target and surrounding main lobe clutter. Using standard transformation rules, this expression is given in Cartesian coordinates by

$$n_D(\mathbf{x}_k, \mathbf{r}_k^S) = \frac{\mathbf{r}_k - \mathbf{r}_k^S}{||\mathbf{r}_k - \mathbf{r}_k^S||} \dot{\mathbf{r}}_k \tag{12.84}$$

and is thus equal to the target velocity projected onto the line-of-sight vector between sensor and target. Another important quantity is the already mentioned width of the blind zone given by the MDV. In general, the MDV is not a constant sensor parameter for a given scenario setup [48] but depends on a possible spacial separation between transmit and receive unit of the radar (bistatic setup), the array antenna configuration and the look angle of the receive antenna towards the target. But in the following, the MDV will be assumed constant which holds for the monostatic sideways-looking case.

An appropriate modeling of the detection probability impacted by the Doppler blind zone has to account for the following implications:

1. The detection probability P_d has to depend on the state vector of the target, i.e., $P_d = P_d(\mathbf{x}_k)$.
2. P_d has to be small or even vanish if $|n_D(\mathbf{x}_k, \mathbf{r}_k^S)| < \text{MDV}$.
3. For $|n_D(\mathbf{x}_k, \mathbf{r}_k^S)| \gg \text{MDV}$, i.e., far away from the blind zone, P_d has to depend solely on the directivity pattern of the antenna and the distance between sensor and target.

To meet the above condition while preserving the Gaussian framework of (extended) Kalman filtering, the following functional form of the detection probability P_d has been proposed [47]:

$$P_d(\mathbf{x}_k, \mathbf{r}_k^S) = p_d(r_k, \varphi_k, \theta_k) \left[1 - e^{-\log 2 \left(\frac{n_D(\mathbf{x}_k, \mathbf{r}_k^S)}{\text{MDV}} \right)^2} \right], \tag{12.85}$$

where $p_d(r_k, \varphi_k, \theta_k)$ accounts for the receive directivity pattern which depends on the Rx azimuth angle towards the target and the target range. The particular form of the detection probability is chosen to approximately resemble the influence of the STAP clutter suppression. If the Doppler notch function equals the current width of the blind zone, then $P_d = p_d(\varphi_k, \theta_k, r_k)/2$. Hence, target detections become more and more unlikely as the target moves deeper into the blind zone region and vanish at the blind zone center where the target's range-rate matches the range-rate of the main lobe clutter.

Filter Implementation: Inclusion of Doppler Blind Zones

The knowledge on the Doppler blind zone is incorporated into the Bayesian tracking filter by expanding (12.84) in first order around the predicted target state and, then, substituting the target state-dependent detection probability (12.85) into the likelihood function (see [47]). This yields a fictitious measurement $\tilde{z}_f$ and fictitious observation matrix $\tilde{\mathbf{H}}_f$:

$$\tilde{z}_f = n_D(\mathbf{x}_{k|k-1}, \mathbf{r}_k^S) + \tilde{\mathbf{H}}_f \mathbf{x}_{k|k-1} \tag{12.86}$$

$$\tilde{\mathbf{H}}_f = -\frac{\partial}{\partial \mathbf{x}_k} n_D(\mathbf{x}_k, \mathbf{r}_k^S)|_{\mathbf{x}_k = \mathbf{x}_{k|k-1}}. \tag{12.87}$$

In that way, the exponential in (12.85) can be rewritten as a Gaussian which linearly depends on the target state vector $\mathbf{x}_k$, yielding

$$P_d(\mathbf{x}_k, \mathbf{r}_k^S) = p_d(r_k, \varphi_k, \theta_k) \left[1 - c_D \mathcal{N}(\tilde{z}_f; \tilde{\mathbf{H}}_f \mathbf{x}_k, v_D) \right], \tag{12.88}$$

where $c_D = \mathrm{MDV}/\sqrt{\log(2)/\pi}$ is a normalization factor and $v_D = \mathrm{MDV}^2/(2\log 2)$ is the variance of the fictitious measurement $\tilde{\mathbf{z}}_f$ in the range-rate domain.

The implications of this detection probability, representing a refined GMTI sensor model, can easily be illustrated by calculating the likelihood function which is now a function of the measurement and the constraint:

$$p(C_k, \mathbf{z}_k | \mathbf{x}_k) = \left(1 - P_d(\mathbf{x}_k, \mathbf{r}_k^S) \right) + \frac{P_d(\mathbf{x}_k, \mathbf{r}_k^S)}{\rho_f} \mathcal{N}(\mathbf{z}_k; \mathbf{H}_k \mathbf{x}_k, \mathbf{R}_k), \tag{12.89}$$

similar as in (12.8), but with a state-dependent detection probability. With the standard expression for P_d, this yields a Gaussian mixture posterior density consisting of two components, representing the following possible sensor data interpretations:

1. The detection belongs to the target, a regular filtering is executed.
2. The detection is due to a false alarm, the target was not detected.

On the other hand, if the refined GMTI sensor model is considered by inserting (12.88) into (12.89), then due to the $(1 - x)$ structure, each previous mixture component now splits into two components. The resulting four mixture components contain two additional components which can be interpreted as follows:

3. The detection belongs to the target, it is not masked by the Doppler blind zone, removing probability mass out of the blind zone region.
4. The detection is due to a false alarm because the target is masked by the Doppler blind zone.

In other words, the hypothesis that the target is masked (not masked) by the Doppler blind zone induces an inequality constraint on the target state, as the radial velocity has to be smaller (larger) than MDV. As P_d describes a statistical detection probability, the constraint is *soft*. This example makes clear that due to the increased number of hypotheses established in the filter update step, a tracking filter utilizing the refined GMTI sensor model is able to interpret the sensor output in a more sophisticated manner compared to a standard tracking filter and is capable of handling a sequence of missed detections arising due to Doppler blind zone masking. Numerical examples are given in Sect. 12.5.2.

12.5 Numerical Results

In this chapter, some results related to various tracking algorithms described in the previous section are reported.

12.5.1 Sea-Lane Assisted Tracking

This section compares the performance of the two tracking filters (SL-CV-CT-EKF and SL-CV-CT-PF) described in Sect. 12.4.2.2, which resort to a priori knowledge of the sea lanes to support the tracking task in specific observation conditions (i.e., lack of sensor measurements). The presented analysis has two objectives. The first one (Objective A) is to assess the improvement coming from the use of the route information. Specifically, we want to demonstrate how the filters follow more reliably the evolution of the track if the knowledge information is used when the measurements fail. The second objective (Objective B) aims at comparing the predisposition of the tracking filters to easily incorporate the context information, i.e., which of the considered knowledge-based filters maintains the track more faithfully in presence of measurement gaps. Given these considerations, the Objective A requires the comparison of each filter (SL-CV-CT-EKF and SL-CV-CT-PF) with its standard counterpart (EKF or PF); the Objective B resorts on the their direct comparison.

The assessment is given in terms of *Kullback-Leibler Divergence*—KLD, denoted by $D_{KL}(p,q)$, which generally allows the comparison between two continuous density p and q. Specifically, the KLD estimator $\hat{D}_{KL}(p,q)$ [49] is used to compare EKF and PF distributions, as follows:

- A reference distribution (PF_{Ref}) is generated using a PF with a high number of samples $N_{p_{Ref}}$;
- A PF with $N_{p_{PF}}$ particles, such that $N_{p_{PF}} \ll N_{p_{Ref}}$, is considered and the KLD between PF and PF_{Ref} distributions is calculated, $\hat{D}_{KL}(PF, PF_{Ref})$;

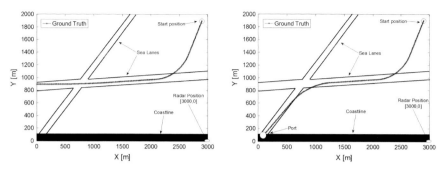

Fig. 12.6 Simulated scenarios. *Left* Single-maneuver target tracking in proximity of the coast accordingly to one sea lane. *Right* Multi-maneuver target tracking for approaching the port area, accordingly to two sea lanes

- The EKF distribution is sampled for comparison. To limit the effect of this approximation we choose a high number of samples $N_{p_{EKF}} = N_{p_{Ref}}$ for computing the $\hat{D}_{KL}(\text{EKF}, \text{PF}_{Ref})$;
- Finally $\hat{D}_{KL}(\text{PF}, \text{PF}_{Ref})$ and $\hat{D}_{KL}(\text{EKF}, \text{PF}_{Ref})$ are compared in terms of mean value.

The scenarios used for simulations are depicted in Fig. 12.6. In the first one, the vessel (i.e., ground truth) approaches the coast, enters the closest sea lane and proceeds along the lane direction, which is approximately parallel to the coastline. The turning maneuver starts roughly 450 m before the lane. The second scenario deals with more complex observation conditions, since the vessel performs a double maneuver to approach the port, which comprises two changes in direction to follow the depicted sea-lanes. For both scenarios, the vessel travels at speed $v = 16$ knots along the path indicated by the red line in an area of [3km × 2km]. The sensor (e.g., a coastal radar providing measurements of range and azimuth) is considered static and positioned at [3000, 0] m. This position was selected in order to offer different degrees of nonlinearity along the target trajectory. The standard deviations of the measurement error are $\sigma_r = 10$ m and $\sigma_\theta = 1°$ in range and azimuth, respectively. The vessel is monitored for a total of $T_{obs} = 420$ s and the collected information is processed each $T = 2$ s (i.e., update rate for the tracking filter). The probability of detection is assumed $P_d = 1$, but drops to zero when gaps of measurement are simulated in T_{obs}. Specifically, only one gap of measurement ($\Delta_{GAP} = 60$ s in the time interval $TI = [80, 140]$s), is generated for Scenario I. Conversely, many gaps of $\Delta_{GAP} = 72$ s are simulated randomly for Scenario II.

A number of 50 Monte Carlo trials have been run per each analysis. Random measurements with zero-mean Gaussian errors are generated in accordance to the sensor model and the observation conditions described above. The measurement vector is $\mathbf{z}_k = [\rho_k, \theta_k]$, where ρ_k and θ_k are range and azimuth estimates at time instant t_k. The target state vector is $\mathbf{x}_k = [x_k, y_k, \dot{x}_k, \dot{y}_k]$ in the Cartesian space. Finally, the process noise value of $\sigma_a = 0.3$ m/s^2 is considered. This parameter

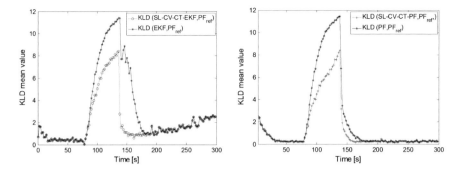

Fig. 12.7 KLD mean value for scenario I, evaluated with $\Delta_{GAP} = 60$ s, $T = 2$ s and $T_{OBS} = 300$ s. *Left* EKF case. *Right* PF case

contributes both to the covariance matrix prediction in the EKF, and the particle cloud prediction for PF case.

Simulation Results—Objective A

The SL-CV-CT-EKF and SL-CV-CT-PF are compared with the standard EKF and PF to assess the improvement coming from the exploitation of the sea lanes. The reference distribution PF_{Ref}, with $N_{p_{Ref}} = 10^5$ is generated without exploiting the context information, since it runs over the continuous set of measurements (i.e., estimation with no measurement gaps as it is the ideal situation we tend to). The posterior pdf of the EKF is generated with $N_{p_{EKF}} = N_{p_{Ref}}$. The PF filter is run with $N_{p_{PF}} = 3000$.

Figure 12.7 shows the results of the comparison for the Scenario I. In the time interval (TI) in which the measurement gap occurs and in which the target maneuvers, the KB filters outperform EKF and PF. The performance is based on the assumption of perfect knowledge of the maneuver (ω, start-end points) by the filters.

Figure 12.8 reports the results for Scenario II. In this case, measurement gaps of 72 s have been randomly inserted over the entire observation period of 420 s. Additional losses are inserted by randomly mismatching the used maneuver model with respect to the true trajectory. The performance improvement due to the use of the context (i.e., the two sea lanes and the port location) is still very high. The robustness of the SL-CV-CT filters to the model mismatch is promising.

Simulation Results—Objective B

Finally, the comparison between the SL-CV-CT-EKF and the SL-CV-CT-PF is here reported. For computing the KLD, a reference distribution SL-CV-CT-PF$_{Ref}$, with $N_{p_{Ref}} = 10^5$ is generated over an intermittent set of measurements. The distribution for the SL-CV-CT-EKF is generated with $N_{p_{EKF}} = N_{p_{Ref}}$ and the SL-CV-CT-PF filter is run with $N_{p_{PF}} = 3000$ particles.

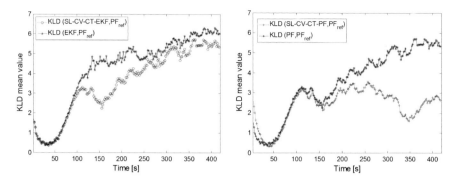

Fig. 12.8 KLD mean value for scenario II, evaluated with $\Delta_{GAP} = 72$ s, $T = 2$ s and $T_{OBS} = 420$ s. *Left* EKF case. *Right* PF case

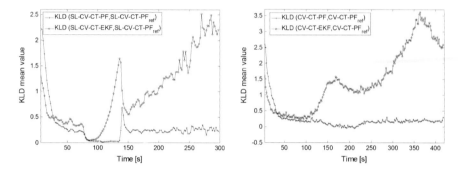

Fig. 12.9 Comparison between the SL-CV-CT-EKF and the SL-CV-CT-PF. *Left* KLD mean value for scenario I, evaluated with $\Delta_{GAP} = 60$ s, $T = 2$ s and $T_{OBS} = 300$ s. *Right* KLD mean value for scenario II, evaluated with $\Delta_{GAP} = 72$ s, $T = 2$ s and $T_{OBS} = 420$ s

Figure 12.9 reports the filter comparison in terms of KLD mean value over both scenarios. The measurement gaps (fixed for Scenario I and variable for Scenario II) are considered for all filters, so that the approximation loss for SL-CV-CT-PF and SL-CV-CT-EKF can be observed. Apart from the initial settling phase of the filter, it is evident that the knowledge-based PF technique largely outperforms the EKF counterpart, yielding a much better capability in approximating the asymptotically true posterior pdf.

12.5.2   *Improved Ground Target Tracking with GMTI Radar*

In the ground moving targets domain, several studies based on simulations demonstrated that the exploitation of road information (Sect. 12.4.3.1) and Doppler

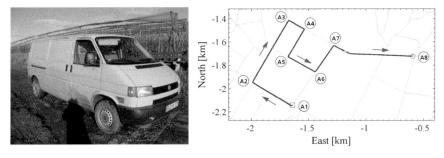

Fig. 12.10 *Left* The GPS equipped VW transporter utilized as ground target. *Photo* © M. Mertens 2013. *Right* True target trajectory based on GPS data. For explanations of the different segments see text. Road network data © OpenStreetMap contributors, CC-BY-SA

blind zones (Sect. 12.4.3.2) in tracking algorithms yields a significant improvement in performance [50, 51, 42]. In this section, the performance of a multi-hypotheses tracking (MHT) filter [52] augmented by road information and Doppler blind zones is evaluated. Example results are provided under realistic conditions based on experimental data acquired by the *phased-array multifunctional imaging radar* (PAMIR) system [53, 54] during a flight campaign [55]. The PAMIR was mounted in the (open) rear side door of a Transall C-160 transport aircraft and thus in a sideways-looking configuration. A detailed description of PAMIR operational parameters as well as the signal processing scheme are reported in [55]. The radar system illuminated a specific region on the ground in which targets (e.g., transporter, car, and bicycle) equipped with GPS receivers moved along predefined trajectories. The context information on the road network in the area of interest is obtained from *OpenStreetMap* (OSM) and is available in form of digitized data. Specifically, the hereafter data evaluation focuses on the transporter, shown in the left plot of Fig. 12.10. Target trajectory is presented in the right plot, where the symbols □ and ○ refer to the individual start and final stop positions, respectively. The trajectory is quite complex and characterized by turns, stops, and periods of unobservability. It is noteworthy to point out the following distinctive features. After turning right at waypoint (A2), the target was masked by the Doppler blind zone for about 15 s. In the course of time, the transporter performed additional turns at waypoints (A3), (A4), (A5), (A6), and (A7), yielding the already mentioned high agility. It is also important to notice that the road segment between (A4) and (A5) was not contained in the digitized road network data.

Three different variants of the MHT filter were utilized in order to analyze the impact of different filter extensions: the MHT filter with no extension (denoted by **Standard MHT**), the MHT with Doppler blind zone information processing (denoted by **MHT + DBZ**), and the MHT filter with Doppler blind zone and road network information (denoted by **MHT + DBZ + Road**). For the radar data processing, a constant detection probability of $P_d = 0.8$ was used in the MHT and for the determination of the measurement error covariance matrix $\mathbf{R}_k$, the variances in each spherical dimension were chosen to be $(3.5\,\mathrm{m})^2$ in range, $(0.2°)^2$ in angle and $(1\,\mathrm{m/s})^2$ in Doppler. The width of the Doppler blind zone, i.e., the MDV, was assumed to be $3\,\mathrm{m/s}$ and the process noise, governing the compatible deviations from the assumed linear motion with constant velocity in the target dynamics model, was chosen to be $0.4\,\mathrm{m/s}^2$ for off-road and $0.2\,\mathrm{m/s}^2$ for road targets, respectively.

The generated tracks associated with the ground target for the three different MHT filters are presented in Fig. 12.11 and the averaged values for the true and estimated position and speed errors as well as other relevant measures of performance are given in Table 12.1. Finally, the evolution of the absolute and estimated errors in position and speed are shown as function of time in Fig. 12.12. It should be noted that for the track coverage calculation, the time of the first target detection was chosen as initial time instance (not the true time of the first considered dwell), corresponding to $5.0\,\mathrm{s}$ in both cases. In the following, the performance of each tracking filter variant is analyzed and discussed individually.

The MHT filter without exploiting any additional information (**standard MHT**) was able to cover most parts (93.2 %) of the true target trajectory. However, this

Fig. 12.11 Extracted, maintained and deleted tracks associated with each ground target for different MHT filter variants. Symbols □ and ◯ refer to track extraction and deletion, respectively. Positions at final time instance are also indicated by ◯. Road network data © OpenStreetMap contributors, CC-BY-SA

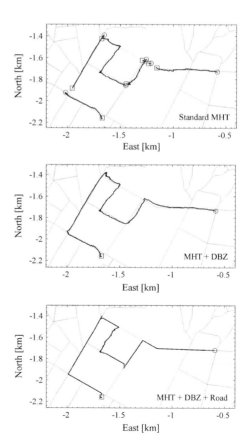

Table 12.1 Averaged true and estimated position and speed errors as well as other relevant measures of performance

MHT filter variant	Absolute position error (m)	Estimated position error (m)	Absolute speed error (m/s)	Estimated speed error (m/s)	No of extracted tracks	Mean track length (s)	Track coverage (%)
Standard MHT	17.6	18.1	3.2	4.4	7	30.5	93.2
MHT + DBZ	24.5	15.1	3.3	2.3	1	228.2	99.5
MHT + DBZ + Road	10.1	14.9	2.2	2.4	1	228.2	99.5

filter was unable to follow the target's path apart from straight line motions which is clearly visible in the corresponding plot of Fig. 12.11. Whenever the target made a turn or disappeared for several revisits due to Doppler blind zone masking, the associated track was extrapolated to regions without any data support and therefore deleted. As soon as new detections became available, a new track was extracted. This track deletion /extraction interplay also resulted in strongly degraded speed

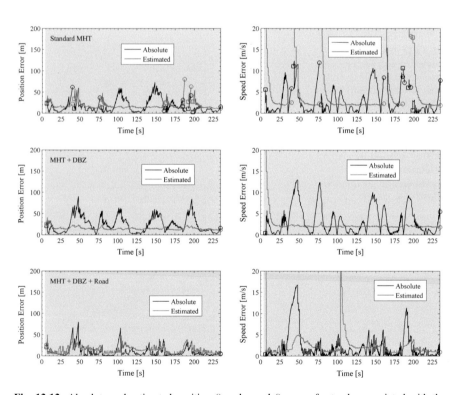

Fig. 12.12 Absolute and estimated position () and speed () errors for tracks associated with the ground target. Each row refers to different MHT filter variants. Symbols □ and ○ refer to track extraction and track deletion, respectively. Values at final time instance are also indicated by ○. The *gray* shaded area indicates the visibility of the ground target at each time step, i.e., if the target is located within the scan area of the PAMIR sensor

error estimation because immediately after track initiation, the uncertainty in velocity is generally large. This effect is clearly visible in Fig. 12.12.

In contrast, by incorporating the information on the Doppler blind zone of the sensor into the tracking filter (**MHT + DBZ**), the performance could be strongly improved. After track extraction, the MHT filter was able to maintain the single track until the final dwell based on the additionally generated hypotheses, despite maneuvers, and blind zone masking. Thus, a track coverage of almost 100 % could be achieved. A closer look at the evolution of the corresponding position and speed errors in Fig. 12.12 for the highly agile transporter reveals the strong mismatch, and thus inconsistency between the utilized dynamics model and the true motion of the target. This is particularly visible by the distinct peaks of the absolute errors corresponding to maneuvering phases of the target, in contrast to the roughly constant estimated position and speed errors during most of the scenario. The tracking filter was therefore too optimistic. But this model mismatch obviously did not lead to a deteriorated tracking performance but was counterbalanced by the exploitation of blind zone information, yielding an optimal track continuity.

The overall best performance in terms of track precision and track continuity (100 % track coverage) was achieved by the tracking filter that exploited all available sources of information, i.e., also the knowledge on the underlying road network. Compared to the also well performing previous MHT filter, the **MHT + DBZ + Road** variant yielded reduced absolute and estimated average position and speed errors. The tracking algorithm was able to correctly handle all occurring target maneuvers and missed detection sequences due to blind zone masking. In addition, the transition between road and off-road track was also accomplished successfully which occurred between waypoints (A4) and (A5), leading to the high peak of the estimated speed error at 105 s in Fig. 12.12.

The discoveries can be summarized as follows: a strong improvement in tracking performance could already be reached by exploiting Doppler blind zone information. The overall best tracking performance, however, was achieved by the fusion of complementary Doppler blind zone and road network information. Therefore, the expected improvement potential from simulation studies could be confirmed.

12.6 Summary

The chapter gave a brief recall of some common approaches to solve the nonlinear recursive filtering within the Bayesian statistical framework for target tracking. Specifically, the extended Kalman filter and the particle filter formulations have been taken into consideration. Then, the general Bayesian recursion has been modified in order to include information about external context in terms of constraints on target motions and/or measurement process (Sect. 12.3.2). Specifically, we demonstrated how the constraints can be exploited either in the prediction step or in the update step of the tracking algorithm. The derivation of sample constrained filters has been presented in Sect. 12.4. Finally, the exploitation of the context led to enhanced performance of the tracking filters, as reported in the numerical examples of Sect. 12.5.

References

1. D. Hall, S. McMullen, *Mathematical Techniques in Multisensor Data Fusion* (Artech House, 2004)
2. Y. Bar-Shalom, X.-R. Li, T. Kirubarajan, *Estimation with Applications to Tracking and Navigation: Theory, Algorithms and Software* (John Wiley & Sons, 2001)
3. S. Blackman, R. Popoli, *Design and Analysis of Modern Tracking Systems* (Artech House, Norwood, MA, 1999)
4. W. Koch, *Tracking and Sensor Data Fusion—Methodological Framework and Selected Applications* (Springer, Berlin, 2014)
5. W. Koch, On Bayesian tracking and data fusion: a tutorial introduction with examples. IEEE Aerosp. Electron. Syst. Mag. **25**(7), 29–52 (2010)
6. A. Benavoli, L. Chisci, A. Farina, L. Timmoneri, G. Zappa, Knowledge-based system for multi-target tracking in a littoral environment. IEEE Trans. Aerosp. Electron. Syst. **42**(3), 1100–1119 (2006)
7. E. Blasch, J. G. Herrero, L. Snidaro, J. Llinas, G. Seetharaman, K. Palaniappan, Overview of contextual tracking approaches in information fusion, in *Proceedings of SPIE Geospatial InfoFusion III*, 2013
8. C. Yang, M. Bakich, E. Blasch. Nonlinear constrained tracking of targets on roads, in *8th International Conference on Information Fusion*, 2005
9. W. Koch, On exploiting 'negative' sensor evidence for target tracking and sensor data fusion, in *Proceedings of 10th International Conference on Information Fusion* (Quebec, Canada, 2007)
10. O. Loffeld, *Estimationstheorie, Bd.1, Grundlagen und stochastische Konzepte*. R. Oldenbourg Verlag GmbH, Muenchen, 1990
11. O. Loffeld, *Estimationstheorie, Bd.2, Anwendungen, Kalman-Filter*. R. Oldenbourg Verlag GmbH, Muenchen, 1990
12. W. Koch, Advanced target tracking techniques, in *Advanced Radar Signal and Data Processing*, Educational Notes RTO-EN-SET-086, Paper 2, France, 2006
13. T. Kirubarajan, Y. Bar-Shalom, K. Pattipati, I. Kadar, Ground target tracking with variable structure IMM estimator. IEEE Trans. Aerosp. Electron. Syst. **36**(1), 26–46 (2000)
14. B. Ristic, S. Arulampalam, N. Gordon. *Beyond the Kalman Filter: Particle Filters for Tracking Applications*. Artech House, 2004
15. S.J. Julier, J.K. Uhlmann, A new extension of the kalman filter to nonlinear systems, in *Proceedings of 11th International Symposium Aerospace/Defense Sensing, Simulation and Controls (AeroSense)*, 1997
16. S.J. Julier, J.K. Uhlmann, Unscented filtering and nonlinear estimation. Proc. IEEE **92**(3), 401–422 (2004)
17. A. Doucet, N.D. Freitas, N. Gordon. *Sequential Monte Carlo Methods in Practice* (Springer, Berlin, 2001)
18. H. Tanizaki. *Nonlinear Filters: Estimation and Applications*. 2nd edn. (Springer, Berlin, 1996)
19. G. Battistello, M. Ulmke. Exploitation of a priori information for tracking maritime intermittent data sources, in *Proceedings of 14th International Conference on Information Fusion* (Chigago, 2011)
20. D. Simon, Kalman filtering with state constraints: a survey of linear and nonlinear algorithms. IET Control Theory Appl. **4**(8), 1303–1318 (2010)

21. D. Simon, T.L. Chia, Kalman filtering with state equality constraints. IEEE Trans. Aerosp. Electron. Syst. **38**(1), 128–136 (2002)
22. N. Gupta, R. Hauser, Kalman filtering with equality and inequality state constraints. Source: http://arxiv.org/pdf/0709.2791.pdf, page URL last checked December 2014, 2007
23. D. Simon, D.L. Simon, Constrained kalman filtering via density function truncation for turbofan engine health estimation. Int. J. Syst. Sci. **41**(2), 159–171 (2010)
24. B. Bell, J. Burke, G. Pillonetto, An inequality constrained nonlinear kalman-bucy smoother by interior point likelihood maximization. Automatica **45**(1), 25–33 (2009)
25. W. Ward, H. Durrant-Whyte, Model-based multi-sensor data fusion, in *Proceedings of IEEE International Conference on Robotics Automation* (Nice, France, 1992)
26. L. Wang, Y. Chiang, F. Chang, Filtering method for nonlinear system with constraints. IEE Proc. Control Theory Appl. **149**(6), 525–531 (2002)
27. S. Ko, R. Bitmead, State estimation for linear system with state equality constraints. Automatica **43**(8), 1363–1368 (2007)
28. C. Yang, E. Blasch, Kalman filtering with nonlinear state constraints. IEEE Trans. Aerosp. Electron. Syst. **45**(1), 70–84 (2008)
29. C. Rao, J. Rawlings, J. Lee, Constrained linear state estimation—a moving horizon approach. Automatica **37**(10), 1619–1628 (2001)
30. C. Rao, J. Rawlings, D. Mayne, Constrained state estimation for nonlinear discrete-time systems: stability and moving horizon approximations. IEEE Trans. Autom. Control **48**(2), 246–258 (2003)
31. F. Papi, M. Podt, Y. Boers, G. Battistello, M. Ulmke, On constraints exploitation for particle filtering based target tracking, in *Proceedings of the 15th International Conference on Information Fusion*, 2012
32. M. Vespe, M. Sciotti, F. Burro, G. Battistello, S. Sorge. Maritime multi-sensor data association based on geographic and navigational knowledge, In *Proceedings of IEEE Radar Conference* (Rome, 2008)
33. G. Battistello, M. Ulmke, F. Papi, M. Podt, Y. Boers, Assessment of vessel route information use in Bayesian non-linear filtering, in *Proceedings of 15th International Conference on Information Fusion* (Singapore, 2012)
34. G. Pallotta, S. Horn, P. Braca, K. Bryan, Context-enhanced vessel prediction based on Ornstein-Uhlenbeck processes using historical AIS traffic patterns: real-world experimental results, in *Proceedings of the 17th International Conference on Information Fusion*, 2014
35. C. Agate, K.J. Sullivan, Road-constraint target tracking and identification using a particle filter, in *Proceedings of Signal and Data Processing of Small Targets,* vol. 5204, SPIE, 2003
36. M.S. Arulampalam, N. Gordon, M. Orton, B. Ristic, A variable structure multiple model particle filter for GMTI tracking, in *Proceedings of 5th International Conference on Information Fusion* (Annapolis, 2002)
37. W. Koch, J. Koller, M. Ulmke, Ground target tracking and road map extraction. ISPRS J. Photogrammetry Remote Sens. **61**, 197–208 (2006)
38. U. Orguner, T. Schon, F. Gustafsson, Improved target tracking with road network information, in *Aerospace conference, 2009 IEEE*, pp. 1–11, March 2009
39. D. Streller, Road map assisted ground target tracking, in *Proceedings of 11th International Conference on Information Fusion* (Cologne, 2008)
40. M. Zhang, S. Knedlik, O. Loffeld, An adaptive road-constrained IMM estimator for ground target tracking in GSM networks, in *11th International Conference on Information Fusion* (Cologne, 2008)
41. W. Koch, Tracking and data fusion applications. *Advanced Radar Signal and Data Processing*, Educational Notes RTO-EN-SET-086, Paper 9 (France, 2006)
42. M. Ulmke, W. Koch, Road-map assisted ground moving target tracking. IEEE Trans. Aerosp. Electron. Syst. **42**(4), 1264–1274 (2006)
43. Y. Bar-Shalom, X.-R. Li, *Multitarget-Multisensor Tracking: Principles and Techniques* (YBS Publishing, Storrs, CT, 1995)
44. M. Skolnik. *Radar Handbook*. 3rd edn. (McGraw-Hill, 2008)

45. J.R. Guerci, *Space-Time Adaptive Processing for Radar* (Artech House, Boston, London, 2003)
46. R. Klemm, *Principles of Space-Time Adaptive Processing*, 3rd edn. IET Radar, Sonar and Navigation, Series 21, 2006
47. W. Koch, R. Klemm, Ground target tracking with STAP radar. IEE Proc. Radar, Sonar Navig. **148**(3), 173–185 (2001)
48. M. Mertens, T. Kirubarajan, W. Koch, Exploiting doppler blind zone information for ground moving target tracking with bistatic airborne radar. IEEE Trans. Aerosp. Electron. Syst. **50**(1), 130–148 (2014)
49. Q. Wang, S. Kulkarni, S. Verdu, Divergence estimation for multidimensional densities via k-nearest-neighbor distances. IEEE Trans. Info. Theory **55**(5), 2392–2405 (2009)
50. M. Mertens, M. Feldmann, M. Ulmke, W. Koch, Tracking and data fusion for ground surveillance, chapter 6, in *Integrated Tracking, Classification, and Sensor Management: Theory and Applications*, ed. by M. Mallick, V. Krishnamurthy, B.-N. Vo (IEEE, Wiley, 2012)
51. M. Mertens, M. Ulmke, Ground moving target tracking with context information and a refined sensor model, in *Proceedings of the 11th International Conference on Information Fusion* (Cologne, 2008)
52. S. Blackman, Multiple hypothesis tracking for multiple target tracking. IEEE Aerosp. Electron. Syst. Mag. **19**, 5–18 (2004)
53. D. Cerutti-Maori, J. Klare, A.R. Brenner, J.H.G. Ender, Wide-area traffic monitoring with the SAR/GMTI system PAMIR. IEEE Trans. Geosci. Remote Sens. **46**(10), 3019–3030 (2008)
54. J.H.G. Ender, A.R. Brenner, PAMIR—a wideband phased array SAR/MTI system. IEE Proc. Radar, Sonar Navig. **150**(3), 165–172 (2003)
55. M. Mertens, R. Kohlleppel, Ground target tracking with experimental data of the pamir system, in *Proceedings of the 17th International Conference on Information Fusion* (Salamanca, 2014)

Chapter 13
Contextual Tracking in Surface Applications: Algorithms and Design Examples

Adam M. Fosbury, John L. Crassidis and Jemin George

Abstract In this chapter, contextual information is discussed for improving tracking of surface vehicles. Contextual information generally involves any kind of information that is not related directly to kinematic sensor measurements. This information, termed trafficability, is used to incorporate constraints on the vehicle that ultimately deflect the tracks to areas that provide the highest trafficable regions. For example, local terrain slope, ground vegetation and other factors that put constraints on the vehicles can be considered as contextual information. Both kinematic sensor data and contextual information are tied into the overall tracker design through the use of trafficability maps. Two specific design examples are summarized in this chapter. The first example involves ground tracking of vehicles where the contextual information exploits terrain information to aid in the tracking. The second example involves a sea-based maritime application where the contextual information exploits depth, marked shipping channel locations, and high-value unit information as contextual information. Both examples show that the use contextual information can significantly improve tracking performance.

Keywords Contextual tracking · Trafficable · Kalman filtering · Contextual-based tracker (ConTracker)

A.M. Fosbury
Space Exploration Sector, Johns Hopkins University, Applied Physics Laboratory,
Laurel, MD, USA
e-mail: Adam.Fosbury@jhuapl.edu

J.L. Crassidis (✉)
Department of Mechanical and Aerospace Engineering, University at Buffalo,
State University of New York, Amherst, NY, USA
e-mail: johnc@buffalo.edu

J. George
U.S. Army Research Laboratory, Adelphi, MD, USA
e-mail: jemin.george.civ@mail.mil

© Springer International Publishing Switzerland (outside the USA) 2016   339
L. Snidaro et al. (eds.), *Context-Enhanced Information Fusion*,
Advances in Computer Vision and Pattern Recognition,
DOI 10.1007/978-3-319-28971-7_13

13.1   Introduction

While early tracking algorithms have relied almost exclusively on target location measurements provided by sensors such as radars [1, 2], more advanced techniques have incorporated information pertaining to the orientation, velocity, and acceleration of the target [3–6]. This progression suggests that increasing the amount of information incorporated into the algorithm can improve the quality of the tracking process. In ground-based target tracking, a map of terrain features affecting target motion is usually available. A terrain-based tracking approach which accounts for the effects of terrain on target speed and direction of movement is presented in Ref. [7]. In Ref. [8], it has been shown that the incorporation of local contextual information, such as the terrain data, can significantly improve the tracker performance.

There exist several constraint target tracking algorithms. The kinematic constraint on target state provides information that can be processed as a pseudomeasurement to improve tracking performance. For example, Alouani [9] shows that the filter utilizing the kinematic constraint as a pseudomeasurement is unbiased when the system with the kinematic constraint is observable and the use of the kinematic constraint can increase the degree of observability of the system. Alouani and Blair [10] propose a new formulation of the kinematic constraint for constant speed targets which is shown to be unbiased and, under mild restriction, uniformly asymptotically stable. Though the proposed approach exploits contextual information to place constraints on target velocity, an explicit expression for the kinematic constraints on target state cannot easily obtained since the contextual information depends on the current target position. Also, the use of a kinematic constraint as a pseudomeasurement would severely degrade the performance of the proposed anomaly detection scheme.

In recent years, researchers have explored the overt use of contextual information for improving state estimation in ground target tracking by incorporating them into the tracking algorithm as potential fields to provide a repeller or an attractor characteristic to a specific region of interest [11]. In Ref. [12], the local contextual information, termed "trafficability," incorporates local terrain slope, ground vegetation, and other factors to put constraints on the vehicle's maximum velocity. This was extended to maritime tracking applications in Ref. [13] where depth, marked shipping channel locations, and high-value unit information are as contextual information.

The rest of the chapter is structured as follows. Section 13.2 gives a comparison between air and surface tracking. Section 13.3 provides a summary of trafficability and terrain characteristics. Section 13.4 provides information on target behavior. Section 13.5 summarizes measurement sources. Section 13.6 summarizes a generic target tracking algorithm. Section 13.7 provides an overview on single target tracking approaches, and Sect. 13.8 provides an overview on multiple target tracking approaches. A ground tracking application using contextual information is shown in Sect. 13.9. A maritime tracking application is shown in Sect. 13.10. Finally, Sect. 13.11 provides conclusions and future work.

13.2 Air Versus Surface Tracking

A majority of target tracking literature has focused on airborne targets. The motivation was generally for general aviation radar or military fighter applications. Due to the decades of research, the tracking of airborne targets has become a mature subject area. The focus shift from air to ground targets yields the question of how much material can be directly applied from the former to the latter. In order to answer this question, a qualitative analysis must be done on the subject. A thorough discussion, including a comparison table, is provided by Ref. [14]. The material will be repeated here. Table 13.1 provides a summary on the differences between airborne and surface target tracking.

The environment defines the area that the target can travel in. Aircraft move in three-dimensional space, free of constraints. Surface targets are limited to motion in two dimensions. Even though most terrain contains variations in elevation, planar coordinates can be defined with respect to the surface. For cases of travel on roads, the motion simplifies to one dimension. If these constraints can be successfully incorporated into an estimator, the results will be inherently more accurate.

Target dynamics govern the type of maneuvers that a vehicle can perform. Aircraft mostly fly in straight lines, and will also climb, descend, and make turns. All of these maneuvers will be relatively gradual. Sharper maneuvers are possible for fighters, but they will still not be sudden. Also, excluding helicopters and a few vertical take-off and landing aircraft, airplanes cannot stop in one place. On the other hand, surface targets can make very sharp turns, are capable of significant changes in acceleration, and are able to stop in place. The greater ability of a surface target to perform maneuvers makes it more difficult to track them.

The density of targets will also play an important role in the effectiveness of a tracking system. Aircraft will generally be spaced far apart. When this is true, a measurement taken in the area of the aircraft will almost always be guaranteed to be of that target. The density of surface-based vehicles will be much higher. This results in the need for data association algorithms, which will not be discussed here. The more uncertainty that exists between a measurement and the true identity of the target it is measuring, the greater the errors in state estimation will become.

The ability of a standard sensor to even detect a target differs for the two types of tracking. Except for aircraft maneuvering within mountain ranges, the view between the target and sensor will be unobstructed, resulting in a very high detection

Table 13.1 Airborne versus surface target tracking

Target type	Airborne targets	Surface targets
Environment	3D	1D or 2D
Dynamics	Low mobility, cannot stop	High mobility, can stop
Target density	Low	High
Detection probability	High	Low
Clutter	Low	High

probability. Surface targets can be obscured by a variety of different terrain types. The sensors used for this type of tracking add additional difficulties. Ground moving-target indication (GMTI) radars can only detect targets that have a radial velocity with respect to the sensor. Even more limiting is that this velocity must be greater than some minimum value in order for the target to be detected. The amount of clutter around the two types of targets is also different. The realm of aircraft motion is mostly clutter free, with the exception of birds and clouds. Surface targets move in a high-clutter environment, primarily due to the nature of the terrain.

13.3   Trafficability and Terrain Characteristics

This chapter will later use the term "trafficability" to help aid the tracking performance of the vehicle. Trafficability is concisely defined as the ability of a given vehicle to traverse a specified terrain. This term is used mostly in the context of the soil capability, without degrading soils and ecosystems, in agricultural machinery applications [15]. Water content in the soil is crucial for the trafficability in agricultural applications. Some form of an index, such as the "consistency index," is often used to describe the behavior of the soil dependence on water content. Mathematical models are often used to define the moisture-dependent soil strength of indices, which in turn are used to define trafficability criteria. There are two main differences for the definition of trafficability between agricultural applications and its use in this chapter. Firstly, in this chapter trafficability is a more broadly used term to relate how well any type of vehicle can transverse any terrain. Secondly, in this chapter, a specific trafficability index value is defined that may be a combination of a number factors other than soil characteristics. This can include road obstructions, elevation, surface quality, and well as sea constraints for naval applications to name a few.

Roads are the primary terrain feature in most target tracking studies. Vehicles traveling on a road are often assumed to remain on the road. Those that are traveling off-road but come within certain proximity are expected to seek entrance to the road. The benefit of a vehicle traveling on a road is that the geometric shape of the road becomes a constraint to the two-dimensional target tracking problem. This reduces it to a single dimension tracking problem. They are characterized by several different factors.

- Type. Differences between highways, major town roads and residential streets will affect the motion of a target. The latter is not suited to large vehicles, such as trucks, nor can it handle convoys. Residential streets are very likely to have lots of stop-and-go motion along with multiple exit and entrance points, while highway travel generally has constant velocity motion with few exits.
- Location. The exits of a city road will generally be other roads. In the country, there is a much greater possibility that roads can be exited at any point resulting in unconstrained off-road travel.

- Surface material. Vehicles speed will be affected by the type of surface that it travels on. The most commonly encountered surfaces are asphalt, concrete, and simple dirt roads.
- Surface quality. This is primarily for man-made road types such as asphalt or concrete. As the surface becomes older, it will be more prone to pot holes and other loose debris, forcing vehicles to travel at reduced speeds.

Varying elevation is another important factor in target tracking. Vehicles climbing an incline will generally do so with a reduced speed. If the incline is too steep, some vehicles will be unable to move through that area. Conversely, a vehicle traveling down an incline will move at a greater speed than normal.

For off-road travel, the type of terrain is necessary knowledge. Forests can have varying densities with some allowing large vehicles through, and others preventing everything except people from traversing. A road passing through a forest acts somewhat like a tunnel, keeping the vehicle from leaving the road at any point. Non-shallow bodies of water will be impassable for most vehicles. Swamps and wetlands will also place constraints on the types of vehicles that can travel through them. Canyons and cliffs will act as barriers to vehicle travel. An open level plain is the most unconstrained terrain that is likely to be encountered.

The presence of man-made objects is also significant. Buildings will be considered impenetrable by the vehicle, requiring an alternate trajectory in order to pass. Bridges will allow movement over areas that were once impassable, such as canyons and bodies of water. Some of these may have weight restrictions preventing vehicles of certain size from using them. Overpasses on roads will also produce a limit on vehicle size.

Weather can also play a role in terrain effects. Rain and snow storms will make roads more slippery and reduce visibility, forcing vehicles to travel more slowly. An impassable shallow stream can be frozen during the winter allowing some targets to cross. Rain can turn dirt roads to mud, significantly reducing the speed of vehicles that traverse them.

The above definition of trafficability is specific to ground vehicles, but the definition is actually broader, as mentioned at the beginning of this section. This can also be applied to other domains. For example, a maritime example will be shown in this chapter that relates trafficability to sea surface characteristics such as depth information, marked channel information, anti-shipping reports, and locations of high-value units.

13.4 Target Behavior

The more information known about a target, the more accurate a tracking algorithm will become. For instance, a truck is most likely to stay on highways and large roads, simply due to its size. Cars, jeeps, and other wheeled vehicles prefer traveling on roads, but can still maneuver on some types of off-road terrain. Tracked vehicles such as tanks have significant mobility in open off-road areas.

Different types of vehicles also have varying kinematic constraints. Trucks will have large masses preventing them from making rapid changes in speed or direction. Cars will have greater maneuverability and acceleration ranges. Tracked vehicles can stop, rotate in place, and begin moving in a direction that is not parallel to their previous line of motion. People will have significantly lower maximum speeds, but possess much greater ability to change heading.

The location of possible target goals is also important. Knowing where a vehicle might go reduces the number of paths that it is likely to take. When road intersections occur, the probability of a vehicle changing from one to the other will be greatly increased, or greatly decreased depending on whether the intersecting road leads to or away from these possible goals.

Models for target motions can have a significant impact on tracking performance as well. Reference [16] provides a summary of the most widely used target motion models. The simplest ones assume linear dynamics, such as constant velocity or constant acceleration. The resulting trajectories are straight-line in nature. The linearity of these models greatly simplifies the tracking design, but these types of models may not be suited well for targets undergoing rotational motion. Rotational-based models, known as "curvilinear models," are much more complex than straight-line models but can provide improvement in tracking performance for targets undergoing rotational motions. Examples include constant-turn-rate and velocity (CTRV) models, and constant-turn-rate and acceleration (CTRA) models. The difference between CTRV and CTRA models is the acceleration is defined to be a constant variable in the CTRA model, while the velocity is defined to be a constant variable in the CTRV model. Both these models assume no correlation between the rotational motion and the linear motion. Models that account for this correlation include the constant-steering-angle and velocity (CSAV) model, and the constant-curvature and acceleration (CCA) model. The difference between the CSAV and CCA models is the steering angle is a constant variable and the yaw rate is derived from the velocity and steering angle in the CSAV model, while velocity assumed is assumed to change linearly in the CCA model. Choosing which target motion model to choose is highly problem dependent. For example, aircraft tracking systems are modeled well by the CTRV model, but this model is not well suited for ground vehicles.

13.5 Measurement Sources

The system being used to measure target position is an important factor in target tracking design. Each system will have its own level of accuracy and associated probability of being able to detect a target. The primary method for ground-based surveillance by the U.S. Air force is currently the JSTARS aircraft. It uses both GMTI radar and synthetic aperture radar (SAR). The former is for detection over large areas, while the latter is for imaging in small areas. This type of surveillance system is also used aboard the U.K. ASTOR, the French HORIZON, and the Italian CRESCO [17].

Forward Looking Infrared (FLIR) systems use cameras to take pictures using the infrared portion of the electromagnetic spectrum. Basically, this captures a picture of the thermal output of all objects within the field of view. Versions exist for multiple detection ranges.

The simplest classes of measurement sources are from human observers. One of the primary advantages of this type is that a measurement is considered to always be associated with a real target. Environmental clutter would not result in a significant number of false measurements. The disadvantage of this type is that range and bearing information will be highly inaccurate.

13.6 Generic Target Tracking Algorithm

A generalized structure for a target tracking algorithm is shown in Fig. 13.1. First, a set of measurements are input to a data association algorithm along with a prediction of the current state values. This block will either associate each measurement with a specific target, or assign probabilities for measurement-to-target matching. The associated measurements along with the current predicted state values are then sent to the estimator, which will update the predicted states and output the current location of each target. The tracks are then available for use by external sources. They are also sent to the prediction block, which will propagate the tracks forward one time step according to the assumed kinematic model. The main focus of this chapter involves using contextual information on the estimation block in Fig. 13.1. Specifically, contextual information will be used to provide enhanced state estimates for better tracking characteristics. Using contextual information to enhance data association will not be discussed here.

Note that not all tracking algorithms require a data association stage. For example, recursive expectation maximization (EM) [18] algorithms use an iterative procedure that estimate both the parameters and the missing or unobservable data during an iteration. First an approximation to the expectation of the log-likelihood functional of the complete data conditioned on the current parameter estimate is done, which is called the expectation step (E-step). Then a new parameter estimate is computed by finding the value of the parameter that maximizes the functional found, which is called the maximization step (M-step). Another example is a class

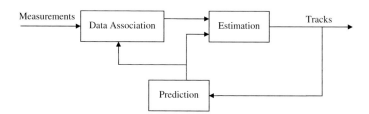

Fig. 13.1 Block diagram of target tracking algorithm

of filters that fall in the category of intensity filters [19], which in general do not explicitly compute associations. Rather, intensity functions are computed that estimate the density of the number of targets.

13.7 Single Target Tracking

Single target tracking problems form the foundation of ground target tracking. Algorithms focus on the ability to track a vehicle during a variety of maneuvers under the influence of different constraints. Kastella and Kreucher [20] use real data of battle simulations for its tests. A description of the terrain was not provided, but it is assumed to be non-road based. Layne and Piyasena [21] simulate a single target maneuvering in the X–Y plane with no terrain features. Yan et al. [22] use a continuous path of three straight line segments separated by constant-turn-rate maneuvers. Kim and Lee [23] simulate a target with varying velocity, sinusoidal acceleration, and coordinated turning. Enders [24] looks at road target tracking. Trajectories consist of consecutive straight line segments where intersections are hard angles. A combination of on and off-road terrain is used by Reid and Bryson [7]. The exact makeup of the terrain is not provided, though it is modeled by a potential field approach. Payne and Marrs [25] examine a four-road network that is broken up into six segments. The four roads intersect each other at the same location. A grid-style road network is simulated by Hernandez [26]. It is described as a Manhattan style network, where all roads form a grid of square cells. At each intersection, a probability is defined to indicate whether the vehicle will continue straight, or make a turn. Arulampalam et al. [27] study a simple three-road network, where all roads converge at the same point. Cheng and Singh [28] simulate a continuous three-road network. The first turn is acute, while the second turn is ninety degrees.

13.7.1 Multiple Model Algorithms

Different types of motion require different types of constraints. The Multiple Model (MM) family of algorithms works on the idea that no single filter can accommodate all types of motion within one framework. Instead, it proposes that each type of motion has a filter, or set of filter parameters, that are tailored to work best for that specific motion type. The MM algorithm then uses a combination of results from those filters to determine the best estimate for position. Several different classes of MM algorithms exist, and will be discussed in the following sections.

13.7.1.1 Interacting Multiple Model (IMM)

One of the earliest discussions of the IMM algorithm is given by Blom and Bar-Shalom [29]. There are three steps:

1. Beginning with N weights, means and covariances, the mixed initial conditions are computed for the filters.
2. The new initial conditions are used as input to their respective filters. Standard update and prediction equations are used.
3. Weights are updated from the innovations of the filters, and then normalized.

A brief discussion is also provided of when hypotheses can be pruned from the system.

The IMM is compared to first and second order generalized pseudo Bayes (GPB) algorithms. The higher the order of the GPB algorithm, the more accurate it is, but at a cost of higher complexity. The IMM is shown to perform nearly as well as the GPB2 while retaining the lower computational cost of the GPB1. For higher complexity systems (i.e., larger model set), a GPBn ($n \geq 2$) algorithm is recommended when the IMM shows less than suitable performance.

Li and Bar-Shalom [30] discuss a performance prediction algorithm. The motivation behind this work is to develop a method for predicting the performance of an IMM algorithm without resorting to computationally expensive series of computer simulations. The general algorithm is as follows. See Ref. [30] for a full description.

1. Compute the true mode residual covariance, and the standard covariance given the true mode sequence and the optimal filter that is matched to it.
2. Compute quantities related to each mode-matched filter in the IMM. This includes mixing probabilities, mode probabilities, likelihood functions and filter gain deviations.
3. Compute values of various quantities for each mode pair. This includes relative mixed residual, its covariance, and the difference in state estimates.
4. Compute the combination covariance.
5. Compute the mean-squared error.

Two simulations are performed. The first involves an aircraft control problem. The aircraft under examination flies straight, makes a ninety degree turn at three degrees per second, and then continues to fly straight. The derived algorithm is shown to accurately predict the average errors calculated by the IMM in real-time. Mode probabilities are accurately determined, and the position and velocity estimation errors are also predicted well.

The second simulation involves the identification of non-stationary noise with rapidly varying statistics. The IMM algorithm used for this problem contained two models, one corresponding to the lower bound of the noise, and the other corresponding to the upper bound. Once again, the predictor algorithm is shown to accurately determine the performance of the IMM algorithm.

Kim and Lee [23] discuss an extension to the IMM algorithm based on the steady-state Kalman filter. The previous algorithms calculated the covariance matrix off-line. In reality, the covariance matrix is a function of range and bearing, so the off-line computed matrix will not always be correct. This paper uses the analytic solution of the steady-state Kalman filter in order to compensate for the variation in the steady-state gain and covariance. The analytic solution given is based on the Castella-Dunnebacke model (see Ref. [31]) and the Ramachandra II model (see Ref. [32]). The core of the IMM algorithm remains the same. The simulated target has varying velocity, sinusoidal acceleration and coordinated turning. Radar measurements are assumed Gaussian with standard deviations of 130 m for range, and one degree for bearing. The root-mean-square (RMS) errors of position and velocity are calculated for the standard IMM, and the IMM proposed in this paper. While the former converges a little quicker, the new algorithm shows significantly lower errors.

An improvement to the standard IMM is given by Johnston and Krishnamurthy [33], and is termed the reweighted IMM (RIMM). This new algorithm uses a bank of Kalman filters, just like the standard IMM. The primary difference is that the RIMM uses a recursive version of the alternating EM algorithm developed by Meng and Van Dyk [34]. The RIMM algorithm is derived from a maximum a posteriori (MAP) algorithm. One of the primary results is that the Markov chain weights are filtered instead of smoothed.

A simulation is performed consisting of a ninety degree turn in a two-dimensional region. The trajectory consists of constant speed straight-line motion before and after the turn. Three methods are considered: a two-model IMM, a three model IMM, and a two-model RIMM. The two-model algorithms use constant velocity and Wiener acceleration with process noise. For the three model case, a constant acceleration term without process noise is added. The RMS error is calculated over fifty runs of each algorithm. The RIMM has slightly lower position errors than the other two, except during the middle of the maneuver. However, it still recovers from the maneuver more quickly during the other two algorithms. Velocity errors are lower for the RIMM for the entire duration of the simulation.

A combination of the IMM with a particle filter (PF) is shown by Boers and Driessen [35]. The IMM is used for switching between models, while the PF is used for the actual state estimation. There are three stages to the algorithm presented.

1. Interaction. Initial densities are computed on the basis of the Markov model, model likelihoods, and a posteriori probabilities. This differs from the standard IMM where only the mean and covariance are calculated. Mixing probabilities are also computed.
2. Filtering. Samples of the probability density are taken; Predicted samples and output are then computed. Particle weights are calculated and normalized. The mean and covariance are then computed over the sample set. Innovations and their respective probability densities are then determined. Finally, likelihoods and mode probabilities are calculated.

3. Combination. The conditional probability density is calculated, and then used to determine an estimate of the state.

The IMM-PF is compared to a standard IMM using three models: straight-line motion, circular motion, and constant acceleration. Measurements of range, bearing, elevation, and range-rate are taken, each with Gaussian white measurement noise. One thousand runs of the same trajectory but with different levels of measurement noise were performed. The two methods were shown to perform equally well twenty-five percent of the time. For all other cases, the standard IMM diverges resulting in tracking failure. The IMM-PF maintains effective tracking capability for all cases.

13.7.1.2 Adaptive Interacting Multiple Model (A-IMM)

An extension to the IMM algorithm is discussed by Laybe and Piyasena [21]. Here, an adaptive acceleration model is used to track dynamics that do not fall into the realms covered by the fixed dynamics models. Three different methods are described. The first was developed by Munir and Atherton in Ref. [36]. The first step of their algorithm is to estimate the current acceleration of the target. The bank of acceleration filters is then moved so that it is centered on this estimated value. The second method, called the Moving-Bank Multiple Model Adaptive Estimator (MBMMAE), was taken from Gustafson and Maybeck [37], and Maybeck and Hentz [38]. In this algorithm, all acceleration models are assumed to be fixed. At each time step, a window is placed around the estimated acceleration. Only models falling within this window are used for estimation at that step.

A new A-IMM approach is proposed Ref. [38]. The bank of filters in acceleration space is reduced when compared to the other algorithms. The five filters used result in a much coarser coverage of acceleration space. A single adaptive acceleration model is then added to compensate for dynamics that do not fall within one of the five fixed models.

The three previously mentioned algorithms are compared to a base IMM algorithm consisting of nine acceleration models. The target is maneuvering within the X–Y plane. The average RMS errors were computed for one hundred Monte Carlo runs of each algorithm. Efficiency of the algorithms was gaged by counting the number of Matlab FLOPS required by each algorithm. The Munir and Atherton technique was shown comparable in error to the classical IMM, but required additional computations. The MBMMAE has less computational requirements than the previous two algorithms, but has greater errors. The A-IMM algorithm proposed in this reference showed lower errors and lower computational costs when compared to the other three algorithms.

An application of an A-IMM algorithm to targets performing maneuvers with varying turn rates in given by Efe and Atherton [39]. Acceleration is estimated based upon the current and previous velocity estimates. The magnitude of this acceleration is then divided by the current speed to provide an estimate of the turn rate. The estimated turn rate is then used to calculate the process noise covariance level for the filter. The relation between turn rate and necessary process noise was determined by creating ten target trajectories and then testing each with Kalman filters of different process noise levels.

This algorithm is compared to two other methods. The first is a three model IMM, where each model has a different level of process noise to account for different levels of acceleration. The other method is a second order Kalman filter. Three different scenarios were simulated, each with an initial two degree per second turn, followed by a maneuver with different turning rates. The A-IMM is shown to have lower overall errors than that of the other two algorithms, while maintaining a low computational cost.

A review of the design of A-IMM algorithms is provided by Yan et al. [22]. There are three primary components to this type of filter: parameter estimation, model set adjustment, and the standard IMM. This paper focuses on the first two components. The most significant parameter for target tracking is the turn rate. Estimation of this parameter is accomplished through a combination of standard Kalman filters and an unscented transform [40]. The model set is shown to be optimal when a single model is used with an assumed turning rate equal to that of the mean of the true turning rate. Since this is generally not feasible, it is recommended to use as few models as possible. A three model set centered on the estimated turning rate is proposed, where the additional two models differ from the estimate by a small quantity that is a function of the turn rate variance.

A simulation is performed with a target initially moving in a straight line, followed by a constant turn, a second straight line, another constant turn maneuver, and lastly a straight line. Five algorithms are studied: a standard IMM, and four A-IMM algorithms, while four different turn rates are assumed. For the turn rate closest to that of the actual, the standard IMM showed the best performance. Position errors increased for all algorithms as the estimated turn rate increased. However, these errors increased far more rapidly for the standard IMM, showing that the A-IMM algorithms are more adept at handling unknown turn rates.

13.7.1.3 Multiple Model Nonlinear Filter (MMNF)

Kastella and Kreucher [20] introduce the multiple model nonlinear filter (MMNF) for ground target tracking using ground target indicator (GMTI) measurements. Previous work has used the variable-structure interacting multiple model Kalman filters (VS-IMM-KF). In this approach, there is no incorporation of vehicle inputs for preferred heading and speed, nor is there a restoring force to constrain the vehicle to remain on the road segment. The motivation of the MMNF is to incorporate terrain information directly into the kinematics of the model. Target dynamics for each of the models are described by the Ito stochastic differential equation. Equations that couple the target dynamics to terrain-based motion preferences are created using inhomogeneous integrated Ornstein–Uhlenbeck (IIOU) models.

Three different estimators are tested on real battle simulation data: a near constant velocity model (NCV), an IIOU model, and an MMNF that combines the two. Multiple examples are given, demonstrating the strengths and weaknesses of the individual filter types. The MMNF is shown to retain the strengths of both. It also shows a significant performance enhancement over the NCV model for cases with low signal to noise ratio in the measurements.

13.7.1.4 Variable-Structure Interacting Multiple Model (VS-IMM)

One of the disadvantages of the IMM is that large quantities of models are required to accurately handle a variety of motion characteristics. The concept behind the VS-IMM is to vary the number of models used within the IMM at any given time in order to estimate the states more efficiently. This method is first introduced by Li and Bar-Shalom in Ref. [41]. A description of the standard IMM along with its limitations is discussed. The theoretical basis for the VS-IMM is given.

Kirubarajan et al. [42] provide another description of the VS-IMM algorithm, consisting of five steps.

1. Update the mode set based on the current state estimate and topography.
2. Mix state estimates and covariances for use in mode-matched filters.
3. Propagate mode-specific estimates and covariances.
4. Update mode probabilities.
5. Combine mode-specific states to form overall state estimate.

Examples of how topographic elements affect the mode set are given. The simulations performed show that the VS-IMM is superior to that of the fixed structure IMM.

Kirubarajan and Bar-Shalom [43] design a VS-IMM specifically for tracking evasive move-stop-move maneuvers. Measurements are taken using Ground Moving Target Indicator (GMTI) sensors. This presents a problem since GMTI sensors will not register movement when a target is stationary. The primary issue is to have a consistent set of likelihood functions for both moving and stationary models. This is accomplished by including the probability of detection within the likelihood functions. Simulations are performed of a target moving within a plane. Three models were used: stopped, constant velocity, and white noise acceleration with high process noise. The VS-IMM was shown to effectively track the target, even when it performed move-stop-move maneuvers. It should be noted that this paper does discuss a multi-target tracking problem. However, the specific data association algorithms are not discussed. The VS-IMM filter is derived for a single target, and then applied to each of the targets individually. It is for that reason that this reference is provided in this chapter.

Another discussion of VS-IMM algorithms is provided by Kirubarajan et al. in Ref. [4]. Three disadvantages of the standard IMM are given.

1. All models are used throughout the entire tracking period. This results in an increased computational load and reduced estimation accuracy.
2. In a multi-target case, the same estimator is used for all targets. No consideration is taken for the different motions of individual targets.
3. A fixed structure does not allow for dependence on external factors. This is significant since these factors can vary with both position and time.

The VS-IMM algorithm presented in this paper adds and removes filter modules based on topography. A simulation of a three-road network is performed, where the possibility of off-road motion exists. The VS-IMM is shown to be more effective at track formation and termination. Error performance with respect to RMS position and RMS velocity is also better for the new algorithm.

A solution to GMTI tracking using an unscented PF approach is discussed by Payne and Marrs in Ref. [25]. Previous approaches relied on variable-structure interacting multiple model extended Kalman filter (VS-IMM-EKF) approaches and variable-structure multiple model particle filter (VS-MM-PF) approaches. Both of these approaches attempt to model the uncertainty of the target state and the uncertainty of the current motion model regime governing the evolution of that target state. For the VS-IMM-EKF approach, the uncertainty is accounted for by taking the probabilistically weighted sum of a bank of EKFs, with each filter being conditional upon one of the model regimes in the model set. However, the EKF assumes that the model is linearized well and that the resulting Gaussian mixture is approximated by a single Gaussian function, both leading to error sources. The VS-MM-PF approaches accounts for the uncertainty by letting each particle follow its own trajectory through the state space defined by the target position and velocity. This approach has been shown to outperform tracking filters based on extended Kalman filters for several scenarios; however, a relatively large number of particles (on the order of one thousand) are needed to capture the joint model regime/target state probability density, as well as constraints on the target's speed.

This paper uses an unscented Kalman filter (UKF) in the place of an EKF as the means to approximate the joint model regime/target state probability density. This leads to a variable-structure multiple model unscented particle filter (VS-MM-UPF) approach. The assumed measurements for the two-dimensional motion are range, azimuth and range-rate. The advantage of the VS-MM-UPF is that only twenty particles are used with no speed constraints. Simulation results indicated that in regions where this is a non-null measurement the VS-MM-UPF gives similar performance to the VS-MM-PF and better performance than the VS-IMM-EKF. The authors note that it seems likely that a more marked improvement in the performance of the VS-MM-UPF may be apparent when the road network is generalized to be nonlinear.

Hernandez [26] derives the Posterior Cramr-Rao Lower Bound (PCRLB) for tracking road-based vehicles using GMTI sensors. This poses a challenging problem the structure of the road network must be accounted for, as well as the concurrent constrained applied with it. Since an analytical solution for the PCRLB is intractable, the bound is instead computed via Monte Carlo simulation. However,

Table 13.2 Comparison of reviewed literature for single target tracking algorithms

Ref. #	[20, 29, 30, 33, 35, 42]	[21, 22, 36, 37–39]	[4, 25–28,41, 43, 44]	[8, 11, 24, 45, 46]
Approach	MM	A-IMM	VS-IMM	Other
Data type	GPS, radar	–	GMTI	GMTI
	Vertical acceleration			
	NCV	Constant acceleration		
System hypotheses	Circular motion	NCV	NCV	NCV
			Move-stop-move	
	Constant acceleration	Constant turn rate		
	Wiener acceleration			
Terrain	Road, none, off-road	None	Road, off-road	Road, none, off-road

because problems associated with multi-modality of the target distribution at each junction, the resulting computed PCRLB may be over-optimistic. Hence, an alternative performance measure (APM) is introduced that resembles the error covariance of an extended Kalman filter with measurements linearized around the true target state and known target maneuvers. The assumed measurements are bearing, range and range-rate. Simulation results are provided using a Manhattan road network in two-dimensional space. A variable structure, multiple model particle filter (VS-MM-PF) is used to rest the performance of the Monte Carlo-based PCRLB solution and the APM. The PCRLB is shown to be hugely over-optimistic, while the APM is shown to accurately predict the performance of the VS-MM-PF (Table 13.2).

A variable-structure multiple model particle filter (VS-MM-PF) for tracking using GMTI sensors is derived by Arulampalam et al. in Ref. [27]. Previous work has used a variable-structure interacting multiple model (VS-IMM) approach. The primary drawback is that the non-standard terrain information will lead to non-Gaussian probability density functions which are approximated by Gaussian pdf's. The VS-IMM also lacks a mechanism for incorporating hard constraints on position and velocity.

The algorithm presented in this paper is based on Sequential Monte Carlo Methods. Random samples are used to represent the posterior density of the target states. Particle filtering methods have no restrictions on the type of models. This allows complex models to be used to represent ground vehicle motion. The non-standard terrain information is modeled by a generalized Jump Markov system with constraints on the states. Transition probabilities of the Markov process are designed to be state dependent, allowing for realistic characterization of ground vehicles.

Simulation results show a significant reduction in error of the VS-MM-PF when compared to the VS-IMM. The reduction primarily occurs for the on-road portion of the simulation, both outside and inside the measurement-free tunnel zone. The two algorithms show equivalent performance during constraint-free off-road travel. The addition of velocity constraints in the VS-MM-PF shows a further increase in performance throughout the entire simulation.

Kravaritis and Mulgrew [44] apply a VS-MM-PF to a road tracking problem. The new contribution from this paper is to create a varying particle VS-MM-PF (VP-VS-MM-PF). The number of particles changes based on the complexity of the tracking problem at that time. Another algorithm is used to force particles to lie in the center of the road segments with velocities directed along the road. A multi-road segment is simulated in conjunction with GMTI sensors. The vehicle under consideration travels both on- and off-road. Three filters were compared

1. VS-MM-PF with 100 particles.
2. VS-MM-PF with 1000 particles.
3. VP-VS-MM-PF that varies between 100 and 1000 particles.

RMS errors were calculated for each of the filters. Errors for all filters were significantly higher off-road than they were on-road. The VS-MM-PF with 100 particles showed the worst performance, while the other two filters were similar in effectiveness. The primary advantage of the VP-VS-MM-PF is that when it is using fewer particles, its computational cost will be reduced, even though it will maintain the same accuracy of the higher PF.

Cheng and Singh [28] apply a VS-MM-PF to a road-constrained tracking problem. All motion is assumed parallel to the direction of the road segments. A three mode MM algorithm was used: NCV, maneuvering, or stopped. GMTI measurements are assumed, so there will be a minimum velocity threshold for detection. Due to this factor, the NCV and maneuvering modes will be active at all times, while the stopped mode will only be active when no detection is received. The only difference between the first two modes is in the process noise, which is larger for the maneuvering mode to account for greater possible accelerations. Process noise and target velocity are set to zero in the stopped model.

Two particle filters are discussed in Ref. [28]. The first is a standard bootstrap filter. The second is the primary contribution of this paper, a computationally efficient particle filter designed for road-constrained tracking. Refer to that actual paper for a full description of the bootstrap and efficient particle filters.

Simulations are performed of a continuous three-road network. The GMTI sensor is assumed stationary with range standard deviation of 20 m, azimuth standard deviation of 0.01 rad/s, and Doppler standard deviation of 1 m/s. Thirty runs are performed for a fifty particle efficient PF and for a one-thousand particle bootstrap PF. The former was shown to have RMS errors equivalent to that of the latter, while requiring less than one-third of the total computational time.

13.7.2 Other Algorithms

This section contains reviews of papers that do not fall into the categories of the prior sections. The methods described are not necessarily related to each other, but it was felt that the topics contained were relevant to this document.

Yang et al. [45] study the use of the Extended Kalman Filter (EKF), the UKF, the particle filter (PF) and the Gaussian mixture sigma-point particle filter (GMSPPF) to track road-based targets. The road is parameterized as segments which are linear and arcs of circles. The measurement equation which represents range and bearing are modified to include road constraints which results in a 1-D tracking problem. They compare the performance of the four filters on a road network which include two straight line segments connected with an arc of a circle. They illustrate that the EKF, UKF, and the GMSPPF have comparable performance. The performance of the particle filter deteriorates when the numbers of particles are small. They do not include road intersections, multiple targets, or stop-and-go modes of motion. They propose to study the effect of these additional complexities in the near future.

A PF approach is applied to out-of-sequence measurements (OOSMs) in multi-sensor target tracking by Mallick et al. in Ref. [46]. The OOSMs may be due to varying data preprocessing times and/or communication delays in the tracking system. Most previous work on filtering with OOSMs uses linear dynamic models and linear/nonlinear measurement models with no uncertainty in the origin of the measurements. Unlike previous approaches, the new OOSM PF algorithm developed in this paper does not require storage of the particle states and weights for a maximum number of past scans. This is accomplished by exploiting the structure of the linear kinematic model. Simulation results incorporate a two-dimensional ground tracking scenario with range, azimuth and range-rate measurements. A PF with ten thousand particles is used with one-, two-, and three-lag problems. The simulation results indicate that the approximate OOSM PF algorithm results compare well with a multiple-lag extended Kalman filter-based OOSM algorithm.

The final three papers both explicitly deal with some form of terrain handling. Enders [24] examines on-road tracking. Vehicle trajectories are assumed to be composed of distinct straight-line segments that connect end-to-end. Target positions are assumed to be given by a Gaussian probability density function. Measurement noise is described by a zero-mean distribution. Three estimation techniques are given as being commonly applied to this problem.

1. Linear least squares.
2. Bayes a posteriori mean (also called Bayes least squares).
3. Bayes maximum a posteriori (MAP).

The latter approach is used throughout the development of the paper. For motion on a road, the prediction covariance will become singular with its column space along the direction of the road. This singular matrix is then defined as a function of the angle that the road makes with the coordinate axes.

When the road segment is not a simple straight line, a more complex update procedure is required. Consider a pair of straight-line road segments intersecting. The probability density function for the target is still a Gaussian, but it now covers portions of both road segments. A predicted location is determined on each segment, with each location being equidistant from the bend. The following conditions determine the choice of the correct solution.

- If both solutions lie on the road, the one that minimizes the statistical distance between the measurement and the proposed target is the MAP solution.
- If neither solution lies on the road, then the location of the bend is the optimal solution.
- If only one solution lies on the road, then that is the optimal solution.

It is noted that when a measurement occurs inside of a bend, the a posteriori probability density becomes multi-modal. In this case, the Bayes least squares estimate is a reasonable alternative to determine an estimate of the position.

Tenne et al. [11] look at the use of a velocity field (VF) for ground target tracking. This field is designed to store local information about the probable velocity of a vehicle. Three objectives are provided for the design of the VF.

1. Avoidance of obstacles.
2. Attraction to goals.
3. Vehicle type, which can specify speed and whether or not there is a preference of on-road or off-road travel.

It is proposed that a potential field is used for construction of the VF.

The region of interest is given as two-dimensional field containing a road network that is divided into small cells. For on-road locations, the VF is parallel to the road direction. The off-road VF assumes that the vehicle will attempt to return to the road network. Vehicle position is modeled by a probability density function which is propagated in time by a hyperbolic partial differential equation, called the linear transport equation. See Ref. [11] for the complete mathematical explanation of this method.

In the final paper, Nougues and Brown [8] look at an all-terrain scenario. The environment is two-dimensional and is represented by a rectangular grid with square elements of predetermined size. The side length of these squares will usually lie between ten and one hundred meters. A mobility factor ranging from zero to one is determined for each grid cell. This number gives the ratio of the actual speed of the target in that terrain compared to the maximum possible speed of the target. Several assumptions are made.

1. There are no goal states known beforehand.
2. Targets have a tendency to move in a constant direction. A set of five probabilities is used to quantify whether the target will alter its trajectory, with each probability corresponding to a multiple of a course alteration of forty-five degrees (beginning at zero, ending at 180).
3. If a vehicle is traveling on a road, it is very likely to remain on the road.

4. If the vehicle is only one cell away from a road segment, it is likely to move onto the road.
5. A vehicle is either moving or stationary. There is a known position-dependent probability of it switching between these states.

See Ref. [8] for the eight step algorithm used to propagate the probability densities forward in time.

A brief discussion on the use of potential surfaces for path planning in the presence of obstacles is provided. These objects are given a potential such that the resulting force will be repulsive. Goal locations, if known, will be given potentials that result in attractive forces. One of the problems that occur in target tracking is that there is great difficulty in creating an analytic potential to mimic the irregular boundaries of geographic objects. The two main requirements for building a potential function are

1. Developing an efficient computation of the distance from an point to significant terrain features (roads, rivers, etc.).
2. Creating the functional form attractive and repulsive potential fields. This is complicated by the fact that different terrain types will have different regions of influence.

It was decided that the attractive potentials should not be felt through obstacles. In light of this, a Euclidean distance from the current point to the goal was replaced by a minimum distance to goal that is achievable without crossing the obstacle. An algorithm based on diffusion or wavefront expansion is used.

The method developed in this paper is compared to two other approaches, a method developed by Reid and Bryson in Ref. [7], and a Kalman filter approach. Sensor reports were received every 100 seconds. Analysis of these methods was done by computing RMS errors. The new algorithm is shown to outperform the other two in terms of this metric.

13.8   Multiple Target Tracking

This section focuses on the problems of multiple target tracking, whose goal is to track multiple vehicles undergoing a wide range of possible maneuvers.

13.8.1   Commonly Studied Problems and Tracking Methods

This section will provide an overview for the various problems and tracking methods examined by current literature. A road network with five entry/exit points is used by Edlund et al. in Ref. [47]. The interior of the network is a single loop of road segments, with each segment being a straight line. All entrance/exit points intersect the interior loop at different points. Simulations use between one and five vehicles. Giannopolous et al. [48] and Rago et al. [49] use a pair of targets moving in close parallel paths with constant velocity. Jing and Vadakkepat [50] track five ground-based targets moving randomly on open terrain. Real measurements of people walking in a random manner are used by Frank et al. in Ref. [51]. The most prominent method for ground-based tracking is the MM algorithm, which was introduced in the previous section.

13.8.2 Multiple Model Algorithms

One of the earliest discussions of an IMM algorithm for Multi-Target Tracking (MTT) is provided by Bar-Shalom et al. [52]. The following six models are used:

1. Undetectable Target
2. Near Constant Velocity
3. Motion with large Acceleration Increment
4. Near Constant Acceleration
5. "Just Split" Target
6. "Split Targets"

The first model is the simple case where no targets are observable. Model two is the standard case of a target moving with constant velocity. The third and fourth models cover different acceleration behaviors. The final two models correspond to the possibility of a single target splitting into two. This will most commonly occur in the tracking of convoys. Model five occurs when a minimum of two validated measurements occurs, and leads directly to model six. Probabilities for switching between the various models are provided by a Markov chain transition matrix.

Initially, each target will be tracked by its own filter. A split target mode will occur when either two validated measurements occur for a single target, or the validation ranges for two separate targets overlap. The estimation of states for split targets are coupled together with a Joint Probabilistic Data Association Filter (JPDAF) used to update the states based on multiple measurements.

A Multi-Rate Interacting Multiple Model (MRIMM) algorithm is introduced by Hong and Ding in Ref. [53]. The primary goal of the MRIMM is to reduce computational needs by updating individual models at a rate proportional to the target's dynamics. Two categories of motion are created, one that is to be updated at a full-rate, and the other at a half-rate. The former will includes maneuvers such as constant acceleration, large acceleration increment, or a constant-turn-rate model. The latter category will contain stationary, NCV, and slowly maneuvering targets. A JPDA algorithm is used for combining measurements during the split target mode.

An IMM algorithm using a Modified Approximate JPDA (MAJPDA) is applied to multiple aircraft tracking by Hwang et al. in Ref. [54]. The MAJPDA is described as computationally abbreviated version of a standard JPDA. When the determined probabilities fall below a designer-specified threshold, often occurring when two or more target paths cross, a Multiple Hypothesis Tracker (MHT) is used to determine additional local information. The explicit decision logic used by the MHT is not provided.

A simulation is performed using four aircraft, and a two-model IMM. One model is for straight motion, while the other is for turning maneuvers and uses a process noise several orders of magnitude larger than that of the first model. Accurate tracking of the aircraft is shown in the presence of clutter during large overlapping maneuvers. One negative aspect of the paper is that velocity information is not included in the state model. If it were, the reliance on the MHT for crossing targets could be reduced.

Singh and Sood [55] test a two-model IMM algorithm with two different data association methods. The algorithms are JPDAF and neural network fusion (NNF). Measurement to target associations are performed jointly across all targets, while state estimation for each target is done individually. Several assumptions are made.

1. The number of targets is N, with each track initialized.
2. Each of the targets are detected independently at each scan.
3. All of the sensors are synchronized.
4. Each target can be the origin of only one measurement. All excess measurements are assumed to be false alarms, or to have arisen from clutter.
5. The number of false measurements obeys a Poisson distribution with known mean.
6. Target originated measurement noise is Gaussian with known mean and covariance.

The two IMM models differ only be the amount of process noise. The model with lower noise is for straight-line motion, while the other is for turning motion.

The NNF algorithm is a feed forward back propagation network with linear transfer functions. Weight and bias values are updated according to Levenberg–Marquardt optimization. A single hidden layer is used with a number of hidden nodes equal to the number of scans for which the target is simulated.

Two scenarios of interest are simulated. The first is two objects whose paths cross. The second involves three objects moving within the same region without having their paths cross. Both the JPDAF and NNF algorithms were shown to be effective in tracking for both scenarios. The latter is said to have lower errors, which can be somewhat inferred from the plots showing estimated and true trajectories. Error plots are only shown for the NNF, so a strict comparison of the two algorithms cannot be made.

Hwang et al. [54] applied a Residual Mean IMM (RMIMM) to aircraft tracking. Data association is performed using a JPDAF algorithm. This is augmented by the multiple target identity management (MTIM) algorithm developed by Hwang et al. (Ref. [56]). The MTIM was developed using Identity-Mass Flow to overcome the computational complexity that normally occurs in managing multiple targets.

Within the RMIMM, mode likelihood functions are computed based on the residuals of the Kalman filter. These are then used to calculate the mode probabilities. Ideally, the mode probability for the true mode will be one, while all others are zero. Tracking difficulties will occur when the computed probabilities deviate significantly from the ideal case. The RMIMM uses a new likelihood function based on the idea that the residual for the correct mode should be a white zero-mean Gaussian process, while the other residuals should be zero-mean. Additional details of the RMIMM are provided by Hwang et al. [57].

Simulations are performed involving the motion of three aircraft in a no-clutter environment. Trajectories of the aircraft are designed such that each path crosses that of the other two. Tracks and identities are estimated accurately throughout the simulation.

Jouan and Michalska [58] introduce the IMM-JVC algorithm, which couples the Joncker-Volgenant-Castanon (JVC) optimization scheme with an IMM. The JVC algorithm, developed by Castanon [59], uniquely associates measurements with individual targets. The estimates for each track are then updated separately using a two-model IMM which assumes either constant velocity or constant acceleration. A simulation of two closely maneuvering aircrafts demonstrates the effectiveness of this filter with and without clutter.

Hadzagic et al. [60] perform a comparison of the IMM-JVC and IMM-JPDA algorithms. A simulation of two closely maneuvering aircraft is performed. The IMM-JVC is shown to be superior in terms of overall tracking, accuracy of maneuver detection, and identity resolution. The IMM-JPDA has better performance in terms of state component errors. A significant weakness of this algorithm was demonstrated in that it merged tracks when the two targets were within close proximity.

Multiple target intensity filters have also been used to track multiple targets. A common filter in this class is the probability hypothesis density (PHD) filter [61], which is based on the random finite set (RFS) formulation. In particular, the collection of individual targets is treated as a set-valued state and the collection of observations is treated as a set-valued observation. The PHD filter propagates the intensity of the targets' RFS instead of the full multi-target posterior density. This makes it suitable to operate in cluttered environments. Several variants of the PHD filter exist, such as the Monte Carlo PHD filter and the Gaussian Mixture PHD filter, each with their advantages and disadvantages.

13.8.3   *Symmetric Measurement Equation Filter*

The previous section highlighted one of the main differences between MTT techniques, namely the data association technique used in conjunction with the estimator. Sastry and Kamen [62] propose the Symmetric Measurement Equation (SME) Filter, an alternative method that provides target estimation without

considering measurement-to-target association. This is accomplished by creating a
new set of measurement equations from the initial Cartesian measurements:

$$\tilde{q}_i(k) = h_i(x_{m1}(k), x_{m2}(k), \ldots, x_{mN}(k)), \quad i = 1, \ldots, N \tag{13.1a}$$

$$\tilde{q}_i(k) = h_i(y_{m1}(k), y_{m2}(k), \ldots, y_{mN}(k)), \quad i = N+1, \ldots, 2N \tag{13.1b}$$

$$\tilde{q}_i(k) = h_i(z_{m1}(k), z_{m2}(k), \ldots, z_{mN}(k)), \quad i = 2N+1, \ldots, 3N \tag{13.1c}$$

These measurements are described as symmetric because the order of arguments
within each h_i does not affect its value. This results in the new set of measurements
being independent of the target-to-measurement association.

$$\tilde{q}_i(k) = h_i(x_1(k) + u_{x1}(k), x_2(k) + u_{x2}(k), \ldots, x_N(k) + u_{xN}(k)), \quad i = 1, \ldots, N \tag{13.2a}$$

$$\tilde{q}_i(k) = h_i(y_1(k) + u_{y1}(k), y_2(k) + u_{y2}(k), \ldots, y_N(k) + u_{y3}(k)), \quad i = N+1, \ldots, 2N \tag{13.2b}$$

$$\tilde{q}_i(k) = h_i(z_1(k) + u_{z1}(k), z_2(k) + u_{z2}(k), \ldots, z_N(k) + u_{z3}(k)), \quad i = 2N+1, \ldots, 3N \tag{13.2c}$$

where $u_{ji}, j \in \{x, y, z\}, i = 1, \ldots, N$ are zero-mean white noise processes. The
symmetric functionals (h_i) are required to satisfy three conditions

1. The original measurement vectors can be reconstructed from the new
   measurements.
2. The new measurements can be expressed in the form

$$\tilde{q}_i(k) = h_i(x_{m1}(k), x_{m2}(k), \ldots, x_{mN}(k) + v_{xi}(k)), \quad i = 1, \ldots, N \tag{13.3a}$$

$$\tilde{q}_i(k) = h_i(y_{m1}(k), y_{m2}(k), \ldots, y_{mN}(k) + v_{yi}(k)), \quad i = N+1, \ldots, 2N \tag{13.3b}$$

$$\tilde{q}_i(k) = h_i(z_{m1}(k), z_{m2}(k), \ldots, z_{mN}(k) + v_{zi}(k)), \quad i = 2N+1, \ldots, 3N \tag{13.3c}$$

where $v_{ji}(k)$, $j \in \{x, y, z\}$ are zero-mean white noise processes that are
independent of the measurement-to-target association.
3. The following observability condition must be satisfied.

$$\text{rank}\left[H^T(k) A^T H^T(k) (A^T)^2 H^T(k) \ldots (A^T)^{6N-1} H^T(k) \right] = 6N \tag{13.4}$$

where $H(k) = [\Gamma(k) 0_{3N}]$, and $\Gamma(k)$ is the $3N \times 3N$ Jacobian matrix of the functionals h_i, and A is the standard continuous-time state space matrix.
    The kinematics are given by the discrete kinematic

$$\begin{bmatrix} \mathbf{r}(k+1) \\ \dot{\mathbf{r}}(k+1) \end{bmatrix} = A \begin{bmatrix} \mathbf{r}(k) \\ \dot{\mathbf{r}}(k) \end{bmatrix} + Bw(k) \tag{13.5}$$

where

$$\mathbf{r}(k) = [x_1(k)\, y_1(k)\, z_1(k) \dots x_N(k)\, y_N(k)\, z_N(k)]^T \tag{13.6a}$$

$$A = \begin{bmatrix} I_{3N} & \Delta t I_{3N} \\ 0_{3N} & I_{3N} \end{bmatrix} \tag{13.6b}$$

$$B = \begin{bmatrix} \frac{1}{2}\Delta t^2 I_{3N} \\ \Delta t I_{3N} \end{bmatrix} \tag{13.6c}$$

and $w(k)$ is a zero-mean Gaussian random process noise vector with covariance Q_k. The update equation for an extended Kalman filter (EKF) is

$$\begin{bmatrix} \hat{\mathbf{r}}(k+1) \\ \dot{\hat{\mathbf{r}}}(k+1) \end{bmatrix} = A \begin{bmatrix} \hat{\mathbf{r}}(k) \\ \dot{\hat{\mathbf{r}}}(k) \end{bmatrix} + K_k[\mathbf{q}_k - \mathbf{h}_k] \tag{13.7}$$

where K_k is the Kalman gain.

The functionals are then defined as sums of products of the Cartesian measurements. An EKF is derived based on the above model and the nonlinear symmetric measurement equations. A simulation is performed with six targets moving through three-dimensional space. Initial positions were known with initial velocities assumed zero. The SME filter was shown to accurately track each of the targets. The algorithm was then shown to handle small initial position errors, though its effectiveness degraded as these errors grew (Table 13.3).

Table 13.3 Comparison of reviewed literature for multiple target tracking algorithms

Ref. #	[52–54, 55, 57, 60]	[58, 60, 68]	[62, 63]	[47, 48, 49, 69, 70]	[50, 51, 71]
Approach	JPDA	NN	SME	DLT	PF-JPDA
Data type	–	–	–	Human bearing	Range bearing laser
System hypotheses	NCV				
	CA				
	Large increment acceleration change	NCV	NCV	Not provided	Random motion
		CA			
	Splitting targets				
	Merging targets				
Terrain	None	None	None	Road	None

The SME approach is explored in conjunction with an UKF and a PF by Leven and Lanterman in Ref. [63]. A prominent difficulty in using a Kalman Filter with the SME approach is identified in that the nonlinear transformations create measurements that cannot be perfectly modeled as simple additive noise. This fact is what leads the authors to apply the UKF to the SME approach.

Two sets of SME's are presented *sum of products* and *sum of powers*.

$$\tilde{y}_{\text{prod}} = \begin{pmatrix} y_1 + y_2 + y_3 \\ y_1 y_2 + y_1 y_3 + y_2 y_3 \\ y_1 y_2 y_3 \end{pmatrix} \tag{13.8a}$$

$$\tilde{y}_{\text{pow}} = \begin{pmatrix} y_1 + y_2 + y_3 \\ y_1^2 + y_2^2 + y_3^2 \\ y_1^3 + y_2^3 + y_3^3 \end{pmatrix} \tag{13.8b}$$

Previous research had shown that the sum of products worked better than the sum of powers with the EKF. Overviews of the UKF and PF are then given. The UKF is actually shown to break down when combined with the sum of products. Due to the mathematical form of the equations, the covariance matrix becomes singular when two targets cross. This demonstrates that the performance of an SME approach is dependent on the interaction between itself and the nonlinear filter, and not the effectiveness of each component separately.

A simulation is performed with three targets moving in one dimension with constant velocity and known process noise. Initial states were chosen so that the target tracks would cross. The primary factor of interest was whether filters were able to maintain correct target association. The EKF was once again shown to perform better using the sum of products than the sum of powers. The converse was shown true for the UKF, mainly due to the break down mentioned above. The UKF using the sum of powers maintained better association than the EKF for either set of SME's. The PF performed well for both types of SME's.

13.9 Ground-Based Tracking Application

This section shows the use of contextual information in the form of terrain information in the estimation of a ground vehicle's position. The filter is known as the Contextual-based Tracker (ConTracker) [12]. Terrain slope and other data is used to generate trafficability values between 0 and 1, corresponding to the percentage of maximum velocity that a vehicle can achieve at that particular location. The estimated velocity vector is then deflected based upon the trafficability in the local region. A hybrid filter is used combining the update steps of the EKF with the propagation steps of the UKF. Other filters, such as a PF discussed previously, can also be used if desired instead. In this section and the next, perfect data association

of the objects is assumed. It should be noted that the strategy detailed in Sect. 13.8.3
could be applied to the tracking application in this section, but will not be shown
here specifically.

The state vector used in the filter is given by

$$\mathbf{x} = [\lambda \, \phi \, v_n \, v_e]^T \tag{13.9}$$

where v_n and v_e are the northward and eastward velocities given in an
North-East-Down (NED) reference frame [64]. The standard "$\alpha - \beta$" tracker
approach assumes a first-order random-walk process for the accelerations [65]. The
approach modifies this concept by using the following model:

$$\mathbf{x}_{k+1} = \begin{bmatrix} \lambda + \frac{v_n \Delta t}{R_\lambda + h} \\ \phi + \frac{v_e \Delta t}{(R_\phi + h)\cos\lambda} \\ v\sqrt{v_n^2 + v_e^2}\cos\theta \\ v\sqrt{v_n^2 + v_e^2}\sin\theta \end{bmatrix}\Bigg|_k + \mathbf{w}_k \tag{13.10}$$

where R_λ and R_ϕ are defined in Ref. [64] as

$$R_\lambda = \frac{a(1 - e^2)}{(1 - e^2 \sin^2 \lambda)^{3/2}} \tag{13.11a}$$

$$R_\phi = \frac{a}{(1 - e^2 \sin^2 \lambda)^{1/2}} \tag{13.11b}$$

and

$$E\{\mathbf{w}_k \mathbf{w}_k^T\} = \Delta t \Upsilon \begin{bmatrix} q_x & 0 \\ 0 & q_y \end{bmatrix} \Upsilon^T \tag{13.12}$$

with

$$\Upsilon \equiv \begin{bmatrix} 0 & 0 \\ 0 & 0 \\ 1 & 0 \\ 0 & 1 \end{bmatrix} \tag{13.13}$$

The angle θ, which is the angle between the velocity vector and the local x-axis,
defines the assumed direction of motion of the vehicle. This is determined by use of
the trafficability matrix. The coefficient v is a number between zero and one that
defines the velocity constraint in that region. This will be explained further in the
next section. The $\sqrt{v_n^2 + v_e^2}$ term is simply the magnitude of the vehicle velocity.
The trigonometric terms are used to project this value onto the North and East axes.

When no terrain information is present, v defaults to one, and the trigonometric terms are given by

$$\cos \theta = \frac{v_n}{\sqrt{v_n^2 + v_e^2}} \tag{13.14a}$$

$$\sin \theta = \frac{v_e}{\sqrt{v_n^2 + v_e^2}} \tag{13.14b}$$

which reduces to the standard $\alpha - \beta$ form. Note that the first two states of Eq. (13.10) represent a simple first-order discrete-time propagation of the kinematic models, which is valid for small Δt. A higher-order integration can be employed if needed.

The filter model in Eq. (13.10) represents a highly nonlinear model. Specifically, as will be shown later, the variable θ is a function of the filter states. The EKF requires taking partial derivatives of the model for the state and covariance propagation, which is intractable due to θ. Hence, a hybrid UKF/EKF is chosen for the filter design. The EKF is used for the update state, given by the following equations [65]:

$$K_k = P_k^- H_k^T(\hat{\mathbf{x}}_k^-)[H_k(\hat{\mathbf{x}}_k^-)P_k^- H_k^T(\hat{\mathbf{x}}_k^-) + R_k]^{-1} \tag{13.15a}$$

$$\hat{\mathbf{x}}_k^+ = \hat{\mathbf{x}}_k^- + K_k[\hat{\mathbf{y}}_k - h(\hat{\mathbf{x}}_k^-)] \tag{13.15b}$$

$$P_k^+ = [I - K_k H_k(\hat{\mathbf{x}}_k^-)]P_k^- \tag{13.15c}$$

The UKF is used for the propagation stage, given by the following equations [66]:

$$\boldsymbol{\sigma}_k \leftarrow 2n \text{ columns from } \pm \gamma \sqrt{P_k^+ + \Upsilon_k Q_k \Upsilon_k^T} \tag{13.16a}$$

$$\boldsymbol{\chi}_k(0) = \hat{\mathbf{x}}_k^+ \tag{13.16b}$$

$$\boldsymbol{\chi}_k(i) = \boldsymbol{\sigma}_k(i) + \hat{\mathbf{x}}_k^+ \tag{13.16c}$$

and

$$\boldsymbol{\chi}_{k+1}(i) = \mathbf{f}(\boldsymbol{\chi}_k(i), \mathbf{u}_k, k) \tag{13.17a}$$

$$\hat{\mathbf{x}}_{k+1}^- = \sum_{i=0}^{2n} W_i^{\text{mean}} \boldsymbol{\chi}_{k+1}(i) \tag{13.17b}$$

$$P_{k+1}^- = \sum_{i=0}^{2n} W_i^{\text{cov}} [\boldsymbol{\chi}_{k+1}(i) - \hat{\mathbf{x}}_{k+1}^-][\boldsymbol{\chi}_{k+1}(i) - \hat{\mathbf{x}}_{k+1}^-]^T \tag{13.17c}$$

The weights are defined by

$$W_0^{\text{mean}} = \frac{\lambda}{n+\lambda} \tag{13.18a}$$

$$W_0^{\text{cov}} = \frac{\lambda}{n+\lambda} + (1 - \alpha^2 + \beta) \tag{13.18b}$$

$$W_i^{\text{mean}} = W_i^{\text{cov}} = \frac{1}{2(n+\lambda)}, \quad i = 1, 2, \ldots, 2n \tag{13.18c}$$

where β is used to incorporate prior knowledge of the distribution (a good starting guess is $\beta = 2$).

Two types of measurements are expected: latitude-longitude pairs and lines of bearing (ψ). The measurement ellipsoid of the former is given in terms of Cartesian position in the NED reference frame. The two measurement models are given by

$$\mathbf{h}_1 = \begin{bmatrix} \lambda \\ \phi \end{bmatrix} \tag{13.19}$$

$$h_2 = \psi$$
$$= \tan^{-1}\left(\frac{y}{x}\right) \tag{13.20}$$

where x and y are the local NED positions [64].

The measurement vector $\tilde{\mathbf{y}}$ will either be equal to $\mathbf{h}_1$ or h_2, depending on the type of measurement. The Kalman update equations require the partial derivatives of these terms with respect to the states:

$$H_1 = \frac{\partial \mathbf{h}_1}{\partial \mathbf{x}} = \begin{bmatrix} 1 & 0 \\ 0 & 1 \end{bmatrix} \tag{13.21a}$$

$$H_2 = \frac{\partial h_2}{\partial \mathbf{x}} \tag{13.21b}$$

The calculation of the partial derivative of h_2 is not shown for brevity.

13.9.1 Trafficability

The trafficability matrix is a grid where local terrain traversability information is stored. This includes terrain slope, soil information, vegetation, weather conditions, etc. Each square for this example in this chapter contains information for a 90 m by 90 m area of land. The size of the grid is problem dependent, and may vary due to the degree of trafficability within a desired region. This information is given by the

Fig. 13.2 Velocity constraint
for cutoff. a Velocity
constraint for trafficability
matrix. b Cutoff for
velocity-based direction
determination

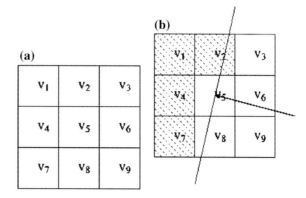

variable v_i, which is a decimal value between 0 and 1. This corresponds to the fraction of maximum velocity that the vehicle can achieve in that grid location.

This data will be used to deflect the direction of motion given by past state information. A generic representation of velocity constraint information in a trafficability matrix is shown in Fig. 13.2a. The vehicle is assumed to be located in square 5 of the 3×3 grid. This results in the coefficient v being given the value of v_5. The 3 by 3 grid will be continually re-centered about the vehicle as it moves throughout the region so that it is always located in square 5. A preferred direction based on the velocity constraint will be calculated based upon the equation

$$\hat{\mathbf{G}}_{tg} = \frac{\sum_j (v_j \hat{\mathbf{G}}_j)}{\left\| \sum_j (v_j \hat{\mathbf{G}}_j) \right\|} \tag{13.22}$$

where $j \, \varepsilon \, J$ is a set of feasible directions. The unit vector $\hat{\mathbf{G}}_j$ points from the center of square 5 to the center of square j. It is assumed that a vehicle's velocity will not change its direction by more than ninety degrees between two consecutive time steps. Thus, cutoff lines perpendicular to the previous direction of motion will be used, extending from the center of square 5. An example is shown in Fig. 13.2b. A square is assumed feasible if its centroid is contained within the feasible region. For this example, squares 1, 2, 4, and 7 are feasible and therefore included in set J. It should be noted that this method will always result in four feasible squares.

This technique for determining the cutoff was chosen because it is least expensive in terms of computational requirements. Another possible solution is to use the current estimated target position instead of the location of the center of square 5 for the above calculations. The unit vectors to the centers of other squares along with the tangent cutoff lines would then require more computational cost. This is demonstrated in Fig. 13.3a, b, where a vehicle is close to the border of the central square. In both cases, the number of feasible squares to be used for direction determination differs from the previous standard of four. A possible advantage is that the set of feasible adjacent squares would be more accurate for cases when the vehicle is near the border of square 5.

Fig. 13.3 Different feasible
regions. **a** Small feasible
region. **b** Large feasible
region

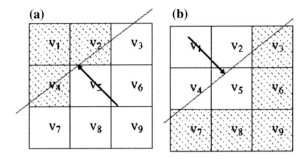

Fig. 13.3 Different feasible regions. **a** Small feasible region. **b** Large feasible region

The assumed direction of motion will be given by

$$\hat{\mathbf{G}}^{+} = \hat{\mathbf{G}}^{-} + \alpha_1 \hat{\mathbf{G}}_{tg} \tag{13.23}$$

where $\hat{\mathbf{G}}^{-}$ is the direction of motion at the previous time step, and α_1 is a weighting coefficient that is a function of v_j.

The functional form for α_1 is based on the average difference in velocity constraint between the current location and the surrounding feasible locations.

$$\mu = \frac{\sum_j (v_j - v_5)}{\sum_j (1)} \tag{13.24}$$

The plot of α_1 is shown in Fig. 13.4. Since the goal is to use velocity information to slightly alter the assumed direction, the maximum magnitude of α_1 was chosen to be 0.5. Several cases can be discussed from this plot. First, consider the scenario where all feasible cells have the same velocity constraint coefficient as the current location. When that occurs, each of the cells is equally probable and should have no

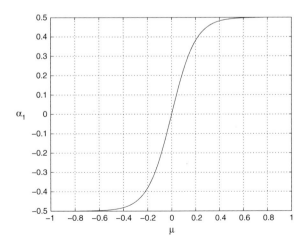

Fig. 13.4 Proposed form for coefficient α_1

influence on the overall direction. From the plot, this scenario corresponds to $\mu = 0$, which yields $\alpha_1 = 0$. Another scenario is when the vehicle is facing impassable territory in all feasible directions (velocity coefficients of zero). This will result in a negative μ, corresponding to a negative α_1. This causes the assumed direction to be directed away from the impassable regions.

The case may also arise where goal information is present. Designate $\hat{\mathbf{G}}_{ob}$ as the unit vector pointing from the center of square 5 (or current estimated location if higher complexity is desired) to the location of the goal, and let d_{ob} be the distance between the two locations. The assumed direction can then be written as

$$\hat{\mathbf{G}}^+ = \hat{\mathbf{G}}^- + \alpha_1 \hat{\mathbf{G}}_{tg} + \alpha_2 \hat{\mathbf{G}}_{ob} \qquad (13.25)$$

where the positive coefficient α_2 is a function of d_{ob}. If goal information is withdrawn for a given target, α_2 is set to zero, and Eq. (13.23) is recovered. A proposed form for α_2 is

$$\alpha_2(r, s) = \frac{1}{\left(1 + \frac{d_{ob}}{90}\right)^n} \qquad (13.26)$$

where n is a positive user-defined coefficient. The "1" in the denominator ensures that a singularity will not occur if the target is located within a region containing a goal. Dividing the distance-to-object by 90 normalizes that value with respect to the grid size. When the goal is far away, this will have a small effect on the overall direction. As the target approaches the goal, the influence of that goal will increase more rapidly. The coefficient n will be best determined by testing after real traversability and goal information have been provided. At this time, a value of $n = 1$ is recommended.

13.9.2 Experimental Results

Based on trafficability data for the Austin, Texas area, a test case was generated to illustrate the performance of the trafficability-based filter. The trafficability data ranges from 0 to 1, where 0 for any region corresponds to infeasibility of the vehicle traversing that region and a 1 corresponds to no constraints on the motion of the vehicle. The trafficability data is provided for a grid of cells where each cell corresponds to a 90 m by 90 m area. A test case which corresponds to a vehicle traveling toward a gully and subsequently making a sharp right turn and following the gully as shown in Fig. 13.5a, is created. The black line is the true path of the vehicle and the diamonds represent the periodic measurements of the vehicle. The additive Gaussian noise is the reason why the magenta diamonds do not lie on the black line. A sampling time of 10 s or a sampling rate of 6 measurements per minute is selected for sampling the position of the vehicle.

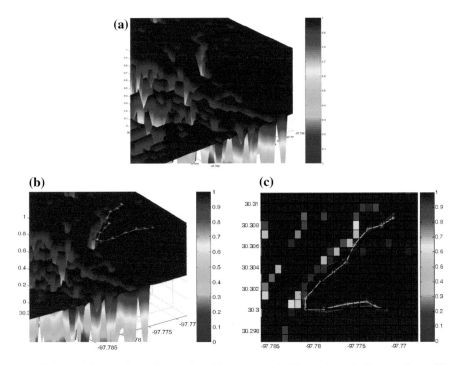

Fig. 13.5 Tracking results. **a** 3D terrain with trajectory. **b** 3D terrain with filter results. **c** 3D terrain with filter results

A UKF is used to predict the motion of the ground vehicle and the resulting trajectory is illustrated by the blue line in Fig. 13.5b. The UKF filter does not exploit knowledge of the trafficability and therefore, as the vehicle approaches the gulley, the velocity vector of the vehicle prior to the sharp turn, predicts the motion of the vehicle to lie in the gulley. The following measurements coax the UKFs trajectory out of the gulley. In contrast, the UKF which exploits the trafficability data to nudge the velocity vector of the UKF is illustrated by the green line. The benefit of knowledge of the trafficability is illustrated by the trajectory which avoids motion in the gulley.

Figure 13.5c illustrates the benefit of using the trafficability data to modify the velocity vector in a planar view of the terrain. The colorbar on the right which ranges for a numerical value of 0 to 1 provide the context for the trafficability of the vehicle. The x and y axes represent the latitude and longitude, respectively, with units of degrees.

This example illustrates the potential of using the trafficability data to enhance the performance of traditional filtering approaches. It should be pointed out that since the proposed approach to nudge the velocity vector is ad hoc, with many tuning parameters, numerical studies are necessary for the appropriate selection of the tuning parameters to optimize the performance of the proposed filter.

13.10 Maritime-Based Tracking Application

In the previous section the ConTracker is used to strictly to improve tracking performance. In this section the ConTracker is further expanded for anomaly detection in a maritime application, as shown in Refs. [13, 67]. For maritime applications considered here, these trafficability values are based on local traversability information and accounts for the following four "contextual" data:

- Depth information
- Marked channel information
- Anti-shipping Reports (ASR)
- Locations of High-Value Units (HVU)

The individual trafficability values corresponding to each contextual information are combined into a single value which is used to indicate the repeller or the attractor characteristic of a specific region. Details of this procedure are given next.

First, a particular area of interest is first divided into a grid-field, similar to a 15×20 grid-field as shown in Fig. 13.6. In Fig. 13.6, the purple channels indicate marked shipping lanes. The area of interest contains three high-value units centered around cells $(2, 11)$, $(6, 14)$, and $(11 \ldots 15, 8)$. The area also contains two anti-shipping areas centered about cells $(4, 2)$ and $(5, 17)$. Finally, low depth areas

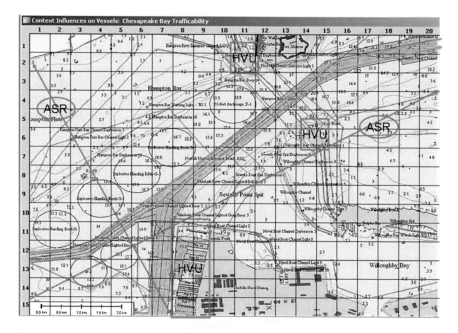

Fig. 13.6 Maritime trafficability values database

are mainly indicated using different shades of brown. According to the vehicle type that is being tracked, a single trafficability value, v_i, is assigned to each cell. This variable is a decimal value between 0 and 1 and corresponds to the fraction of maximum velocity that the vehicle can attain in that grid location. For example, the grid cell $(10, 17)$ has a trafficability of zero due to the depth information and therefore the vessels are supposed to avoid and navigate around this particular cell.

Trafficability data will be used to deflect the direction of target motion given by the past velocity information. In order to implement this, at each propagation stage in the ConTracker, we consider a 3×3 trafficability grid-field that depends on the current vehicle position. For example, if the vehicle is located in cell $(13, 3)$, the 3×3 trafficability grid-field consists of cells $(12, 2), (12, 3), (12, 4), (13, 2), (13, 3), (13, 4), (14, 2), (14, 3),$ and $(14, 4)$. The vehicle is assumed to be located in square 5 of the 3×3 grid. The 3×3 grid will be continually re-centered about the vehicle as it moves throughout the region so that it is always located in the center (square 5) of the 3×3 trafficability grid-field.

In the propagation stage of the ConTracker, vehicle states are propagated according to the repeller or the attractor characteristic of the current location of the vehicle. Any behavior of the vehicle that is inconsistent with the repeller or the attractor characteristic of the current location would be classified as suspicious. Such an inconsistent vehicle behavior would be directly indicated by a high measurement residual which may be used to estimate the process noise covariance associated with the target model. Thus ConTracker accuracy is not only a function of the contextual information provided, but its performance also depends on the usual Kalman "tuning" issue, i.e., determination of the process noise covariance [65]. The tuning process is a function of the actual vehicle motion, which can vary.

The aforementioned tuning issue is usually done in an ad hoc manner. However, mathematical tools can be used to automatically tune the tracker. Multiple model estimation schemes are useful for the process noise identification (tuning) problem. Multiple Model Adaptive Estimation (MMAE) approaches run parallel trackers, each using a different value for the process noise covariance [65]. The tuning process is a function of the actual vehicle motion, which can vary. This variation is the key to the hypothesis generator. This is best explained by an example; suppose that a vehicle is heading toward a high-value unit, the contextual information incorporated into the ConTracker would repel the vehicle away from the high-value unit during the propagation stage of the tracker. However, if the vehicle still proceeds toward the high-value unit, which is shown directly through the measurements of the vehicle location, then in order to provide good tracker characteristics a large value of process noise covariance must be chosen, i.e., tuned.

The MMAE scheme implemented here consists of a bank of ConTrackers each with a different process noise covariance. Assuming the estimated process noise covariance values are consistent with the truth, a small value of process noise covariance correspond to a case where the context-aware target model is an accurate representation of the true target and a large value of process noise covariance indicates that the context-aware target model is a poor representation of the truth and the target does not comply with the available contextual information.

The process noise covariance is estimated as a weighted sum of all the process noise covariances used and the weight associated with each covariance is calculated using the likelihood of the process noise covariances conditioned on current-time measurement-minus estimate residual. The estimated covariance is incorporated into a hypothesis scheme that provides a hypothesis on whether or not a vehicle motion should be alerted to an analyst. The hypothesis generator "red-flags" the vehicle based on the rate of change of the process noise covariance and the contextual information provided.

13.10.1   Simulation Results

In order to evaluate the performance of the a priori subsystem, a test case scenario is developed where we consider Hampton Roads Bay, Virginia, near the Norfolk Naval Station. The area of interest is first divided into a 15×20 grid-field as shown in Fig. 13.6. Afterwards a trafficability value is assigned to each cell based on the target vessel type and the individual contextual data. Since we consider four different contextual data here, a combined trafficability value is also assigned to each cell by combining the four individual trafficability value. As shown in Fig. 13.6, the harbor area contains three high-value units centered around cells $(2, 11)$, $(6, 14)$, and $(11…15, 8)$. The harbor area also contains two anti-shipping areas centered about cells $(4, 2)$ and $(5, 17)$. There are several marked shipping lanes in the harbor area that are indicated by shaded purple channels. Here Ski boat 1 results are shown. It 1 starts in cell $(15, 8)$ and travels toward cell $(2, 1)$. Ski boat 1 crosses over two different marked channels at cells $(14, 7)$ and $(11, 5)$. Finally, the ski boat 1 crosses over a anti-shipping area located around cell $(14, 2)$ and travels toward cell $(2, 1)$.

Figure 13.7 shows the measured and estimated trajectories for ski boat 1. Figure 13.7 contains the estimated trajectories from both context-aided ConTracker

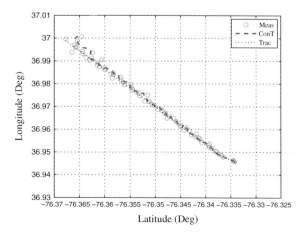

Fig. 13.7 Ski boat 1 Trajectories: Measured Position (Meas), ConTracker Estimate (ConT) & Tracker Estimate (Trac)

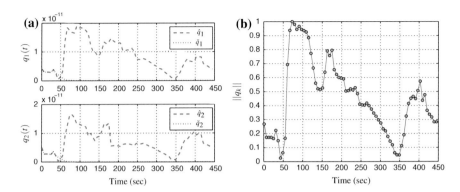

Fig. 13.8 ConTracker & tracker estimated process noise covariance and normalized norm for ski boat 1. **a** Estimated q_1 and q_2. **b** Normalized process noise covariance norm

(denoted as ConT) and the traditional Kalman filter-based tracker (denoted as Trac). The performance difference between the ConTracker and the traditional Kalman filter is not investigated here though, because the ConTracker is used strictly for anomaly detection in this maritime-based application. Figure 13.8a shows the estimated process noise covariance variance values from the ConTracker/MMAE $\{\hat{q}_{1_k}, \hat{q}_{2_k}\}$ and the Kalman filter tracker/MMAE $\{\breve{q}_{1_k}, \breve{q}_{2_k}\}$. The normalized process noise covariance norm, $\|q_k\|$, is given in Fig. 13.8b. Note the sudden increase in $\|q_k\|$ at times 50, 150, and 350 s. The first increase in the process noise covariance values occur when the ski boat crosses over the marked channel located about cell $(14, 7)$. The second increase in process noise covariance values occur when the ski boat crosses over the second marked channel located about the cell $(11, 5)$ around 145 s. The final increase in the process noise covariance values occurs when the ski boat enters the anti-shipping area located about cell $(4, 2)$ around 350 s. It should be noted that the actual state estimates are not as important as the change in the estimate of the process noise because the ConTracker/MMAE is used for anomaly detection here.

Figure 13.9 shows the rate of change of the normalized process noise covariance norm, Δq_k, and the trafficability values, v, for ski boat 1. The target vehicle (ski boat 1) is red-flagged based on the rate of change of normalized process noise covariance norm. The maximum allowable Δq_k is selected to be $\Delta q_{max} = 0.8$. Note that at times 50, 150, and 350 s, Δq_k is higher than its threshold value and therefore the target vehicle is red-flagged at these instances. Also note the low trafficability values at these instances as shown in Fig. 13.9b.

Figure 13.10a shows θ, which is the angle between the velocity vector and the local y-axis, for the ConTracker and the traditional Kalman filter-based tracker. The angle is measured positive clockwise and negative counter clockwise. Note that the angle obtained from the Kalman filter-based tracker is much smoother compared to the one obtained from the ConTracker. The discrepancy in the ConTracker's angle is due to the velocity nudging that occurs when the target vehicle encounters a

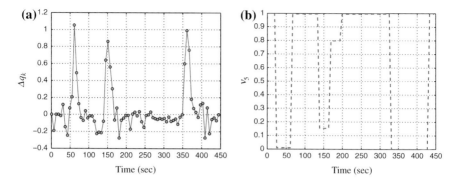

Fig. 13.9 Rate of change of normalized process noise covariance norm and trafficability values for ski boat 1. **a** Rate of change of $\|qk\|$. **b** Trafficability values

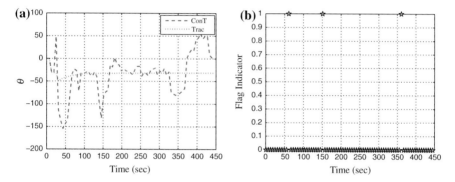

Fig. 13.10 ConTracker and tracker estimated direction and *Red-Flag* Indicator for ski boat 1. **a** Boat direction. **b** *Red-Flag* indicator

zero-trafficability area. Also note that when the boat is traveling in a completely traversable region, θ obtained for the ConTracker and the traditional Kalman filter-based tracker are very similar. Figure 13.10b shows the red-flag alerts for ski boat 1. Here zero indicates a no red-flag alert and one indicates a red-flag occurrence. Note that the red-flag occurrence and the large deviations in θ are consistent with the results shown in Fig. 13.9.

13.11 Conclusions and Future Work

In this chapter, we have presented various research examples for context-based target tracking. The applications shown here indicate that good performance can be achieved to both provide better estimated tracks, and provide a means to generate a hypothesis on whether or not a target should be red-flagged for violating certain pre-described conditions. The accuracy of the any context-based target estimates depends on the usefulness of the contextual data. In this chapter the contextual information is assumed to be static. For example, the ground terrain information is assumed to be the same for any tracking application in the particular area. However, this may not be true for a variety of reasons, such as vegetation growth or changing ground conditions due to weather. Future designs should incorporate more dynamic-based contextual information as well as other sources of information, such as human reports.

Acknowledgments This work was supported in part by funding provided by Overwatch Systems and Silver Bullet Solutions through an Office of Naval Research grant.

References

1. R. Moose, H. Vanlandingham, D. Mccabe, Modeling and estimation for tracking maneuvering targets. IEEE Trans. Aerosp. Electron. Syst. **15**(3), 448–456 (1979)
2. R. Singer, Estimating optimal tracking filter performance for manned maneuvering targets. IEEE Trans. Aerosp. Electron. Syst. **6**(4), 473–483 (1970)
3. R.J. Fitzgerald, Simple tracking filters: position and velocity measurements. IEEE Trans. Aerosp. Electron. Syst. **18**(5), 531–537 (1982)
4. T. Kirubarajan, Y. Bar-Shalom, K.R. Pattipati, I. Kadar, Ground target tracking with variable structure IMM estimator. IEEE Trans. Aerosp. Electron. Syst. **36**(1), 26–46 (2000)
5. D.D. Sworder, R.G. Hutchins, Maneuver estimation using measurements of orientation. IEEE Trans. Aerosp. Electron. Syst. **26**(4), 625–638 (1990)
6. M. Ulmke, W. Koch, Road-map assisted ground moving target tracking. IEEE Trans. Aerosp. Electron. Syst. **42**(4), 1264–1274 (2006)
7. D.B. Reid, R.G. Bryson, A non-Gaussian filter for tracking targets moving over terrain, in *Proceedings of the 12th Annual Asilomar Conference on Circuits, Systems, and Computers* (Pacific Grove, CA, 1978), pp. 112–116
8. P.O. Nougues, D.E. Brown, We know where you are going: Tracking objects in terrain. IMA J. Math. Appl. Bus. Ind. **8**, 39–58 (1997)
9. A.T. Alouani, W.D. Blair, G.A. Watson, Bias and observability analysis of target tracking filters using a kinematic constraint, in *Proceedings of the Twenty-Third Southeastern Symposium on System Theory*, 1991, pp. 229–232
10. A.T. Alouani, W.D. Blair, Use of a kinematic constraint in tracking constant speed, maneuvering targets. IEEE Trans. Autom. Control **38**(7), 1107–1111 (1993)
11. D. Tenne, B. Pitman, T. Singh, J. Llinas, Velocity field based tracking of ground vehicles. in *RTO-SET-059: Symposium on "Target Tracking and Sensor Data Fusion for Military Observation Systems"*, 2003
12. A.M. Fosbury, T. Singh, J.L. Crassidis, C. Springen, Ground target tracking using terrain information, *10th International Conference on Information Fusion*, 2007
13. J. George, J.L. Crassidis, T. Singh, A.M. Fosbury, Anomaly detection using context aided target tracking. J. Adv. Inf. Fusion **6**(1), 39–56 (2011)
14. C.Y. Chong, D. Garren, T. Grayson, Ground target tracking-a historical perspective. IEEE Aerosp. Conf. **3**, 433–448 (2000)
15. L. Müller, J. Lipiec, T.S. Kornecki, S. Gebhardt, Trafficability and workability of soils, in *Encyclopedia of Agrophysics*, ed. by J. Gliński, J. Horabik, J. Lipiec (Springer, The Netherlands, 2011), pp. 912–924

16. R. Schubert, E. Richter, G. Wanielik, Comparison and evaluation of advanced motion models for vehicle tracking, in *Eleventh International Conference on Information Fusion*, 2008
17. M. Hura, G. McLeod, E. Larson, J. Schneider, D. Gonzales, D. Norton, J. Jacobs, K. O'Connell, W. Little, R. Mesic, L. Jamison, Interoperability: A Continuing Challenge in Coalition Air Operations, Chapter 8. Rand Corporation, 2000
18. A.P. Dempster, N.M. Laird, D.B. Rubin, Maximum likelihood from incomplete data via the EM algorithm. J. Roy. Stat. Soc.: Ser. B (Methodol.) **39**(1), 1–38 (1977)
19. L.D. Stone, R.L. Streit, T.L. Corwin, K.L. Bell, *Bayesian Multiple Target Tracking*, 2nd edn. (Artech House, Norwood, MA, 2013)
20. K. Kastella, C. Kreucher, Multiple model nonlinear filtering for low signal ground target applications. IEEE Trans. Aerosp. Electron. Syst. **41**(2), 549–564 (2005)
21. J.R. Layne., U.C. Piyasena, Adaptive interacting multiple model tracking of maneuvering targets, in *Digital Avionics Conference*, 1997
22. H.E Yan, G. Zhi-Jiang, J. Jing-Ping, Design of the adaptive interacting multiple model algorithm, in *American Control Conference*, 2002, pp. 1538–1542
23. B. Kim, J.S. Lee, IMM algorithm based on the analytic solution of steady state Kalman filter for radar target tracking, in *IEEE International Radar Conference*, 2005, pp. 757 7622
24. R. Enders, Fundamentals of on-road tracking, in *SPIE Conference on Aquisition, Tracking and Pointing*, 1999
25. O. Payne, A. Marrs, An unscented particle filter for GMTI tracking, in *Proceedings of the 2004 IEEE Aerospace Conference*, vol. 3, 2004, pp. 1869–1875
26. M. Hernandez, Performance bounds for GMTI tracking. Proc. Sixth Int. Conf. Inf. Fusion **1**, 406–413 (2003)
27. A. Arulampalam, N. Gordon, M. Orton, B. Ristic, A variable structure multiple model particle filter for GMTI tracking, in *5th International Conference on Information Fusion*, vol. 2, 2002, pp. 927–934
28. T. Cheng, T. Singh, Efficient particle filtering for road-constrained target tracking, in *Eighth International Conference on Information Fusion*, 2005
29. H.A. Blom, Y. Bar-Shalom, The interacting multiple model algorithm for systems with markovian switching coefficients. IEEE Trans. Autom. Control **33**(8), 780–783 (1988)
30. W.R. Li, Y. Bar-Shalom, Performance prediction of the interacting multiple model algorithm. IEEE Trans. Aerosp. Electron. Syst. **29**(3), 755–771 (1993)
31. F. Castella, F. Dunnebacke, Analytical results for the x, y Kalman tracking filter. IEEE Trans. Aerosp. Electron. Syst. **1**, 891–895 (1974)
32. K. Ramachandra, *Kalman Filtering Tachniques for Radar Tracking* (Marcel Dekker Inc. 2000)
33. L.A. Johnston, V. Krishnamurthy, An improvement to the interacting multiple model (IMM) algorithm. IEEE Trans. Sig. Process. **49**(12), 2909–2923 (2001)
34. X. Meng, D.V. Dyk, The EM algorithm-an old folk song sung to a fast new tune. J. R. Stat. Soc. B. **59**(3), 511–567 (1997)
35. Y. Boers, J.N. Driessen, Interacting multiple model particle filter. Radar, Sonar and Navigation, IEE Proc. **150**(5), 344–349 (2003)
36. A. Munir, D. Atherton, Maneuvering target tracking using and adaptive interacting multiple model algorithm, in *Proceedings of the American Control Conference*, 1994
37. J. Gustafson, P. Maybeck, Control of a large flexible space structure with moving-bank multiple model adaptive algorithms, in *Proceedings of the 31th Conference on Decision and Control*, 1992, pp. 1273–1278
38. P. Maybeck, K. Hentz, Investigation of moving-bank multiple model adaptive algorithms. AIAA J. Guidance, Navig., and Control **10**(1), 1273–1278 (1987)
39. M. Efe, D. Atherton, Maneuvering target tracking with an adaptive Kalman filter, in *IEEE Conference on Decision and Control*, 1998, pp. 737–742
40. S.J. Julier, J.K. Uhlmann, H.F. Durrant-Whyte, A new method for the nonlinear transformation of means and covariances in filters and estimators. IEEE Trans. Autom. Control **AC-45**(3), 477–482 (2000)

41. X.R. Li, Y. Bar-Shalom, Multiple model estimation with variable structure. IEEE Trans. Autom. Control **41**(4), 478–493 (1996)
42. T. Kirubarajan, Y. Bar-Shalom, K.R. Pattipati, Topography based vs. IMM estimator for large scale ground target tracking, in *IEEE Colloquium on Target Tracking: Algorithms and Applications*, 1999, pp. 11/1–11/4
43. T. Kirubarajan, Y. Bar-Shalom, Tracking evasive move-stop-move targets with a GMTI radar using a VS-IMM estimator. IEEE Trans. Aerosp. Electron. Syst. **39**(3), 1098–1103 (2003)
44. G. Kravaritis, B. Mulgrew, Ground tracking using a variable structure multiple model particle filter with varying number of particles, in *IEEE International Radar Conference*, 2005, pp. 837–841
45. C. Yang, M. Bakich, E. Blasch, Nonlinear constrained tracking of targets on roads, in *Eigth International Conference on Information Fusion*, 2005
46. M. Mallick, T. Kirubarajan, S. Arulampalam, Out-of-sequence measurement processing for tracking ground target using particle filters. IEEE Aerosp. Conf. **4**, 1809–1818 (2002)
47. J. Edlund, C. Setterlind, N. Bergman, Branching ground target tracking using sparse manual observations, in *Seventh International Conference on Information Fusion*, 2004
48. E. Giannopolous, R. Streit, P. Swaszek, Probabilistic multi-hypothesis tracking in multi-sensor, multi-target environment, in *First Australian Data Fusion Symposium*, 1996, pp. 184–189
49. C. Rago, P. Willett, R. Streit, A comparison of the JPDAF and PMHT tracking algorithm. Int. Conf. Acoust., Speech, and Sig. Process. **4**, 3571–3574 (1995)
50. L. Jing, P. Vadakkepat, Multiple targets tracking by optimized particle filter based on multi-scan JPDA, in *Instrumentation and Measurement Technology Conference*, 2004, pp. 303–308
51. O. Frank, J. Nieto, J. Guivant, S. Scheding, Multiple target tracking using sequential Monte Carlo methods and statistical data association, in *International Conference on Intelligent Robots and Systems*, 2003, pp. 2718–2723
52. Y. Bar-Shalom, K.C. Chang, H.A. Blom, Tracking of splitting targets in clutter using an interacting multiple model joint probabilistic data association filter, in *30th Conference on Decision and Control*, 1991, pp. 2043–2048
53. L. Hong, Z. Ding, Multiple target tracking using a multirate IMMJPDA algorithm. Am. Control Conf. **4**, 2427–2431 (1998)
54. I. Hwang, H. Balakrishnan, K. Roy, C. Tomlin, Multiple target tracking and identity management in clutter, with application to aircraft tracking, in *American Control Conference*, 2004, pp. 3422–3428
55. A.K. Singh, N. Sood, Modeling multi target multi sensor data fusion for trajectory tracking. Defence Sci. J. **59**(3), 205–214 (2009)
56. J. Shin, L. Guibas, F. Zhao, A distributed algorithm for managing multi-target identities in wireless ad-hoc sensor networks, in *Information Processing in Sensor Networks*, 2003, pp. 223–238
57. I. Hwang, J. Hwang, C. Tomlin, Flight-mode-based aircraft conflict detection using a residual-mean interacting multiple model algorithm, in *AIAA Guidance, Navigation and Control Conference*, 2003
58. A. Jouan, H. Michalska, Tracking closely maneuvering targets in clutter with an IMM-JVC algorithm, in *Third International Conference on Information Fusion*, vol. 1, 2000
59. D. Castanon, New assignment algoriths for data association. Proc. SPIE **1698**, 313–323 (1992)
60. M. Hadzagic, H. Michalska, A. Jouan, IMM-JVC and IMM-JPDA for closely maneuvering targets. Sig., Syst. Comput. **2**, 1278–1282 (2001)
61. R. Mahler, The multisensor PHD filter, I: General solution via multitarget calculus, in *Proceedings of SPIE*, vol. 7336, 2009
62. C.R. Sastry, E.W. Kamen, SME filter approach to multiple target tracking with radar measurements. Radar and Sig. Process., IEE Proc. **140**, 251–260 (1993)

63. W.F. Leven, A.D. Lanterman, Multiple target tracking with symmetric measurement equations using unscented Kalman and particle filters, in *36th Southeastern Symposium on System Theory*, 2004, pp. 195–199
64. J. Farrell, M. Barth, *The Global Positioning System and Inertial Navigation* (McGraw-Hill, New York, NY, 1998)
65. J.L. Crassidis, J.L. Junkins, *Optimal Estimation of Dynamic Systems*, 2nd edn. (CRC Press, Boca Raton, FL, 2012)
66. E. Wan, R. van der Merwe, *The Unscented Kalman Filter*, ed by S. Haykin, chap. 7 (Wiley, New York, NY, 2001)
67. E.D. Martí, J. García, J.L. Crassidis, Improving multiple-model context-aided tracking through an autocorrelation approach, *16th International Conference on Information Fusion*, 2012
68. H. Leung, Z. Hu, M. Blanchette, Evaluation of multiple target track initiation techniques in real radar tracking environments. Radar, Sonar, and Navig., IEE Proc. **143**, 246–254 (1996)
69. S. Oh, S. Russell, S. Sastry, Markov chain Monte Carlo data association for general multiple target tracking problems, in *Conference on Decision and Control*, 2004, pp. 735–742
70. S. Gattein, P. Vannoorenberghe, M. Contat, Prior knowledge integration of road dependant ground target behaviour for improving tracking reliability. in Multisensor, Multisource Information Fusion: Architectures, Algorithms and Applications, 2005, pp. 138–149
71. J. Vermaak, S.J. Godsill, P. Perez, Monte carlo filtering for multi-target tracking and data association. IEEE Trans. Aerosp. Electron. Syst. **41**(1), 309–332 (2005)

Chapter 14
Context Relevance for Text Analysis and Enhancement for Soft Information Fusion

Michael Kandefer and Stuart C. Shapiro

Abstract Soft information fusion, fusing information from natural language messages with other soft information and with information from physical sensors is facilitated by representing the information in the messages as a formally defined propositional graph that abides by the uniqueness principle—the principle that every entity or event that is mentioned in the message is represented by a unique node in the graph, or, at worst, by several nodes connected by co-referentiality relations. To further facilitate information fusion, information from the message is enhanced with relevant information from background knowledge sources. What knowledge is relevant is determined by also representing the background knowledge as a propositional graph, embedding the knowledge graph from the messages into the background knowledge graph using the uniqueness principle to fuse a message graph node with a background knowledge graph node, and then using spreading activation to find subgraphs of the background knowledge graph. This combination of the message graph with the retrieved subgraphs is considered the "relevant information." In this chapter, we discuss, evaluate, and compare two techniques for spreading activation.

Keywords Context · Relevance · Information fusion · Soft information fusion · Spreading activation · Graph knowledge representation · Propositional graphs · Tractor · SNePS

M. Kandefer
Applied Sciences Group, Inc., Buffalo, NY 14225, USA
e-mail: mkandefer@asgrp.com

S.C. Shapiro (✉)
University at Buffalo, Buffalo, NY 14260-2500, USA
e-mail: shapiro@buffalo.edu

© Springer International Publishing Switzerland (outside the USA) 2016   381
L. Snidaro et al. (eds.), *Context-Enhanced Information Fusion,*
Advances in Computer Vision and Pattern Recognition,
DOI 10.1007/978-3-319-28971-7_14

14.1 Introduction

Tractor is a system for message understanding within the context of a multi-investigator, multidisciplinary, multi-university effort on "Hard and Soft Information Fusion" [1]. Information obtained from physical sensors such as pan tilt zoom (PTZ) cameras, light detection and ranging (LIDAR) sensors, and acoustic sensors are considered hard information. Information from humans expressed in natural language is considered soft information. Tractor [2, 3] is a computational system that understands isolated English intelligence messages in the counterinsurgency (COIN) domain for later fusion with each other and with hard information, all to aid intelligence analysts to perform situation assessment. In this context, "understanding" means creating a knowledge base (KB), expressed in a formal knowledge representation (KR) language that captures the information in an English message.

Tractor takes as input a single English message. The ultimate goal is for the Tractor to output a KB representing the semantic information in that message. Later systems of the larger project fuse these KBs with each other and with hard information. Fusing KBs from different messages and different hard sources is done via a process of data association [1, 4] that operates by comparing the attributes of and relations among the entities and events described in each KB. It is therefore important for Tractor to express these attributes and relations as completely and accurately as possible. Doing this requires the use of background knowledge— knowledge that is not explicitly included in the text. Background knowledge includes: knowledge of how the natural language is used; knowledge of the world; knowledge of the domain being discussed in the text; and knowledge of the axioms of the relations that are used (explicitly or implicitly) in the text. Rather than including all available background knowledge in the KB created from the message, it is important to include only background knowledge that is relevant to the context of the message.

To investigate the relevant meaning of "context," we review the approaches of several cognitive science disciplines, and identify factors that can serve various uses among embodied cognitive architectures. We capture the notion of "relevance" by representing both the information from the messages and the background knowledge as propositional graphs. We embed the message graph in the background knowledge graphs and spread activation from the former into the latter. Spreading activation finds related information, while limiting the spread makes sure that the related information remains relevant. In this chapter, we discuss and evaluate several approaches to spreading activation.

Tractor and the larger information fusion system of which it is a part have been developed by experimenting with several datasets, particularly the Synthetic Counterinsurgency (SYNCOIN) [5] dataset. All examples in this chapter have been drawn from these datasets.

14.2   Propositional Graphs

In the tradition of the SNePS family [6–8], propositional graphs are graphs in which every well-formed expression in the KB, including those that denote individuals, events, relations, or propositions, are represented by nodes in the graph. In particular, every relation normally used in natural language discussions, whether unary, binary, or n-ary, is represented by a node, and propositions (sometimes called "facts," "beliefs," etc.) are also represented by nodes. From a logical point of view, nodes that represent propositions are terms, rather than formulas, in the logic and relations are proposition-valued functions. Arcs in the graph go from nodes representing functional terms, including propositions, to nodes that represent the arguments in those terms, including the function itself.

Every node is labeled with an identifier. Atomic nodes, nodes corresponding to individual constants, proposition symbols, function symbols, or relation symbols, are labeled with the symbol itself. Molecular nodes, nodes corresponding to functional terms, are labeled wft$i$, for some integer, i. (wft for "well-formed term.") An exclamation mark, "!," is appended to the label if its node represents a proposition that is asserted (taken to be true) in the KB. Every arc is labeled with a symbol that indicates the argument position of the node it points to in the functional term that it points from. It may be that more than one node occupies the same argument position of some functional term [6, 9]. For example, in Fig. 14.1, the node labeled wft5! represents an asserted propositional term whose member argument is filled by the atomic node

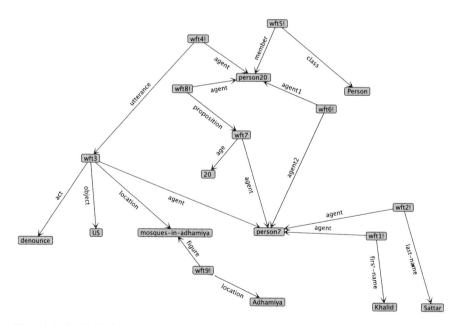

Fig. 14.1 A SNePS 3 propositional graph of STEF message 2

labeled `person20`, and whose class argument is filled by the atomic node labeled `Person`. The node labeled `wft3` represents an unasserted propositional term with four arguments. Its `agent` argument is filled by the node labeled `person7`; its `act` argument by the node labeled `denounce`; `object` argument, `US`; and `location`, `mosques-in-adhamiya`. The node labeled `wft4!` represents an asserted propositional term whose agent argument is filled by the node labeled `person20`, and whose `utterance` argument is filled by the node labeled `wft3`.

SNePS graphs obey the "uniqueness principle" [10], namely no two nodes represent syntactically identical expressions; rather, if there are multiple occurrences of one subexpression in one or more other expressions, the same node is used in all cases. More precisely, the KB does not contain two atomic nodes with the same label, and, if we consider the pair consisting of an arc label and a node pointed to by an arc with that label to be a "wire," the KB does not contain two molecular nodes with the same set of wires emanating from them. If there is an attempt to create a node that is syntactically identical to an already existing node, then the already existing node is used instead. For example, in Fig. 14.1, the node labeled `person20` is an argument in the propositional terms represented by the nodes labeled `wft4!`, `wft5!`, `wft6!`, and `wft8!`, and the node labeled `person7` is an argument of five different propositional terms.

Propositional graphs have several properties that make them useful for information fusion:

- The uniqueness principle establishes a base case for data association—multiple mentions in a message that are worded identically are represented by the identical node in the graph.
- Co-referential mentions that are not identical are represented by different nodes, but a proposition asserting their co-referentiality is put into the graph, thus connecting them.
- All assertions about an entity or event, whether from the message or from background knowledge, are connected to the node representing it.
- Since propositions are represented as terms in the representational language and by nodes in the graph, propositions about propositions can be represented in the graph. This is useful for asserting the pedigree of information, including the name of the informant.
- Relationships are *n*-ary (i.e., they can have any number of arguments) [11, 12], which makes it easier to formalize the complex actions described in soft information.

Because of these advantages, we have used propositional graphs for representing the messages and background knowledge sources, and use the SNePS 3 knowledge representation system [6, 13] for the implementation of the representation. Figure 14.1 is an example of a SNePS 3 propositional graph representing the STEF message 2,

Source said a Sunni youth he knows to be about 20 years old, Khalid Sattar, has become increasingly vocal in denouncing the U.S. at 4 or 5 mosques in Adhamiya.

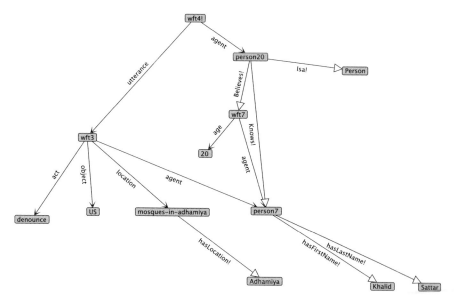

Fig. 14.2 The collapsed version of Fig. 14.1

The exact proposition represented by each propositional term is specified by a caseframe definition, which may vary from application to application. Each caseframe definition specifies a set of argument position labels and the relation thereby represented. The propositions represented by the propositional terms of Fig. 14.1 are

wft1!: The first name of person7 is Kalid
wft2!: The last name of person7 is Satter
wft3:   Person7 performed the act of denouncing on US at mosques-in-adhamiya
wft4!: Person 20 said that person7 performed the act of denouncing on US at mosques-in-adhamiya
wft5!: Person20 is a Person
wft6!: Person20 knows person7
wft7:   Person7 is 20 years old
wft8!: Person20 believes that person7 is 20 years old
wft9!: Mosques-in-adhamiya are located in Adhamiya

Binary relations that are not arguments of other relations may be drawn in a "collapsed" [6] format by drawing an arc labeled with the relation from the node representing the first argument to the node representing the second argument, drawing the arrowhead as an open triangle, and omitting the intervening wft node. If there was an exclamation mark on the wft label, it is shown on the relation instead. Figure 14.2 is the collapsed version of Fig. 14.1, collapsing nodes wft1!, `wft2!`, `wft5!`, `wft6!`, and `wft9!`.[1] Notice that the underlying graph is not changed—only the way it is drawn.

14.3   Merging with the Global Graph

The information in any information source can be represented by a propositional graph. Since information from all available background knowledge sources can be combined into a single global propositional graph that satisfies the uniqueness principle, each new message being processed can also be merged into this global graph using the same process. Afterwards, every node from the message would be connected to nodes from the global graph that provide background information about them.

   The propositional graph constructed from a message, enhanced by the connected information from the global graph of background information, can then be used by the data association process [1, 4] to associate entities and events from different messages. One question, however, is how much of the global graph should be included in the enhanced graph for input to the data association process. This is the subject of the rest of this chapter.

14.4   Theories of Context

We will take context to be the structured set of variable, external constraints to some (natural or artificial) cognitive process that influences the behavior of that process in the agent(s) under consideration. By reviewing the cognitive science disciplines of linguistics, psychology, human–computer interaction, and knowledge representation, we have identified contextual factors that can serve several uses among embodied cognitive architectures, such as knowledge acquisition, knowledge partitioning, and context switching.

   Linguistics approaches the study of context as an influence on the processes of interpreting an utterance and producing an utterance. A type of process that is useful, but still a form of interpretation, is constructing a mental context for interpretation (e.g., when reading a work of fiction) [14].

   Cognitive and experimental psychology, hereafter, "psychology," examines contextual influence on the cognitive processes, such as perception, learning, and memory [14]. While each of these is a process of its own, the interplay of each process can fall under the general process, cognition. In this sense, each cognitive process can act as a constraint on another cognitive process, and thus, the former is a contextual constraint on the latter. This notion is exemplified in experiments that

---

[1]Node `wft4!` has been left uncollapsed in preparation for Fig. 14.3.

study the influence of environment on the recall process [15, 16], and those that demonstrate the effects of mental reinstatement of environment, demonstrating how another cognitive process, namely "imagination," can serve as a constraint on the recall process [16, 17].

Human–computer interaction (HCI) examines the influence of contextual constraints on computational devices that interact with a user. This research endeavor falls under the broad category of "context-aware computing," which uses context to provide relevant services and information to a user [18]. Typical processes in HCI include: user preference learning and selection, autobiographical construction, providing relevant information based on context, and relevant operations [14, 19, 18].

Knowledge representation and reasoning (KRR) seeks to formalize context, a need that grew out of the identification of the problem of generality, which is essentially the notion that any representation of knowledge can be criticized as eliminating some influential properties useful to other domains not (yet) represented in the current knowledge base [20]. As such, one process that context can constrain is the process of representation itself,[2] where the context determines how general or specific a logical representation can be. Furthermore, the process of developing the logic used for reasoning is also constrained by contextual aspects, such as: the locality of logical semantics and syntax, and a priori considerations that effect initial relationships between contexts [21–23]. Other processes that can be constrained by context in KRR include; knowledge acquisition [24, 25], large-scale knowledge base partitioning [22, 26, 27], providing relevant information [28], and providing semantic interpretation [26].

14.5 Using Spreading Activation to Find Relevant Information

14.5.1 General Spreading Activation and Propositional Graphs

Spreading activation is an information retrieval procedure that was developed for propositional graphs, and based on models of cognition [29–31].

Since we are using propositional graphs for the representation of information in the domain, and given the volume of the background knowledge anticipated for working in this domain, it was practical to explore and evaluate retrieval operations that were designed for propositional graphs, like spreading activation. Spreading activation works by retrieving those nodes in a graph that achieve a specified activation value using this general algorithm

---

[2]More appropriately, this can be viewed as constraining the memory encoding process of some agent, though a knowledge engineer is performing the encoding process.

1. Initiate a pulse into the propositional graph at specified nodes. This is called a "cue" and sets these nodes to have an activation value higher than the threshold.[3]
2. Spread this pulse throughout the graph while it has energy to activate nodes.
3. The pulse dies when the activation energy runs out, and the algorithm terminates.
4. Activated proposition nodes are considered retrieved for use in future processing, like reasoning.

The key step in this process is determining whether a node is active or not (Step 2), which allows the algorithm to spread the activation throughout the graph. This is accomplished through an *activation function*, which calculates the *activation level* of a node and compares this value to an *activation threshold* parameter. If the value is above the threshold the node is considered active. If no more nodes can be activated, the algorithm terminates; this is called the *terminating condition*. *Activation functions* and *terminating conditions* vary between algorithms, and all spreading activation algorithms permit setting parameters, like the *activation threshold*. In the algorithms covered in this paper *activation levels* are real values in the closed interval between 0.0 and 1.0. The *activation threshold* parameter is crucial to the performance of the algorithms, and determines how much information is retrieved, as such it is a crucial variable to the evaluation. Other crucial variables (and those less so), will be discussed as encountered.

Fine tuning the algorithms to retrieve enough information to be useful without retrieving too much is crucial to the successful use of the process. Figure 14.3 shows the collapsed version of a propositional graph with retrieved information added after using the Texai algorithm (discussed below) and the graph of Fig. 14.1 as a "cue". The algorithm spread outward conservatively with the settings given[4] and retrieved from the background knowledge sources three propositions[5]:

wft10!: "Khalid Sattar is a Person."

wft11!: "Khalid Sattar's denouncing the US at mosques at Adhamiya is an indicator of terrorist activity."

wft13!: "If someone is engaged in a type of terrorist activity, they may be an insurgent."[6]

---

[3]A value of 1.0 is used for the initial activation value since it is recommended in the Texai approach, and will always be greater than or equal to the *activation threshold*.

[4]The *activation threshold* was 0.5 and *decay* was 0.9 (c.f., Sect. 14.5.1.1).

[5]These rules are provisional ones created for testing purposes, and are probably not those a SME would come up with for this domain.

[6]The actual representation of this reasoning rule is much more specific.

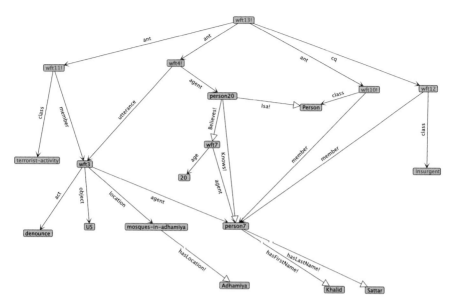

Fig. 14.3 The SNePS 3 propositional graph of Fig. 14.2 after Texai spreading activation. The *green* nodes, and the wires emanating from them, were added as a result of spreading activation

14.5.1.1   Texai Algorithm

The Texai knowledge representation and natural language processing system [32] uses a spreading activation algorithm on a propositional graph. The Texai system uses a simple activation function to calculate the activation of a node (A'_j) given the set of adjacent nodes (N):

$$A'_j = A_j + \sum_{i \in N} A_i * W_{ij} * D$$

The *activation function* takes into account any previous activation the node may have received (A_j), the activation of adjacent nodes (A_i), the weights of the edges between nodes (W_{ij}), and a decay factor (D). The Texai spreading activation algorithm does not specify a means of calculating weights, but does specify that they are values in the closed interval between 0.0 and 1.0. An approach similar to ACT-R will be used. The technique uses the degree of the node to calculate weighting between nodes. Each arc connected to the node i is given the value of 1.0 divided by the number of arcs pointing to the node. In Texai, the *decay factor,* a value also in the closed interval between 0.0 and 1.0, is used to impact how quickly the pulse decays as it spreads through the graph, it is not to be confused with the concept of decay as a constraint [31] in constrained spreading activation algorithms. The Texai *decay factor* is a variable of interest for evaluation. Texai uses the same *terminating condition* as the general algorithm given previously (i.e., the nodes

recently spread into do not exceed the *activation threshold*). With these parameters
and ranges explained the Texai *activation function* evaluated is

$$A'_j = A_j + \sum_{i \in N} A_i * \frac{1}{|N|} * D$$

14.5.1.2 ACT-R Declarative Memory Activation Algorithm

ACT-R is a modular cognitive architecture that models the cognitive process of
humans [33] and its *declarative memory module* is a frequent example of spreading
activation in cognitive psychology textbooks [34]. ACT-R's modules communicate
information to a central production system, that in turn places information in their
buffers to determine how they operate. When the production system places information into the declarative buffer the declarative memory module uses the information as a "cue" into a spreading activation algorithm on a propositional graph to
retrieve one memory "chunk" (i.e., proposition) that best matches the "cue" after
ranking all of the "chunks" with their *activation value*. Despite only using it to
retrieve one chunk, the activation calculation can still be used as a means of
retrieving multiple chunks by using it as the *activation function* in the general
spreading activation algorithm.

The spreading activation algorithm for ACT-R is specified in [29, 35]. The
specification does not provide a *terminating condition* for using the algorithm as a
means of information retrieval in large-scale knowledge bases.[7] To alleviate this,
we used the general spreading activation *terminating condition*.

Activation Equation: The ACT-R spreading activation algorithm requires a set of
nodes that will contribute to the activation of other nodes, called the "context" (C).
Initially, these will be the nodes contained in the pulse. If more nodes fire as a result
of the activation calculation, they will become to new "context." This process
repeats until termination. ACT-R uses the following *activation function* for calculating the *activation level* of a node (A_i) given initial "context" nodes C:

$$A_i = B_i + \sum_{j \in C} W_j * Sj$$

To calculate the activation of the node (i) the *activation function* takes into
account the *base-level activation* (B_i), the attentional weighting of "context" nodes
C, and the *associative strength* (S_j) of the connection between nodes in the "context" C and i. B_i, W_j, and S_j are explained more fully below.

---

[7]ACT-R representations typically use smaller knowledge bases than those in large-scale systems,
like Cyc [36], that require information retrieval techniques. As such, the activation calculation used
in ACT-R gives a ranking to all the information in declarative memory and then selects the best
ranked results as a match.

Base-level Activation Equation: The *base-level activation* models the effect of past usage of a memory "chunk" and how those uses influence the retrieval of that "chunk" later. The following is used to calculate *base-level activation*:

$$B_i = \ln \left(\sum_{k=1}^{n} t_k^{-d} \right)$$

Here, t_k indicates the time since the kth usage of the term (out of n usages). Neither the ACT-R specification nor the manual describe how times are stored. In the implementation used for evaluation, we assume a new cycle (i.e., every time a pulse is encountered) indicates the passage of one time increment and all prior knowledge in the background knowledge sources occurred at the first time period. A pulse is used to add new times encountered to those "chunks" contained in the pulse. These assumptions are listed for completeness and replicability, but do not offer a variable of interest for the evaluation since the evaluation evaluates pulses as retrieval queries from system start up and no new timestamps will be provided for the "chunks" as a result. The d indicates a *decay* parameter, a positive real value[8] that determines how much influence time passage has on the base-level activation. The *decay* has negligible influence on the algorithm performance in the evaluation since no new timestamps are created.

Attentional Weighting Equation: The *attentional weighting* models a form of context sensitivity in memory retrieval (i.e., that certain "cues" contribute more to retrieval than others). This is done by associating the "chunks" in the "context" with the individual ACT-R buffers that they originated from and calculating their weight as a percentage of the number of other chunks that originate from that buffer. To calculate the *attentional weighting* (W_j), the following is used:

$$W_j = \frac{1}{n}$$

where n is the number of nodes that come from the same buffer as j. However, in the implementation used for our evaluation we do not have buffers like ACT-R, and thus all nodes will be considered as originating from the same buffer. Because of this assumption all nodes in the "context" contribute equally to the *attentional weighting* factor, and n is the cardinality of C, $|C|$.

Associative Strength Equation: The *associative strength* is used to model how strong the associations are between the "context" nodes and i. To calculate the *associative strength* a heuristic from the ACT-R manual [35] is used instead of the underspecified equation discussed in [29].[9] The equation from [35] is as follows:

---

[8]The ACT-R specification [29] recommends a value of 0.5 for d after numerous tests, but this was for the retrieval of one chunk and may be different for using the spreading activation algorithm for information retrieval.

[9]The equation provided in [29] calculates the *associative strength* as $S_{ji} \approx ln(prob(i|j)/prob(i))$, but provides no specification for calculating the probabilities in a propositional graph.

$$S_j = S - \ln(fan(j))$$

Here, S is the *maximum associative strength* parameter, a value that can be any real number, and is a variable of interest for evaluation. The $fan(j)$ is the number of arcs in the propositional graph connected to j.

With the parameters and assumptions explained, the ACT-R *activation function* evaluated is

$$A_i = \ln\left(\sum_{k=1}^{n} t_k^{-0.5}\right) + \frac{1}{|C|} * \sum_{j \in C}(S - \ln(degree(j)))$$

14.6 Evaluating Spreading Activation

14.6.1 *Methodology*

A preliminary effort was made to evaluate the Texai and ACT-R spreading activation algorithms using the limited amount of background knowledge and messages handcrafted for the domain.[10] The evaluation of the spreading activation algorithms in the COIN domain took part in two phases. In **Phase I,** we examined how changes in the parameters affect the performance of the algorithms. In **Phase II,** we compared the algorithms with their best parameter settings using the information gathered from the first phase. To evaluate the algorithms we use the following:

- A propositional graph knowledge representation and reasoning (KRR) system, SNePS 3 [6, 13],
- The two algorithms implemented to work with the SNePS 3 graph structure,
- Four messages from the STEF dataset represented in SNePS 3 to be used as "cues" into the spreading activation algorithms,
- A subset of the National Geospatial-Intelligence Agency: GEOnet Names Server (NGA: GNS) [37] and hand crafted background information about people in the domain represented in SNePS 3. These represent the background knowledge sources (BKS) for the domain, and
- Seven hand crafted reasoning rules for reasoning about the COIN domain that rely on information from the messages and the BKS. These are also considered part of the BKS.[11]

---

[10]At the time of this study, Tractor was in its infancy, and thus the messages had to be manually translated into SNePS 3 propositional graphs. This limited the number of examples we could use in the evaluation.

[11]The SNePS 3 KRR system, background knowledge sources and means of loading them into SNePS 3, message representations, and code for evaluating the algorithms is available at http://www.cse.buffalo.edu/∼mwk3/Papers/evaluation.html.

Table 14.1 Variables and ranges evaluated

Texai algorithm		
Variable	Range	Increment
Activation threshold	0.0–1.0	0.1
Decay of pulse (D)	0.0–1.0	0.1
ACT-R declarative memory algorithm		
Variable	Range	Increment
Activation threshold	0.0–0.19	0.01
Maximum associative strength (S)	0.5–5.0	0.5

The four messages were

- Message 1: Approximately 40 worshipers outside the Imam Shaykh Hadid shrine in Adhamiya expressed increased hostile sentiment against U.S. troops yesterday.
- Message 2: Source said a Sunni youth he knows to be about 20 years old, Khalid Sattar, has become increasingly vocal in denouncing the U.S. at four or five mosques in Adhamiya.
- Message 3: Bookstore owner on Dhubat Street in Adhamiya said about a dozen customers are asking if he has any books, magazines, or other material on al-Qaeda.
- Message 4: Large gathering of 20 to 30 teenagers ages 15–19 chanted anti-U.S. slogans outside the Jami al Kazimiyah mosque in Adhamiya.

Phase I consisted of sampling the performance of the spreading activation algorithms on these messages over a range of values to approximate the best settings for the various parameters in the COIN domain. The process is as follows:

1. Iterate over the variable settings using the selected range and increments,
2. A single message will be given to the algorithm and the results evaluated,
3. The system will then be reset, and the next message will be evaluated, and
4. Repeat the previous steps for all the parameter settings in the iteration.

The variables of interest and ranges used in the evaluation are given in Table 14.1.

We chose the Texai values and ranges because these are the ranges these values can take on as specified for the *Texai* algorithm [32]. The ACT-R values were chosen after preliminary testing demonstrated that the algorithm did not return any results outside of this range.

To score the variable sampling of the two spreading activation techniques we used the accepted practice for evaluating information retrieval results, the calculation of an *f-measure* [38]. An *f-measure* score is between 0.0 and 1.0, with 0.0 indicating the poorest result and 1.0 a perfect retrieval. The calculation of an *f-measure* requires a set of *retrieved propositions,* which will be the result of the spreading activation algorithms in this evaluation, and a set of *relevant propositions.*

Table 14.2 Formulas for computing the f-measure [38]

Recall (r)	$r = \frac{|\{relevant\ propositions\} \cap \{retrieved\ propositions\}|}{|\{relevant\ propositions\}|}$
Precision (p)	$p = \frac{|\{relevant\ propositions\} \cap \{retrieved\ propositions\}|}{|\{retrieved\ propositions\}|}$
F-measure (F)	$F(r,p) = \frac{2rp}{r+p}$

The set of *relevant propositions* represent what the desired results should be. For our evaluation, we used a technique based on the *distance from the optimal* [39]. This technique uses the input "cue" (*I*) and the contents of the background knowledge sources (*BKS*) to determine which portion of the *BKS* will be used as part of an inference (forward or backward). Those propositions that contribute to any inferences made, excluding those from *I*, are considered the *relevant propositions*, since they are the only propositions from the *BKS* necessary for drawing the conclusions, we want in the domain. This method of establishing relevancy is useful for a domain that uses reasoning, like the COIN domain, since it will necessarily indicate as relevant all the information needed to reason about a given input. However, some domains may consider relevant information to be more than that which is used in the reasoning processes. For example, it is possible that a suspect may be a known insurgent in the background knowledge sources, but if no reasoning rule uses that information the information will not be considered relevant by the distance from the optimal technique. The *distance from the optimal* offers an objective means of establishing what is relevant from the background knowledge sources, but does not take into account the subjective opinions of COIN experts.

The *distance from the optimal* technique described by Kandefer and Shapiro [39] also requires a reasoner capable of maintaining origin sets,[12] and performing reasoning to populate the origin sets of some query proposition, and using that as the *relevant propositions*. However, SNePS 3 currently lacks origin sets and the numbers of rules were small, so we chose to determine manually what the origin sets are for each "cue" encountered.

With the *relevant propositions* established for each message the *f-measure* can be calculated. An *f-measure* is the harmonic mean of two other calculations (not shown in the results). The first calculation is the *recall*. The *recall* is also a value between 0.0 and 1.0 and is the fraction of the *relevant propositions* that are included in the *retrieved propositions*. The second calculation is the *precision*. The *precision* is the fraction of the *retrieved propositions* that are *relevant propositions*. These calculations are depicted in Table 14.2.

To learn the best settings for the algorithms we calculated the *f-measure* for each algorithm on the four messages using the parameter ranges and increments in Table 14.1. Since two parameters were evaluated per algorithm, this resulted in four *f-measure* matrices per algorithm. We took the mean of the four matrices and then selected the cell in the resulting matrix with the highest *f-measure*. The parameter

---

[12]An origin set for a proposition is the set of propositions used in the derivation of that proposition. Origin sets originate from *relevance logic* proof theory [40].

settings corresponding to this cell were used as the "best" settings for **Phase II**. For Texai the best parameter settings were an *activation threshold* of 0.5 and decay of 0.9. For ACT-R, this was an *activation threshold* of 0.04 and *maximum associative strength* of 2.0.

Phase II uses the results of best settings learned from *Phase I* to compare the two algorithms with these settings. This was done to test how well the algorithms can be trained using an initial sample set, and comparing their performance using the learned settings. Since only four messages were hand crafted, the four messages are used again for the comparison.

14.6.2   Evaluation Results

14.6.2.1   Phase I—Parameter Learning

Texai Algorithm
Figure 14.4 shows the average *f-measure* results of varying the *activation threshold* from 0.0 to 1.0 and the *decay* from 0.0 to 1.0 using the Texai spreading activation algorithm on the four messages. The average maximum *f-measure* of 0.375 occurred when the *activation threshold* was 0.5 and the *decay* was 0.9.

ACT-R Declarative Memory Activation Algorithm
Figure 14.5 shows the results of varying the *activation threshold* from 0.0 to 0.19 and the *maximum associative strength* from 0.5 to 5.0 using the ACT-R declarative memory activation function on the four messages. The maximum average *f-measure* of 0.375 occurred when the *activation threshold* was set to 0.04 and the *maximum associative strength* was set to 2.0.

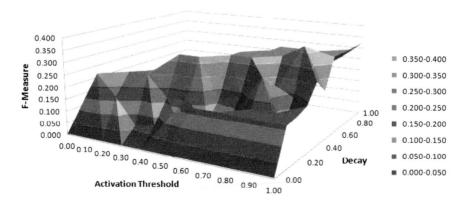

Fig. 14.4 Average f-measures for Texai

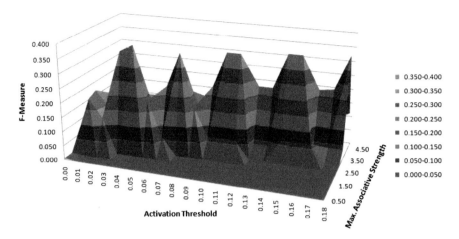

Fig. 14.5 Average f-measures for ACT-R declarative memory

Table 14.3 F-Measures for the predicted parameter settings	Message	Texai	ACT-R
	Message 1	0.5	0.0
	Message 2	1.0	0.75
	Message 3	0.0	0.5
	Message 4	0.0	0.25
	Mean	0.375	0.375
	Standard deviation	0.41	0.28

Phase II—Comparison

The results of using the best average settings for the two algorithms on the four messages are shown in Table 14.3. For Texai the *activation threshold* was set to 0.5 and the *decay* was set to 0.9. For ACT-R the *activation threshold* was set to 0.04 and *maximum associative strength* to 2.0. These were chosen since they were where the maximum average *f-measure* occurred as depicted in Fig. 14.5, and are the best settings using the method discussed in Sect. 14.6.1.

14.6.3 Discussion

Phase I was successful in establishing an understanding of how the variables of interest influenced the spreading activation algorithms in question. In the Texai spreading activation algorithm the *activation threshold* had its best performance when set to 0.5 (Fig. 14.4). It was at this point that there was a balance between the *precision* and *recall*. As the threshold increased the *recall* was worse; when it was decreased *precision* was worse. The *decay* tended to cause poorer performance as its value decreased (meaning it had greater impact on the spread of the pulse). As such, higher values tended to result in better *recall* without influencing *precision* greatly, which results in better *f-measures.*

In the ACT-R declarative memory spreading activation algorithm, the *activation threshold* functioned similarly to Texai. The algorithm tended to generate its best results at an average *activation threshold* of 0.04 and a *maximum associative strength* of 2.0 (Fig. 14.5). Like with Texai these values offered the best balance of *precision* and *recall,* though *precision* was frequently poor. Unlike Texai's *decay,* deviations from 2.0 would cause sharp deceases in the *f-measure* unless the threshold was also adjusted. Though a maximum *f-measure* average was found among the four messages, ACT- Rs declarative memory module can perform successfully under multiple *maximum associative strength* settings (as seen by the numerous peaks), so long as the spreading activation threshold is adjusted as well.

The results of **Phase II** show that when using the best average parameter values learned from **Phase I** that the ACT-R declarative memory module and Texai's spreading activation algorithm have the same average performances. However, ACT-Rs declarative memory algorithm has a lower standard deviation, suggesting that its settings would have performance closer to the shared average performance with other inputs. This difference was mostly due to poor performance with messages 3 and 4 by Texai. Messages 3 and 4 did not differ considerably from the other messages representationally and all messages required different reasoning rules, but approximately the same amount. These results also show that even with a few messages a learning phase can be used to generate parameters that result in good performance for the algorithms (an *f-measure* as high as 1.0) in this domain. If more messages were used using a similar propositional network representation it is not expected that they would change the results of this evaluation (particularly for ACT-R), so these four messages serve as a small, but useful predictive set for the domain.

14.7 Conclusions

Soft information fusion, fusing information from natural language messages with other soft information and with hard information, is facilitated by representing the information in the messages as a formally defined propositional graph that abides by the uniqueness principle, the principle that every entity or event that is mentioned in the message is represented by a unique node in the graph, or, at worst, by several nodes connected by co-referentiality propositions. To further facilitate information fusion, information from the message is enhanced with relevant information from background knowledge sources. What knowledge is relevant is determined by also representing the background knowledge as a propositional graph, embedding the knowledge graph from the messages (called the "message graph") into the background knowledge graph using the uniqueness principle to fuse a message graph node with a background knowledge graph node, and then using spreading activation to find subgraphs of the background knowledge graph. This combination of the message graph with the retrieved subgraphs is considered the "relevant information."

Spreading activation operates by first setting the activation level of the nodes in the message graph, and then spreading the activation to connected nodes in the background knowledge graph, activating them if their own activation levels exceed some threshold. As the activation level spreads its signal weakens and eventually dies out, causing no new nodes to activate. After the activation spread terminates those nodes in the background knowledge graph that were successfully activated are considered to be relevant to the message.

Two spreading activation algorithms we evaluated are the Texai algorithm and the ACT-R spreading activation algorithm. The Texai activation function we evaluated is

$$A'_j = A_j + \sum_{i \in N} \frac{DA_i}{|N|}$$

where:

- A'_j is the new activation level of node j;
- A_j is the old activation level of node j;
- N is the set of nodes adjacent to node j;
- A_i is the old activation level of node i;
- D is the decay factor,

and the ACT-R spreading activation function we evaluated is

$$A_i = \ln\left(\sum_{k=1}^{n_i} t_{ik}^{-0.5}\right) + \frac{\sum_{j \in C}(S - \ln(degree(j)))}{|C|}$$

where:

- A_i is the new activation level of node i.
- n_i is the number of times node i has been pulsed.
- t_{ik} is the number of pulse cycles since the kth time that node i was pulsed.
- C is the set of currently activated nodes.
- S is the maximum associative strength parameter.

Evaluation of the Texai algorithm found that the average maximum *f-measure* of 0.375 occurred when the activation threshold was 0.5 and the decay factor, D, was 0.9. Evaluation of the ACT-R algorithm found that the maximum average *f-measure* of 0.375 occurred when the activation threshold was set to 0.04 and the maximum associative strength was set to 2.0.

A comparison of the two algorithms shows that when using the best average parameter values learned from earlier evaluations the ACT-R declarative memory module and Texai's spreading activation algorithm have the same average performances, but ACT-R's declarative memory algorithm has a lower standard deviation, suggesting that its settings would have performance closer to the shared average performance with other inputs from our domain.

Spreading the activation of nodes of a message graph into the connected background knowledge graph is a promising technique for automatically identifying contextually relevant background knowledge, and is worthy of further investigation.

Acknowledgements This work was supported in part by the Office of Naval Research under contract N00173-08-C-4004, and by a Multidisciplinary University Research Initiative (MURI) grant (Number W911NF-09-1-0392) for "Unified Research on Network-based Hard/Soft Information Fusion," issued by the US Army Research Office (ARO) under the program management of Dr. John Lavery. The work describe here was done while both authors were in the Department of Computer Science and Engineering, University at Buffalo, Buffalo, NY. Parts of this paper were taken from [39, 41, 42].

References

1. G.A. Gross, R. Nagi, K. Sambhoos, D.R. Schlegel, S.C. Shapiro, G. Tauer, Towards hard + soft data fusion: processing architecture and implementation for the joint fusion and analysis of hard and soft intelligence data, in *Proceedings of the 15th International Conference on Information Fusion (Fusion 2012)* (ISIF, 2012), pp. 955–962
2. M. Prentice, M. Kandefer, S.C. Shapiro, Tractor: a framework for soft information fusion, in *Proceedings of the 13th International Conference on Information Fusion (Fusion2010)* (2010), pp. Th3.2.2
3. S.C. Shapiro, D.R. Schlegel, Natural language understanding for soft information fusion, in *Proceedings of the 16th International Conference on Information Fusion (Fusion 2013)* (ISIF, 2013), 9 p (unpaginated)
4. A.B. Poore, S. Lu, B.J. Suchomel, Data association using multiple frame assignments, in *Handbook of Multisensor Data Fusion* (chapter 13), 2nd ed. ed. by M. Liggins, D. Hall, J. Llinas (CRC Press, 2009), pp. 299–318
5. J.L. Graham, A new synthetic dataset for evaluating soft and hard fusion algorithms, in *Proceedings of the SPIE Defense, Security, and Sensing Symposium: Defense Transformation and Net-Centric Systems 2011* (2011), pp. 25–29
6. D.R. Schlegel, S.C. Shapiro, Visually interacting with a knowledge base using frames, logic, and propositional graphs, in *Graph Structures for Knowledge Representation and Reasoning*, vol. 7205, Lecture Notes in Artificial Intelligence, ed. by M. Croitoru, S. Rudolph, N. Wilson, J. Howse, O. Corby (Springer, Berlin, 2012), pp. 188–207
7. S.C. Shapiro, Belief spaces as sets of propositions. J. Exp. Theor. Artif. Intell. (JETAI), **5**(2 and 3):225–235 (1993, Apr–Sept)
8. S.C. Shapiro, W.J. Rapaport, The SNePS family. Comput. Math. Appl. **23**(2–5):243–275 (1992, Jan–Mar) Reprinted in [24, pp. 243–275]
9. S.C. Shapiro, Symmetric relations, intensional individuals, and variable binding. Proc. IEEE **74**(10), 1354–1363 (1986)
10. A.S. Maida, S.C. Shapiro, Intensional concepts in propositional semantic networks. Cogn. Sci. **6**(4):291–330 (1982, Oct–Dec). Reprinted in [7, pp. 170–189]
11. S.C. Shapiro, Cables, paths and "subconscious" reasoning in propositional semantic networks, in *Principles of Semantic Networks: Explorations in the Representation of Knowledge*, ed. by J. Sowa (Morgan Kaufmann, Los Altos, CA, 1991), pp. 137–156

12. A.N. Steinberg, G. Rogova, Situation and context in data fusion and natural language understanding, in *Proceedings of the 11th International Conference on Information Fusion (Fusion2008)* (IEEE, 2008, June), pp. 1–8
13. S.C. Shapiro, An introduction to SNePS 3, in *Conceptual Structures: Logical, Linguistic, and Computational Issues*, vol. 1867, Lecture Notes in Artificial Intelligence, ed. by B. Ganter, G. W. Mineau (Springer, Berlin, 2000), pp. 510–524
14. N.A. Bradley, M.D. Dunlop, Toward a multidisciplinary model of context to support contextaware computing. Hum. Comput. Interact. **20**(4), 403–446 (2005)
15. D. Godden, A. Baddeley, Contextdependent memory in two natural environments: on land and underwater. Br. J. Psychol. **66**, 325–332 (1975)
16. S. Smith, E. Vela, Environmental context-dependent memory. Psychon. Bull. Rev. **8**(2), 203–220 (2001)
17. S. Smith, Remembering in and out of context. J. Exp. Psychol. Hum. Learn. Memory **5**(5), 460–471 (1979)
18. A.K. Dey, Understanding and using context. Pers. Ubiquit. Comput. **5**(1), 4–7 (2001)
19. G. Chen, D. Kotz, A survey of context-aware mobile computing research. Technical Report TR2000–381, Department of Computer Science, Dartmouth College, Hanover, NH, November 2000
20. J. McCarthy, Generality in artificial intelligence. Commun. ACM **30**(12), 1030–1035 (1987)
21. M. Benerecetti, P. Bouquet, C. Ghidini, Contextual reasoning distilled. JETAI **12**(3), 279–305 (2000)
22. P. Bouquet, C. Ghidini, F.O. Giunchiglia, E. Blanzieri, Theories and uses of context in knowledge representation and reasoning. J. Pragmat. **35**(3), 403–446 (2003)
23. S. Buvač, Quantificational logic of context, in *Proceedings of the Thirteenth National Conference on Artificial Intelligence (AAAI-96)*, Menlo Park, CA (AAAI Press, 1996), pp. 600–606
24. P. Brézillon, Context in artificial intelligence: I. A survey of the literature. Comput. Artif. Intell. **18**(4), 321–340 (1999)
25. P. Brézillon, Context in problem solving. Knowl. Eng. Rev. **14**(1), 47–80 (1999)
26. P. Brézillon, Context in artificial intelligence: II. Key elements of contexts. Comput. Artif. Intell. **18**(5), 425–446 (1999)
27. D. Lenat, The dimensions of context-space. Technical report, Cycorp, October 1998
28. R.P. Arritt, R.M. Turner, Situation assessment for autonomous underwater vehicles using a priori contextual knowledge, in *Proceedings of the Thirteenth International Symposium on Unmanned Untethered Submersible Technology (UUST)* (2003)
29. J. R. Anderson. Human associative memory. In *How Can the Human Mind Occur in the Physical Universe?* (Oxford University Press, New York, 2007), pp. 91–134
30. A.M. Collins, E.F. Loftus, A spreading activation theory of semantic processing. Psychol. Rev. **82**(6), 407–428 (1975)
31. F. Crestani, Application of spreading activation techniques in information retrieval. Artif. Intell. Rev. **11**(6), 453–482 (1997)
32. S.L. Reed, Texai (2010). http://sourceforge.net/projects/texai/
33. J.R. Anderson, Cognitive architecture, in *How Can the Human Mind Occur in the Physical Universe?*, pages 3–43. Oxford University Press, New York, 2007
34. M.B. Howes, Long-term memory: ongoing research, in *Human Memory: Structures and Images* (SAGE Publications, Thousand Oaks, 2007)
35. D. Bothell. *ACT-R 6.0 Reference Manual* (2010)
36. D.B. Lenat, Cyc: a large-scale investment in knowledge infrastructure. Commun. ACM **38**(11), 33–38 (1995)
37. National Geospatial-Intelligence Agency. NGA GEOnet Names Server (2014). http://earth-info.nga.mil/gns/html/
38. C.J. van Rijsbergen, *Information Retrieval* (Butterworths, London, second edition, 1979)
39. M. Kandefer, S.C. Shapiro, An F-measure for context-based information retrieval, in *Commonsense 2009: Proceedings of the Ninth International Symposium on Logical*

Formalizations of Commonsense Reasoning, ed. by G. Lakemeyer, L. Morgenstern, M.-A. Williams (The Fields Institute, Toronto, CA, 2009), pp. 79–84

40. S.C. Shapiro, Relevance logic in computer science, in *Entailment*, volume II, ed. by A.R. Anderson, N.D. Belnap Jr, M. Dunn (Princeton University Press, Princeton, 1992), pp. 553–563

41. M. Kandefer and S. C. Shapiro. Evaluating spreading activation for soft information fusion, in *Proceedings of the 14th International Conference on Information Fusion (Fusion 2011)*, pages 498–505. ISIF, 2011

42. M.W. Kandefer, S.C. Shapiro, A categorization of contextual constraints, in *Biologically Inspired Cognitive Architectures: Papers from the 2008 AAAI Fall Symposium*, ed. by A. Samsonovich (AAAI Press, Menlo Park, CA, 2008), pp. 88–93

43. R.J. Brachman, H.J. Levesque (eds.), *Readings in knowledge representation* (Morgan Kaufmann, San Mateo, 1985)

44. F. Lehmann (ed.), *Semantic Networks in Artificial Intelligence* (Pergamon Press, Oxford, 1992)

Chapter 15
Algorithms for Context Learning and Information Representation for Multi-Sensor Teams

Nurali Virani, Soumalya Sarkar, Ji-Woong Lee, Shashi Phoha and Asok Ray

Abstract Sensor measurements of the state of a system are affected by natural and man-made operating conditions that are not accounted for in the definition of system states. It is postulated that these conditions, called contexts, are such that the measurements from individual sensors are independent conditioned on each pair of system state and context. This postulation leads to kernel-based unsupervised learning of a measurement model that defines a common context set for all different sensor modalities and automatically takes into account known and unknown contextual effects. The resulting measurement model is used to develop a context-aware sensor fusion technique for multi-modal sensor teams performing state estimation. Moreover, a symbolic compression technique, which replaces raw measurement data with their low-dimensional features in real time, makes the proposed context learning approach scalable to large amounts of data from heterogeneous sensors. The developed approach is tested with field experiments for multi-modal unattended ground sensors performing human walking style classification.

Keywords Context awareness · Feature extraction · Machine learning · Pattern recognition · Support vector regression · Sensor fusion

N. Virani · S. Sarkar · A. Ray
Department of Mechanical and Nuclear Engineering, Pennsylvania State University, University Park, PA, USA

J.-W. Lee
State College, University Park, PA, USA

S. Phoha (✉)
Applied Research Laboratory, Pennsylvania State University, University Park, PA, USA
e-mail: sxp26@arl.psu.edu

© Springer International Publishing Switzerland (outside the USA) 2016
L. Snidaro et al. (eds.), *Context-Enhanced Information Fusion*,
Advances in Computer Vision and Pattern Recognition,
DOI 10.1007/978-3-319-28971-7_15

403

15.1 Introduction

In realistic scenarios with data-driven systems, sensor measurements and their interpretation are affected by various environmental factors and operational conditions, which we call contexts [1–3]. For example, factors that determine ground conditions—such as the soil type, moisture content, permeability, and porosity—form the set of contexts for seismic sensor measurements, because they affect the propagation of surface and sub-surface seismic waves [4]. A reliable, high-performance inference engine for pattern recognition, state estimation, etc., must therefore be based on a sensor measurement model that takes into account the effects of the context. For example, in dynamic data-driven application systems (DDDAS) [5], modeling context helps not only in the information fusion as a part of the forward problem, but it is also relevant for obtaining the value of information for selecting relevant sources of information in the inverse problem. However, it is an often onerous and arbitrary task to identify the context set for every sensing modality in a multi-sensor team or to develop a physics-based measurement model that accounts for all contextual effects. This chapter focuses on the forward problem of multi-modal sensor fusion in the DDDAS framework, and develops a systematic machine learning method for the context.

The notion of context is task-specific in nature, and often differs across sensing modalities. For example, research in image processing generally assumes the visual scene to be the context for object recognition [6]; for natural language processing tasks such as speech recognition, handwriting recognition, and machine translation, the intended meaning of an ambiguous word might depend on the text which precedes the word in question, thus the preceding text would be considered as context [7]; and, for ubiquitous or mobile computing, the context set consists of the user location as well as activity attributes [8]. In a multi-sensor operational environment, involving both hard and soft sensing modalities, a broad unified notion of context is needed. This notion should characterize situations in the physical, electronic, and tactical environments that affect the acquisition and interpretation of heterogeneous sensor data for machine perception and adaptation. Furthermore, it is often necessary to iteratively update the belief about the spatio-temporal context automatically and treat it as a latent variable to be estimated.

Different clustering techniques [1, 9] and mixture modeling methods [10] were previously developed and used to identify the context set from measurements. In [1], the authors presented a supervised context learning technique via finding all maximal cliques from an undirected graph [11, 12]. An unsupervised context learning approach using the concept of community detection as in social networks [13] was also presented in [1]. These approaches, however, push the burdensome task of characterizing the size of the context set to the user, the resulting context set is different for each modality in the system, and the context model is not suitable for sequential decision-making and multi-modal fusion problems [3].

The main focus of this chapter is to present an unsupervised context-learning approach that addresses, or mitigates, the aforementioned issues. This approach is based on the postulation that the context of a system, along with the system state, completely conditions sensor measurements. That is, extending the common, but often incorrect, assumption that the measurements are conditionally independent given the system state, we hypothesize that the sensor measurements are independent conditioned on the state-context pair. This postulation allows for a definition of context that is application-specific, and yet uniform across different sensor modalities. Moreover, the arbitrary nature of clustering and mixture modeling approaches is avoided through a kernel-based unsupervised context learning, where the context set and a context-aware measurement model are automatically generated by the machine. In particular, the machine-generated measurement model automatically guarantees the required conditional independence of sensor measurements, which is crucial for tractable sequential inference.

Aside from sequential inference and multi-modal sensor fusion with heterogeneous sensor teams, the developed context-aware measurement model finds application in the problem of in situ measurement system adaptation for improved state estimation performance [3]. In addition to cheap, persistent sources of information, it allows more expensive, higher-fidelity sensors to be activated and added to a team of active sensors in a sequential manner. Changes in the sensor team are tantamount to adjusting decision boundaries in accordance with the contextual interpretation of data, and to exploiting the expected complementarity between available and new sensor measurements, in order to optimally trade off the accuracy of situation assessment against the cost of sensor activation. Realistic scenarios in multi-modal surveillance, health monitoring, target localization, etc., can employ these context-aware techniques for improved system performance. In this work, the context-aware decision-making framework in which the forward process leads to state estimation and the inverse process involves measurement system adaptation was developed as a dynamic data-driven application system (DDDAS) [5] and a schematic view of the system is shown in Fig. 15.1.

In order for the overall system to handle large amounts of data from multiple sources in real time, raw measurements are normally replaced with their

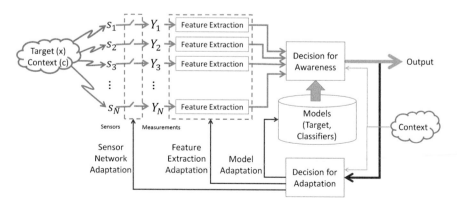

Fig. 15.1 Schematic of a dynamic data-driven application system (DDDAS) with in situ, context-aware, sequential decision-making

low-dimensional features, which are in the form of probabilistic finite state automata (PFSA) and their synchronous compositions and cross machines; otherwise, the context learning algorithm and resulting measurement model remain valid. A realistic numerical example verifies the effectiveness of the context learning and context-aware sensor fusion approaches in combination with the PFSA feature extraction technique.

The organization of this chapter is as follows. Section 15.2 mathematically formalizes the notion of context, presents an approach to automatically identify the context set from heterogeneous sensor data, and shows a context-aware technique that can be used for sequential and multi-modal information fusion and decision adaptation. Section 15.3 presents powerful tools for extracting, refining, and combining features from data. These tools enable the application of the context-aware approach in Sect. 15.2 to realistic situations. A realistic numerical example in Sect. 15.4 assesses the performance of the proposed approach. Lastly, concluding remarks are made in Sect. 15.5.

15.2 Context Learning

Existing context modeling techniques [1, 9, 10] do not guarantee that the measurement sequences from a single or multiple sensors are conditionally independent given the system state and context pair. The inability to guarantee conditional independence of measurements limits the applicability of these techniques in sequential analysis and decision-making. In this section, we mathematically formalize the notion of context and present a context-learning approach that automatically guarantees conditional independence of measurements.

15.2.1 Mathematical Formalization of Context

Let S be a nonempty finite set of sensors, possibly with different modalities, and let X be the random system state that takes values in a finite set $\mathcal{X}$. For each sensing modality $s \in S$, let $Y(s)$ be the random measurement, or the feature vector obtained as in Sect. 15.3, associated with the observation of the system state X from sensor s. Before introducing a modality-independent context notion suitable for unsupervised, machine-generation of the context set, let us present a modality-specific context definition, and context types (i.e., intrinsic and extrinsic contexts), that are suitable for supervised learning.

Definition 1 (*Context Elements*) For each $s \in S$, let $\mathcal{L}(s)$ be a nonempty finite set of labels. Each element of $\mathcal{L}(s)$ is called a *context element*. Every context element is a natural or man-made physical phenomenon, which is relevant to the sensing modality s used to observe the system state. It is assumed that the context elements are enumerated in $\mathcal{L}(s)$ in such a way that no two elements can occur simultaneously.

The assumption in this definition is not restrictive. If it is possible for two context elements l and m to occur simultaneously, then a new context element k representing l and m occurring together can be added to $\mathcal{L}(s)$. For $s \in \mathcal{S}$ and $l \in \mathcal{L}(s)$, let $p(Y(s)|X, l)$ be the probability density of sensor measurements of modality s for the state X under a given context element l.

Definition 2 (*Extrinsic and Intrinsic Subsets of Contexts*) For $s \in \mathcal{S}$, a nonempty set $\tilde{C} \subseteq \mathcal{L}(s)$ is called *extrinsic* relative to the state $X = x$ and its measurement $Y(s) = y$ if

$$p(y|x, l) = p(y|x, \tilde{l}) \quad \text{for all } l, \tilde{l} \in \tilde{C}.$$

Otherwise, the set $\tilde{C}$ is called *intrinsic* relative to the state $X = x$ and its measurement $Y(s) = y$.

It is sometime impractical to precisely distinguish extrinsic context elements from intrinsic ones. If the observation densities are overlapping and very close to each other under different context elements, then it is deduced that these context elements have nearly the same effect on the sensor data. Thus, an alternative approach is to obtain sets of context elements that are approximately indistinguishable for a given threshold parameter $\varepsilon > 0$ and a metric $d(\cdot, \cdot)$ on the space of observation densities, and let them define contexts.

Definition 3 (*Modality-Specific Context and Context Set*) For $s \in \mathcal{S}$ and $x \in \mathcal{X}$, let $C(s, x)$ be a set cover of $\mathcal{L}(s)$. Then, the collection $\mathcal{C}(s, x)$ is called a *context set* and each (nonempty) set $c(s, x) \in \mathcal{C}(s, x)$ is called a *context* provided that $c(s, x)$ is a maximal set satisfying the following condition:

$$d(p(Y(s)|x, l), p(Y(s)|x, m)) < \varepsilon \quad \text{for all } l, m \in c(s, x).$$

In order to obtain a context set $\mathcal{C}(s, x)$ based on Definition 3, the set $\mathcal{L}(s)$ of all context elements must be known a priori, in which case a supervised context modeling approach [1] can be used to reduce the problem of context learning to that of finding all maximal cliques in an undirected graph [11]. However, in many cases, the set $\mathcal{L}(s)$ is unknown, and thus unsupervised context modeling techniques must be used to directly obtain $\mathcal{C}(s, x)$ from the data. In [1], a fast community detection algorithm for social networks [13] was used for unsupervised extraction of context. The resulting context sets are modality-specific as in Definition 3.

The rest of this subsection is aimed at presenting an alternative definition of contexts, which facilitates learning a unified, modality-independent, context set from a multi-modal sensor set [14]. This approach of context learning does not need a defined set of context elements and thus it is an unsupervised way of context modeling. Let $Y_1 = Y(s_1)$ and $Y_2 = Y(s_2)$ be random measurements of the state X from sensors s_1, $s_2 \in \mathcal{S}$. Let $p(Y_1, Y_2|X)$ denote the joint likelihood function of the pair (Y_1, Y_2). For $i - 1, 2$, let $p_i(Y_i|X)$ denote the marginal likelihood function of Y_i. A common practice in sequential, statistical inference tasks is to assume, for the sake of convenience, that the measurements are statistically independent conditioned on the state [15]. Clearly, this assumption is incorrect unless the state X completely determines all factors that condition the measurements. That is, in general, we have

$$p(Y_1, Y_2 \,|\, X) \neq p_1(Y_1 \,|\, X)p_2(Y_2 \,|\, X).$$

For example, two seismic sensor measurements in binary location testing are expected to be correlated, even if they are conditioned on the true location of a target, because the location alone does not specify the target type, soil conditions (e.g., moisture and porosity), etc., that affect seismic sensor measurements.

Therefore, we define the context as a parameter that, together with the system state, completely conditions the measurements.

Definition 4 (*Context and Context Set*) Suppose that the measurements Y_1 and Y_2 take values in $\mathcal{Y}_1$ and $\mathcal{Y}_2$, respectively. Suppose that the state X takes values from a finite set $\mathcal{X}$. Then, a nonempty finite set $\mathcal{C}(X)$ is called the *context set* and each element $c \in \mathcal{C}(X)$ of the set is called a *context*, if the measurements Y_1 and Y_2 are mutually independent conditioned on the state-context pair (x, c) for all $x \in \mathcal{X}$ and for all $c \in \mathcal{C}(X)$.

According to this definition, the following relation holds:

$$p(Y_1, Y_2 \,|\, X, c) = p_1(Y_1 \,|\, X, c)p_2(Y_2 \,|\, X, c) \quad \text{for all } c \in \mathcal{C}(X). \tag{15.1}$$

Here, the left-hand side of (15.1) denotes the conditional density of (Y_1, Y_2) given (X, c), and the right-hand side gives the product of conditional densities of Y_1 and Y_2 given (X, c). It is now of interest to generate a context set $\mathcal{C}(x)$ for each $x \in \mathcal{X}$, so that (15.1) holds.

15.2.2 Learning Context-Aware Measurement Models

A novel machine learning approach to identifying contexts and determining their prior probabilities (which reflect one's prior knowledge about the true context) in a modality-independent manner is described in this subsection (See [14] for more details). The resulting model treats the context as a random variable and explicitly takes into account the effect of contexts on sensor measurements. The task of identifying all contexts is done by the machine in an unsupervised setting, and thus the extracted contexts need not have a human-understandable meaning associated with them.

15.2.2.1 Mathematical Formulation

Let $p(Y_1, Y_2 \mid X)$ denote the joint density of the pair (Y_1, Y_2) conditioned on the state X; for $i = 1, 2$, let $p_i(Y_i \mid X)$ denote the marginal density of Y_i conditioned on X. The measurement modeling problem that we are concerned with is to estimate these conditional densities, called likelihood functions, based on a training sample consisting of realizations of the triple (Y_1, Y_2, X). In view of Definition 4, a context-aware measurement model gives a likelihood function of the form

$$
\begin{aligned}
p(Y_1, Y_2 \mid X) &= \sum_{c \in \mathcal{C}(X)} \pi_c(X) p(Y_1, Y_2 \mid X, c) \\
&= \sum_{c \in \mathcal{C}(X)} \pi_c(X) p_1(Y_1 \mid X, c) p_2(Y_2 \mid X, c),
\end{aligned}
\tag{15.2}
$$

where $\pi_c(X)$ is the prior probability that, conditioned on the state X, the true context is c. It is immediate from (15.2) that the marginal likelihoods are given as

$$
p_i(Y_i \mid X) = \sum_{c \in \mathcal{C}(X)} \pi_c(X) p_i(Y_i \mid X, c) \quad \text{for } i = 1, 2.
$$

In general, it is a difficult task to identify a nontrivial context set and a probability distribution on it, so that the prior information about all possible contexts is correctly represented by the measurement model. This task is addressed using a special type of mixture models, where each component density is a product of marginal component densities. For example, Gaussian mixture models with block diagonal covariance matrices are of this type. More specifically, we propose that mixture models of the form (15.2) be used conditioned on the state X, where the context set $\mathcal{C}(x)$ is finite for all $x \in \mathcal{X}$:

$$
\mathcal{C}(X) = \{1, 2, \ldots, N(X)\}.
\tag{15.3}
$$

Conditioned on the state X, the latent variable plays the role of a machine-defined context variable C that takes values in $\mathcal{C}(X)$ and satisfies the conditional independence requirement (15.1) by construction. Here, $N(X)$ is the cardinality of the finite context set $\mathcal{C}(X)$.

15.2.2.2 Kernel-Based Approach

If the marginal component densities $p_i(Y_i \mid X, C)$ are assumed Gaussian, then the expectation maximization algorithm [16] or the variational Bayesian method [17] can be used to obtain a mixture model of the form (2). In this case, the number of contexts $N(x)$ may be determined for each state value $x \in \mathcal{X}$ based on a model selection criterion such as the Akaike and Bayesian information criteria [18, 19]. Alternatively, a Dirichlet process prior can be put over $N(X)$ and then a Gaussian

mixture density model can be estimated together with the optimal number of
component densities [20]. However, these parametric estimation approaches do not
scale up to high-dimensional measurement spaces, especially with small sample
sizes, and also their applicability is limited to Gaussian component densities.

We suggest that a kernel-based nonparametric method be used to overcome this
limitation. A kernel function defines an inner product on an implicit, possibly
infinite-dimensional, feature space. The standard topology of such a feature space is
that of the reproducing kernel Hilbert space induced by a (continuous) Mercer
kernel [21, 22]. On the other hand, it is shown in [23] that, if one uses a discon-
tinuous kernel, the resulting feature space can be taken to be the space ℓ^2 (of
square-summable sequences) endowed with its weak topology [24]. Let K :
$(\mathcal{Y}_1 \times \mathcal{Y}_2)^2 \to \mathbb{R}$ be a kernel function of the form

$$K\left(\begin{bmatrix} s_1 \\ s_2 \end{bmatrix}, \begin{bmatrix} y_1 \\ y_2 \end{bmatrix}\right) = K_1(s_1, y_1)K_2(s_2, y_2), \tag{15.4}$$

with

$$\int_{\mathcal{Y}_i} K_i(s_i, z_i)\, dz_i = 1 \quad \text{for } i = 1, 2 \text{ and } s_i, y_i \in \mathcal{Y}_i. \tag{15.5}$$

Then, conditioned on the state X, a support-vector regression method [25, 26] with
the kernel K leads to a mixture model of the form

$$p(Y_1, Y_2|X) = \sum_{c=1}^{N(X)} \pi_c(X) K_1(s_1^{(c)}(X), Y_1) K_2(s_2^{(c)}(X), Y_2) \tag{15.6}$$

where $(s_1^{(c)}(X), s_2^{(c)}(X))$, $c = 1, \ldots, N(X)$, are the support vectors chosen by the
machine from the available data, and the number of support vectors $N(X)$ can be
controlled by tuning the underlying insensitivity factor [27]. Note that, with (15.3)
and

$$K_i(s_i^{(C)}(X), Y_i) = p_i(Y_i | X, C) \quad \text{for } i = 1, 2, \tag{15.7}$$

the kernel-based model (15.6) leads to a mixture model of the desired form (15.2)
and the support vectors can be taken to be the machine-defined contexts, provided
that the following extra constraints are satisfied in addition to (15.4) and (15.5):

$$\sum_{c=1}^{N(X)} \pi_c(X) = 1, \quad \pi_c(X) \geq 0, \quad c = 1, \ldots, N(X). \tag{15.8}$$

15.2.2.3 Support Vector Density Estimation

For the purpose of learning a context-aware measurement model, support vector regression has a clear advantage over other nonparametric approaches like the Parzen density estimation method [28]. Depending on the insensitivity factor utilized in support vector regression, it is possible that only a few key data points contribute to the density estimate and become the support vectors, resulting in a sparse representation without much loss in accuracy. Support vector density estimation (SVDE) [29, 30] is a version of the support vector regression method appropriate for our purpose. Since the cumulative distribution of (Y_1, Y_2) conditioned on X is unknown at the outset, one cannot directly estimate the likelihood function. Instead, one approximates the cumulative distribution function with its empirical approximation formed by the sample of measurements $(y_1^{(1)}, y_2^{(1)}), \ldots, (y_1^{(L)}, y_2^{(L)})$ available for the given value of X [29]. For example, if $\mathcal{Y}_1 = \mathcal{Y}_2 = \mathbb{R}$, then the true distribution F and the empirical distribution $\widetilde{F}$ are

$$F(y_1, y_2|X) = \int_{-\infty}^{y_1} \int_{-\infty}^{y_2} p(z_1, z_2|X)\, dz_1 dz_2,$$

$$\widetilde{F}(y_1, y_2|X) = \frac{1}{L} \sum_{j=1}^{L} \theta(y_1 - y_1^{(j)}) \theta(y_2 - y_2^{(j)}),$$

where $\theta(\cdot)$ is the unit step function. In order for the empirical distribution to be a consistent estimator of the true distribution (i.e., for the convergence of $\widetilde{F}$ to F as the sample size L tends to infinity), it is assumed in the literature that the available data $(y_1^{(1)}, y_2^{(1)}), \ldots, (y_1^{(L)}, y_2^{(L)})$ form an i.i.d. sample of the pair (Y_1, Y_2) conditioned on X [29]. Note that this assumption is a reasonable one even if Y_1 and Y_2 are correlated conditioned on X.

For simplicity, assume $\mathcal{Y}_1 = \mathcal{Y}_2 = \mathbb{R}$. Let $\mathbf{G} = (G_{ij})$ be a matrix whose entry (i, j) is

$$G_{ij} = K_1(y_1^{(i)}, y_1^{(j)}) K_2(y_2^{(i)}, y_2^{(j)})$$

for $i, j = 1, \ldots, L$. Let

$$\widetilde{F}_i = \widetilde{F}(y_1^{(i)}, y_2^{(i)}|X),$$

$$K_{ij} = \int_{-\infty}^{y_1^{(i)}} \int_{-\infty}^{y_2^{(i)}} K_1(y_1^{(j)}, z_1) K_2(y_2^{(j)}, z_2)\, dz_1 dz_2$$

for $i, j = 1, \ldots, L$. Then, taking note of the extra constraint (15.8), and introducing an insensitivity factor $\sigma > 0$, our SVDE problem is translated to the following constrained optimization problem:

Minimize the cost

$$\pi^{\mathrm{T}} \mathbf{G} \pi$$

over column vectors $\pi = (\pi_i)$ subject to the constraints

$$\left| \tilde{F}_i - \sum_{j=1}^{L} \pi_j K_{ij} \right| \leq \sigma,$$

$$\pi_i \geq 0, \quad \sum_{j=1}^{L} \pi_j = 1, \quad i = 1, \ldots, L.$$

Matrix $\mathbf{G}$ is symmetric and positive definite, and thus this is a convex optimization problem with a quadratic cost function and affine constraints. If the problem is feasible, then a unique solution is guaranteed. If there are a few kernel parameters to be tuned, then the admissible set of these parameters is identified by checking the feasibility of the problem. One can perform a grid search over this admissible set to find the parameters that minimize the cost function. Conditioned on X, the set of support vectors obtained by solving the above optimization problem is the context set. The product form of the kernel guarantees conditional independence of Y_1 and Y_2 given X for each support vector.

15.2.2.4 Extension to Multiple Measurements

It is straightforward to extend the proposed approach to the case of $M(> 2)$ sensor measurements. In this case, the context-aware measurement model (15.2) becomes

$$p(Y_1, \ldots, Y_M \mid X) = \sum_{c \in \mathcal{C}(X)} \pi_c(X) p(Y_1, \ldots, Y_M \mid X, c)$$

$$= \sum_{c \in \mathcal{C}(X)} \pi_c(X) \prod_{k=1}^{M} p_k(Y_k \mid X, c),$$

and its kernel-based approximation (15.6) will be of the form

$$p(Y_1, \ldots, Y_M \mid X) = \sum_{c=1}^{N(X)} \pi_c(X) \prod_{k=1}^{M} K_k(s_k^{(c)}(X), Y_k).$$

As in the case of $M = 2$, these equations are related via (15.3) and (15.7).

15.2.3 Context-Aware In Situ Decision Adaptation

In this subsection, an in situ decision adaptation scheme with multi-modal sensor fusion and sensor selection is proposed as a major application of the context-aware measurement model. The key enabler of the proposed application system is that the measurement model guarantees the conditional independence of sensor measurements given the state and context of the system.

15.2.3.1 Context-Aware Sensor Fusion for Multi-Sensor Teams

In the context-aware sensor fusion approach, the following relation holds for multi-sensor teams with M (possibly heterogeneous) measurements:

$$p(Y_1, \ldots, Y_M \mid X, C) = \prod_{i=1}^{M} p_i(Y_i \mid X, C).$$

If the state space $\mathcal{X}$ is finite, then the following sequential update rule for the posterior distribution of the state-context pair (X, C) is used:

$$P(X, C \mid Y_1, \ldots, Y_{i-1}, Y_i) = \frac{p_i(Y_i \mid X, C) P(X, C \mid Y_1, \ldots, Y_{i-1})}{\sum_{x \in \mathcal{X}} \sum_{c \in \mathcal{C}(x)} p_i(Y_i \mid x, c) P(x, c \mid Y_1, \ldots, Y_{i-1})} \quad (15.9a)$$

for $i = 2, 3, \ldots, M$, where

$$P(X, C \mid Y_1) = \frac{p_1(Y_1 \mid X, C) \pi_C(X) P(X)}{\sum_{x \in \mathcal{X}} \sum_{c \in \mathcal{C}(x)} p_1(Y_1 \mid x, c) \pi_c(x) P(x)}. \quad (15.9b)$$

This update rule plays a crucial role in sequential inference and decision-making problems. In a sequential state estimation problem, for instance, one keeps track of the posterior probability of the state-context pair $P(X, C \mid Y_1, \ldots, Y_i)$, updates it to $P(X, C \mid Y_1, \ldots, Y_i, Y_{i+1})$ as a new sensor measurement Y_{i+1} becomes available, and marginalizes out the context variable to obtain the posterior probability of the state $P(X \mid Y_1, \ldots, Y_i, Y_{i+1})$, from which an updated state estimate can be deduced.

15.2.3.2 Multi-Modal Context-Aware Sensor Team Formation

Suppose now that a set of sensors of possibly different modalities are available for the purpose of sequential state estimation, where the state space $\mathcal{X}$ is finite. Some of these sensors are of high fidelity and generate quality measurements under most contexts, but are costly and need more computational power for operation. On the other hand, some of the sensors are inexpensive to operate, but yield relatively poor measurements. Sensor fidelity, however, is a relative measure. Under some contexts, low-cost sensor measurements can be effective and show good reliability; likewise, sensors that are generally of high quality can be cost-ineffective and/or unreliable depending on the context. For example, while an inexpensive acoustic sensor on a calm summer day can give good human-vehicle classification results, an expensive camera may not be very useful in poor visibility conditions.

A dynamic sensor team formation framework was proposed in [3]. It integrates the aforementioned contextual effects and their impact on hypothesis testing performance in a systematic manner using dynamic programming. In this framework, the number and types of selected sensors are determined in a data-driven fashion in order to achieve an optimal compromise over estimation performance, cost effectiveness, and contextual awareness. The state as well as the context is assumed to be fixed and unknown and the aim of the sensor team is to estimate the state. The dynamic sensor selection framework enables us to sequentially select sensors and sample their measurements until either sufficient information about the state is gathered or adding an additional sensor is deemed too costly. What makes this framework unique is that the measurement model avoids, without significantly increasing computational burden, the often incorrect assumption that the measurements are independent conditioned on the state. Further details beyond the early conference presentation in [3] are currently being developed and will appear elsewhere.

15.3 Semantic Information Representation of Multi-Modal Signals

This section develops an efficient approach to extract low-dimensional features from heterogeneous signals. This approach facilitates the real-time applicability of the context-aware measurement and fusion models introduced in the previous section. PFSA, along with their Hilbert space framework, form the basis for the approach.

15.3.1 Structure of Probabilistic Finite State Automata

The generative, low-dimensional model to be discussed in this section is the probabilistic finite state automaton (PFSA). The rationale for having the PFSA structure as a semantic model, as opposed to other models such as hidden Markov models (HMM) [31], is that, in general, PFSA is easier to learn and may also perform better in practice. For example, experimental results [32] show that the usage of a PFSA structure could make learning of a pronunciation model for spoken words to be 10–100 times faster than a corresponding HMM, and yet the performance of PFSA is slightly better. Rao et al. [33] and Bahrampour et al. [34] have shown that the performance of PFSA-based tools for feature extraction in statistical pattern recognition is comparable, and often superior, to that of other existing tools such as Bayesian filters, artificial neural networks, and principal component analysis. This leads to a very wide usage of PFSA in many areas such as pattern classification [35, 36] and anomaly detection [37, 38].

In formal language theory, an alphabet Σ is a (non-empty finite) set of symbols. A string s over Σ is a finite-length sequence of symbols in Σ. The length of a string s, denoted by $|s|$, represents the number of symbols in s. The Kleene closure of Σ, denoted by $\Sigma^{\star}$, is the set of all finite-length strings including the null string ε; the cardinality of $\Sigma^{\star}$ is $\aleph_0$. The set Σ^{ω} denotes the set of all strictly infinite-length strings over Σ; the cardinality of Σ^{ω} is $\aleph_1$. See [39, 40] for more details. The following is a formal definition of the PFSA.

Definition 5 (*PFSA*) A probabilistic finite state automaton is a tuple $G = (Q, \Sigma, \delta, q_0, \Pi)$, where

- Q is a (nonempty) finite set, called the set of states;
- Σ is a (nonempty) finite set, called the input alphabet;
- $\delta : Q \times \Sigma \to Q$ is the state transition function;
- $q_0 \in Q$ is the start state;
- $\pi : Q \times \Sigma \to [0, 1]$ is an output mapping which is known as a probability morph function and satisfies the condition $\sum_{\sigma \in \Sigma} \pi(q_j, \sigma) = 1$ for all $q_j \in Q$. The morph function π has a matrix representation Π, called the *(probability) morph matrix* $\Pi_{ij} = \pi(q_i, \sigma_j)$, $q_i \in Q$, $\sigma_j \in \Sigma$.

Note that Π is a $|Q|$-by-$|\Sigma|$ stochastic matrix; i.e., each element of Π is non-negative and each row sum of Π is equal to 1. While the morph matrix defines how a state sequence leads to a string of symbols, a PFSA gives rises to another stochastic matrix that defines how state sequences are formed. That is, every PFSA induces a Markov chain.

Definition 6 (*State Transition Probability Matrix*) Associated with every PFSA $G = (Q, \Sigma, \delta, q_i, \Pi)$ is a $|Q|$-by-$|Q|$ stochastic matrix P, called the *state transition (probability) matrix*, which is defined as follows:

$$P_{jk} = \sum_{\sigma:\delta(q_j,\sigma)=q_k} \pi(q_j, \sigma).$$

We are only interested in PFSA where all states are reachable (or accessible) from the initial state q_0. In particular, we focus on the following class of PFSA:

$$\mathscr{A} = \{(Q, \Sigma, \delta, q_0, \Pi) : \pi(q, \sigma) > 0 \text{ for all } q \in Q \text{ and for all } \sigma \in \Sigma\}.$$

We say that two PFSA are structurally similar if their graph representations have the same connectivity. Structurally similar PFSA only differ in the probabilities on the directed edges.

Definition 7 (*Structural Similarity*) Two PFSA $G_i = (Q_i, \Sigma, \delta_i, q_0^{(i)}, \Pi_i)$ $\in \mathscr{A}$, $i = 1, 2$, are said to be *structurally similar* if $Q_1 = Q_2$, $q_0^1 = q_0^2$, and $\delta_1(q, \sigma) = \delta_2(q, \sigma)$ for all $q \in Q_1$ and for all $\sigma \in \Sigma$.

One can always bring two arbitrary PFSA into the common structure without loss of information by composing the two PFSA in a time-synchronous manner.

Definition 8 (*Synchronous Composition*) [35] The *synchronous composition* $G_1 \otimes G_2$ of two PFSA $G_i = (Q_i, \Sigma, \delta_i, q_0^{(i)}, \Pi_i) \in \mathscr{A}$, $i = 1, 2$, is defined as

$$G_1 \otimes G_2 = (Q_1 \times Q_2, \Sigma, \delta', (q_0^{(1)}, q_0^{(2)}), \Pi'),$$

where

$$\delta'((q_i, q_j), \sigma) = (\delta_1(q_i, \sigma), \delta_2(q_j, \sigma)),$$
$$\Pi'((q_i, q_j), \sigma) = \Pi_1(q_i, \sigma)$$

for all $q_i \in Q_1$, $q_j \in Q_2$, and $\sigma \in \Sigma$.

It was shown in [35] that $G_1 \otimes G_2$ and $G_2 \otimes G_1$ describe the same stochastic process as G_1 and G_2, respectively, and yet $G_1 \otimes G_2$ and $G_2 \otimes G_1$ are structurally similar. Synchronous composition is an efficient procedure for fusing the information contents of individual PFSA into a single PFSA representation. It is, however, limited to PFSA sharing a common alphabet.

15.3.2 Hilbert Space Construction

This subsection describes the construction of a PFSA Hilbert space, which allows algebraic manipulations and comparison of PFSA. The space $\mathscr{A}$ of PFSA is a vector space with vector addition $\oplus$ and scalar multiplication $\odot$ defined as follows.

Definition 9 [40] For $G_i = (Q, \Sigma, \delta, q_0, \Pi_i) \in \mathscr{A}$, $i = 1, 2$ and for $k \in \mathbb{R}$, define operations $\oplus$ and $\odot$ as

- $G_1 \oplus G_2 = (Q, \Sigma, \delta, q_0, \Pi)$ where

$$\pi(q, \sigma) = \frac{\pi_1(q, \sigma)\pi_2(q, \sigma)}{\sum_{\alpha \in \Sigma} \pi_1(q, \alpha)\pi_2(q, \alpha)}; \qquad (15.10a)$$

- $k \odot G_1 = (Q, \Sigma, \delta, q_0, \Pi')$ where

$$\pi'(q,\sigma) = \frac{(\pi_1(q,\sigma))^k}{\sum_{\alpha \in \Sigma}(\pi_1(q,\alpha))^k}. \tag{15.10b}$$

Theorem 1 [40] The triple $(\mathscr{A}, \oplus, \odot)$ forms a vector space over the real field $\mathbb{R}$.

In addition, the space $\Sigma^{\star}$ is measurable. A probability measure on $\Sigma^{\star}$ leads to a definition of inner product.

Definition 10 (*Measure* μ) [40] The triple $(\Sigma^{\star}, 2^{\Sigma^{\star}}, \mu)$ forms a measure space, where $\mu : 2^{\Sigma^{\star}} \to [0,1]$ is a finite measure satisfying the following:

- $\mu(\Sigma^{\star}) = 1$;
- $\mu(\bigcup_{k=1}^{\infty}\{s_k\}) = \sum_{k=1}^{\infty}\mu(\{s_k\})$ for all $s_k \in \Sigma^{\star}$.

For each PFSA $G = (Q, \Sigma, \delta, q_0, \Pi) \in \mathscr{A}$, denote the row vector of the morph matrix Π for a particular state q_i by Π_i, so that Π_i is a probability vector with $|\Sigma|$ components. Denote the componentwise natural logarithm of Π_i by

$$f(\Pi_i) = \begin{bmatrix} \log \Pi_{i1} & \cdots & \log \Pi_{i|\Sigma|} \end{bmatrix} \quad \text{for } i = 1,\ldots,|Q|.$$

Define $g : \mathbb{R}^{|\Sigma|} \to \mathbb{R}^{|\Sigma|-1}$ by

$$g(x) = x - \left(\frac{1}{|\Sigma|}\sum_{i=1}^{|\Sigma|}x_i\right)1_{|\Sigma|} \quad \text{for } x \in \mathbb{R}^{|\Sigma|},$$

where $1_{|\Sigma|}$ denotes the vector in $\mathbb{R}^{|\Sigma|}$ whose components are all equal to 1. Then, overload the composition $F = g \circ f$ on the stochastic matrix as

$$F(\Pi) = \begin{bmatrix} F(\Pi_1) \\ \vdots \\ F(\Pi_{|Q|}), \end{bmatrix}$$

and define the set

$$\mathscr{H} = \{(Q, \Sigma, \delta, q_0, K) : (Q, \Sigma, \delta, q_0, \Pi) \in \mathscr{A}, K = F(\Pi)\}.$$

It is readily seen that the sets $\mathscr{H}$ and $\mathscr{A}$ are isomorphic to each other. According to (10), the linear operations on $\mathscr{A}$ involve normalization steps. We can avoid these steps if we work on $\mathscr{H}$ instead. The space $\mathscr{H}$ turns out to be a Hilbert space with inner product defined as follows.

Proposition 1 *For any $h_i = (Q, \Sigma, \delta, q_0, K^i) \in \mathcal{H}$, $i = 1, 2$, we have*

- $h_1 + h_2 = (Q, \Sigma, \delta, q_0, K^1 + K^2)$;
- $k \cdot h_1 = (Q, \Sigma, \delta, q_0, kK^1)$.

Proposition 2 *The function $\langle \cdot, \cdot \rangle : \mathcal{H} \times \mathcal{H} \to \mathbb{R}$ defined by*

$$\langle h_1, h_2 \rangle = \sum_{j=1}^{|Q|} \mu(q_j) \langle K_j^1, K_j^2 \rangle \quad \text{for } h_i = (Q, \Sigma, \delta, q_0, K^i) \in \mathcal{H}, \ i = 1, 2,$$

is an inner product on $\mathcal{H}$.

The Hilbert space–structure of the space of PFSA makes it possible to speak of comparison, reduction, refinement, etc., of PFSA, which are essential operations for ensuring the scalability of PFSA-based features to data size.

15.3.3 Extension to Cross Machines

The construction in the previous subsection naturally extends to cross machines. Cross machines are obtained from two symbol sequences s_1 and s_2 associated with two different sensors, possibly of different modalities, and capture the symbol-level cross-dependence of sensor measurements.

Definition 11 (*Cross Machine*) The cross machine of two sensor measurements is defined as $(Q, \Sigma_1, \Sigma_2, \delta, q_0, \Psi)$, where

- Q is a (nonempty) finite set, called the set of states;
- Σ_1 is a (nonempty) finite set, called the alphabet of sensor 1;
- Σ_2 is a (nonempty) finite set, called the alphabet of sensor 2;
- $\delta : Q \times \Sigma_1 \to Q$ is the state transition function;
- $q_0 \in Q$ is the start state;
- $\psi : Q \times \Sigma_2 \to [0, 1]$ is the output morph function satisfying the condition $\sum_{\sigma \in \Sigma_2} \psi(q_j, \sigma) = 1$ for all $q_j \in Q$. The output morph function ψ has a matrix representation Ψ, called the *output (probability) morph matrix* $\Psi_{ij} = \psi(q_i, \sigma_j), q_i \in Q, \sigma_j \in \Sigma_2$.

One can define a Hilbert space of cross machines as well. Define

$$\mathcal{R} = \{R = (Q, \Sigma_1, \Sigma_2, \delta, q_0, \Psi) : \psi(q, \sigma) > 0 \text{ for all } q \in Q \text{ and all } \sigma \in \Sigma_2\}.$$

We will focus on the cross machines in $\mathcal{R}$.

Definition 12 (*Synchronous Composition*) The synchronous composition $R_1 \otimes R_2$ of two cross machines $R_j = (Q_j, \Sigma_1, \Sigma_2, \delta_j, q_0^{(j)}, \Psi_j) \in \mathcal{R}$, $j = 1, 2$, is defined as

$$R_1 \otimes R_2 = (Q_1 \times Q_2, \Sigma_1, \Sigma_2, \delta', (q_0^{(1)}, q_0^{(2)}), \Psi'),$$

where

$$\delta'((q_i, q_j), \sigma) = (\delta_1(q_i, \sigma), \delta_2(q_j, \sigma))$$
$$\Psi'((q_i, q_j), \tau) = \Psi_1(q_i, \tau)$$

for all $q_i \in Q_1$, $q_j \in Q_2$, $\sigma \in \Sigma_1$, and $\tau \in \Sigma_2$.

This definition ensures that $R_1 \otimes R_2$ is a non-minimal realization of R_1, and that $R_1 \otimes R_2$ and $R_2 \otimes R_1$ describe the same process. This also implies that, without loss of generality, we can consider structurally similar cross machines that only differ in their output morph matrices. As in Sect. 3.2, one can obtain a space $\mathcal{H}$ isomorphic to $\mathcal{R}$ by considering a mapping $\Psi \mapsto K$ that involves the logarithm of the output morph matrix, and then by defining the inner product of two cross machines as in Propositions 3.2 and 3.2. See [39, 40] for more details.

15.3.4 PFSA Feature Extraction: Construction of D-Markov Machine

This subsection briefly describes the procedure for constructing PFSA features from time series data. More details can be found in [38, 41].

15.3.4.1 Symbolization of Time Series

Time series data, generated from a physical system or its dynamical model, are symbolized by using a partitioning tool—e.g., maximum entropy partitioning (MEP)—based on an alphabet Σ whose cardinality $|\Sigma|$ is finite. MEP maximizes the entropy of the generated symbols, where the information-rich portions of a data set are partitioned finer and those with sparse information are partitioned coarser. That is, each cell contains (approximately) equal number of data points under MEP. The choice of $|\Sigma|$ largely depends on the specific data set and the trade-off between the loss of information and computational complexity.

15.3.4.2 D-Markov Machine Construction

A *D-Markov Machine* is a special class of PFSA [38], where a state is solely dependent on the most recent history of at most D symbols, where the positive integer D is called the depth of the machine. That is, each state of a *D-Markov Machine* is a string of D symbols, or less, in alphabet Σ. In general, we have $|Q| = |\Sigma|$ when $D = 1$, and $|Q| \leq |\Sigma|^{|D|}$ for $D \geq 1$.

The construction procedure for *D*-Markov Machines consists of two major steps; namely, *state splitting* and *state merging*. In general, state splitting increases the number of states to achieve more precision in representing the information content in the time series. Conceptually, state splitting should reduce the entropy rate, thereby, focusing on the critical states (i.e., those states that carry more information). On the other hand, state merging is the process of combining the states, often resulting from state splitting, that describe similar statistical behavior. The similarity of two states, $q, q' \in Q$, is measured in terms of the conditional probabilities of future symbol generation. A combination of state splitting and state merging is performed in order to trade off information content against feature complexity, and leads to the final form of the *D*-Markov Machine, possibly with $|Q| \ll |\Sigma|^{|D|}$.

15.3.4.3 Feature Extraction

Once a *D*-Markov Machine is constructed based on quasi-stationary time series data, the associated state probability vector is computed by frequency counting. Let $N(q)$ be the number of times state $q \in Q$ occurs in the state sequence associated with the constructed *D*-Markov Machine. Then the probability of state q is estimated as

$$\widehat{P}(q) = \frac{1 + N(q)}{|Q| + \sum\limits_{q' \in Q} N(q')} \quad \text{for all } q \in Q.$$

The resulting vectors $\widehat{P}(q_j)$ can be used as stationary features representing the sensor measurements for statistical inference and decision-making purposes. These feature vectors serve the role of low-dimensional versions of raw data. That is, they replace all the sensor measurements $Y_1, \ldots, Y_M$ (in the case of a team of M sensors) that appear in Sect. 15.2.

15.4 Experiments and Results

The methods presented in Sect. 15.2 for context learning, and in Sect. 15.3 for multi-modal feature extraction, were validated using a binary target classification scenario. The details are presented in this section.

15.4.1 Experimental Scenario and Data Collection

The experiment aims to identify the walking gait of a human target and classify it as normal walking or stealthy walking. The dataset used in this work was collected in

(a)   **(b)**   **(c)**

Fig. 15.2 Sensors used in the experiment. **a** PIR, **b** acoustic and **c** seismic

a field experiment conducted with the U.S. Army Research Lab. There were in total 160 observations, each collected at 4 kHz for 10 s; i.e., 40,000 data points in a time series. For each observation, the following 4 sensors recorded measurements at different locations: one passive infrared (PIR) sensor, one acoustic sensor, and two seismic sensors. These sensors are shown in Fig. 15.2.

Out of total 160 observations, there were 80 observations under each hypothesis. Hypothesis 1 (i.e., $X = 1$) corresponds to the event of a human walking with a normal gait, and hypothesis 2 (i.e., $X = 2$) corresponds to a human walking with a stealthy gait. Typical signals from the 4 sensors under each hypothesis are shown in Fig. 15.3. Out of the 80 samples for each hypothesis, 40 samples were collected in a region which had moist soil, and 40 samples in another region which had gravel soil. The response of the seismic sensors was affected by different soil conditions. If soil conditions at the sensor deployment site are unknown at the outset, then context estimation and context-aware pattern classification become important tools for measurement system modeling.

15.4.2 Data Preprocessing and Feature Extraction

In the signal preprocessing step, each time-series signal is down-sampled by a factor of 4 to give a time series of 10,000 data points. The DC component (i.e., the constant offset) of a seismic signal was eliminated by subtracting the average value, resulting in a zero mean signal. Then, the signal was partitioned using the MEP approach with a symbol size of 7. The maximum number of allowable states was varied, and the classification performance on a validation test set was found under each hypothesis using individual sensors. This process was repeated three times to obtain average error. The number of states was then chosen to be 10 for the PIR sensor and 14 for other sensors, as these numbers resulted in the minimum average error. After partitioning, symbolization was done and the feature vectors were extracted as explained in Sect. 15.3. The feature vectors constructed in this fashion replace the (down-sampled) raw sensor measurements for the purpose of target classification.

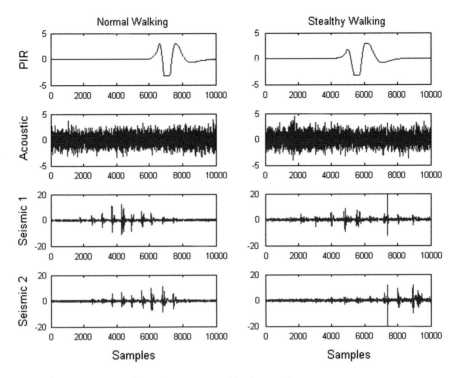

Fig. 15.3 Typical signals from the sensors used in the experiment

15.4.3 Performance Assessment

We now compare the following two approaches:

1. *Naïve Bayes approach.* This is the usual approach, where the sequential measurements are assumed to be independent conditioned on the state.
2. *Context-aware approach.* This is the proposed approach, where the sequential measurements are assumed to be independent conditioned on the state-context pair and the context is allowed to be dependent on the state.

The naïve Bayes approach assumes

$$p(Y_1, \ldots, Y_M | X) = \prod_{i=1}^{M} p_i(Y_i | X),$$

and so, as new measurements are being sampled sequentially, updates the posterior distribution of X via the standard update rule given by

Table 15.1 Confusion matrix result for target walking-type classification

(a) Naïve Bayes approach (Acc: 85.61 %)

X	1	2
1	191	50
2	9	160

(b) Context-aware approach $\sigma = 0.01$, $\gamma = 0.01$ (Acc: 89.02 %)

X	1	2
1	184	29
2	16	181

(c) Context-aware approach $\sigma = 0.01$, $\gamma = 0.05$ (Acc: 88.29 %)

X	0	1
0	179	27
1	21	183

$$P(X \mid Y_1) = \frac{p_1(Y_1 \mid X)P(X)}{\sum_{x=0}^{1} p_1(Y_1 \mid x)P(x)}$$

and

$$P(X \mid Y_1, \ldots, Y_{i-1}, Y_i) = \frac{p_i(Y_i \mid X)P(X \mid Y_1, \ldots, Y_{i-1})}{\sum_{x=0}^{1} p_i(Y_i \mid x)P(x \mid Y_1, \ldots, Y_{i-1})}$$

for $i = 2$, 3, M, where $P(x)$ is the prior probability that $X = x$. The marginal likelihood $p_i(Y_i \mid X)$ for each i is estimated by computing the sample mean and sample covariance from the available data.

The context-aware approach fuses the information from sequential multi-modal measurements using the context-aware sensor fusion rule given in (15.9a, b). The context set $\mathcal{C}(X)$, as given in Definition 4, is constructed from Sect. 15.2.2.3. The SVDE approach has one user-defined parameter $\sigma > 0$ and also the kernel parameters can be chosen suitably. It was found that the results were sensitive to the choice of kernel parameters and the results shown here are not for the optimal choice of these parameters. The dataset was partitioned into randomly drawn training (75 %) and test (25 %) sets. The partitioning of the dataset was repeated 10 times and the overall classification performance is reported below. The D-Markov Machine construction-based feature extraction technique, as shown in Sect. 15.3.4, was used for extracting features from the sensor time-series data. Assuming that the D-Markov Machine feature vector from each modality has a multi-variate Gaussian distribution, the context-aware approach shows a 10.98 % error and the naïve Bayes approach gives 14.39 % error. Thus, the context-aware approach yields a 24 % reduction in classification error over that of the naïve Bayes approach. See Table 15.1 for a summary of the result.

15.5   Summary and Conclusions

In this chapter, the notion of context in the multi-modal sensor framework is mathematically formalized, and then a novel, kernel-based context learning approach is presented. Based on the resulting context-aware measurement model, a multi-modal sensor fusion approach for sequential statistical inference is discussed. A powerful feature extraction technique results in a low-dimensional feature of sensor measurements in the form of PFSA (or, in particular, the D-Markov Machine), which replaces the raw data set and yet captures the information from, and the dynamics of, the heterogeneous sensor system. The superior performance of the context learning approach is validated on a real-world sensor data set, whose feature is extracted through a D-Markov Machine.

Our major innovation consists of two sets of algorithms. One set of algorithms is for unsupervised learning of the context and for context-aware multi-modal sensor fusion. The context-learning algorithm is based on a kernel machine that yields an estimate of the joint density of multi-modal measurements, so that the support vectors serve the role of machine-generated contexts, and that the conditional independence of sensor measurements given the state-context pair, which is crucial for sequential inference, is automatically satisfied. The algorithm for context-aware sensor fusion suggests the potential of the proposed context-aware approach in realistic scenarios. The other set of algorithms is for symbolic compression–based feature extraction, which yields an attractive and scalable low-dimensional PFSA features. These features are attractive because they are endowed with a Hilbert-space structure, which enables us to replace the raw measurement data with their low-complexity features and carry out feature comparison (i.e., inner product), reduction (i.e., state merging), and refinement (i.e., state splitting) operations. Owing to these operations defined on the space of PFSA (and, in particular, the D-Markov Machine–based features), PFSA features are, in principle, scalable to any desired level of description.

A research direction in the immediate future is to fully develop the proposed sensor fusion and decision-making system, and demonstrate it in a scenario more complicated than those of binary hypothesis testing. The experimental validation described in Sect. 15.4 used a limited amount of data, which was obtained from a test performed by the Army Research Lab. A border-control testbed being set up at Penn State would allow collection of much larger amounts of data from several heterogeneous sensors and enable a more detailed and systematic validation of the presented techniques. Other future research paths include optimizing the proposed kernel machine for the purpose of unsupervised context learning (in terms of sparsity, generalization ability, etc.), and developing a method that unifies the context learning and feature extraction steps, which are currently separate and hence suboptimal.

Acknowledgments The work reported in this chapter has been supported in part by U.S. Air Force Office of Scientific Research (AFOSR) under Grant No. FA9550-12-1-0270 and by the Office of Naval Research (ONR) under Grant No N00014-11-1-0893. Any opinions, findings, and conclusions or recommendations expressed in this paper are those of the authors and do not necessarily reflect the views of the sponsoring agencies.

References

1. S. Phoha, N. Virani, P. Chattopadhyay, S. Sarkar, B. Smith, A. Ray, Context-aware dynamic data-driven pattern classification. Procedia Comput. Sci. **29**, 1324–1333 (2014)
2. N. Virani, S. Marcks, S. Sarkar, K. Mukherjee, A. Ray, S. Phoha, Dynamic data-driven sensor array fusion for target detection and classification. Procedia Comput. Sci. **18**, 2046–2055 (2013)
3. N. Virani, J.W. Lee, S. Phoha, A. Ray, Dynamic context-aware sensor selection for sequential hypothesis testing, in *2014 IEEE 53rd Annual Conference on Decision and Control (CDC)*, 2014, pp. 6889–6894
4. D.K. Wilson, D. Marlin, S. Mackay, Acoustic/seismic signal propagation and sensor performance modeling, in *SPIE*, vol. 6562, 2007
5. F. Darema, Dynamic data driven applications systems: new capabilities for application simulations and measurements. In: Computational Science–ICCS 2005, Springer, 2005, pp. 610–615
6. A. Olivaa, A. Torralba, The role of context in object recognition. Trends Cogn. Sci. 520–527 (2007)
7. R. Rosenfield, Two decades of statistical language modeling: Where do we go from here? (2000)
8. B. Schilit, N. Adams, R. Want, Context-aware computing applications, in *Mobile Computing Systems and Applications, 1994. WMCSA 1994. First Workshop on, IEEE*, 1994, pp. 85–90
9. H. Frigui, P.D. Gader, A.C.B. Abdallah, A generic framework for context-dependent fusion with application to landmine detection, in *SPIE Defense and Security Symposium, International Society for Optics and Photonics*, 2008, pp. 69,531F–69,531F
10. C.R. Ratto, Nonparametric Bayesian context learning for buried threat detection. Ph.D. thesis, Duke University, (2012)
11. C. Bron, J. Kerbosch, Algorithm 457: Finding all cliques of an undirected graph. Commun. ACM **16**(9), 575–577 (1973)
12. E. Tomita, A. Tanaka, H. Takahashi, The worst-case time complexity for generating all maximal cliques and computational experiments. Theor. Comput. Sci. **363**(1), 28–42 (2006)
13. M. Newman, Fast algorithm for detecting community structure in networks. Phys. Rev. E. **69** (2003)
14. N. Virani, J.W. Lee, S. Phoha, A. Ray, Learning context-aware measurement models, in *Proceedings of the 2015 American Control Conference*, IEEE 2015, pp. 4491–4496
15. P.R. Kumar, P. Varaiya, Stochastic systems: estimation, identification and adaptive control, Prentice-Hall, Englewood Cliffs, NJ, 1986
16. A.P. Dempster, N.M. Laird, D.B. Rubin, Maximum likelihood from incomplete data via the EM algorithm. J. Roy. Stat. Soc. B **39**(1), 1–38 (1977)
17. C.R. Ratto, P.A. Torrione, L.M. Collins Context-dependent feature selection using unsupervised contexts applied to GPR-based landmine detection, in *SPIE Defense, Security, and Sensing, International Society for Optics and Photonics*, 2010, pp. 76,642I–76,642I

18. H. Akaike, A new look at statistical model identification. IEEE Trans. Autom. Control **19**(6), 716–723 (1974)
19. G. Schwarz, Estimating the dimension of a model. Ann. Stat. **6**(2), 461–464 (1978)
20. C.R. Ratto, K.D. Morton, L.M. Collins, P.A. Torrione Contextual learning in ground-penetrating radar data using dirichlet process priors, in *Proceedings of SPIE, the International Society for Optical Engineering, Society of Photo-Optical Instrumentation Engineers*, 2011
21. F. Cucker, S. Smale On the mathematical foundations of learning. Bulletin (New Series) of the Am. Math. Soc. 39(1):1–49 (2001)
22. B. Schölkopf, C.J.C. Burges, A.J. Smola (eds.), *Advances in Kernel Methods: Support Vector Learning* (MIT Press, Cambridge, MA, 1999)
23. J.W. Lee, P.P. Khargonekar, Distribution-free consistency of empirical risk minimization and support vector regression. Math. Control Sig. Syst. **21**(2), 111–125 (2009)
24. J.L. Kelley et al., *Linear Topological Spaces* (Springer, New York, NY, 1976)
25. A.J. Smola, B. Schölkopf, A tutorial on support vector regression. Stat. Compu. **14**(3), 199–222 (2004)
26. V.N. Vapnik, *Statistical Learning Theory* (Wiley, New York, NY, 1998)
27. C.C. Chang, C.J. Lin, Training v-support vector regression: theory and algorithms. Neural Comput. **14**(8), 1959–1977 (2002)
28. E. Parzen, On estimation of a probability density function and mode. Ann. Math. Stat. 1065–1076 (1962)
29. S. Mukherjee, V. Vapnik, Support vector method for multivariate density estimation. Cent Bio. Comput. Learn. Dept Brain and Cogn. Sci., MIT CBCL **170** (1999)
30. J. Weston, A. Gammerman, M.O. Stitson, V. Vapnik, V. Vovk, C. Watkins, Support vector density estimation. (Advances in kernel methods, MIT Press, 1999), pp. 293–305
31. L. Rabiner, A tutorial on hidden markov models and selected applications in speech proccessing. Proc. IEEE **77**(2), 257–286 (1989)
32. D. Ron, Y. Singer, N. Tishby, On the learnability and usage of acyclic probabilistic finite automata. J. Comput. Syst. Sci. **56**(2), 133–152 (1998)
33. C. Rao, A. Ray, S. Sarkar, M. Yasar, Review and comparative evaluation of symbolic dynamic filtering for detection of anomaly patterns. SIViP **3**, 101–114 (2009)
34. S. Bahrampour, A. Ray, S. Sarkar, T. Damarla, N.M. Nasrabadi, Performance comparison of feature extraction algorithms for target detection and classification. Pattern Recogn. Lett. **34**, 2126–2134 (2013)
35. I. Chattopadhyay, A. Ray, Structural transformations of probabilistic finite state machines. Int. J. Control **81**(5), 820–835 (2008)
36. X. Jin, S. Sarkar, A. Ray, S. Gupta, T. Damarla, Target detection and classification using seismic and PIR sensors. IEEE Sens. J. **12**(6), 1709–1718 (2012)
37. S. Gupta, A. Ray, Statistical mechanics of complex systems for pattern identification. J. Stat. Phys. **134**(2), 337–364 (2009)
38. A. Ray, Symbolic dynamic analysis of complex systems for anomaly detection. Sig. Process. **84**(7), 1115–1130 (2004)
39. P. Adenis, Y. Wen, A. Ray, An inner product space on irreducible and synchronizable probabilistic finite state automata. Math. Control Sig. Syst. **23**(4), 281–310 (2012)

40. Y. Wen, S. Sarkar, A. Ray, X. Jin, T. Damarla, A unified framework for supervised learning of semantic models, in *Proceedings of the 2012 American Control Conference*, pp. 2183–2188, IEEE, (2012)
41. K. Mukherjee, A. Ray, State splitting and merging in probabilistic finite state automata for signal representation and analysis. Sig. Process. **104**, 105–119 (2014)

Part V
Context in Hard/Soft Fusion

Chapter 16
Context for Dynamic and Multi-level Fusion

Lauro Snidaro and Ingrid Visentini

Abstract The understanding and principled exploitation of contextual information in fusion systems is still very limited. Domain knowledge is generally acquired from an expert and applied to stove-piped solutions that can hardly scale or adapt to new conditions. However, "context" can play a vital role at any level of a modern information fusion system: from object recognition through physical context exploitation, to intention estimation through linguistic communication analysis. In this work, a few important elements that should be considered in designing a context-aware system are discussed including: context refinement using terrain information, context to promote fusion results to higher levels of abstraction, and context for resource management. We highlight concepts of context sifting, shifting, and adaptation for multi-level fusion.

Keywords Multi-level fusion · Resource management · Context-aware fusion · Context sifting · Context switching · Surveillance

16.1 Introduction

In modern surveillance environments, the amount of incoming information is exponentially growing driven by the expansion and availability of sensors and hardware; more and new sensors produce more data. Combined with these sensor-based data, inputs can also come from Open Sources and from human observers [1, 2]. In domains where a lot of raw data is available, the general trend is to develop technological tools that can act in real-time, condensing the raw sensory output into meaningful information. There is an increasing global trend: while in the past the monitoring systems were focused on the extensive use of single-type

L. Snidaro (✉) · I. Visentini
Department of Mathematics and Computer Science, University of Udine, Udine, Italy
e-mail: lauro.snidaro@uniud.it

I. Visentini
e-mail: ingrid.visentini@gmail.com

© Springer International Publishing Switzerland (outside the USA) 2016
L. Snidaro et al. (eds.), *Context-Enhanced Information Fusion*,
Advances in Computer Vision and Pattern Recognition,
DOI 10.1007/978-3-319-28971-7_16

sensors, modern systems aim to fuse multi-cued information coming from different types of sources [3, 4]. For example, cities are more and more permeated by pervasive and smart sensors that can track and identify people. The focus is shifted from only the use of cameras to the aggregation of information provided by radio-frequency identification (RFID) sensors, lasers, infrared (IR) cameras, human intelligence (HUMINT) information, and chemical, biological, radiological, and nuclear (CBRN) sensors to improve the coverage, the detection rate and the recognition accuracy and to provide richer hypotheses regarding situational conditions. In the maritime domain, cooperative sources, such as automatic identification system (AIS) transponders, are coming to be coupled with non-cooperative sensors, such as synthetic aperture radar (SAR) imagery, shore-based or over-the-horizon high-frequency radars to cite some. However, sensory data alone can not describe the situation or its background in detail.[1] On the contrary, the contextual information (CI) that surrounds an event describes its "setting" and the relations between the entities observed by the sensors.

Context is being exploited in a wide spectrum of research fields, from pervasive computing [5], to face identification [6], from target tracking [7, 8], to sensor fusion [9] just to name a few. CI is a precious source of information in every automatic system for situation awareness since it provides a powerful way to semantically bind sensor measurements and real-world observables. As we will discuss, CI can play different roles at different fusion levels, providing significant cues that can range from ancillary data to human-provided information. A survey on the use of CI for information fusion can be found in [10].

16.1.1 Multi-sensor Multi-cue Fusion

Modern multi-source multi-sensor fusion deals with different data types that have to be merged together in a coherent decision support process for providing better estimates or more precise operational picture description. It is generally agreed that any process can benefit from a combination of data coming from different and complementary sources [11], and that this benefit involves at the low-level and the high-level fusion operations [12]. Multi-modal systems, even more often used for biometric identification and recognition [13], or multi-sensor multi-cue approaches [4], which fuse heterogeneous data provided by multiple sensors, are deemed to be a powerful tool to provide a more robust response and enhanced awareness. For instance, in a maritime scenario an AIS contact can be associated with a detection provided by space-based SAR snapshot, and the resulting estimate could be fused

---

[1]Conventional electromechanical sensors ("physics-based or hard" sensors) fundamentally provide attributes of the various entities observed, they do not provide (are not capable of providing) first-order evidence about inter-entity relationships, which are the basis of situational compositions.

with a track obtained by over-the-horizon (OTH) radar [14]. In a surveillance scenario, an IR processed contact can be associated with a detection provided by an RGB camera snapshot, and the resulting estimate could be fused with a track obtained by radar [3, 4, 15]. In these cases, the fusion of multi-sensor information can resolve many data-related issues, as detection imprecisions and difficulties in object association.

Evolving from the multi-sensor concept, the multi-cue approach couches the requirements of representing the object of interest with a collection of distinct and complementary pieces of information at multiple abstraction levels. Fusing information is a matter of reducing the complexity of the domain we want to observe, obtaining an information space of tractable size, and preserving the integrity and the semantics of the data. However, the richness of the domain can be prohibitive to encapsulate in a *single* piece of information. To give an example, a single sensor can be limited with respect to a space and time, a single feature can be insufficient to describe the appearance of an object, and one sentence to depict a certain situation can be not sufficiently descriptive. Fusion must consider a multi-cue approach, where the object of interest is described by more than one aspect at once. Moreover, the information we obtain from sensors, wherever they are deployed, is often imprecise, incomplete, ambiguous, unresolved, deceptive, hard-to-be-formalized, or contradictory. Fusing and comparing redundant and heterogeneous data could allow for improvement in addressing the challenges in various environments. In fact, it is deemed that heterogeneity of input data can improve the accuracy and the robustness of an inferencing system [11].

It is evident that the multi-sensor multi-cue approach forces the fusion process designer to consider nonhomogeneous data. In particular, we can observe two types of heterogeneity, as shown in Fig. 16.1. The first is "horizontal", in the sense that refers to same-level information produced or extracted by concurrent or cooperative sources which operate in the same environment. For instance, an object appearance can be described by features as color, shape, velocity, or class, which are at the same abstraction level.

The second is "vertical", in the sense that considers that fusion can take place between different levels of information abstraction, from sensory data to features, from features to decisions [16], including also high-level layers. In this case, the object of interest can be represented by multi-layered information with different degrees of refinement and detail. In a fusion process sense, "complementary" can be taken to mean "associable", and refers to a single given entity, which could be a physical object, an event or a situation. The higher the levels, the more general and abstract the information.

This general taxonomy can be seen as a low-to-high refining process, from a low-level fusion that involves raw data coming straight from sensors to high-level combination of abstract and processed information. The flow through the levels can also be generally considered as a fan-in tree, because each step provides a response to the higher levels receiving the input data from the previous ones. However, it must be noticed that sometimes it is possible to merge non-adjacent levels.

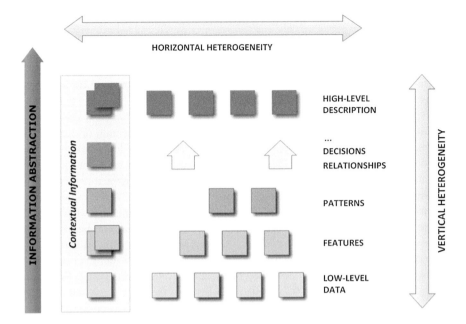

Fig. 16.1 Exemplification of data and context heterogeneity at different abstraction levels

For example, heterogeneous data can imply non-commensurate data, data that do not have a common physics and/or semantic foundation, such as imagery and radar, or soft (human-generated) data and hard (sensor-generated) data. Relating and associating such data requires some type of semantic transform or some strategy by which to develop a semantic relation in order to associate them (e.g., ontology).

Frameworks for fusing heterogeneous information have been proposed in the past (e.g., [17, 18]), but no architecture has become a standard yet, mainly due to the complexity of the problem. According to the previously described taxonomy of complementarity, each level can be considered as a black box, in which different fusion methods can be transparently employed for combining input information. Fusing intra-layer information is a transparent and stand-alone process: multiple and diverse techniques can be alternated without influencing the other layers input/output. For instance, several classifiers working on different features [19] can be combined by voting techniques; in another situation boosting techniques can be used instead.

Interlayer fusion is also promoted with context [20, 21]: low-level data can be fused with high-level information if properly formatted. For instance, the position of a moving car can be fused with online reports or ancillary information on its status to assess if potentially in a threatening situation or compared with a city map to signal the risk of violation of sensitive areas. To provide a concrete example, we consider a tracking system that has to cope with unidentified objects detected by physical sensors and with uncertain information coming from human intelligence.

- The data level can be constituted, for instance, of different measurements of the object position provided by different sensors (geolocation given by camera, radar, etc.).
- The feature level comprises different object characteristics, basic pieces of information (Haar features output, color, class, etc.) which describe the object's physical appearance.[2]
- The next opportunity includes the contextualization of the object in a network of entities and relationships, which may be built on a priori knowledge or obtained by data mining. Entities involved in the urban domain are, for instance, much more than just pedestrians and cars, as they can include sensitive targets, resources, and assets, in the form of CI or a priori abstract entities.
- One level above we can find trajectories and historical motion patterns that are structured pieces of information obtained by exploiting features and data at lower level. From trajectories and formatted knowledge provided by operators or intelligence, we move one step up, and include information regarding the object's capabilities, its behavior, or even its future intent.

16.1.2 Heterogeneity in Contextual Information

The taxonomy introduced in the previous section can be translated to context in order to structure the knowledge. Context, in fact, can contain several elements which can have the same or different degree of abstraction, and can comprise redundant or complementary information. Context, defined as [22]

- a collection of objects or properties or features of the world exploited to define or recognize and label simple or complex events or situations.
- a collection of various data, sensed in a subset of the world, exploited to build a correct or reliable perception of objects or events.
- a collection of possibly wide-ranging types of data that can be said to be adjunct to certain focal conditions of interest, and depict the "setting" or "surroundings" in which the focal information unfolds; they are complementary to the focal information but are not the focal information of interest. Thus, such information can be helpful toward understanding the focal states of interest or for describing these states, or yet other purposes.

In Fig. 16.2 we give a concrete example of how context can span at every level of abstraction: CI of a chemical plant, for instance, can include low-level

---

[2]In the literature, many different descriptors have been devised for describing an object, but inevitably no one emerged as the most effective as none of them cannot guarantee superiority over the others in every condition. This fact stresses the need to combine the descriptive power of several different features to represent the appearance of an object and to exploit them in a synergistic way.

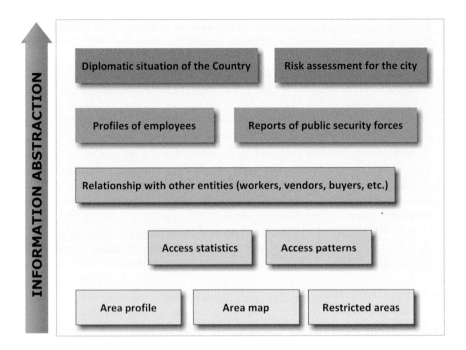

Fig. 16.2 Examples of CI at several levels of abstraction

information (i.e., the geographical location, its perimeter and area, restricted areas, etc.), and features, which include statistics on the accesses and the patterns associated with people entering and leaving. At higher levels of information fusion, we find the relationship with other entities (vendors, buyers or plant's workers, etc.) and other entities information (intelligence reports on a specific situation in a certain period of time, military assets, etc.). In the example of Fig. 16.2, the highest-level descriptions are for diplomatic situation of the Country and the assessment of the risk level of the city where the plant is built. The latter describes a more general picture and helps the operator to place the situation in a global context.

Contextual knowledge binds sensor measurements and real-world observables; an evident example is provided by for low-level checking in surveillance systems, where the measured position of a target is matched against the location of sensible areas, triggering an alarm if a suspicious event is recognized [23]. According to the

	Level	Context	Effect
Table 16.1 Example of effect of CI (weather) on JDL levels	0	Rainy/darkness	Reduced camera signal quality
	1	Rainy weather	Reduced objects' speed
	2	Rainy weather	Traffic more intense
	3	Clear/full daylight	Reduced likelihood of car thefts

JDL [24] data fusion model,[3] this kind of inferences belong to Levels 2 and 3. A description of context integration in low level processing can be found in [8].

As already observed in [26], context may be exploited in data fusion at different levels, even if, up to now, its most wide use is to support the development of inferences on the current or future (focal) situation. In the broadest sense, CI can be viewed as having influences on features, relations, behaviors, and/or events, and knowledge of such influences can aid in situational estimation and understanding; knowledge of such influences can also be exploited in a consistency-checking or anomaly-detecting scheme for given situational hypotheses. Table 16.1 shows how weather/visibility can have an impact at different levels in the observed environment, that is: signal acquisition (Level 0), objects' features (Level 1), relations/situation (Level 2), and possible threats (Level 3).

16.2 Context as Binding Element for Multi-level Fusion

As discussed in [20], Information Fusion processes and systems have been traditionally designed to fit low-level observational data with a priori models, often at one information fusion level only. These approaches have shown to work well for static and predictable domains where a priori knowledge is rich, but are not fully capable to solve problems in which the global behavior is very complex or multifaceted, or where contextual influences are clearly evident. These issues can be addressed exploiting contextual knowledge to enhance the performance and capabilities of a fusion system. An integrated approach should extend problem-space modeling with a structured multi-level representation of semantically rich domain knowledge, which describes situations and possible entities interactions of the observed scenario. From the literature, high-level information is not often merged with sensory data, even if its richness and completeness are extremely useful to properly interpret the available stream of data. Qualitative high-level knowledge can help to infer hidden states from low-level data generated by sensors, other fusion processes, or human reports. In other words, it can reduce uncertainties in problems where normally experts would need to be consulted.

The main concepts remarked here are the following:

- Context allows for improving the associability between problem-space knowledge and models and observational data, increasing fusion performance. The a priori model can be better fit to data exploiting the semantics provided by CI.
- Context can be provided at different information fusion levels. Different types of context, from coarse to refined information, can be injected at different stages of the fusion process, overlapping or overriding each other.

---

[3]Here and in the remainder of the chapter we refer to the classical hierarchical partitioning of data fusion problems into levels. However, other partitioning schemes can be considered as recently proposed in [25].

16.3   Context and JDL Level 4

The topic of Resource Management (RM) is recently attracting a significant amount of interest as it is considered a key factor for the development of next generation automatic Situation Assessment systems [27]. These systems should be able to organize themselves to collect data relevant to the objectives specified by the operator [28]. The process of managing available resources falls in the fourth level of the JDL model, also called Process Refinement (or sensor management) step as it implies adaptive data acquisition and processing to support mission objectives. Conceptually, this refinement step should be able to manage the system in its entirety: from controlling hardware resources (e.g., sensors, processors, storage, etc.) to adjusting the processing flow in order to optimize the behavior of the system to best achieve the mission goals. It is therefore apparent that the Process Refinement step encompasses a broad spectrum of techniques and algorithms that operate at very different logical levels. In this regard, an implemented full-fledged Process Refinement would provide the system a form of awareness of its own capabilities and how they relate and interact with the observed environment. The Process Refinement part dedicated to sensors and data sources is often called Sensor Management and it can be defined as "a process that seeks to manage, or coordinate, the use of a set of sensors in a dynamic, uncertain environment, to improve the performance of the system" [28]. In other words, a Sensor Management process should be able to, given the current state of affairs of the observed environment, translate mission plans or human directives into sensing actions directed to acquire needed additional or missing information in order to improve situational awareness and fulfill the objectives.

As mentioned above, and as already pointed out in [28], RM is a complex under-researched process that can be subdivided in different layers: from translation of mission objectives to the actual control of available sensors. Most of the literature on RM is dedicated to the optimal allocation of scarce resources (generally sensors) to carry out a given task while being subject to certain cost constraints (e.g., power consumption for sensor activation, repositioning cost, etc.) (see for example [29] for comprehensive coverage of the subject).

Other works are directed to the unconstrained analysis of the optimal set of measurements to be fused. When redundant observations (per time instant) are available on a given target both the reliability of the sources [30], and the quality of their data [31] should be taken into account to regulate the fusion process accordingly. As a consequence, fusing all available data might be not always a good idea [32] as better performance could be achieved by discarding measurements coming from faulty sensors. In this spirit, other works analyze how to evaluate, weight, and possibly discard sensor readings. The concepts of Information Theory have been used in the literature in this sense [33] to perform sensor selection according to the information gain that a given source or set of sources can provide [34].

In [35] the tradeoff between sensor cost and information gain is explored. In particular, the authors propose a heuristic method for efficient computation of

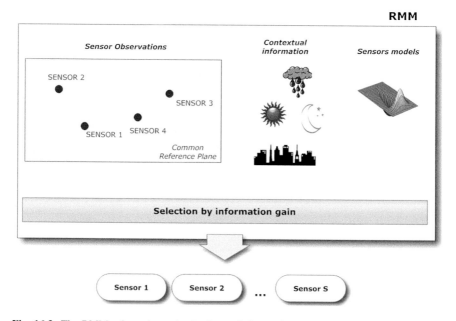

Fig. 16.3 The RMM selects the optimal subset of observations according to CI, sensor models, and the information gain provided to the fused result

information gain, calculating the synergy among pairs of sensors, and building a graph consisting of couples of them that are pruned exploiting the mutual information properties. A different technique that is also based on cost is detailed in [36], where the selection procedure is driven by battery constraints and energy savings, and a tradeoff between benefits (in speed, accuracy, etc.) and energy consumption is the key factor of the paper. Another approach, by Das and Kempe [37], treats sensors subsets like clusters, grouped using efficient approximation algorithms with the aim to minimize the prediction error.

The fusion engine is supposed to perform tracking and classification tasks by combining data coming from multiple, (partially) redundant, and possibly heterogeneous sources. These JDL Level 1 tasks provide the building blocks for higher level reasoning processes and situation assessment routines. In this work, we will discuss how a resource management module (RMM) can actively influence the fusion engine by hinting the most rewarding measurements to be fused in terms of information gain.[4] The role of the RMM is illustrated in Fig. 16.3.

---

[4]The RMM module described here is broken down in a more detailed architecture in Chap. 8.

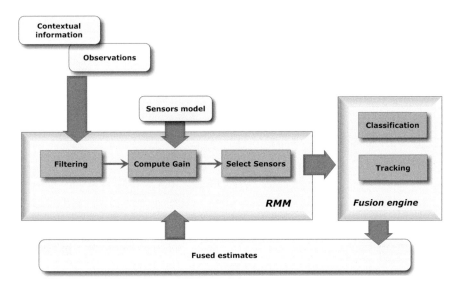

Fig. 16.4 Data flow through RMM and fusion modules

16.3.1 Architecture

The RMM is intended to be part of an engine for multi-sensor fusion which is able to combine observations from multiple and possibly heterogeneous sensors for tracking and classification. These two tasks are the main duties of the engine supported by a contextual database that encodes a priori knowledge of the observed environment (e.g., map of the area, weather map, etc.)

The overall RMM processing chain is shown in Fig. 16.4. The RMM receives observations from sensors and CI as inputs. A first selection step is performed at this point by discarding sensor measurements that are likely to be false alarms (e.g., noise, reflections, etc.). This is particularly true for tracking as a position measurement can be easily checked against spatial and structural constraints (see Sect. 16.3.2). Observations validated by context are then evaluated for the information gain that they could provide to the estimate computed by the engine at the previous time instant regarding a given target. According to their informative value, a subset of all the measurements is selected and passed to the fusion engine that will generate the new estimate. This loop is repeated for each collection of new observations received by the sensors.

16.3.2 Filtering Step

Considering the available scenario information, a prefiltering phase can be used to remove very uncertain observations, considering variables as weather or time.

Imagine, for instance, the case of a target moving along a city street and suppose that we want to estimate its state $\mathbf{x}$ as the vector of Cartesian bidimensional coordinates. Suppose now that the observation $\mathbf{z}(t)$ at time t is checked against an urban map of the monitored area resolving $\mathbf{z}(t)$ as falling inside a building. Now, given the fact that we know that the sensor has no see-through-walls capability, this could be explained as an occasional quirk of the sensor and could be easily filtered out by the tracking algorithm (e.g., Kalman filter, particle filter, etc.). Especially if $\mathbf{z}(t)$ resolves inside a building while both the previous state $\mathbf{x}(t-1)$ and the next measurement $\mathbf{z}(t+1)$ do not.

Unfortunately, in real-world monitoring applications it often happens that a sensor provides a sequence of unreliable observations due to partial occlusion of the target, unfavourable weather conditions, sun blinding, persistent reflections, etc. [38]. In these cases tracking can be severely disrupted providing an unreliable estimate of the target's position and trajectory.

The prefiltering step exploits, therefore, different and diversified CI as a means to filter observations, as shown in Fig. 16.5. The aim of integrating CI into tracking

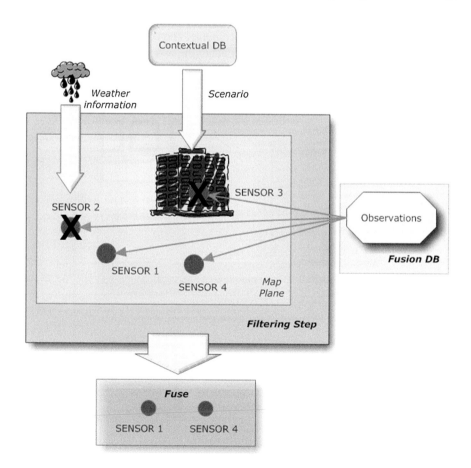

Fig. 16.5 CI integration in the filtering step

systems is to better refine and optimize the task according to the observations provided by the sensors and to prior high-level knowledge of the environment that is coded as context. CI can be a key factor in determining the state of an entity of interest, as it can dramatically impact on the reliability of an observation. Checking the measurements against a map of the monitored area is a form of contextual knowledge inclusion that could, as in the latter example, provide an insight on the reliability of the sensor in a specific situation. Knowing the sensing capabilities of a sensor is another form of contextual knowledge that could be exploited conveniently. In the previous example, knowing that the sensor has no see-through-walls capability *and* the fact that the last few measurements fall inside a building can help us in concluding that those measurements may be affected by a form of bias and thus be unreliable. The sensor may be in fact persistently experiencing one or more of the disturbing conditions mentioned above.

To be pragmatic, one can discard the sensors that give measurements not compatible with the reliability assigned by CI, adopting thus a *pruning* strategy [30]. Alternatively, instead of getting rid of sensors observations, the measurements can be combined by weighting them with respect to the reliability factor given by context analysis. This strategy is called *discounting*, and is less drastic than pruning because it allows to include also uncertain data in the fusion. A detailed description

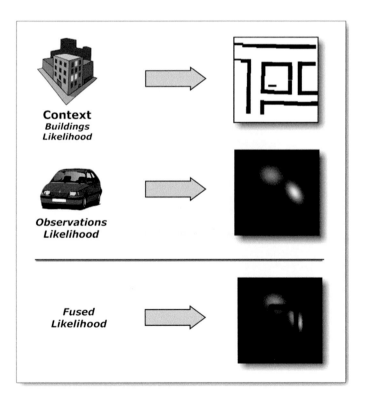

Context
Buildings
Likelihood

Observations
Likelihood

Fused
Likelihood

Fig. 16.6 Example of likelihood masks for topological information that is fused in the last line with the observations likelihood

of how context can be included in tracking systems to improve localization is given in [8]. CI takes here the form of likelihood maps, as in Fig. 16.6, to be fused with the sensor's likelihood function for tracking purposes. The masks are concretely conceived as 2D matrices with values in the [0,1] interval, that are combined by Hadamard product. These likelihood masks provide the reliability factor that can be employed to regulate the measurements error covariance matrix as in [3]. In our case, the discounting strategy has proved to work better than pruning.

16.4 Design Directions for Context-Aware Systems

Before designing or implementing a fusion system, we must remember that domain context plays a vital role at any level of a fusion model, from object detection through geographical context exploitation, to intention estimation through linguistic communication analysis [22]. Context awareness allows the possibility for a system to change and adapt to better react to unpredictable or potentially harmful events. The system should not only adapt to changes in the availability of resources, but also to the presence of new or updated CI, such as time of the day or adapting the exploitation of the information a sensor has about the object being observed. This form of adaptation is pertinent to JDL model Level 4 optimization schemes and policies [24]. In the following, concepts relevant to a context-aware fusion system able to adapt to changing context conditions are discussed. Since such a wide-spread commercial system has yet to be developed, the following suggestions could be considered for developing a context-aware architecture.

16.4.1 Context Sifting

Contextual elements can be defined in different ways in a fusion system. As already mentioned in Sect. 16.1.2, knowledge about a particular domain can have effects at different fusion levels. It could be of interest to the system designer or from an algorithmic point of view to understand how CI can be decomposed, possibly translated, and exploited at different levels. For example, a surveillance application for the security of an enterprise or public building could have information, provided by a domain expert or automatically acquired [23], regarding the activity of the parking lot attached. Information could be in the form of overall working hours of the employees in the building. This could suggest the typical arrival and departure hours for vehicles in the parking lot thus providing a way for detecting unusual activity outside of the normal working hours time window. This kind of information would therefore be exploited at high level (Levels 2 and 3) in a fusion system. Other information could comprise the map of the area, entrance and exit gates, allowed parking slots, etc. This kind of information could be useful to constrain vehicles' movements in that area and thus be exploited by Level 1 algorithms for target

Fig. 16.7 Sifting of CI to
JDL Levels

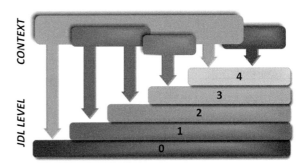

Table 16.2 Online and
offline context sifting

Sifting	When	Data source	Data type
Online	System running	Incoming flow	Hard/soft
Offline	Design time	Repository	Hard/soft

tracking. At the same time, this information could be exploited at high level to detect unusual movement patterns. The simple parking-lot example shows how contextual knowledge could affect a different number of levels depending on the entities involved. The process by which the entirety of the domain knowledge acquired is fractured into pieces and assigned to the proper algorithms is here referred to as *context sifting* and illustrated in Fig. 16.7.

The problem is relevant for both offline repositories and online flows of information which could carry relevant cues of the domain at hand. While in the former case contextual factors could be assigned by the system designer offline, the mechanism for sifting CI online is of particular interest. In both cases, CI can be provided by collected sensory data or expert knowledge. These concepts are summarized in Table 16.2.

Figure 16.8 illustrates a possible process by which domain knowledge, possibly in the form of soft data reports [39], is first stored in computable form (knowledge structuring) and then actually sifted to the proper algorithms. Rich domain knowledge can comprise descriptions of entities and their features and relations, rules describing typical entity behavior, regulations, constraints, uncertainties, etc. Different representations can be used for such wealth of knowledge. For example, in [8] an urban area map was used to weigh noisy sensor measurements of vehicles

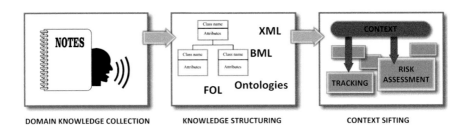

Fig. 16.8 Representation and sifting of CI

and pedestrians. In [23] the Markov Logic Networks framework was used leveraging both the expressive power of first order logic and the probabilistic uncertainty management of Markov networks to encode high-level knowledge in maritime domain.

The process by which online CI is dynamically exploited at different fusion levels has not seen, to our knowledge, practical implementation yet. To dynamically sift incoming contextual knowledge a context-aware architecture would be needed where the internal parameters of the algorithms (e.g., tracking, event detection, etc.) would be bound to concepts expressed in the contextual knowledge repository. The idea could be seen from the perspective of an agent-based architecture, where agents register/offer their functions and services to the system and could actively search for updated relevant contextual knowledge [40].

16.4.2 Context Switching

CI, as the name implies, has local scope and validity and is thus pertinent to the scenario at hand. The granularity of the scope of certain information can be more fine-grained and be applicable only to sub-areas of the observed environment. Figure 16.9 illustrates the case of two cameras observing the activities of two different parking lots.

Take for example the case of two different parking areas for a public/enterprise building. The first is for visitors/customers and allows free parking while the second is dedicated to staff personnel only. Activity in the two areas is likely to be different, for example knowing that working hours should be in the 0800–1900 time range, the system could exploit this information to detect anomalous events (Sect. 16.4.1). This knowledge does not necessarily apply to the first parking area. How much of the knowledge that applies to one area applies also to the second one? Given the effort required to build an effective knowledge base (made of expert provided notions or learnt online by the system), from a knowledge engineering perspective it would be interesting to know how much of a certain context knowledge can be

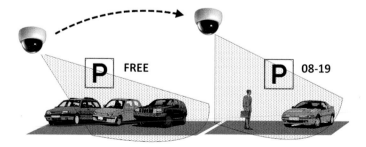

Fig. 16.9 Context switching, and *shallow transfer*. Source and target domain are the same. Source and target tasks are the same

reused and applied in another situation. This of course is not only related to the effort or cost in building the knowledge base, it directly determines the capability of a system to adapt to changing domain conditions, and also it affects its capability to be redeployed in another scenario.

The context switching capability discussed here is inspired by available literature on *transfer learning* [41]. Transfer learning deals with transferring classification knowledge and capability from a source domain to a target domain or from a source task to a target task. The idea here is brought even further by postulating a transfer of the entire system capabilities from a scene to another or from a domain to another. In Fig. 16.9, the source and target domain are the same (parking lot) and the source and target task are also the same (surveillance). Nonetheless, the two parkings have different maps, different patterns of activity, different entrance and exit gates, etc. However, in both cases the expected entities are vehicles and pedestrians with their known typical (for such scenario) movement speeds. Also models of usual and unusual behavior are likely to be transferable between the two scenes. In the transfer learning literature this type of transfer is often referred to as *shallow transfer* [42].

A more drastic context switch is illustrated in Fig. 16.10. Even though source and target tasks are the same (detecting unusual activity) here very few contextual knowledge is likely to be transferred between domains. This is often called *deep transfer*. However, a fusion system with context adaptable architecture should be able to be easily redeployed in a different scenario without much retraining and reconfiguring. For example, normal patterns of activity in a surveillance scenario can be relearnt online [23]. Domain knowledge and rules should easily be swapped by changing knowledge repositories [23]. Deep transfer can also be performed automatically by inductively learning knowledge from data in a target domain starting from the knowledge base of a source domain. Deep Transfer via Markov logic [42], for example, starts by lifting knowledge bases expressed within the Markov Logic Networks framework to second-order clauses where domain-specific predicates have been replaced by predicate variables. This second-order set of clauses represents domain-independent knowledge that can be exploited as

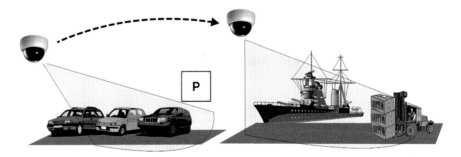

Fig. 16.10 Context switching, *deep transfer*. Source and target domain are different. Source and target tasks are the same

declarative bias that is a starting point, while learning knowledge in the target domain. This allows to both reducing the computational burden of automatically learning new knowledge and producing a more refined and accurate knowledge base [42].

16.5   Discussion

This chapter has presented several design and engineering issues that should be considered for the effective integration of contextual knowledge in a fusion system. The following subsections comment the main strands addressed along with the potential beneficial outcomes in terms of system functionality and performance.

16.5.1   A Priori Knowledge, Context, and Adaptability

First of all, a first step that can help the design phase of a context-aware fusion system is a clear separation between what should be considered as an always-valid static a priori knowledge and what could instead be relevant to the specific domain at hand. This allows to develop knowledge repositories in a modular way, thus allowing easier context switching and system redeployment. Also understanding what kind of knowledge is of dynamic nature allows to develop systems that can automatically exploit a change in the observed environment. This understanding brings in the concept of context sifting that was described in Sect. 16.4.1. Channeling CI to the proper algorithms can easily be done at design time or while the system is offline with the help of a human expert. More complicated is the case of online context exploitation. However, it should be noticed that the sifting procedure would work differently depending on the type of context received by the system while online. If context is received as *value* of a known *property/attribute*, then the value is exploited by the system according to the existing system design. Take for example, the case of weather conditions: this is dynamic contextual knowledge that can be provided both by human observers and sensors. Supposing that weather can take values in a predefined set of strings like {Rainy, Stormy, Sunny, Cloudy,...}, then online processing of this CI occurs as per the existing architecture. If context is instead provided, typically by a human expert, as a new *relation or rule* such as ``is$(w, \text{Rainy}) \land \text{event}(x, w, \text{sensor}) \Rightarrow$ confidence$(\text{sensor}, ``\text{low}")$'' then this kind of knowledge could simply be added to the contextual knowledge base and immediately produce effects on entailed predicates. A much more advanced architecture would need to reason on CI, system capabilities, and scenario entities in terms of causes and effects as mentioned in Sect. 16.5.3.

16.5.2 Context Heterogeneity and Information Fusion Levels

CI can be represented with different and inhomogeneous information tokens; each of these depicts a snippet of background, which is associated to a situation or an event, or a physical object. Heterogeneity is a fundamental requirement in fusion, since it provides complementary, redundant, and rich information at different levels of abstraction, which can be helpful toward understanding the focal states of interest or for describing these states, or other purposes. No single sensor is currently capable to capture the complexity and vastness of a domain, but expert knowledge and, more in general, high-level soft (e.g., text) data should be blended together with low-level hard (e.g., physical measurements) information to obtain a more comprehensive, timely, and accurate situational awareness picture. A synergistic exploitation of available contextual pieces is demanded, both for intra-level and inter-level fusion: fusion can take place between information produced or extracted by concurrent or cooperative sources which operate in the same environment, and between different abstraction levels as well.

16.5.3 Middleware

A context-aware fusion architecture needs to be designed to be able to incorporate the capabilities above mentioned to properly exploit contextual knowledge both for understanding better the observed domain entities and to automatically regulate the system itself to cope better with changes in the environment. A form of middleware layer would be required as the means of access to the contextual databases and of binding system capabilities to context as well. This layer would also be responsible to perform the context sifting and switching capabilities described in this chapter. However, a significant additional effort is required to properly formalize such an architecture and the representation of all aspects of CI, some of which have been highlighted in this work. Further insights to the middleware concept for context-aware information fusion can be found in [10] and in Chap. 8.

16.6 Conclusions

There is a need for the fusion community to develop an engineering and design methodology for the inclusion and exploitation of CI. This chapter tries to move a step forward in the understanding of several top-level issues in approaching fusion process design challenges for the incorporation of CI. We highlighted forms of contextual refinement for multi-level fusion and discussed the need for context sifting, switching, and adaptation for multi-level fusion in a site surveillance application.

Acknowledgments This work was partially supported by ONRG Grant N62909-14-1-N061.

References

1. J. Biermann, V. Nimier, J. Garcia, K. Rein, K. Krenc, L. Snidaro, Multi-level fusion of hard and soft information, in *Proceedings of the 17th International Conference on Information Fusion* (ISIF, Salamanca, Spain, 2014)
2. E. Blasch, J. Nagy, A. Aved, E.K. Jones, W.M. Pottenger, A. Basharat, A. Hoogs, M. Schneider, R. Hammoud, G. Chen, D. Shen, H. Ling, Context aided video-to-text information fusion, in *Proceedings of the 17th International Conference on Information Fusion* (Salamanca, Spain, 2014)
3. L. Snidaro, R. Niu, G. Foresti, P. Varshney, Quality-based fusion of multiple video sensors for video surveillance. IEEE Trans. Syst. Man Cybern. B **37**(4), 1044–1051 (2007)
4. L. Snidaro, I. Visentini, G. Foresti, Fusing multiple video sensors for surveillance. ACM Trans. Multimedia Comput. Commun. Appl. **8**(1), 7:1–7:18 (2012)
5. N. Roy, T. Gu, S.K. Das, Supporting pervasive computing applications with active context fusion and semantic context delivery. Pervasive Mob. Comput. **6**(1), 21–42 (2010)
6. W.J. Scheirer, N. Kumar, K. Ricanek, P.N. Belhumeur, T.E. Boult, Fusing with context: a Bayesian approach to combining descriptive attributes, in *International Joint Conference on Biometrics (IJCB)* (IEEE, 2011)
7. E. Blasch, J. García Herrero, L. Snidaro, J. Llinas, G. Seetharaman, K. Palaniappan, Overview of contextual tracking approaches in information fusion (2013), pp. 87, 470B–87, 470B–11. doi:10.1117/12.2016312
8. I. Visentini, L. Snidaro, Integration of contextual information for tracking refinement, in *14th International Conference on Information Fusion* (Chicago, Illinois, 2011)
9. A. Padovitz, S.W. Loke, A. Zaslavsky, B. Burg, C. Bartolini, An approach to data fusion for context awareness, in *Proceedings of the 5th international conference on Modeling and Using Context* (Springer, Berlin, 2005), pp. 353–367
10. L. Snidaro, J. García, J. Llinas, Context-based information fusion: a survey and discussion. Inf. Fusion **25**, 16–31 (2015). doi:10.1016/j.inffus.2015.01.002
11. L.I. Kuncheva, *Combining Pattern Classifiers: Methods and Algorithms* (Wiley-Interscience, 2004)
12. E. Blasch, D. Lambert, P. Valin, M. Kokar, J. Llinas, S. Das, C. Chong, E. Shahbazian, High level information fusion (hlif): survey of models, issues, and grand challenges. IEEE Aerosp. Electron. Syst. Mag. **27**(9), 4–20 (2012). doi:10.1109/MAES.2012.6366088
13. N. Poh, A. Merati, J. Kittler, Heterogeneous information fusion: a novel fusion paradigm for biometric systems, in *Proceedings of the International Joint Conference on Biometrics (IJCB)* (Washington, DC, 2011). doi:10.1109/IJCB.2011.6117494
14. I. Visentini, L. Snidaro, New trends for enhancing maritime situational awareness, in *Prediction And Recognition Of Piracy Efforts Using Collaborative Human-Centric Information Systems*, NATO Science for Peace and Security Series (IOS Press, 2013), pp. 193–200
15. L. Snidaro, I. Visentini, G., Foresti, Data fusion in modern surveillance, in *Studies in Computational Intelligence*, vol. 336, chap. 1 (Springer, Germany, 2011), pp. 1–21
16. D.L. Hall, J. Llinas, An introduction to multisensor data fusion. Proc. IEEE **85**(1), 6–23 (1997)
17. A.C. Boury-Brisset, Ontology-based approach for information fusion, in *the 6th International Conference on Information Fusion* (2003), pp. 522–529
18. A. Hunter, W. Liu, Merging uncertain information with semantic heterogeneity in xml. Knowl. Inf. Syst. **9**, 230–258 (2006)
19. I. Visentini, L. Snidaro, G.L. Foresti, Diversity-aware classifier ensemble selection via f-score. Inf. Fusion **28**, 24–43 (2016). doi:10.1016/j.inffus.2015.07.003

20. J. García, L. Snidaro, I. Visentini, Exploiting context as binding element for multi-level fusion, in *Proceedings of the 15th International Conference on Information Fusion*. Panel Session on Multi-Level Fusion: Issues in Bridging the Gap between High and Low Level Fusion (2012)
21. L. Snidaro, I. Visentini, J. Llinas, G.L. Foresti, Context in fusion: some considerations in a JDL perspective, in *Proceedings of the 16th International Conference on Information Fusion* (IEEE, Istanbul, Turkey, 2013)
22. G. Ferrin, L. Snidaro, G. Foresti, Contexts, co-texts and situations in fusion domain, in *14th International Conference on Information Fusion* (Chicago, Illinois, USA, 2011)
23. L. Snidaro, I. Visentini, K. Bryan, Fusing uncertain knowledge and evidence for maritime situational awareness via markov logic networks. Inf. Fusion 21, 159–172 (2015). doi: 10.1016/j.inffus.2013.03.004
24. J. Llinas, C.L. Bowman, G.L. Rogova, A.N. Steinberg, E.L. Waltz, F.E. White, Revisiting the JDL data fusion model II, in *Proceedings of the 7th International Conference on Information Fusion*, vol. II (Stockholm, Sweden, 2004), pp. 1218–1230
25. A. Steinberg, L. Snidaro, Levels? in *Proceedings of the 18th International Conference on Information Fusion* (Washington, D.C., USA, 2015). pp. 1985–1992
26. A. Steinberg, G. Rogova, Situation and context in data fusion and natural language understanding, in *Proceedings of the 11th International Conference on Information Fusion* (Cologne, Germany, 2008)
27. E. Blasch, I. Kadar, K. Hintz, J. Biermann, C. Chong, J. Salerno, S. Das, Resource management and its interactions with level 2/3 fusion from the fusion06 panel discussion, in Proceedings *of the 10th International Conference on Information Fusion* (Québec, Canada, 2007)
28. N. Xiong, P. Svensson, Multi-sensor management for information fusion: issues and approaches. Inf. fusion **3**(2), 163–186 (2002)
29. A.O. Hero, D.A. Castan, D. Cochran, K. Kastella, *Foundations and Applications of Sensor Management*. (Springer Publishing Company, Incorporated, 2008)
30. G. Rogova, V. Nimier, Reliability in information fusion: literature survey, in: *Proceedings of the 7th International Conference on Information Fusion*, ed. by ISIF (2004), pp. 1158–1165
31. G. Rogova, E. Bossé, Information quality in information fusion, in *Proceedings of the 13th International Conference on Information Fusion* (Edinburgh, U.K., 2010)
32. L. Kuncheva, Switching between selection and fusion in combining classifiers: an experiment. IEEE Trans. Syst. Man Cybern. B **32**(2), 146–156 (2002). doi:10.1109/3477.990871
33. J. Aughenbaugh, B. La Cour, Metric selection for information theoretic sensor management, in *International Conference on Information Fusion* (2008)
34. B. Fassinut-Mombot, J. Choquel, A new probabilistic and entropy fusion approach for management of information sources. Info. Fusion **5**, 35–47 (2004)
35. Y. Zhang, Q. Ji, Sensor selection for active information fusion, in *Proceedings of the 20th national conference on Artificial intelligence*, Vol. 3 (AAAI Press, 2005), pp. 1229–1234. URL http://portal.acm.org/citation.cfm?id=1619499.1619531
36. F. Bian, D. Kempe, R. Govindan, Utility based sensor selection, in *Proceedings of the 5th international conference on Information processing in sensor networks, IPSN '06* (ACM, New York, NY, USA, 2006), pp. 11–18. doi:http://doi.acm.org/10.1145/1127777.1127783. URL http://doi.acm.org/10.1145/1127777.1127783
37. A. Das, D. Kempe, Sensor selection for minimizing worst-case prediction error, in *International Conference on Information Processing in Sensor Networks*, vol. 0 (2008), pp. 97–108. doi:http://doi.ieeecomputersociety.org/10.1109/IPSN.2008.40
38. B. Kahler, E. Blasch, Sensor management fusion using operating conditions, in *Proceedings of the IEEE National Aerospace and Electronics Conference (NAECON)* (IEEE, 2008), pp. 281–288
39. G. Ferrin, L. Snidaro, S. Canazza, G. Foresti, Soft data issues in fusion of video surveillance, in *Proceedings of the 11th International Conference on Information Fusion* (Cologne, Germany, 2008), pp. 1882–1889

40. A.V. Smirnov, M.P. Pashkin, N.G. Chilov, T.V. Levashova, A.A. Krizhanovsky, Ontology-driven information integration for operational decision support, in *Proceedings of the Eighth international conference on Information Fusion* (International Society of Information Fusion, Philadelphia, PA, 2005)
41. S.J. Pan, Q. Yang, A survey on transfer learning. IEEE Trans. Knowl. Data Eng. **22**(10), 1345–1359 (2010). doi:10.1109/TKDE.2009.191
42. J. Davis, P. Domingos, Deep transfer via second-order Markov logic, in *Proceedings of the 26th annual international conference on machine learning* ACM, 2009), pp. 217–224

Chapter 17
Multi-level Fusion of Hard and Soft Information for Intelligence

Joachim Biermann, Jesús García, Ksawery Krenc, Vincent Nimier, Kellyn Rein and Lauro Snidaro

Abstract Driven by the underlying need for an as yet undeveloped framework for fusing heterogeneous data and information at different semantic levels coming from both sensory and human sources, we present some results of the research conducted within the NATO Research Task Group IST-106/RTG-051 on "Information Filtering and Multi Source Information Fusion." As part of this ongoing effort, we discuss here a first outcome of our investigation on multi-level fusion. It deals with removing the first hurdle between data/information sources and processes being at different levels: representation. Our contention here is that a common representation and description framework is the premise for enabling processing overarching different semantic levels. To this end, we discuss here the use of the Battle Management Language (BML) as a way ("lingua franca") to encode sensor- and text-based data and a priori and contextual knowledge, both as hard and soft data. We here expand on our previous works [1, 2] further detailing and exemplifying the

J. Biermann
SDF, Fraunhofer FKIE, Wachtberg, Germany
e-mail: joachim.biermann@fkie.fraunhofer.de

J. García
GIAA, Universidad Carlos III de Madrid, Colmenarejo, Spain
e-mail: jgherrer@inf.uc3m.es

K. Krenc
C4I Research and Development Department, OBR CTM S.A, Gdynia, Poland
e-mail: ksawery.krenc@ctm.gdynia.pl

V. Nimier
Department of Information Processing and Modelling, ONERA,
Palaiseau CEDEX, France
e-mail: Vincent.Nimier@onera.fr

K. Rein
ITF, Fraunhofer FKIE, Wachtberg, Germany
e-mail: kellyn.rein@fkie.fraunhofer.de

L. Snidaro (✉)
Department Mathematics and Computer Science, University of Udine, Udine, Italy
e-mail: lauro.snidaro@uniud.it

© Springer International Publishing Switzerland (outside the USA) 2016   453
L. Snidaro et al. (eds.), *Context-Enhanced Information Fusion*,
Advances in Computer Vision and Pattern Recognition,
DOI 10.1007/978-3-319-28971-7_17

use of BML and clarifying aspects related to the use of contextual information and
the exploitation of uncertain soft input along with sensor readings.

Keywords Multi-level fusion · Hard and soft fusion · Intelligence · BML ·
Controlled language · Uncertainty

17.1 Introduction

Effective exploitation of all relevant information originating from a growing mass
of heterogeneous sources, both device-based (video, radar, etc.) and
human-generated (largely expressed in natural language), is a key factor for the
production of reliable descriptions of a situation or phenomenon. There is a
growing need to efficiently identify relevant information from the mass available,
and exploit it through automatic fusion for timely, comprehensive, and accurate
situation awareness. Even when exploiting multiple sources, most fusion systems
have been developed for combining just one type of data (e.g., positional data) in
order to achieve a certain goal (e.g., accurate target tracking). This approach does
not consider other relevant information that could be of different origin, type, and
with possibly very different representations (e.g., a priori knowledge, contextual
knowledge, mission orders, risk maps, availability and coverage of sensing
resources, etc.) but that are still very significant to augment the knowledge about
observed entities. Very likely, this latter type of information could be considered to
be of different fusion levels that rarely end up being systematically exploited
automatically. The result is often stovepiped systems dedicated to a single fusion
task with limited robustness. This is caused by the lack of an integrative approach
for processing sensor data (low-level fusion) and semantically rich information
(high-level fusion) in a holistic manner thus effectively implementing a multi-level
processing architecture and fusion process.

17.2 Background

The notion of "levels" of fusion was introduced by the well-known JDL model one
of the most frequently referred approaches to a categorization of methods for the
association and combination of data and information. It originates from the Data
Fusion Group of the US Joint Directors of Laboratories (JDL) and was proposed in
1985. After its first publication in 1988 [3], the JDL model has undergone two
major revisions in 1998 [4], 1999 [5], and 2004 [6].

The JDL model is a functional model and its levels were defined to provide a
distinction between different degrees of problem-space complexity indicating
changing grades of abstraction. It does not define the architecture or model of a
fusion system and it does not imply a strict sequential processing within or across

its levels. Processing at these levels is not necessarily performed in a fixed order and any one of the JDL fusion levels can be processed on its own given its corresponding input [6].

The generation and maintenance of comprehensive and up-to-date situation awareness is one of the major tasks within military Command and Control. The cyclic running process chain of Boyd's OODA (Observe, Orient, Decide, and Act) loop and the cyclic nature of the UK intelligence cycle, both interacting with each other [7], are models of important aspects of this military area. They are fed by different types of input data and information gained from different phases of military action and command. The process chain across these phases, having different complexity and timescales, is a good example for a JDL multi-level fusion task as will be shown later in Figs. 17.1 and 17.2.

Bedworth and O'Brian [8] discuss the association of JDL fusion levels and distinct fusion functionality to the process phases of the OODA loop. Table 17.1 is derived from the relations between JDL Model and OODA Loop presented in [8] differing in the association of the functionality of JDL level 1 to the "Observe" and not to "Orient."

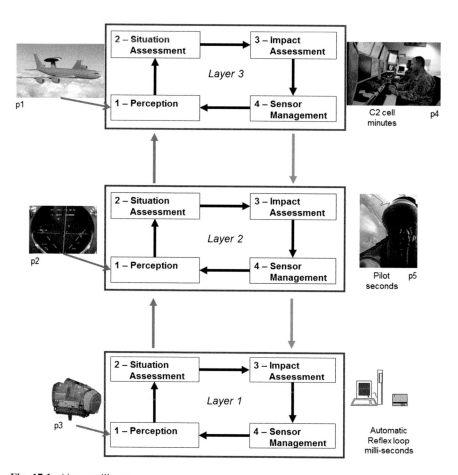

Fig. 17.1 Air surveillance

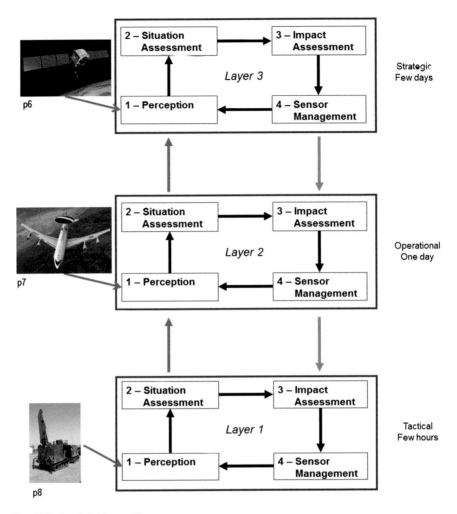

Fig. 17.2 Battlefield surveillance

Table 17.1 Association of JDL levels to OODA loop phases [8]

Levels of the JDL model	Phases of the Boyd OODA loop
	Act
Level 4 Process refinement; resource (sensor) management	Decide
Level 3 Impact assessment; Treat evaluation	Orient
Level 2 Situation assessment	
Level 1 Object assessment; perception	Observe
Level 0 Signal assessment	

The "Act" phase has no corresponding JDL level. JDL level 5 ("Human (or User) Refinement"), which was introduced in 2003 by Blasch and Plano [9] does not address real-life activities in military operations but is only related to the human interface to and control of the data fusion process.

As mentioned previously, in an operational environment, JDL multi-level information processing (fusion) for situation awareness is not limited to one loop of the OODA cycle but defines continuously running processes shown in Figs. 17.1 and 17.2. For the sake of simplicity, only JDL levels 1–4 are taken into account in these examples of multi-level fusion. The different JDL level functions supporting the OODA process cycle will be activated in a repeated way and will communicate according to their own objectives and the requirements of the respective OODA process phases.

Figure 17.1 gives a typical example of air surveillance with airborne sensors. There are three layers of data processing but there can be more if we include, for example, ground sensors. The first layer (at the bottom) is a reflex loop where all information is pure numerical. Information processing and decision-making are automatic at this level. The semantic level of information is very poor (limited mainly to kinematics and, sometimes, some identity attributes). It is important to note that at this layer the time to react is very short (milliseconds) so there is no possibility to have a human interaction. The second layer has the pilot involved. He observes the current situation presented on a screen showing the results of some data processing software (fusion JDL level 1), he understands the situation (level 2), and then, he predicts the enemy's action (level 3) and orients his sensor to have new information (level 4). In this layer, the information is more elaborate: both the situation on the screen but also human information provided by pilots of others aircrafts. Here, the time to react is short (few seconds) but the human is in the loop and he is in charge of taking a decision. The third level is at the C2 level, for example in an AWACS. The situation picture generated in this layer is the result of fusing the individual situation pictures provided by fighters of the lower layer plus additional information provided by the AWACS sensors. In this layer, the time to react is longer (few seconds to minutes). Part of the processing is automatic (fusion) and a second part is manual (track management). In this example, the information in the first layer is done by a network internal to the aircraft. However, communications between layer 2 and layer 3 are done using Link 16. The local situations from the individual aircrafts are communicated to the C2 where they are fused. The fused situation is pushed back from the C2 to each aircraft and this situation is then considered as the reference situation.

For copyright information concerning the pictures in Fig. 17.1.[1]

---

[1] p1: http://www.defenceimagery.mod.uk/fotoweb/Grid.fwx?search=%28IPTC020%20contains%20%28Sentry%29%29 file is available for reuse under the OGL (Open Government License) http://www.nationalarchives.gov.uk/doc/open-government-licence/.

p2: http://commons.wikimedia.org/wiki/File:F-14_Radar_TID.jpg#filelinks; public domain.

p3: http://commons.wikimedia.org/wiki/File:AN-APG-63V3.jpg, by 'Raytheon', freely reproducible.

Figure 17.2 gives an example of ground surveillance. In the first layer, the information may be both numerical provided by sensors and verbal (human) provided by operators.

For copyright information concerning the pictures in Fig. 17.2.[2]

The main part of the processing is done by operators. The time to react is much longer than in the first layer of Fig. 17.1: it can vary from a few hours to a day. The semantic value of information is greater than the one of the first layer in Fig. 17.1 because the information includes text reports provided by human.

In the second layer of Fig. 17.2, information is provided by different sources of the lower layer and data from sensors directly assigned to this layer. The information can be structured, based on a data model like JC3IEDM (Joint Consultation Command and Control Information Exchange Data Model) based on a fixed and limited vocabulary, unstructured, provided by humans reports, and numerical data. This heterogeneous input has to be fused with the situation provided by layer 1. The third layer is similar to the second one but covers a much longer period of time.

The language to carry the information between layers can be Battle Management Language (BML) in the same way as it is shown in the examples in Sect. 17.6. Figures 17.1 and 17.2 depict only one loop in each layer. However, in a real scenario, there are many loops in a layer as it is shown in Fig. 17.3.

In a single layer, the processing loops can communicate between themselves (horizontal arrows) and can send the results of their fusion processes to the immediate upper layer (upward arrows). A loop within a layer can also represent fusing the result from a lower loop and its own direct data and information input and send back the result to the lower layer (downward arrows) as a reference situation. As discussed in the next sections, the intercommunication between processes at different levels of abstraction can be seen as contextual feedback.

(Footnote 1 continued)

p4: http://www.army.mil/media/226029/ by Staff Sgt John H. Johnson III 11042011-A-zv120-001) public domain.

p5: http://www.defenceimagery.mod.uk/fotoweb/Grid.fwx?position=65&archiveid=5036&columns= 8&rows=1&sorting=ModifiedTimeAsc&search=%28IPTC020%20contains%28Royal%20Air%20Force %29%29 file is available for reuse under the OGL (Open Government License) http://www. nationalarchives.gov.uk/doc/open-government-licence/.

[2]p6: http://www.gps.gov/multimedia/images/IIF.jpg United States Government; public domain.

p7: http://en.wikipedia.org/wiki/Boeing_E-3_Sentry, public domain

p8: http://www.defenceimagery.mod.uk/fotoweb/Grid.fwx?archiveId=5042&search=451483 29.jpg available for reuse under the OGL (Open Government License) http://www. nationalarchives.gov.uk/doc/open-government-licence/.

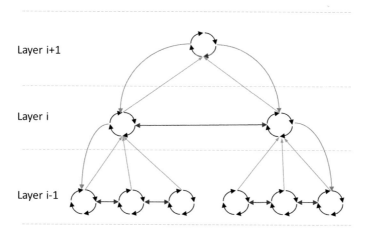

Fig. 17.3 Processing loops between layers

17.3 Previous Works

In this section, we highlight some related research that appeared in recently organized events around the multi-level fusion topic and other closely related areas of
research.

At the higher levels, an important input is soft data, consisting of
human-generated information in natural language as either written text or spoken
(voice). Soft data is unstructured and therefore needs preprocessing in order to be
usable for automated fusion processes. At present, there is much work in various
types of text analytics going on, some of it with a focus on the needs of fusion
algorithms. One example of such a focused system is the Tractor system [10],
developed for text understanding in situation assessment problems. Analogously,
soft data processing has been proposed in counterinsurgency examples, such as
[11]. An important initiative to test with real data set by fusing soft (natural language) information with hard (signal) information is called Mixed Initiative Soft
Fusion Implementation Testbed (MISFIT) [12]. In this chapter, the objective is to
integrate the content of hard data sources with soft sources (mainly texts in
unconstrained natural language), trying to define a whole "machine-processable"
representation.

In the ambient intelligence domain, multi-level architectures for the computation
of contextual data in a "smart home" environment are presented in [13] and different methods at different levels of abstraction are addressed. Here, belief functions
theory is applied to measures included in stable abstractions, at the highest layer,
and contextual data is exploited to provide adapted services. Other areas where
multi-level integration has shown itself to be of interest are business intelligence
and decision support products [14, 15].

A fundamental aspect to injecting high-level information is representation of uncertainty, which will be discussed later in this chapter. As previous work in this area, we can mention the analysis on absolute and relative conditioning rules for multi-level conditioning in a threat assessment problem [16, 17].

We here expand on our previous works [18, 19] further detailing and exemplifying the use of BML and clarifying aspects related to the use of contextual information and the exploitation of uncertain soft input along with sensor readings.

17.4 Multi-level Fusion

The general goal of multi-level fusion is making simultaneous use of sensor data processing techniques along with high-level processes working on symbolic elements of a situation such as relationships, categories, etc. It seems clear that the ability to interconnect and make interactions among processes working at different levels will bring opportunities to successfully address challenging applications. However, the interconnection of information fusion processes operating at different levels is a quite recent research topic in information fusion, with a limited number of research works being published until now.

17.4.1 An Example Scenario

In order to illustrate the discussion of multi-level fusion concepts in this chapter, particularly with consideration of device-generated and human-generated input from diverse sources, we present a small example scenario below. In particular, we wish to show how HUMINT can be combined with sensor-derived data.

A small military facility situated at the edge of a small town is bordered by a perimeter fence. A portion of the fence borders onto a small woods on one side, while other sides face onto open fields. Where the fence borders on fields, it is outfitted with an array of acoustic sensors which track activity outside the perimeter. Entrance to the facility is via a gate with a guard shack which is continuously staffed. There is also a routine human patrol along the perimeter. Within the compound itself there are various different surveillance motion sensors such as video and motion detection. One of the buildings on the facility is a lock-up for hazardous substances.

Because of its location close to the town, it is not unusual for there to be normal, unthreatening civilian activity outside of the perimeter of the fence. In particular, along one portion of the fence there is a footpath used by local residents to walk their dogs. Children play in the fields and woods near the facility. At night, wild animals living in the vicinity including deer and fox can be seen outside the perimeter.

Two weeks before the initial time of the scenario (t_0), a general alert was sent out to military installations in the region by the regional intelligence unit that their sources indicated that there was indications that an attack on a military facility would take place in the near future; the target facility was unknown, so all facilities in the region were on alert.

The day before t_0 a hole was discovered in the perimeter fence near the woods. it is uncertain whether this is indicative of a potential attack or not, because there have been incidents in the past where the local children have caused minor damage to the facility (throwing rocks, digging holes, etc.) as pranks and dares. The fencing cannot be immediately replaced, and, since there is, in addition to the intelligence alert, a further danger of unwanted human or animal entry, a robot outfitted with various sensors (camera, motion detectors) is placed near the hole for surveillance purposes.

At night under cover of darkness, the acoustic sensors pick up a metallic sound from the perimeter fence which is initially identified with a high probability as wire cutters snipping fencing. This information is transmitted to a second robot which is sent to the coordinates of the possible entry to gather information, as the patrolling guard is on his rounds at the other end of the facility. He is also notified of the unusual reading and abandons his usual round to investigate the event.

In the meantime, motion detectors report movement inside of the facility, the synthesis of which indicates that something or someone is moving in the general direction of the HAZMAT storage facility. The IR camera on the robot which was sent for surveillance transmits the information that the moving object is large, probably human. Shortly, thereafter, the patrol arrives and verifies it is human and also reports that he observes the intruder drop something next to the HAZMAT facility and sends a report to that effect to the watch station at the guard shack who requests assistance. The robot is then tasked to investigate the object dropped by the intruder and reports, via chemical sensor, that there is explosive present.

All communications within this scenario, whether between humans and robots, robots and sensors, is via BML (Battle Management Language) which we will describe in more detail in Sect. 17.6.

17.4.2 "Multi-level" Is not "Hard+Soft" Fusion

The scenario described above shows the case of a significant amount of data collected over a time span of several days from multiple sources comprising sensor arrays, robots, and human observations. These data are meant to be received by a surveillance processing node able to fuse it and reason about possible suspicious activities. For the sake of simplicity, we are assuming here a single processing node resembling a centralized architecture. The ultimate goal of the system is to assist human security operators by pointing out unusual patterns that might deserve further human analysis and validation. The amount of data is potentially very large as the scenario describes illicit activities that require several preparation steps several days before the actual breach into the monitored area is performed. In any case, such a system is supposed to be continuously running collecting both live signals from sensors and human observations. In addition to this live flow of data, the system is supposed to be able to take advantage of static information contained in repositories comprising: (1) a priori knowledge of the system (such as onto-logical knowledge supporting the general objectives and goals of the system), (2) contextual information relevant to the specific site and entities (and their pos-sible relations) being monitored, (3) historical observations, that is significant past events that are logged into the system and build up as time passes forming the information the system has accrued so far during its operation.

The data and information just described and available to the system encompass a wide range of different pieces, going from positional data, to classification labels, to detection of events and situations, etc. The live stream from sensors is not assumed to be sent directly as raw signals to the processing node but messages are sent only upon the detection of simple events of interest [7]. This means that a first level of processing is performed by the various platforms in order to send formatted mes-sages to the fusion node. However, the message maintains links to the original signals that can be accessed by the fusion node upon request.

To further clarify the nature of the data/information that the system is called to process, it should be noted that in our case here data is not only "hard" or "soft", that is, coming from sensors or humans, but it belongs to different JDL (and semantic) levels. As a matter of fact, the level of the data and the type (hard/soft) represent different dimensions and Table 17.2 Low- and high-level data versus hard and soft sources exemplifies all four combinations that can hold.

Table 17.2 Low- and high-level data versus hard and soft sources

	Low-level	High-level
Hard	Typically, raw numerical data such as positional data provided by sensors	Sensor or system outputs with high semantic value such as detection of events or situations which are typically underpinned by relations holding between the elements involved in the detected pattern (e.g. relations among detected entities, relations between entities and context, etc.)
Soft	Typically numerical information (e.g., figures giving number of observed entities) or text labels regarding entities	Semantically rich observations typically couched in natural language

In particular, what is referred to in Table 17.2 as "Low-level" fusion comprises JDL levels 0-1, while "High-level" is considered level 2 and above.

It is clear then that the first step for this significant heterogeneity of static and inflowing data and information, both hard and soft, has to be couched in a common representation means in order to be exploited in a principled way thus allowing real multi-level fusion. As we will see in the following sections, these messages are encoded according to the BML [20–22].

17.5 Use of Context in Multi-level Fusion

Context has been identified as one of the key binding elements to integrate information at different levels [1, 2, 23, 24]. An analysis of context operations to integrate JDL levels is given in [23]. Contextual knowledge can be adapted to adjust parameters of the algorithms at different levels (e.g., tracking, event detection, etc.), according to the subareas of the observed scenario where this context can be applicable. Some possible extensions of the JDL model are analyzed in [6] and [25] to address new requirements including contextual information. The aspect of interlevel information and control flow has been first discussed in [6]. The distinction of the levels of different fusion processes in order to define interactions and potential advantages is recently considered in [26].

An integrated approach to context exploitation should extend problem modeling with representations of domain knowledge, which describe situations and possible entities' interactions in the observed scenario. As mentioned, multi-level fusion approaches integrating high-level information with sensory data can be extremely useful to properly interpret the available stream of data. The role of context can be very relevant with the following considerations:

- Context is an important source of semantics, providing means to bind data and models and thus increasing fusion performance. A priori models can be better fit to the data exploiting the semantics provided by contextual information;
- Context can be provided at different JDL levels. Different types of context, from coarse to refined information, can be injected at different stages of the fusion process, possibly overlapping or overriding each other.

A general workflow of context exploitation for dynamic situational picture formation was presented in [1]. There, two strategies were pointed out to integrate context in multi-level approaches:

- *Ontology-based models* provide a formal and uniform way for specifying concepts, facts and their interrelationships to enable realistic representation of contextual knowledge. An example of contextual information represented with ontologies [27] is modeling the heterogeneous entities present in the domain and the "normal" situations (the "normalcy" model). Context of normal operations can be specified by a set of rules and axioms to classify behaviors as compliant to the operational rules or not. However, ontological reasoning by default is not well suited to deal with uncertain or imprecise knowledge, so some extensions are needed to deal with this issues appearing in any real application.

- *Markov Logic Networks* (MLNs) [28] is a statistical relational learning technique that attempts to unify the world of logic and probability by representing, reasoning, and learning in domains with complex relational and rich probabilistic structure. They are able to encode expressive domain knowledge through FOL formulas, and handle typically uncertain sensory data in a probabilistic framework that takes into account relations and dependencies through a graphical model (Markov Networks).

Both approaches are examples with very strong potential of application to situational awareness systems integrating data at different levels for their ability to model dependencies between related instances [29].

The topic of contextual information in multi-level problems has been also discussed in [30–32], basically proposing that higher level state estimates can be considered a form of "contextual feedback" for lower level processes that can be adapted accordingly. However, the multi-level incorporation of uncertain contextual information in IF processes is quite preliminary yet and can be considered an open area of research.

17.6 BML-Enabled Fusion

One of the major hurdles in fusing device-derived data, which is predominantly quantitative in nature, and human-generated data, which is produced in natural language, is finding a representation which can easily and effectively handle data and information from all types of sources in a standardized manner. Within the context of our work, we are using BML, developed under the aegis of NATO and used for military communications (orders, requests, and reports) [21].

BML was created as an unambiguous language which allows automatic processing of statements, including information gathered by both humans and by devices, therefore making it an ideal vehicle for fusion. It is a controlled language [20] based on a formal grammar, Lexical Functional Grammar (LFG) [33, 34] from the field of computation linguistics. While the original goal of BML was to facilitate the exchange of orders and requests between C2 systems of various NATO countries, it was later expanded to include various types of reports [22]. These report types include not only HUMINT information on own and enemy activities, but also status reports, location reports, task completion reports, etc. While such reports may be generated directly in BML via an interface, there has been considerable work on the automatic analysis of natural language text (HUMINT, OSINT, etc.) and conversion into BML [35]. Furthermore, BML statements can be generated uniformly even when underlying natural languages are different [36], easing cross-border communications.

The next step from communications between human players on the battlefield was the extension of BML to include communications with robotic forces [37], including swarms, drones, and unmanned vehicles. Because the robotic forces are outfitted with sensors of various types, BML report types were developed (e.g., sensor readings) [38] or extended (e.g., location report). The BML statements are generated by middleware or by algorithms reporting data or results.

The end result is that all information flowing between humans and devices in the area of endeavor can be represented in the same standardized automatically processable format. The difference between a location report from a human patrol and a location report from a robot will be essentially identical: only the identity of the report (mechanical or flesh and blood) will be different [39], and so their associated uncertainties (as discussed in the following subsections).

This means that the fusion algorithms working upon received data need only to "understand" (i.e., be able to parse BML statements for the relevant data needed) and to be able to produce their results as BML statements for use within the complex system of humans and devices to support multi-level fusion.

17.6.1 BML in Action

BML has been designed to represent orders, requests, and reports for military operations. It is also in the process of being adapted for use in a number of civilian domains such as crisis management and police investigative work.

An order is a directive for action given by a (hierarchically) superior person or unit to a subordinate unit or person. In general, the subordinate is expected to carry out to the best of its ability the action requested, unless there are extenuating circumstances. A request is similar to an order, in that it is a directive to a person or unit; however, this person or unit is not subordinate to the requester in the chain of command and therefore has the option to refuse (with or without extenuating circumstances). For example, in multinational operations, a request may be made by a unit commander of one nation to a commander of another nation's forces during a joint endeavor. Another instance would be a request from a military commander to a nonmilitary organization such as the Red Cross for assistance in a particular situation.

Reports in BML were designed to convey information from the theater of operations for the purposes of situational awareness. There are several different types of reports, including status reports which provide updates on manpower, equipment, facilities, etc., intelligence reports which deliver information on enemy movements, capabilities, etc., as well as reports on (non-military) events of importance for the field of operation (e.g., road intersection blocked due to a traffic accident, civilian protest in the town square, etc.)

Originally, reports in BML were designed for input from human sources such as units reporting updates on equipment, supplies and location, or intelligence operatives reporting on enemy movements and locations. For example, in (1a) the basic form of a unit report on equipment is presented, while in example (1b), the second company of PzGrenBtl 391 (*Coy_391_2*) reports that it has three Dingos which are operational. The report refers to the current point in time (*now*) and is reported as fact (*RPTFCT*).

(1a) [report] *own* whoRef *has* EquipmentIdentifier operational count When Certainty Label

(1b) [report] *own Coy_391_2 has Dingo operational 3 at now RPTFCT report-196;*

However, it was quickly evident that the standardized representation of information in BML statement would lend itself well to adaption for use with robotic forces. Using BML it is possible to give orders to single robots or to swarms of robots, which is processed by middleware to direct the robots to move, stop, patrol, and so on.

In example (2b) below, the robot called *Longcross* reports being ready (operational = *OPR*) at the given location identified by the coordinates *50.123,7.123* (2a is the generalized report form). The report refers to the current point in time (*now*) and is reported as fact (*RPTFCT*).

(2a) [report] *own status-gen* ReporterIdentification Status-Value AtWhere When Certainty Label

(2b) [report] *own status-gen Longcross OPR at [50.123,7.123] at now RPTFCT report-169;*

From there, the next logical step was the creation of middleware for sensors located on the robots to report their readings via BML for display on the C2 system. For example, the GPS system would report location, fuel sensors would report supply, chemical sensors would report on substances detected, etc.

In the example (3b), robot Longcross reports that the temperature at Hades is currently 16.5°. This is reported as fact for the point in time "year = 2014, month = 01, day = 31, hour = 12, minute = 00, second = 00". (Again, (3a) is the generalized form of the report.)

(3a) [report]   Phenomenon   ReporterIdentification   SensorIdentification MeasuredValue AtWhere When Certainty Label

(3b) [report] *Temperature Longcross Weather-Sensor0815 16.5degree at Hades ongoing at 20140131120000 RPTFCT report-256;*

Once BML was able to support the expression of both natural language-based (human-derived) information and sensor (device-derived) information, it was clear that BML could be used as a vehicle to support the fusion of hard and soft data, which would be represented in a similar format regardless of the source.

However, there has been one piece that has been missing: speculative and future events.

HUMINT quite often contains speculation and inference on the part of the reporter. Consider the following short HUMINT report:

(4)   "A convoy of armed vehicles was observed in the valley heading west along the river. They appear to be heading for the harbor."

The first sentence reflects an actual event, which can be considered "historical," as the observation reports actions which occurred in the past. The second sentence, however, speculates on the destination of the convoy, based upon an inference on the part of the observer. The two pieces of information cannot be treated identically: one reflects fact, one reflects possibility.

Device-derived data is always "historical," in that the sensor data are actual readings which have been gathered in the past, and therefore, are never speculative and never project future results. Algorithms operating on this sensor-derived data may utilize data collected to project into the (generally short-term) future, for example, extrapolating a possible extension of a track from a series of readings by radar devices.

When considering nonfactual (speculative, future) information such as the second sentence of the HUMINT report above, and the result of an algorithm which uses device-derived information to project the (possible, future) movement of a vehicle based upon collected data, it is clear that both pieces of information can be useful for situation awareness. However, since neither is fact, one cannot consider this information as entirely reliable (maybe the convoy turns off and heads up into the hills again), and for decision must be designated as not "true" but "possible" or "probable" based upon the opinion of the observer, an analyst or an algorithm.

Using the STANAG 2025 and the JC3IEDM A1–F6 assignment of source reliability and information credibility a weight can be assigned which reflects an assessment of the veracity of the information. In BML until now, this is the system which has been used for both historical and future/speculative information.

However, there are instances in which there may be more than one possible interpretation: for example, algorithms may produce multiple hypotheses. Suppose the HUMINT report above read

(5)   "A convoy of armed vehicles was observed in the valley heading west along the river *toward the intersection with the coastal road.*
(6)   They appear to be *either heading for the harbor in X, or backtracking to meet up with units already in Y.*"

In this case, the observer has indicated that there are two potential conclusions that could be drawn from this observation. Because the behavior at this point is unknown, we would want to capture both possible outcomes, as both could be important for situation awareness. Likewise, we would want to capture multiple interpretations of data from sensor data fusion algorithms.

Furthermore, intelligence officers often receive tips from informants which are added to the mix. For example, a report is issued containing the following statements:

(7) "According to our sources in the region, the leader of the radical extremists will be in X on Tuesday to meet with deputies.
(8) They are planning an attack on an as yet unidentified allied facility in the province, probably within the next three weeks."

This is a report of possible future actions, passed on by human informants (hearsay), which is neither inferred by the reporter, nor a result of algorithmic analysis, but "information" which may be needed for more complete situation awareness.

Originally, BML's reports were conceived to represent "real" information about movements, status, pertinent environmental information, etc. about own, allied and enemy forces in the theater of operations. Any uncertainty about the veracity of the information is represented by assigning a value representing the level of confidence in the source of the information and in the credibility of the information itself.

One solution for dealing with "non-factual" information is to continue to use the existing report structure, and adjust the weighting of the uncertainty of the information received, such that speculative or future statements are assigned a lower weighting to reflect the higher uncertainty.

There are several problems with this. One is that it may prove impossible to differentiate between "real" and "speculative" intelligence. In the case of (7), the first statement would be date-time stamped for when it was reported (today) but with a "start" time of "next Tuesday," making it clear that this concerns a future action, and therefore the information is speculative (in the future). However, in the first HUMINT example (5, 6) above, both the actual observation and the speculative statement would end up with "start" times of "now" with a certainty assignment determined by the reporter and thus would appear in BML to be indistinguishable except for content. Even should the above statements be placed in a standardized format and an uncertainty weight assigned (such as the A1—F6 scale from the JC3IEDM), it would difficult or impossible to ensure that the second statement is not in the future (e.g., during mission debriefing) viewed as "historical" and that the weighting is based on an assessment of source reliability and content credibility, rather than because the assertion is speculative.

However, it is the second statement in (8) that presents a more difficult problem to resolve, namely, how can multiple hypotheses for the same observation(s) be represented for use in threat and fusion models? The existing structures in BML could be used by weighting uncertainties, but the result is likely inelegant and, for later debriefing and analysis, confusing and unwieldy.

Therefore, we propose extending BML to add another statement type, namely "hypothesis" which would capture (multiple) speculative or future outcomes, and would be useful for "what-if" analysis. For example, the reference in (8) above to the (possible) future action of an attack on a (unspecified) military facility in the next 3 weeks could be represented as a hypothesis (which may or may not actually happen). The multiple suggestions expressed in (6) could be either expressed as two separate hypotheses for use in threat modeling.

Using the scenario described in Section 4a, the original HUMINT report (warning) will have already been converted into BML for fusion processing. As a result, the "perimeter breach" threat model has been activated but has not reached critical mass (i.e., is "humming" in the background). A patrol registered the first fence break-in via BML, as the patrolling soldier has been fitted with a tablet fastened to his arm with a BML interface for reporting. This statement has been processed automatically by the system and the warning level in the threat model has climbed slightly, but is not yet registering actual danger (the hole may have been the work of local children, who have pulled pranks before). Then the acoustic sensor array picks up noises, which are conveyed to the low-level fusion algorithm which identifies the sound as a metal-on-metal, likely wire cutters, at a location calculated by the algorithm and that algorithm delivers its results to the system. This time the threat model kicks up to a higher threat level and begins to transmit warnings of a possible perimeter breach along the fence to the human (guard) at the guard shack. At the same time, the system issues an automatic order to the closest patrol robot to proceed to the location identified by the acoustic sensor array algorithm, and likewise sends the (BML) notification to the (foot) patrolling guard who also proceeds to investigate. When the robot approaches the specified location, its motion detector/IR camera verifies the presence of movement and a large object, possibly human, and again the system is notified so that the threat model kicks up yet another notch (i.e., the "yellow" warning turns to "orange"). Stationary motion detectors located on various buildings register movement, each movement is processed and from that the probable direction of the movement is identified by another algorithm as being in the direction of a sensitive facility and that result is sent via BML to the system and distributed to the humans (guard and patrol). The patrolling solder verifies via his forearm-tablet using BML that the "large object" detected by the robot are two humans inside the perimeter fence who are carrying something toward the building which the motion detector algorithm has identified as the possible target and the threat model moves to "red alert" mode and an automatic transcript of the system proceedings is forwarded to the next level of contact within the command (e.g. to HQ). Once the threat level has reached the point that this information goes up the line, the upline center would receive real-time information forwarded by the local system (which consists of men and machines). This process is similar to the OODA processes described in Sect. 17.2.

When fusing information from ontologically different sources, uncertainty of information, obtained from the particular sources, plays an important role. When, additionally, these sources produce information on different processing levels, the importance of the uncertainty raises significantly.

One of the hurdles for the analysis of uncertainty of information derived from multiple types of sources, and in particular, when fusing device-based and human-based information is how to harmonize the uncertainty in order to make it appropriate and useful. Much of the uncertainty in device-based data can be handled by knowledge of calibration, previous performance, environmental factors, etc.

Uncertainty in human language may be based upon perception, intention and motivation of the source, and as well as the interpretation of the words themselves by the receiver of the information, factors which may be much more slippery to determine.

In such case, information uncertainty must undergo scrutiny, being examined on many points. Also the uncertainty representation should be a subject of extensive analysis in order to guarantee that: *If one source is "better" than others then uncertainty representation has to be able to indicate that.*

17.6.2 Expressing Uncertainty in BML

C2LG introduces a possibility to examine information provided by a source on many points. At present, each report line is tagged with "Certainty" attribute, which consists of three constituents: one mandatory: "Credibility," and two optional: "InformationSource" and "Reliability" [20].

"Credibility" expresses the degree of the trustworthiness of the information reported as evaluated by reporter [20]. By definition, it may be either: "reported as fact," "reported as plausible," and "reported as uncertain" or "indeterminate".

$$Cr = \{RPTFCT, RPTPLA, RPTUNC, IND\} \qquad (17.1)$$

"InformationSource" denotes the type of source from which the reporter obtained the information [20]. By definition it may be either: "eyeball observation," "forward observer," "human intelligence," or "prisoner of war."

$$IS = \{EYOBSN, REFUGEE, POW\} \qquad (17.2)$$

"Reliability" expresses the degree by which source can be trusted according to the reporter [20]. By definition it can be either: "completely reliable," "usually reliable," "fairly reliable," "not usually reliable," "unreliable," or "reliability cannot be judged."

$$R = \{A, B, C, D, E, F\} \qquad (17.3)$$

17.6.3 Exploiting BML Representations for Uncertainty Management

"Certainty" information expressed in BML may be used effectively in order to manage uncertainty in multi-level fusion system. "Credibility," "InformationSource," and "Reliability" attributes provide a descriptive view of vagueness of both: the source and the information it is providing. Even though some of the relationships among these different constituents of "certainty" may be easily drawn based on logic or common sense, e.g. *"...if "InformationSource" is set to EYOBSN it is unlikely that "Reliability" will be given as D (unreliable)..."* [20], it is important to have them defined explicitly.

In order to define the precise relationships, the most convenient way is to convert them into numbers, and then to establish the necessary dependencies.

Transforming Labels Into Numbers

For two of the attributes (Cr and *R*) transformation of qualitative descriptions, expressing information uncertainty into quantitative ones may be easily achieved by selecting appropriate number intervals (for each of the attribute values), and then simple assignment of medians of these intervals to the particular labels, e.g., for (1) it may be:

Note that "InformationSource" attribute cannot be transformed in such a way due to the fact it refers to different observation means, not to the degree of trust. Fortunately, this attribute is highly correlated with "Reliability" attribute, which undergoes the mapping mentioned above. Therefore, even if "InformationSource" is omitted while assessing quantitative uncertainties it does not matter due to the fact that its meaning for manageable uncertainty resides mainly in reliability of the source it is indicating.

Modification of Uncertainty

While discussing label-to-number transformation of the uncertainty attributes a question may be raised: Why medians, not maximal (or minimal) values, have been taken as representatives of the particular value intervals? The answer is that this kind of solution enables easy modification, both: increasing and decreasing their values in the subsequent stages of information processing.

The mentioned modification may have two origins: intrinsic and extrinsic. The intrinsic origin may be conditioned by specific algorithms of quality degradation, mostly as a function of elapsing time. The extrinsic origin may result from fusion when additional information is available. In both cases, precise determination of the uncertainty changes can be performed only if appropriate process specification is delivered.

In general, one may deduce that intrinsic degradation pace depends on the particular source, which can be reasoned from "InformationSource" attribute. This may perform a sort of application of this attribute that even though it is not directly mapped like "Credibility" and "Reliability" it affects the quality degradation pace. It is worth of notice that the quality affection may refer to "Credibility," which is a requirement very often stated in specifications for C2 systems, as well as to "Reliability" if appropriate amount of statistic data is collected.

Example Let *Certainty* be expressed by *Credibility* attribute consisting of two other attributes: *Reliability* and *Commonness* in such a way that:

Certainty → Credibility(Reliability, Commonness)

Assume, that *Commonness* is an attribute expressing usualness of occurrence of the considered event, and it is defined as follows:

$$\textbf{Commonness} = \left\{ \begin{array}{l} \text{ALWAYS\_HAPPENING, USUAL, FREQUENT, OCCURRING,} \\ \text{UNUSUAL, RARE, NEVER\_OCCURRED} \end{array} \right\}$$

When no hypothesis is privileged over another, according to Laplace's principle of insufficient reason labels-to-numbers transformation of Credibility may be performed with application of uniform distribution as presented in Table 17.3. Labels-to-numbers transformations of Reliability and Commonness may also be achieved in the same manner, which is shown in Tables 17.4, 17.5.

Certainly, if additional knowledge about superiority of any hypothesis is accessible, e.g., regarding statistics, it may be applied resulting in diversified value ranges.

Table 17.3 Example of label-to-value transformation of the "Credibility" attribute

Labels	RPTFCT	RPTPLA	RPTUNC	IND
Intervals	0.75–1	0.5–0.74	0.25–0.49	0–0.24
Values	0.875	0.625	0.375	0.125

Table 17.4 Label-to-value transformation of the "Reliability" attribute

No.	Reliability label	Value range
1	A	0.86–1.0
2	B	0.69–0.85
3	C	0.52–0.68
4	D	0.35–0.51
5	E	0.18–0.34
6	F	0–0.17

Table 17.5 Label-to-value transformation of the "Commonness" attribute

No.	Commonness label	Value range
1	ALWAYS_HAPPENING	0.85–1.0
2	USUAL	0.71–0.84
3	FREQUENT	0.57–0.70
4	OCCURRING	0.43–0.56
5	UNUSUAL	0.29–0.42
6	RARE	0.15–0.28
7	NEVER_OCCURRED	0–0.14

Table 17.6 Expected relations among reliability, commonness, and credibility

Reliability	Commonness	Credibility
1	1	1
1	7	2–3
2	1	1
2	7	2–3
3	1	2
3	7	3
4	1	3
4	7	3
5	1	3
5	7	3
6	1	4
6	7	4

The next step is to define basic relations among these three attributes, which should be taken after analysis of the edge cases. This step is typically intuitive and it is suggested to utilize any existing expert knowledge in order to model the changeability of Credibility reasonably. An example of such relation, expressed in hypothesis numbers, has been shown in Table 17.6.

After drawing the basic relations, which may be regarded as the relation frame, the next step is to define all the rest ones. Depending on the strictness of the frame elements, they can be regarded as nodes of approximation or interpolation. If precisely defined by the expert, the interpolation process seems to be a reasonable choice. In other case, e.g. where the basic relations are only roughly drawn, the approximation should be adequate enough.

In the presented example (Table 17.7), Credibility has been estimated using polynomial approximation. Particularly, the second-order approximation has been used. Thus, Credibility may be calculated in the following manner:

$$\mathrm{Cr} = a_1 \cdot R^2 + a_2 \cdot R + b_1 \cdot C^2 + b_2 \cdot C \qquad (17.4)$$

where coefficients: a_1, a_2, b_1, and b_2 may be calculated using the least squares method.

For the presented example (with the covariance Cov = 0.007791), these values may be estimated as follows:

$$a_1 = 0.0095; \quad a_2 = 0.799$$
$$b_1 = 0.05; \quad b_2 = 0.095$$

When adding some additional information, the total Credibility may be calculated according to the following formula:

$$\mathrm{Cr_T(k)} = 1 - (1 - \mathrm{Cr(k)}) \cdot (1 - \mathrm{Cr_{add}(k)}) \qquad (17.5)$$

This may be regarded as an example of extrinsic modification.

Table 17.7 Approximation of "Credibility" attribute

Reliability	Commonness	Credibility (aproximated)	Credibility (expected)	Square error: $(Cr_{approx} - Cr_{expct})^2$
0.93	0.925	0.881943	0.875	4.82E−05
0.93	0.07	0.758182	0.62	0.019094
0.77	0.925	0.751519	0.875	0.015248
0.77	0.07	0.627758	0.62	6.02E−05
0.6	0.925	0.613476	0.62	4.26E−05
0.6	0.07	0.489715	0.37	0.014332
0.43	0.925	0.475983	0.37	0.011232
0.43	0.07	0.352222	0.37	0.000316
0.26	0.925	0.339038	0.37	0.000959
0.26	0.07	0.215277	0.37	0.023939
0.085	0.925	0.19864	0.12	0.006184
0.085	0.07	0.074879	0.12	0.002036

$$E\left[(Cr_{approx} - Cr_{expct})^2\right] = 0.007791$$

Regarding the intrinsic modification, the following simple degradation formula may be applied:

$$\begin{aligned}
&\texttt{if (!Cr(k)) \{}\\
&\quad \texttt{Cr(k) = Cr(k - 1) - }\Delta\texttt{Cr(R);} \qquad (17.6)\\
&\texttt{\}}
\end{aligned}$$

which means that if at the given moment of time (k), the Credibility values cannot be calculated (due to the lack of the current measurements) they may be estimated based on the previous values, degraded with the predefined pace.

The particular values of ΔCr act as parameters and depend on reliabilities of the considered sources.

17.6.4 Harmonization of Multisource BML Information

When integrating complex fusion subsystems, one has to be aware that information being used for the fusion process may come from different processing levels. In practical terms, that means that "a common denominator" is required in order to establish the contribution weights properly with respect to their informational incomes, and uncertainties of information they are providing.

Having "Credibility" and "Reliability" attributes expressed in numbers together with paces of degradation of each one of them, one may assume to have in their hands a well-defined "common denominator". For example, if one source provides information with an error smaller than another, the "Credibility" of information from this source should be relatively greater. On the other hand, when two sources provide information of the similar "Credibility," and one source is a complex system while the other is a radar, the "Reliability" of the former may (but does not necessarily have to) be greater than the latter's but the pace of information degradation of the first one is expected to be much slower than the other's.

In the above case, harmonization of the uncertainty information may be achieved by appropriate processing of "Credibility" and "Reliability" values of the elements in the fusion. There are diverse techniques which can be applied starting with weighted averaging, through probabilistic arithmetic, and finalizing with evidential techniques.

However, the most problematic seems to be the transformation of uncertainty information to the numerical forms of "Credibility" and "Reliability." In the previous subsection, it was presented how values of these two attributes may be retrieved based on their label substitutes. Nevertheless, in case of specific low-level fusion subsystems there is a need for defining "Credibility" and "Reliability" based on estimation errors and possibly on covariance matrices. At present, BML has not yet been fully expanded to cover all necessary representation types for uncertainties generated via lower level fusion processes; this work, however, has already begun and will be further developed in the near future in the follow-on Task Group IST-132.

It is worth of noticing that one of the basic reasons for uncertainty management is decision-making. Thus, the uncertainty information is important not only due to the fact it supports the fusion of various diverse pieces of information properly and dealing with intrinsic and extrinsic modifications, but also that it allows the operator of the fusion system to make decisions upon the results.

Sophisticated algorithms for data association may produce seemingly useful information; however, if this information is to be utilized effectively its certainty (expressed in terms of the introduced measures of "Credibility" and "Reliability") must be above the predefined thresholds. In other cases, the decision should be deferred.

17.7 Conclusions

In this chapter, we have discussed the use of BML as a *lingua franca*, which is a common communication mechanism to interface fusion processes at different levels and to deal with data and information coming from both human- and device-based sources. Illustrative examples have been developed to show the capability to integrate information from multi-level hard and soft sources, and we have discussed also how uncertainty could be encoded in the corresponding messages. Further work will be directed to the algorithmic exploitation of the messages generated for a surveillance scenario being developed within the NATO Research Task Group IST-106/RTG-051 on "Information Filtering and Multi Source Information Fusion."

Acknowledgments This work was partially supported by ONRG Grant N62909-14-1-N061 and project MINECO TEC2014-57022-C2-2-R.

References

1. J. Garcia, L. Snidaro, I. Visentini, exploiting context as binding element for multi-level fusion, in *15th International Conference on Information Fusion* (Singapore, July 2012)
2. L. Snidaro, J. Garcia, J. Llinas, Context-based information fusion: a survey and discussion. Inf. Fusion **25**, 16–31 (2015). doi:10.1016/j.inffus.2015.01.002
3. E.E. White, A model for data fusion, in *Proceedings of 1st National Symposium on Sensor Fusion*, vol. 2, 1988
4. A.N. Steinberg, C.L. Bowman, F.E. *White, revisions to the JDL data fusion model, presented at the Joint NATO/IRIS Conference* (Quebec, October 1998)
5. A.N. Steinberg, C.L. Bowman, F.E. *White, sensor fusion: architectures, algorithms, and applications*, in *Proceedings of the SPIE*, vol. 3719, 1999
6. J. Llinas, C.L. Bowman, G.L. Rogova, A.N. Steinberg, E.L. Waltz, F.E. White, revisiting the JDL data fusion model II, in *Proceedings of the Seventh International Conference on Information Fusion*, vol. II (Stockholm, Sweden, June 2004), pp. 1218–1230
7. J. Biermann, P. Hörling, L. Snidaro, Experiences and challenges in automated support for intelligence in asymmetric operations. J. Adv. Inf. Fusion **8**(2), 101–118 (2013)
8. M. Bedworth, J. O'Brien, The omnibus model: a new model of data fusion?, IEEE Aerosp. Electron. Syst. Mag., **15**(4), (2000)
9. E.P. Blasch, S. Plano, Level 5: user refinement to aid the fusion process, *in Multisensor, Multisource Information Fusion: Architectures, Algorithms, and Applications 2003*, vol. 5099, ed by B. Dasarathy (Proceedings of the SPIE, 2003)
10. S.C. Shapiro, D.R. Schlegel, natural language understanding for soft information fusion, in *16th International Conference on Information Fusion* (Istanbul, July 2013)
11. K. Date, G.A. Gross, S. Khopkar, R. Nagi, K. Sambhoos, Data association and graph analytical processing of hard and soft intelligence data, in *16th International Conference on Information Fusion* (Istanbul, July 2013)
12. H. Köhler, D.A. Lambert, J. Richter, G. Burgess, T. Cawley, implementing soft fusion, in *16th International Conference on Information Fusion* (Istanbul, July 2013)
13. B. Pietropaoli, M. Dominici, F. Weis, Virtual sensors and data fusion in a multi-level context computing architecture, in *16th International Conference on Information Fusion* (Istanbul, July 2013)
14. M.A. Solano, J. Carbone, Systems engineering for information fusion: towards enterprise multi-level fusion integration, in *16th International Conference on Information Fusion* (Istanbul, July 2013)
15. M. Haberjahn, K. Kozempel, Multi level fusion of competitive sensors for automotive environment perception, in *16th International Conference on Information Fusion* (Istanbul, July 2013)
16. K. Krenc, Updating attribute fusion results with additional evidence using DSmT, in *15th International Conference on Information Fusion* (Singapore, July 2012)
17. K. Krenc, F. Smarandache, application of new absolute and relative conditioning rules in threat assessment, in *16th International Conference on Information Fusion* (Istanbul, July 2013)
18. J. Biermann, V. Nimier, J. Garcia, K. Rein, K. Krenc, L. Snidaro, Multi-level fusion of hard and soft information, in *Proceedings of the 17th International Conference on Information Fusion* (Salamanca, Spain, July 7–10, 2014)
19. J. Biermann, V. Nimier, J. Garcia, K. Rein, K. Krenc, L. Snidaro, Standardized representation via BML to support multi-level fusion of hard and soft information, in *Proceedings of the NATO IST/SET-126 Symposium on "Information Fusion (Hard and Soft) for Intelligence,*

Surveillance & Reconnaissance (ISR)", Joint Symposium IST-106 and SET-189 (Norfolk, Virginia, US, May 04–05, 2015)
20. U. Schade, M. Hieb, M. Frey, K. Rein, Command and Control Lexicon Grammar (C2LG) Specification. ITF/2012/02, pp. 33–34
21. U. Schade, M.R. Hieb, Development of formal grammars to support coalition command and control: a battle management language for orders, requests, and reports, in *11th ICCRTS* (Cambridge, UK, 2006)
22. U. Schade, M.R. Hieb, battle management language: a grammar for specifying reports, in *2007 Spring Simulation Interoperability Workshop (Paper 07S-SIW-036)* (Norfolk, VA, Mar 2007)
23. L. Snidaro, I. Visentini, J. Llinas, G.L. Foresti, Context in fusion: some considerations in a JDL perspective, in *16th International Conference on Information Fusion* (Istanbul, July 2013)
24. L. Snidaro, L. Vaci, J. García, E. Marti, A.-L. Jousselme, K. Bryan, D.D. Bloisi, D. Nardi, A framework for dynamic context exploitation, in *Proceedings of the 17th International Conference on Information Fusion*, July 6–9, 2015, (Washington, D.C., USA, 2015), pp. 1160–1167
25. E.P.Blasch, A. Steinberg, S. Das, J. Llinas, C. Chong, O. Kessler, E. Waltz, F. White, revisiting the JDL model for information exploitation, in *16th International Conference on Information Fusion* (Istanbul, July 2013)
26. K. Rein, J. Biermann, Your high-level information is my low-level data. A new look at terminology for multi-level fusion, in *16th International Conference on Information Fusion* (Istanbul, July 2013)
27. J. Gómez-Romero, M.A. Serrano, J. García, J.M. Molina, G. Rogova, Context-based multi-level information fusion for harbor surveillance. Inf. Fusion **21**, 173–186 (2015)
28. M. Richardson, P. Domingos, Markov logic netwoks. Mach. Learn. **62**, 107–136 (2006)
29. L. Snidaro, I. Visentini, K. Bryan, Fusing uncertain knowledge and evidence for maritime situational awareness via Markov Logic Networks. Inf. Fusion **21**, 159–172 (2015). doi:10.1016/j.inffus.2013.03.004
30. R. Glinton, J. Giampapa, K. Sycara, A markov random field model of context for high-level information fusion, in *Proceedings of the 9th International Conference on Information Fusion* (Florence, Italy, July, 2006)
31. A.N. Steinberg, C.L. Bowman, adaptive context discovery and exploitation, in *Proceedings Of the 16th International Conference on Information Fusion* (Istanbul, Turkey, July 9–12, 2013)
32. A.N. Steinberg, L. Snidaro, Levels?, in *Proceedings of the 18th International Conference on Information Fusion*, July 6–9, 2015, (Washington, D.C., USA, 2015), pp. 1985-1992
33. W.-O. Huijsen, Controlled language—an introduction, in *proceedings of the Second International Work-shop on Controlled Language Applications (CLAW98)* (Language Technologies Institute, Carnegie Mellon University, Pittsburgh, PA, May 1998), pp. 1–15
34. J. Bresnan, *Lexical-Functional Syntax* (Blackwell, Malden, MA, 2001)
35. C. Jenge, S. Kawaletz, U. Schade, *Combining Different NLP Methods for HUMINT Report Analysis* (NATO RTO IST Panel Symposium, Stockholm, Sweden, 2009)
36. S. Kawaletz, K. Rein, Methodology for standardizing content for fusion of military reports generated in different natural languages, in *Proceedings of MCC 2010* (Wroclaw, Poland, 2010)
37. T. Remmersmann, B. Brüggemann, M. Frey, Robots to the ground, in *Concepts and Implementations for Innovative Military Communications and Information Technologies* (Military University of Technology, Sept 2010), pp. 61–68
38. T. Remmersmann, B. Brüggemann, reporting sensor information using battle management language, in *Proceedings of MCC2011* (Amsterdam, 2011)
39. K. Rein, U. Schade, T. Remmersmann, using battle management language to support all source integration, in *Proceedings of NATO Joint Symposium SET-183 and IST-112* (Quebec City, 2012)

Chapter 18
Context-Based Fusion of Physical and Human Data for Level 5 Information Fusion

Erik Blasch, Riad I. Hammoud, Haibin Ling, Dan Shen, James Nagy and Genshe Chen

Abstract Information fusion consists of organizing a set of data for correlation in time, association over collections, and estimation in space. There exist many methods for object tracking and classification; however, video analytics systems suffer from robust methods that perform well in all operating conditions (i.e., scale changes, occlusions, high signal-to-noise ratios, etc.). Challenging scenarios where context can play a role includes: object labeling, track correlation/stitching through dropouts, and activity recognition. In this chapter we propose a novel framework to fuse video data with text data for enhanced simultaneous tracking and identification. The need for such methodology resides in answering user queries, linking information over different collections, and providing meaningful product reports. For example, text data can establish that a pedestrian is crossing the road in a low-resolution video and/or the activity type is the object turning. Together, physics-derived and human-derived fusion (PHF) enhances situation awareness, provides situation understanding, and affords situation assessment. PHF is an example of hard (e.g., video) and soft (i.e., text) data fusion that links Level 5 user

E. Blasch (✉) · J. Nagy
Air Force Research Lab, Rome, NY, USA
e-mail: erik.blasch@gmail.com

J. Nagy
e-mail: james.nagy.2@us.af.mil

R.I. Hammoud
BAE Systems, Burlington, MA, USA
e-mail: riad.hammoud@baesystems.com

H. Ling
Department of Computer and Information Science, Temple University, Philadelphia, PA, USA
e-mail: hbling@temple.edu

D. Shen · G. Chen
Intelligent Fusion Technology, Germantown, MD, USA
e-mail: dshen@intfusiontech.com

G. Chen
e-mail: gchen@intfusiontech.com

© Springer International Publishing Switzerland (outside the USA) 2016   479
L. Snidaro et al. (eds.), *Context-Enhanced Information Fusion*,
Advances in Computer Vision and Pattern Recognition,
DOI 10.1007/978-3-319-28971-7_18

refinement to Level 1 object tracking and characterization. A demonstrated example for multimodal text and video sensing is shown where context provides the means for associating the multimode data aligned in space and time.

Keywords Level 5 user refinement · High-level information fusion · Semantic label · L1 tracker · Hard–soft fusion · Data dictionary · Target template

18.1 Introduction

Information fusion has a long history of development starting from data and sensor fusion to information fusion and management [1]. Low-level information fusion (LLIF) consists of filtering, estimation, and control for target tracking and classification. High-level information fusion (HLIF) consists of sensor, user, and mission (SUM) management [2]. Management of information includes resource data (e.g., text) that can be gathered a priori or developed from external sources that is matched to current collections (e.g., video).

Figure 18.1 highlights the elements of information fusion from which context is provided from the user (e.g., mission) to the machine and the machine provides analytics (e.g., visual) to perform functions of object tracking and classification (LLIF) as well as situation and impact assessment (HLIF) [3, 4]. To support both assessment and analysis, context provides information from the sensor, target, and environment operating conditions [5]. The user must use judgment (e.g., intuition,

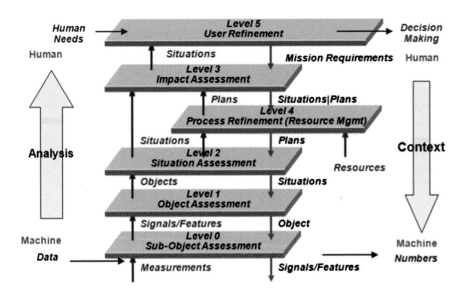

Fig. 18.1 Information fusion levels

Fig. 18.2 Multi-intelligence system

experience, decision making, trust, etc.) in the analysis [6] that comes from contextual understanding of the situation [7, 8]. Contextual assessment is an important concept that needs to be matched with context management [9].

Context information includes geospatial intelligence (such as road networks [10] and locations of interest), target types (such as vehicles), cultural factors (social networks), and mission objectives. In each case, context provides information to guide the assessment of real-time collected information for such applications as target tracking [11] and classification [12]. Likewise, new information (such as target intent classification from text reports) could be associated for target tracking and identification [13, 14] from multiple observations [15].

For multi-intelligence gathering systems, such as in Fig. 18.2, there is a need to understand, integrate, and deduce the situation from multiple types of information [16, 17]. Typically, geographical information provides a unifying picture for video and text analytics.

The rest of the chapter is organized as follows. Section 18.2 discusses the physical (hard) and human-derived (soft) analytics. Section 18.3 describes methods of physical- and human-derived fusion. Section 18.4 discusses the tracker and 18.5 presents an example. Section 18.6 provides a discussion and 18.7 concludes the chapter.

18.2   Video and Text Analytics

There are many cases in which video and text are collected together, yet few approaches in combing these modalities. In the following, we describe the elements of physical-based sensing using video tracking and human-based sensing with textual data as an example.

18.2.1 *Physical-Based Sensing—Video Tracking*

Obvious examples of hard measurements from radar, electro-optical, and biomedical data are widely available. Video tracking has been widely studied so we focus on activity analysis through multi-intelligence fusion for context assessment. Standard methods such as appearance-based (e.g., color, structure, etc.) image tracking support activity analysis.

One approach is to bridge the gap between low-level image features and high-level semantic representations [18] such as extracting keywords from a news broadcast. Capturing relevant text attributes in the video can provide audio (linguistic semantics) and video (image features) for context. Likewise, semantic video modeling [19] could include objects (e.g., person), verbs (e.g., motion), pruning (scene descriptors), and attributes (fast, slow, north). Results demonstrated the ability to identify relevant videos related to semantic concepts.

Pattern analysis includes many forms of data aggregation such as motion information detected from tracking using a dynamic Bayesian network (DBN) [20]; in [21], a hidden Markov model (HMM) to determine complex events based on tracks. They use a spatial distance as a semantic relationship "close" to link when a vehicle is close to an airplane. Additional developments [22] include a DBN as a generalization to a HMM to model events, and when tracks are fragmented can better link objects with observed recognition (or identity). Using semantic labels for events (e.g., truck is close to plane), then the tracklets can be combined for a complex event (e.g., plane refueling) through analysis of an event log-likelihood score.

Pixel level probability density functions (pdfs) of object tracks can be modeled as a multivariate Gaussian mixture model (GMM) of the motion (destination location and transition time) and the size (width and height) parameters of the objects at that location [23]. Track outputs, with unsupervised expectation-maximization-based learning of every GMM and scene modeling, detect local as well as global anomalies in object tracks. Other techniques include clustering [24, 25], histogram of gradients [26, 27], and bag of visual words [28] that can label pattern of life [29] activities.

The semantic differences between people and vehicles can be modeled using their size and movement characteristics. A good example is the human-behavior markup language (HBML) based on the environment, entities, behaviors, and observations [30]. Behaviors come from cyber (websites), social (interaction), spatial (proximity), and logistics (transactions). Likewise, audiovisual features labeling over vehicles [31] and people activities for video indexing and retrieval [32]. Together, the use of context, [33], from the machine or human helps refine and highlight activities in video tracking [34].

18.2.2 Human-Based Sensing—Text Processing

Soft data (not to be confused with soft processing such as fuzzy logic) typically includes text [35]. One common example of text data is the synthetic counterinsurgency (SYNCOIN) data set [36]. Other text data collections analysis includes Twitter [37].

Clustering is a popular detection method for imagery (pixels), tracks (groups), and text (topics) to bin content into classes for labeling. For the text, however, we first seek information extraction (IE) from a chat message (i.e., microtext) or a document (e.g., using Sphynx or Apache NLP) as an automated approach [38]. In addition to employing information extraction, the use of text analytics techniques for prediction (classification) enhances content extraction [36]. Prior work in relational learning has demonstrated that significant improvements in model accuracy are possible by leveraging feature relations [39], including when modeling microtext. For example, recent work with microtext has demonstrated that higher order Naive Bayes (HONB) statistically significantly outperforms learning approaches based on a non-relational feature space [40, 41]. HONB is a relational learning approach based on higher order learning™ [42]. For the analyst, the goal is useful text analytics to provide semantic indications and warnings to video data [43].

Given the developments in video and text processing, we seek to combine these for effects-based analysis.

18.3 Physical to Human Data Fusion

PHF fusion includes determining the attribute (signal, feature), classification (type), and identification (allegiance) from video or text data. Notions of hard–soft fusion include filtering, correlation, and association of data types.

18.3.1 Effects-Based Labeling

Many times an operator desires not only the type/allegiance semantic label, but also the impact that the target might have on their operations. The threat can come from many sources:

- Spatial (location relative to own forces),
- Speed (method of travel),
- Equipment (types of weapons), or
- Intent (a prior known interests).

Figure 18.3 demonstrates information fusion of multi-INT data from a paradigm of effects-based operations (EBO) [44]. The data fusion information group (DFIG)

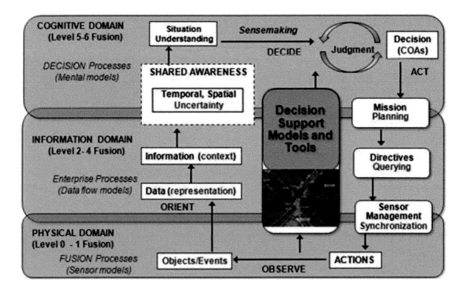

Fig. 18.3 Fusion of information using effects-based reasoning

process model [45] levels (L) are indicated on the left, over cognitive, information, and physical domains.

The physical domain includes data characterization (L0) and object assessment (L1). The information domain builds on the data from the physical domain for situation (L2) and impact (L3) assessment with sensor management (L4). The cognitive domain includes user (L5) and mission (L6) refinement.

From Fig. 18.3, information fusion progresses from object analysis to shared awareness through context. A key issue in the analysis is uncertainty reduction that comes from tracking spatial accuracy [46] and temporal context [47]. A shared ontology [48] is needed to characterize the uncertainty reduction in decision making [49]. The uncertainty reduction can be determined from the planning, querying, and sensor management over situation beliefs [50], measures of performance [51], and measures of effectiveness [52, 53].

18.3.2   Query-Based Analysis

When a user is processing a video, there are multiple ways they can interact such as passive (autonomy) and interactive (automation). If the user interacts with the video system, they are reasoning over the image, providing annotations, and assessing the exploitation results. Future systems would allow the user to manually query over the image to request more information such as filtering, highlighting, and call-outs to prescribed events. Another option is to allow the user to audibly query the image

Table 18.1 Semantic query analysis

Semantic label	Question	Information
Image label	Who	EEI
Object label	What	PVO
Edge label	Where	Space
Track label	When	Time
Track and ID label	Why	Intent

analytics, such as for requesting a label. The difficulty then is to determine where and what the audible query is referring to. One could call out a semantic label (e.g., white car), but then image processing system needs to know where in the image the semantic entity is. One proposed method is to provide location-specific labels. These types of queries need to be refined over the questions being asked.

Table 18.1 provides a framework for video-based processing with text information. For the image label, it is a contextual analysis which can be gathered from the essential elements of information (EEI) requests for the image location and abstracted from the metadata. Within the image there would need to be descriptors of the person, vehicle, and others (PVO) designation of the object of interest. In the image, references are needed as to the pixel location for spatial analysis. The spatial call-out provides notions of edge detection for the imaging routine. Likewise, the time of the event is needed to highlight interactions for the tracking such as track start and kinematic behavior. Given the various classification labels, there is still a meta-reasoning needed as to the track and identification analysis. Identification, as opposed to classification looks at the behavioral analysis to determine the intent. Intent is usually associated with an activity [such as positioning an improvised explosive device (IED) as per the example in the SYCOIN challenge problem].

Since we are concerned with V2T (Video-to-Text) versus static imagery analysis, the labels will change due to the dynamic context in the image. The querying analysis must allow for stimulus–response capabilities. One good example of man–machine interaction is a check list (e.g., pilot check list). A goal is to then design both a check list for the machine to refine estimates as well as an annotation system where the user can associated information based on their intuitive knowledge, experience, and reasoning. The V2T fusion is thus a systems approach in which a user can call out key information they are interested in as well as manual refined the annotated information (Level 5 fusion).

Our design is shown in Fig. 18.4. On the lower right, the user interacts with the system through a user-defined operating picture (UDOP) [1] viewer. In a passive mode, the user can accept the autonomy of the video exploitation and text extraction results. However, for automation, the user would start by providing query requests. These queries become part of the text data (i.e., chats or external reports). Both the video and the text then need to have space–time designations. With V2T synchronization and alignment through filtering, V2T is enabled. Given multiple possibilities, V2T reasons over events and activities of interest (AOI) to

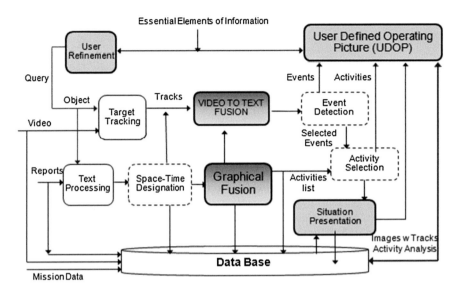

Fig. 18.4 Physical and human-derived information fusion design

find the salient requests that respond to the queries. Then, a video clip is provided over the time–space analysis and place in a database for continuity.

18.3.3 Video and Text Descriptors for Analytics

We want to enable *dynamic* adaptation to changing mission requirements or operating conditions. The first concern is to determine the usefulness of the *audile* information which is relevant, irrelevant, and clutter. Additionally, there are call-outs to the video, discussions with multiple users, and then text that is collected from outside. For example, when watching a sports game, the announcer calls out what is happening in the game, provides internal discussions with the other commentator, and then brings in outside facts of previous performances of the players. Sometimes, there are discussions associated with the microphone which is clutter, but a call-out. Internal clutter discusses the scene between users and external clutter might be how the team got to the game. Nonrelevant information also has to be designated. Table 18.2 then lists the key concepts for text.

The text information can be mapped to the video constructs. Table 18.3 lists some designations between relevant and nonrelevant information. The typical analysis for the image processing community is to key the target credibility results with high probability.

Clutter includes spurious signals inducing change detection, many short tracks, low probability of classification, false alarms, and neutral or routine activities.

Table 18.2 Text descriptor categories

Text	Relevant	Clutter
Call-outs	Player, other	How do I use the mic?
Internal	Clarifications	How to zoom camera?
External	Commercial break	Score of other game?

Table 18.3 Video descriptor categories

Video	Relevant	Nonrelevant
Detections	Players, ball location	Birds, people on sidelines
Tracks	Those players in the designated area	Other team members, referees
Classes	Home, Away	Other teams in audience
IDs	Offense, Defense, Other (threats based on activity)	Distant actions not in designated areas
Credibility	High probability	Low probability

18.3.4   Context as a Means of Correlation of Video and Text

The use of context can be of many forms such as context aware tracking. A scenario is defined as $\pi = f(s, t, g, c)$, where s is the spatial location, t is the time, g is the geography, and c is the culture. Given some context (g, c) from historical analysis, we need to determine if the hypothesis is true for an association. The hypothesis assessment is done over the relevant information which has been decomposed from the text and video observable quantities. Context, such as roads (g), can refine the hypothesis space for targets and tracks. To determine the validity of the hypothesis, we can use context information in relation to the utility of the information against the query (c) from the text information (s, t). A detailed example of these attributes of context is shown in Fig. 18.19 as revealed to an operator, while Fig. 18.14 highlights the graphical association of (s, t) with (g, c).

Other approaches include graphical fusion methods that link tracking networks to semantic networks. For example, if a semantic network links people from a social network, then it is likely that these people move together. With text extraction of external reports and video detections of suspicious activities, a positive tracking and identification could be rendered as to an activity of interest. We highlight these results in Sect. 18.5.5.

Given space limitation, we next describe only the video tracking method used for the V2T association, where the HONB for text extraction is described in [40–43]. Specifically, the tracking details are highlighted as to where the context extracted from the text content is used to refine the track estimate.

E. Blasch et al.

18.4 L1 Tracking Framework

The L1 particle filter tracker [54–57] takes advantages of the sparse representation and compressive sensing techniques. The original L1 tracker was computationally expensive due to the intensive computation of L1 solutions. But several techniques have been developed to speed up the process for near real-time analysis. In this section, we highlight the particle filtering approach in Sect. 18.4.1 followed by sparse representation in Sect. 18.4.2, a method to deal with occlusion and noise in Sect. 18.4.3, and then a minimum bound to remove particles associated with objects in Sect. 18.4.4. Using the results presented in Sect. 18.5 with the text call-outs, we highlight the correspondence to the tracker.

18.4.1 Particle Filter

The particle filter provides a means to sequentially estimate the posterior distribution of random variables related to Markov chains. In visual tracking, it serves as an important tool for estimating the target in the next frame without knowing the concrete observation probability. It consists of two steps: prediction and update. Specially, at the frame t, denote x_t as the state describing the location and the shape of the target, $y_{1:t-1} = \{y_1, y_2,..., y_{t-1}\}$ the observation of the target from the first frame to the frame $t - 1$. Particle filter proceeds in two steps with following two probabilities:

Given a set I of T consecutive frames, we need to remove the camera motion

$$p(x_t|y_{1:t-1}) = \int p(x_t|x_{t-1})p(x_{t-1}|y_{1:t-1})\mathrm{d}x_{t-1} \tag{18.1}$$

$$p(x_t|y_{1:t}) = \frac{p(y_t|x_t)p(x_t|y_{1:t-1})}{p(y_t|y_{1:t-1})} \tag{18.2}$$

The optimal state for frame t is obtained according to the maximal approximate posterior probability: $x_t^* = \arg\max_x p(x|y_{1:t})$. The posterior probability is approximated using finite samples $S_t = \{x_t^1, x_t^2,...x_t^N\}$ with different weights $W = \{w_t^1, w_t^2,...w_t^N\}$, where N is the number of samples. The samples are sampled according to the sequential importance distribution $\Pi(x_t|y_{1:t}, x_{1:t-1})$ and weights are updated by

$$w_t^i \propto w_{t-1}^i \frac{p(y_t|x_t^i)p(x_t^i|x_{t-1}^i)}{\Pi(x_t|y_{1:t}, x_{1:t-1})} \tag{18.3}$$

When $\Pi(x_t|y_{1:t}, x_{1:t-1}) = p(x_t|x_{t-1})$, the above equation takes a simplified form $w_t^i \propto w_{t-1}^i p(y_t|x_t^i)$. Then, the weights of some particles may keep increasing and fall into the degeneracy case. To avoid such a case, in each step, a resampling strategy is used to generate samples with equal weights according to previous sample weights distribution.

18.4.2 Sparse Representation

The sparse representation model aims at calculating the observation likelihood for sample state x_t, i.e., $p(z_t|x_t)$. The observation likelihood can be related to the target template such as person, vehicle, or other. At the frame t, given the target template set $T_t = [t_t^1, t_t^2, \ldots t_t^n]$, let $S_t = \{x_t^1, x_t^2, \ldots x_t^N\}$ denote the sampled states and $O_t = \{y_t^1, y_t^2, \ldots y_t^N\}$ the corresponding candidate target patch in target template space. The sparse representation model can then be written as

$$y_t^i = T_t a_T^i + I a_I^i, \quad \forall y_t^i \in O_t, \tag{18.4}$$

where I is the trivial template set (identity matrix) and $a_t^i = [a_T^i, a_I^i]$ is sparse in general. Additionally, nonnegative constraints are imposed on a_T^i for the robustness of the L1 tracker. Consequently, for each candidate target patch y_t^i, the sparse representation of y_t^i can be found via solving the following L1-norm related minimization with nonnegative constraints:

$$\min_a \frac{1}{2} \|y_t^i - Aa\|_2^2 + \lambda \|a\|_1, \quad a \succcurlyeq 0, \tag{18.5}$$

where $A = [T_t, I, -I]$.

Finally, the observation likelihood of state x_t^i is given as

$$p(z_t|x_t^i) = \frac{1}{\Gamma} \exp\left\{-a\|y_t^i - T_t c_T^i\|_2^2\right\}, \tag{18.6}$$

where a is a constant controlling the shape of the Gaussian kernel, Γ is a normal factor, and c_T^i is the minimizer of the L1-norm minimization restricted to T_t. The parameters of the observation state can be related to the call-out information such as a text call provided by the user in designation a person (versus vehicle) which identifies the shape. Likewise, the target designation from the text is modified by c_T^i, in relation to the text action such as running. Together the context of the call-out target and its changes in appearance relative to the text modify the likelihood update.

Then, the optimal state x_t^* of frame t is obtained by

$$x_t^* = \arg \max_{x_t^i \in S_t} p(z_t|x_t^i). \tag{18.7}$$

In addition, a template update scheme is adopted to overcome pose and illumination changes.

18.4.3 A Modified Version to Deal with Occlusion and Noise

There are two types of dictionary templates: target and trivial templates. The dictionary templates derive from the text-based templates of person, vehicle, and other as described in Sect. 18.4.2. The target templates are updated dynamically for representing target objects during the tracking process. The trivial template (identity matrix I) is for representing occlusions, background, and noise. However, since parts of objects may also be represented by the trivial templates, the region detected by the original tracker sometimes does not fit the target very accurately. However, the user call-out provides some context as to when the target template is not occluded (or in full view) as called out by the user. Likewise, the user can call out descriptive information as to the impending target occlusion such as the "target is going behind the building."

We use a modified version for improving tracking accuracy. The new model is based on the following observation. When there are no occlusions, the target in the next frame should be well approximated by a sparse linear combination of target templates with a small residual. Thus, the energy of the coefficients in a associate with trivial templates, or trivial coefficients, should be small. On the other hand, when there exist noticeable occlusions, the target in the next frame cannot be well approximation by any sparse linear combination of target templates; the large residual (corresponding to occlusions, background, and noise in an ideal situation) will be compensated by the part from the trivial templates, which leads to a large energy of the trivial coefficients. The minimization is obviously not optimal since it does not differentiate these two cases.

To optimize the usage of the trivial templates in the tracking, we need to adaptively control the energy of the trivial coefficients, that is, when occlusions are negligible, the energy associated with trivial templates should be small. When there are noticeable occlusions, the energy should be allowed to be large. This motivation leads to the following minimization model for the L1 tracker:

$$\min_a \frac{1}{2}\|y - A'a\|_2^2 + \lambda\|a\|_1 + \frac{\mu_t}{2}\|a_I\|_2^2, \quad \text{s.t. } a_T \succeq 0, \qquad (18.8)$$

where $A' = [T_t, I]$, $a = [a_T; a_I]$ are the coefficients associated with target templates and trivial templates, respectively, and the parameter μ_t is a parameter to control the energy in trivial templates. In our implementation, the value of μ_t for each state is automatically adjusted using the occlusion detection method, that is, if occlusions are detected, $\mu_t = 0$; otherwise, μ_t is set as some pre-defined constant. The benefit of the additional L2 norm regularization term is that the trivial template coefficients from minimization are small and lead to better tracking results.

18.4.4   Minimum Error Bound

A minimal error bounding method is proposed to reduce the number of needed L1
minimizations. For reducing the processing, some of the call-outs can be used to
reduce the minimization by the target template call-out. Actually, the method is
based on the following observation:

$$\|T_t a - y\|_2^2 \geq \|T_t \hat{a} - y\|_2^2, \quad \forall a \in \mathbb{R}^N, \tag{18.9}$$

where

$$\hat{a} = \arg \min_a \|T_t a - y\|_2^2 \tag{18.10}$$

Consequently, for any samples x_t^i, its observation likelihood has the following
upper bound:

$$p(z_t|x_t^i) = \frac{1}{\Gamma} \exp\left\{-a\|y_t^i - T_t c_T^i\|_2^2\right\} \triangleq q(z_t|x_t^i) \tag{11}$$

where $q(y_t^i|x_t^i)$ is the probability upper bound for state x_t^i. It is seen that if
$q(z_t|x_t) < \frac{1}{2N}\sum_{j=1}^{i-1} p(z_t|x_t^j)$, then the sample x_t^i will not appear in the resample set. In
other words, x_t^i can be discarded without being processed. Thus, a two-stage
resample method is used to significantly reduce the number of samples needed in
tracking.

The L1 tracker outputs the results in the form of tracks that need to be associated
with the text processing. The text processing analysis is described in [38].

18.5   Physical and Human-Derived Example

For our example, we describe the context architecture that uses the context information to integrate the text and video information. The results are presented as to
the graphical text information in Sect. 18.5.1 as well as the video analytics of the
tracking results in Sect. 18.5.2. Then, in Sect. 18.5.3 we show how the data is
integrated in time followed by integration in time in Sect. 18.5.4. Section 18.5.5
shows the combined results of graphical fusion in time and space where context is
established from the added information from the text information.

For many cases, there is cultural information available either from video sensing
(geography) or human reports (text and situation call-outs). Figure 18.5 highlights
the association where HLIF includes the mission requirements that the user is
interested in. The LLIF is the tracker and text information. For the text, there is both
an individual user (call-outs), a team (internal text), and then external messages.
Shown on the left is context management [8]. Together the V2T must output a

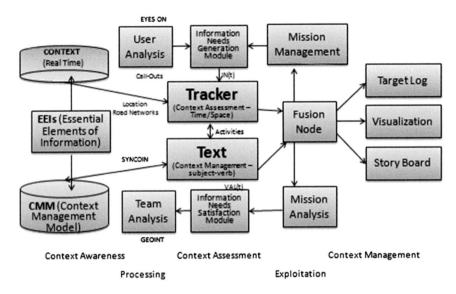

Fig. 18.5 PHF system description

target log of processing, situation awareness visualization, and any related story content.

18.5.1 Text from SYNCOIN

The story content we use comes from the SYNCOIN data. Methods of SYNCOIN analysis have been reported for vehicle-borne IED that we leverage use cases. From the SYNCOIN data, text information is associated with the activities of interest. For example, from SYNCOIN [36]:

Citizen tip	A local citizen in Rashid states that a ***group of people*** were seen loading a large tank onto a ***Toyota flatbed*** truck in the early afternoon
Tipline call	line ***caller*** from Qadisiya says, "Everyone inside (the Green Zone) has lights and air-conditioning, fresh produce and we have none of that…when will Baghdad again be enjoyed by Iraqis?"
TUAS video	***T-UAS observes*** a white truck matching the description of one of ***two Toyotas*** in the designated area. The truck turns and parks at a gas station in a parking lot near a coalition checkpoint
IED attack	A large explosion occurred outside of the Green Zone some 500 m from the US checkpoint

Note that the italics text refers to a text report and/or a video report. We seek to associate activities extracted from the text and the video so as to improve situation understanding. The first step is data *registration* (synchronization, alignment) to *correlate* information in time and space [58]. For *associating* the text to the video we utilize semantic descriptions to link entities in space (e.g., near) [59] and form activity patterns (e.g., kinematic movement and semantic labels) with *event* demarcations in time.

We perform semantic labeling by extracting information from text to form an activity pattern. An activity pattern is a graph in which we represent the activities, entities, and relations between them that form the pattern. In this case, we have a *loading pattern*, as shown in the left side of Fig. 18.6. In a similar fashion, we process the video to track and characterize objects in the scene. For example, a white pick-up truck is detected as stopping, resulting in the activity pattern on the right side of Fig. 18.6. From this representation, we can form a semantic track whereby activity patterns derived from text and video are associated to each other based on correlations between kinematic and attribute information, such as color and type of vehicle. We also use the activity patterns to learn patterns of life with our multi-intelligence activity pattern learning engine (MAPLE) for rendering activity density heat maps of detected activities (e.g., vehicle stops) and alerting to activities that are spatially or temporally anomalous.

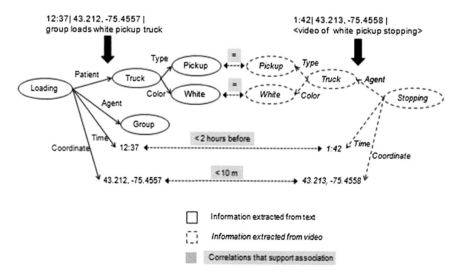

Fig. 18.6 PHF association

18.5.2   *Video Analysis*

Using the SYNCOIN example, the mission storyboard identifies that something is happening corresponding with the video exploitation. Using the L1 tracker, we can get track information on people and vehicles in the videos. Shown in Figs. 18.7, 18.8, and 18.9 are the results using the DARPA VIRAT data set (http://www. viratdata.org/). The video analysis labels the relevant objects and the associated activities (walking, stopped) as well as people activities (groups). As a use case, only part of the SYNCOIN scenario provides information as to the surveillance up to the story board analysis (for example, not a video with exploitation). Here, we have a forensic analysis of the attributes of key observations between the times of

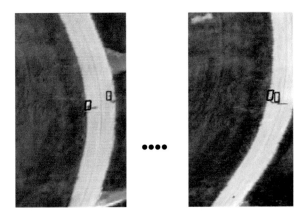

Fig. 18.7 People movement detection (person–person interaction)

Fig. 18.8 People activity detection (person–environment interaction)

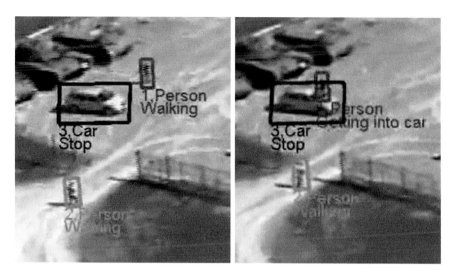

Fig. 18.9 People getting into car (person–object interaction)

the video collection. With the SYCOIN, we can initiate tracks and determine a time, location, and set of activities for analysis. For the V2T association between the video and the SYNCOIN external text, there are also call-outs associated with someone watching the video.

18.5.3 Video–to–Text Correlation in Space

For the videos, we have designated call-outs that provide metadata for time and space:

0:08–0:18	People walking on road,
0:30–1:15	People enter parking lot,
1:55–1:96	People milling around a building,
2:39–2:50	Person running,
2:56–3:15	Person gets into a parked car (near gas station),
3:22–4:26	Person gets out of car, with others,
5:05-5:08	Black car drives away.

Using the SYNCOIN format, we can correlate in space and time the tracks and the text that relates to the information needs. Figure 18.10 overlays the information from a database that provides context information. The contextual information includes building numbers and relevant information such as roads, buildings, and water towers. The listed semantic information represents significant activity.

Fig. 18.10 Visualization with Google earth

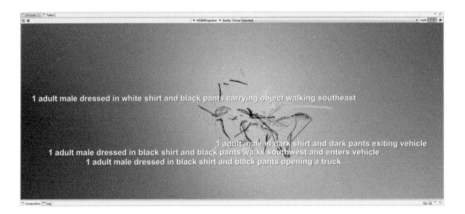

Fig. 18.11 Track data with semantic call-outs for space correlation

Figure 18.11 shows the extended tracks with the key semantic associations where the video events are plotted in JVIEW [60]. The JVIEW UDOP affords data rendering, filtering, and analysis for a user to confirm V2T-associated relevant activities, filter over results, and make annotations. The geospatial information provides situation awareness, while the text overlaid cues a user to key attributes. Together the context perspective allows a user to refine estimates of key events in space where entities of interest support the analysis.

The information presented for correlation of data in space can be depicted for local analysis but also be rendered for a situation awareness *global* display as shown in Fig. 18.12. The elements of the text can be plotted on the global coordinates along with the track data to see the emerging context of the multimodal analysis. Thus, a user can decide which perspective they are interested.

Another component is that the various windows with the text, video, local, or global awareness can be configured by an operator in a user-defined operating

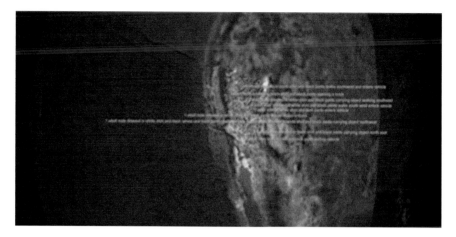

Fig. 18.12 Video–text fusion rendered in a situation awareness UDOP

picture (UDOP). The tailoring of the display affords ease of situation and context understanding.

18.5.4   *Video-to-Text Association in Time*

Fusing the text reports (e.g., SYNCOIN) with the video data affords a joint probability density fusion (pdf) analysis. The reports cue video collections and the user exploiting the video provides call-outs of significant activities. When these events happen together, there is a weighted function of their associations. A measure of significance is implied from the joint PDF in time (Fig. 18.13). Just by correlating the timelines of events (MOP) from video and text report activities and doing a sum of Gaussians, we can determine when significant (MOE) activity is happening and segmentation between activities. Further explanation is provided in [61].

Fig. 18.13 Multimodal PHF in time

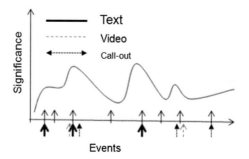

18.5.5   Video-to-Text Graphical Association in Space
          and Time

Figure 18.14 shows an example where the text is used to call out the significant events and reduce the false alarms associated with the track data. The context of the call-out indicates the importance of certain cues and elements within the analysis. The graphical representation of the call-out highlights both time (e.g., 00:23) and space (e.g., middle) information as linked to the attributes needed for the video processing (e.g., template vehicle and moving), as shown in Fig. 18.14. Figure 18.15 then shows a video matched to the selected graphical representation. Finally, Fig. 18.16 shows an example taken from the same data set as shown in Sect. 18.5.3.

Using the association of the chats to tracks (ACT) shown in Fig. 18.14, reports can be combined with a relevance factor. By fusing the report timelines, we can weigh the automated V2T product as a relevant. Assume we are looking for a target turning (e.g., SYNCOIN TUAS), then by collection association, we can rank the videos of importance shown in Fig. 18.17. The text with video exploitation offers a semantic ranking of relevant video collections cue a user as to which clips are important [64]. The designated video clips can be selected for video compression, indexing, storing, and archiving. From the indexed clips, a user can extract previous video collections annotated with the relevant semantic overlays from the continuity folder.

Figure 18.18 shows an example of videos that were identified as having significant content related to the context of a vehicle turning. The re-ranking of the videos allows a user to only have to attend the videos with significant activity.

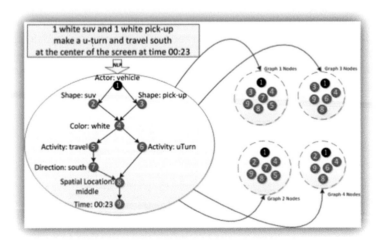

Fig. 18.14 Video and text data representation as graphs of attributes for the probabilistic graph matching to perform associations over a time/space interval

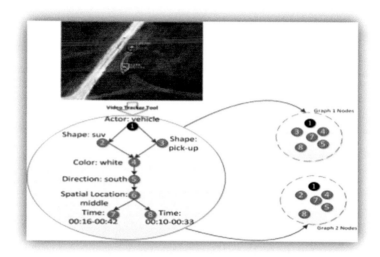

Fig. 18.15 Video correspondence to the selected graph

Fig. 18.16 Successful identifications of target of interests in exemplar clips from the VIRAT aerial dataset using our multi-source association framework. Multiple vehicle tracks and a single chat message being called out are shown, where the tracks in *white circles* (*1, 2, 3, and 4*) were highly matched with the chat message graphs, while targets in other *circles* (*A; B; C; and D*) scored low matching probabilities [62, 63]

Fig. 18.17 Multimodal time analysis

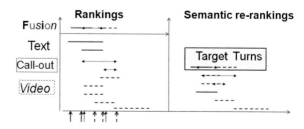

Fig. 18.18 Illustration of an exemplar target track (from the VIRAT aerial dataset) being matched to the proper activity pattern model (a *u-turn* in this example) learned using the training data (video segments being associated activity labels form text) generated by the probabilistic graph-based multi-source association approach briefly presented above [62, 63]

The results of the analysis with context provide both qualitative and qualitative analyses as shown in Table 18.4. The combination of quantitative analysis can be determined from the qualitative results of query satisfaction.

The combined results for video and text analytics are featured in a UDOP window we call multimedia indexing and explorer (MINER) that calls video-indexed by voice annotations (VIVA) results. The UDOP local awareness display is featured in Fig. 18.19. Note, Fig. 18.12 shows the global situation awareness, while Fig. 18.19 shows the local situation awareness. Figure 18.19 (middle) shows a zoom-in from the global situation awareness which provides context as to the location of the video collection.

It is then noted that the ability to use text information as associated chat with tracks utilizes context of information (e.g., space, appearance, occlusions, etc.) to reduce the uncertainty. An example is getting the events (time) of activities (kinematic movements in space) provides *situation context* in the analysis of the scene. The target footprint can be featured as a plotted over the *scene context* to determine the accuracy of the track (and inherently the correctness and accuracy of the results). Finally, it is to be noted that there are user queries to get the information requested which is *mission context*.

The user refinement of the information fusion (video and text association) results in a combing contextual association. If the presented information is slightly incorrect, the user can adjust the results, correctly label the associations, and/or add content to extracted product. Together the user interacts in multiple ways with fusion results through contextual information.

Table 18.4 Qualitative performance analysis

	Targets (%)	Patterns (%)
Detections	83.77	70.60
Miss detections	06.39	09.00
False alarms	09.84	20.40

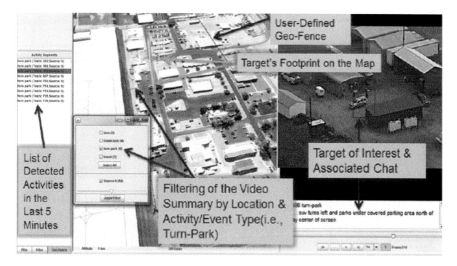

Fig. 18.19 Event-reporting UDOP interface [multimedia indexing and explorer (MINER)] allowing users to visualize and query correlated chats, pattern of life, and activity-labeled track segments

18.6 Discussion

A current theme in multimedia is *big data*. Big data (as shown in Fig. 18.20) includes volume, variety, velocity, and veracity. Volume is the amount of data which can include large images. Likewise, variety includes the multimodal data types which have been presented as video and text data. The velocity of data is inherent the video streams and text data being presented to the user that can overwhelm them. Finally, veracity includes the uncertainty of the data for which an easy example is unregistered video providing a difficult situation for the user to assess. Bringing together the elements of big data, context can provide a means to deal with all of these issues.

To deal with uncertainty, context provides a means of determining the accuracy of the data over time and space for which errors can be reduced. Context can deal with the speed of the data by only rendering the new information. For example, a streaming video being exploited for moving targets only needs to plot the changes and not the entire new set of data. The different types of data can be associated to determine the related content, much as the situation awareness UDOP provides a means to reference all the data to a common frame of reference. Finally, the volume of data, while originally large, can be filtered as to the salient content given the context of the situation. For example, much of the chat text from a variety of source (e.g., twitter) can be removed as irrelevant to the user-desired situation analysis. Together then, context-enhanced information fusion provides a basis to deal with the big data problem while leveraging the opportunities provided by big data to increase the knowledge and situation assessment.

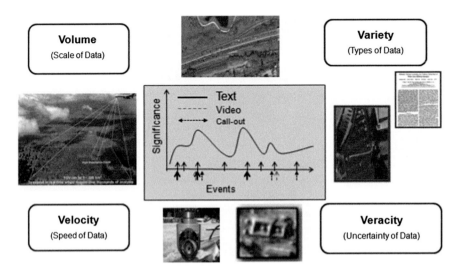

Fig. 18.20 Elements of big data: volume, variety, velocity, and veracity

18.7 Conclusions

We demonstrated a methodology for doing physics-derived and human-derived information fusion (PHF) that incorporates hard (e.g., video) and soft (e.g., text) data. The video exploitation produces tracks and the text content extraction supports semantic labels. Together, these are fused for activity and event characterization to provide a more meaningful understanding of the situation. Context (from text) provides the mission needs, utility function, and narrative to augment real-time PHF analysis.

The next phases include information management [65], pattern learning over contextual operating conditions [66], and performance evaluation over contextual information to include cyber [67] and satellite imagery [68].

Acknowledgments This work is partly supported by the Air Force Office of Scientific Research (AFOSR) under the Dynamic Data Driven Application Systems program and the Air Force Research Lab. Contracts for the work were supported by the Air Force Research Lab (RIEA). Additional technical thanks go to Steve Scott, Alex Aved, William M. Pottenger, Michael K. Schneider, Eric K. Jones, Hillary Holloway, Arslan Basharat, and Anthony Hoogs.

References

1. E. Blasch, E. Bosse, D. Lambert, *High-Level Information Fusion Management and Systems Design* (Artech House, Norwood, 2012)
2. E. Blasch, Sensor, user, mission (SUM) resource management and their interaction with level 2/3 fusion, in *International Conference on Info Fusion*, 2006

3. E. Blasch, D.A. Lambert, P. Valin, M.M. Kokar, J. Llinas, S. Das, C.-Y. Chong, E. Shahbazian, High level information fusion (HLIF) survey of models, issues, and grand challenges, in *IEEE Aerospace and Electronic Systems Magazine*, vol. 27, No. 9, Sept. 2012

4. P. Foo, G. Ng, High-level information fusion: an overview. J. Adv. Inf. Fusion **8**(1) (2013)

5. B. Kahler, E. Blasch, Sensor management fusion using operating conditions, in *Proceedings of IEEE National Aerospace Electronics Conference*, 2008

6. M.R. Endsley, D.J. Garland (eds.), *Situation awareness analysis and measurement* (Lawrence Erlbaum Associates, Mahwah, 2000)

7. E. Blasch, S. Plano, Level 5: user refinement to aid the fusion process, in *Proceedings of SPIE*, vol. 5099, 2003

8. A. Steinberg, C. Bowman, et al., Adaptive context assessment and context management, in *International Conference on Information Fusion*, 2014

9. E. Blasch, I. Kadar, J. Salerno, M.M. Kokar, S. Das et al., Issues and challenges in situation assessment (Level 2 Fusion). J. Adv. Inf. Fusion **1**(2), 122–139 (2006)

10. C. Yang, E. Blasch, Fusion of tracks with road constraints. J. Adv. Inf. Fusion **3**(1), 14–32 (2008)

11. Y. Bar-Shalom, P.K. Willett, X. Tian, *Tracking and Data Fusion* (YBS Publishing, 2011)

12. M. Mallick, V. Krishnamurthy, B.-N. Vo, *Integrated Tracking, Classification, and Sensor Management, Theory and Applications* (Wiley, New York, 2012)

13. E. Blasch, *Derivation of a Belief Filter for High Range Resolution Radar Simultaneous Target Tracking and Identification*, Ph.D. Dissertation, Wright State University, 1999

14. E. Blasch, S. Plano, JDL Level 5 Fusion model 'user refinement' issues and applications in group Tracking, in *Proceedings of SPIE*, vol. 4729, 2002

15. E.T. Senlap, Coordination of sensor platforms for tracking and identifying objects: performance measures, in *International Conference on Information Fusion*, 2013

16. E. Blasch, Z. Wang, H. Ling, K. Palaniappan, G. Chen, D. Shen, A. Aved, G. Seetharaman, Video-based activity analysis using the L1 tracker on VIRAT data, in *IEEE Applied Imagery Pattern Recognition Workshop*, 2013

17. E. Blasch, G. Seetharaman, K. Palaniappan, H. Ling, G. Chen, Wide-area motion imagery (WAMI) exploitation tools for enhanced situation awareness, in *IEEE Applied Imagery Pattern Recognition Workshop*, 2012

18. A. Hoogs, J. Mundy, G. Cross, Multi-modal fusion for video understanding, in *IEEE Applied Imagery Pattern Recognition Workshop*, 2001

19. A. Hoogs, J. Rittscher, G. Stein, J. Schmiederer, Video content annotation using visual analysis and a large semantic knowledgebase, in *IEEE CVPR*, 2003

20. N. Denis, E. Jones, Spatio-temporal pattern detection using dynamic bayesian networks, in IEEE Conference on Decision & Control, 2003

21. M.T. Chan, A. Hoogs, J. Schmiederer, M. Petersen, Detecting rare events in video using semantic primitives with HMM, in *International Conference on Pattern Recognition*, 2004

22. M.T. Chan, A. Hoogs, Z. Sun, J. Schmiederer, R. Bhotika, G. Doretto, Event recognition with fragmented object tracks, in *International Conference on Pattern Recognition*, 2006

23. A. Basharat, A. Gritai, M. Shah, Learning object motion patterns for anomaly detection and improved object detection, in *IEEE CVPR*, 2008

24. E. Swears, A. Hoogs, A.G.A. Perera, Learning motion patterns in surveillance video using HMM clustering, in *IEEE WMCV*, 2008

25. E. Blasch, C. Banas, M. Paul, B. Bussjager, et al., Pattern activity clustering and evaluation (PACE), in *Proc. SPIE*, vol. 8402, 2012

26. K.K. Reddy, N. Cuntoor, et al., Human action recognition in large-scale datasets using histogram of spatiotemporal gradients, in *IEEE International Conference on Advanced Video and Signal-Based Surveillance*, 2012

27. P. Liang, et al., Multiple kernel learning for vehicle detection in wide area motion imagery, in *International Conference on Information Fusion*, 2012

28. C. Yuan, X. Li, W. Hu, H. Ling, S. Maybank, 3D R transform on spatio-temporal interest points for action recognition, in *IEEE Conference on Computer Vision and Pattern Recognition (CVPR)*, 2013
29. J. Gao, H. Ling, et al., Pattern of life from WAMI objects tracking based on visual context-aware tracking and infusion network models, in *Proceedings of SPIE*, vol. 8745, 2013
30. N.F. Sandell, R. Savell, D. Twardowski, G. Cybenko, HBML: a representation language for quantitative behavioral modeling in the human terrain, in *Social Computing and Behavioral Modeling*, eds. by H. Liu, J.J. Salerno, M.J. Young (Springer, Berlin, 2009)
31. T. Wang, Z. Zhu, R. Hammoud, Audio-visual feature fusion for vehicles classification in a surveillance system, in *IEEE Conference on Computer Vision and Pattern Recognition (CVPR)*, 2013
32. I. Kim, S. Oh, B. Byun, A.G.A. Perera, C.-H. Lee, Explicit performance metric optimization for fusion-based video retrieval, in *European Conference on Computer Vision (ECCV)*, 2012
33. J. Garcia Herro, L. Snidaro, I. Visentini, Exploiting context as a binding element for multi-level fusion, in *International Conference on Information Fusion*, 2012
34. E. Blasch, J. Garcia Herrero, L. Snidaro, J. Llinas, G. Seetharaman, K. Palaniappan, Overview of contextual tracking approaches in information fusion, in *Proceedings of SPIE*, vol. 8747, 2013
35. M.A. Pravia, O. Babko-Malaya, M.K. Schneider, et al., Lessons learned in the creation of a data set for hard-soft information fusion, in *International Conference on Information Fusion*, 2009
36. J.L. Graham, D.L. Hall, J. Rimlan, A synthetic dataset for evaluating soft and hard fusion algorithms, in *Proceedings of SPIE*, vol. 8062, 2011
37. A. Panasyuk, et al., Extraction of semantic activities from Twitter data, in *Semantic Technology for Intelligence, Defense, and Security*, 2013
38. T. Wu, W.M. Pottenger, A semi-supervised active learning algorithm for information extraction from textual data. J. Am. Soc. Inf. Sci. Tech. **56**(3), 258–271 (2005)
39. M.C. Ganiz, C. George, W.M. Pottenger, Higher order Naïve Bayes: a novel non-iid approach to text classification. IEEE Trans. Knowl. Data Eng. **23**(7), 1022–1034 (2011)
40. B. Liu, E. Blasch, Y. Chen, D. Shen, G. Chen, Scalable sentiment classification for big data analysis using Naive Bayes classifier, in *IEEE International Conference on Big Data*, Oct. 2013
41. C. Nelson, H. Keiler H., W.M. Pottenger, Modeling Microtext with higher order learning, in *AAAI Spring Symposium*, 2013
42. www.intuidex.com. Accessed 13 March 2014
43. A. Preece, D. Pizzocaro, D. Braines, D. Mott, G. de Mel, T. Pham, Integrating hard and soft information sources for D2D using controlled natural language, in *International Confernece on Information Fusion*, 2012
44. E.A. Smith, Effects based operations: applying network centric warfare in peace, crisis, and war, Command and Control research Programs (CCRP), 2003
45. E. Blasch, et al., DFIG Level 5 (User Refinement) issues supporting situational assessment reasoning, in *International Conference on Information Fusion*, 2005
46. O. Straka, J. Duník, M. Šimandl, Randomized unscented Kalman Filter in target tracking, in *International Conference on Information Fusion*, 2012
47. P. Liang, H. Ling, E. Blasch, G. Seetharaman, D. Shen, G. Chen, Vehicle detection in wide area aerial surveillance using temporal context, in *International Conference on Information Fusion*, 2013
48. P.C.G. Costa, K.B. Laskey, E. Blasch, A.-L. Jousselme, Towards unbiased evaluation of uncertainty reasoning: the URREF ontology, in *International Conference on Information Fusion*, 2012
49. J. Dezert, D. Han, Z.-G. Liu, J.-M. Tacnet, Hierarchical DSmP transformation for decision-making under uncertainty, in *International Conference on Information Fusion*, 2012
50. A. Josang, P.C.G. Costa, et al., Determining model correctness for situations of belief fusion, in *International Conference on Information Fusion*, 2013

51. E. Blasch, K.B. Laskey, A.-L. Joussselme, V. Dragos, P.C.G. Costa, J. Dezert, URREF reliability versus credibility in information fusion (STANAG 2511), in *International Conference on Information Fusion*, 2013
52. E. Blasch, P. Valin, E. Bossé, Measures of effectiveness for high-level fusion, in *International Conference on Information Fusion*, 2010
53. E. Blasch, R. Breton, P. Valin, Information fusion measures of effectiveness (MOE) for decision support, in *Proceedings of SPIE, 8050*, April 2011
54. H. Ling, L. Bai, et al., Robust infrared vehicle tracking across target pose change using L1 regularization, in *International Conference on Information Fusion*, 2010
55. X. Mei, H. Ling, et al., Minimum error bounded efficient L1 tracker with occlusion detection, in *IEEE Computer Vision and Pattern Recognition* (2011)
56. X. Zhang, W. Li, W. Hu, H. Ling, et al., Block covariance based L1 tracker with a subtle template dictionary, in *Pattern Recognition* (2012)
57. X. Mei, H. Ling, Y. Wu, E. Blasch, L. Bai, Efficient minimum error bounded particle resampling L1 tracker with occlusion detection, IEEE Trans. Image Process. (T-IP) **22**(7), 2661–2675 (2013)
58. E. Blasch, Enhanced air operations using JView for an air-ground fused situation awareness UDOP, in *AIAA/IEEE Digital Avionics Systems Conference*, Syracuse, NY, Oct. 2013
59. R.T. Antony, J.A. Karakowski, First-principle approach to functionally decomposing the JDL fusion model: emphasis on soft target data, in *International Conference on Information Fusion*, 2008
60. R.T. Antony, J.A. Karakowski, Homeland security application of the Army Soft Target Exploitation and Fusion (STEF) system, in *Proceedings of SPIE*, vol. 7666, 2010
61. E.P. Blasch, S.K. Rogers, H. Holloway, J. Tierno, E.K. Jones, R.I. Hammoud, QuEST for information fusion in multimedia reports. Int. J. Monit. Surveill. Technol. Res. (IJMSTR) **2**(3), 1–30 (2014)
62. R.I. Hammoud, C.S. Sahin, E.P. Blasch, B.J. Rhodes, T. Wang, Automatic association of chats and video tracks for activity learning and recognition in aerial video surveillance. Sens. Spec. Issue Target Track. FLIR Imagery **14**, 19843–19860 (2014)
63. R.I. Hammoud, et al., Multi-source multi-modal activity recognition in aerial video surveillance, in *IEEE Conference on Computer Vision and Pattern Recognition (CVPR 2014)*, 2014
64. E. Blasch Introduction to level 5 fusion: the role of the user, Chap. 19, in *Handbook of Multisensor Data Fusion*, 2nd edn., by M.E. Liggins, D. Hall, J. Llinas (CRC Press, Boca Raton, 2008)
65. E. Blasch, A. Steinberg, S. Das, J. Llinas, et al., Revisiting the JDL model for information Exploitation, in *International Conference on Information Fusion*, 2013
66. B. Kahler, E. Blasch, Sensor management fusion using operating conditions, in *Proceedings of IEEE National Aerospace Electronics Conference (NAECON)*, July 2008
67. G. Chen, D. Shen, C. Kwan, J. Cruz et al., Game theoretic approach to threat prediction and situation awareness. J. Adv. Inf. Fusion **2**(1), 1–14 (2007)
68. E. Blasch, Z. Liu, LANDSAT satellite image fusion metric assessment, in *Proceedings of IEEE National Aerospace Electronics Conference*, 2011

Chapter 19
Context Understanding from Query-Based Streaming Video

Alex J. Aved and Erik Blasch

Abstract Context understanding is established from the content, analysis, and guidance from query-based coordination between users and machines. In this chapter, a live video computing (LVC) structure is presented for access of a database management of information for context assessment. Context assessment includes multimedia fusion of query-based text, images, and exploited tracks which can be utilized for content-based image retrieval (CBIR). In this chapter, we explore the developments in database systems to enable context to be utilized in user-based queries (e.g., Level 5 fusion) for information fusion content extraction. Using a common video dataset, we demonstrate time savings in the analysis from user queries to provide a context, privacy, and semantic-aware information fusion.

Keywords Query-based computing · Content-based image retrieval · Context-aware computing · Semantic-aware information fusion · Privacy-aware processing

19.1 Introduction

Utilization of contextual information by a machine includes the database system, the sensor type (e.g., video), the extracted features (e.g., the target), and the scenes (e.g., the environment). These operating conditions of the sensor, target, and environment need to be established together to support information exploitation and contextual analysis [1]. Note, that we use *context data* as the scene and meta-information while the *context features* are the extracted elements from the target detection and activities.

Early database systems were designed to efficiently manage the storage, retrieval, and querying of alphanumeric data [2]. Figure 19.1 compares a traditional

A.J. Aved · E. Blasch (✉)
Air Force Research Lab, Rome, NY, USA
e-mail: erik.blasch@gmail.com

A.J. Aved
e-mail: alexaved@yahoo.com

© Springer International Publishing Switzerland (outside the USA) 2016   507
L. Snidaro et al. (eds.), *Context-Enhanced Information Fusion*,
Advances in Computer Vision and Pattern Recognition,
DOI 10.1007/978-3-319-28971-7_19

Fig. 19.1 A typical database
architecture (*left*) versus a
multimedia database (*right*)

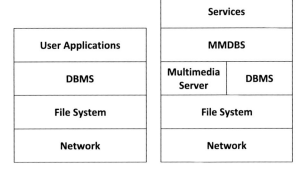

database management system (DBMS) with a multimedia database system
(MMDBS). A typical DBMS implementation, Fig. 19.1 (left), supports business
applications by persisting application state, resolving queries, and facilitating
transactions to mitigate concurrency errors. Figure 19.1 (right) illustrates a
MMDBS, which can utilize a traditional DBMS to manage metadata and indices,
but also encompasses additional technologies and services not typically present in
DBMSs which include: video on demand, document management and imaging,
spatial data, specialized query languages, face recognition and relevance feedback,
to name a few. Because multimedia content, and video in particular, can be quite
large and its communication bandwidth intensive, MMDBS are often paired with
specialized communication frameworks, such as the HeRO protocol discussed in
[3], in order to provide content delivery to a multitude of concurrent users without
overwhelming the physical communication medium. Content delivery could
include contextual information passed as content from one user and used as context
for another user. The user queries themselves constitute context, where a query is
indicative of some pattern the user is interested in observing or finding. The corresponding contextual information is a function of the query, i.e., the result, indicating the presence or absence of the pattern, or a numerical quantity (such as the
number of individual objects corresponding to the pattern).

Multimedia constructs include content (data), entities (features), and scenes
(context). Context-enhanced information fusion examples include imagery [4], user
queries [5], text and tracking [6], and content-based image retrieval (CBIR) [7].
The multiple applications of fusion require resource management [8] to facilitate the
ability of the user-defined queries to be determined from the information management system.

In the remainder of this section, context is described in terms of data, features,
and scenes. Contextual information can be used to refine data to actionable
knowledge. Contextual analysis is not simply a series of filters applied at different
stages in a hierarchical reduction, but the process is more intricate. Data transformation with contextual information also entails other inputs (not present in the
initial dataset) such as goals and historical trends (i.e., transformations, relationships, ontologies). In the fusion process, "outside knowledge" is induced in the
form of contextual queries, which a user can create, observe, and change. In the

query-based information fusion scheme, context is included as (1) the user crafts the query for data adding outside knowledge, goals, and guidance, (2) the fusion processing transforms raw data to features using details from the environment, metadata, and spatial–temporal analysis; and (3) the interface provides query-based interactions through visualization, performance, and acceleration of results relevancy within the selected scene.

19.1.1   Context Data

Data can be classified as *structured* or *unstructured*. Structured data is organized in accordance with a data model [9]. Some examples of structured data include tabular data stored in a relational database or in an Extensible Markup Language (XML) file. Structured data is recognizable (by both humans and computers) in accordance with an ontology. With structured information, the schema can be used as context information. Unstructured data is not inherently organized by an identifiable structure. Examples of unstructured data include audio (e.g., MP3 format files), images, and video.

Unstructured data can be categorized by its inherent dimensionality. The simplest type of unstructured data consists of alphabet characters, and the more complex is video. Table 19.1 provides a list of different types of unstructured data. If the data is not temporally realted, it is listed as "discrete." Data listed as "Continuous" in the state column consists of data that is related temporally, and one or more of these classifications (or types) of data may be combined and still be considered multimedia [10].

As previously stated, features represent a measurable property of a type of data that can be observed. Typically, more than one feature is extracted to represent an item of multimedia data, and taken together these features form a vector which can correspond to a point in a multidimensional Euclidean feature space. The process of identifying and calculating features from multimedia data is called feature extraction. The features selected enable contextual understanding of the data.

19.1.2   Context Features

MMDBS frameworks typical consist of three primary components, or phases that include feature extraction, knowledge representation, and information analysis [11].

Table 19.1 Unstructured data by state	Data dimensionality	Example of data	State
	0	Characters, text	Discrete
	1	Audio, output from sensor	Continuous
	2	Image, graphics	Discrete
	3	Video, animations	Continuous

At each stage, context can be used; for example, when determining which features to extract, the knowledge ontology, and the analysis needed.

The first component entails representing the raw multimedia data as a point in an abstract, n-dimensional space termed a feature space, where n is the number of features that describes some aspect of the data item. The process of representing the data as a point in the feature space is called *feature extraction*. Similar items should be grouped together (e.g., Figure 19.2), thus, the feature selection and extraction methods affect the grouping and compactness of the data points. The data compactness in the feature space can have ramifications pertaining to the effectiveness of retrieval (e.g., k-nearest neighbor (k-NN)) and classification (e.g., the application of support vector machines).

The second component of the framework is ***knowledge representation***. A feature represents a measurable property of the multimedia data item (e.g., the number of target pixels in an image [12]), and are typically represented as numeric data, though they can be a string or also a graph representation. Numeric features are usually chosen, as they can be operated upon mathematically. Discriminative features should be chosen, and the effectiveness by which the multimedia data may be represented by the selected features will have a significant impact on the performance of the MMDBS.

The third framework component performs some ***type of analysis or retrieval*** on the multimedia data that is represented in the feature space, for example, categorization (applying class labels or keywords), retrieval (k-NN), data mining, image fusion [13], etc.

Each phase is dependent of the feature type; and some features are applicable only to certain modalities of data. Three types of features are described here: *geometric*, *statistical*, and *meta*. Typically, extracted geometric and statistical

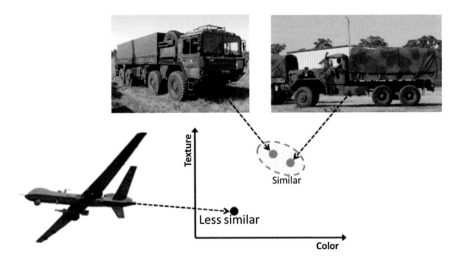

Fig. 19.2 Multimedia data (*images*) represented as points in a two-dimensional feature space

features are associated with the objects; while meta-features are associated with contextual information. Contextual information (calculated or known a priori) can be leveraged to guide the feature extraction. For example, as a function of context some information may not need to be persisted in the feature and can be discarded. This reduction of unnecessary data will result in a more concise and compact representation.

Geometric **features** apply to specific objects that have been identified within a unit of multimedia data (such as a frame of video). Before objects can have features calculated for them, a previous processing step must have been executed to identify the objects contained in the data item. An example of a geometric feature is a moment. In image processing, a moment is a weighted average of the intensities of the pixels that represent the appearance of an object. Features that can be derived from the moment include area (the number of pixels that contribute to the object's representation) and also the centroid (or, the coordinates of the center of the object) [14]. Another simple geometric feature is the shape number [15]. The shape number represents the contour of a shape, and is a sequence that describes the directions of line segments that one would encounter when tracing the shape of an object, having started from some particular boundary point. For details about shape and image processing the reader is referred to a computer vision text, for example [16].

A *statistical* **feature** is another type of feature that can describe an image. Statistical features are generally applied to the image as a whole. A histogram is an example of a statistical feature that can represent a property of an image, for example, the intensities of the pixel values that represent the appearance of the image. Consider, for example, a grayscale image, which is a two-dimensional image whose pixels represent shades of gray with intensities ranging from 255 (white) to 0 (black). A histogram representing a particular grayscale image could have 256 bins, one for each possible pixel intensity, and the value of each bin would be the number of pixels contained in the image with that particular value. To make the histogram more compact, the bins can be generalized to represent nonoverlapping ranges of pixel values. Other features that could fit into the statistical category are edges (e.g., the number of pixels that represent edges in the image, as outputted by some edge detection algorithm [17]), and interesting points within the image [18].

*Meta-***features** are another class of features that can describe data. Meta-features apply to the data as a whole. For example, for an audio recording of music a meta-feature could be the name of the artist who recorded the work. For an image, a meta-feature could be the focal length of the lens used to capture the image, or the model of camera. For video, frame rate, aspect ratio, language, producer, etc., are all examples of meta-features.

As indicated in Table 19.1, the term multimedia encompasses a number of different modalities of data. In the remainder of this chapter, the modalities of data that are of primary consideration are video, and the images (i.e., frames) extracted from the video. It is important to also note that the data (and metadata) generation techniques considered here are those that are primarily automated. For example, some algorithms for image segmentation require a human to provide "seed" parameters, but we would still consider such a technique to be automated; as opposed to a technique in which a human observes some data and performs some manual transformation such as determining relevant labels to associate with the said data. This includes user correction (such as correcting a metadata value that is incorrect) or applying (i.e., associating) context with an object (e.g., marking whether or not a video sequence contains a representation of a particular person), other than for purposes such as determining a ground truth baseline. The features are dependent on the contextual scene [19].

19.1.3 *Context Scenes*

Background subtraction is the process of identifying objects (or portions thereof) of interest in an image, from the rest of the image [20]. Background information is the context of the scene. The output from the background segmentation process is a mask image of binary values that indicates which pixels (in the corresponding image) represent the foreground object (or said another way, the pixels which are detected to not represent the scene background). Frame differencing is the simplest case of background subtraction, in which the foreground pixels of a scene can be determined by taking two images and converting them to gray scale images to simplify handling the separate color channels and subtracting (or, finding the absolute difference) between the pixels in the images. Frame differencing can be improved by computing the average pixel value from the last n frames, and slowly updating the background model over time to account for slow changes to the illumination of the scene.

The background models just discussed characterize each pixel independently from its neighbors and base the color model on each pixel's recent history, such as the weighted average of the previous n frames. These do not take into account complex scenes with moving objects, like branches moving in the wind, moving water, or clouds passing overhead. Background subtraction methods base the value of background pixels on a *probably distribution function* (*PDF*) that follows a Gaussian distribution [21] or a *Mixture of Gaussians* (*MOG*) [22]. The downside of MOG is that it does not adapt well to fast-changing backgrounds like waves, or to cases where more than a few Gaussians might be required. The codebook [23] background segmentation model takes into consideration periodic background variations over a long period of time. In order to conserve the amount of memory required to implement the algorithm, a codebook is constructed by associating with each pixel one or more code words which can be thought of as clusters of colors at each pixel (e.g., each pixel may be associated with one or more code words), and the clusters may not necessarily correspond to a Gaussian distribution or any other parametric distribution. That is, a codebook still encodes the background representation on a pixel-by-pixel basis. Classification of a pixel as background or

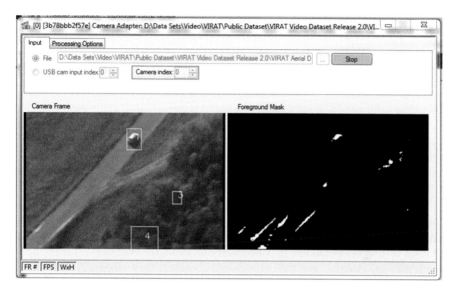

Fig. 19.3 Aerial surveillance scene from the VIRAT dataset (*left*), and the corresponding foreground mask (*right*)

foreground is done by comparing a pixel's value to the corresponding code words; if its color distribution is sufficiently close to one of the code words and its brightness is within a range of the corresponding code word, the pixel is considered to be part of the background, else it is classified as a foreground pixel. For additional information pertaining to background subtraction methods the reader is referred to the works of [24] and [25].

It should also be noted that the pixels in the foreground mask might not always represent the object completely; that is, there may be some error due to noise. For example, as can be observed in Fig. 19.3, in some situations the pixels that represent the appearance of the object can match the color of the background. This type of error can be mitigated by introducing a post-processing step to reduce noise in the binary foreground mask image, or also group together nearby disconnected components that could correspond to the same object [26]. Further information on context scenes is discussed in [27].

The remainder of this chapter proceeds as follows. Section 19.2 describes the live video computing database management system (LVCDMS) starting with the data representation for indexing and retrieval. Section 19.3 describes database systems that enable context analysis, while Sect. 19.4 describes the system, model, and query language. Section 19.5 provides an example and Sect. 19.6 conclusions.

19.2 Multimedia Data Representation for Context Indexing

Multimedia constructs include content (data), entities (features), and scenes (context) that are utilized through indexing and retrieval. To explore how to utilize contextual information in information fusion, it is important to understand indexing of information for storage and retrieval. For example, indexing of entities in an image is akin to Level 1 information fusion object assessment; while the indexing of scenes provides context for Level 2 information fusion situation assessment. Furthermore, an index can be construed as a reduction of information whereby the reduction that is applied is context dependent. Note that multiple indices can exist for an item, and thus the object can be represented as a function of multiple contexts; for example, in terms of color, shape, size, or combinations thereof. In order to fully understand high-level concepts such as the performance of indexed retrieval or fusion operations, it is necessary to know the indexing schemes upon which they are derived, and the corresponding context they inherently construe.

Collections of multimedia information can grow to very large sizes, consuming many gigabytes of storage space. In order to utilize multimedia content it must be retrieved; whether the retrieval is to find a movie based upon its title, or one is looking for images, clips of audio, or video segments showing a particular subject or class of objects. As an example, consider a table of records in a traditional relational database. Each record in the table can be considered as a point in a multidimensional space [28]. Consider a record for an employee–department relation with the following fields: {*employee_id, department_id, manager_id, start_date, end_date*}. In this case, records in this table correspond with points in a five-dimensional space, where three of the dimensions refer to, say, integers (*employee_id, department_id and manager_id*) and the other two dimensions are of type date–time (i.e., *start_date, end_date*). The DBMS manages the collection of these records and stores them in a file on some persistent media as contextual information. In order to facilitate efficient retrieval of records in the database, *indexes* can be created.

The index itself is simply another table (or, correspondingly, a file created and maintained by the DBMS). For example, an index over the field *employee_id* could contain only *employee_id*'s and the location of associated records in the corresponding employee–department file. By utilizing the index file in order to resolve queries, less data would need to be loaded and processed, since the index file contains primarily *employee_id* data (and not other data fields such as *manager_id*). To further enable efficient retrieval, an ordering can be imposed upon the records, either in the primary data file or in the index. However, to accommodate future record operations to the primary data table (e.g., delete, insert, update) it is often more efficient to impose the ordering only on the data in the index files. For numeric fields, the ordering can be based upon numeric value. For character fields, the order can be based upon corresponding ASCII or UNICODE numeric values, or based upon lexicographic order. For other types of data, such as color, the ordering could be based upon the corresponding hexadecimal value (e.g., red is "ff0000") or the color's wavelength.

Samet [29] identifies five key questions that should be considered when deciding how to represent a dataset:

1. What is the type of the data; continuous, discrete?
2. Which operations will be performed, e.g., a log file might only have data appended to its end?
3. How should the ordering of the data be applied; should the data in the primary file be ordered, or only the index files? How should attributes be included in the ordering?
4. Will more data be added or removed? Will additional attributes be added in the future? and
5. Is the quantity data sufficiently small such that all of it will fit into the primary memory of the computer hosting the database, or will disk-resident data access algorithms need to be utilized?

There are many different ways data can be represented, and considering questions such as these can guide the process of designing an implementation as well as identifying and using data for context.

When considering multimedia for browsing and searching for contextual data, an index is also required. Some fundamental question pertaining to multimedia data are *what*, *which,* and *how*. At *what* granularity should the item be indexed; as a whole or by frame or a clip of frames? *Which* refers to those items that should be indexed; should all pixels shown in each frame of video be represented somewhere in an index, or should only moving objects be stored? Should the time index of an object that appears or disappears be recorded? *How* to index an item pertains to selecting and extracting features to be indexed. Data indexing, and more specifically multimedia data indexing, is a multifaceted and difficult problem, and as such, there is a significant quantity of research and correspondingly, solutions and indexing algorithms and data structures. Some works that address the issues of multimedia indexing holistically are [30–33].

To illustrate multimedia indexing, consider the information that can be extracted from a video: the visual component (the visual content represented by pixels in the frames), the auditory information (i.e., audio tracks), and text (words that can be extracted; and metadata pertaining to the video itself such as genre, actors, etc.). A multitude of semantic properties of the video can be extracted from the metadata pertaining to its content for context: the type of video (e.g., education, training, entertainment), the time period the video covers; major actors who appear, and so forth [34, 35]. To index content that is depicted visually in the video, pattern recognition approaches can be employed, for example, template matching (e.g., Bayes classifier, decision trees, Hidden Markov Models, face and people detection [36]). The reader is referred to [37] for a comprehensive review of pattern recognition techniques. To index videos, they can be decomposed into a series of semantic shots, and each shot can be individually indexed [38]. Pertaining to audio data, a number of different techniques can be employed, for example, sounds can be analyzed to detect musical instruments or talking [39, 40].

19.2.1 Multimedia Index and Retrieval

To index multimedia content, first, it is decomposed and segmented and features which correspond to points in a multidimensional space are extracted. The next step is to efficiently store and retrieve those points and correspondingly, the associated multimedia content. Some of the questions raised in the previous section are also relevant to how data will be represented for storage and retrieval. The retrieved data is used for contextual understanding (e.g., scene content).

Storage of data on a disk implies that it is organized; logically the data is organized into buckets and physically the buckets are oriented in *pages*. Pages (and correspondingly, the buckets containing data points) are stored in files. The simplest way to store a set of points in a file is as an unordered sequential list. The downside is that in order to do an equality search on the file for a particular attribute value, the entire file must be processed. Thus, if there are N records stored in the file and each file has d attributes, the processing will be of order $O(Nd)$. With this simple organization as a starting point, there are numerous structures (and corresponding algorithms) that facilitate indexed storage and retrieval, one example is the Grid File [41].

Another straightforward technique to organize data in a file is to utilize a *hash function*. The concept behind a hash function is to utilize a mathematical function to distribute items (i.e., key/value pairs) into buckets which are stored on persistent media in a file (or files, depending upon the implementation). Given a key, the hash function can suggest which bucket to store the value into. In the case that the bucket is at capacity, there are various algorithms that determine how to manage the overflow (collision resolution, load factor, etc.) [42–44].

When choosing an index structure it is important to consider the type of data that will be stored, for example, strings or numbers, point data, lines (or line equations), rectangles, regions, surfaces, volumes, etc., and the types of queries that will be performed; point queries, range queries, window queries, etc. For point data one can utilize index structures like the binary search trees [45], B-Tree [46] or B$^+$-Tree, etc.

The *tree structures* discussed thus far are referred to as space-partitioning structures; they are hierarchical data structures that decompose the space into disjoint partitions. A downside is that if they become unbalanced then their implementation suffers in terms of I/O. The SP-GiST index is a space-partitioning index that is designed to be input–output, even in the case where the tree structure is unbalanced [47].

When working with high-dimensional data, one method of data management is to reduce the dimensionality and utilize one of the hierarchical data structures discussed previously, such as an R-tree [48] illustrated in Fig. 19.4. Alternatively, there exist indices that are not based upon the dimensions (i.e., features) of the objects, but on the distances between them (the interobject distances), e.g.,

Fig. 19.4 Example of an
R-tree spatial index

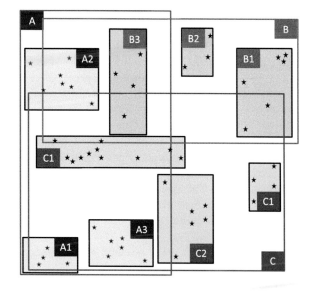

SparseMap [49], FastMap, and MetricMap [50]. Some types of data cannot be represented by bounding boxes, for example, the representation of a plane or surface. In this case, these types of objects can be decomposed into a smaller volume, for example, a cube, and the corresponding cubes indexed (or for query purposes, a cube can be queried and then determined which object(s) it corresponds to). The R^+-Tree index structure can accommodate these types of items, but the downside is that one object can be represented by multiple blocks and can thus potentially lead to duplicated results being reported. To accommodate this, algorithms have been developed that take into account duplicate objects in the search space, for example [51–53].

Indexing is based on the data content, the situation context, and the need for information retrieval as described in the next section.

19.2.2   Content-Based Image Retrieval

Multimedia context is established through content (data) which has been termed CBIR. In literature there are many ways in which CBIR described. In particular, it is the application of computer vision techniques to extract information from an image in an automated fashion for the purposes of retrieval. Also referred to as *query by image content* (*QBIC*) [54], it pertains to the retrieval of images based upon what they visually depict; not by metadata or human-ascribed annotations, whose assignment can vary from person to person, culture to culture, reflect personal biases, etc. In CBIR systems, image data is represented by features corresponding to its visual appearance; color, texture, shape, edges, etc. Early work in CBIR was done with pictorial databases [55, 56].

Present day CBIR systems facilitate retrieval by accommodating a variety of query methods, to include query by example, sketching an image by hand, random browsing, text search (i.e., keyword, speech/voice recognition), and hierarchical navigation by category [57]. Objects in CBIR systems are represented by features associated with their content. As such, feature extraction is an important step inherent to CBIR systems. Features (color, shape, texture, edges, regions, etc.) are extracted and stored in a multidimensional index (feature vectors can range from very few to hundreds of dimensions). Figure 19.5 provides an example of a system architecture for generic CBIR systems. A user submits an image as a query through a user interface. The query image is parsed and its representative features are extracted. The features from the query image are mapped to a multidimensional query point in the index, and similar images are returned back to the user as the query result.

There are presently many research and commercial CBIR systems; a few representative examples include QBIC, Virage [58], Photobook [59], and Multimedia analysis and retrieval system (MARS) [60], to name a few. Additionally, there are many good surveys on CBIR techniques and systems [61–63].

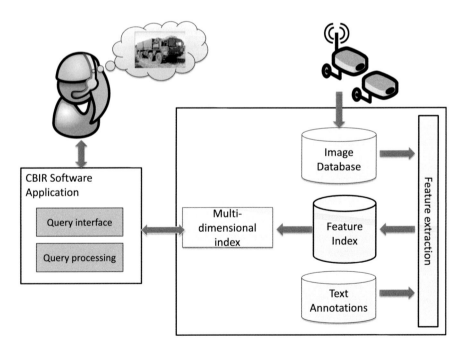

Fig. 19.5 Representative architecture of a typical CBIR system. The context within which an object exists can either guide the exploration or form a portion of the query result

Although originally applied to images, *content-based video retrieval (CBVR)* is another active area of research due to the commoditization of compute and storage capacity [64]. CBVR is semantically similar to CBIR except its domain is that of video, rather than images. Hence, context is retrieved over space and time, and can be utilized as a guide in the exploration of the data. Videos are segmented into shots, which may be represented by key frames [65], features are extracted and indexed. At that point retrieval is similar to the workflow presented in Fig. 19.5 for [66]. Of course, video adds the potential to fuse additional data modalities not available in traditional CBIR into the indexing and retrieval process, such as correlation with audio tracks [67–69].

CBIR is enabled by the database structure for contextual analysis.

19.3 Database Systems in Support of Context Analysis

Various diagrams of information fusion models typically include a database for the collection of data and information (e.g., see the JDL/DFIG information fusion model [1]). Traditional DBMSs orient data in tables, such that each table contains records (or tuples in the relational vernacular). Each record in a table has a common attribute structure, illustrated in the right side of Fig. 19.6. LVC is stream oriented;

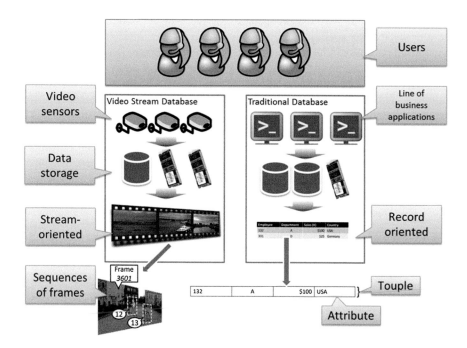

Fig. 19.6 LVC stream data model contrasted with relational record and disk data model

operating over video streams. That is, the video streams are queried for their content conceptually similar to how files residing in disk drives are also queried for the content they hold. A comparison of concepts between traditional database computing and LVC is presented in Table 19.2, extending what is presented in Fig. 19.6 with additional comparisons of similar concepts that exist between these two platforms. *Live Video Query Language* (*LVQL*) is the query language of the LVC prototype implementation. It can specify *events* in terms of spatiotemporal observations, correlations of objects in video streams, and as contextual activities.

LVC is the theoretical framework upon which the LVDBMS prototype system is based on which there are silo and repository types. Traditional video stream processing applications (e.g., depicted in Fig. 19.7a) are designed specifically to solve a particular problem, termed *siloed*. In this context siloed systems are those that are designed to work with a specific set of cameras or sensor hardware. The result of siloed application development is applications that are not capable of operating with each other in a reciprocal fashion to share information and provide additional value and value-added opportunities such as contextual interpretations. If context data developed from one application needs to be combined for auditing, reporting, or other purposes, additional software (middleware) must be purchased and interfaced with these applications, resulting in a higher cost of ownership. Exploiting contextual knowledge helps to align different systems for data assimilation, integration, and analysis.

However, the downside is that this middleware must be installed and configured on a case-by-case bases and "adapters" for each application must be configured or developed to provide application-specific interfaces to the middleware. The middleware must then perform an *extract, transform, and load* (*ETL*) process to transform data received from the application-specific adapters into a common data format that is amenable to further processing. The result is additional middleware software that must be purchased and maintained and also staff resources to install, configure, maintain, and upgrade, as appropriate. Figure 19.7b highlights the common repository approach with middleware.

Note that libraries such as OpenCV [70] and *Integrated Performance Primitives* (*IPP*) [71] are commonly used by programmers when developing repository applications, to provide basic data-handling functionality. The OpenCV library provides a comprehensive assortment of image processing and data management routines and data structures. For example, the IPP library provides functions and associated data structures that are specifically tuned to take advantage of features

Table 19.2 Comparison of LVC and traditional DBMS concepts		LVC	DBMS
	Storage	Camera	Hard drive
	Relation	Video stream	Record
	Data unit	Video frame	Tuple
	Data granularity	Object	Attribute
	Query language	LVQL	SQL

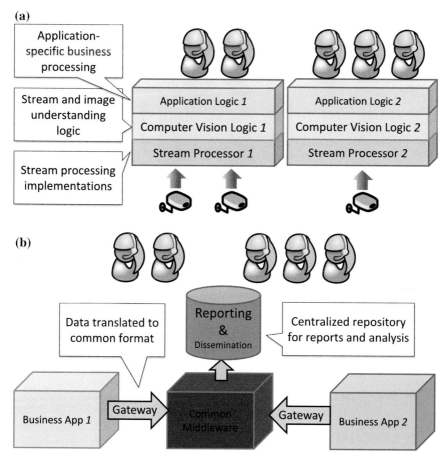

Fig. 19.7 Applications built as information silos utilizing middleware and application-specific data adapters. **a** Siloed applications and data. **b** Siloed applications, common repository

provided by modern multicore processors such as parallel data processing instructions. However, these common libraries provide low-level functionality that programmers use as conveniences, and do not generally provide out-of-the-box high-level application functionality. (For example, OpenCV routines could be used to read in frames from a camera, and other routines would need to be called in the proper order with the proper parameters and settings in order to interpret imagery depicted in the frames.)

The Live Video Computing (LVC) approach leverages a common video processing software infrastructure to provide a common programmable interface to clients and a shareable pool of camera resources to share context data, illustrated in Fig. 19.8. The goal is to create an ecosystem for collaboration and sharing of contextual information to allow users to draw new insights that are not possible with siloed information frameworks. The LVC approach facilitates rapid

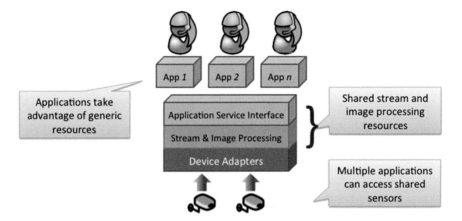

Fig. 19.8 LVC approach showing common core software stack and shared sensor resources

application development by allowing application architects and software developers to focus their time and resources on the business problem, rather than having to devote time and resources to develop core stream processing functionality for each application. The LVC approach is similar to how business application software leverages a common database platform allowing the application designers and programmers to focus their efforts on the business problem and rely on the programmatic interface and SQL to persist business data and retrieve data for reporting purposes.

19.4   LVC-DMBS for Context Analysis

The components of the LVDBMS are logically grouped into four tiers, as illustrated in Fig. 19.9. Each tier defines one or more web service interfaces to facilitate communication between the tiers. The four tiers include:

- The *camera layer*, which encompasses cameras and their corresponding adapters. Camera adapters are conceptually similar to device drivers in computer systems, allowing for disparate camera device hardware to connect with a standard LVDBMS interface.
- The *spatial processing layer*, which processes the metadata and video streams from the camera adapters, passes results to the stream processing layer. A host in this layer communicates with multiple camera adapters, but a camera adapter communicates with only a single spatial processing layer host.
- The *stream processing layer* receives subquery evaluation streams from spatial processing layer hosts and computes final query results for delivery to clients. The query results include object detections, contextual information, and semantic descriptions. As this interfaces with end users and applications (i.e.,

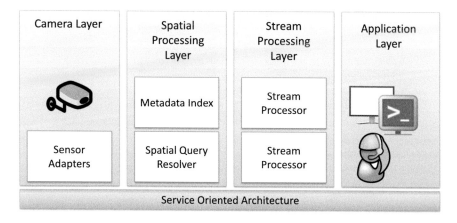

Fig. 19.9 Logical 4-tier architecture of the LVDBMS prototype and major components of the framework encapsulated in each tier

the client layer), it contains logic for managing authentication, connections, and session state with LVDBMS clients.

- The *client layer* encompasses LVDBMS end users and client applications. Clients authenticate and interact with the LVDBMS by browsing the catalog of cameras, submitting queries, and receiving query results. Representative images of the LVDBMS graphical user interface (GUI) are depicted in Fig. 19.9. Queries are specified in the area "Query Description" and buttons "Query 1," "Query 2,", etc., recall prewritten queries. The "Send Query" button submits a query for evaluation.

The LVDBMS illustration is depicted in Fig. 19.9 and is refined in Fig. 19.10, which illustrates how a query flows down through the LVDBMS architecture, and then how data and query results flow back up through the layers and back to the client.

An initial query (including contextual queries) is posed by an end user or client application to the LVDBMS. The initial query is submitted to the stream processing layer host to which the client is connected. The stream processing layer host maintains a catalog of available spatial processing layer hosts (also referred to as camera servers, as they interface with cameras via their adapters and perform processing) and their associated cameras. Contextual information available at each tier and host can guide the stream processing layer host as it translates a query into one or more subqueries. Each subquery corresponds to a particular camera server host, where it will be sent for evaluation. Camera adapters process imagery from camera sensors and translate it into a stream of images and corresponding metadata, which is sent to its respective camera server. *Metadata*, as contextual information, associated with each video frame from the camera adapter includes information pertaining to the frame itself (i.e., timestamp, sequence number, etc.) and to objects observed within the frame and segmented out by the camera adapter (i.e., object

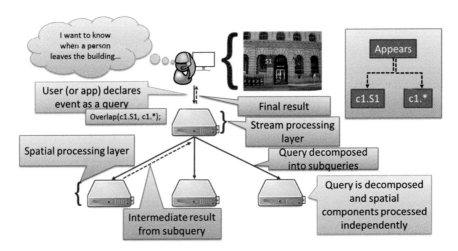

Fig. 19.10 LVDBMS query and subsequent decomposition

identifier, a bounding box identifying the location of the object within the frame, etc.). Subqueries evaluate LVQL expressions over video streams (specifically, over the intersection of video streams specified by the query and video streams managed by a particular camera server to which the subquery was sent) and stream subquery evaluation results back to the respective stream processing layer host. The stream processing layer host receives one or more intermediate results for each evaluation time step and computes a final query result (for the particular point in time), which is then delivered back to the end user or client application. The query information is based on the data model.

19.4.1 LVC-DMBS Data Model

LVC, and correspondingly the LVDBMS, is concerned with computation over video streams. As such, the event and data models revolve around objects that are observable by imaging sensors and depicted in temporally oriented frames in the video streams that emanate from these sensors. Therefore, it follows that an event (i.e., a *simple event*) is defined to be occurrence of an action that may be observed by one (or more) cameras and represented in frame data in corresponding data streams. We note that in this work, the terms video stream and camera stream are used interchangeably, as are enabling hardware device terms such as camera and imaging sensor. Also, an analyzed event includes the data and context information (e.g., contextual information).

From the perspective of an LVDBMS client, events may be specified in LVQL using a combination of spatial and temporal components, or operators. Thus, a user can leverage the LVQL to specify a *complex event* in terms of simple events that are related temporally. For example, a simple event could be a person (or more generally some object) appearing in a scene or moving in front of a desk (where the term scene refers to some portion of the real world that is observed by a camera and rendered into a sequence of frames in a video stream). A complex event, or *activity*, relates simple events with temporal operators [72]. For example, a complex event could be defined as a person first appearing in a scene and then, within some threshold of time, moving in front of a desk. (Since the LVQL presented here is two-dimensional, there is no distinction between touching and in-front-of, as that type of scene information is not captured by the cameras.)

A *spatiotemporal contextual query* is formulated in LVQL. This query specification defines which video streams will be monitored for the occurrence of an event. That is, if the query specifies that a particular video stream will be monitored for the appearance of an object, if an object subsequently appears in a different video stream, there will be no impact upon the query result. An object is a fundamental component of an event specification. As indicated in Table 19.3, there are two basic types of objects that are recognized: *dynamic objects* are detected automatically by the image processing software, and *static objects* are indicated by users of the system. The third class of objects are *cross-camera* dynamic objects. These are dynamic objects that were first recognized in one video stream and subsequently recognized in a second stream. The inclusion of the cross-camera object class simplifies the expression of queries that define events correlating objects that appear in multiple video streams. Note that in each respective stream these objects also qualify as dynamic objects.

Another view of the data flow in the LVDBMS is presented as an example in Fig. 19.11. Starting from the left, two cameras observe the same scene from different vantage points, but contain similar contextual information. Two frames are depicted at a particular point in time, from the two cameras. Within the scene two objects are observed, assigned identifiers (unique to the video stream), and tracked within their respective video streams. Within each stream these objects are dynamic objects. However, a query may be defined specifying an event that involves both cameras, for example, the event may be that an object appears in both the first camera stream and then the second stream. In that case, these two objects are also considered to be cross-camera dynamic objects. Hence, the *context* (geometry, resolution, and target speed) enables the efficient handoff between cameras.

Continuing with the example in Fig. 19.11, the scene is segmented and objects are tracked by each camera's respective camera adapter and sent to the camera server, which resides in the spatial processing layer. The camera server uses the metadata received from the camera adapter to process the spatial operators and send the stream of results to the stream processing server residing in the stream processing layer. The final query result is streamed to the user from the stream processing layer host.

Additionally, there is *permission context*. When a user requests to monitor the imagery from a video stream, the images come from the camera server. This allows the user to observe the same images in sequence with query evaluation results and eliminates a potential capacity bottleneck if multiple users view images from the

Table 19.3 Comparison classes of LVC objects

Object class	Description
Static	Objects of this class are defined by the user and do not move within the scene. For example, a static object may be defined (drawn) over a window or door for subsequent use in a query
Dynamic	Salient objects that are detected automatically within a video stream. A model of the scene background is maintained and as an object passes through the scene, its appearance is distinguished from the background. If its size is beyond a threshold it is segmented, assigned a unique identifier, and tracked
Cross-camera dynamic	Static objects detected in one video stream and subsequently matched to an object in a second video stream are classified as cross-camera dynamic objects

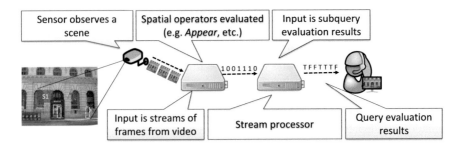

Fig. 19.11 Depiction of the data flow in the LVDBMS, from sensor to frames to query result

same camera simultaneously. Also, by serving the pictures from an LVDBMS host (rather than the camera hardware directly), authorization information pertaining to the user's session may be consulted in order to determine if the user should have direct viewing access to the raw imagery of the scene.

19.4.2 LVC-DMBS Query Language

LVQL is the query language of the LVDBMS that enables contextual acquisition of information. Analysts and programmers may leverage this query language to develop applications that interact with video streams. As such, the programmers and application designers need only know the details of the query language, and do not need to spend time developing stream processing algorithms or low-level details of the LVDBMS. LVQL permits for the specification of an event and a corresponding action to be defined over a video stream (or a set of video streams). It is a declarative language, meaning that the user defines a logical event specification and not the particular flow of control or algorithms that will be executed to determine the query result. An LVQL expression specifies a spatiotemporal event, and an action that is to be triggered when the event is recognized. The basic form of a query (specifically, an *ActionEvent*) is as follows:

ACTION *UserSpecifiedAction*

ON EVENT *EventSpecification*

which signifies that an action *UserSpecifiedAction* corresponds with *EventSpecification* and will be executed the first time a query evaluation result of *true* is returned. *EventSpecification* is an event specification that is generated by a context-free grammar which consists of a set of rules, or productions, which can be utilized to express (describe) an event. A simplified set of LVQL productions is presented in Fig. 19.12; items shown in **bold** represent reserved words recognized by the language.

As shown in Fig. 19.12, an LVQL statement consists of either an *ActionEvent* or a *View Definition Language* (*VDL*) production. In the case of an *ActionEvent*, which specifies a query, the event definition must contain a spatial operator (e.g., *Appear, North, Meet*, etc.) The VDL is used to define privacy filters and views over video streams, and is discussed in [73].

Declaring an event in LVQL entails expressing the event in terms of contextual spatial, temporal, and Boolean operators. The simplest event that can be expressed is the appearance of an object in a video stream using the *Appear()* operator. The *Appear()* operator accepts two arguments (i.e., operands) where the first operand specifies the video stream, the object class (and possibly filter criteria) that the operator will be applied to, and the second is a threshold. (All spatial operators accept a threshold argument.) The threshold for the *Appear()* operator specifies the minimum size of an object that will satisfy the appearance condition, in terms of the

```
Lvql := ActionEvent | VDL
ActionEvent := [action UserSpecifiedAction] on EventSpecification
EventSpecification := NotSpTmplEvent ( BooleanOperator NotSpTmplEvent )
NotSpTmplEvent := [not] SpatialTemporalEvent
SpatialTemporalEvent := CompositSpatialEvent | CompositTemporalEvent
CompositSpatialEvent := appear | north | northwest | inside | meet | ...
CompositTemporalEvent := before | meets
BooleanOperator := and | or | not BooleanOperator
VDL := VCmdType view ViewIdentifier over VStreamIdent [set VPrivFilter ]
VCmdType := create | update | delete
VTargetStmt := target eq ( querytargets | nonquerytargets | previouslymasked | none )
VTmpScpStmt := temporalscope eq ( querynonactive | queryactive |
    permanent | none )
VObjScpStmt := objectscope eq ( static | dynamic | crosscameradynamic | none )
VStreamIdent := ( Cameraidentifier | ViewIdentifier )
Cameraidentifier := camIdent
ViewIdentifier := viewIdent
```

Fig. 19.12 A simplification of the LVQL grammar, including privacy *view definition language* (*VDL*) productions

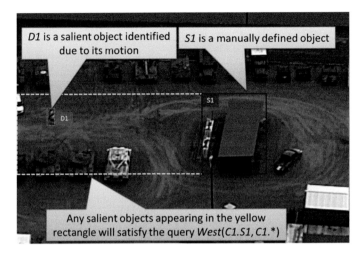

Fig. 19.13 Illustration depicting salient and manually defined objects to determine *West*

area of the *minimum bounding rectangle* (*MBR*) that contains the object. For example, *Appear(s1.*, 200)* will return true each time it is evaluated if a dynamic object with an MBR of area greater than or equal to 200 is observed in the current video frame. In the case of a spatial operator such as *West()*, three arguments are accepted; the first two correspond to objects in the video stream, and the third is again a threshold. *West()* returns true if the object specified by the first operand is to the left of the object specified by the second operand, in a stream (e.g., see Fig. 19.13). The third argument, the threshold, specifies the amount of separation between these objects (i.e., the distance between the bottom of the upper object's MBR and the top of the lower object's MBR). For example, a value of 10 pixels means the upper object must be at least 10 pixels above the lower object. Note that this threshold can be negative, allowing MBRs to overlap.

The ability to ascertain properties of the target resolves context such as geometry, orientation, intensity, etc., for context assessment.

19.4.3 Context Assessment

In this chapter, we have made use of context data from metadata and scenes and contextual features from the target and activities. Using the contextual metadata, the video was aligned with geographical information, coordinated with the user mission as related to the contextual goals for queries, and correlated with the space/time information of entities (e.g., buildings). Since the metadata is included in the analysis, it is understood to help as context-enhanced information fusion. Thus, we focus on the context features as supporting enhanced analytics for temporal efficiency of activity analysis.

Each instance (were feature vector and instance are used interchangeably) contained in a bag can be interpreted as a data point in a multidimensional feature space (where the dimensionality of the feature space is the number of components in the feature vector). In the LVDBMS, bags have a maximum capacity. At the onset, when an object first appears in a video stream, its bag will contain a single instance. As the object is observed in subsequent frames additional instances are added to the bag.

A *distance function* is applied to a pairing of bags to determine their similarity; if the distance between the bags (i.e., a smaller distance means they share more similarity) is below a threshold then the bags (corresponding to objects observed in different video streams) are considered to represent the same physical object, and the bags are merged. Each bag (i.e., its centroid) can be mapped to a point in a feature space, and the assumption is that bags corresponding to similar objects (based upon their modeled appearances) are located closely in this feature space (i.e., cluster analysis). The pairing of bags that will be matched can be modeled as a bipartite graph [74]. Note that as the bags initially contain only one instance and an object may appear in one stream before it appears in another. Bags with differing number of instances may be compared. The actual comparison is dependent upon the particular distance function that the system is configured to apply; however, there is a system-defined minimum threshold such that if a bag contains fewer instances than this "lower watermark" it will not be considered for matching. The idea being that if a bag contains too few instances, the instances it contains may not be sufficiently representative of the object for cross-camera matching purposes.

More formally, the stream matching problem can be formulated as follows. Given the appearance of an object O_a in stream A, the problem is to determine if some object O_b appearing in some stream B corresponds to the same physical entity. The corresponding contextual query is approximately formulated as *when some object O_a appearing in α correlates with an object O_b in stream β, execute the specified action.* Thus, the search space for the object matching can be constrained to objects observed in streams α and β, and the issue is how to measure the similarity between O_a and O_b.

Let A and B represent point sets to O_a and O_b, respectively, such that $A = \{\vec{x}_1, \vec{x}_2, \ldots, \vec{x}_k\}$ and $B = \{\vec{x}'_1, \vec{x}'_2, \ldots, \vec{x}'_{k'}\}$, where $\vec{x} \in O_a$, $\vec{x}' \in O_b$, $k = |O_a|$, $k' = |O_b|$, and k is not necessarily equal to k', k is the number of objects (represented as a feature vector x) within a time window, where $\|$ is the cardinality. Let G be a bipartite graph $G = (V, E)$ where $V = A \cup B$ and V consists of the vertices in G and E, the edges. There are a number of distance functions that can be applied to G. For example, one may measure the distance between the two farthest points (the point in A and the point in B that result in a maximal Euclidean distance), the distance between the two closest points, or the distance from the centroid of each point set, etc. The *normalized distance* between the two point sets may be defined as follows:

$$\mathrm{Dist}(O_a, O_b) = \frac{\sum_{e \in E} \sqrt{e}}{|V|}$$

such that the sum of lengths of edges in E, is the minimum possible when considering all mappings from A to B. Objects are matched from A to B (without loss of generality) by comparing each unmatched object in A to each unmatched object in B that exist (i.e., may be observed) in the current frames of each respective stream. Therefore, if all objects in both streams were to be unmatched at some particular time, the number of comparisons taking place would be at most $(|k| + |k'|)^2$, where $|k|$ and $|k'|$ are the number of dynamic objects in the latest frame of each respective stream. The Hungarian algorithm [75–77] may be used to determine the edges in E to which the distance function is applied. Note that in the circumstances that $k \neq k'$, 0 vectors may be injected, or the farthest instances in the set with larger cardinality may be ignored, etc.

Having defined the LVC-DBMS and the context assessment, the next section provides an example where context is established from one camera to another.

19.5 Results

The LVC-DMBS uses a context query optimizer and associated execution environment that is designed for the LVC environment (Fig. 19.14). It performs query optimization at runtime, taking a new query and finding any possible overlap with the existing queries in the system and rewriting the new query in order to minimize duplicate subexpressions and optimize the utilization of the query execution engine (Fig. 19.15). Results presented in this chapter show that the query optimization methods that were designed for the LVC environment and implemented in the LVC-DMBS prototype reduce context query execution overhead by merging the

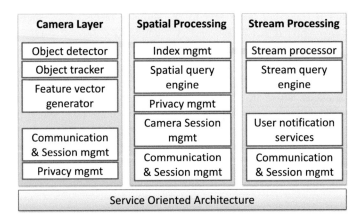

Fig. 19.14 LVC-DMBS major system components

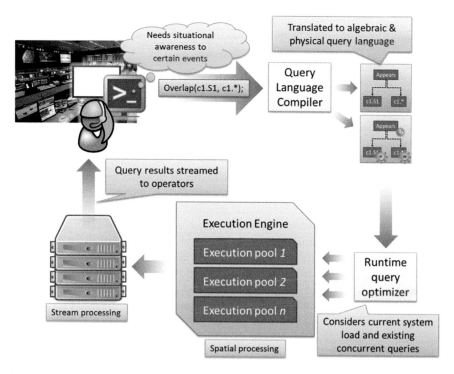

Fig. 19.15 Query lifecycle, from the inception of a query to results delivered to the issuer

physical algebra query trees. The merging of query trees is done through context associations. To facilitate the performance evaluation and the impact of the query optimization, a query cost metric was derived and used to present optimization performance results.

In the example, the camera adapter receives the raw imagery from the camera and adds **_contextual metadata_** pertaining to the frames and objects observed. The raw imagery is a temporally ordered series of frames of video that is simply data; a two-dimensional matrix of pixel values corresponding to what was sensed by the imaging device. The camera adapter implements algorithms to model the scene background. As salient objects move across the background, a segmentation algorithm attempts to determine which pixels belong to the scene background and which pixels do not. Pixels that are not recorded as part of the background are grouped together into a blob. Enhanced methods can make use of context to more accurately determine the pixels that belong to the target.

Blobs are assigned an identifier that is unique to each instance of a camera adapter (and thus, unique to each video stream). A frame-to-frame tracker maintains correspondences between objects, as they move, from one frame to the next. By maintaining these correspondences, the image analysis module computes a feature vector corresponding to the visual appearance of each object in each frame of video. The output of the image analysis module is contextual metadata describing each frame, e.g., a monotonically increasing frame number, timestamp when the frame was received, the number of objects in the frame and their identifiers, privacy filters associated with the camera, etc.

To evaluate the performance of the cross-camera tracking, videos from the CAVIAR [78] project are utilized. The CAVIAR collection of videos show a number of different scenarios observing humans (leaving an object, walking, fighting, etc.) from multiple vantage points. The scenes with two perspectives are used in this study to measure the cross-camera tracking functionality and gauge the merits of the bag comparison technique when an object is observed from different angles. The results presented indicate that the bag comparison is robust to these differences in angles, and also the slight differences in scene lighting observed in these videos. Note also that the timing of occurrences of objects in these videos are not temporally aligned, which also would simulate an object being observed by one camera and then later observed by a second. In addition to the CAVIAR videos (Fig. 19.16), some scenes were created to test specific scenarios; these additional scenes have a first camera positioned in a room and a second camera located in a hallway. These scenes have different backgrounds but the same objects moving about in them, being observed from different angles.

The continuous contextual queries (i.e., subqueries) in the LVDBMS are evaluated periodically. The interval in which they are evaluated is referred to as the resolution of the query. The amount of time required to evaluate each subquery should be less than its resolution, else the subquery evaluations will be missed due

Fig. 19.16 Sample frames from CAVIAR dataset

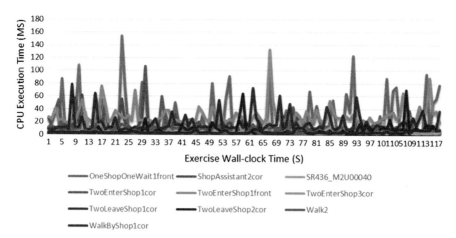

Fig. 19.17 Evaluation costs select queries

to its evaluation time running over into the next evaluation time slot. To test the subquery evaluation performance of the execution engine and related metadata structures, an evaluation scenario comprised of executing five subqueries simultaneously for a period of 120 s over ten randomly selected videos was performed. The test was repeated for ten different videos, with a query resolution of one second. The time taken for the evaluation procedure to conclude is recorded at one-second intervals. These evaluation times are plotted for each video in Fig. 19.17. Additional detail pertaining to the evaluation times is presented in Table 19.4. In order to simplify the information presented in Table 19.4, it has been normalized relative to a single video by dividing the values by five. The evaluation times are significantly less than the query resolution, and in most cases the standard deviation is larger than the average execution time. The use of query-based assessment provides rapid analytics for context understanding.

Table 19.4 Average query evaluation in milliseconds of Central Processing Unit (CPU) time, by video

Movie	Performance			
	Min	Max	Std Dev.	Average
SR436_M2U00040 (3)	0.40	5.60	0.73	0.78
OneShopOneWait1front (2)	0.40	30.81	6.26	4.58
ShopAssistant2cor (2)	0.40	21.24	2.72	2.49
TwoEnterShop1cor (2)	1.60	12.00	1.68	2.42
TwoEnterShop1front (2)	3.40	26.60	3.05	5.97
TwoEnterShop3cor (2)	0.40	7.00	0.90	0.87
TwoLeaveShop1cor (2)	1.40	15.60	2.75	3.47
TwoLeaveShop2cor (2)	0.40	14.00	1.86	1.38
Walk2 (2)	0.40	1.80	0.40	0.72
WalkByShop1cor (2)	0.40	3.00	0.49	0.73

19.6 Conclusions

As cameras and imaging sensors continue to be installed, more and more of our lives can be captured, analyzed, and correlated by computer systems. Video tracking, especially between distributed cameras, can be enhanced with contextual analysis. Contextual analysis includes feature extraction, scene content, and target handoff. To efficiently transfer contextual data for information fusion exploitation, information management was developed using CBIR and live query computing (LVC). The LVC also enables policies (e.g., privacy and permissions) to determine access of the contextual information in the live video streams. Together, the LVC enables a context-aware, privacy-aware, and semantic-aware video content. Context-aware tracking is established with the tracking methods. Privacy-aware comes with access to the camera information. Finally, the ability to map features and linguistic queries facilitates semantic-aware information fusion.

The LVC-DBMS includes efficient query processing techniques, web service communication, and a scalable 4-tier application architecture that can scale and accommodate large camera networks. Experimental results show that the LVC-DBMS can effectively recognize events observed in video streams, implement privacy policies and efficiently processing semantic queries. The key elements described include a prototype LVC implementation including:

- *Context-aware*: a high-level query language for specifying events and interacting with the LVDBMS,
- *Privacy-aware*: infrastructure permitting for the specification of privacy policies and their implementation in a real-time stream processing environment, and
- *Semantic-aware*: efficient query processing and execution techniques to maximize compute memory resource usage over a large set of linguistic information.

Future efforts include using the information exploitation system for big data problems, including physics-based and human-based video-to-text information fusion. Large-scale multimedia applications will require dynamic-driven application systems approaches that bring together the context, privacy, and semantic-aware analysis.

Acknowledgments This work is partly supported by the Air Force Office of Scientific Research (AFOSR) under the Dynamic Data Driven Application Systems program and the Air Force Research Lab.

References

1. E. Blasch, A. Steinberg, S. Das, J. Llinas, C.-Y. Chong, O. Kessler, E. Waltz, F. White, Revisiting the JDL model for information exploitation, in *International Conference on Info Fusion* (2013)
2. C.J. Date, *An Introduction to Database Systems*, 2nd edn. (Addison-Wesley Publishing Company Inc, 1977)

3. M.A. Tantaoui, K.A. Hua, T.T. Do, BroadCatch: a periodic broadcast technique for heterogeneous video-on-demand. Broadcast. IEEE Trans. **50**(3), 289–301 (2004)
4. Z. Liu, E. Blasch, Z. Xue, E. Langaniere, W. Wu, Objective assessment of multiresolution image fusion algorithms for context enhancement in night vision: a comparative survey. IEEE Trans. Pattern Analysis Mach. Intell. **34**(1), 94–109 (2012)
5. E. Blasch, S. Plano, Cognitive fusion analysis based on context, in *Proceedings of SPIE*, vol. 5434 (2004)
6. E.P. Blasch, E. Bosse, D.A. Lambert, *High-Level Information Fusion Management and Systems Design* (Artech House, Norwood, MA, 2012)
7. S. Ezekiel, M.G. Alford, D. Ferris, E. Jones et al., Multi-scale decomposition tool for content based image retrieval, in *IEEE Applied Imagery Pattern Recognition Workshop* (2013)
8. E. Blasch, I. Kadar, K. Hintz, J. Biermann, C. Chong, S. Das, Resource management coordination with level 2/3 fusion issues and challenges. IEEE Aerosp. Electron. Syst. Mag. **23**(3), 32–46 (2008)
9. S. Hoberman, *Data Modeling Made Simple: A Practical Guide for Business and Information Technology Professionals* (Technics Publications, 2005)
10. J. Grimes, M. Potel, What is multimedia? Comput. Graph. Appl. IEEE **11**(1), 49–52 (1991)
11. Z. Zhang, R. Zhang, *Multimedia Data Mining: A Systematic Introduction to Concepts and Theory* (Chapman & Hall/CRC, 2008)
12. H. Ling, L. Bai, E. Blasch, X. Mei, Robust infrared vehicle tracking across target pose change using L_1 regularization, in *International Conference on Info Fusion* (2010)
13. Z. Liu, E. Blasch, Z. Xue, R. Langaniere, W. Wu, Objective assessment of multiresolution image fusion algorithms for context enhancement in night vision: a comparative survey. IEEE Trans. Pattern Anal. Mach. Intell. **34**(1), 94–109 (2012)
14. M.K. Hu, Visual pattern recognition by moment invariants. Inf. Theory IRE Trans. **8**, 179–187 (1962)
15. E. Bribiesca, A. Guzman, How to describe pure form and how to measure differences in shapes using shape numbers. Pattern Recogn. **12**, 101–112 (1980)
16. M. Nixon, A.S. Aguado, *Feature Extraction and Image Processing for Computer Vision* (Academic Press, 2012)
17. C. Harris, M. Stephens, A combined corner and edge detector, in *Alvey Vision Conference*, (Manchester, UK, 1988) p. 50
18. D.G. Lowe, Object recognition from local scale-invariant features. *IEEE International Conference on Computer Vision* (1999), pp. 1150–1157
19. Y. Wu, E. Blasch, G. Chen, L. Bai, H. Ling, Multiple source data fusion via sparse representation for robust visual tracking, in *International Conference on Info Fusion* (2011)
20. H. Ling, Y. Wu, E. Blasch, G. Chen, L. Bai, Evaluation of visual tracking in extremely low frame rate wide area motion imagery, in *International Conference on Info Fusion*
21. C.R. Wren, A. Azarbayejani, T. Darrell, A.P. Pentland, Pfinder: real-time tracking of the human body. IEEE Trans. Pattern Anal. Mach. Intell. **19**, 780–785 (1997)
22. C. Stauffer, W.E.L. Grimson, Adaptive background mixture models for real-time tracking. in *IEEE Conferernce on Computer Vision and Pattern Recognition* (1999)
23. K. Kim, T.H. Chalidabhongse, D. Harwood, L. Davis, Real-time foreground–background segmentation using codebook model. Real-Time Imaging **11**, 172–185 (2005)
24. M. Piccardi, Background subtraction techniques: a review, in *Presented at the 2004 IEEE International Conference on Systems, Man and Cybernetics* (IEEE, 2004), pp. 3099–3104
25. S.C.S. Cheung, C. Kamath, Robust techniques for background subtraction in urban traffic video, in *Presented at the Proceedings of SPIE* (2004) pp. 881–892
26. D.H. Parks, S.S. Fels, Evaluation of background subtraction algorithms with post-processing, in *Presented at the IEEE Fifth International Conference on Advanced Video and Signal Based Surveillance* (IEEE, 2008), pp. 192–199
27. R.O. Duda, P.E. Hart, D.G. Stork, *Pattern Classification and Scene Analysis*, 2nd edn. (1995)
28. H. Samet, *The Design and Analysis of Spatial Data Structures* (Addison-Wesley Reading MA, 1990)

29. H. Samet, *Foundations of Multidimensional and Metric Data Structures* (Morgan Kaufmann, 2006)
30. R.M. Bolle, B.L. Yeo, M. Yeung, Video query: research directions. IBM J. Res. Dev. **42**, 233–252 (1998)
31. R. Brunelli, O. Mich, C.M. Modena, A survey on the automatic indexing of video data. J. Vis. Commun. Image Represent. **10**, 78–112 (1999)
32. C.G.M. Snoek, M. Worring, Multimodal video indexing: a review of the state-of-the-art. Multimed. Tools Appl. **25**, 5–35 (2005)
33. Y. Wang, Z. Liu, J.C. Huang, Multimedia content analysis-using both audio and visual clues. Signal Process. Mag. IEEE **17**, 12–36 (2000)
34. J.M. Boggs, *The Art of Watching Films* (ERIC, 1996)
35. R. Jain, A. Hampapur, Metadata in video databases. ACM Sigmod Rec. **23**, 27–33 (1994)
36. R. Brunelli, O. Mich, C.M. Modena, A survey on the automatic indexing of video data. J. Vis. Commun. Image Represent. **10**, 78–112 (1999)
37. A.K. Jain, R.P.W. Duin, J. Mao, Statistical pattern recognition: a review. Pattern Anal. Mach. Intell. IEEE Trans. **22**, 4–37 (2000)
38. I. Ide, K. Yamamoto, H. Tanaka, Automatic video indexing based on shot classification. Adv. Multimed. Content Process. 87–102 (1999)
39. J. Foote, An overview of audio information retrieval. Multimed. Syst. **7**, 2–10 (1999)
40. E. Wold, T. Blum, D. Keislar, J. Wheaten, Content-based classification, search, and retrieval of audio. Multimed. IEEE **3**, 27–36 (1996)
41. J. Nievergelt, H. Hinterberger, K.C. Sevcik, The grid file: an adaptable, symmetric multikey file structure. ACM Trans. Database Syst. TODS **9**, 38–71 (1984)
42. A.V. Aho, J.E. Hopcroft, J. Ullman, *Data Structures and Algorithms* (Addison-Wesley Longman Publishing Co., Inc, 1983)
43. T.H. Cormen, C.E. Leiserson, R.L. Rivest, C. Stein, Introduction to Algorithms. MIT press
44. Pieprzyk, J., Sadeghiyan, B. *Design of Hashing Algorithms* (Springer, New York, 2001)
45. J.L. Bentley, Multidimensional binary search trees used for associative searching. Commun. ACM **18**, 509–517 (1975)
46. P. Scheuermann, M. Ouksel, Multidimensional B-trees for associative searching in database systems. Inf. Syst. **7**, 123–137 (1982)
47. W.G. Aref, I.F. Ilyas, Sp-gist: an extensible database index for supporting space partitioning trees. J. Intell. Inf. Syst. **17**, 215–240 (2001)
48. A. Guttman, R-trees: a dynamic index structure for spatial searching (ACM, 1984)
49. G. Hristescu, M. Farach-Colton, Cluster-preserving embedding of proteins. Technical Report 99-50, Computer Science Department, Rutgers University
50. J.T.L. Wang, X. Wang, K.I. Lin, D. Shasha, B.A. Shapiro, K. Zhang, Evaluating a class of distance-mapping algorithms for data mining and clustering, in *Presented at the Proceedings of the Fifth ACM SIGKDD International Conference on Knowledge Discovery and Data Mining* (ACM, 1999), pp. 307–311
51. W. Aref, H. Samet, Uniquely reporting spatial objects: yet another operation for comparing spatial data structures, in *Presented at the Proceedings of the Fifth International Symposium on Spatial Data Handling* (1992) pp. 178–189
52. W.G. Aref, H. Samet, Hashing by proximity to process duplicates in spatial databases, in *Presented at the Proceedings of the Third International Conference on Information and Knowledge Management* (ACM, 1994), pp. 347–354
53. H. Samet, Spatial data structures. Mod. Database Syst. Object Model Interoperability Beyond, 361–385 (1995)
54. M. Flickner, H. Sawhney, W. Niblack, J. Ashley, Q. Huang, B. Dom, M. Gorkani, J. Hafner, D. Lee, D. Petkovic, Query by image and video content: the QBIC system. Computer **28**, 23–32 (1995)
55. A. Blaser, *Data base techniques for pictorial applications* (Springer, Florence, 1979)

56. N.S. Chang, K.S. Fu, Query-by-pictorial-example. IEEE Trans. Softw. Eng. 519–524 (1980)
57. S.F. Chang, A. Eleftheriadis, R. McClintock, Next-generation content representation, creation, and searching for new-media applications in education. Proc. IEEE **86**, 884–904 (1998)
58. J.R. Bach, C. Fuller, A. Gupta, A. Hampapur, B. Horowitz, R. Humphrey, R. Jain, C.F. Shu, The virage image search engine: an open framework for image management, in *Presented at the SPIE Storage and Retrieval for Image and Video Databases IV* (1996) pp. 76–87
59. A. Pentland, R.W. Picard, S. Sclaroff, Photobook: content-based manipulation of image databases. Int. J. Comput. Vis. **18**, 233–254 (1996)
60. T. Huang, S. Mehrotra, K. Ramchandran, Multimedia analysis and retrieval system (MARS) project
61. Y. Rui, T.S. Huang, S.F. Chang, Image retrieval: current techniques, promising directions, and open issues. J. Vis. Commun. Image Represent. **10**, 39–62 (1999)
62. R. Zhao, W.I. Grosky, Negotiating the semantic gap: from feature maps to semantic landscapes. Pattern Recognit. **35**, 593–600 (2002)
63. Y. Liu, D. Zhang, G. Lu, W.Y. Ma, A survey of content-based image retrieval with high-level semantics. Pattern Recognit. **40**, 262–282 (2007)
64. D. Durkee, Why cloud computing will never be free. Queue **8**, 20 (2010)
65. T. Sato, T. Kanade, E.K. Hughes, M.A. Smith, S. Satoh, Video OCR: indexing digital news libraries by recognition of superimposed captions. Multimed. Syst. **7**, 385–395 (1999)
66. P. Geetha, V. Narayanan, A survey of content-based video retrieval. J. Comput. Sci. **4**, 474–486 (2008)
67. J. Foote, Content-based retrieval of music and audio, in *Presented at the Proceedings of SPIE* (1997) pp. 138–147
68. Z. Liu, Q. Huang, Content-based indexing and retrieval-by-example in audio, in *Presented at the IEEE International Conference on Multimedia and Expo* (IEEE, 2000), pp. 877–880
69. J. Makhoul, F. Kubala, T. Leek, D. Liu, L. Nguyen, R. Schwartz, A. Srivastava, Speech and language technologies for audio indexing and retrieval. Proc. IEEE **88**, 1338–1353 (2000)
70. G. Bradski, *The OpenCV Library*. Dr Dobbs J. Software Tools (2000)
71. S. Taylor, *Optimizing Applications for Multi-Core Processors, Using the Intel Integrated Performance Primitives* (Intel Press, 2007)
72. E. Blasch, Z. Wang, H. Ling, K. Palaniappan, G. Chen, D. Shen, A. Aved, G. Seetharaman, Video-based activity analysis using the L1 tracker on VIRAT data, in *IEEE Applied Imagery Pattern Recognition Workshop* (2013)
73. A.J. Aved, *Scene Understanding for Real Time Processing of Queries over Big Data Streaming Video*. Ph.D. dissertation, University of Central Florida, 2013
74. H. Zha, X. He, C. Ding, H. Simon, M. Gu, Bipartite graph partitioning and data clustering, in *Presented at the Proceedings of the Tenth International Conference on Information and Knowledge Management* (ACM, 2001), pp. 25–32
75. H.W. Kuhn, The Hungarian method for the assignment problem. Nav. Res. Logist. Q. **2**, 83–97 (1955)
76. J. Munkres, Algorithms for the assignment and transportation problems. J. Soc. Ind. Appl. Math. **5**, 32–38 (1957)
77. G.A. Mills-Tettey, A. Stentz, M.B. Dias, *The Dynamic Hungarian Algorithm for the Assignment Problem with Changing Costs* (No. CMU-RI-TR-07-27) (Robotics Institute, Pittsburgh, PA, 2007)
78. R. Fisher, CAVIAR: context aware vision using image-based active recognition (WWW Document). URL http://homepages.inf.ed.ac.uk/rbf/CAVIAR/. Accessed 11 Dec 2011

Part VI
Applications of Context Approaches to Fusion

Chapter 20
The Role of Context in Multiple Sensor Systems for Public Security

Wolfgang Koch

Abstract The informational basis for making appropriate decisions is provided by situation pictures that electronically represent a dynamically evolving real-world scenario. For the rapidly growing area of civil security applications, exploitation of observational information, sensor data as well as textual reports, critically depends on the availability and the quality of appropriate context information as well as on the underlying data fusion algorithms that take them into account. Often, sensor signals and measurements are referred to as "hard" data, while observer reports and context information are considered to be "soft" pieces of information. Besides speaking of "hard" and "soft" data, one may also characterize the data to be fused with respect to the timescale they are referring to. In this sense, we distinguish between "close-to-object evolution data," where the informational content of the data streaming in possibly change on a relatively short-time scale, from data with a more stable or slowly changing informational content. Emerging assistance systems for safety and security applications are driven by algorithms for extracting high-value information from data streams of even poor quality. Due to the complexity of the real-world phenomena to be observed, however, and their inherently unpredictable nature, context information and its integration is crucial. Also legal and moral constraints can be viewed as context information shaping informational decision support for public safety and security. In this chapter, fusion applications are exemplarily discussed as well as more general design principles of future security assistance systems.

Keywords Decision support systems · Assistance systems · Public/civil security · Sensor data · Observer reports · Context information · Data fusion algorithms · Hazardous materials · Person tracking and classification

Context Enhanced Information Fusion. Improving real world performance with domain knowledge, editors: Lauro Snidaro, Jesús García, James Llinas, Erik Blasch.

W. Koch (✉)
Fraunhofer FKIE, Wachtberg, Germany
e-mail: w.koch@ieee.org

© Springer International Publishing Switzerland (outside the USA) 2016
L. Snidaro et al. (eds.), *Context-Enhanced Information Fusion*,
Advances in Computer Vision and Pattern Recognition,
DOI 10.1007/978-3-319-28971-7_20

20.1 Introduction

The exploitation of observational data in decision support systems that are collected from networks of physical sensors and provided by human observers critically depends on the quality of appropriate context information as well as on the underlying fusion algorithms that take them into account. It seems reasonable to distinguish between *physical context* information, derived from facts of the natural and engineering sciences, *environmental context* information, determined typically while operating the system, *partially known context* information, often described by statistical models, and, last but not least, *language-encoded context* information.

In many cases, these categories of context information do not appear isolated from each other. Sensor models, for example, combine physical and partially known context for describing imprecise sensor measurements with environmental context, e.g., when a clutter background has to be estimated online. Besides a human observer report, an example for language-encoded context information is a plan to be followed by certain objects of interest in the course of time. A plan, i.e., a certain mode of expected motion, comprises the description of geographical way-point coordinates to be passed at a given instants of time via particular paths along with quantitative measures of tolerance.

The informational basis for making appropriate decisions in a given situation is in many cases provided by so-called "situation pictures" that electronically represent a dynamically evolving "real-world" scenario in a decision support system. Situation pictures are produced by fusing sensor signals and preprocessed sensor measurements from various sensors as well as textual information from many sources, differing in relevance and reliability, that are typically stored in database systems. Often, signals and measurements are referred to as "hard" data, while observer reports and context information are considered to be "soft" pieces of information [1]. Besides speaking of "hard" and "soft" data, one could also characterize the data to be fused with respect to the timescale they are referring to. In this sense, we may distinguish between "close-to-object evolution data," where the informational content of the data streaming in may change on a relatively short timescale, from data with a more stable or slowly changing informational content.

The technology of sensor data and information fusion aims at the development of mathematically formulated algorithms for extracting information from both, hard and soft data, collected on all relevant timescales. What cannot be processed algorithmically on principle, cannot be transformed in a technical assistance system for decision support at all. We thus have nearly always to deal with "hybrid systems" or "assistance systems" that combine algorithmic, i.e., automated, reasoning with characteristically human thought and judgment not replaceable by any form of "artificial intelligence."

In emerging informational assistance systems designed for safety and security applications, all forms of information, including context information, are of critical importance. Such systems aim at a basic human desire with many facets, i.e., living safely and securely. Its satisfaction has psychological and societal, but also technical, legal, and economic implications. On the other hand, rapid progress in networking sensors and distributed database systems producing an ever-increasing diversity of information has profoundly transformed the very notion of public security and its appreciation in modern liberal societies.

This technological revolution is in particular driven by algorithms for extracting high-value information from sensor data streams of even poor quality. Due to the complexity of the real-world phenomena to be observed, however, and their inherently unpredictable nature, the role context information and its integration on various levels in systems engineering are particularly crucial. In a sense, also legal and moral constraints can be viewed as context information shaping the very design of informational decision support for public safety and security. We here exemplary discuss data fusion methodologies having their roots in "classical" tracking and sensor data fusion applications and some more general design principles of future multiple source security assistance systems. A preliminary version of the following considerations has been published in [2].

20.2 Safety and Security—Approach and Preliminaries

Safety and security are basic requirements for preserving personal life and physical integrity, but also for guaranteed and calculable economic and societal processes, for providing services of public interest, or even for achieving proper social balancing. In addition, modern industrialized societies fundamentally depend on inherently risky technologies. Corresponding safety and security technologies are thus enabling technologies for stability and prosperity in modern societies. Not unexpectedly, the fundamental human desire for safety and security, taken as an individual and societal phenomenon, has been an object of philosophical, psychological, and historical speculation for a long time.

Since safety and security are basic human desires [3], their satisfaction is expected to be a major political, societal, legal, and psychological factor of governmental and private agency that is creating a corresponding and rapidly evolving safety and security industry. How can safety and security be improved by morally, legally, and societally acceptable, as well as economically affordable "products" or "services" to be offered on appropriate markets, i.e., by putting this technology into a proper context, e.g., by integrating properly language-encoded context information. Needless to say, the "Edward Snowden effect" has made a wide public aware of these issues—not only in Europe.

To provide possible contributions for answering these difficult questions from a systems engineering point of view and emphasizing context information, this chapter basically follows three lines of thought:

1. In a sociopolitical perspective, we consider the desire for safety and security as a fundamental function or responsibility of government introducing the problem

of reconciling the value of greater safety and security with the value of the liberty, freedom, personal dignity, or privacy that an individual foregoes.

2. In a systems engineering and architectural perspective, we discuss principles that allow the design of effective safety and security systems that are scalable and adaptable, and may facilitate the assessment of the value of the additional safety and security against the liberty, freedom, and privacy lost.

3. Guided by the spirit of Concept Development and Experimentation [4], we consider a modular, prototypical realization as a "concrete example" that is addressing on hazardous material localization in public infrastructures along with the concepts and principles previously discussed.

Since any systems engineering approach to public safety and security is at least implicitly embedded in a more general framework of thought, i.e., in a language-encoded context according to our four categories of context information, we should stress some basic elements.

Besides being capable of "insight," human beings, and partly even other living creatures, are often said to be characterized by their ability of using tools for interacting with their environment and of communicating with other entities that may provide additional insight. This very general observation seems to be visible in the polarity of Western civilization with its technology-driven and language-encoded strands of thought. From these two cultural branches, even the different types of context information have evolved that are considered here. On the systemic level of safety and security systems engineering, the different types of context information besides observational data produced by sensors, human beings or living creatures, have to be fused synergistically and are expected to yield more robust and informative results, improving real-world performance in the domain considered.

The "tools" for improving safety and security seems to be the emerging sociotechnical infrastructures that massively gather data and transform them into information, the basis for decision-making and governmental as well as private agency. Quite obviously, such technological systems have normative impacts and are intimately related to legal systems to be seen as a language-encoded "repository of knowledge, a formal accumulation of practical judgments. The law embodies the core insights about the way the world works and how we evaluate it" [5].

In other words, the issues of safety and security enforce a joint effort of the two polar strands of Western civilization. Of crucial importance is the relation between the emerging safety and security technology and the notion of an individual human subject born with freewill, capable of and accountable for deliberate intentional action, and entitled to "inalienable fundamental rights to which a person is inherently entitled simply because she or he is a human being" [6]. This very hallmark of Western democracy and the basic assumption of Western legal systems is the guiding principle and a most important context information to be integrated also into our approach, where we consider liberty, freedom, personal dignity, or privacy, etc., as "inalienable fundamental rights."

The organization of the chapter is as follows: Sect. 20.3 links the need for safety and security technology to economy and traces hidden links to law and statistical approach back in history. Based on the discussion so far, Sect. 20.4 introduces "the three pillars of public safety and security" to which technology can contribute. Section 20.5 identifies requirements regarding information fusion in support of these three pillars, while section VI focuses on a specific example: localization of hazardous materials. Section 20.6 presents a state-of-the-art technology in support of hazard materials localization, which is integrated into an experimental system sketched in Sect. 20.7. How this technological development should be supported by timely developments in law is explained in Sect. 20.8, opening the view to more general systems. Sections 20.9 and 20.10 discuss the role of various types of context information for formulating appropriate sensor models and detecting anomalies in person flows. The notion of security assistance systems is compared with the emerging paradigms of autonomic computing in Sect. 20.11. We finally attempt to draw some conclusions in Sect. 20.12.

20.3 Context of Insurance, Law, and Information Fusion

Some historical reflections on the more general context of safety and security, a look at the parallels between insurance industry and emerging safety and security technologies provide a starting point and initial insight.

Insurance companies improve safety and security for individuals or legal entities by providing financial compensation of contingent, uncertain losses. This is made possible by collecting relatively small monetary contributions from a large number of insurees. Consequently, the methodological basis of this business model is mathematical statistics for calculating appropriate premiums, while its modern enabling technology is provided by information engineering due to its nature as a mass business. Already in the 1950s, insurance industry began to introduce computers [7], invented in the 1940s by Konrad Zuse (1910–1995) [8] and others in the USA and the United Kingdom. Needless to say, insurance industry is of high economic importance for modern societies.

Statistics and informatics, however, are also the backbones of the emerging and rapidly evolving safety and security technologies for reducing risks caused by contingent, uncertain threats. In contrast to insured events, where *post-loss compensation* is contracted, *loss prevention* is in the focus here. By analyzing uncertain, incomplete, imperfect, and massively collected sensor and context data, safety and security threats are to be recognized *before* injuries and damages have occurred or at least mitigated in their effects. Along with technological progress, a specialized industry is marketing safety and security products or services with an ever-increasing economic impact. A recent study of the German Federal Ministry of Economics and Technology anticipates for the German safety and security market in 2015 a value of more than 30 billion Euros [9], already the sixth part of the total German premium income in 2012 [10]. Moreover, in analogy to insurance law, legal structures for supervising safety and security technologies are currently framed [11].

Perhaps rather surprisingly, the notion of "subjective probabilities" and their fusion by uncertain reasoning have been developed in medieval rabbinic jurisdiction, where even a first idea of the *Bayesian formalism* has been developed [12]. Analysis of evidence, methodical questioning, calculation of risks, and evaluation of uncertain data, reports, and particular circumstances—all these tasks to be solved wherever human beings form a society—in one way or other involve accumulation of individual probabilities. According to modern terminology, this reasoning is called "information fusion" and enables the design of assistance systems for computer-aided reasoning and decision-making [13]. In analogy to mechanical tools facilitating human labor and enhancing human physical strengths, informational assistance systems serve as "cognitive tools" that enhance our mental capabilities to deal with uncertain data that may massively be streaming in by providing "situation pictures" of possibly dynamically evolving phenomena.

First philosophical reflections along these lines have already been made in medieval scholasticism, culminating in the work of the logician, philosopher, theologian, and poet Raymundus Lullus (c.1232-1315), one of the early ancestors of modern computer science. His *Ars generalis ultima*, published in 1305, is considered as the first idea of a general purpose computer [14]. It influenced the thinking of Athanasius Kircher SJ (1602–1680) [15] and Gottfried Wilhelm Leibniz (1646–1716), who contributed to the intellectual foundations of modern computer science. Interestingly enough, Leibniz is also among the founders of modern actuarial science [16].

A pioneer of modern sensor data and information fusion is Thorvald Nicolai Thiele (1838–1910), an outstanding Danish astronomer, actuarian, and mathematician, who is perhaps not adequately remembered. In his famous textbook Statistical Methods (1932), the mathematician Ronald A. Fisher (1890–1962) provides a list of the main contributors to statistics containing only six names: Bayes, Laplace, Gauß, K. Pearson, Student (Gosset), and Thiele [17]. While Fisher's *information matrix* is a fundamental notion in information fusion as well, Thiele's extensive paper *The general theory of observations: Calculus of Probability and the method of least squares* (1889) contains many ideas shaping modern sensor data and information fusion, e.g., a complete version of the Kalman filter and smoother, a clear and distinct expression of the idea of likelihood, and an instance of what is now called the Expectation–Maximization algorithm that is useful, e.g., for solving data association problems in fusion applications [18]. Among his many other activities, Thiele was the founder and mathematical director of the *Hafnia* insurance company, Copenhagen, which existed until 1992. Also a large portion of Harald Cramé's (1893–1985) work, whose famous *Cramér-Rao-Lower-Bound* using Fisher's information matrix is a key tool in current fusion research, concerned the field of mathematical risk theory, actuarial science, and insurance mathematics [19]. Obviously, insurance and information fusion are the two major ways to do business with statistics, where fusion still has an enormous potential of development, scientifically and economically.

20.4 Notion and Particulars of Public Safety and Security

Before any further considerations on safety and security technology evolving from these roots, a look at the concise definition of public safety and security in juridical handbooks might provide some clarity: "The notion of public safety and security covers the integrity of the ... fundamental institutions ... of the state as well as the integrity of health, honor, freedom, property, and related objects of legal protection of its citizens. Defense against endangerment of public safety and security is the task of public safety and security authorities" [20].

Considering a familiar example, "integrity of health and property of citizens" is certainly affected by automotive traffic, for in the European Union alone more than 28,000 traffic deaths have been reported in 2012 [21], while globally 1.2 million persons have lost their lives due to traffic accidents. According to the previous definition, public safety and security authorities should actually forbid private transport in view of these facts. Nevertheless, individual mobility is a desirable good of high public and economic interest. To find a reasonable compromise between the competing goods of public safety and security on one side and individual mobility on the other, a triple strategy, based on the three pillars of technology, law, and insurance, has been developed over decades:

1. Primarily, injuries and damages are prevented or mitigated in their effects by a hierarchy of technological measures, such as vehicle inspections, robust vehicle bodies, passenger belts, air bags, or by the most recent advance, multiple sensor driver assistance systems.
2. This engineering work is accompanied by developing appropriate legal structures comprising road traffic law, including mandatory seat belt wearing or banning of mobile phone use by drivers, etc. In addition, proper police authorities enforce such regulations.
3. Since the financial loss by traffic accidents may easily exceed individual fortunes, the monetary aspects of affecting "integrity of health and property of citizens," is covered by a specialized traffic insurance industry, which has a large economic impact itself.

In this more general systemic approach, technology is put in context with complementary, non-technological elements. Obviously, this approach is practically proven and effective. From its maximum of more than 20,000 traffic deaths on German roads in the early 1970s, this number dropped down to 3340 in 2013, while the number of registered vehicles has grown from 14 million in 1970 to 52 million [22]. A quite analogous triple strategy based on technological, legal, and actuarial measures, has been developed for other risky technologies as well, such as air traffic control, offshore or chemical industry, and even nuclear industry, while in the latter case this strategy certainly reaches its limitations because of the sheer size of potential harm.

The discussion of the individual mobility example also illustrates that individuals often appear to take a comparatively simple utilitarian view placing a subjective value upon the benefit and cost–loss considerations, which can lead to a substantially different stance when compared to government surveillance. Internet platforms such as *Google* and *Facebook* or smartphone tracking provide examples in the ICT domain where individuals appear to be perfectly content to surrender substantial privacy in exchange for a "no-cost service" that provide benefits they value.

In the 9/11 attacks, 2976 citizens died. The attacks in Madrid on March 11, 2004, and in London, July 7, 2005, cost 191 and 56 lives of citizens, respectively. According to the previous definition, defense against endangerment of public security by such attacks is the task of public authorities. Even more than mobility as in the previous example, liberality, privacy, informational self-determination, civil rights, preservation of respectful treatment, and personal dignity are (highly!) desirable goods, even natural rights.

Why should not we react in a similarly unexcited manner to resolve this dilemma? Why should not we following the well-proven triple strategy with its three pillars, i.e., a combination of preventive or mitigating measures of risk management (technologically and legally based), which is complemented by financial residual risk compensation, i.e., by insurance? As the individual mobility example shows, this approach may increase the value that both society and an individual can derive from a risky activity that involves a large number of organizations and individuals whilst simultaneously bounding cost and risk. The "point of balance," however, is not necessarily static over time: the perceived level of terrorist risk/activity, for example, may cause it to move.

One might argue that terrorist events are essentially deliberate acts in contrast to merely "accidental" traffic accidents. Since this systemic approach is undoubtedly effective also in case of other deliberate acts, such as speeding or drunk driving, and even in crime prevention, e.g., housebreaking, we expect *The Three Pillars of Public Safety and Security* to be an effective strategy even in case of terrorist crimes and other safety and security applications. In particular, this strategy is a good example to inserting fundamental context knowledge into systems engineering for applications in the public domain.

20.5 Context-Derived Design of Public Security Systems

In the domain of public security, multiple sensor security assistance systems are expected to play a role comparable to existing car driver assistance systems, i.e., contributing to the first, the technological pillar of a triple strategy.

Considering a concrete example, let us focus on detecting and preventing harm caused by hazardous materials in public infrastructures, e.g., by explosives or radioactive substances. The related events are contingent, uncertain, and rare, when happening, however, resulting in serious injuries of the "integrity of health, honor, and property" of a large number of citizens. Such events may even threaten "fundamental institutions of the state." Typically, security contractors, a new and

Fig. 20.1 A public infrastructure with security personnel (© by drp under CC BY-NC-ND 2.0)

highly specialized profession, are responsible for countering such threats, thereby acting on behalf of public authorities. Let us consider a departure hall such as shown in Fig. 20.1. Obviously, the security forces need support to fulfill their duty in such scenarios. Desirable are informational assistance systems that pinpoint potential threats, such shown in Fig. 20.2, where a person is labeled as a potential threat, e.g., as carrying homemade explosives similar to the London attacks in 2005. In a couple of minutes after this video sequence has been taken, the suspect may bring death to many citizens.

More generally speaking, automated recognition of security relevant features in public scenarios is a key functionality of security assistance systems. It has to fulfill several overall requirements that need to cover a broader range of issues than conventional engineering standards such as:

1. Unburden from routine and mass tasks to gain room for human expertise and insight.
2. Focus human attention to potential threats, hazards, or anomalies as a key functionality.
3. Preserve dignity and informational self-determination by collecting threat-relevant data only.
4. Operate permanently without interfering with or annoying everyday public life.
5. Exploit sensors enabling apprehension beyond natural senses for threat recognition.
6. Indicate properly the possibly limited quality of inferences from inaccurate and incomplete data.
7. Profit from technology trends (sensors, communications, databases, processors).

Fig. 20.2 Potential terrorist such as in the London tube attack 2005 (labeled red, © by drp under CC BY-NC-ND 2.0)

8. Fuse multiple sensor data and context information to the extent that is allowed.
9. Guarantee constant and standardized quality levels for any module used in public security applications.
10. Design scalable architectures to be adapted to large diverse networks of sensors and databases.
11. Enable the utility–cost–privacy balance of each module be understood and its impact assessed.
12. Provide intuitive interfaces to human decision-makers, adapted to their specific needs.

Essentially, multiple sensor security assistance systems that are designed along these lines combine the strengths of automated and human data exploitation by:

• real-time analysis of large streams of multiple sensor data and context databases,
• while enabling high decision competence in individual situations by expert knowledge.

Security assistance systems may thus be considered as "cognitive tools" for providing awareness of threats that enhance our natural mental capabilities of dealing with large amounts of security relevant sensor and context data in an analogous way as mechanical tools enhance our physical capabilities. Their development should be accompanied by considering technology-driven legal aspects and covering residual risks by properly designed insurance products. Moreover, by identifying fundamental technological limitations of preventive measures and quantitative performance analysis of modular and standardized security assistance systems, the residual risks and therefore even corresponding insurance premiums may become calculable, which would otherwise hardly be possible.

20.6   The Problem of Hazardous Material Localization

Returning to the "London terrorist" example shown in Fig. 20.2—what makes the labeled person suspicious? Is there a chance to sense the threat connected to him to single him out in a crowd of non-suspects?

There is certainly little chance of threat recognition by video analytics alone. Probably, the suspect has not shown any type of individual behavior not being shared with many other persons. What makes him different, however, is the very fact of carrying a significant amount of explosives, homemade explosives that to a certain extent "smell," not to human noses, but to dogs' noses, for example, and olfactory chemical sensors. While in the biosphere "noses" are among the oldest of senses, their technical equivalents are still subject to a rapid technological development. Only recently, they have reached a level of maturity that making their operational use in open systems an option for a growing number of hazardous materials. Chemical sensors detecting even traces of popular explosives in open systems, however, are still in an experimental state and not yet available as stable products. In 3–5 years, however, this situation will have changed completely. System design considerations taking these new sensing options into account should thus start right now (Fig. 20.3).

The design principle of a potentially inexpensive class of chemical sensors with enormous market potential, so-called quartz microbalances, is quite intuitive [23]. Basically, they consist of an oscillating quartz crystal coated with a macromolecular

© Fraunhofer FKIE, all rights reserved
© AK Waldvogel, University of Mainz
© Fraunhofer FKIE, all rights reserved

(**a**) MOx semi-conductor gas sensors   (**b**) QMB array for gas sensing   (**c**) Scintillation counter

Fig. 20.3 *Detection of gases and radiation in open systems.* The semiconductor sensors in (**a**) adsorb molecules on a metal oxide (MOx) coating. The sensor in (**b**) uses coated quartz micro balances (QMB). The scintillation counter in (**c**) counts gamma quanta from radioactive sources. (© by Fraunhofer FKIE)

receptor substance that selectively absorbs particular substances to be detected. Even a few absorbed molecules cause an increase of mass attached to the oscillating crystal, which is sufficient for inducing a tiny, but measurable frequency shift. Quartz microbalances can thus be highly *sensitive*. By considering crystal arrays with different coatings, a significant *selectivity* can be reached as well. With this principle, even sensors for detecting biological agents are within reach, where enzymatic coatings are reversibly reacting with particular proteins, viruses, or even bacteria.

Apart from all physiological or chemical differences in olfactory senses or sensors, a fundamental commonality of all *attribute sensors* of this type can be identified, i.e., their *inherently limited space-time resolution capability*. While attribute sensors are able to detect the presence of a particular substance or classes of substances among a variety of alternatives, they on principle are unable to provide useful information on their location. They neither enable any association of the sensed signature to a particular carrier, nor any tracking of its position over time if the substance is carried on. The same observation is valid for wider classes of attribute sensors such as radioactive sensors. Context information on these fundamental sensor properties is thus a highly critical component of system design.

Obviously, the situation in Fig. 20.1 is by far too complex to provide any reasonable technological aid, at least in the foreseeable future. To enter public places like this, however, persons often have to pass well-defined access areas, skywalks, or escalators such as shown in Fig. 20.2, where the complexity of the surveillance task is much reduced. Tunnel-type areas, where persons enter, stroll along, and finally leave, enable a space-time approach for tracking-aided hazardous material localization. We may span a temporal basis to collect data over time and exploit "space" by spatially distributing attribute sensors along the walls. The temporal dimension is used by video cameras or laser scanners for tracking each person. By fusing measurements of each chemical sensor over time with the tracking data of all potential carriers of hazardous materials, we get a chance to overcome the limited space-time resolution capability of attribute sensors. More abstractly speaking, we wish to learn from uncertain data, which time-varying object can be classified as suspect or non-suspect [24].

20.7 HAMLeT—Discussion of an Experimental Example

To illustrate tracking-aided multiple object, multiple sensor classification for informational security assistance systems, we discuss an experimental setup called HAMLeT (Hazardous Material Localization and Person Tracking) [25]. A prototypical demonstration system like HAMLeT may serve as an example of how taking sensors plus associated system components, including a walkway, for example, creates a safety and security assistance module that conforms to the design principles identified earlier.

First, relevant object properties are to be identified and modeled, e.g., by random vectors and their kinematical characteristics, by random matrices and their shape, by discrete random variables and the class they belong to, such as "non-suspect" or "suspect" along with the potential type of threat. The collection of such quantities referring to a particular object at a given time defines the object state at this very time. For dealing with uncertain knowledge on objects states, appropriate functions of them are considered, mainly probability density functions, but also proper generalizations of this notion, such as probability hypothesis densities [26] or intensity functions [27]. Spiky functions of this type indicate precise information on the states, while multimodal or "broad" functions represent ambiguous or imprecise knowledge. Data-driven "learning" of object properties is essentially an iterative updating of such functions. For doing so, the relationships between sensor data and objects states are to be modeled, as well as possible errors and uncertainties attached to them. Formally, this is described by functions of the object states, measurements, and sensor parameters, called likelihood functions, which reflect the physical characteristics of the sensor data to be processed in the updating procedure. For initiating or terminating this learning iteration, statistical decision-making is required.

A key problem in hazardous material localization is uncertainty on which position and attribute measurements are to be associated to which individual object. Among several solutions, *Expectation–Maximization* methods prove to be of particular value providing a unified and actually very beautiful framework. According to this methodology, each measurement is associated to all persons of interest with appropriate weighting factors. Ideally, measurements actually originating from a particular person have weight One, all other measurements Zero weight. Expectation–Maximization serves as a method to estimate the weighting factors from the measured data iteratively. In other words, joint estimation of objects' states and data association weights is considered.

Chemical sensors are influenced by numerous external factors, i.e., context information, that is not easily modeled. Of strong impact on the data quality and time delays involved are the distances between potential carriers, their velocities, temperature, humidity, and other environmental parameters such as the degree of turbulence, etc. For designing overall system parameters and quantitative performance predictions, experimental investigations are therefore inevitable. Figure 20.4 shows the experimental system HAMLeT, wherein corridor persons are entering and leaving. Three laser range scanners, four chemical sensors and three miniaturized gamma spectrometers are collecting data. For a detailed description of the mathematical methodology used (based on expectation maximization) and experimental results obtained see the dissertation [28]. Figure 20.5 provides an impression of the system's operation.

Of growing concern for public safety and security are so-called "dirty bombs," where radioactive materials, readily available for medical or commercial use, are combined with conventional explosives [29]. Their damage potential is high in view of contamination, health damage, and the psychological and societal impact in general [30]. There is also an ever-increasing need for localizing radioactive

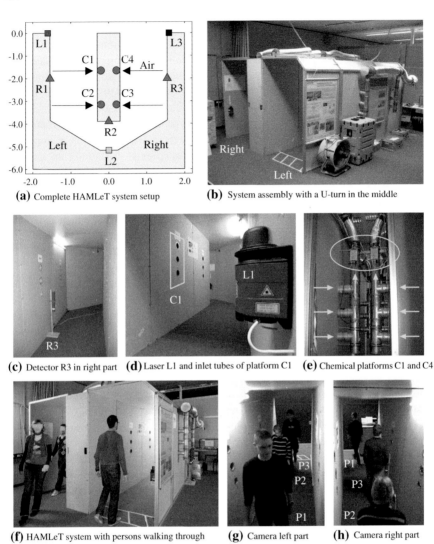

(a) Complete HAMLeT system setup

(b) System assembly with a U-turn in the middle

(c) Detector R3 in right part   (d) Laser L1 and inlet tubes of platform C1   (e) Chemical platforms C1 and C4

(f) HAMLeT system with persons walking through   (g) Camera left part   (h) Camera right part

Fig. 20.4 *Views of the HAMLeT system.* In the *upper row*, **a** and **b** show the system plan and a photo of the system assembly. The *middle row* is dedicated to the sensors that are integrated with the system. In particular, **e** sketches the airstream which blows molecules toward the chemical sensors hooked into the tubes. The *lower row* shows people walking through the system corridor. (© by Fraunhofer FKIE)

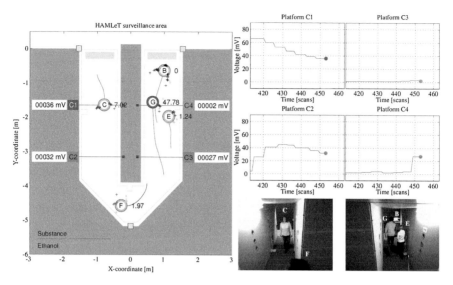

Fig. 20.5 Persons walking arbitrarily, carrier has a test tube (snapshot 2). The *left plot* shows the surveillance corridor, the sensor placement, the signals of the chemical sensor platforms and the person tracks with their carrier potential. The four plots on the *right* visualize the development of the voltage signals over time. The video snapshots show the current person constellation. (© by Fraunhofer FKIE)

materials in logistic chains or when deconstructing nuclear plants, where millions of tons of radioactively contaminated concrete and other debris have to be transported safely. A mobile version of the HAMLeT tunnel may be helpful even in case of catastrophes where incidents at chemical or nuclear plants are involved.

To sum up: by quantitatively analyzing the performance characteristics of an experimental system such as HAMLeT, it is in particular possible to assess the utility–cost–privacy balance, to define information needs and information outputs, to define the usual engineering interfaces and standards, and to define contractual interfaces. It also provides a means to measure or assess the marginal impact upon utility/cost/privacy of providing access to additional background, context, or historical information, or of providing additional output information. Systems like HAMLeT thus provide a means to test emerging architectures for security assistance systems.

20.8   Context Integration: Law Compliance by Design

Besides its use for system design considerations and quantitative performance prediction and evaluation, HAMLeT may also serve as a concrete example to raise societally relevant aspects of security assistance systems and to discuss "The Three

Pillars of Public Safety and Security" on a more systemic level, i.e., the interrelations of their technological, legal, and actuarial elements.

First of all and on principle, systems like HAMLeT do not collect any biometrically relevant parameters and therefore preserve the anonymity of the observed individuals by their very technical design. Only positional data in the corridor are collected for tracking-aided association of chemical or radioactive signatures to a distinct carrier. At least in the foreseeable future, chemical sensors are not capable to sense olfactory signatures characteristic of individuals. HAMLeT is thus "blind for normal people," i.e., for the vast majority of persons not carrying hazardous materials. Even though false alarms and manual inspection of a few remaining persons cannot be avoided, such systems may enable "normal" public life without extensive security checks at an ever-increasing number of occasions that consider everybody as a "suspect." Moreover, multiple sensor security assistance systems may seamlessly be embedded in public infrastructures making them essentially "invisible". Since the airflow in public infrastructures, for example, can often be modeled fairly well, chemical sensors could be part of the air-conditioning system of a public building.

There are, however, numerous procedurally and societally relevant questions in the context of security assistance systems that still have to be answered:

1. How to act when a threat is recognized? This task is by no means easy in cases as shown in Fig. 20.2, where any open police action is likely to trigger an explosion. This question raises the problem of automated or semiautomated actions involving possibly even lethal effects and serious legal problems [31].
2. Which domains of life will be safe and secure? Security assistance systems are opening a "security umbrella," wherever the necessary investments are made. Will countering security threats remain the task of public authorities? Will living safely and securely remain an affordable public good?
3. How to certify security assistance systems? As demonstrated by systems such as HAMLeT, certain aspects of law compliance are "inbuilt" technical features. Is this to be formalized to cover more features for wider classes of assistance systems? Are there procedures for certification and verification?
4. How to standardize security assistance systems? Calculation of residual risks and design of more intelligent legal measures for event prevention and actuarial residual risk compensation seem to become possible by standardized quality measures and quantitative performance evaluation for such systems.
5. What is the legal role of security contractors? New treat recognition technologies are likely to change traditional roles, since specialized technical understanding and training are required. In which way do security contractors participate in "public authority"? Who is controlling and limiting them in their actions?
6. How to check system integrity? Security assistance systems cannot exist in hermetic environments and thus need a sort of "immune system," since they are predictably targets in cyber-attacks or subject to varying and unpredictable conditions or malfunctions and must be capable to reconfigure themselves.

At any rate, such questions among others have a significant societal and political impact, they involve even psychoemotional and cultural apprehension, interpretation and reaction patterns, and should therefore be discussed publicly. Interestingly enough, these topics are already present in early science fiction novels [32] and recent movies.

It seems worth mentioning that the technical term *Information Fusion* was coined in George Orwell's very year 1984 in the defense domain, when the first attempt to scientifically systematize this emerging technology was made [33]. Orwell's warning "Don't let it happen!" may call us to think of potential threats to human society that may be related to this technology having reached a fairly mature level in the meantime. Attempts to identify and to counter undesirable developments will have to comprise interdisciplinary efforts by engineers, computer scientists, philosophers, sociologists, and, last but not least by lawyers and actuaries, "the engineers of ethics" that frame robust legal systems from more theoretical ethical insights and calculate residual risks based on statistical considerations.

20.9 Context Integration: Appropriate Sensor Models

So far, we have addressed context information that is language-encoded and even formalized to a certain degree in rule-based documents, e.g., basic legal notions on privacy, etc., or even standardization and certification issues or rule of engagement that are crucial for the deployment and day-to-day operation of assistance systems for public security. According to our introductory discussion this type of context information may be called "soft". As we have shown, it is highly relevant for any systems design considerations and security systems engineering in general.

Of no less importance is "hard" context information at various levels. Let us define the "hardness" of such information by the possibility of describing it quantitatively. "Hard" information in this sense can thus be encoded in mathematical models and directly enters into the mathematically formulated data fusion algorithms for combining observational data produced by physical sensing devices. The complexity of the context information entering the design of appropriate sensor models to develop well-adapted likelihood functions may substantially vary for different sensor types.

In Fig. 20.4, the placement of three scintillation sensors for detecting illicitly transported radioactive materials by their gamma radiation emitted is indicated by red triangles. Note that alpha and beta rays can be easily shielded: alpha rays are stopped by a sheet of paper and beta rays are stopped by a few millimeters of aluminum. Therefore, it is not possible to detect a shielded alpha or beta radiator within the HAMLeT concept. Gamma rays, in contrast, have the ability to penetrate matter and are merely attenuated. One of the aim of the HAMLeT system is thus to localize a person carrying a weak gamma radiation source.

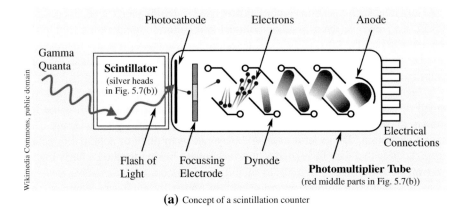

Wikimedia Commons, public domain

(a) Concept of a scintillation counter

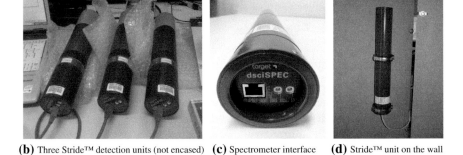

(b) Three Stride™ detection units (not encased) **(c)** Spectrometer interface **(d)** Stride™ unit on the wall

Fig. 20.6 Radiation detectors used in the HAMLeT system. The radiation detection in the HAMLeT system is realized by gamma scintillation counters. The concept of this technology is explained by (**a**), while (**b**)–(**d**) refer to the detection units integrated with the system. (© by Fraunhofer FKIE)

"Scintillation counting" is a robust sensing principle that is illustrated in Fig. 20.6. The device consists of a scintillator (yellow) and a photomultiplier tube (white). When gamma quanta of a radioactive source strike the scintillator, they are absorbed by the scintillation material. Due to the special characteristics of the material, this process causes small flashes of light: the scintillations. The number of flashes is proportional to the number of emitted gamma quanta. Counting the number of flashes over a certain period of time is therefore a means to estimate the source intensity. In Fig. 20.6a the gamma quanta are represented by red arrows. Within a scintillation counter, the produced flashes of light are emitted toward a photocathode. The photocathode converts the flashes into electrons (blue), which are focussed by an electrode and then multiplied within a system of dynodes. At the end of the tube, the generated avalanche is strong enough to be registered as a signal. At the anode, the generated signals are collected and summed up. Figure 20.6b shows three devices without enclosure. The silver head of each device comprises the scintillator (with diameter 2″ and length 3″), whereas the red part corresponds to the photomultiplier tube connected to the scintillator. A scintillation counter requires a computation and communication module to provide the data over an appropriate interface. Figure 20.6c shows a close-up view with the communication interface in the front. The component provides functions for digital signal processing and multichannel analyzing. Therefore, in addition to the registered counts and the count rate, the device is also capable of deriving a spectrum from the measurements. The spectrum can be exploited to identify the detected radionuclide. The device is sensitive enough to detect a radioactive source of 220 kBq while it is carried through the experimental corridor.

In view of sensor data fusion, this discussion of an advanced sensing device makes clear that non-sensor, "hard" context information is critically required at three different levels. (1) We need a clear statistical model of the underlying physics of radioactive decay (physical context). (2) We need an equally clear statistical model of the observable quantities that are related to the physical phenomena and of the errors involved in each measurement processes (partially known context). (3) We finally need a dispersion model of Gamma radiation when propagating though media (environmental context). Also here statistical approaches are needed to cover partially unknown effects. For a more detailed discussion see [28, p. 166 ff.].

While the dispersion of Gamma radiation within the HAMLeT system is not influenced by dynamically changing environmental factors, such as air turbulence, environmental context information is of critical relevance for chemical sensors. In open systems, molecules of the hazardous material to be detected and localized need gas as a carrier medium for being transported from their source toward the chemical sensor, where the detection is initiated. Therefore, an air ventilation system has been integrated. In Fig. 20.4a, the chemical sensor systems are indicated as red circles, i.e., they are placed in the center of HAMLeT, between the two halves of the U-shape. For each sensor system the ventilation system generates an air stream, which is represented by a black arrow. The air stream works like a barrier. When a person crosses the barrier, the streaming air immediately directs adhering molecules from the person toward the sensor triggering the detection process with a relatively small time delay and establishing a causal relation between the person movement and the sensor reaction.

The air barriers are generated by the combination of a sucking and a blowing component. In Fig. 20.4d the inlet tubes of the chemical platform C1 are surrounded by a yellow rectangle. Figure 20.4e shows how the sensors C1 and C4 are installed. The air stream is indicated by yellow arrows. From this perspective, the sensors C2 and C3 are not visible. The exit of the ventilation system is on the top of the corridor. Molecules that have not been absorbed, leave the system via the roof tubes.

To provide context information for appropriate sensor models, anemometer measurements of the velocity of the airflow were carried out on a dense grid of measurement positions. The high density of the grid requires a high-precision instrument. The anemometer was shifted stepwise along a twine that was tautened

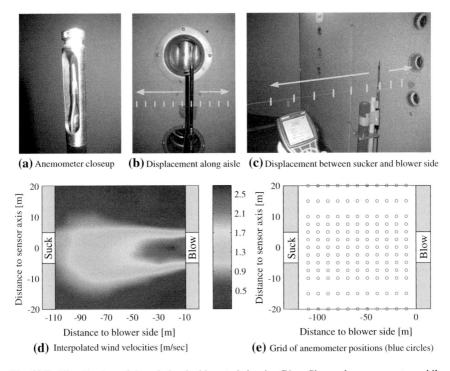

(**a**) Anemometer closeup   (**b**) Displacement along aisle   (**c**) Displacement between sucker and blower side

(**d**) Interpolated wind velocities [m/sec]   (**e**) Grid of anemometer positions (blue circles)

Fig. 20.7 Visualization of the wind velocities at air barrier C1. **a** Shows the anemometer, while (**b**) and (**c**) show the experimental setup according to the grid in (**e**) to provide environmental context information. In (**d**) the measured and interpolated velocity distribution between the blower and the sucker side is depicted. (© by Fraunhofer FKIE)

between the sucker and the blower side of the air barrier. Figure 20.7c shows the experimental setup. At each measuring point the anemometer provides the magnitude of the wind velocity vector. In Fig. 20.7d the measured and interpolated velocity distribution between the blower and the sucker side is depicted. The vertical extent of the area ranges from −20 to 20 cm. The visualization proves that the coaction of a sucking and a blowing component indeed generates an air barrier, which is able to remove molecules from a person and transport them to the sensor.

Since the air stream serves as a transportation medium for the molecules, the measured wind field can be used to estimate the travel time of molecules from the source to the sensor. Obviously, this is critical context information, since that the detection delay is essential for correctly associating chemical detections to person tracks, and thus for correctly localizing the source carrier. For a more detailed discussion see [28, p. 210 ff.].

20.10 Context Integration: Information on Person Flows

HAMLeT may serve a module in a larger overall security assistance system that monitors person flows in public infrastructures. In a view, hazardous material localization is an example of the more general notion of *anomaly detection*. It can be regarded as a process of information fusion that combines incomplete and imperfect pieces of mutually complementary sensor data and context information in such a way that the attention of human decision-makers or decision-making systems is focused on particular events that require special actions [34]. Fusion-based anomaly detection thus improves situational awareness. What is actually meant by "regular" or "irregular" events is higher level information itself that critically depends on the context of the underlying application. Here, it is either assumed to be a priori known or to be learned from statistical long-time analysis of typical situations. We thus may consider it as another example of environmental context information.

20.10.1 Integration of Regularity Patterns

In complex surveillance applications, we can often take advantage of context information on the environment to be insofar as it is the stationary or slowly changing "stage" where a dynamic scenario evolves. Typical examples of such environmental information are digital maps of roads, sea-/air-lane, or regions where people in a public infrastructure typically move. Context information of this type can essentially be regarded as spatial motion constraints. Another category of context information that can be relevant in certain applications is provided by visibility models indicating regions, where sensor coverage is low. Moreover, rather detailed planning information or knowledge of prescribed motion is often available, e.g., for passengers after they have left the check-in counter. This category of information can be used to decide whether an object is moving on allowed path within a plausible time frame or leaving it, for example. In addition, map and behavior pattern information can be used to improve the track accuracy and enhance track continuity. See [13, p. 188ff.] for a more detailed discussion.

Often rather detailed information on the overall behavior of person flows is available, which provides valuable context knowledge on the temporal evolution of their motion. In a sense, it is "hard" context information and can be incorporated into the tracking and classification algorithms. Person flow patterns can in certain situations approximately be described by space-time waypoints that have to be passed by the individual objects while reaching their destination, e.g., an airport gate. The waypoints are a set of position vectors to be reached at given instants of time and via particular routes between the waypoints within an infrastructure that are known in advance. In addition, we assume that the acceptable tolerances related to the arrival of the objects at the waypoints are characterized by known error covariance matrices, possibly individually chosen for each waypoint and object, and that the association between the waypoints and the objects is predefined.

The impact of waypoints on the trajectory to be estimated from future sensor data (under the assumption that the regular pattern is actually preserved) can simply be obtained by processing the waypoints as additional artificial "measurements" via the standard Bayesian tracking paradigm, where the tolerance covariance matrices are taken into account as the corresponding "measurement error covariances." If this is done, the processing of sensor measurements with a younger time stamp are to be treated as "out-of sequence" measurements with respect to the artificial waypoint measurements processed earlier. For dealing with out-of-sequence measurements see, for example [13, p. 95ff.] and the literature cited therein. According to these considerations, planning information can well improve both track accuracy and continuity as well as facilitate the sensor-data-to-track association problems involved, provided behavior pattern is actually kept.

20.10.2   Detecting Regularity Pattern Violation

A practically important class of anomalies results from a violation of regularity patterns such as those previously discussed. An anomaly detector thus has to decide between two alternatives:

- The observed objects obey an underlying pattern.
- The pattern is not obeyed (e.g., passengers not aiming at the gate).

Decisions of this type are characterized by decision errors of first and second. In most cases, it is desirable to make the decisions between both alternatives for given decision errors to be accepted. A sequential likelihood ratio test fulfills this requirement and has enormous practical importance. For a more detailed discussion see [13, p. 199ff.]. As soon as the test decided that the pattern is obeyed, the calculation of the likelihood ratio can be restarted since it is more or less a by-product of track maintenance. The output of subsequent sequential ratio tests can serve to reconfirm "normality" or to detect a violation of the pattern at last. The most important theoretical result on sequential likelihood ratio tests is the fact that the test has a *minimum decision length on average* given predefined statistical decision errors of first and second kind.

We have discussed moving objects that obey certain space-time constraints that are a priorly known (paths, waypoints). A violation of these constraints was quite naturally interpreted as an anomaly. Seen from a different perspective, however, moving objects that are assumed to obey a priorly *unknown* space-time constraints and to be observed by appropriate sensors produce large data streams that can also be used for extracting the underlying space-time constraint. After a suitable post-processing, the produced tracks of motion-constrained objects define the corresponding constraints and can thus be extracted from tracking-based results. See [13] for a more detailed discussion.

20.11   Assistance Systems Versus Autonomic Computing

It might be instructive to compare the context-derived design of security assistance system serving as a cognitive tool for human security personal, such as previously discussed, with an influential computing paradigm called *Autonomic Computing*. Launched in 2001 by IBM, Paul Horn, Senior Vice President, IBM Research, explains the underlying idea by an intuitive metaphor [35]:

> Think for a moment about one such system at work in our bodies, one so seamlessly embedded we barely notice it: the autonomic nervous system. It tells your heart how fast to beat, checks your blood's sugar and oxygen levels, and controls your pupils so the right amount of light reaches your eyes as you read these words. It monitors your temperature and adjusts your blood flow and skin functions to keep it at 98.6 °F. It controls the digestion of your food and your reaction to stress—it can even make your hair stand on end if you're sufficiently frightened. It carries out these functions across a wide range of external conditions, always maintaining a steady internal state called homeostasis while readying your body for the task at hand.

> But most significantly, it does all this without any conscious recognition or effort on your part. This allows you to think about what you want to do, and not how you'll do it: you can make a mad dash for the train without having to calculate how much faster to breathe and pump your heart, or if you'll need that little dose of adrenaline to make it through the doors before they close.
> It is as if the autonomic nervous system says to you, 'Don't think about it—no need to. I've got it all covered'. That's precisely how we need to build computing systems – an approach we propose as autonomic computing.

In a self-managing autonomic system, the human operator takes on a new role: instead of controlling the system directly, he or she defines general policies and rules that guide the self-management process. For this process, IBM has defined the following four functional areas, which critically depend on the availability and proper integration of context information [36]:

1. Self-configuration: Automatic configuration of components;
2. Self-healing: Automatic discovery, and correction of faults;
3. Self-optimization: Automatic monitoring and control of resources to ensure the optimal functioning with respect to the defined requirements;
4. Self-protection: Proactive identification and protection from arbitrary attacks.

There seems to be a hidden or conscious link between these considerations and notion of "cognitive" sensor systems, such as *cognitive radar*, a notion that among others was coined by Simon Hykin, see, for example, [37].

Philosophers of law and technology argue, however, that this emerging paradigm and the sociotechnical infrastructures it supports are expected to have serious implications for the notion and the experience of human agency, where we follow the discussion in [5]. The development of autonomous computing and ambient intelligence may challenge traditional conceptions of human self-constitution and agency, with significant consequences for the theory and practice of constitutional self-government. Ideas of identity, subjectivity, agency, personhood, intentionality, and embodiment are all central to the functioning of modern legal systems. How "distinctly human" can human agency be in a world of autonomic computing?

While skepticism with respect to the performance of these systems has become quite, its central paradigm calls for scrutiny. Even if a smart environment does not adequately infer our preferences, we will never find out, insofar as intelligent environments operate at a subliminal level. Even if they are based on inaccurate and incomplete data or on inadequate inferences, we may end up with accepting decisions taken by the smart infrastructure as a convenient shortcut in the labyrinth of options provided by our ICT infrastructures. It might thus be that *subliminal intervention* is the primary novel paradigm of autonomic computing, next to its claimed *self-awareness*.

The subliminal operation of autonomic computing raises issues of our notion of human agency. Apparently, the philosophical concept of "human agency" underlying our legal systems is a prime example of an essentially contested concept, meaning that there is no consent about the content of the notion between different users of the term. Post-structural orientations, for example, seem to discard the notion of human agency altogether, declaring the "death of the subject," a position often attributed to Michel Foucault [38].

Autonomic computing may thus create a situation in which smart computing environments decide what is reasonable, without them being capable of explaining their behaviors in terms of reason, since their decisions are based on calculations and correlations. The issue that is at stake is whether this is a problem, how it could affect the kind of agency the law presupposes, i.e., accountability, autonomy, and identity in the era of autonomic computing.

Quite obviously, any beneficial use of "cognitive tools," such as the type of security assistance systems discussed here, that augment human capabilities beyond their "natural" range sensitively depends on a commonly agreed idea of what human beings actually are and what is right for them to do, in other words, on the very foundations of law. According to what has been recalled in the very beginning, the notion of an individual human subject born with freewill, capable of and accountable for deliberate intentional action, and the idea of inalienable fundamental rights to which a subject is inherently entitled simply because she or he is a human being are the very hallmarks of Western democracy and the basic assumption of Western legal systems.

Only if these foundations are really clear, commonly agreed upon and societally conscious, their transformation in a legal system, the second pillar of the triple strategy for safety and security, is possible. Embedded into appropriately framed and truly human legal structures, however, and along with actuarial residual risk assessment, properly designed law-compliant technologies such HAMLeT may indeed become key modules of comprehensive systems that satisfy the quite legitimate desires for individual and societal safety and security without implying the risks of careless "autonomic computing."

And in a safe and secure and truly human society we may harvest the fruits that are only ripening in protected habitats: mental liberality, cultural achievements, calculable economic and societal processes, social balancing, and stable industries, the sources of material prosperity. Therefore, it does not seem unrealistic to anticipate a significant need for security assistance systems and related "big business" finding its path between the Scylla and Charybdis of utopian [39] or dystopian [40] visions.

20.12   Conclusion

We thus naturally conclude that a modular approach for safety and security assistance systems needs to be encouraged that explicitly includes context information at all levels and of all types. Particularly important is language-encoded context related to legal and other metadata to assess the utility–cost–privacy impact for each system module and the overall system. Only then we will be able to exploit the rapidly increasing number of sensors, volume of information, and processing capabilities within a framework that recognized the essential need to respect the privacy, dignity, and other fundamental rights of the individual.

References

1. See, e.g., in *Proceedings of the NATO STO* Symposium on *Information Fusion (Hard and Soft) for ISR*, SET-IST-126, Norfolk, VA, USA, 4–5 May 2015
2. W. Koch, Towards cognitive tools: systems engineering aspects for public safety and security. IEEE Aerosp. Electron. Syst. Mag. **15**(9), 14–26 (2014)
3. A. Maslow, A theory of human motivation. Psychol. Rev. **50**(4), 370–396 (1943) (available online)
4. R.E. Hayes (ed.), *Campaigns of Experimentation: Pathways to Innovation and Transformation* (CCRP Publication Series, Washington, DC, 2005). See also: W. Honekamp, *Experimentieren in komplexen Organisationen—Ein Update der Erfahrungen aus der praktischen Anwendung von Concept Development & Experimentation (Experimentation in Complex Organizations—Practical Applications of Concept Development & Experimentation)* (Remscheid, 2010)
5. M. Hildebrandt, A. Rouvroy (eds.), *Law, Human Agency and Autonomic Computing: The Philosophy of Law Meets the Philosophy of Technology* (Routledge, 2011), p. 3
6. *Human rights*. From Wikipedia, the free encyclopedia. http://en.wikipedia.org/wiki/Human_rights. Retrieved 25 Mar 2014
7. The first digital computer in insurance industry was introduced in 1954 by the *Metropolitan Life Insurance Company*, New York, while the first computer for German insurance applications was installed by Allianz in 1956. See: P. Koch, *Geschichte der Versicherungswirtschaft in Deutschland (History of Insurance Industry in Germany)*. (Karlsruhe, 2012), p. 379f
8. K. Zuse, *The Computer—My Life*. Transl. by P. McKenna, J.A. Ross (Springer, Berlin, 1968)
9. *Master Plan Civil Safety & Security Industry*. Released 20 Sept 2013, ed. by Bundesministerium für Wirtschaft und Technologie. http://www.bmwi.de/DE/Mediathek/publikationen,did=600562.html. Retrieved 25 Mar 2014

10. *Die deutsche Versicherungswirtschaft.* Jahrbuch 2012 (German Insurance Economy. Year Book 2012), ed. by Gesamtverband der Deutschen Versicherungswirtschaft e.V. (available online)
11. See for example: U. von Drobnig, *Principles of European Law: Security Rights in Movables. Law, Human Agency and Autonomic Computing* (Oxford University Press, UK, 2014)
12. N. Rabinovitch, *Probability and Statistical Inference in Ancient and Medieval Jewish Literature* (University of Toronto Press, Toronto, 1973)
13. For example: W. Koch, *Tracking and Sensor Data Fusion. Methodological Framework and Selected Applications* (Springer Mathematical Engineering Series, 2014)
14. *The Ultimate General Art.* See: W. Künzel, H. Cornelius, *Die Ars generalis ultima des Raymundus Lullus: Studien zu einem geheimen Ursprung der Computertheorie* (*The Ars generalis ultima of Raymundus Lullus. Studies on an Unknown Origin of Computer Theory*). Advanced Studies in Modern Philosophy and Computer Science (Berlin, 1989). Lullus is honored a catholic martyr, beatified in 1857 by Pope Pius IX
15. R. Buonanno, *The Stars of Galileo Galilei and the Universal Knowledge of Athanasius Kircher*, Vol. 399 (Springer Astrophysics and Space Science Library, 2014)
16. E. Knobloch et al., *Gottfried Wilhelm Leibniz. Hauptschriften zur Versicherungs- und Finanzmathematik* (*Main Works on Actuarial and Financial Mathematics*) (Oldenbourg, 2000). See also: P. Koch, *Geschichte der Versicherungswissenschaft in Deutschland [History of Actuarial Science in Germany]* (Karlsruhe, 1998), p. 58ff
17. S. Lauritzen, *Thiele. Pioneer in Statistics* (Oxford University Press, Oxford, 2002), p. 249
18. Op. Cit., p. 57ff
19. See, for example: *On the Mathematical Theory of Risk (1930) and Collective Risk Theory (1955).* In: *Harald Cramér. Collected Works I.* Springer Collected Works in Mathematics, 2013
20. C. Creifelds et al. (eds.), *Rechtswörterbuch* (*Juridical Dictionary*) (MÃijnchen, 2007)
21. *Road Safety.* European Commission—Mobility and Transport. http://ec.europa.eu/transport/road_safety/specialist/statistics/. Retrieved 25 Mar 2014
22. *Verkehrsunfälle.* Statistisches Bundesamt. https://www.destatis.de/DE/ZahlenFakten/Wirtschaftsbereiche/TransportVerkehr/Verkehrsunfaelle/Verkehrsunfaelle.html. Retrieved 25 Mar 2014
23. S. Waldvogel et al., Simple and sensitive online detection of triacetone triperoxide explosive. Elsevier J. Sens. Actuators B Chem. **143**(2), pp. 561–566 (2010)
24. M. Wieneke, W. Koch, Combined person tracking and classification in a network of chemical sensors. Elsevier Int. J. Crit. Infrastruct. Prot. **2**(2009), 51–67 (2009)
25. W. Koch et al., A Security Assistance System Combining Person tracking with Chemical Attributes and Video Event Analysis, in *Proceedings of the 11th International Conference on Information Fusion* (Cologne, 2008)
26. R. Mahler, *Statistical Multisource-Multitarget Information Fusion* (Artech House, 2007)
27. R. Streit, *Poisson Point Processes: Imaging, Tracking, and Sensing* (Springer, 2010) and M. Schikora, W. Koch, R. Streit, D. Cremers, *A Sequential Monte Carlo Method for Multi-target Tracking with the Intensity Filter.* Chapter 3 in: *Advances in Intelligent Signal Processing and Data Mining. Theory and Applications*, eds. by Mila Mihaylova et al. (Springer, 2013)
28. M. Wieneke, Hazardous material localization and person tracking, in *Advances in Sensor Data and Information Fusion*, ed. by Wolfgang Koch, Vol. 3, PhD thesis at Bonn University, 2013. ISBN 978-3-89863-256-0
29. M. Wieneke, W. Koch, Localization and Tracking of Radioactive Source Carriers in Person Streams, in *15th International Conference on Information, Fusion* (Singapore, 2012)
30. See, for example, the European Union project CATO (A comprehensive holistic answer centered on an integrated CBRN toolbox). http://www.cato-project.eu. Retrieved 25 Mar 2014
31. R.C. Arkin, *Governing Lethal Behavior in Autonomous Robots* (CRC Press, 2009)
32. For example: Isaac Asimov's Three Laws of Robotics. In: I. Asimov (1941). *Runaround.* Short story published in: A. Asimov (1950). *I, Robot.* HarperVoyager 2013

33. M.E. Liggins, D.L. Hall, J. Llinas (eds.), *Handbook of Multisensor Data Fusion—Theory and Practice*, 2nd edn.(CRC Press, 2008), p. 24

34. W. Koch, J. Biermann, Anomaly detection from tracking-derived situation elements, in *Proceedings of the NATO Workshop on Data Fusion and Anomaly Detection for Maritime Situational Awareness—MSA 2009*, La Spezia, Italy, Sept 2009

35. P. Horn, *Automomic Computing: IBM's Perspective on the State of Information Technology* (2001).   Available   at: http://people.scs.carleton.ca/ ∼ soma/biosec/readings/autonomic_computing.pdf. Retrieved 25 Mar 2014

36. *Autonomic computing*. From Wikipedia, the free encyclopedia. http://en.wikipedia.org/wiki/Autonomic_computing. Retrieved 25 Mar 2014

37. S. Haykin, Cognitive radar: a way of the future. IEEE Signal Process. Mag. **23**(1), 30–40 (2006)

38. "Nobody needs to be particularly upset about the 'end of man'; this is only a special case, or if you like, one of the visible forms of a far more general death. I do not mean the 'death of God', but the death of the subject, the subject as the origin and basis of knowledge, freedom of speech, and history." This often cited statement was made in an interview between Michel Foucault and Jean-Michel Palmier on May 3, 1969, published in *Le Monde*. In: Michel Foucault. *Schriften in vier Bänden. Dits et Ecrits*. Hrsg. von Daniel Defert und François Ewald. Frankfurt am Main 2003. Bd. I, S. 1002. Compare, e.g., with: C. S. Lewis (1943). *The Abolition of Man*. Lits 2010

39. R. Kurzweil, *The Singularity is Near: When Humans Transcend Biology* (Viking, New York, 2005)

40. M. Heidegger, *The Question Concerning Technology, and Other Essays* (Garland, New York, 1953) (1977)

Chapter 21
Entity Association Using Context for Wide Area Motion Imagery Target Tracking

Erik Blasch, Pengpeng Liang, Xinchu Shi, Peiyi Li and Haibin Ling

Abstract Entity estimation includes tracking the numbers and types of targets in a scene and is challenging in large area surveillance due to high target density, severe similar target ambiguity, and a low sensor frame rate. Moving vehicle detection from wide area aerial surveillance can be aided by context information. In this paper, we utilize the maximum consistency context (MCC) as spatiotemporal information to estimate multiple targets, and temporal context (TC) to capture the road information. For a candidate association, the MCC is defined as the most consistent association in its neighborhood. Such a maximum selection chooses the reliable neighborhood context information while filtering out noisy and distracting data. In contrast with previous methods to exploit road information, TC does not need to get the location of the road first or use the geographical information systems' (GIS) information. We first use background subtraction to generate the candidates and then build MCC/TC based on the candidates that have been classified as positive by histograms of oriented gradient (HOG) with multiple kernel learning (MKL). For each positive candidate, a region around the candidate is divided into several subregions based on the direction of the candidate, then each subregion is divided into 12 bins with a fixed length; and finally the TC, a histogram, is built according to the positions of the positive candidates in eight consecutive frames. In order to benefit from both the appearance and context information, we use MKL to combine MCC/TC and HOG. We demonstrate the usefulness

E. Blasch (✉)
Air Force Research Lab, Rome, USA
e-mail: erik.blasch@gmail.com

P. Liang · X. Shi · P. Li · H. Ling
Department of Computer and Information Sciences,
Temple University, Philadelphia, USA
e-mail: pliang@temple.edu

X. Shi
e-mail: xcshi@temple.edu

P. Li
e-mail: peiyili@temple.edu

H. Ling
e-mail: hbling@temple.edu

© Springer International Publishing Switzerland (outside the USA) 2016   569
L. Snidaro et al. (eds.), *Context-Enhanced Information Fusion*,
Advances in Computer Vision and Pattern Recognition,
DOI 10.1007/978-3-319-28971-7_21

of context modeling on multi-target tracking using three challenging wide area motion imagery (WAMI) sequences using the publicly available Columbus Large Image Format (CLIF) 2006 dataset. Both quantitative and qualitative results show clearly the effectiveness of using MCC and TC information, in comparison with algorithms that use no context information. Likewise, the experiments demonstrate that the proposed MCC/TC are useful to remove the false positives that are away from the road and the combination of TC and HOG with MKL outperforms the use of TC or HOG only.

Keywords Wide area motion imagery · Temporal context · Spatial context · Maximum consistency context · Background subtraction · Histogram of gradients · Multiple kernel learning · Target tracking · Road abstraction

21.1 Introduction

Context, specifically for tracking, incorporates attributes from the sensor, target, and environment. For the sensor, the context could be the frequency, modality, and field of view. With the contextual knowledge, algorithms are designed for specific sensor modalities. One obvious example is using visual cameras for daytime and infrared for nighttime. For the target, context could be speed, density, and obscurations. Targets that can maneuver fast, such as a car would change the nature of the models used in the tracking algorithms. Finally, the environment, which typically is associated with context includes weather, terrain, and illumination. Recent examples have explored road networks to augment track estimation errors. To explore the nature of context, we select a difficult problem of tracking many vehicles with a wide area imagery sensor for targets assumed to be moving on roads.

Surveillance over wide area motion imagery (WAMI) has recently been attracting increasing amount of research attention due to its wide range of applications and the advance in acquisition techniques [1–11]. However, tracking and detection of multiple moving vehicles in such scenes is challenging, since a wide area traffic scene usually contains more moving targets than traditional visual tracking scenarios with a narrow field of view. These targets are often hard to distinguish from each other due to similar appearances and small sizes in images. In addition, the low frame rate, which is typical in WAMI applications, brings extra ambiguity for associating targets over long time periods. To address such ambiguity, researchers have investigated ways to integrate additional information, such as prior knowledge [1], scene structures [6], and target context [7, 10, 11].

21.1.1 Spatial Context

Using target context to improve multiple target tracking in wide area traffic scenes is of special interest because it is relatively domain independent and therefore

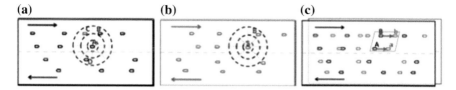

Fig. 21.1 Spatial context (**a**, **b**) and maximum consistency context (**c**). **a** Traffic scene in frame *t*. Circular-polar histogram centered at object '**A**' represents its spatial context. **b** Traffic scene in frame *t* + 1. Circular-polar diagram denotes the spatial context of object '**a**'. **c** Traffics in frame **t** and *t* + 1 are overlapped. Association (**B**, **b**) is the maximum consistency context of association (**A**, **a**)

applicable to various situations. For a target under investigation, existing methods [7] usually model its context by the spatial distribution of other targets within its neighborhood. Such modeling implicitly assumes that the neighborhood context is reliable, which for example is true for a group of targets moving together.

However, in traffic scenes it is common to see vehicles with opposite directions are spatially close to each other due to the juxtaposition of two-way lanes. Furthermore, the false positives in target detection often introduce noises into the spatial context. An example is illustrated in Fig. 21.1a, b.

Motivated by the above observation, we developed a new model named maximum consistency context (MCC), which is a spatiotemporal context (TC) and is robust to noises in target neighborhood. For a potential association from two consecutive frames, e.g., (**A**, **a**) in Fig. 21.1c, the idea is to extract context information from only the most consistent association in (**A**, **a**)'s neighborhood, e.g., (**B**, **b**) in Fig. 21.1c. Assuming that we use environmental context of road networks, there are still difficult tasks for highly accurate tracking. With contextual information, MCC effectively reduces the disturbance from neighbor targets which either head in different directions or are false detections. Meanwhile, MCC provides strong discriminative features to guide multi-object association across frames.

21.1.2 Temporal Context

Moving vehicle detection in WAMI is an important task, the result of which can be applied to monitoring traffic flow, identifying illegal behavior, etc. A common approach to detect moving vehicles in WAMI is to generate candidates using background subtraction [12, 13]; as WAMI frame rates increase the flux tensor model, which can be used as a more reliable motion detector [14]. Nevertheless, due to the large camera motion, 3D parallax, and the low contrast between the vehicles and the background, there are many false positives among the candidates resulting from background subtraction.

Beyond using the appearance information, recent work has demonstrated that the contextual information is useful to boost the object detection task [15–17]. One reason for the effectiveness of context information is that objects in a scene always

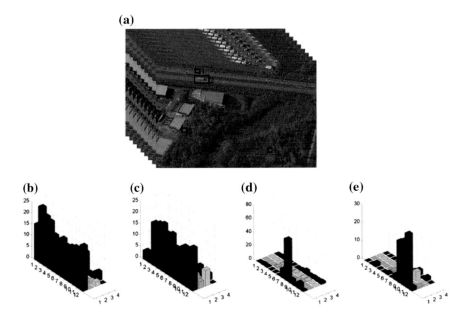

Fig. 21.2 An example of TC. **a** shows the classification result of HOG with MKL, the bounding boxes indicate the candidates classified as positive and negative respectively. **b–e** are the histograms for candidates *1*, *2*, *3*, *4* in (**a**) respectively

have a physical and reasonable layout, i.e., situation context. Intuitively, for moving vehicle detection, the most useful context information is the road, if we have information about the road, we can eliminate the false positives which do not directly appear on the road.

One common way to explore the situation context is to use a graphical method to model the relationships among objects or regions in the scene, such as [15, 16, 18–22]. A common requirement of these approaches is that in order to learn the relationships among objects or regions in a scene, we need to model objects or regions in the scene globally, i.e., objects or regions are used as context for each other. More specifically, for the vehicle detection task, if we want to use the road as context for vehicles, we need to first know where the road is.

In this chapter, based on the motivation that along the direction of the road we can find a relatively large number of vehicles in several consecutive frames and these vehicles will cover a continuous region of the road, we propose a novel TC method, which can capture the road information without detecting the road. In order to build TC, we first use a background subtraction technique to generate the candidates, then, we build TC for those candidates that have been classified as positives by histograms of oriented gradient (HOG) [23] with multiple kernel learning (MKL) [24–27]. For each such candidate, we divide a region around the candidate into several subregions based on the direction of that candidate, and each subregion is divided into 12 bins. Finally, the TC, a histogram, is built by calculating the number of positive candidates in eight consecutive frames lying in each bin. Figure 21.2 gives an example of the histograms of TC for positive and negative candidates classified by HOG with MKL, from which we can see that the TC for true positives have smooth consecutive bins that have relatively large values while the false positives do not. In order to benefit from both the appearance and context information, MKL [24] is used to combine TC and HOG. Our experiment is conducted on the Columbus Large Image Format (CLIF) 2006 dataset [28]. In order to get both qualitative and quantitative results, vehicles in 102 frames which are 2672×1200 subregions that contain the expressway road of the original 2672×4008 image are labeled for ground truth. The experiment demonstrates that with the same recall, the combination of TC and HOG outperforms the use of TC or HOG only, and TC is useful to remove the false positives that are away from the road.

The rest of the chapter is organized as follows: Section 21.2 discusses the related work. Section 21.3.2 presents the proposed TC method. Section 21.4 gives the details of the approach for vehicle detection. Section 21.5 experimentally demonstrates the effectiveness of the proposed TC and Sect. 21.6 provides conclusions.

21.2 Background on Entity Estimation

Multiple target tracking (MTT) is a widely studied topic in computer vision (e.g., [29, 30]) and tracking estimation. The focus of this paper is on the context modeling in MTT. Contextual information plays a critical role in visual tracking. Yang et al. [31] proposed to explore the auxiliary objects which have persistent co-occurrence and consistent motion correlation with the target object, to help localize and reacquire targets. However, it is hard to mine the auxiliary objects. In Reilly's work [7], the context is the representation of geometric relationships of objects with their respective neighbors. Grabner et al. [32] proposed to use local features, which have some temporal relations with the target, to predict the target position. However, the method is computationally expensive on finding and matching features, and it is neither suitable for traffic scene. In [11], Ali et al. propose to use similar objects to predict and reacquire targets after occlusion, but they assume object detections are good enough. Compared with aforementioned work, the main contribution is the novel context model, which fits well the task of tracking closely-spaced targets with mixed local motion patterns.

The research about understanding of WAMI has become increasingly popular. Zhao and Nevatia [33] used the boundary of the car, the boundary of the front windshield and the shadow as features and integrated these features in the structure of the Bayesian network. Also, several papers about vehicle detection and tracking have been published in recent years [12, 13]. These papers mainly focus on the tracking task as detection is just conducted as a prerequisite for tracking. Reilly et al. [12] used background subtraction to generate the candidates by modeling the background with 10 consecutive stabilized images using a median background model. Prokaj et al. [13] adopted the similar method as [12] to perform vehicle detection, while at the same time; they refined the detected vehicles using the tracking result. Shi et al. [34] first used the vehicle detection result to construct trajectories, then road information was estimated by these trajectories and used to refine the detection result. Xiao et al. [35] used a three-frame subtraction scheme to initialize the tracking, and the road information from an additional coregistered geographical information systems (GIS) database as a constraint. Aside from the above work, other studies on general moving object detection and analysis in WAMI using a variety of methods can be found in [36–41].

The effectiveness of context for object detection tasks has been well explored and studied in the computer vision community. Divvala et al. [17] gave an empirical study of context for the object detection task. Besides the spatial layout, the area surrounding the objects or the neighborhood of the objects can provide useful information [42, 43]. However, for moving vehicle detection in WAMI, the area surrounding the candidates of vehicles cannot provide enough information, due to the low contrast between the candidates and the background. Different approaches to explore contextual information have also been recently proposed; Song et al. [44] proposed the Context-SVM (support vector machine) to boost the object classification and detection using the outputs from one task as the context of the other one. Context-SVM is not suitable for the vehicle detection task in WAMI, since it is hard to categorize this kind of imagery into different categories. Felzenszwalb et al. [45] selected the highest score of detections from each of the k different models (for different object categories) to form a k-dimensional vector and rescoring a detection using this k-dimensional feature vector plus the original score, the position of the bounding box and the image context.

21.3 Multiple Vehicle Tracking

21.3.1 Framework Overview

Following the general tracking-by-detection framework [46, 47], we treat multi-vehicle tracking as a target association problem. We roughly divide the tracking framework into three consecutive stages: preprocessing, detection, and

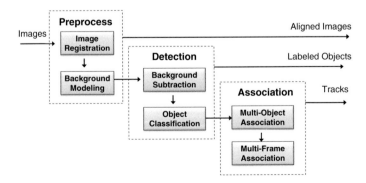

Fig. 21.3 The framework of wide area surveillance

association. The flowchart is summarized in Fig. 21.3. This section briefly introduces the first and second stages. Then we will elaborate in detail the proposed context model and association algorithms, which are the focus of the chapter. In the preprocessing, similar as in [7], registration is used for image alignment. In particular, Speeded Up Robust Features (SURF) [48] features are used for the efficiency to fit affine models for image warping. After the alignment, background modeling is achieved through a standard median filter.

In the detection, instead of directly using the results from background subtraction, a vehicle classifier cascade is applied on the results in order to eliminate noises. The cascade is composed of two support vector machines (SVMs): the first SVM uses simple shape features (dimensions of a candidate target); and the second SVM uses the histogram of oriented gradient (HOG) [49] features.

21.3.2 Temporal Context

Given T consecutive segmented frames as target templates, augment the information with positive and negative trivial templates as $I = \{I_1, I_2, I_3, …, I_T\}$, as shown in Fig. 21.4. A candidate token pixel p in frame i which is from the result of background subtraction and has been classified as positive target templates by HOG [23] with MKL [24], of which the results are shown in Fig. 21.2. Note that the context comes from the temporal consistency of each frame to contain the target after background subtraction and learning. The aggregation of the token pixel information p is related by the histograms.

A region around p is divided into m subregions of the target template based on the estimated direction characterizing a manifold centered at p. Algorithm 1 explains the method for building TC for a candidate. Each subregion is similar to a fan and all the subregions have the same angle at the center θ as shown in Fig. 21.5. m is determined by θ, and $m = 360/\theta$. Then, each subregion is divided into 12 consecutive bins with a fixed length ℓ. In the contextual tracking approach, every candidate obtained from background subtraction technique is a rectangle, and the direction d_p of a candidate is estimated using the direction of the longer edge of the

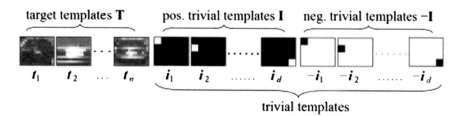

Fig. 21.4 Selection of target and trivial templates

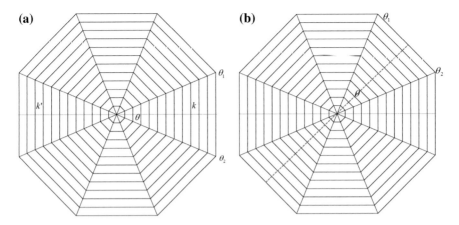

Fig. 21.5 Diagram of the histogram bins of TC. **a** The difference between the estimated direction of a candidate and the direction of the road is not greater than a threshold, the *horizontal green line* is the estimated direction of the candidate; **b** the difference between the two directions is greater than the threshold, the *horizontal green line* is the estimated direction of the candidate and the *red dashed line* is the direction of the road (Color figure online)

rectangle. The value of each bin is the number of candidates lying in the region associated with each bin and satisfying a constraint. The constraint is that the difference between the estimated direction d_p of the candidate p and the estimated direction d_i of a candidate i that is not greater than a threshold ε, or d_i is between θ_1 and θ_2, the angles of the two edges of the subregion as shown in Fig. 21.5a. The second part of the constraint aims at solving the problem that the directions of a small number of candidates on the road might be quite different from most of the candidates on that road. In order to decrease the difference of TC between a candidate at the center of a frame and a candidate at the border of a frame, two bins which are symmetric, e.g., the bin k and bin k' in Fig. 21.5a, are combined into one bin k. The value of the kth bin of candidate p is

$$h_p(k) = \#\{i \in C \wedge i \neq p \wedge i \in R(k) \wedge (|d_p - d_i| \leq \varepsilon \vee \theta_1 \leq d_i \leq \theta_2)\}, \quad (21.1)$$

$$h_p(k') = \#\{i \in C \wedge i \neq p \wedge i \in R(k') \wedge (|d_p - d_i| \leq \varepsilon \wedge \theta_1 \leq d_i \leq \theta_2)\}, \quad (21.2)$$

$$h_p(k) = h_p(k) + h_p(k'), \quad (21.3)$$

where C is the set of candidates of I, $\#$ is the cardinality function, and $R(k)$ is the region associated with the kth bin.

So, given the number of subregions m, the dimension of TC is $(m \times 12)/2$.

Algorithm 1: Building TC for a Candidate

Input:
    p: a candidate
    $I = I = \{I_1, I_2, I_3, \ldots, I_T\}$,: T consecutive frames
    C: the set of candidates of I
    ε: a threshold
Output:
  h: the TC, a histogram, for p

1: **for** each bin k of h **do**
2:    $count \leftarrow 0$; $count' \leftarrow 0$
3:    **for** each i 2 C do
4:        **if** $i \in C \wedge i \neq p \wedge i \in R(k) \wedge (|d_p - d_i| \leq \varepsilon \vee \theta_1 \leq d_i \leq \theta_2)$,**then**
5:            $count \leftarrow count + 1$
6:        **end if**
7:        $k' \leftarrow$ the symmetric bin of k
8:        **if** $i \in C \wedge i \neq p \wedge i \in R(k') \wedge (|d_p - d_i| \leq \varepsilon \vee \theta_1 \leq d_i \leq \theta_2)$ **then**
9:            $count' \leftarrow count' + 1$
10:      **end if**
11:    **end for**
12:    $h(k) \leftarrow count + count'$
13: **end for**
14: **return** h

Figure 21.5 is the situation that the direction of most candidates on a road cannot be estimated correctly because of the shadow. In this case, the road direction might be quite different from the estimated direction of candidates, but with some rotation of the estimated direction of the candidate; however, the road direction can still be found using contextual information. The reason for using the candidates in T consecutive frames is that even when the traffic is not busy, the candidates in consecutive frames will be able to cover some consecutive bins, which correspond to a consecutive region of the road due to the movement of the vehicles. Also, the subregion is similar to a fan, with the increase of distance from the center of a candidate, where the width of the region associated with a bin also increases, which allows a moderate change in the direction of road. Fig. 21.2 demonstrates that positive candidates have obvious patterns. The TC has only two parameters, the number of subregions m which can be determined by θ, the angle at the center, and the length ℓ for dividing each subregion. Experiment in Sect. 21.5 tests several θ and ℓ, and there is a large range for choosing these two parameters.

21.3.3 Multiple Object Association

Some notations are given first. Denote the image sequences as $\{I_t: t = 1, \ldots, n_I\}$, such that I_t is the frame at time t. The detected candidates at time t are denoted as $O^t = \{\mathbf{o}_i^t : i = 1, \ldots, n_i\}$, containing n_i candidate targets (objects).

A target $\mathbf{o}$ is defined as a vector $\mathbf{o} = (\mathbf{x}(\mathbf{o}), \mathbf{h}(\mathbf{o}), \theta(\mathbf{o}), a(\mathbf{o}))$ or simply $(\mathbf{x}, \mathbf{h}, \theta, a)$, where $\mathbf{x}$, $\mathbf{h}$, θ, and a denote the location, appearance histogram, orientation, and area of $\mathbf{o}$ respectively.

Without loss of generality, assume that two frames to be associated are frames 1 and 2. To handle the missing targets and false detections in O^1 and O^2, we introduce dummy targets into the two sets and then assume they have the same number of targets, i.e., $n_1 = n_2 = n$. The multi-object association can be defined as to find the assignment $\Pi = \{\pi_{i:j}\} \in \{0, 1\}^{n \times n}$ to maximize certain total association score, denoted as $\mathcal{E}(\Pi; O^1, O^2)$. The problem is formulated as

$$\max_{\Pi_n} \mathcal{E}\left(\Pi; O^1, O^2\right) = \max_{\Pi} \sum_{i=1}^{n} \sum_{j=1}^{n} \pi_{ij}\left(s_{ij} + c_{ij}\right) \tag{21.4}$$

$$\text{s.t.} \sum_{i=1}^{n} \pi_{ij} = 1 \quad \text{and} \quad \sum_{j=1}^{n} \pi_{ij} = 1$$
$$\pi_{ij} \in \{0, 1\}; \quad i, j \in \{1, \ldots, n\}, \tag{21.5}$$

where $\pi_{ij} = 1$ (or 0) indicates there is an (or no) association between $\mathbf{o}_i^1$, $\mathbf{o}_j^2$; sij measures the *affinity* between $\mathbf{o}_i^1$, $\mathbf{o}_j^2$; and c_{ij} represents the *context similarity* between $\mathbf{o}_i^1$, $\mathbf{o}_j^2$.

The association without context modeling can be viewed as a special case where $c_{ij} = 0$, $\forall i, j$. The association problem turns to a standard integer assignment, where the Hungarian algorithm [50] provides the optimum solution.

The item s_{ij} measures the similarity between targets $\mathbf{o}_i^1 = (\mathbf{x}_i, \mathbf{h}_i, \theta_i, a_i) \in O^1$ and $\mathbf{o}_j^2 = (\mathbf{x}_i, \mathbf{h}_i, \theta_i, a_i) \in O^2$, in terms of appearance, area, and orientation. Specifically, it is defined as

$$s_{ij} = \alpha s_{\mathrm{h},ij} + \beta s_{\mathrm{o},ij} + (1 - \alpha - \beta)s_{\mathrm{a},ij}, \tag{21.6}$$

where s_{h}, s_{o}, and s_{a} denote, respectively, for similarities in appearance, orientation, and area; and α, β are weight factors.

21.3.3.1 Spatial Context

At frame t, for a target candidates $\mathbf{o}_i^t = (\mathbf{x}_i, \mathbf{h}_i, \theta_i, a_i) \in O^t$, its spatial context (SC), denoted by $\mathbf{o}_i^t$, measures the spatial distribution of other candidates in O^t.

Specifically, it divides the neighborhood of $\mathbf{o}_i^t$ into $n_d \times n_o$ distance-orientation bins, and SC_i^t is then defined as a weighted $n_d \times n_o$ histogram as

$$SC_i^t(p,q) = \frac{1}{Z} \sum_{o_k \in \mathcal{N}_i^t} \exp\left[-\left(\mathbf{v}_{ik} - \mathbf{u}_{pq}\right)^\top \Sigma^{-1}\left(\mathbf{v}_{ik} - \mathbf{u}_{pq}\right)\right] \qquad (21.7)$$

where $\mathcal{N}_i^t = \{\mathbf{o}_k^t : \mathbf{o}_k^t \in O^t, \|\mathbf{x}_i - \mathbf{x}_k\|_2 \leq r\}$ defines the neighborhood of $\mathbf{o}_k^t$ with radius r; $\mathbf{v}_{ik} = (\|\mathbf{x}_i - \mathbf{x}_k\|_2, \text{atan2}(\mathbf{x}_k - \mathbf{x}_i)^\top$ calculates the relative distance and orientation of $\mathbf{o}_k^t$ with respect to $\mathbf{o}_i^t$; $\mathbf{u}_{pq} = (p\Delta d, q\Delta\theta)^\top$ represents the bin (p, q) such that Δd and $\Delta\theta$ are the distance and angle interval respectively; Σ is the estimated covariance matrix; and, finally, Z is the normalization constant. An illustration of spatial context is shown in Fig. 21.1a, b.

With SC_i^t, c_{ij} in Eq. (21.4) is represented as $c_{ij} = \text{sim}(SC_i^1, SC_j^1)$, where $\text{sim}(\cdot, \cdot)$ defines the similarity between two histograms, which is computed using histogram intersection [51].

21.3.3.2   Maximum Consistency Context

The spatial context captures rich statistics that is powerful when the target's neighborhood remains stable over time.

However, in the wide area traffic environment, this can be violated since vehicles moving in opposite directions are often close to each other. Likewise, SC can be vulnerable by inaccurately taking such noises into account. In the following, we present an alternative context modeling, which captures only the most reliable information in a target's spatial–temporal neighborhood.

First, for two association pairs $(\mathbf{o}_i^1, \mathbf{o}_j^2)$ and $(\mathbf{o}_{i'}^1, \mathbf{o}_{j'}^2)$, the consistency between pairs is as follows:

$$\varphi\left(\left(\mathbf{o}_i^1, \mathbf{o}_j^1\right), \left(\mathbf{o}_{i'}^1, \mathbf{o}_{j'}^1\right)\right) = \gamma \cos 2(\theta_{ij} - \theta_{i'j'}) + (1 - \gamma)\frac{2\ell_{ij}\ell_{i'j'}}{\ell_{ij}^2 + \ell_{i'j'}^2}, \qquad (21.8)$$

where $\theta_{ij} = \text{atan2}(\mathbf{x}(\mathbf{o}_i^1) - \mathbf{x}(\mathbf{o}_j^2)$, $\ell_{ij} = \left\|\mathbf{x}(\mathbf{o}_i^1) - \mathbf{x}(\mathbf{o}_j^2)\right\|^2$ are the orientation and length of $(\mathbf{o}_i^1, \mathbf{o}_j^2)$, respectively, $\theta_{i'j'}$, $\ell_{i'j'}$ have similar definitions; and γ is the weight parameter. With this definition, we define the MCC for an association $(\mathbf{o}_i^1, \mathbf{o}_j^2)$ as

$$\text{MCC}\left(\left(\mathbf{o}_i^1, \mathbf{o}_j^1\right), \Pi\right) = \underset{\left(\mathbf{o}_{i'}^1 ; \mathbf{o}_{j'}^1\right)\mathcal{N} \in \left(\mathbf{o}_i^1 ; \mathbf{o}_j^1 ; \Pi\right)}{\arg\max} \varphi\left[\left(\mathbf{o}_i^1, \mathbf{o}_j^1\right), \left(\mathbf{o}_{i'}^1, \mathbf{o}_{j'}^1\right)\right] \qquad (21.9)$$

where $\mathcal{N}(\mathbf{o}_i^1, \mathbf{o}_j^2, \Pi) = \{(\mathbf{o}_{i'}^1, \mathbf{o}_{j'}^2) : \mathbf{o}_{i'}^1 \in \mathcal{N}(\mathbf{o}_i^1), \mathbf{o}_{j'}^2 \in \mathcal{N}\left(\mathbf{o}_{ij}^1\right), \pi_{i'j'} = 1$ defines the spatio-temporal neighborhood of $(\mathbf{o}_i^1, \mathbf{o}_j^2)$, which depends on the association Π.

The proposed MCC is more flexible as it does not request the majority consistency in a target's neighborhood. In contrast, it extracts context information only from the most reliable neighbor association. Such a scheme makes MCC robust to distractions of inconsistent motions in a target's neighborhood, e.g., the vehicles running in opposite lanes in the highway scenario. It also performs robustly against false detections, as illustrated in Fig. 21.1.

To integrate MCC in track association, define c_{ij} in Eq. (21.4) as $c_{ij} = \varphi \, [(\mathbf{o}_i^1, \mathbf{o}_j^2)$, $\mathrm{MCC}(\mathbf{o}_i^1, \mathbf{o}_j^2)]$. As a result, the following MCC-based association problem is

$$\max_{\Pi_n} \varepsilon\left(\Pi; O^1, O^2\right) = \max_{\Pi} \sum_{i=1}^{n} \sum_{j=1}^{n} \pi_{ij} \left(s_{ij} + \varphi\left[\left(\mathbf{o}_i^1, \mathbf{o}_j^2\right), \mathrm{MCC}\left(\mathbf{o}_i^1, \mathbf{o}_j^2\right)\right]\right) \quad (21.10)$$

Considering the fact that $\pi_{ij} \in \{0, 1\}$, rewrite (Eq. 21.10) as

$$\max_{\Pi} \sum_{i,j=1}^{n} \pi_{ij} \left\{ s_{ij} + \max_{\left(\left(\mathbf{o}_{i'}^1; \mathbf{o}_{j'}^1\right) \mathcal{N} \in \left(\mathbf{o}_i^1; \mathbf{o}_j^1\right)\right)} \pi_{i'j'} \left[\left(\mathbf{o}_i^1, \mathbf{o}_j^1\right), \left(\mathbf{o}_{i'}^1, \mathbf{o}_{j'}^1\right)\right] \right\} \quad (21.11)$$

The formulation is a quadratic integer optimization with non-smooth component (i.e., 'max'). The global optimal solution is unfortunately computationally expensive. In line with the interlocked property of this formation, an iterated algorithm is devised to optimize it, which is given in Algorithm 2.

Algorithm 2: Multi-object association with MCC

1: Input: two consecutive candidate target sets O^1 and O^2
2: Output: association matrix Π
3: Calculate affinities $S = \{s_{ij}\}$ according to Eq. (3)
4: Initialization $\Pi = \mathbf{0}$; $\varepsilon_{max} = 0$; $C = \{c_{ij}\} = \mathbf{0}$
5: **for** $i = 1, 2, \ldots, n_{it}$ **do**
6:    Compute the integrated similarities $d_{ij} = s_{ij} + c_{ij}$
7:    Solve Eq. (9) using the Hungarian algorithm

$$\max_{\Pi} \varepsilon\left(\Pi; O^1, O^2\right) = \max_{\Pi} \sum_{i=1}^{n} \sum_{j=1}^{n} \pi_{ij} d_{ij} \quad (12)$$

   Denote the solution and score by $\hat{\Pi}$ and $\hat{\varepsilon}$ respectively.
8:    Update C using $\hat{\Pi}$ according to Eq. (6)
9:    **if** $\hat{\varepsilon} > \varepsilon_{max}$ **then**
10:      $\varepsilon_{max} = \hat{\varepsilon}$, $\Pi = \hat{\Pi}$.
11:   **end if**
12: **end for**

21.3.4 Multiple Frame Association

We treat multi-frame tracking as a task of associating short reliable tracklets into long tracks, in a similar framework used in [52, 53]. Two procedures, reliable tracklets acquisition and tracklet-to-tracklet association, are performed iteratively. Reliable tracklets are obtained by checking the motion smoothness of trajectories. Suppose a basic tracklet is $M_{1:t}^k = \{\mathbf{o}_k^1, \mathbf{o}_k^2, \ldots, \mathbf{o}_k^t\}$, which is reliable only if

$$\theta_{t-1;t}^k - \theta_{t;t+1}^k < \theta_0; \quad \text{and} \tag{21.13a}$$

$$\min\left\{\frac{\ell_{t-1;t}^k}{\ell_{t;t+1}^k}; \frac{\ell_{t;t+1}^k}{\ell_{t-1;t}^k}\right\} > \ell_0 \tag{21.13b}$$

where $\theta_{t-1;t}^k$, $\ell_{t-1;t}^k$ are the orientation and length of association $(\mathbf{o}_k^{t-1}, \mathbf{o}_k^t)$, respectively; θ_0 and $\ell_0 c$ are corresponding thresholds. In this way, if association $(\mathbf{o}_k^{t-1}, \mathbf{o}_k^t)$ has inconsistency with adjoining associations, trajectory $M_{1:t}^k$ is divided into two short tracklets by breaking the association $(\mathbf{o}_k^{t-1}, \mathbf{o}_k^t)$.

Tracklet-to-tracklet association follows the similar manner as two-frame multi-target association. First, the affinity between two tracklets is constituted of appearance, motion, and temporal similarities. Later, Hungarian algorithm is used here again to associate the two tracklets into the long one. Finally, isolated detections and too short tracklets after multi-frame association are discarded as false alarms.

21.4 Implementation

21.4.1 Registration

Given a set I of T consecutive frames, we need to remove the camera motion first. As in [1], we use point-matching based algorithm. Given a reference frame t and another frame $t + i$, we first detect the keypoints in both t and $t + i$ using the scale-invariant feature transform (SIFT) [54] and extract a SIFT descriptor at each keypoint. Then, the keypoints in $t + i$ are matched with keypoints in t with FLANN (Fast Library for Approximate Nearest Neighbors) [55]. Finally, a robust homography d_p is estimated using RANSAC (random sample consensus) [56]. We use the first frame in I as the reference frame. Other piecewise simplex-based approaches are also possible [57].

21.4.2 Generating Candidates

In order to detect the moving vehicles, background subtraction is used to first generate the candidate detections. As in [12], we use median image filtering to model the background. Due to the motion of camera, the more frames we use to build the background model, the smaller the active area is. To keep the active area as large as possible and also get a relatively satisfying background model, eight consecutive frames model the background B. Then, we can obtain the difference image $I_{dt} = |I_t - B|$. Since we use homography for registration, an assumption is that the scene is planar which is not true for WAMI. So, pixels belonging to the areas that contain out of plane objects, e.g., trees, tall buildings, cannot be well aligned. There is a lot of noise along the edges of these out of plane objects due to parallax error. The work in [1] alleviated this problem by subtracting the gradient of the media background ∇B, i.e., $I_{dt}^r = I_{dt} - \nabla B$. Since we found that due to the misalignment, there is an offset between the pixels in ∇B that have obvious response and the pixels in I_{dt} where noise exists, we adopt a different approach. Given I_{dt} and ∇B, if the value of a pixel at position (i, j) of ∇B is greater than a threshold, we set the value of the corresponding pixel at (i, j) of I_{dt}^r to 0,

$$I_{dt}^r(i,j) = \begin{cases} 0 & \text{if } \nabla B > \delta \\ I_{dt}(i,j) & \text{otherwise} \end{cases} \tag{21.14}$$

In our implementation, we found that our TC approach is better than the approach used in [1]. After getting I_{dt}^r, we filter out the blobs that are too large or too small, and the remaining blobs are used as the candidates.

21.4.3 Classification of Candidates

1. *Generalized Multiple Kernel Learning*: In order to benefit from both the appearance information and context information, MKL [24, 25] is used for classification. The main idea of MKL is to learn an optimal combination of a set of kernel matrices,

$$K_{\text{opt}} = \prod_k K_k(d_k) \tag{21.15}$$

The objective of the generalized MKL [24, 25] is to learn a function $f(x) = w^t \phi_d(x) + b$ with the kernel $k_d(x_i, x_j) = \phi_d^t(x_i)\phi_d(x_j)$. The MKL not only estimates w and b which is the goal of SVM, but also estimates the kernel parameters d from the training data. The above problem can be formulated as the following optimization problem,

$$\underset{d}{\text{Min}} \quad T(d) \text{ subject to } d \geq 0 \tag{21.16a}$$

$$\text{where } T(d) = \underset{w;d}{\text{Min}} \frac{1}{2} w^t w + \sum_i \ell(y_i, f(x_i)) + r(d) \tag{21.16b}$$

where ℓ is the loss function and r is a regularizer for d. The optimization includes two steps, in the outer loop, the kernel parameter d is estimated, and in the inner loop, the parameters of SVM are estimated with fixed kernel. Varma et al. [25] used projected gradient descent approach for the optimization. In order to deal with the inefficiency of the projected gradient descent optimizer, spectral projected gradient (SPG) was proposed in [24] which can handle millions of kernels. In this chapter, we choose to use SPG-GMKL (Generalized MKL), and each dimension of the feature vector is treated as a radial basis function (RBF) kernel. Assuming the combination of HOG and TC as M dimensions, the optimal kernel is

$$k_d(x_i, x_j) = \prod_{m=1}^{M} e^{-d_m}(x_{im} - x_{jm})^2 \tag{21.17}$$

2. *Classification*: After background subtraction, there is a set C of candidates for $I = \{I_1, I_2, I_3, \ldots, I_T\}$. To keep consistent with background subtraction, T is set to 8. For each candidate, we normalize it to 24(width) by 32(height) and use HOG with SPG-GMKL [24] to classify them first, and then only build TC for those candidates that have been classified as positive; and for those candidates that have been classified as negative, the value of each dimension of TC is 0. Then, TC with HOG is combined through SPG-MKL.

21.5 Experiment

21.5.1 Temporal Context

The dataset includes WAMI images from CLIF 2006 [58]. The scene of this dataset is a flyover of the Ohio State University (OSU) from a large format monochromatic electro-optical platform, which is comprised of a matrix of six cameras and the size of each image is 2672(width) by 4008(height) pixels.

Our experiments are conducted on the CLIF dataset [59]. CLIF is challenging with following features:

1. Large image format (4008×2672);
2. Large camera and target motion;
3. Tiny target occupancy (4×70 pixels);

4. Similar target appearance;
5. Low frame rate sampling (2 fps); and
6. A large amount of targets (hundreds).

Since there is a large area in each image that does not contain an expressway road, a 2672 × 1200 subregion is used as shown in Figs. 21.6 and 21.7. The subregion is very challenging, including not only horizontal and vertical express ways, but also an overpass. For the test data, we labeled the vehicles in 102 frames of camera 3, and there are 9364 vehicles in total. For training, we labeled 1730 candidates obtained from background subtraction from 16 frames of camera 1.

In our experiment, three kinds of classifiers are built, using TC only, using HOG only, and combing TC and HOG. For HOG, the block size is 12 × 12, the block stride is 4 × 4, the cell size is 6 × 6, and the number of bins is 6. The dimension of HOG is 576. To build the classifiers evaluated on the test data, all the 1730 candidates from camera 1 are used. Since the classification result of HOG is used to build TC, if we use 1730 candidates to train a classifier with HOG which is used to classify the same data to build TC, overfitting exists. So, we select 367 candidates from the 1730 candidates labeled by hand to build the classifier with HOG and

(a)   **(b)**

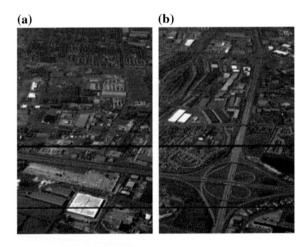

Fig. 21.6 **a**, **b** are the original images, where the region between the two lines is the subregion

(a)   **(b)**

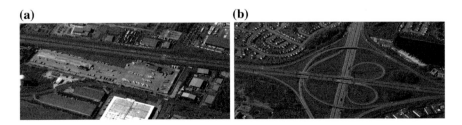

Fig. 21.7 **a**, **b** are subregions for Fig. 21.5a, b, respectively

MKL, which is used for building TC of the training data. After building TC, we linearly scale each attribute to the range [0, 1] using the tool "svm-scale" provided by LIBSVM [60]. For the regularizer of the kernel weights d of the SPG-GMKL [24], we choose ℓ_2 regularization. ε used in Eq. 21.4 and Eq. 21.5 is $10°$.

21.5.1.1 Evaluation Metrics: Choosing θ and ℓ for TC

To obtain the ground truth, we labeled by hand the ground truth detections. The ground truth included the labeled vehicles in 102 frames, which are 2672×1200 subregions that contain expressway of the original 2672×4008 images. The distance between a positive candidate and the ground truth is used to judge whether it is a true positive. Given the ground truth $G = \{g_1, g_2, g_3, \ldots, g_S\}$, for a true positive candidate c, there exists $g \in G$ and the distance between the center of g and the center of c is not greater than 10. The value of $c < 10$ was chosen as a reasonable estimate relative to the ground sampling distance of a rough estimate of road width. For the evaluation of classifiers built with different kinds of features, we use a precision–recall curve and area under the curve (AUC) to evaluate the performance. Since we classify the candidates obtained from background subtraction, the recall can be calculated in two different ways. One way is to use the number of the actual ground truth, S, i.e., the actual number of vehicles in each image; while another way is to use the number of candidates which are indeed vehicles as ground truth, S'. In the following comparisons, both kinds of precision–recall curves are given. Without classification, the performance of background subtraction with the size and the gradient constraint is not satisfying, as the precision is only 0.398 at the recall 0.854.

TC has two parameters, the angle at the center of the subregion θ and the length ℓ used to divide each subregion. To seek the best θ, we test $15°$, $30°$, $45°$, and $60°$ with fixed $\ell = 50$. Figure 21.8 and Tables 21.1 and 21.2 summarize the results. From the results we can see that when only TC is used, $45°$ performs the best. One reasonable explanation is that small θ makes the pattern of TC too complicated, while large θ cannot capture enough information. So, a moderate θ performs the best. When the combination of TC and HOG are used automatically by the machine, $45°$ also performs the best, but the advantage is not obvious.

To seek the best ℓ, we test 30, 40, 50, 60, 70 with fixed $\theta = 45°$. From Tables 21.3 and 21.4, 30 performs best when only TC is used, and 40 performs best when TC and HOG are combined. However, from Fig. 21.9c, Tables 21.5 and 21.6, we can see that when the recall is high, the precision of 50 is a little better. Since a better performance at low recall does not have practical use in the vehicle detection application, 50 is chosen for ℓ. Though 50 is chosen for ℓ, TC is not very sensitive to ℓ, when the recall is high, the difference among 30, 40, and 50 is small.

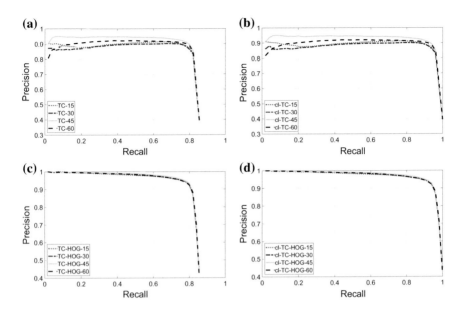

Fig. 21.8 The precision–recall *curves* for different θ. **a**, **b** Use only TC and are plotted based on S and S' respectively; **c**, **d** use the combination of TC and HOG and are plotted based on S and S0 respectively

Table 21.1 The AUC for different θ of TC

	15°	30°	45°	60°
S	0.738	0.729	**0.773**	0.748
S'	0.867	0.856	**0.908**	0.878

Table 21.2 The AUC for different θ of TC + HOG

	15°	30°	45°	60°
S	0.807	0.808	**0.811**	0.808
S'	0.958	0.950	**0.953**	0.949

Table 21.3 The AUC for different ℓ of TC

	30	40	50	60	70
S	**0.783**	0.779	0.773	0.760	0.743
S'	**0.920**	0.915	0.908	0.892	0.873

Table 21.4 The AUC for different ℓ of TC + HOG

	30	40	50	60	70
S	0.812	**0.813**	0.811	0.802	0.783
S'	0.954	**0.955**	0.953	0.941	0.920

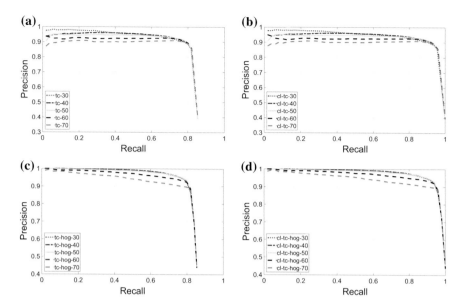

Fig. 21.9 The precision–recall curves for different ℓ. **a, b** Use only TC and are plotted based on S and S0, respectively; **c, d** use the combination of TC and HOG and are plotted based on S and S0, respectively

Table 21.5 The precision for three different recalls of TC with different ℓ using S

	30	40	50	60	70
0.78	0.899	0.905	**0.912**	0.906	0.898
0.80	0.886	0.891	**0.894**	0.893	0.888
0.82	0.856	0.854	0.854	**0.859**	0.854

Table 21.6 The precision for three different recalls of TC + HOG with different ℓ using S

	30	40	50	60	70
0.78	0.942	0.945	**0.946**	0.931	0.900
0.80	0.923	0.928	**0.934**	0.923	0.896
0.82	0.863	0.873	0.881	**0.887**	0.886

21.5.1.2 Quantitative and Qualitative Comparison

To demonstrate that TC is useful to remove false positive candidates away from the road, the performance of TC, HOG, and the combination of TC and HOG are evaluated using SPGGMKL [13]. We normalize the candidates from background subtraction to 24×32, and compute the HOG for each candidate. For TC, $45°$ and $50°$ are used for θ and ℓ, respectively. The dimension of TC is 48. Figure 21.10, Tables 21.7 and 21.8 list the quantitative results. The combination of TC and HOG

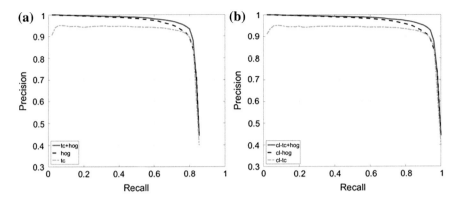

Fig. 21.10 The precision–recall curve for TC, HOG, and the combination of TC and HOG: **a** is plotted based on S, **b** is plotted based on S'

Table 21.7 The AUC for TC, HOG, and TC + HOG

	TC	HOG	TC + HOG
S	0.773	0.805	**0.811**
S'	0.908	0.955	**0.953**

Table 21.8 The precision of TC, HOG, and TC + HOG at different recalls using S

	TC	HOG	TC + HOG
0.700	0.932	0.953	**0.970**
0.720	0.929	0.947	**0.966**
0.740	0.925	0.937	**0.960**
0.760	0.920	0.926	**0.955**
0.780	0.912	0.915	**0.946**
0.800	0.894	0.893	**0.934**
0.820	0.854	0.841	**0.881**
0.854	0.399	0.442	**0.442**

which can make use of both the appearance and context information outperforms the only use of TC or HOG. When comparing AUC, the advantage of TC + HOG is tiny. However, Fig. 21.10 and Table 21.7 shows that the advantage is obvious when the recall rate is high, which is useful in practice. Compared to the performance of background subtraction with the constraints on the size of candidates and the gradient of background model, the classification can obviously boost the detection performance. Using the combination of TC and HOG with SPG-GMKL [24], the precision can boost to 0.881 at the recall 0.82.

Figures 21.11 and 21.12 are some qualitative results. There are very few false positives on the road for TC, HOG, and the combination of TC and HOG. TC is useful to remove false positives that are away from the road with a very small number of misclassified candidates on the road; while HOG can almost capture all

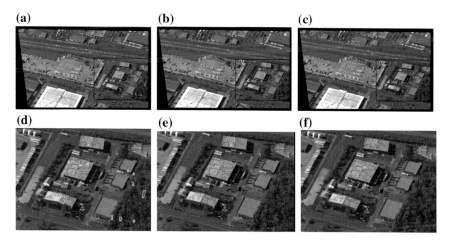

Fig. 21.11 The classification result. The *green, yellow, red,* and *blue* bounding boxes indicate true positive, false positive, true negative, false negative, respectively: **a–c** are the results of TC, HOG, TC + HOG, respectively; **d–f** are the enlargement for the part in the *black* bounding box in (**a–c**). respectively

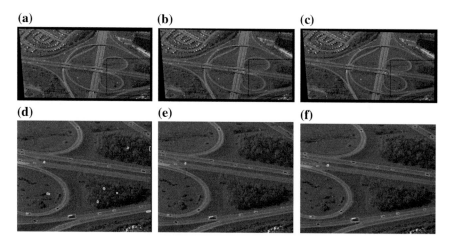

Fig. 21.12 The classification result. The *green, yellow, red,* and *blue* bounding boxes indicate true positive, false positive, true negative, false negative respectively: **a–c** are the results of TC, HOG, TC + HOG, respectively; **d–f** are the enlargement for the part in the *black* bounding box in (**a–c**), respectively

the vehicles on the road with some false positives away from the road. Figures 21.11c, f, 21.12c, f demonstrate the benefit of the combination of TC and HOG. By making use of both the appearance and context information, we can obviously reduce the number of false positives without sacrificing recall.

21.5.2 Consistency Spatial Context

Three sequences with 80 frames (40 s), 50 frames (25 s), and 100 frames (50 s), respectively, are used to evaluate the proposed approach.

To study the effectiveness of the proposed context, we evaluate three types of associations: association without context (NoCon), with the spatial context (SC), and with the proposed MCC. Furthermore, for each method, we test two different affinity models: with appearance features and without. In all cases, Hungarian algorithm is used as the basic assignment solution. The parameters are set as follows: α in (Eq. 21.6) is set as 0.5 in the first sequence and 0.8 in the other two sequences. If appearance feature is used, both α and β in (Eq. 21.6) are set as 0.3 in all sequences. Otherwise, α and β are set as 0.5 equally. The maximum iteration number (*nit* in Algorithm 2) is 10. We use the precision, $100\Sigma_t\, c(t)/\Sigma_t\, g(t)$, to measure the association performances. $c(t)$ and $g(t)$ in the precision measure denote the numbers of correct and ground truth association respectively. Results are summarized in Table 21.9.

From the results, we have the following observations. First, the proposed MCC performs the best in general. Furthermore, if no appearance is used in the association, all methods have degenerated performances, yet our method is affected least. This confirms that the proposed context plays an important role in handling the motion ambiguity. Second, spatial context helps little in performance. This seemingly contradicting phenomenon can be attributed to two factors: (1) the scenes we selected contain mainly two-direction highways, which largely confuses local context as we conjectured; and (2) the vehicle detection is rather noisy, leading to unstable spatial distributions. Third, the method without using context obtains the moderate results, which attributes to kinds of well-designed affinity measures. However, when excluding the appearance information, the performance drop of NoCon is much larger than those of SC and MCC.

Qualitative results of three methods on sequence 1 are shown in Fig. 21.13, which is a snapshot of two-frame association. Associations with SC are distracted by those cars moving in opposite directions. While NoCon is vulnerable to ambient similar objects, after embedding MCC, the motion ambiguity is greatly alleviated. With the help of neighbor association, confused object succeeds in finding true associated target, it can be seen from Fig. 21.13.

Table 21.9 Precisions of multi-object association

	Sequence 1		Sequence 2		Sequence 3	
	A+	A−	A+	A−	A+	A−
No Con	92.1	88.5	89.5	77.8	90.7	86
SC	86.8	86.1	84.8	76.2	75.2	72.9
MCC	**92.5**	**90.5**	89.6	80.5	91.3	89.6

'A+' appearance features are used; and 'A−' no appearance features are used

Fig. 21.13 Associations with different contexts on sequence 1. *Top:* NoCon. *Middle:* SC. *Bottom:* MCC. *Black*(*White*) *rectangle*: detection in the last(current) frame. *Red*(*blue*) *line*: rightward (leftward) association output

Results of multiple object tracking are shown in Fig. 21.14. It can be seen that, the approach has two merits. First, there are few wrong two-frame associations. Second, the approach associates the track fragments into long tracks, which is especially useful in the case of occlusion and missing detections. We do not have quantitative evaluation on multiple object tracking, as no ground truth data is available. The labeling of associations in wide area traffic scenes is a time-consuming work, which we will consider in the future.

Fig. 21.14 Multiple object tracking results, *Top* sequence 3; *Middle* sequence 2; *Bottom* sequence 1

21.6 Conclusions

We propose using the TC which can capture the road information in the moving vehicle detection task of WAMI. To make use of both the appearance and context information for classification, we use MKL to combine these two kinds of features. In order to demonstrate the effectiveness of the proposed TC, we label 9364 vehicles in 102 frames of the CLIF 2006 dataset, and the experimental results show that TC is very useful to remove false positives away from the road.

In this chapter, we also extended TC for a novel spatial–temporal context, MCC, to assist multi-object tracking in wide area traffic scenes. By selecting the most reliable ingredient in the spatial–temporal neighborhood of an association, MCC leverages the discriminative power and robustness against clutter distractions. Experiments using challenging wide area surveillance videos validate the effectiveness of the proposed approach.

Results demonstrated the TC method, a combined spatial–temporal MCC method, as well as use of contextual information. Examples of contextual benefits were demonstrated by: (a) HOG had eight incorrect detections, (b) context methods had four missed detections, while (c) combining context and HOG resulted in only one detection error. The benefits of using context in many forms have increased the robustness, accuracy, and reliability of target tracking methods for real-world applications.

Acknowledgments This work is partly supported by the Air Force Office of Scientific Research (AFOSR) under the Dynamic Data Driven Application Systems program and the Air Force Research Lab. The work was supported in part by NSF Grants IIS-1218156 and IIS-1350521.

References

1. S. Pellegrini, A. Ess, K. Schindler, L. Van Gool, You'll never walk alone: modeling social behavior for multi-target tracking, in *IEEE International Conference on Computer Vision* (2009) pp. 261–268
2. J. Xiao, H. Cheng, F. Han, H. Sawhney, Geo-spatial aerial video processing for scene understanding and object tracking, in *IEEE Conference on Computer Vision and Pattern Recognition* (2008), pp. 1–8
3. J. Xiao, H. Cheng, H.S. Sawhney, F. Han, Vehicle detection and tracking in wide field-of-view aerial video, in *CVPR*, 2010
4. E. Blasch, G. Seetharaman, K. Palaniappan, H. Ling, G. Chen, Wide-area motion imagery (WAMI) exploitation tools for enhanced situation awareness, in *Proceedings of IEEE Applied Imagery Pattern Recognition (AIPR) Workshop: Computer Vision: Time for Change*, 2012
5. J. Prokaj, X. Zhao, G.G. Medioni, Tracking many vehicles in wide area aerial surveillance, in *CVPR Workshops* (2012), pp. 37–43
6. J. Prokaj, G. Medioni, Using 3D scene structure to improve tracking, in *IEEE Conference on Computer Vision and Pattern Recognition* (2011), pp. 1337–1344
7. V. Reilly, H. Idrees, M. Shah, Detection and tracking of large number of targets in wide area surveillance, in *European Conference on Computer Vision* (2010), pp. 186–199
8. H. Ling, Y. Wu, E. Blasch, G. Chen, L. Bai, Evaluation of visual tracking in extremely low frame rate wide area motion imagery, in *Proceedings of the International Conference on Information Fusion (FUSION)*, 2011
9. K. Palaniappan, F. Bunyak, P. Kumar, I. Ersoy, S. Jaeger, K. Ganguli, A. Haridas, J. Fraser, R. M. Rao, G. Seetharaman, Efficient feature extraction and likelihood fusion for vehicle tracking in low frame rate airborne video, in *Proceedings of the International Conference on Information Fusion (FUSION)*, 2010
10. X. Shi, H. Ling, E. Blasch, W. Hu, Context-driven moving vehicle detection in wide area motion imagery, in *International Conference on Pattern Recognition (ICPR)*, 2012
11. S. Ali, V. Reilly, M. Shah, Motion and appearance contexts for tracking and re-acquiring targets in aerial videos, in *IEEE Conference on Computer Vision and Pattern Recognition* (2007), pp. 1–6
12. V. Reilly, H. Idrees, M. Shah, Detection and tracking of large number of targets in wide area surveillance, in *ECCV (3)*, 2010
13. J. Prokaj, M. Duchaineau, G. Medioni, Inferring tracklets for multi-object tracking, in *Workshop of Aerial Video Processing Joint with IEEE CVPR*, 2011

14. F. Bunyak, K. Palaniappan, S.K. Nath, G. Seetharaman, Flux tensor constrained geodesic active contours with sensor fusion for persistent object tracking. J. Multimedia **2**(4), 20–33 (2007)
15. G. Heitz, D. Koller, Learning spatial context: using stuff to find things, in *ECCV (1)*, 2008
16. A. Jain, A. Gupta, L.S. Davis, Learning what and how of contextual models for scene labeling, in *ECCV (4)*, 2010
17. S.K. Divvala, D. Hoiem, J. Hays, A.A. Efros, M. Hebert, An empirical study of context in object detection, in *CVPR*, 2009
18. H. Myeong, J.Y. Chang, K. M. Lee, Learning object relationships via graph-based context model, in *CVPR*, 2012
19. C. Galleguillos, B. McFee, S.J. Belongie, G.R.G. Lanckriet, Multi-class object localization by combining local contextual interactions, in *CVPR*, 2010
20. Z. Niu, G. Hua, X. Gao, Q. Tian, Context aware topic model for scene recognition, in *CVPR*, 2012
21. J. Porway, K. Wang, B. Yao, S.C. Zhu, A hierarchical and contextual model for aerial image understanding, in *CVPR*, 2008
22. A. Rabinovich, A. Vedaldi, C. Galleguillos, E. Wiewiora, S. Belongie, Objects in context, in *ICCV*, 2007
23. N. Dalal, B. Triggs, Histograms of oriented gradients for human detection, *in CVPR (1)*, 2005
24. A. Jain, S.V.N. Vishwanathan, M. Varma, Spg-gmkl: generalized multiple kernel learning with a million kernels, in *KDD*, 2012
25. M. Varma, B.R. Babu, More generality in efficient multiple kernel learning, in *ICML*, 2009
26. M. Varma, D. Ray, Learning the discriminative power invariance trade-off, in *ICCV*, 2007
27. M. G¨onen, E. Alpaydin, Multiple kernel learning algorithms. J. Mach. Learn. Res. **12**, 2211–2268 (2011)
28. O. Mendoza-Schrock, J.A. Patrick, E. Blasch, Video image registration evaluation for a layered sensing environment, in *Proceedings of IEEE National Aerospace Electronics Conference (NAECON)*, 2009
29. Y. Bar-Shalom, T. Fortmann, *Tracking and Data Association* (Academic Press, 1988)
30. D. Reid, An algorithm for tracking multiple targets. TAC **24**(6), 843–854 (1979)
31. M. Yang, Y. Wu, G. Hua, Context-aware visual tracking. IEEE Trans. Pattern Anal. Mach. Intell. **31**(7), 1195–1209 (2009)
32. H. Grabner, J. Matas, L. Van Gool, P. Cattin, Tracking the invisible: learning where the object might be, in *IEEE Conference on Computer Vision and Pattern Recognition* (2010), pp. 1285–1292
33. T. Zhao, R. Nevatia, Car detection in low resolution aerial image, in *ICCV*, 2001
34. X. Shi, H. Ling, E. Blasch, W. Hu, Context-driven moving vehicle detection in wide area motion imagery, in *International Conference on Pattern Recognition (ICPR)*, 2012
35. J. Xiao, H. Cheng, H.S. Sawhney, F. Han, Vehicle detection and tracking in wide field-of-view aerial video, in *CVPR*, 2010
36. P. Liang, G. Teodoro, H. Ling, E. Blasch, G. Chen, L. Bai, Multiple kernel learning for vehicle detection in wide area motion imagery, in *International Conference on Information Fusion (FUSION)*, 2012
37. K. Palaniappan, F. Bunyak, P. Kumar, I. Ersoy, S. Jaeger, K. Ganguli, A. Haridas, J. Fraser, R. M. Rao, G.S. Seetharaman, Efficient feature extraction and likelihood fusion for vehicle tracking in low frame rate airborne video, in *Proceedings of the International Conference on Information Fusion (FUSION)*, 2010
38. R. Pelapur, S. Candemir, F. Bunyak, M. Poostchi, G. Seetharaman, K. Palaniappan, Persistent target tracking using likelihood fusion in wide-area and full motion video sequences, in *Proceedings of the International Conference on Information Fusion (FUSION)*, 2012
39. H. Ling, Y. Wu, E. Blasch, G. Chen, L. Bai, Evaluation of visual tracking in extremely low frame rate wide area motion imagery, in *Proceedings of the International Conference on Information Fusion (FUSION)*, 2011

40. E. Blasch, G. Seetharaman, S. Suddarth, K. Palaniappan, G. Chen, H. Ling, A. Basharat, Summary of methods in wide-area motion imagery (WAMI), in *Proceedings of SPIE*, vol. 9089, 2014
41. X. Shi, P. Li, W. Hu, E. Blasch, H. Ling, Using maximum consistency context for multiple target association in wide area traffic scenes, in *Proceedings of International Conference on Acoustics, Speech and Signal Processing (ICASSP)*, 2013
42. W.-S. Zheng, S. Gong, T. Xiang, Quantifying and transferring contextual information in object detection. IEEE Trans. Pattern Anal. Mach. Intell. **34**(4), 762–777 (2012)
43. Y. Ding, J. Xiao, Contextual boost for pedestrian detection, in *CVPR*, 2012
44. Z. Song, Q. Chen, Z. Huang, Y. Hua, S. Yan, Contextualizing object detection and classification, in *CVPR*, 2011
45. P.F. Felzenszwalb, R.B. Girshick, D.A. McAllester, D. Ramanan, Object detection with discriminatively trained part-based models. IEEE Trans. Pattern Anal. Mach. Intell. **32**(9), 1627–1645 (2010)
46. M. Andriluka, S. Roth, B. Schiele, People-tracking-by-detection and people-detection-by-tracking, in *IEEE Conference on Computer Vision and Pattern Recognition* (2008), pp. 1–8
47. M.D. Breitenstein, F. Reichlin, B. Leibe, E. Koller-Meier, L. Van Gool, Online multiperson tracking-by-detection from a single, uncalibrated camera. IEEE Trans. Pattern Anal. Mach. Intell. **33**(9), 1820–1833 (2011)
48. H. Bay, T. Tuytelaars, L. Van Gool, Surf: speeded up robust features, in *European Conference on Computer Vision* (2006), pp. 404–417
49. N. Dalal, B. Triggs, Histograms of oriented gradients for human detection. IEEE Conf. on Comput. Vis. Pattern Recogn. **1**, 886–893 (2005)
50. H.W. Kuhn, The hungarian method for the assignment problem. Naval Res. Logistics Quart. **2**(1–2), 83–97 (1955)
51. M.J. Swain, D.H. Ballard, Color indexing. Int. J. Comput. Vis. **7**(1), 11–32 (1991)
52. C. Huang, B. Wu, R. Nevatia, *Robust Object Tracking by Hierarchical Association of Detection Responses* (2008), pp. 788–801
53. C.H. Kuo, C. Huang, R. Nevatia, Multi-target tracking by on-line learned discriminative appearance models, in *IEEE Conference on Computer Vision and Pattern Recognition* (2010), pp. 685–692
54. D.G. Lowe, Distinctive image features from scale-invariant keypoints. Int. J. Comput. Vis. **60**(2), 91–110 (2004)
55. M. Muja, D.G. Lowe, Fast approximate nearest neighbors with automatic algorithm configuration, in *International Conference on Computer Vision Theory and Application*, 2009
56. M.A. Fischler, R.C. Bolles, Random sample consensus: a paradigm for model fitting with applications to image analysis and automated cartography. Commun. ACM **24**(6), 381–395 (1981)
57. E.C. Cho, S.S. Iyengar, G. Seetharaman, R. Holyer, M. Lybanon, Velocity Vectors for Features of Sequential Oceanographic Images
58. AFRL: Columbus large image format (clif) 2006, https://www.sdms.afrl.af.mil/index.php?collection=clif2006
59. O. Mendoza-Schrock, J.A. Patrick, E. Blasch, Video image registration evaluation for a layered sensing environment, in *Proceedings of IEEE National Aerospace Electronics Conference (NAECON)*, 2009
60. C.-C. Chang, C.-J. Lin, LIBSVM: a library for support vector machines, ACM Trans. Intell. Syst. Technol. **2**, 27:1–27:27 (2011), software available at http://www.csie.ntu.edu.tw/cjlin/libsvm

Chapter 22
Ground Target Tracking Applications. Design Examples for Military and Civil Domains

Jesús García, Tarunraj Singh and Dirk Tenne

Abstract This chapter presents two examples of Ground Target Tracking (GTT) designs. There has been a notable interest in GTT algorithms and applications among estimation and sensor fusion research communities; a survey describes recent strategies for GTT algorithms in different fields. In the chapter, the objective is to present in detail some real experiences of the authors in developing approaches for GTT which include modeling and exploitation of available ground contextual information in two representative examples: battlefield situations and airport surface, indicating the common aspect and peculiar algorithms exploited in each case.

Keywords Ground target tracking · Physical context formalization · Terrain constraints · Velocity field filter · Road-based tracking · Applications

22.1 Introduction

The distinguishing difference of GTT domain with respect to 3D scenarios such as aerial or underwater, is the available knowledge of surface constraints and limitations which may restrict the targets mobility and also the conditions of sensors. Sometimes it can be due to pure physical conditions, such as topographical constraints restricting the target mobility as well as degrading the quality of the measurements, as for example with hidden targets like tanks under trees. In other

J. García (✉)
Computer Science Department, Universidad Carlos III de Madrid, Madrid, Spain
e-mail: jgherrer@inf.uc3m.es

T. Singh
Department of Mechanical and Aerospace Engineering, University at Buffalo, Amherst, NY, USA
e-mail: tsingh@buffalo.edu

D. Tenne
Varian Medical Systems, Seattle, Washington, USA
e-mail: tenne.eng@gmail.com

© Springer International Publishing Switzerland (outside the USA) 2016   597
L. Snidaro et al. (eds.), *Context-Enhanced Information Fusion*,
Advances in Computer Vision and Pattern Recognition,
DOI 10.1007/978-3-319-28971-7_22

cases it can be due to procedural constraints, such as roads or channels, speed limitations, restricted areas, etc. This circumstance allows the opportunity of using knowledge that may help to refine the sensors data and also the objects dynamics, accordingly to the constraints of the topography and the mobility of the target as a function of road and off-road conditions.

Regarding the type of context information available, static physical files is the most usual, such as geographic data files, road maps, etc. The use of tactical or procedural information besides physical is also an option; predictions can be also refined by using tactical rules, and operational domain knowledge. Finally, dynamic context variables such as meteorological conditions, ground state (dry, wet, mud, etc.), situation variables or human inputs can be also considered. In the case of logical knowledge (such as entities engaged in a coordinated trajectory, warning, mission goals, etc.), context can come from human reports, learned from data or the result of indirect inference processes from other pieces of information.

In the first scenario, ground information is used to refine the dynamic models for ground targets. The available information includes terrain databases, obstacle goal intelligence, and characteristics of vehicle. This information is used to process radar surveillance data to get the estimated trajectory of the vehicle. The approach is a Bayesian estimator with a velocity field (VF) built from terrain information and obstacle goal intelligence to model the vehicle behavior. The approach to estimate the probability density function (pdf) of the vehicle location is propagated using partial differential equations (PDEs) which represent the transport model, driven by this VF, which influences the tracking algorithm. The design goals of the VF contain three objectives (i) avoidance of obstacles or unattractive areas, (ii) attraction to certain regions (as influenced by intention and goal), and (iii) vehicle type (speed, on-road, off-road). Regarding the measurement fusion of arbitrarily shaped probability density distributions, it is addressed by discretizing the pdf's and applying Bayes' rule of conditional probability. In contrast to the classical approaches such as Kalman or Covariance Intersection, this method utilizes the complete pdf and does not introduce approximations on the probability distribution.

In the second scenario, the design of sensor fusion for airport surface surveillance is addressed, what is known as advanced surveillance monitoring guidance and control system (A-SMGCS). On airport surface it is important to track aircraft with highest priority, but also any others as far as they can compromise safety: fuel trucks, luggage convoys, buses, cars, etc. The targets move constrained to the physical shapes of airport roads, represented in the map, and follow predefined procedures (types of motion patterns, acceleration magnitudes, etc.), so the tracking procedures should be quite different from a free environment. A simplified representation of the airport map is used, where each element in the map (road, runway, taxiway) is defined by a collection of waypoints and a given width. The tracking algorithm is an IMM filter (Interacting Multiple Model) whose modes are designed to exploit the available surface information: motion aligned with the taxiways orientation; segment transition filter for transversal maneuvers when the target approaches branching areas; longitudinal transition areas in stop-and-go areas, runway accelerations, etc. With respect to sensor inputs, they are classified into cooperative, such as multilateration or D-GPS transponder systems, and nonco-operative, such as surface radar or videos. The Surveillance function integrates sensor data and takes into account surface constraints to refine the information, the pdf of the sensor provided positions are conditioned to physical area of airport surface element and masks with sensor performance.

The rest of the chapter is structured as follows. Section 22.2 overviews recent developments in GTT applications and representation of ground information in level-1 fusion systems, surveying how other works represent ground information to develop tracking techniques based on contextual surface information. Section 22.3 presents a military application, the ground battlefield surveillance, and Sect. 22.4 a civil application, the airport surface environment. Finally, Sect. 22.5 develops the conclusions closing the chapter.

22.2   Related Works. Representation of Ground Information and Ground Target Tracking Techniques

The use of ground context in sensor fusion has been a very active research area in the last fifteen years; a recent survey on contextual tracking approaches is in [1, 2]. Physical context has been profusely employed to refine state estimators, and model the behavior of targets. It is quite usual modeling geographic data in the format of GIS files [3] with information in DTED format (Digital Terrain Elevation Database). Maps are usually represented as waypoints and junctions to describe the roads, or sets of linear segments between the points [4].

Regarding the specific alternatives to integrate the context knowledge (roads, maps, airways, etc.), it can be divided into two groups [5]: post-processing techniques, which apply corrections to the estimates accordingly to context information; and pre-processing methods integrating the context information into the estimation algorithms. Several approaches are in the second strategy: motion model tuned with the road map, measurements projection along map, extrapolation accordingly to the roadways, etc.

To include constraints, the IMM approach has been one of the most extended approaches, although other approaches in discrete spaces have been also explored [6]. The Variable Structure Multiple Model (VS)-IMM, has been widely used in ground target tracking (GTT) [7]. The basic idea is that the active model set varies in an adaptive manner and thus only a small number of active models are needed to be maintained at each time. Nonlinear approaches to exploit context are the particle filter and unscented Kalman filter, which keep a Bayesian formulation applied over the constrained subspace [8], and hard constraints available in ground information are naturally integrated on the state vector or the measurement process during the estimation process. For instance, in [9], a constrained unscented Kalman filter is used in GPS/INS fusion integrating state constraints from the surface geometry.

Combined with multiple mode approach, particle filters lets the different modes within the estimator framework be represented by constrained likelihood models. An example is [10], where the Gaussian sums are used in the jump Markov framework solved by the aforementioned VS-IMM algorithm.

Another frequent strategy to employ ground information is weighting sensor inputs with quality factors. Nimier et al. [11], proposed a method to combine symbolic and numerical information, favoring measurements provided by the sensors well adapted to the context and minimizing the impact of those sensors that are not well adapted. Caron et al. [12], Wang and Gao [13] present similar approaches for GPS quality assessment and weigh the observations.

Finally, using tactical or procedural information (not only physical), target prediction can be also refined, accordingly to the operational domain. This is the case in some ground military scenarios such as convoy targets following certain tactical rules [14].

22.3 Ground Target Tracking

This section details an algorithm to estimate the position of a ground vehicle. The PDF of the vehicle location is propagated using a hyperbolic PDE, which is driven by a VF. This VF reflects the maneuverability of the ground vehicle. It can result from a mapping algorithm based on the gradient field obtained from the potential surface. It can also result from the representation of the domain of interest as being on-road or off-road, where the VF in the off-road grid points have a local VF which points toward the road, so as to quickly guide the vehicle onto the road. The VF considered models terrain information, obstacle goal intelligence and the type of the vehicle. Additional information such as radar surveillance observations of the vehicle location are used to update the target position via the Bayes' rule.

22.3.1 Velocity Field Generation

The VF stores local information about the travel direction and speed of a vehicle. Thus it greatly influences the proposed tracking algorithm. The design goals of the VF may contain the following:

- Avoidance of obstacles or unattractive areas
- Attraction to certain regions (intention, goal)
- Vehicle type (speed, on-road, off-road)

22.3.1.1 Potential Field

To construct such a VF we may use the advantages of a potential field. Sethian [15] applied the method of potential surfaces to various applications such as path planning in robot navigation, evolving interfaces in geometry and fluid mechanics. The potential field models obstacles and goals as opposite electrostatic charges and maps the space between them. The potential field can be constructed as the sum of the attractive potential due to goals and the repellent potential due to obstacles. The negative gradient of the potential field can be seen as a "force" acting on the considered object at a specific location. It also can be used to construct the VF, since the negative gradient of the potential field points toward attractive regions and away from obstacles.

Potential surfaces are commonly generated in path planning approaches as a function of the distance to the goal or obstacle. The attractive potential consists of a generalized distance d from each location to the goal. Whereas the repellent potential is generated by the inverse distance to the obstacles. The obstacles are usually approximated by compact regions enclosed in linear borders, and the resulting repellent potential can be calculated as:

$$\frac{1}{\epsilon + \sum_{j=1}^{n} g_j[d(x)]}$$

where n is the number of boundaries surrounding the obstacles, $g_j[d(x)]$ is a linear function of the distances and ϵ is a small positive constant to avoid singularity. There are several known disadvantages of the above generation of the potential field:

1. A robot can oscillate between obstacles.
2. High number of algebraic calculations for irregular entities.
3. The potential field can contain local minima.
4. To close obstacles might prevent passage between them.

The oscillations are due to the dynamics of the robot and are therefore not addressed for the generation of the VF. The second item is also of less concern since the VF is calculated a priori. The last two items are addressed by an approach presented by Plumer [16]. His algorithm is a two-stage recursive algorithm computing first the repellent potential and secondly augmenting this result to obtain the overall potential field. The recursive algorithm ensures locally an increase in the repellent potential and a decrease in the attractive potential. Plumer has shown that this algorithm converges rapidly to a surface without local minima. In addition, the number of calculations is also reduced.

The application of the potential field approach in target tracking notes one difficulty, that a single goal is not known. Generally, the intention of the target is unknown, although it is often possible to determine regions to which the target is attracted to move. Assuming prior knowledge about the terrain, one may identify areas of interest such as bases, covered areas, etc. Furthermore, information about the type of the vehicle triggers the generation of an on-road or off-road potential field model. A road vehicle is most likely to travel toward the next road, whereas an off-road vehicle may use plain terrain instead.

22.3.1.2 Gradient-Based Velocity Mapping

The propagation technique developed in the proceeding text requires a VF reflecting the trafficability of the ground vehicle. This section explores an intuitive concept of generating the VF. It is the result of a mapping algorithm based on the gradient field obtained from the potential surface. As an extension to this method the gradient of topographical information could be used likewise.

The gradient mapping algorithm is based on the following concept, which is illustrated in Fig. 22.1. Assuming a flat terrain $\nabla \Phi = 0$, the vehicle would travel with a nominal speed v_{nom}. While the slope descends the vehicle's traveling speed increases until it reaches the maximum speed v_{max}. Further decent constraints the vehicle to smaller speed. Similarly, if the slope is increasing the speed gradually reduces.

22.3.1.3 On-Road Velocity Field

The following describes an algorithm to develop a VF assuming an on-road vehicle. Suppose a two-dimensional region of interest (ROI) containing a road network is divided into small cells. The road is approximated by piecewise linear functions, and we know the on-road and off-road speed capabilities of the vehicle. Therefore, the ROI can be divided in on-road and off-road cells or grid points. The VF for

Fig. 22.1 Gradient-based velocity mapping

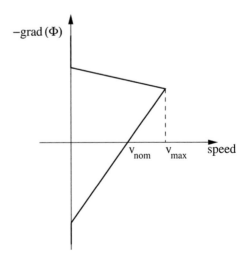

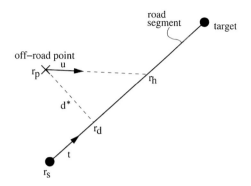

Fig. 22.2 Optimal velocity direction of an off-road location to minimize the time of arrival

on-road points is generated parallel to the direction of the road pieces with a magnitude of the on-road speed. The generation of the VF of the off-road grid points assumes that the vehicle "tries" to get back onto the road. Certainly, the driver of the vehicle will choose a path minimizing the travel time to a point on the road rather than driving the shortest distance. Thus, the generation of the off-road grid point velocity becomes a simple optimization procedure. Figure 22.2 shows a road segment beginning at r_s and with the normalized direction t. The optimal direction from the off-road point r_p can be calculated as the normalized distance between the location, where the vehicle hits the road r_h and the location of the vehicle r_p. The interception location with the road (r_h) is the result of an optimization scheme minimizing the travel time between the off-road location and the target location, which is assumed to be the end of the road segment. Considering the vehicle travels on straight line segments partially off-road and on-road, the optimal interception on the road can be calculated as:

$$\overrightarrow{r_h} = \overrightarrow{r_d} + \frac{v_r d^*}{\sqrt{1 - v_r^2}} t$$

where d^* is the shortest distance from the off-road location to the road and r_d is the position vector to this interception. v_r is the off-on-road speed ratio v_{off}/v_{on}. Figure 22.3 shows the VF generated with the described on-road assumption.

22.3.2 Computational Method of Solving the Linear Transport Equation

The location of the vehicle is described by its position pdf. The pdf is a continuous function associating a certainty of the containment of the vehicle to every location. The proposed algorithm, however, discretizes the pdf in space and also in time to numerically solve the governing equations. The desired behavior to be simulated is the continuous motion of a vehicle on the ground. In this special case, it is the

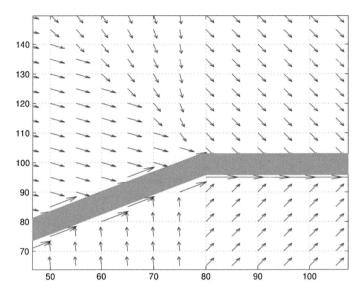

Fig. 22.3 Velocity field assuming an on-road vehicle. The *solid line* indicates two road segments

motion of the position pdf in the considered environment. Its movement is influenced by the terrain and the vehicle type and therefore controlled by the aforementioned VF.

The dynamics of the vehicle are described by a hyperbolic PDE expressing its location in the ROI. The proposed algorithm employs a numerical algorithm the so-called ENO scheme to simulate the continuous vehicle motion. The ENO scheme (Essentially Non-Oscillatory) has been introduced by Harten and Osher [17], Shu and Osher [18] and applied to various applications such as the simulation of propagating concentration profiles in renal tubulus by Pitman et al. [19]. The solution to the hyperbolic PDE expresses the motion of the vehicle influenced by the VF, which in turn is generated with the terrain information. While propagating the position pdf, its shape is formed according to the local velocity information and is not restricted to any probabilistic modeling assumptions. For example, an initial observation (assumed to be a normal distribution) propagated with the on-road velocity model stretches along the road and does not retain the initial shape.

The following text explores the numerical method, which has been employed to solve the hyperbolic PDE. The basic concepts are derived on a one-dimensional simplification and expanded to the two-dimensional case.

22.3.2.1 The Basic Concept

This section explores the computational method which has been used to solve the linear transport equation. The basic concepts are derived on a one-dimensional

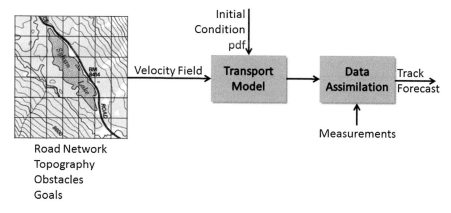

Road Network
Topography
Obstacles
Goals

Fig. 22.4 Ground target tracking

simplification and expanded to the two-dimensional case. Figure 22.4 is a block diagram illustration of the flow of information to generate a forecast track pdf.

The method applied to the transport equation exhibits the following characteristics:

- Second-order accuracy in time and space
- variable sampling rate
- semi-direction flow rate
- preserving the flux continuity at the "sonic points"

The linear transport equation is given in Eq. 22.1.

$$\frac{\partial}{\partial t}u(x,t) + a\frac{\partial}{\partial x}u(x,t) = 0 \tag{22.1}$$

where $u(x, t)$ is a density variable which is a function of space and time, and a is the velocity which can be a function of space and time. In general, the numerical solution of Eq. 22.1 is propagated in time after evaluating the spatial derivatives. If numerical efficiency is required, these operations can be separated. The above equation may be rewritten as follows in order to utilize the benefit of operator splitting.

$$\frac{\partial}{\partial t}u(x,t) = -a\frac{\partial}{\partial x}u(x,t) = L[u(x,t)] \tag{22.2}$$

where L is an operator used for brevity. The framework of time integration is derived using Eq. 22.2. Sampling the function $u(x, t)$ at time steps of Δt, denoting u^n as $u(x, t + n\Delta t)$, and applying the trapezoidal integration rule, yields the prediction equation in time:

$$u^{n+1} = u^n + \frac{\Delta t}{2}(L[u^{n+1}] + L[u^n]) \tag{22.3}$$

Equation 22.3 is a recursive algorithm of the prediction u^{n+1}. A first-order approximation of the solution at the time step $n + 1$ is obtained by propagating with a simple Euler predictor, which solution is denoted by u^*. The Euler prediction is used to estimate the right-hand side of $L[u^{n+1}]$ in the recursive algorithm. The two equations called the prediction and correction equations are written as follows:

$$\text{Prediction:} \quad u^* = u^n + \Delta t L[u^n] \tag{22.4}$$

$$\text{Correction:} \quad u^{n+1} = u^n + \frac{\Delta t}{2}(L[u^*] + L[u^n]) \tag{22.5}$$

This set of equations may be rewritten in a numerical efficient form such that the function calls of the right-hand side are reduced.

$$u^{n+1} = \frac{1}{2}(u^n + u^*) + \frac{\Delta t}{2}L[u^*] \tag{22.6}$$

where

$$u^* = u^n + \Delta t L[u^n] \tag{22.7}$$

The above set of equations is the framework of the time propagation with a second-order accuracy. Next we will describe the computation of the right-hand side $L[.]$, which reverts essentially the space derivative.

The space derivatives are approximated by a second order scheme, which is conceptualized in the subsequent text. The applied method addresses positive and negative flow, where the positive flow is referred to as the flow from *left* to *right* and the negative flow vice versa. A second order upwind scheme may be written as:

$$\begin{aligned} -\Delta x L[u_j^n] = a\Delta x u_x = a^+ &\left[\left(u_j + \frac{1}{2}\Delta u_j\right) - \left(u_{j-1} + \frac{1}{2}\Delta u_{j-1}\right)\right] \\ + a^- &\left[\left(u_{j+1} + \frac{1}{2}\Delta u_{j+1}\right) - \left(u_j + \frac{1}{2}\Delta u_j\right)\right] \end{aligned} \tag{22.8}$$

Where

$$a^+ = \max(a, 0)$$
$$a^- = \min(a, 0)$$

The subscript "j" symbolizes the space grid point after discretizing the ROI. This scheme combines a first-order upwind scheme with a higher order approximation which is giving by:

$$\Delta u_j = \frac{1}{2} \left[sgn(u_{j+1} - u_j) + sgn(u_j - u_{j-1}) \right] \cdot \min\left(|u_{j+1} - u_j, u_j - u_{j-1}| \right) \quad (22.9)$$

Equations 22.6–22.9 state the desired algorithm to solve the linear transport equation. It is noteworthy to observe the physics behind the prediction and correction Eqs. 22.4 and 22.5. The operator L is a representation of the net flux, which is the difference between the incoming flow and the outgoing flow at the intermediate grid points. Now, the solution u at time $n + 1$ is the previous solution at time n updated by the net flux of the previous solution and the predicted solution u^*. This observation may be helpful in understanding the numerical scheme, validating the solution and deriving methods for the so-called sonic points.

22.3.2.2 The Two-Dimensional Representation

The basic concept of the one-dimensional algorithm can be extended to the two-dimensional case, where the problem formulation is stated as follows:

$$\frac{\partial}{\partial t} \Phi(x, y, t) = -u \frac{\partial}{\partial x} \Phi(x, y, t) - v \frac{\partial}{\partial y} \Phi(x, y, t) = L[\Phi, u, v] \quad (22.10)$$

The function Φ depends on the position in the x-y coordinate system and on the time t. The variables u and v are the VFs in each coordinate direction.

The numerical solution to the two-dimensional transport equation can be obtained by adjusting Eqs. 22.6–22.9 as follows:

$$\text{Prediction:} \quad \Phi_{ij}^* = \Phi_{ij}^n - \Delta t u_{ij} \Phi_x \Big|_{ij}^n - \Delta t v_{ij} \Phi_y \Big|_{ij}^n$$
$$= \Phi_{ij}^n + L[\Phi_{ij}^n, u_{ij}, v_{ij}] \quad (22.11)$$

$$\text{Correction:} \quad \Phi_{ij}^{n+1} = \frac{1}{2} \left(\Phi_{ij}^* + \Phi_{ij}^n \right) + \frac{\Delta t}{2} L\left(\Phi_{ij}^*, u_{ij}, v_{ij,} \right), \quad (22.12)$$

where the subindices (ij) denote the spatial grid points and the superscripts $n,^*$ indicate the time step similar to the one-dimensional solution. The space derivatives in the two coordinate directions are abbreviated by the subscripts x and y. The operator $L[.]$ is evaluated likewise the Eqs. 22.8 and 22.9.

Figure 22.5 shows an example of the function Φ at the initial time and the propagated function at later time steps. In this example the VF has been changed in time in order to predefine the path of the function Φ.

(a) (b)

(c) (d)

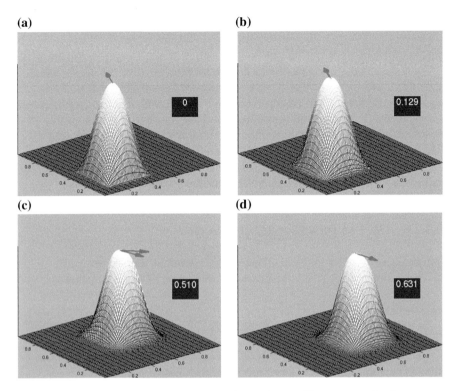

Fig. 22.5 The propagation of the function Φ in time and space. The vector on the *tip* represents the velocity assigned to the corresponding grid point and the number in the *blue* box represents time (Color figure online)

22.3.3 Numerical Example

A GUI which permits generating road maps using linear line segments is used to generate a tracking scenario as shown in Fig. 22.6. The blue circle represents the location of a radar and the five red ellipses represent the measurements generated with their associated covariances.

The GUI permits generating of the velocity filed using a mouse click resulting in a VF illustrated in Fig. 22.7 where the arrows pointing left to right at the bottom quarter of the figure represents the VF on the road. Note that the VF in the proximity of the road point toward the road prompting any target location off the road to be guided toward the road.

Figure 22.8 illustrates the time evolution of a road-based target traversing the illustrated domain from left to right. The red circles represent the five radar measurements that are used in the filtering process for the estimation of the pdf of the road-based target. The blue line corresponds to the time history of the true position of the target and the red line corresponds to the filtered/forecast position of the

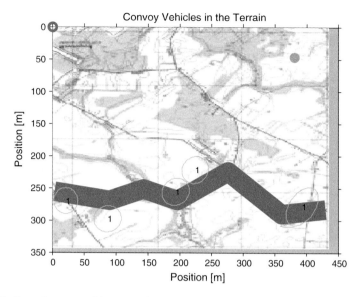

Fig. 22.6 Ground target tracking scenario (Color figure online)

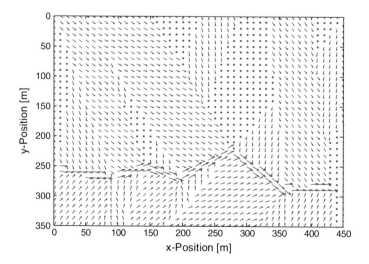

Fig. 22.7 Velocity field generated based on the on-road assumption

target illustrating the ability of the context-based tracker to forecast the position of the road-based target using a VF which guides the estimated position of the target to lie on the road.

Figure 22.9 illustrate the evolution of the pdf of the position estimate of the target. The first panel ($i = 1$) corresponds to the initial location initial pdf of the

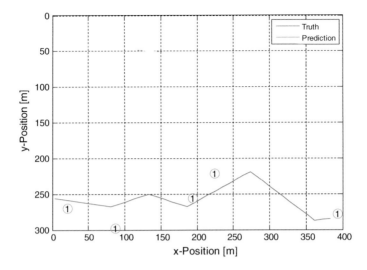

Fig. 22.8 Predicted and true track of a road-based target (Color figure online)

position of the road-based target. The index at the top of each of the panel corresponds to the time index of the evolution of the pdf of the position estimate of the target. Note that in the first column of the second row, the pdf of the position of the target is highly peaked with small variance. This is attributed to the fact that a measurement has been integrated with the forecast pdf, reducing the uncertainty of the estimate of the target location. Also, note panels with indices $i = 60$ and $i = 136$ illustrate a pdf which conforms to the curved road (or the intersection of two piecewise linear segments of the road) helping illustrate the potential of the ENO scheme to propagate the pdf of the target location.

22.4 Airport Surface Example

This section describes sensor fusion algorithms proposed for a prototype implementation in Spanish airports, illustrated in Madrid/Barajas airport [20]. Airport domain is a representative example of ground knowledge exploitation, addressed by some other authors like [21] besides the example developed here.

The application of sensor fusion techniques to airport surveillance is inside the A-SMGCS concept (Advanced Surface Movement Guidance and Control Systems (A-SMGCS) [22, 23], oriented to monitoring all aircraft and vehicles in the airport movement area (see Fig. 22.10). The system provides controllers and pilots with a periodically updated synthetic image reflecting the current traffic state on the airport surface and close airspace. This output is used besides by other functions of the A-SMGCS, such as displaying the location of all surface traffic, enabling its

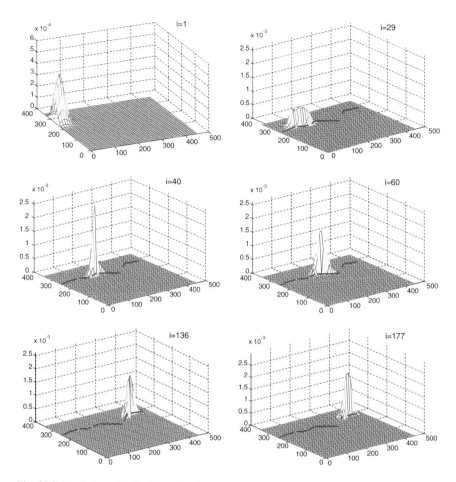

Fig. 22.9 Evolution of pdf of target tracks

separation and guidance in all types of weather conditions without reducing the number of operations or the level of safety.

To do that, these systems usually integrate a diverse range of detection technologies, together with contextual information about ground configuration and operational rules, as depicted in Fig. 22.11. In this work the types of sensors considered were: ASDE radar (Airport Surface Detection Equipment) [24, 25], ASR radar (Approach Surveillance Radar), Mode S multilateration systems (Mode Selective), and short-range MWS radars (Millimeter Wave Sensors) [26], connected through the *ASTERIX* protocol as indicated in the figure, although later appeared other alternatives as video surveillance [27]. In the fusion center, the data fusion combines detections from sensors in an optimal way. This is the first step, used to merge the information necessary to develop the perception of the traffic situation. The monitoring function will make use of the data fusion output together with the

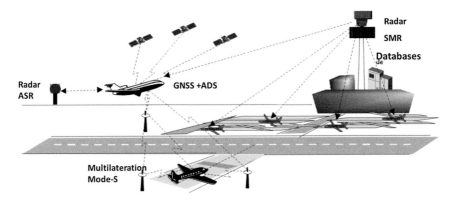

Fig. 22.10 The airport surface scenario

airport representation, available routes, and operational rules in order to detect potential conflicts and hazardous situations [25, 28]. Analogously, the planning function [29] takes the available routes and plans together with surveillance output to refine the surface movement plans.

22.4.1 Airport Layout Representation

One of the most important context sources is the airport configuration and layout of ground paths. This configuration includes description of taxiways, runways and stand areas, the actual routing strategy for commercial flights and the location and characteristics of the available sensors [23]. The airport layout is stored in a data base that contains all the necessary information to define the physical layout and the arrival/departure routes defined by operator. There are tables and attributes reflecting the physical and procedural information:

- Ground points
- Segments
- Intersection ground points and intersection segments
- Runways, taxiways, taxilanes
- Standlanes
- Departure and arrival ground routes

The basic elements of airport layout are 2D points forming the segments used by the tracking filter. The original representation considers ground segments composed by pairs of ground points, and intersection segments composed by one ground point and one intersection point (auxiliary computed point), as can be seen in Fig. 22.12.

Analogously, a runway is defined by set of points and several taxiways intersecting on it. In order to be used by the data processing methods, all the points that define the intersections along the runway are computed and linked to the runway.

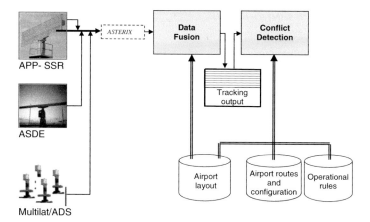

APP- SSR

ASDE

Multilat/ADS

Fig. 22.11 Structure of A-SMGCS prototype

Fig. 22.12 Original segment
representation in airport
layout data base

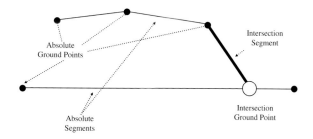

The information is stored in a relational database with different levels. Absolute
ground points (the original ground points and the intersection ground points that
have been transformed) forms a first level. The second file contains all the segments
of the airport defined by two absolute points. The third file contains all the taxis (the
original taxilanes, standlanes, taxiways and the transformed runways) to use the
route definition stored in the departure/arrival ground routes tables. Integrity rules
are defined in order to assure the completeness and coherence of the data stored. For
instance, the segment table is related with the point table and if any segment is
defined with a point that is not contained in the segment table. In the same way,
taxilanes, taxiways, and standlanes must be defined using the defined segments in
the segment table. It is an object-oriented design of the airport database with pointer
to access all necessary information, as depicted in Fig. 22.13.

22.4.2 Data Fusion Solution

The data fusion architecture is depicted in Fig. 22.14 [29], it integrates several processes to carry out the estimation of all objects of interest. The first step is data preprocessing and bias removal, where operations are performed to align data from information sources to be fused, and bias is a key to guarantee the matching from different sensors and avoid fusion errors. Then, data association determines correspondence among observations with targets. The tracking filter exploits prediction models and estimation/inference processes. Besides, the tracking management controls the output of fusion processes, such as creation, deletion, merging, etc.

We will comment two of the functions employing context information to adapt the process, bias correction and tracking filter.

22.4.2.1 Bias Estimation

Regarding the bias correction, it is based on the assumption that objects usually tend to follow taxiways axes [3, 5]. Using the information contained in the airport map, we could calculate a "separation distance" (d). For instance, with an ASDE sensor, we can compute how far is the measured position from the axis of the segment where the aircraft is located and relate with biases in the measured magnitudes (range and azimuth). Figure 22.14 shows how the "separation distance" is obtained.

For instance, the ADE error can be modeled with ith range-azimuth measurement $(R_{\mathrm{measure}}(i), \theta_{\mathrm{measure}}(i))$ including the following terms:

$$R_{\mathrm{measure}}(i) = R_{\mathrm{ideal}}(i) + b_{\mathrm{R}} + n_{\mathrm{R}}(i) \tag{22.13}$$

$$\theta_{\mathrm{measure}}(i) = \theta_{\mathrm{ideal}}(i) + b_{\theta} + n_{\theta}(i) \tag{22.14}$$

Fig. 22.13 Airport database design

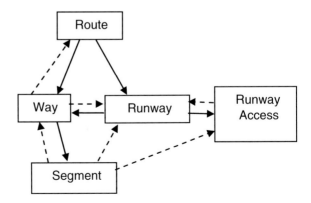

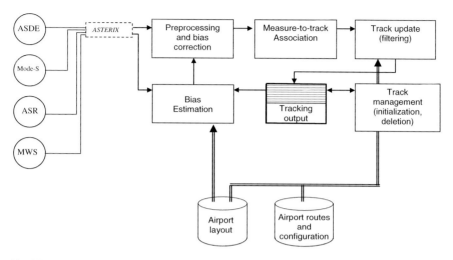

Fig. 22.14 Data processing architecture for airport surveillance

The ideal aircraft position for the ith measurement is corrupted with two types of erros. $(n_R(i), n_\theta(i))$ are measurement noise errors, considered as a random white process with associated constant covariance matrix R:

$$R = \begin{bmatrix} \sigma_R^2 & 0 \\ 0 & \sigma_\theta^2 \end{bmatrix} \qquad (22.15)$$

being σ_R and σ_θ the standard deviation of the range and azimuth noises, and (b_R, b_θ) the sensor bias terms (Fig. 22.15). More details on bias computation are in [30].

In any case, the first step to exploit the map information to improve the estimation processes is the location of targets on airport structure, determining the closest segments to current measurement accordingly to the uncertainty (Fig. 22.16), ranked by their transversal distances [25, 30].

22.4.2.2 Tracking Filter

Regarding the tracking filter design, the basic assumption is that interesting objects move accordingly to physical shapes of the airport roads contained in the map, and follow certain procedures (types of motion patterns, acceleration magnitudes, etc.), so the tracking procedures can be different from those used in other free environments. As mentioned above, the implemented solution is an IMM filter with modes exploiting the available surface information. The proposed filter is composed of three modes: constant speed motion, aligned with the segment orientation where target is currently located; segment transition filter, performing transversal maneuvers in order to move to close segments when the target crosses branching areas; and

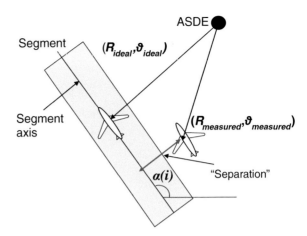

Fig. 22.15 "Separation distance" due to biases

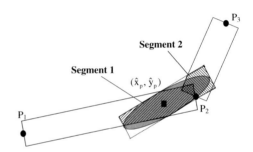

Fig. 22.16 Uncertainty in segment location

longitudinal-transition filter, adapting to stop and go, or runway acceleration maneuvers. They provide a considerable improvement in the accuracy of the estimates, due to continuous correction on heading which leads to good smoothing in segments at constant velocity.

To do that, the closest segment to current position is selected to define orientation of principal mode (mode "constant velocity") and the second one to define the adjacent mode (mode "segment transition"). This information of segment orientation is directly integrated in the prediction structures for motion prediction, considering two aspects. First, uncertainty in target maneuvers is projected along road axis so that the target may accelerate or stop depending on traffic conditions. Second, the predicted course is corrected to follow the road axis, in order to improve the reaction time in transitions for turns or branches:

$$\hat{x}_p[k+1] = F[k, \alpha]\,\hat{x}_f[k]$$
$$P_p[k+1] = F[k, \alpha]\,P_f[k]\,F[k, \alpha] + Q[k, \alpha] \tag{22.16}$$

being $\hat{x}_p[k+1]$ the predicted state vector to time $k+1$, from last update at k, $\hat{x}_f[k]$, and covariance matrices associated to both vectors are $P_p[k+1]$ and $P_f[k]$. So, the

Fig. 22.17 Difference between map orientation and track course

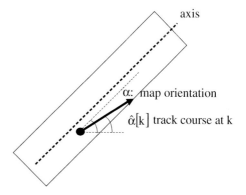

transition matrix F during time interval $\Delta t[k]$ integrates corrections to align the track course with axis, using the difference between road orientation, α, and estimated course, $\hat{\alpha}$ (see Fig. 22.17):

$$F[k, \alpha] = \begin{bmatrix} 1 & 0 & \Delta t[k]\cos((\alpha - \hat{\alpha})/2) & \Delta t[k]\mathrm{sen}((\alpha - \hat{\alpha})/2) \\ 0 & 1 & \Delta t[k]\mathrm{sen}((\alpha - \hat{\alpha})/2) & \Delta t[k]\cos((\alpha - \hat{\alpha})/2) \\ 0 & 0 & \cos(\alpha - \hat{\alpha}) & -\mathrm{sen}(\alpha - \hat{\alpha}) \\ 0 & 0 & -\mathrm{sen}(\alpha - \hat{\alpha}) & \cos(\alpha - \hat{\alpha}) \end{bmatrix} \quad (22.17)$$

The covariance matrix Q integrates map orientation to project the prediction error.

$$Q[k, \alpha] = \sigma_a^2 \begin{bmatrix} \Delta t^4/4 & 0 & \Delta t^3/2 & 0 \\ 0 & \Delta t^4/4 & 0 & \Delta t^3/2 \\ \Delta t^3/2 & 0 & \Delta t^2 & 0 \\ 0 & \Delta t^3/2 & 0 & \Delta t^2 \end{bmatrix}$$

$$+ \sigma_1^2 \begin{bmatrix} \cos(\alpha)^2\Delta t^4/4 & \cos(\alpha)\mathrm{sen}(\alpha)\Delta t^4/4 & \cos(\alpha)^2\Delta t^3/2 & \cos(\alpha)\mathrm{sen}(\alpha)\Delta t^3/2 \\ \cos(\alpha)\mathrm{sen}(\alpha)\Delta t^4/4 & \mathrm{sen}(\alpha)^2\Delta t^4/4 & \cos(\alpha)\mathrm{sen}(\alpha)\Delta t^3/2 & \mathrm{sen}(\alpha)^2\Delta t^3/2 \\ \cos(\alpha)^2\Delta t^3/2 & \cos(\alpha)\mathrm{sen}(\alpha)\Delta t^3/2 & \cos(\alpha)^2\Delta t^2 & \cos(\alpha)\mathrm{sen}(\alpha)\Delta t^2 \\ \cos(\alpha)\mathrm{sen}(\alpha)\Delta t^3/2 & \mathrm{sen}(\alpha)^2\Delta t^3/2 & \cos(\alpha)\mathrm{sen}(\alpha)\Delta t^2 & \mathrm{sen}(\alpha)^2\Delta t^2 \end{bmatrix}$$

$$(22.18)$$

σ_a^2 is the general uncertainty in prediction, while σ_1^2 is the longitudinal uncertainty $(\sigma_1 > \sigma_a)$. As mentioned above, the proposed IMM filter takes both the orientation corresponding to current road segment (mode 1, "constant velocity") and the closest possible deviation, if any (mode 3, "segment transition") (see Fig. 2.18).

Analogously, the mode with longitudinal acceleration (mode 2, "longitudinal") extends the state vector with this component, which is projected along map orientation (and the track course is also corrected):

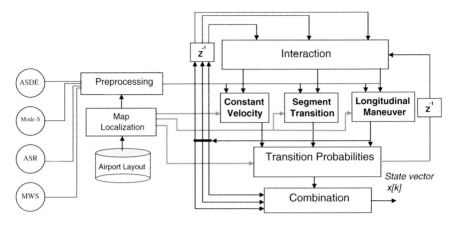

Fig. 22.18 IMM filter for track update in airport surface

$$\hat{x}_2[k] = \begin{bmatrix} x_2[k] & y_2[k] & v_{x2}[k] & v_{y2}[k] & a_1[k] \end{bmatrix}^{\mathrm{t}} \tag{22.19}$$

$$\begin{bmatrix} x_2[k+1] \\ y_2[k+1] \\ v_{x2}[k+1] \\ v_{y2}[k+1] \\ a_1[k+1] \end{bmatrix} = \begin{bmatrix} 1 & 0 & \Delta t_k \cos((\alpha - \hat{\alpha})/2) & \Delta t_k \mathrm{sen}((\alpha - \hat{\alpha})/2) & \cos(\alpha)\Delta t_k^2/2 \\ 0 & 1 & \Delta t_k \mathrm{sen}((\alpha - \hat{\alpha})/2) & \Delta t_k \cos((\alpha - \hat{\alpha})/2) & \mathrm{sen}(\alpha)\Delta t_k^2/2 \\ 0 & 0 & \cos(\alpha - \hat{\alpha}) & -\mathrm{sen}(\alpha - \hat{\alpha}) & \cos(\alpha)\Delta t_k \\ 0 & 0 & \mathrm{sen}(\alpha - \hat{\alpha}) & \cos(\alpha - \hat{\alpha}) & \mathrm{sen}(\alpha)\Delta t_k \\ 0 & 0 & 0 & 0 & 1 \end{bmatrix} \begin{bmatrix} x_2[k] \\ y_2[k] \\ v_{x2}[k] \\ v_{y2}[k] \\ a_1[k] \end{bmatrix}$$
$$\tag{22.20}$$

(covariance matrix has a similar expression as above for other modes).

So, this solutions searches quick transitions in branching points, as detailed next figure, and also a "longitudinal maneuver" is intended to improve performance under longitudinal maneuvers such as acceleration in runways or stop-and-go motion. A practical aspect is the introduction of a specific mode for segment transitions (see Fig. 22.19). When a branching effectively takes place and IMM transition is carried out, the location now will be done over map segment which was previously mode 2, and the closest segment will be the mode previously corresponding to mode 1. From that moment on, it is not applicable the classification before. Modes switch to keep the state and probability computed for mode 2 when it is labeled as mode 1. The switching logic identifies this situation of branch to closest segment. A double condition is checked: first, the probability of mode 2 must be higher than probability of mode 1. Secondly, several (at least two) consecutive locations must be done in the same segment, the one stored as closest segment in last update. More details on this solution for airport surface tracking can be found in [25] (Fig. 22.18).

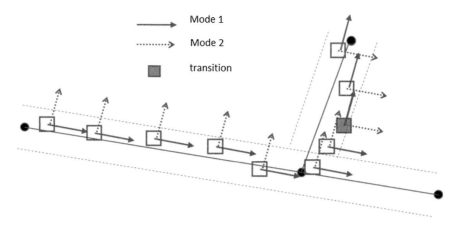

Fig. 22.19 Example of mode1-mode2 switch

22.4.3 Some Results

A series of simulations were carried out in order to analyze results and validate the system developed. To do that, the Barajas–Madrid airport configuration was represented following the scheme mentioned in Sect. 22.4.1 and several operations were simulated, as depicted in Fig. 22.20 with the sensors indicated in Table 22.1.

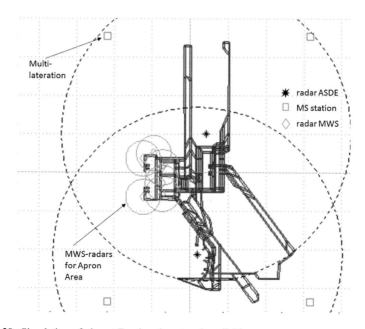

Fig. 22.20 Simulation of airport Barajas airport and available sensors

Table 22.1 Sensor simulated in Barajas–Madrid airport

Sensor	Position	T_{scan}	Error	Range
ASDE1	(−900, 400) m	1 s	$\sigma_\rho = 5$ m, $\sigma_\theta = 0.15°$	5 km
ASDE2	(−600, 3700) m	1 s	$\sigma_\rho = 5$ m, $\sigma_\theta = 0.15°$	5 km
Multimode S	Four stations: {(−4, −2), (3, −2), (3, 7), (−4, 7)} km	1 s	$\sigma_x = 5$ m, $\sigma_y = 5$ m	Quadruple coverage in surface
ASR	(10,000, 0) m	4.8 s	$\sigma_\rho = 10$ m, $\sigma_\theta = 0.09°$	100 km
MWS1	(−2770, 1550) m	1 s	$\sigma_\rho = 5$ m, $\sigma_\theta = 0.15°$	600 m
MWS2	(−2770, 2850) m	1 s	$\sigma_\rho = 5$ m, $\sigma_\theta = 0.15°$	600 m
MWS3	(−2400, 3030) m	1 s	$\sigma_\rho = 5$ m, $\sigma_\theta = 0.15°$	600 m
MWS4	(−2100, 2550) m	1 s	$\sigma_\rho = 5$ m, $\sigma_\theta = 0.15°$	600 m
MWS5	(−2100, 2025) m	1 s	$\sigma_\rho = 5$ m, $\sigma_\theta = 0.15°$	600 m
MWS6	(−2100, 1650) m	1 s	$\sigma_\rho = 5$ m, $\sigma_\theta = 0.15°$	600 m

With this configuration a set of typical operations were simulated to analyze the performance of the tracking system, typically aircraft trajectories between standlines and runways, and vehicles moving on surface. For instance, Fig. 22.21 shows a set of take-off trajectories on different areas of the airport using the four available runways.

The following results show illustrations of fusion system and exploitation of map information for two trajectories. First, the tracking error in position and velocity is depicted in Fig. 22.22 for different sets of sensors, showing the relative improvement when more sensors are integrated in the fusion algorithm.

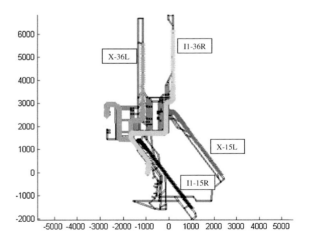

Fig. 22.21 Simulated take-off trajectories

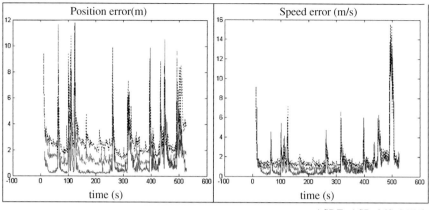

- ASDE+ASR+MS+MWS
-- ASDE+ASR+MS
⋯ ASDE+ASR

Fig. 22.22 Errors in position and velocity for target X-36L with different sets of sensors (Color figure online)

Secondly, the improvement achieved when map information is integrated is depicted in Fig. 22.23, for the situation of all sensors available. It can be seen the improvement in position accuracy and velocity, with the exception of a increase of errors during transitions, due to the filter adaptation during changes of segments.

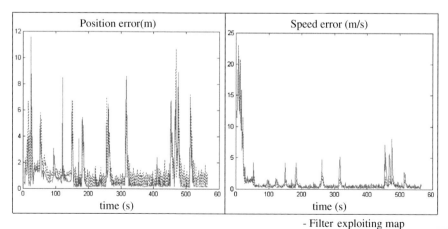

- Filter exploiting map
-- Filter with no map

Fig. 22.23 Errors in position and velocity for target X-36L with all sensors (Color figure online)

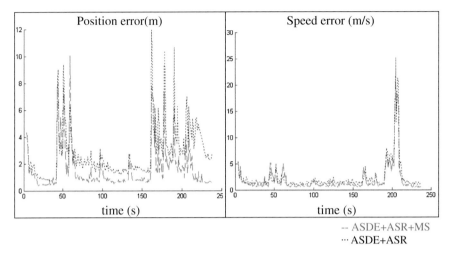

Fig. 22.24 Errors in position and velocity for target I1-15R with different sets of sensors (Color figure online)

Analogous results can be seen with the second trajectory in Figs. 22.24 and 22.25. In this case, the MWS mini-radars are not available and the comparison is with and without multilateration sensor.

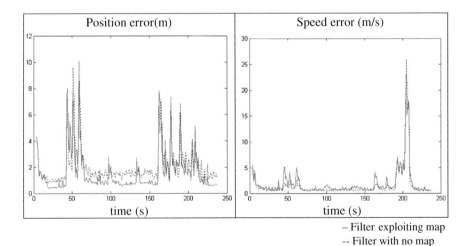

Fig. 22.25 Errors in position and velocity for target I1-15R with all sensors (Color figure online)

The two main aspects in this analysis are:

- A centralized fusion architecture that achieved the best accuracy, and the effect of adding new sensors lead to continuous improvement, especially in the noise reduction.
- The effect of incorporating map information on the filter allowed a significant improvement in the position (cross track error) and heading, mainly due to the corrections applied from available map information. Regarding transitions, improvement depends on the topology, with notable advantage when maneuvers follow the road path, and little effect or sometimes counterproductive under uncertainty in the way to follow in the presence of branching areas.

The above two conclusions for achieved accuracy corresponds to a preliminary and generic design implemented, which could be adjusted to a more detailed specifications of performance.

22.5   Conclusions and Future Work

In this chapter, we have presented two case studies for context-based ground target tracking. For the road-based vehicle tracking, a VF is generated based on the local gradients of the ground surface, and the objective of any road-based vehicle when off-road to move back to the road. This VF in conjunction with a transport equation is used to propagate the pdf of a road-based target. Bayes' rule is used to integrate the measurement pdf with the track pdf to generate a posterior pdf forms the current uncertain target location.

Regarding the airport example, centralized fusion architecture was developed to be used with the available sensors in Spanish airports. It was the first step toward the implementation of an ASMGCS prototype for Madrid/Barajas Airport, composed of a multisensor tracking system and a conflict detection module to alert of unsafe situations. The integration of ground information in the system (including bias estimation and target motion models) lead to improvements. Realistic conditions close to real-world operations were simulated and the analysis showed that: (i) the effect of including additional sensors is significant, with improvement in accuracy reflected in higher smoothing impact; (ii) the use of map information is very positive, outstanding the improvement in transversal and heading accuracy; (iii) the continuity was satisfactory in realistic and hard conditions (such as low separations and presence of noise and false alarms).

Acknowledgments This work was supported in part by projects MINECO TEC2014-57022-C2-2-R, TEC2012-37832-C02-01, and mobility program of Fundacion Caja Madrid.

References

1. E. Blasch, J. Garcia Herrero, L. Snidaro, J. Llinas, G. Seetharaman, K. Palaniappan, overview of contextual tracking approaches in information fusion (2013), in *Proceedings of SPIE 8747*, (Geospatial InfoFusion III, 2013), pp. 87470B
2. L. Snidaro, J. Garcia, J. Llinas, Context-based information fusion: a survey and discussion. Inf. Fusion **25**, 16–31 (2015)
3. J.A. Besada, J. Garcia, J.I. Portillo, J.M. Molina, A. Varona, G. Gonzalez, Airport surface surveillance based on video images. *IEEE Transactions on Aerospace and Electronic Systems* **41**(3), 1075–1082 (2005). Julio 2005
4. G. Ng, C.H. Tan, T.P. Ng, Tracking ground targets using state vector fusion, in *Proceedings of the 8th International Conference on Information Fusion*, vol. 1, (IEEE, 2005)
5. C. Yang, E. Blasch, J. Patrick, D. Qiu, Ground target track bias estimation using opportunistic road information, in *Proceedings of the IEEE Aerospace and Electronics Conference (NAECON)*, 2010 National, pp. 156–163
6. C.C. Ke, J. García, J. Llinas, comparative analysis of alternative ground target tracking techniques, in *Proceedings of 3rd International Conference on Information Fusion*, (Paris, France, July 2000)
7. T. Kirubarajan, Y. Bar-Shalom, K.R. Pattipati, I. Kadar, Ground target tracking with variable structure IMM estimator. Aerosp. Electron. Syst., IEEE Trans. on **36**(1), 26–46 (2000)
8. G. Battistello, M. Ulmke, Exploitation of a priori information for tracking maritime intermittent data sources, in *Proceedings of the 14th International Conference on Information Fusion*, (IEEE, Chicago, USA, 2011), pp. 1–8
9. W. Li, H. Leung, Constrained unscented kalman filter based fusion of GPS/INS/digital map for vehicle localization, in *Proceedings of the IEEE International Conference on Intelligent Transportation Systems*, (IEEE, Shanghai, China, 2003)
10. M. Roth, F. Gustafsson, U. Orguner, On-road trajectory generation from GPS data: a particle filtering/smoothing application, in *Proceedings of the 15th International Conference on Information Fusion*, (IEEE, Singapore, 2012), pp. 779–786
11. V. Nimier, A. Bastiere, N. Colin, M. Moruzzis, MILORD, an application of multifeature fusion for radar NCTR, in *Proceedings of the 3rd International Conference on Information Fusion*, (Paris, France, 2000)
12. F. Caron, E. Duflos, D. Pomorski, P. Vanheeghe, GPS/IMU data fusion using multisensor kalman filtering: introduction of contextual aspects. Inf. Fusion **7**(2), 221–230 (2006)
13. J. Wang, Y. Gao, The aiding of mems INS/GPS integration using artificial intelligence for land vehicle navigation. IAENG Int. J. Comput. Sci. **33**(1), 61–67 (2007)
14. W. Koch, Information fusion aspects related to GMTI convoy tracking, in *Proceedings of the 5th International Conference on Information Fusion*, vol. 2, (IEEE, Annapolis, USA, 2002), pp. 1038–1045
15. J.A. Sethian, Level set methods: evolving interfaces in geometry. *Fluid Mechanics, Computer Vision, and Material Science*. (Cambridge University Press, 1996)
16. E.S. Plumer, Cascading a systolic array and a feedforward neural network for navigation and obstacle avoidance using potential fields. Technical Report 1777575, NASA Contracter Report, 1991
17. A. Harten, S. Osher, Uniformly high-order accurate nonoscillatory schemes I. SIAM J. Numer. Anal. **24**, 279–309 (1987)
18. C.W. Shu, S. Osher, Efficient implementation of essentially non-oscillatory shock capturing schemes II. J. Compt. Phys. **83**, 32–78 (1989)
19. E.B. Pitman, H.E. Layton, L.C. Moore, Numerical simulation of propagating concentration profiles in renal tubules. Bull. Math. Biol. **56**, 567–586 (1994)
20. J. García, J.M. Molina, G. de Miguel, A. Soto Design of an A-SMGCS prototype at Barajas airport: data fusion algorithms, in *8th International Conference on Information Fusion*. (FUSION 2005, Julio, 2005)

21. A. Farina, L. Ferranti, G. Golino, constrained tracking filters for ASMGCS, 2003, in *5th International Conference on Information Fusion*, (2003), pp. 414–421
22. EURCONTROL Operational Concept and Requirements for A-SMGCS Implementation Level 2. Edition 2.1 EUROCONTROL Publications reference 10/07/15-69. 30 Oct 2010
23. M. Molina, J. García, J.A. Besada., J.R. Casar, Design of an A-SMGCS prototype at Barajas airport: available information and architecture, special session data fusion applied to surveillance and monitoring systems for airport surface, in *8th International Conference on Information Fusion,* (FUSION 2005 Pennsylvania, USA, Julio 2005)
24. J. García, J.A. Besada, F. Jiménez, J.R. Casar, Surface movement radar data processing methods for airport surveillance. IEEE Trans. Aerosp. Electron. Syst. **37**(2), 563–586 (2001). April 2001
25. J. García, J.A. Besada, J.R. Casar, Use of map information for tracking targets on airport surface. IEEE Trans. Aerosp. Electron. Syst. **39**(2), 75–694 (2003)
26. J. García, A. Berlanga, J.M. Molina, G. de Miguel, *Data Fusion alternatives for the integration of Millimetric Radar in Airport Surveillance Systems.* (2005 IEEE International Radar Conference, Philadelphia, USA, 2005)
27. J.A. Besada, A. Soto, G. de Miguel, J. Portillo, Design of an A-SMGCS prototype at Barajas airport: airport surveillance sensors bias estimation, in *8th International Conference on Information Fusion,* (FUSION 2005, Julio, 2005)
28. J. García, J.A. Besada, G. de Miguel, J. Portillo, *Data processing techniques for conflict detection on airport surface. Air Traffic Management 2003* (Budapest, Hungary. June 2003)
29. J. García, A. Berlanga, J.M. Molina, J.R. Casar, Methods for operations planning in airport decision support systems. Appl. Intell. **22**(3), 183–206 (2005). Mayo 2005
30. J. García, J.A. Besada, J.R. Casar, On-line multi-sensor registration for data fusion on airport surface. IEEE Trans. Aerosp. Electron. Syst. **43**(1), 356–370 (2007)
31. K. Benameur, B. Pannetier, V. Nimier, A comparative study on the use of road network information in gmti tracking, in *Proceedings of the 8th International Conference on Information Fusion*, vol. 1, (IEEE, Philadelphia, USA, 2005), pp. 8

Chapter 23
Context-Based Situation Recognition in Computer Vision Systems

Juan Gómez-Romero, Jesús García, Miguel A. Patricio, Miguel A. Serrano and José M. Molina

Abstract The availability of visual sensors and the increment of their processing capabilities have led to the development of a new generation of multi-camera systems. This increment has also conveyed new expectations and requirements that cannot be fulfilled by applying traditional fusion techniques. The ultimate objective of computer vision systems is to obtain a description of the observed scenario in terms that are both computable and human-readable, which can be seen as a specific form of situation assessment. Particularly, there is a great interest in human activity recognition in several areas such as surveillance and ambient intelligence. Simple activities can be recognized by applying pattern recognition algorithms on sensor data. However, identification of complex activities requires the development of cognitive capabilities close to human understanding. Several recent proposals combine numerical techniques and a symbolic model that represents context-dependent, background and common-sense knowledge relevant to the task. In this chapter the current challenges in the development of vision-based activity recognition systems are described, and how they can be tackled by exploiting formally represented context knowledge. Along with a review of the related literature, we describe an approach with examples in the areas of ambient intelligence and indoor security. The chapter surveys methods for context management in the literature that use symbolic

J. Gómez-Romero
Department of Computer Science and A.I., CITIC-UGR,
c/Periodista Rafael Gómez Montero, 2, 18071 Granada, Spain
e-mail: jgomez@decsai.ugr.es

J. García (✉) · M.A. Patricio · M.A. Serrano · J.M. Molina
Applied Artificial Intelligence Group, Universidad Carlos III de Madrid,
c/Avenida Gregorio Peces-Barba Martínez, 22, 28270 Colmenarejo, Spain
e-mail: jgherrer@inf.uc3m.es

M.A. Patricio
e-mail: mpatrici@inf.uc3m.es

M.A. Serrano
e-mail: mserrano@inf.uc3m.es

J.M. Molina
e-mail: molina@ia.uc3m.es

© Springer International Publishing Switzerland (outside the USA) 2016   627
L. Snidaro et al. (eds.), *Context-Enhanced Information Fusion*,
Advances in Computer Vision and Pattern Recognition,
DOI 10.1007/978-3-319-28971-7_23

knowledge models to represent and reason with context. Due to their relevance, we will pay special attention to ontology and logic-based models.

Keywords Activity recognition · Computer vision · Context formalization · Description logics · Ontological reasoning

23.1 Introduction

The decrease of the price of visual sensors and the increment of their processing capabilities has led to the development of a new generation of multi-camera systems. These advances have also generated new expectations and requirements that cannot be fulfilled by applying traditional fusion techniques. Specifically, in the video-vigilance domain, the term *third-generation systems* is used to designate systems that resemble the nature of the human process of surveillance, in such a way that they are able to identify what is happening and how it may affect the security [1, 2]. Besides the intrinsic difficulties that providing such cognitive capabilities poses, these systems must also face several technological problems, such as the size of the observed areas, the large number of available sensors, the geographical spread of resources, and the coordination of many monitoring points [3].

This state of affairs is common to the overall Information Fusion research area. Generally speaking, Information Fusion has experienced a similar shift of focus from lower-level problems—e.g., object detection, identification and tracking—to higher-level problems—e.g., situation recognition and assessment—, which demand more sophisticated solutions beyond the classical numerical approaches. The ultimate objective of modern fusion systems, and specifically, of visual data fusion systems, is to obtain an abstract description of the activities developed in the scenario in terms that are both computable and human-readable. This would support users and other processes to understand the ongoing situation and to react consequently.

Activities are mental constructs built up from the perception of a tangible reality. Hence, simple activities can be recognized by applying pattern recognition algorithms on sensor data. However, identification of complex activities, which may include social interactions and group behavior, requires the development of more complex cognitive capabilities. The role of context knowledge here is essential, because it establishes the necessary cognitive frame to complement the perceptions provided by the sensors and to restrict the plausible interpretations. Context can be informally defined as the set of background circumstances that are not of prime interest to the system, but have potential relevance toward optimal estimation [4].

In this chapter, we present various research works on the use and exploitation of context knowledge in visual information fusion. We focus on the combination of sensor-based and context-based knowledge, regardless of the number of cameras involved in the application. (Actually, for the sake of simplicity, we will mostly consider single-camera examples.) Our proposals are based in symbolic knowledge representation models, which are commonly used to represent relevant context-dependent, background and common-sense knowledge necessary for situation assessment. Among them, ontologies have recently received a noticeable attention, since they promote knowledge reuse while offering appropriate computational properties [5].

The chapter describes the current challenges in the area of vision-based activity recognition systems, and how they can be addressed by exploiting formally represented context knowledge. Along with a review of the related literature, we introduce some relevant proposals developed in the last years. We also illustrate the different approaches with examples in the areas of Ambient Intelligence and video surveillance. The main contribution of the chapter is to provide a unified view on recent advances on vision-based activity recognition, as well as several conclusions obtained by our research group after more than a decade of work in these topics.

The structure of the chapter is the following. In Sect. 23.2 we elaborate on the use of symbolic knowledge models to represent and reason with context in vision systems. Due to their relevance, we will pay special attention to ontology and logic-based models. Given the uncertain nature of the input data and the identification process itself, as well as the vagueness of the notion of activity, we also study approaches for context-based imprecise reasoning. In Sect. 23.3, we firstly consider object tracking problems, such as occlusions, unions, deformations and changes in the illumination, and describe an extended tracker that minimizes them. Secondly, we present an architecture and a model for high-level activity recognition. Finally, in Sect. 23.4 we show some application examples of the proposals described in Sects. 23.2 and 23.3. The chapter ends with a summary of the most relevant conclusions, and points to some directions for future work.

23.2 Knowledge Models for Context Management

The concept of context has been studied in many research fields: philosophy, psychology, linguistics, computer science, etc. [6]. Essentially, there are two main perspectives in context-aware computing. One the one hand, context can be considered a first-class modeling object. McCarthy [7] proposed the relation $ist(c, p)$ to represent that a given proposition p is true in the context c. These c's can be manipulated as any other symbol of the representation. On the other hand, more frequently context is implicitly embedded and exploited in the knowledge base [8]. It acts therefore as a structured "set of variable, external constraints [...] that influences the behavior of that process in the agent(s) under consideration" [9].

Context is used in information fusion to refine ambiguous estimates, to define situational hypotheses and explain observations, to constrain processing, and to provide for interrelationship between different fusion levels [10]. For a more comprehensive survey and discussion of the use of context in Information Fusion, we recommend the reader the work by Snidaro et al. [11].

In previous works, we have identified two paradigmatic frameworks of exploitation of contextual information [12]. The "a priori" framework accounts for context that is known at design time and can be integrated into the fusion algorithms, thus leading to hybrid procedures that use this external information to improve estimations. Conversely, the "a posteriori" framework is applied when not all the relevant context information is known at design time, or the nature of context information makes it impossible the integration into fusion algorithm. In both cases, there are additional engineering issues to be considered. We need to allow access to the context information, which may not be straightforward in some cases. Other related question is setting boundaries to context information; i.e., to determine which context is relevant to a given situation. The latter falls into what is called *process refinement*, because it has strong influence in the adaptation of the fusion process itself.

An additional question is selecting a proper formalism for context representation. Steinberg and Rogova [13] enumerate three basic types of context models more applicable to information fusion are: key-value models, ontology-based models, and logic-based models. Key-value models are the simplest ones, but they are not suitable for the complex representations required in higher-level fusion. Ontology-based models allow for the axiomatic description of concepts, relations, and individuals, and they have been used to reason about situations. Nevertheless, they are known to have several limitations to manage temporal and uncertain knowledge. Hence, logic-based models have been proposed as extensions of ontologies especially targeted to domains that require more expressive representation models.

Representing the wider context in which the fusion processes take place has been one of the main concerns addressed by ontology-based models. For example, the Situational Awareness (SAW) core ontology defines abstract concepts used in situation assessment [14]. Similarly, the Situation Theory Ontology (STO) is an upper-model for situation awareness based on the semantics of Barwise and Perry's situation theory [5]. In computer vision, ontologies have been used for deductive reasoning based on context and common-sense knowledge toward situation recognition. As it can be seen in [15], the procedure is insufficient in complex problems, because there is an inherent uncertainty in the recognition process that is omitted.

The logic-based extensions of ontologies proposed in information fusion are mostly based on the probability theory. PR-OWL, an extension of the standard ontology language OWL with Bayesian probabilities, has been used in higher-level fusion in the maritime domain [16]. In the same application area, Snidaro et al. [17] have proposed the use of Markov Logic Networks for context exploitation in seaport vigilance, whereas in [18] we describe a hybrid algorithm that combines deductive reasoning with ontologies and abductive reasoning with the belief-based argumentation system for threat assessment in a similar setup. It is interesting to notice that these approaches concentrate in the high-level, and consequently, they are agnostic of the sensor data used as system input, as long as it can be converted to the underlying symbolic model. Therefore, they could be seamlessly applied in vision-based applications.

23.3   Context for Vision-Based Activity Recognition

According to the JDL model [19], lower-level visual data fusion is focused on the extraction of relevant features and the characterization of moving objects from video streams captured by distributed cameras. The main task at this level is object tracking, which is defined as the estimation of the number of objects in a scene, together with their instantaneous position, speed and other kinematic properties. The objective of higher-level visual data fusion, in turn, is to identify the current scenario and to evaluate whether it poses a threat. There are two major problems that have to be addressed here: object classification, i.e., to determine object types (e.g., car, human, aircraft); and situation recognition, i.e., to determine activity types (e.g., approaching, walking, maneuvering).

Context exploitation in lower-level fusion typically fits into the "a priori" framework described in Sect. 23.2, whilst in higher-level fusion usually falls into the "a posteriori" framework. The reason is that there is a considerable gap between context knowledge and their impact on the behavior of a tracking algorithm. The former is usually defined at a high abstraction level (e.g., "a person is hidden behind a column"), whereas the latter is usually a numerical parameter of a statistical procedure (e.g., noise models or variance matrices). Consequently, in lower-level fusion, the context management logic is incorporated into the process, thus resulting in a hybrid algorithm. We describe this approach in Sect. 23.3.1. In contrast, the heterogeneity of problems and domains of interest in higher-level fusion does not favor "a priori" frameworks. Therefore, the approaches based on symbolic and expressive context representation formalisms, such as the ones described in Sect. 23.3.2, are more common.

23.3.1   Context in Lower-Level Fusion

Most computational techniques applied to understand situations based on video data are founded on probabilistic models for prediction and inference. Some widely used methods are MHT (*Multiple-Hypothesis Tracker*) [20], distributed JPDA (*Joint Probabilistic Data Association*) [21], and distributed Kalman filter [22]. Nevertheless, they have shown insufficient in scenarios that involve interacting objects, deformable objects, occlusions, and dynamic environments with changing setups and illumination conditions [23]. These events produce anomalous tracks splits and merging, as well as track loss.

One way to understand the use of context in the lower-level fusion process is by considering a typical *fusion node*. The fusion node receives data from sensors or from other nodes to provide a unified view on the perceived scenario (Fig. 23.1). Processing in the visual data fusion node encompasses three stages [24]: (i) data alignment or common referencing, which involves coordinate or units

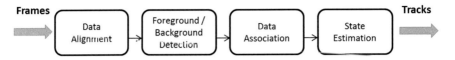

Fig. 23.1 Visual fusion node

transformations, uncertainty normalization, and inter-sensor alignment according to camera calibration; (ii) foreground/background detection for pixel segmentation; (iii) data association to delimit tracks from *blobs*,[1] in particular when new blobs enter the stage; and (iv) state estimation (usually simplified as tracking), which involves the computation of object characteristics: size, position, direction, etc.

The role of context knowledge in the sensor fusion node is improving the accuracy and continuity of tracking estimators. To attain this goal, it is necessary to perform an effective integration of raw sensor data with the contextual sources. Accordingly, the context model is used to reason about the sensed object and to provide feedback to the tracking algorithms, while affecting the initialization and association logic. Context-based reasoning contributes to the track initialization and blob-to-track association processes by providing clues about the number of targets intervening in certain predefined scenarios, the entrance points to the area under observation, and the behavior of static elements, to name some of them. Another key use of contextual information exploitation is to support predictions. For instance, observed individuals may be constrained to follow predefined paths according to practicable walking routes. More generally, feedback strategies—i.e., commands flowing from the higher-level fusion processes to the sensor fusion node–, are expected to yield performance improvements in adverse conditions, such as high occupation or noisy scenarios with small probability of target detection.

The Fuzzy Region Assignment (FRA) algorithm [25] defines a hybrid tracking procedure to initialize and maintain video tracks so that context knowledge can be injected to adapt its performance. This proposal integrates visual information at several levels of granularity: low-level image segmentation operations, medium-level smoothness criteria on target features, and high-level constraints on tracking continuity.

Specifically, FRA addresses the data association problem, for which many approaches using diverse meta-heuristic strategies have been proposed [26, 27]. Data association is the process of assigning each blob to its closest target based on a certain distance measure, which can be very error-prone in multi-target video scenarios with occluding, merging, or overlapping tracks. Internally, FRA uses fuzzy concepts to represent the concepts at different levels and rule-based reasoning to associate blobs to tracks. It allows multiple regions to be associated to multiple

---

[1]A *blob* is a set of pixels included in a connected image area. A *track* is a set of blobs corresponding to a scene object with associated properties: size, position, speed, color, etc. Generally, blobs and tracks are represented by their minimum enclosing rectangles.

tracks, thus extending conventional approaches based on simplified point or centroid representation of targets.

Essentially, FRA implements a Bayesian framework that determines the contribution of each blob to update the target tracks by means of an estimated probability value. The probabilities are calculated by the fuzzy system, which uses the heuristic functions *Overlap*, *Deform*, *Density*, and *Conflict* to update the track situation and its dimensions, and a set of rules derived from experimentation (81) to infer the resulting confidence (Fig. 23.2).

FRA firstly expresses the granules of information with variables extracted from image operations. Next, the rule-based aggregation performs a soft approximation to the likelihood function, which considers at the same time intuitive closeness criteria and exclusion constraints, equivalent to those defined with hard decisions. Finally, the output variable (confidence level) is used to compose a synthesized measurement, named *pseudoblob*, which is assigned to the track.

The rules in the fuzzy inference subsystem have been designed from the behavior of the tracking system after observing the defined input and output data and variables by a human expert. The overall idea is that the result of the fuzzy assignment contains the proper action to take under a set of particular extreme conditions to guarantee track continuity. An example is the following:

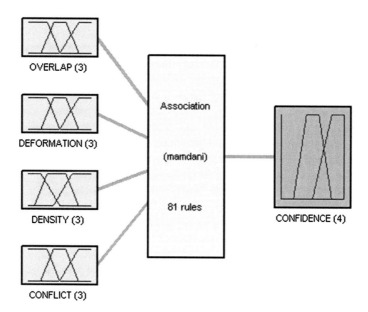

Fig. 23.2 FRA fuzzy inference

```
IF overlap IS <LOW> AND deformation IS <MEDIUM>

THEN confidence is <MEDIUM>



IF conflict IS NOT <LOW>

THEN confidence IS <ZERO>
```

23.3.2   Context in Higher-Level Fusion

Situation interpretation and assessment involves several transformation steps from lower-level numerical data to higher-level descriptive statements. The first one is known as the grounding problem [28], which in video applications is the process of converting tracking information into (atomic) symbols of the abstract representation. If ontologies are used for the representation, we use ontology instances to ground track data produced by real-world moving objects. From this point, deductive reasoning can be applied to classify the object and to determine the situation.

Let us explain this procedure in more detail. Deductive reasoning is the automatic procedure that obtains new implicit axioms that are not in the model but are entailed by the explicit axioms. Basic ontological reasoning includes the inference of subsumption axioms (i.e., determining the implicit taxonomy according to the features of asserted concepts) and instance membership axioms (i.e., determining the type of an instance according to the concepts of the model and the property values and relations of the instance). Thus, a combination of both can be used to classify track instances according to their features into matching classes of a complex taxonomy. For example, we can define a concept for *small objects* to include all tracks with size less that a threshold. Similarly, we can deduce relations for objects that are compulsory for specific object classes. Deductive classification can be also expressed by using rules in the Semantic Web Rule Language (SWRL) [29] under certain safety restrictions—which basically imply that the reasoning process must be monotonic [30].

Deductive reasoning with ontologies has a major limitation: it does not allow us to directly create new ontology instances [31]; i.e., existing instances are reclassified, but new instances are never created. Nevertheless, scene interpretation is a paradigmatic case of abductive reasoning, in which we take a set of facts as input (the observations) and find a suitable hypothesis that explains them (the interpretation)—sometimes with an associated degree of confidence or probability. This kind of reasoning can be simulated by using customized procedures or, alternatively, by relying on the extended features provided by some ontological reasoning engines. To name one of them, RACER supports abductive reasoning by means of production rules expressed in the new RACER query language (nRQL) [32].

Accordingly, it is possible to describe the context of the scene with ontological axioms and rules, and later use this context to: (a) classify entities to infer additional information; (b) infer the current situation, expressed as new ontology instances and relationships. The main advantage of this approach is that we have a common representation and a formal inference procedure to manage different types and sources of information, as long as they are encoded into the ontology.

In previous works, we have proposed a multi-layer model to manage contextual and perceived knowledge for high-level visual information fusion, both in single-camera [33] and multiple-camera configurations [24]. Each layer corresponds to a different abstraction level in the transformation process from tracks to assessments in accordance to the JDL fusion model (Fig. 23.3):

- Tracks sub-ontology: Representation of tracking data (JDL Level 1). Output of the tracking algorithm symbolically represented; i.e., frames, tracks and track properties (color, position, velocity, etc.)

Fig. 23.3 Multilayer context management architecture

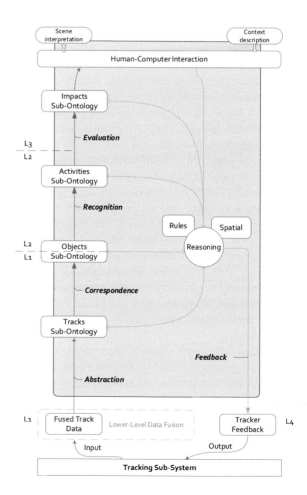

- Objects sub-ontology: Representation of scene objects (JDL Level 1). Objects resulting after track classification; i.e., static and dynamic elements of the scene.
- Situations sub-ontology: Representation of relations between objects that last in time (JDL Level 2); i.e., activities and events.
- Threats sub-ontology: Representation of cost or threat value assigned to activities (JDL Level 3), plus additional information regarding possible contingency actions.
- Feedback and process improvement sub-ontology: Representation of configurations and commands to be issued to the tracker under certain circumstances to improve the overall fusion process (JDL Level 4); e.g., changes in filter parameters, camera movements, etc.

Each sub-ontology of an upper abstraction level is based upon the sub-ontology of the lower abstraction level. Deductive reasoning is performed 'intra-level,' in such a way that context is used to refine the information available. Abductive reasoning is performed 'inter-level,' since it involves the creation of new knowledge of an upper level that explains the facts known at a lower level.

With this architecture, situation assessment is a bottom-up process. First, tracking data is inserted as ontology instances into the tracks sub-ontology. Here, we assume that track data comes from a single sensor, but it could be also the result of multi-camera lower-data fusion. Spatial relations among tracks may be also computed at this point. To do so, it is possible to use a hybrid numerical-symbolical approach based on any topology library (e.g., the Java Topology Suite) and the RCC spatial calculus [34]. Afterwards, tracks are classified according to their features by deductive rules and ontology axioms. Those unclassified tracks can be considered unknown or even suspicious depending on the application domain.

Once track information is symbolically represented and enriched in the tracks sub-ontology, abductive reasoning is applied to identify objects from tracks. For example, a medium-size rectangular track may denote a person in the scene. A proper rule would be created in that case. The procedure continues to the upper levels, thus elaborating more abstract descriptions of the situation at each step. Obviously, not every inter-level transformation would be implementable by only using abductive rules. We consider the possibility of inserting more sophisticated algorithms to carry out this conversion. It is worth to highlight that these algorithms can be transparently integrated into the overall process, as long as they use the well-defined upper and lower sub-ontologies for their input and output, respectively.

Besides bottom-up situation assessment, the model also provides support for top-down process refinement. In both cases, abductive reasoning is carried out to draw new knowledge, but in the latter, the new instances denote actions that could be used to modify the fusion procedure, rather than elaborations on the primitive visual perceptions. For example, in a situation where we detect that there is a person hidden behind a column, the tracker could be notified to not delete the associated track, even if it exceeds the normal track elimination threshold (as shown in the next section). Notice that, in most cases, it will be necessary and additional module to transform ontological descriptions of process feedback to actionable operations. This is not a trivial process that may require a complex logic, a full characterization of processes at each level, and a deep understanding of the application domain. For example, it may be quite complex to selectively modify the covariance matrix of a Kalmar filter to improve track estimations when contextual information warns against adverse weather conditions.

23.4 Examples on Context-Based Activity Recognition

Throughout the last decade of research work our group has developed several proposals focused in surveillance and Ambient Intelligence areas. The common interest that has guided these approaches is the improvement of the quality of human activity recognition processes. The examples described in this section depict real applications in which we incrementally implement a context-based activity recognition system under the theoretical framework introduced in the previous section. The first example introduces a video annotation prototype to interact with video processing, built to validate some key concepts of the systems subsequently developed. The second example extends the system with context input to address occlusion problems. Finally, a generalization and extension for complex situations is introduced to show the capability to handle scene interpretation and process improvement in Ambient Intelligence by integrating the annotation and context reasoning processes.

23.4.1 Video Annotation

The widespread presence of video applications has led to an increase of the amount of raw and unclassified resources. This trend has generated the need to automatically analyze and catalog the resources according to the semantics of their content. This first example describes a semi-automatic tool that extracts lower-level features from video sources and uses them as a basis to annotate the sequences, allowing the user to visualize and edit the annotations. The prototype is composed of three modules: (1) a tracker based on the FRA algorithm; (2) a context information layer; (3) an annotation module, which integrates the other modules and displays the results. We call this tool MViPER.

The annotation software is implemented on top of ViPER (Video Performance Evaluation Resource) [35], a tool that provides support for easily creating and sharing video ground truths in a flexible format. The ViPER GUI enables users to manually annotate spatiotemporal and general information of objects in a single scan of video. It supports frame-by-frame annotation of video metadata and storage in XML format. Annotations describe the object state by means of the values of its attributes, which contain, for instance, its name or its location.

MViPER extends this functionality by adding automating track annotation to video. This is done by the underlying tracking module. In addition, it allows users to edit the automatic track annotations, as well as to add new annotations related with the abstraction levels described in Sect. 23.3.2 (i.e., tracks, objects, and situations) by means of predefined templates. For example, it is possible to define (manually or by using any external algorithm) that a track correspond to a specific entity type (e.g., person), or that two entities are involved in an action (e.g., meeting). Besides, if the human supervisor manually modifies the track properties that have been automatically detected, MViPER sends these changes back to the tracker, which restarts the track analysis process with the new information. For example, if the user changes track size or position, the corresponding track in the FRA tracker is also modified. Such bidirectional interaction allows dynamically repairing tracking errors in real time, with the advantage of modifying the behavior of the tracker when it fails to adapt to the corrected situation. The user can select whether changes in annotations are propagated to the tracker or not, which is useful if we just want to record the ground truth of a video sequence.

The system implementation uses a legacy tracker programmed in C with the OpenCV[2] library, and a Java-based program logic that manages the representation ontology and generates the user interface. The communication between them is realized with the Java Native Interface (JNI) technology. The system has been tested with the Computer Vision Based Analysis in Sport Environments (CVBASE) dataset.[3] Video features are: speed at 25 frames per second, resolution 384 × 576 pixels, and M-JPEG compression. The selected video is a zenithal record of two individuals playing squash. They are in close proximity to each other, dressed similarly, and moving quickly. Therefore, there are constant crossings and occlusions between them, which makes the video an interesting challenge to measure the quality of the tracker.

In our experiments, tracks have been detected quite accurately, and the supervisor user is not required to modify the annotations frequently. In Figs. 23.4 and 23.5, we present two screenshots of the system when it fails. They show an overlapping situation between two close tracks, which results in swapping the object IDs. This would require the participation of the user to modify the automatic annotations.

23.4.2 Reasoning with Context to Improve Tracker Accuracy

We have developed an extension that leverages the basic MViPER capabilities by integrating the tracking system and the context information layer, in such a way that the overall scene is represented with the model at different granularity levels. First, it allows users to annotate any contextual object, in addition to the edition of automatic track annotations. For example, it is possible to annotate an object as a *door* in the same way as track properties can be changed. The possible contextual elements that

---

[2]http://opencv.org/.

[3]http://vision.fe.uni-lj.si/cvbase06/.

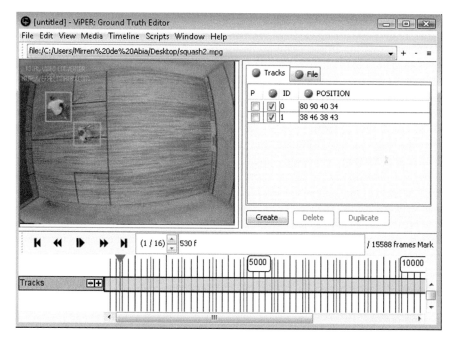

Fig. 23.4 Video analysis. Frame 530

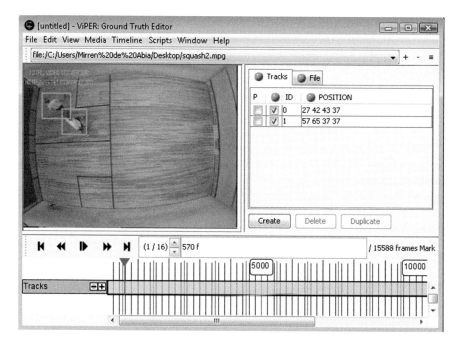

Fig. 23.5 Video analysis. Frame 570

can be used in the annotations are those defined in the complete context representation model (mainly, at the object level). Second, the combined representation of tracks and context information in the ontology is the basis for more complex tasks, such as checking data consistency, making deductive and abductive inference, and providing feedback at different levels. As explained in Sect. 23.3.2, intra and inter-level information transformation is achieved by (extended) ontological reasoning.

The implementation of this platform is based on the RACER reasoner (Renamed ABox and Concept Expression Reasoner).[4] RACER has been chosen because it provides support for different inference paradigms, including deductive and abductive reasoning, and spatial inference.

In the following example, we show a rule in the nRQL language (new RACER query language) that generates new higher-level knowledge by transforming a track in a dynamic scene object of the Person class. The rule antecedent contains perceptual data (such as track identifiers trackID), previously stored queries (such as the current-snapshot function, which retrieves the last occurrence of a track), a priori context knowledge (the condition on the *width* and the *height* of the track), and so forth. The rule consequent generates a new individual classified as Person, declares a specific identifier, and creates a new role that associates the individual to a track entity. (In the example, we use the tren namespace to notate tracking entities, scob for scene objects, and *ind* for new individuals.)

```
(firerule
  (and
    (?track      (equal #!tren:id trackID)
    (?track ?tsnapshot ?dimension current-snapshot)
    (?tsnapshot #!tren:unknown_frame #!tren:isValidInEnd)
    (?dimension (>= #!tren:width 9))
    (?dimension (>= #!tren:height 9)))
  (
    (instance  (new-ind |ind|) #!scob:Person)
    (instance  (individual |ind|)(equal #!scob:id trackID))
    (related   (individual |ind|)?track #!scob:hasAssociatedTrack)))
```

RACER support for reasoning with spatial knowledge is provided by an implementation of the Region Connection Calculus (RCC) theory. However, abductive reasoning with spatial objects is very expensive in terms of the number of required rules and the computation time. Moreover, it grows exponentially with the number of entities, which is a serious drawback in moderately complex scenes. To address these problems, we have developed an optimized geometry model that partitions the scene space to avoid checking all the pair-wise relations between the objects [36]. The RCC-enabled version of the system including the spatial reasoning implements a variation of the schema shown in Fig. 23.3. Essentially, it extends the reasoning module with a geometrical reasoning sub-module, which interacts with the RACER RCC layer and the optimized geometry model.

---

[4]http://www.racer-systems.com/.

Similarly to the basic MViPER, the scene interpretation output in higher-level terms is presented to the user. This allows the user to edit the erroneous semantic conclusions of the system module at different abstraction levels. In addition, the system also provides further recommendations to the tracker, either automatically or after supervisor editions. To do so, we use a specific ontology that abstractly represents actions to improve the accuracy of the tracking system. These actions should be afterwards translated into modifications that the tracker can understand. In the current implementation, this translation is quite straightforward, since the recommended actions directly correspond to tracker parameter modifications.

This general semi-automatic annotation system has been tested in a scenario about recognition and management of occlusions with several static objects and one track. The a priori information is the position and size of static object individuals of type Column. The user annotates the column and a column object; column objects are defined in the object ontology as a subtype of occluding objects. During the analysis of the video, the tracking system detects a track in the scene and updates its position in the scene model. From this features, the reasoning module infers that it is a person, and a corresponding person instance is created at the objects level.

Occlusions are detected when a tracked object in an overlap relation with a static object (in this case a column) is deleted by the tracking system. This situation is represented as follows:

```
(firerule
  (and
    (?track    #!tren:Track)
    (?object   #!scob:StaticObject)
    (?track    (equal #!tren:id trackID))
    (?track    ?person #!scob:isAssociatedToObject)
    (?*object ?*track :po))
  (
    (instance (new-ind |ind|) #!actv:Occlussion)
    (related  (individual |ind|) ?object #!actv:isOccluder)
    (related  (individual |ind|) ?person #!actv:isOccluded)))
```

(Namespaces preceded with #! and variables preceded with * mean that this information is used in the geometrical model; actv namespace notates activities; :po represents the RCC property partial overlap.)

Figure 23.6 shows the processing sequence and the results obtained by the system. In Fig. 23.6a, no occlusion is detected between *static object 2* and *tracked object 1*, because the track associated to the static object is not deleted by the tracking system. In Fig. 23.6b, an occlusion is detected, because the tracker is not detecting the hidden track, and consequently it is deleted. Nevertheless, in this situation the previous rule is triggered, a recommendation for the tracker is generated: recreate the track, keep the last registered size before the deletion, and set the object position to the center of the occluding object. In the next step shown in Fig. 23.6c, the continuity of the object is guaranteed. Table 23.1 shows a simplified view of the context model data managed during of the occlusion situation.

Fig. 23.6 Sequence of the test occlusion situation: **a** beginning of an occlusion; **b** track completely occluded by the column; **c** end of the occlusion

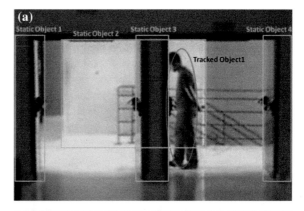

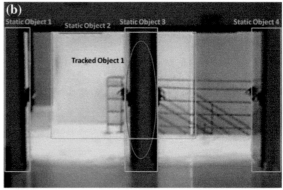

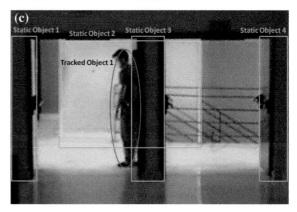

23.4.3 Scene Interpretation in Ambient Intelligence

The context-based reasoning system can be used to provide support beyond correcting tracking errors. One interesting application domain is Ambient Intelligence (AmI), where visual sensors have not received very much attention, but can be used

Table 23.1 Changes in the knowledge model corresponding sequence in Fig. 23.6

Figure 23.6a		
A priori knowledge	Tracks	**Instances:** `Track1` [position and size]
	Objects	**Instances**: `Static_object1,` `Static_object2,` `Static_object3,` `Static_object4` [+ positions and sizes]
Rule fired		`Track_1` matches the 'person detection' rule, and therefore, a new person instance is created (`PersonObj1`)
Asserted knowledge	Tracks	**Relationships:** `Track1 isAssociatedToObject` `PersonObj1`
	Objects	**Instances:** `PersonObj1` **Relationships:** `PersonObj1` `hasAssociatedTrack Track1`
Figure 23.6b		
Tracking event		`Track1` deleted
Knowledge event		`Track1` and `PersonObj1` declared as inactive in knowledge base
Rule fired		'Overlapping' rule is fired with `PersonObj1`
Recommendations asserted	Tracks	**Instances:** `Track1` [+ new position, previous size] **Relationships:** `Track1 isAssociatedToObject` `PersonObj1` [reactivation]
	Objects	**Instances:** `PersonObj1` **Relationships:** `PersonObj1` `hasAssociatedTrack Track1` [reactivation]
Activities asserted (by the 'overlapping' rule)	Activities	**Instances:** `Occlusion_1_3` **Relationships:** `Occlusion_1_3 hasOccluder` `Static_object2,` `Occlusion_1_3 hasOccluded` `PersonObj1`
Figure 23.6c		
Final status	Recommendation	**Instances:** `Reco1` **Relationships:** `Reco1 isConsequenceOf` `Occlusion_1_3`

to complete the information obtained by other sensors. In that regard, in Gomez Romero et al. [37] we propose an extension of our system for the interpretation of the typical situations of interest inside a smart home.

The knowledge model used in this application is the same one depicted in Fig. 23.3, with appropriate extensions to manage the objects and situations of the AmI environment. The instances of the model corresponding to the a priori knowledge are created as seen in Sect. 23.4.2 that is, with the annotation tool. The basic reasoning procedures supported by the system are also similar (i.e., object identification and tracking enhancement), but we have studied in more detail scene identification from single and multiple cameras.

To test the system, we used the video sequences included in the LACE dataset of the University of Rochester.[5] This dataset includes footage taken from several cameras covering a room that reconstructs the living room and the kitchen of a small apartment. Only one moving person is present in the videos. The three cameras are located in the room as depicted in Fig. 23.7. As it can be seen, they have considerably overlapping fields of view.

Before starting the processing, the framework must be configured; particularly, the scenario viewed by each camera must be annotated. Annotations include object position and size, possible occlusions, enter and exit zones, and any other convenient contextual knowledge. For instance, we have used concepts, such as Person, Door, Couch, Table and Fridge, and axioms such as *couch is a static occluding object*, defined in a specific ontology (noted smarthome). Some examples of the ontology instances created after annotation are shown in Fig. 23.8.

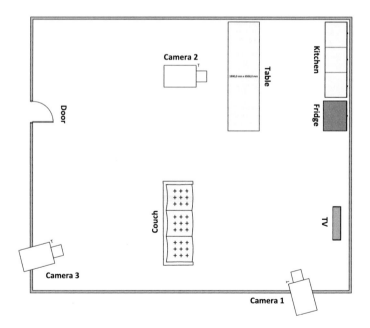

Fig. 23.7 Scenario plane: camera and static objects location

[5]http://www.cs.rochester.edu/~spark/muri/.

Fig. 23.8 Camera 1: contextual objects annotation

We have marked the same objects in cameras 1, 2, and 3: exit door, couch, table, and fridge. The figure depicts the correspondence between ontology instances and scenario information. We show an excerpt of the OWL code corresponding to the definition of `fridge1` as an instance of the `Fridge` class with a point of the bounding polygon at position (687, 144).

It is interesting to highlight that we assign the same identifier to an object regardless of the camera scenario that is being annotated. For example, the fridge has the object identifier 1 in camera 1 and camera 2. Since we have only one moving person, this avoids explicit camera calibration, as explained below.

Rules have been as well defined to create actions to enhance the low-level tracking performance. For example, we have added a general rule to detect an overlapping situation similar to the one described in the previous section. This rule is triggered in frame 118 of the sequence, being `person1` and `couch1` the objects that match the rule antecedent. After the new occlusion situation is detected, the framework watches the changes in the size of the occluded object in order to keep the consistency and avoid the effects due to the occlusion. Figure 23.9 shows the bounding box of the track as calculated by the tracker without context and the bounding box as estimated by the cognitive layer as a result of the reasoning procedure.

Additional abductive rules can be defined in the model to interpret what is happening in the scene from tracking and object data. For example, we have defined

(a)

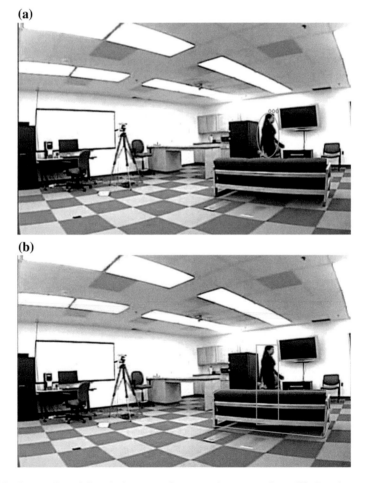

(b)

Fig. 23.9 Camera 3 partial occlusion correction: **a** tracker output; **b** modified tracker output

the rule below in camera 1 to detect if a person is close to the fridge (RCC EC predicate, meaning 'externally connected'). If the rule is triggered, a new instance of the Touch action is created, making a relation between the objects involved in the action with the property touch.

```
(firerule

(and

    (?track         #!tren:Track)

    (?person        #!smarthome:Person)

    (?person    ?track          #!scob:hasAssociatedTrack)

    (and        (?object        #!smarthome:Fridge)

                (?*object       ?*track     :ec)))

(

(instance

(new-ind ind ?person ?object)       #!smarthome:Touch)

(related (individual ind) ?person #!smarthome:touch)

(related (individual ind) ?object #!smarthome:touch)))))
```

It goes without saying that this naive rule can lead to wrong situation identifications. However, we can perform an additional simple confirmation step by taking advantage of the detection obtained by another camera. If camera 2 is detecting a similar situation (with a corresponding rule), then the degree of certainty of the situation can be increased. This mechanism can be extended to multiple situations, thus achieving spontaneous calibration. The processing can be implemented in a central fusion node, and the communication with this node can be done by exchanging messages also expressed in the ontology [38]. It would be also possible to use multiple and heterogeneous sensors in addition to traditional video cameras, such as time-of-flight cameras, as described in [39].

The use of a formal and extensible language allows us to scale the system to more complex situations. For instance, let us imagine that camera 2 detects that a milk bottle has been left on the table after detecting that the fridge has been used (because these situations have been confirmed by several cameras, or because the operator has annotated the scene). At this point of the execution, we would have a previous situation that states that the person was using the fridge, and a situation that states that the bottle is on the table (Fig. 23.10). We could define a rule such as:

(a)

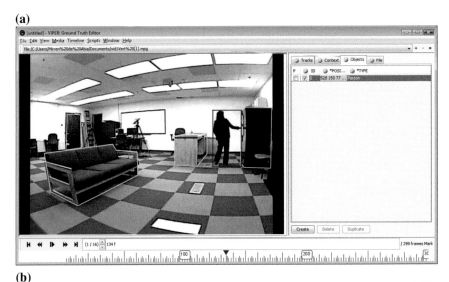

(b)

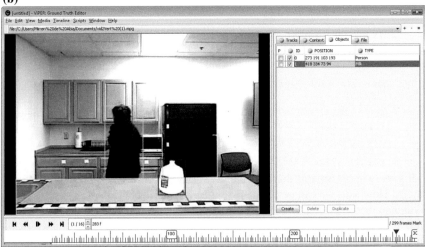

Fig. 23.10 Breakfast situation detection: **a** individual interacts with fridge; **b** milk bottle is on the table

if the person has been (recently) using the fridge and the bottle on the table, then we can infer that the person is preparing breakfast. Obviously, this rule should be improved to avoid false positives (e.g., daytime can be also considered), but it shows the potential of the cognitive model and how the system can be compositionally extended with new situation detection heuristics.

23.5 Conclusions and Future Work

In this chapter, we have presented various research approaches for context-based activity recognition in Computer Vision systems. Context is used as an additional source in Information Fusion that provides a knowledge frame to reduce ambiguity of input data, to limit the possible interpretations, to extend the available information, and in general, to guide the situation interpretation process. Formal languages, mainly ontology and logic-based formalisms, can be used to create flexible representations that assimilate context and perceived information to obtain a global description of the situation in symbolic terms. Our architecture, which defines several layers of knowledge (corresponding to the JDL model layers, ranging from lower-level to higher-level fusion), establishes a bidirectional situation recognition and feedback generation process that provides support for scene identification and fusion improvement. The examples provided in the chapter show an implementation of the framework that supports video annotation, tracking improvement, and situation identification.

There are still several open problems in this domain. Particularly, our proposals are still in the prototype stage, and further developments to prove their scalability in larger setups are necessary. One evident drawback of the presented examples is that they require a considerable manual work to include the background and common-sense knowledge that is necessary for situation recognition. Part of this knowledge can be automatically learned (e.g., it is possible to delimit a door in the field of view of a camera from basic track creation information), but in general terms, this problem gives rise to the epistemological question of which amount of human-generated knowledge is necessary to implement a system that can show cognitive capabilities. There is hardly a definitive answer for this question, but still, we have shown how to formally represent and reason this knowledge, either larger or smaller, and its unquestionable relevance in the situation recognition process.

Acknowledgments This work was supported in part by projects MINECO TEC2014-57022-C2-2-R, TEC2012-37832-C02-01 and TIN2012-30939.

References

1. C.S. Regazzoni, V. Ramesh, G.L. Foresti, Scanning the issue/technology, special issue on video communications, processing, and understanding for 3rd generation surveillance systems. Proc. IEEE, **89**(10), 1355–1367 (2001)
2. M. Valera, S.A. Velastin, Intelligent distributed surveillance systems: a review. IEEE Proc. Vis. Image Sig. Proc. **152**(2), 192–204 (2005)
3. A. Luis Bustamante, J.M. Molina, M.A. Patricio, A practical approach for active camera coordination based on a fusion-driven multi-agent system. Int. J. Syst. Sci. **45**(4), 741–755 (2014)
4. K. Henricksen, A framework for context-aware pervasive computing applications, Ph.D. Thesis, University of Queensland, 2003

5. M. Kokar, M. Matheus, K. Baclawski, Ontology-based situation awareness. Inf. Fusion **10**(1), 83–98 (2009)
6. N.A. Bradley, M.D. Dunlop, Towards a multidisciplinary model of context to support context-aware computing. Hum. Comput. Inter. **20**, 403–446 (2005)
7. J. McCarthy, Notes on formalizing context, in *Proceedings of the 3rd International Joint Conference on Artificial Intelligence (IJCAI'93)* (Chambéry, France, 1993), pp. 555–562
8. T. Stang, C. Linnhoff-Popien, A context modeling survey, in *1st International Workshop on Advanced Context Modeling, Reasoning and Management*, Nottingham, UK, 2004
9. M. Kandefer, S.C. Shapiro, A categorization of contextual constraints, in *Biologically Inspired Cognitive Architectures—Papers from the AAAI Fall Symposium* (Menlo Park, USA, 2008), pp. 88–93
10. J. Gómez-Romero, J. García, J. Kandefer, J. Llinas, J.M. Molina, M.A. Patricio, M. Prentice, S.C. Shapiro, Strategies and techniques for use and exploitation of contextual information in high-level fusion architectures, in *Proceedings of the 13th Conference on Information Fusion (Fusion 2010)*, Edinburgh, UK, 2010
11. L. Snidaro, J. García, J. Llinas, Context-based information fusion: a survey and discussion. Inf. Fusion **25**, 16–31 (2015)
12. J. Gómez-Romero, J. García, M.A. Patricio, J.M. Molina, J. Llinas, High-level information fusion in visual sensor networks, in *Visual Information Processing in Wireless Sensor Networks: Technology, Trends and Applications*, eds. by L.-M. Ang, K.P. Seng (IGI Global, 2012), pp. 197–223
13. A.N. Steinberg, G. Rogova, Situation and context in data fusion and natural language understanding, in *Proceedings of the 11th Conference on Information Fusion (Fusion 2008)*, Cologne, Germany, 2008
14. C.J. Matheus, M. Kokar, K. Baclawski, J. Letkowski, C. Call, M. Hinman, J. Salerno, D. Boulware, SAWA: an assistant for higher-level fusion and situation awareness, in *Proceedings of the SPIE Conference on Multisensor, Multisource Information Fusion* (Orlando, USA, 2005), pp. 75–85
15. B. Neumann, R. Möller, On scene interpretation with Description Logics. Imagine Vis. Comput. **26**, 82–101 (2008)
16. R.N. Carvalho, K.B. Laskey, P.C.G. Costa, PR-OWL 2.0—Bridging the gap to OWL semantics, in *Uncertainty Reasoning for the Semantic Web II*, ed. by F. Bobillo (Springer, Berlin, 2013), pp. 1–18
17. L. Snidaro, I. Visentini, K. Bryan, Fusing uncertain knowledge and evidence for maritime situational awareness via Markov logic networks. Inf. Fusion **21**, 159–172 (2015)
18. J. Gómez-Romero, M.A. Serrano, J. García, J.M. Molina, G. Rogova, Context-based multi-level information fusion for harbor surveillance. Inf. Fusion **21**, 173–186 (2015)
19. A.N. Steinberg, C.L. Bowman, Revisions to the JDL data fusion model, in *Handbook of Multisensor Data Fusion*, eds. by J. Llinas, M. Liggins, D. Hall (CRC Press, 2009), pp. 45–68
20. C.Y. Chong, S. Mori, K.C. Chang, Distributed multitarget multisensor tracking, in *Multitarget-Multisensor Tracking: Advanced Applications*, ed. by Y. Bar-Shalom, Vol. 1 (Artech House, 1990), pp. 247–295
21. K. Chang, C.Y. Chong, Y. Bar-Shalom, Joint probabilistic data association in distributed sensor networks. IEEE Trans. Autom. Control **31**(10), 889–897 (1986)
22. R. Olfati-Saber, Distributed Kalman filtering for sensor networks, in *Proceedings of the 46th Conference in Decision and Control* (New Orleans, USA, 2007), pp. 5492–5498
23. A. Yilmaz, O. Javed, M. Shah, Object tracking: a survey. ACM Comput. Surv. **38**, 1–45 (2006)
24. F. Castanedo, J. Gómez-Romero, M.A. Patricio, J. García, J.M., Molina, Distributed data and information fusion in visual sensor networks, in *Distributed Data Fusion for network-centric operations Hall*, eds. by D. Hall, M. Liggins, C.-Y. Chong, J. Llinas (CRC Press, 2012), pp. 437–467
25. J. García, M.A. Patricio, A. Berlanga, J.M. Molina, Fuzzy region assignment for visual tracking. Soft. Comput. **15**(9), 1845–1864 (2011)

26. I. Dotú, M.A. Patricio, A. Berlanga, J. García, J.M. Molina, Discrete optimization algorithms in real-time visual tracking. Appl. Artif. Intell. **23**(9), 805–827 (2009)
27. I. Dotú, M.A. Patricio, A. Berlanga, J. García, J.M. Molina, Boosting video tracking performance by means of Tabu search in intelligent visual surveillance systems. J. Heuristics **17**(4), 415–440 (2011)
28. A. Pinz, H. Bischof, W. Kropatsch, G. Schweighofer, Y. Haxhimusa, A. Opelt, A. Ion, Representations for cognitive vision. ELCVIA Electron. Lett. Comput. Vis. Image Anal. **7**(2), 35–61 (2008)
29. I. Horrocks, P. Patel-Schneider, Reducing OWL entailment to description logic satisfiability. Web Seman. Sci. Serv. Agents World Wide Web **1**(4), 345–357 (2004)
30. B. Motik, U. Sattler, R. Studer, Query answering for OWL-DL with rules. Web Seman. Sci. Serv. Agents World Wide Web **3**(1), 41–60 (2005)
31. C. Elsenbroich, O. Kutz, U. Sattler, A case for abductive reasoning over ontologies, in *Proceedings of the OWL Workshop: Experiences and Directions (OWLED '06)*, Athens, USA, 2006
32. V. Haarslev, K. Hidde, R. Möller, M. Wessel, The RacerPro knowledge representation and reasoning system. Semant. Web J. **3**(3), 267–277 (2011)
33. J. Gómez-Romero, M.A. Patricio, J. García, J.M. Molina, Communication in distributed tracking systems: an ontology-based approach to improve cooperation. Expert Syst. **28**(4), 288–305 (2011)
34. M.A. Serrano, J. Gómez-Romero, M.A. Patricio, J. García, J.M. Molina, Applying the dynamic region connection calculus to exploit geographical knowledge in maritime surveillance, in *Proceedings of the 15th International Conference on Information Fusion (Fusion 2012)*, Singapore, 2012
35. D. Doermann, D. Mihalcik, Tools and techniques for video performance evaluation, in *Proceedings of the 15th International Conference on Pattern Recognition (ICPR '00)*, Barcelona, Spain, 2000
36. M.A. Serrano, J. Gómez-Romero, M.A. Patricio, J. García, J.M. Molina, Topological properties in ontology-based applications, in *11th International Conference on Intelligent Systems Design and Applications (ISDA 2011)* (Córdoba, Spain, 2011), pp. 1329–1334
37. J. Gómez-Romero, M.A. Serrano, M.A. Patricio, J. García, J.M. Molina, Context-based scene recognition from visual data in smart homes: an information fusion approach. Pers. Ubiquit. Comput. **16**(7), 835–857 (2012)
38. J. Gómez-Romero, M.A. Patricio, J. García, J.M. Molina, Ontology-based context representation and reasoning for object tracking and scene interpretation in video. Expert Syst. Appl. **38**, 7494–7510 (2011)
39. M.A. Serrano, J. Gómez-Romero, M.A. Patricio, J. García, J.M. Molina, Ontological representation of light wave camera data to support vision-based AmI. Sensors **12**, 12126–12152 (2012)

Chapter 24
Data Fusion Enhanced with Context Information for Road Safety Application

Fernando García, Aurelio Ponz, David Martín, Arturo de la Escalera
and José María Armingol

Abstract Traffic accidents are an important socio-economic problem. Every year, their cost to human lives and the economic consequences are inestimable. Efforts to reduce or mitigate this problem have led to a reduction of the death toll in the past years. However, this number is still significant, thus further actions are necessary. Recent advances in computational and information technologies have led to sophisticated applications, which have the ability to warn the driver, or even to take control of the vehicle in case of danger, providing a safer and more efficient driving experience. These advanced and complex systems demand trustable and accurate sensing technologies that are able to provide environment perception and identify all the agents on it. The available sensing technologies are insufficient to provide this accurate environment perception, thus the combination of different technologies available is mandatory in order to fulfill the demanding requirements of these applications. Furthermore, within this scope, contextual information (CI) has a key role to provide complete situation assessment. This chapter describes a road safety application for pedestrian detection, using both laser scanner and optical sensor technologies. CI is used to enhance these detections and provide situation assessment. Both online and offline information are used. Online information is used to obtain the status of the vehicle and its localization. Offline information allows to understand the interaction with the detected targets, i.e., danger involving the interaction with the different users of the roads can be estimated, thanks to the

F. García (✉) · A. Ponz · D. Martín · A. de la Escalera · J.M. Armingol
Intelligent Systems Lab, Universidad Carlos III de Madrid, Leganés, Spain
e-mail: fegarcia@ing.uc3m.es

A. Ponz
e-mail: apv@ing.uc3m.es

D. Martín
e-mail: dmgomez@ing.uc3m.es

A. de la Escalera
e-mail: escalera@ing.uc3m.es

J.M. Armingol
e-mail: armingol@ing.uc3m.es

© Springer International Publishing Switzerland (outside the USA) 2016
L. Snidaro et al. (eds.), *Context-Enhanced Information Fusion*,
Advances in Computer Vision and Pattern Recognition,
DOI 10.1007/978-3-319-28971-7_24

information regarding traffic safety, physical behavior, road localization, etc. Furthermore, CI is also used to enhance the detections, thanks to information such as anthropometric data, pedestrian movement information, etc. The proposed method provides multilevel solution for road safety application, and is able to provide trustable detection, situation assessment, and threat detection.

Keywords Intelligent transport systems · Advanced driver assistance systems · Computer vision · Road safety

24.1 Introduction

Traffic accidents are usually related to human errors, mostly caused by wrong decision making or inattention. Although these errors are associated with the human nature of the drivers and can hardly be eliminated, efforts can lead to decrease them. Recent advances in information technologies (IT) have lead to more advanced and reliable sensing and computing technologies to create new applications that help the driver prevent and avoid dangerous situations in the process of driving. These applications are called Advanced Driver Assistance Systems (ADAS).

Among ADAS applications, sensor reliability is an important matter. To accomplish these strong requirements, the combination of different sensors is mandatory in order to overcome the limitations of each sensor. This way, by the use of advanced fusion technologies, reliable detection is provided, fulfilling road safety and reliability demands.

Contextual information (CI) [1] is a novel topic in data fusion that allows, by the use of specific and expert information, to enhance the classical detection algorithms and improve performance of the fusion process by means of this new information source.

In this chapter, a novel approach for pedestrian detection, based on data fusion, is presented. Both optical sensors and laser scanner are used, providing low level detection. Later, a trustable tracking algorithm is used to track the detected obstacles. This tracking process is based on joint probabilistic data association (JPDA) approach, specifically adapted for automotive environments, based on the laser scanner and optical sensors detection. The application uses CI, including both static knowledge and online information for detection enhancement. By combining advanced detection systems, powerful tracking algorithms, and CI, trustable obstacle detection and tracking are obtained. Four information sources were used in this approach:

- **Laser scanner**. Laser scanner is a well-known sensor in robotic and automotive research fields. Contestants at DARPA Grand and Urban Challenges [2–5] have used laser scanners extensively, proving their suitability for these applications. Although the technology is expensive, recent advances in road safety and autonomous driving have led to sophisticated and advanced applications that add value and are worth including in commercial applications.

- **Optical sensors**. The optical sensors approaches (based on computer vision techniques) are very common in modern road safety applications. Its main limitation is the reliability of its detections, but on the other hand, it provides large amount of data that can be used for obstacle identification. The combination of reliability of the laser scanner and information provided by the optical sensor can lead to robust and trustable applications, as it is proved in the present work.
- **Inertial sensor**. By combining precise inertial correction with advanced GPS technology, inertial sensors can provide information about the movement of the vehicle that can be used in the reconstruction problem. The fusion stage of the process will use this vehicle state information as online contextual knowledge.
- **Contextual information**. Context is a powerful information source that is included in the fusion process in all levels. At low level, statistical information regarding pedestrians' movement and sizes is used. At higher level, CI is used to identify those detections that represent a real threat to road security, i.e., those that may interfere with the vehicle according to the trajectory, velocity, etc.

24.2 Data Fusion in Intelligent Transport Systems

Data fusion works in intelligent vehicles (IV) and intelligent transport systems (ITS), a more general scientific branch that includes all advances in the field of transport related with IT technologies, can be categorized according to the processing architecture.

In **feature fusion** the data are preprocessed independently for each sensor, or combined together in a single data set; the final decision is performed in a single node. In [6] different visual feature extraction methods are used and combined in different ways such as Support Vector Machine (SVM), Naïve Bayesian and Minimum Distance Classifier. In [7, 8] different approaches are presented for feature level fusion, and the final classification is compared in several methods, e.g.: Naïve Bayes, Gaussian Mixture Models, and Neural Networks. **High level fusion** approaches provide detection and identification for each node or sensor, then final classification is made according to the detections' certainty and sensors' reliability. [9] uses region of interest (ROI) detection based on laser scanner, applying later computer vision through optical sensors and CI from digital map Bayesian approach based high level fusion. In [10] Adaboost is used for pedestrian detection based on optical sensors; Gaussian Mixture Model (GMM) is used for laser scanner detection. A Bayesian decisor is finally used to provide high-level detection.

Typically data fusion works in IV and ITS use scanner laser to provide reliable ROI detection and optical sensors to classify among different obstacles in the road. In [11] invariant features, and in [12] histogram of oriented gradients

(HOG) features are used to provide vision detection after laser scanner ROI identification. Although the use of laser scanner helps to improve the computational
costs (optical sensor based approaches can focus in certain regions), and reduce the
false true positives thanks to the reliability of the laser scanner, the information
provided by the fusion is restricted to region of interest identification.

On the other hand, some other works use specific features of the sensors, to
enhance the detection particular applications for automotive environments. [13]
provides detection based on capacitive sensors and optical sensors. Laser scanner is
used in [14] to detect specific regions where pedestrians can be located, later
identification is based on optical sensors. In [15] radar and optical sensors are used
to identify the obstacles in the road, similar to the work in [16], where the raw data
from the radar is used, combined with optical flow for overtaking detection.

Vehicle positioning is another classical data fusion application in the road
environment. By the combination of several positioning techniques, e.g., odometry,
inertial measurements and GPS, limitations of each technology such as GPS sig-
naling problems or odometry cumulative errors, can be overcome by the fusion of
all these sensors, as presented in [17, 18].

Finally, the use of CI can enhance road safety applications. It can be helpful in
the inference process by verifying consistence according to the predefined model,
helping to identify if the provided detections are consistent with the context. Several
of the aforementioned approaches take advantage of this information, such as [9],
which uses digital maps to enhance pedestrian detection, or [18] for vehicle positioning and tracking.

Works commented are different solutions developed for specific sensor inputs
with no information retrieved from the contextual knowledge. In the present work, a
multilevel solution for road safety application is presented. The solution takes
advantage of the CI, both in the inference process and to identify those pedestrians
that represent a potential risk for road safety.

24.3 General Description

The present work provides enhanced pedestrian detection by means of a fusion
procedure with CI. The in-vehicle available sensors are laser scanner, optical
camera, and a GPS with inertial measurements. All these sensors are mounted in the
IVVI 2.0 platform, a test vehicle used to research, test, and develop novel ADAS
applications (Fig. 24.1).

The fusion process presented is mainly based on JPDA approach and the use of
CI for detection enhancement. The different information provided is both online
(e.g., pedestrian detection, vehicle positioning, and velocity) and offline (such as
digital maps and safety regulation).

The application is able to reduce the driver's work load by identifying safety
threats (i.e., pedestrians that interact with the vehicle) according to three factors:
danger estimation as a function of the distance to the vehicle and its velocity, the

location of the pedestrian according to digital maps, and the time to collision. In the present work, a multilevel solution is proposed (Fig. 24.2), giving answer to the fusion process based on the JDL model [19].

- Level 0. At this level, alignment is necessary to synchronize the different sensors. This alignment is mandatory to locate detections in both sensor spaces.
- Level 1. At this level, low-level detections provided by the laser scanner and optical sensors approaches are obtained. Here, CI is used to identify anthropometric and movement information that helps to reduce the amount of false true positives. Besides, CI is used to adapt the estimation filter and the association technique to this specific road safety application.

Fig. 24.1 IVVI 2.0 platform for ADAS test used in the work. External view (*left*) and internal view (*right*)

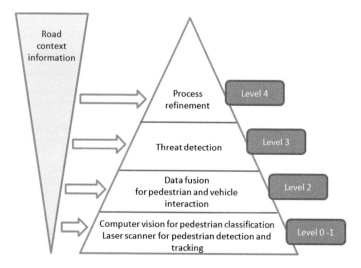

Fig. 24.2 General diagram with the process involved in each level and the relevance of the context information used in each level

- Level 2. Here, interactions of pedestrians–vehicle are studied in order to identify the potential risks at higher level.
- Level 3. At this level, threat detection is performed, identifying those pedestrians that present a potential risk of collision. Here, CI plays an important role in providing both offline and online information. First, it gives information regarding traffic safety regulation, relevant distances, distance maps, etc.; second it refers to all online information provided by the test platform such as vehicle velocity, pedestrian location, time to collision, etc.
- Level 4. Process refinement is also addressed in the work by adapting the system in the tracking process according to the risk information provided in level 3. Thus, the tracking of the system is adapted to the risks (e.g., a high threat is tracked along time with higher priority, avoiding misdetections).

As it is detailed in the aforementioned points, CI is relevant at all levels. However, it is in the highest levels where it acquires an important role. In the lowest levels it is used to enhance sensor detection. This way, this chapter focuses on higher level algorithms, while the low-level detection systems provided by the camera and laser scanner which are presented in [20] are briefly summarized in the following lines.

24.3.1 Laser Scanner Pedestrian Detection

The IVVI 2.0 platform mounts a single-layer SICK laser scanner attached to the front bumper of the vehicle (Fig. 24.3), with an angular resolution of 0.25°, maximal detection distance of 82 m and 100° of field of view and, in our configuration, 401 points per scan.

Fig. 24.3 IVVI 2.0 platform with the sensors mounted in the vehicle

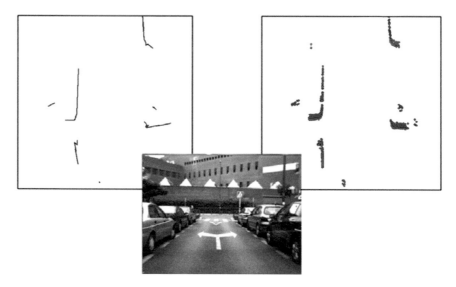

Fig. 24.4 Points detection (*right*) with *blue dots* for original detection and *red* for movement compensated points. Polyline detection (*left*) and polyline projected to the real world

To achieve pedestrian detection, an initial stage of obstacle segmentation is performed, followed by shape estimation (Fig. 24.4), while obstacle classification is completed at a later stage using the previously estimated shape.

After complete reconstruction of the real shape, classification of individual pedestrians is performed in two separate steps. First, narrowing the study to just those obstacles whose size is proportional to a pedestrian. Next, the shapes of the remaining obstacles are compared to the typical shapes of a pedestrian in a way that will be shown next.

There are several models for human body which can be used for the first stage in pedestrian detection. In this application, the [21, 22] models will be used. They model the dressed human body as an ellipse of (0.6 × 0.5) m. Figure 24.5 shows two detection examples of individual pedestrians.

24.3.2   Optical Sensors Based Obstacle Detection and Classification

Classification based on optical sensors is very costly in terms of computing, so the best approach is applying it just in the region of interest (ROI) of the image where the pedestrian is supposed to be, based on laser detections. Later, pedestrian detection in the image is achieved using the HOG descriptor and SVM classification. It is important to remark that in order to use two sensors together, data alignment must be performed to be able to determine the position in a sensor of the obstacle detected in

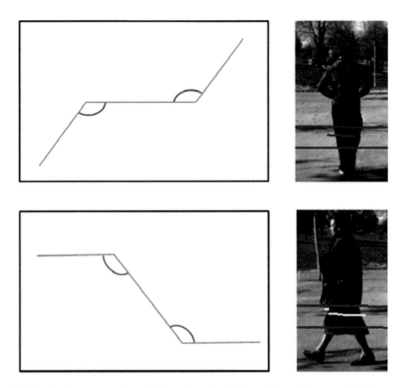

Fig. 24.5 Pedestrian pattern for walking pedestrian, (*left*) and the real image with the example (*right*)

Fig. 24.6 ROI identification with distances highlighted (*left*). Final detections, *red boxes* for optical sensors detection and blue or laser scanner

the other sensor. This alignment is achieved using the rotation and translation matrixes and the pin-hole model for the camera. Thus, ROI detections in the laser scanner coordinates are translated into camera image coordinates (Fig. 24.6).

Fig. 24.7 Example of HOG features calculation (*left*) for a detection (*right*)

After the ROIs are extracted, a HOG features based algorithm is executed as presented in [23] for pedestrian detection (Fig. 24.7).

The descriptors obtained are later trained with a database, obtaining the weights for the different members of the descriptors that identify a pedestrian. This last part is completed using an SVM classifier.

24.4 Fusion System

This section will describe the fusion algorithms at level 1. An exhaustive explanation of pedestrian movement tracking and the estimation filter used is included. Plot to track configuration is explained, detailing both track creation and deletion policy, including gating procedures and data association. This pedestrian tracking algorithm was first presented in [20], where further CI is included in order to provide better situation assessment; besides, further test provides full understanding of the improvement added to the system.

24.4.1 Estimation Filter

The unscented Kalman Filter was used to estimate the movement of the detected pedestrians. A constant velocity system was chosen, and the acceleration has been modeled as process noise, modeling the changes in velocity. In Eq. (24.1) Q represents system error and (R) the measurement error in (24.2).

$$Q = \begin{bmatrix} \frac{a_x^2 t^3}{3} & \frac{a_x^2 t^2}{2} & 0 & 0 \\ \frac{a_x^2 t^2}{2} & a_x^2 & 0 & 0 \\ 0 & 0 & \frac{a_y^2 t^3}{3} & \frac{a_y^2 t^2}{2} \\ 0 & 0 & \frac{a_y^2 t^2}{2} & a_y^2 \end{bmatrix} \tag{24.1}$$

$$R = \begin{pmatrix} \sigma_{\in,x}^2 & 0 \\ 0 & \sigma_{\in,y}^2 \end{pmatrix} \tag{24.2}$$

with $\sigma_{\in,x}^2$ and $\sigma_{\in,y}^2$ as the standard deviation for the measurements for the specific sensors in x, y coordinates. As the ROI coordinates come from the laser scanner, these values are the same, and are provided by the laser scanner. The values a_x and a_y in Eq. (24.2) are the maximum amplitude of acceleration in each axis defined as 11 m/s^2 each.

Equations 24.3–24.6 are also used to define the movement, where X is the state vector, x, y represent the pedestrians location coordinates (in meters), with the vehicle as reference. v_x and v_y represent the velocity of the pedestrians in m/s. Y is the measurements vector, the observation matrix is represented in H and F is the state transition matrix.

$$X = \begin{bmatrix} x \\ y \\ v_x \\ v_y \end{bmatrix} \tag{24.3}$$

$$Y = \begin{bmatrix} x \\ y \end{bmatrix} \tag{24.4}$$

$$H = \begin{bmatrix} 1 & 0 & 0 & 0 \\ 0 & 1 & 0 & 0 \end{bmatrix} \tag{24.5}$$

$$F = \begin{bmatrix} 1 & 0 & t & 0 \\ 0 & 1 & 0 & t \\ 0 & 0 & 1 & 0 \\ 0 & 0 & 0 & 1 \end{bmatrix} \tag{24.6}$$

24.4.2 JPDA for Data Association

First, non-likely pairs are discarded by means of a squared-gate approach (24.7), with σ_r is the residual standard deviation and K_{Gl} a constant:

$$K_{Gl}\sigma_r \tag{24.7}$$

After gating, the association process is based on an adaptation of the JPDA for this specific application.

JPDA is a probabilistic association technique [24 25] which provides higher performance in complex and difficult association situations where the classic approach, based on Global Nearest Neighbors, suffers severe difficulties.

In (24.8) is defined the joint association probability. It represents the probability of a joint association event θ_{kj}^m that associated measurement m to track j at a time k. The association likelihood $g_{i,j}$ is a 2 dimensional Gaussian, as detailed in (24.9).

$$P(\theta|Z_k) = P_D^{M-n}(1-P_D)^n P_{\mathrm{FA}}^{m_k-(1-M)} \prod_{j=1}^{m_k} g_{i,j} \tag{24.8}$$

$$g_{i,j} = \frac{1}{(2\pi)^{N/2}\sqrt{|S_{ij}|}} e^{-\frac{d_{i,j}^2}{2}} \tag{24.9}$$

where $d_{i,j}$ is the distance between the prediction and the observation (Euclidean distance), the residual covariance is represented as $S_{i,j}$, and it is defined as $\sqrt{|S_{ij}|} = \sigma_x \sigma_y$ with $N = 2$.

All the association hypotheses for a specific target are weighted in the estimation filter. Therefore, all possible combinations, weighted with association likelihood, are used to calculate the innovation, as depicted in Eq. (24.10).

$$I_k = \sum_{i=1}^{m} \left[P(\theta|Z_k)\left(Z_{i,k} - H_k \hat{X}_{k|k-1}\right) \right] \tag{24.10}$$

where I_k is the innovation for the KF of a given track.

To reduce the computational costs and allow reliable association, associated track-new detection pairs are removed from the assignation process after they are assigned, and in further assignments the joined probabilities are recalculated taking into account only the remaining detections and tracks. This step helps to avoid unstable behaviors. When several tracks are pointing to a single observation, the clutter is first assigned to the less probable detection, eliminating the weight of this detection in further assignments, and allowing a proper and reliable assignation.

The JPDA solution for road safety application presented allows to improve the performance in certain specific situations, such as clustering errors, double detection (a single pedestrian is detected twice in a frame) and occlusions.

24.4.3   Track Management

Track creation and deletion policy is based on consolidated and not consolidated tracks. The former refers to those tracks detected by both sensors. The latter refers to those pedestrians detected by a single sensor. According to the sensor fields of view, two detection zones are defined. First, (laser scanner zone) where only the laser scanner is available, and second (fusion zone) where both, laser scanner and camera can provide detections. Depending on where the pedestrian is located, different measures may be applied (number of true positive detections before creation or misdetections before deletion), so zone switching has to be managed:

– If a track goes from laser zone to data fusion, it is labeled as not consolidated. It assures that any consolidated detection has to be corroborated by the optical sensors.
– When a track changes from fusion to laser scanner zone, its status is maintained, whether it is consolidated or not.

Only consolidated tracks are reported to higher levels and considered reliable enough to be reported. Not consolidated tracks are maintained to check their evolution over time, they are tracked but not reported to higher levels until they are considered consolidated. Furthermore, the algorithm can track the pedestrians even when it is unreachable from any of the sensors.

24.5   Environment CI for Pedestrian Detection with Danger Estimation

The present section discusses a CI methodology to be included in sensor fusion architecture by means of devices that provide environment data. The collection of CI from in-vehicle devices allows to be used in the data fusion processes to obtain a safe vehicle response. This CI focuses on pedestrian detection and later classification according to danger estimation levels. So, this section depicts pedestrian–vehicle behavior based on the use of in-vehicle sensors to extract reliable CI. CI, such as safety regulation, velocity, and GPS data, enriches the fusion process of sensor fusion architecture, from low to high levels, by the use of a priori knowledge of the domain. Moreover, the use of CI in the fusion levels improves the perception of the road environment and the relations among detections. The CI provides a complete situation assessment which involves any pedestrian detection, with danger estimation.

CI is becoming one of the main subjects for advance driver assistant systems (ADAS) to overcome the limitations of the available sensors and fulfill their requirements. The recent advances in optical sensors, laser scanner, GPS positioning or road map allow to extract and refine CI to be used in ADAS, which helps to detect and warn the driver in advance in case of hazardous situations. So, one of the main topics in ADAS research is the reliable detection of pedestrians, where main work focuses on the signal processing level and does not pay attention to CI from pedestrian detections. The context analysis of real driving situations is important for dealing with complex vehicle environment problems, e.g.: pedestrians merging into groups.

The pedestrian situation and threat assessment are explained, using CI, to enhance the safety of the system in order to detect the pedestrians around the vehicle and estimate their associate levels of danger. The danger estimation in each pedestrian detection is based on two distances: braking distance and response distance. The response distance is the distance covered by the vehicle until it is completely stopped, thus any pedestrian detected farther than this value can be avoided by a braking maneuver. The braking distance is the distance covered in the elapsed time form the trigger of any signal until the driver reacts. These distances are useful CI used for danger estimation; however, further information is necessary to estimate this danger: such as response time and some collision equations that are explained in the following section.

An algorithm for pedestrian danger estimation based on detection zones was first presented in [25]. Based on this research, it has been extended based on time to collision and distance to the road, enhancing the danger estimation by means of CI, as detailed next.

24.5.1 Danger Estimation Based on Detection Zones

Detection zones are available according to the sensor ranges. So, the first zone uses only the laser scanner, and the second one is the fusion zone with both subsystems (laser + camera). Danger estimation takes into account the driving response time as well as the braking time. So according to this, three detection zones have been created; first, a green safe zone in which pedestrian detections are safe, because the speed of the vehicle and the distance to the target are appropriate enough to stop the vehicle avoiding the collision. A second zone is integrated within the limits of the braking distance and the response distance, which is the distance according to the actual speed of the car, where the driver can perform a maneuver to avoid pedestrian collision, so it is called the danger zone. Finally, the closest zone is the danger zone where pedestrian collision is imminent. So, in this zone, collision is not possible to be avoided and only a pre-collision system can try to mitigate pedestrian damage. The detection zones are shown in Fig. 24.8.

Vehicle braking distance, as well as response distance allow to estimate the distances where the vehicle can be stopped or the pedestrian can be avoidable. Response distance is the distance that the vehicle covers meanwhile the driver responses to a stimulus, it can be either audio or visual stimulus. It is generally accepted a response of 0.66 s, as proved Johansson and Rumar [26]. To corroborate this measurement we have performed a statistical test that confirms it, so the response time for drivers is 0.66 s. Other authors have proved this approach [27].

Fig. 24.8 Detection zones
with the relevant pedestrian
distances

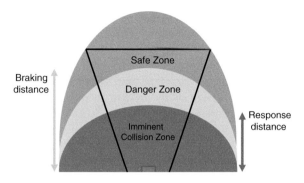

Braking distance is the distance that vehicle takes to stop completely. The distance that vehicles need to brake depends on each vehicle and different external conditions, such as weather, road condition, tires, brake efficiency, among others. The approach that has been used in the presented work is based on the mathematics of basic accident reconstructions [28]. So, the worst-case scenario is a loaded vehicle under normal weather conditions; however, weather conditions can vary by changing the road coefficient like asphalt, concrete, snow, etc. According to traffic accident reconstruction theory, the worst scenario is when only one of the vehicle axes has been blocked, and the forces associated with the weight of the car are displaced to the front. So, different coefficients are applied depending on the distance of the axis to the center of mass. The correction applied to the coefficient is denoted by (24.11).

$$\eta = \frac{b_2}{L - h\mu} \tag{24.11}$$

where b_2 is the mass distance to the rear axis, L is the longitude of the car, h the height of the mass center, μ is the friction coefficient. To calculate the mass center several approaches are possible and some authors give mass center height approximation of 0.4. So, d is the braking distance which is velocity dependant in this way:

$$d = \frac{v^2}{\eta\mu g} \tag{24.12}$$

Finally, the response has to be taken into account; in order to include the time elapsed until the driver presses the braking pedal:

$$d_{\text{braking}} = vt_{\text{response}} + \frac{v^2}{\eta\mu g} \tag{24.13}$$

24.5.2 Pedestrian Detection with Danger Estimation

This subsection presents three aspects that have been taken into account for estimating the threat of a given pedestrian track: danger estimation, distance to the road, and time to collision. The application was developed taking into account the danger zones (Table 24.1). The first zone represents the part of the environment according to the velocity of the vehicle, where it can be stopped before entering this area. The second zone is the area of the road where the driver can perform avoidance maneuvres. The last one is the area of the road where there is no option to avoid the collision.

The actions to perform in each of the zones are out of the scope of this work. So, a first approximation to a real application should be to trigger a visual image, as for example a bounding box, to highlight the pedestrian in the first one. In the danger zone, sound and visual alarm should be necessary to avoid the possible collision. Finally when a pedestrian is detected within imminent collision zone, measures to reduce injuries should be taken.

Besides detection zones, it should be provided a degree of the danger which involves the detections. This way, upper layer applications are provided with a value that gives an estimation of the danger regarding the detected pedestrians. Here, several factors were taken into account. The value provided goes from 0 (no danger) to 1 (high danger). To summarize, Table 24.2 shows the correspondence:

An exponential approximation was selected:

$$f(r) = \begin{cases} e^{-\lambda(r-d_r)}, & \text{for Max\_laser\_range} \leq r \leq d_r \\ 1, & \text{for } d_r < r \leq 0 \end{cases} \tag{24.14}$$

where r is the distance to the detected pedestrian, d_r is the reaction distance and Max_laser_range is the maximum distance provided by the laser scanner. The value of λ is selected to assure a value of 0.6 when the pedestrian is in the braking distance:

$$e^{-\lambda(d_b-d_r)} = 0.6; \quad \lambda = \frac{-\ln 0.6}{(d_b - d_r)} \tag{24.15}$$

where d_b is the braking distance, and r the response distance.

Table 24.1 Correspondence between distances and detections zones

	Starts	Ends
Safe zone	∞	$d_{braking}$
Danger zone	$d_{braking}$	$d_{response}$
Imminent collision zone	$d_{response}$	0 m

Table 24.2 Correspondence between detection zones and danger estimation

	From	To
Safe zone	0	0.6
Danger zone	0.6	1
Imminent collision Zone	1	1

The distance to the road is the second aspect. So, using digital maps and GPS, the distance of a given detection to the road where the vehicle is moving can be calculated. The use of this distance allows to estimate the danger that involves a given track, based on an accurate location of the pedestrian. For this reason, the accurate pedestrian position is obtained from the laser scanner and the vehicle location by GPS with inertial measurement unit available in the IVVI 2.0 Intelligent Vehicle [18].

The estimation est(d) of the danger is modeled in a Gaussian manner, using width of the road as standard deviation:

$$\text{est}(d) = e^{-\frac{d^2}{2\sigma^2}} \tag{24.16}$$

where d is the distance to the center of the road and σ is width/2 of the road. By this estimation, pedestrians inside the road have danger estimation bigger than 0.6.

Collision estimation is the last parameter to take into account, that is, the pedestrian collision time that is calculated by means of the velocities of both the vehicle and the pedestrian. According to [29], the collision solution can be obtained as follows: The estimation of the state of the targets, defined by its position (x, y), and velocity vectors (v_x, v_y) is obtained by the estimation filter. On the other hand, information from the GPS with inertial system allows estimation of the same kinematic information related to the vehicle. Thus, the diagram shown in Fig. 24.9 can be used to calculate the collision using (24.17)–(24.18) based on the afore-mentioned information.

$$x_c = \frac{(y_2 - y_1) - (x_2 \tan\theta_2 - x_1 \tan\theta_1)}{(\tan\theta_1 - \tan\theta_2)} \tag{24.17}$$

$$y_c = \frac{(x_2 - x_1) - (y_2 \cot\theta_2 - y_1 \cot\theta_1)}{(\cot\theta_1 - \cot\theta_2)} \tag{24.18}$$

where x_c and y_c are the coordinates of the collision point.

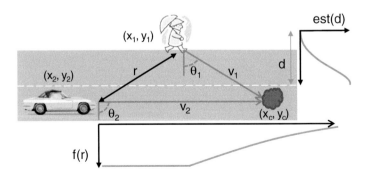

Fig. 24.9 Representation of the trajectories, with the estimation of the danger for road proximity (est(d)) and the danger estimation according to the vehicle velocity ($f(r)$)

Once the collision point has been calculated, the next step is to calculate the time of each of the obstacles to this point according to their respective velocity. If the time coincides, this is considered the time to the collision. But, in order to provide a safety margin, a δ parameter that defines the security margin is established, as depicted in Eq. (24.19). So, the higher the δ parameter, the more conservative is the approach:

$$\text{ttc\_d} = |\text{TX1} - \text{TX2}| < \delta \qquad (24.19)$$

A Gaussian estimation method has been used to determine the danger that involves a given detection, called collision estimation (ce), according to the time distance (ttc_d) and using the security margin δ as the standard deviation:

$$\text{ce}(d) = \begin{cases} e^{-\frac{\text{ttc\_d}^2}{2\delta^2}}, & \text{for collision trajectories} \\ 0.4, & \text{for nocollision trajectories} \end{cases} \qquad (24.20)$$

Moreover, no-collision trajectories are also taken into account with ce = 0.4. This allows the detection of possible danger pedestrians that are not colliding with the vehicle, e.g.: a pedestrian walking parallel to the vehicle within the road.

Finally, the threat priority is provided by means of a decision-making approach, based on the three aspects presented (estimation based on distance, time to collision, and distance to the road). That is, the use of an expert module that includes knowledge, data, and decision-making can be conducted. Thus, the three values are easily combined for estimating the priority classification of a given pedestrian track as low, medium, or high threat. The decision-making allows a safe solution to determine if a given detection represents a threat to the vehicle or not, highlighting the individual knowledge of each danger estimation studied in this work.

24.6 Test and Comparison

24.6.1 Tests Performed

In this section we detail the different tests performed on the algorithms presented. Some of the tests were provided in [20]; here further information of the comparison of the two tests is added, adding relevant information for further discussion.

First a set of tests in controlled scenarios were performed, to allow the set up for the different subsystems and to test the real performance of the whole system. Later, real road scenarios were used to test both low- and high-level algorithms; at this part the tests were divided into urban and interurban scenarios. The first represent more challenging scenarios with more obstacles in the road that may lead to mis-detections and errors. The latter represent scenarios with less obstacles but higher distances and velocities. For the tracking algorithm, first a comparison of the algorithm using KF and UKF is given and finally a comparison of the presented

670   F. García et al.

algorithm (JPDA and UKF) with other well-known approach, based on GNN [30] is provided.

Results of low-level tests (single sensor detection) are depicted in Tables 24.3 and 24.4, and some examples are shown in Fig. 24.10.

Table 24.3 Results for the optical sensors-based detection, with the laser based obstacle segmentation

	Test (%)	Interurban (%)	Urban (%)	Total (%)
True positive rate	78.01	73.19	70.72	73.97
False positive rate	5.19	3.91	6.72	5.27

Table 24.4 Results for the laser scanner pedestrian detection

	Test (%)	Interurban (%)	Urban (%)	Total (%)
True positive rate	79.71	70.35	73.61	74.56
False positive rate	6.23	16.96	16.72	13.3

Fig. 24.10 Detections examples. Laser scanner detections are represented in *blue boxes*. *Red boxes* are for optical sensors detections. Polylines created with laser scanner information are also shown in the images

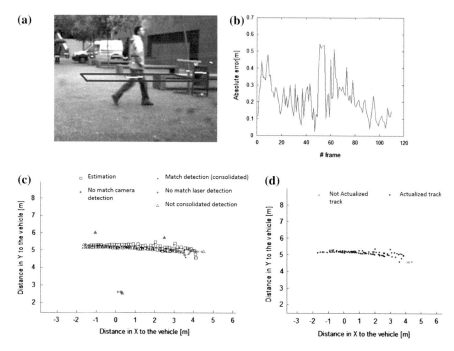

Fig. 24.11 Examples for a test sequence, with a pedestrian performing a lateral movement. **a** Image example of the sequence. **b** Absolute error obtained in the tracking procedure. **c** Low level results displayed for the sensors and the matches with tracking. **d** Tracking detection results

Table 24.5 Results for the KF and UKF tracking comparison for the fusion system

Tacking method	σ [m][1]
KF	0.2058
UKF	0.1591

[1]σ standard deviation in meters. This data was measured with the distance between the predicted values and the laser scanner detections

Test sequences were used to test the performance of the pedestrian tracking algorithm. Movement model and performance was tested, using the UKF predictions and subsequent laser scanner detections as ground truth. Performance is depicted in Fig. 24.11. Table 24.5 depicts the error result of the system, with the comparison between the KF and UKF tracking procedures.

24.6.2   Algorithm Comparison

Table 24.6 provides results for algorithm comparison; the JPDA approach presented was tested in relation to the classical GNN, presented in [30].

Table 24.6 Overall results for all the tests, comparing single sensor performance and the fusion procedures tested, JPDA and GNN

	% True positive rate	% False positive rate
Camera	72.9	5.3
Laser scanner	74.6	13.3
GNN	79.6	2.2
JPDA	82.3	1.1

The advance of the fusion algorithms in relation to single sensor approaches is shown in Table 24.6. Besides, it is proved the JPDA approach represents an improvement to the GNN system. The improvement that JPDA provides in relation to GNN is due to the better performance of the algorithm in specially challenging situations (i.e.: clustering errors, double detections, and occlusions).

24.7 Conclusions

Results obtained in the previous section lead to some conclusions that are here discussed.

The original laser scanner pedestrian detection yields interesting results, given the limited information provided by the laser scanner, although the algorithm lacks reliability due to the 13.3 % of false true positives obtained. On the other hand, performance of the optical sensor system was set up to provide reliable detection in spite of the lower positive rate (i.e., higher detection threshold). This way, the combination of both detections provides interesting and reliable results. It is interesting to mention that the majority of false positive results provided by the camera system are not associated with the HOG features algorithm, but to the nature of the clustering algorithm based on the ROIs identified by the laser system. In certain situations, spurious observations are returned by the laser, thus pedestrians can be included in more than one ROI; if this happens, pedestrians within several bounding boxes are confirmed as pedestrians, thus providing false positive (Fig. 24.12).

This chapter presented a novel multilevel solution for data fusion in road safety applications. The proposed solution takes advantage of the CI to enhance classical pedestrian detection. By means of the fusion of the different information sources, trustable application is able to fulfill the demanding requirements of these applications.

The results provided proved that the JPDA solution presented in this paper, was more reliable than GNN, mainly in difficult situations, such as crossing or misdetections. On the other hand, CI at level 2–4 has been used to provide a novel solution to provide a new CI-based risk identification. The risk identification system allows reducing the stress load of the driver by identifying those detections which represent a real risk to safety.

Fig. 12 Example of camera misdetections due to clustering errors

Thus, based on the aforementioned remarks, the work is a step forward in pedestrian detection for road applications in three fronts: First by using CI to enhance the detections and to provide risk estimation. Second by creating at different levels, that provides solution at all fusion levels. Finally, by adapting powerful association and estimation techniques (i.e., JPDA and UKF) to work with road safety applications.

Acknowledgements This work was supported by the Spanish Government through the CICYT projects (TRA2013-48314-C3-1-R) and DGT project (SPID 2015-01802).

References

1. L. Snidaro, J. García, J. Llinas, Context-based information fusion: a survey and discussion. Inf. Fusion **25**, 16–31 (2015)
2. T. Defense, P. Agency, Foreword for journal of field robotics—special issue on the DARPA grand challenge. J. Field Robot. **23**(9), 657–658 (2006)
3. K. Iagnemma, M. Buehler (eds.), Special issue on the DARPA grand challenge, part 1. J. Field Rob. **23**(8), 461–652 (2006)
4. M. Buehler, K. Iagnemma, S. Singh, S. Thrun, M. Montemerlo, H. Dahlkamp, D. Stavens, A. Aron, J. Diebel, P. Fong, J. Gale, M. Halpenny, G. Hoffmann, K. Lau, C. Oakley, M. Palatucci, V. Pratt, P. Stang, S. Strohband, C. Dupont, L.-E. Jendrossek, C. Koelen, C. Markey, C. Rummel, J. Van Niekerk, E. Jensen, P. Alessandrini, G. Bradski, B. Davies, S. Ettinger, A. Kaehler, A. Nefian, P. Mahoney, DARPA grand challenge 2005. Ind. Robot Int. J., **31**(5), 1–43 (2007)
5. K. Iagnemma, E.M. Buehler, Special issue on the 2007 DARPA urban challenge. J. Field Robot. **25**, 423–860 (2008)
6. J. Zhao, Y. Chen, X. Zhuang, Y. Xu, Posterior probability based multi-classifier fusion in pedestrian detection, in *Genetic and Evolutionary Computing*, eds. by J.-S. Pan, P. Krömer, V. Snášel, SE—35, vol. 238 (Springer International Publishing, Berlin, 2014), pp. 323–329

7. C. Premebida, O. Ludwig, M. Silva, U. Nunes, A cascade classifier applied in pedestrian detection using laser and image-based features, in *IEEE Intelligence Transport System Conference ITSC*, 2010, pp. 1153–1159

8. C. Premebida, O. Ludwig, U. Nunes, LIDAR and vision-based pedestrian detection system. J. Field Robot. **26**(Iv) 696–711 (2009)

9. C. Premebida, U.J.C. Nunes, Fusing LIDAR, camera and semantic information: a context-based approach for pedestrian detection. Int. J. Rob. Res. (2013)

10. L. Spinello, R. Siegwart, Human detection using multimodal and multidimensional features, in *2008 IEEE International Conference on Robotics Automation*, 2008, pp. 3264–3269

11. A. Pérez Grassi, V. Frolov, F. Puente León, Information fusion to detect and classify pedestrians using invariant features. Inf. Fusion **12**(4), 284–292 (2010)

12. O. Ludwig, C. Premebida, U. Nunes, R. Ara, Evaluation of boosting-SVM and SRM-SVM cascade classifiers in laser and vision-based pedestrian detection, in *IEEE Intelligent Transportation Systems Conference ITSC*, 2011, pp. 1574–1579

13. D. Bohmlander, I. Doric, E. Appel, T. Brandmeier, Video camera and capacitive sensor data fusion for pedestrian protection systems, in *2013 Proceedings of the 11th Workshop on Intelligent Solutions in Embedded Systems (WISES)*, 2013, pp. 1–7

14. A. Broggi, P. Cerri, S. Ghidoni, P. Grisleri, H.G. Jung, Localization and analysis of critical areas in urban scenarios, in *IEEE Intelligent Vehicles Symposium*, 2008, pp. 1074–1079

15. M. Bertozzi, L. Bombini, P. Cerri, P. Medici, P.C. Antonello, M. Miglietta, Obstacle detection and classification fusing radar and vision, in *2008 IEEE Intelligence Vehicle Symposium*, 2008

16. F. Garcia, P. Cerri, A. Broggi, A. de la Escalera, J.M. Armingol, Data fusion for overtaking vehicle detection based on radar and optical flow, in *Intelligent Vehicles Symposium (IV), 2012 IEEE*, 2012, pp. 494–499

17. D. Bhatt, P. Aggarwal, V. Devabhaktuni, P. Bhattacharya, A novel hybrid fusion algorithm to bridge the period of GPS outages using low-cost {INS}. Expert Syst. Appl. **41**(5), 2166–2173 (2014)

18. E.D. Martí, D. Martín, J. García, A. de la Escalera, J.M. Molina, J.M. Armingol, Context-aided sensor fusion for enhanced urban navigation. Sensors (Basel) **12**(12), 16802–16837 (2012)

19. D.L. Hall, J. Llinas, An introduction to multisensor data fusion. Proc. IEEE **85**(1), 6–23 (1997)

20. F. García, J. García, A. Ponz, A. de la Escalera, J. M. Armingol, Context aided pedestrian detection for danger estimation based on laser scanner and computer vision, In *Expert Systems with Applications*, vol. 41, Nov 2014, pp. 6646–6661

21. R.J. Skehill, M. Barry, S. Mcgrath, Mobility modelling with empirical pedestrian and vehicular traffic characteristics. WSEAS Trans. Commun. **4**(10) (2005)

22. Highway Capacity Manual 2000, no. 193. Transportation Research Board, National Academy of Sciences, 2000

23. N. Dalal, B. Triggs, Histograms of oriented gradients for human detection, in *Computing Vision Pattern Recognition, IEEE Computing Society Conference, CVPR 2005*, vol. 1, 2005, pp. 886–893

24. S.S. Blackman, *Multiple-Target Tracking with Radar Application*, vol. 1 (Artech House, Norwood, MA, 1986)

25. S. Blackman, R. Popoli, *Design and Analysis of Modern Tracking Systems* (Artech House, Norwood, MA, 1999)

26. G. Johansson, K. Rumar, Drivers' brake reaction times. Hum. Factors **1**, 23–27 (1971)

27. H. Makishita, K. Matsunaga, Differences of drivers' reaction times according to age and mental workload. Accid. Anal. Prev. **40**(2), 567–575(2008)

28. J.C. Collins, *Accident Reconstruction* (Charles C. Thomas Publisher, Limited, 1979)

29. F. Jiménez, J. Naranjo, F. García, An improved method to calculate the time-to-collision of two vehicles. Int. J. Intell. Transp. Syst. Res. **11**(1), 34–42 (2013)

30. F. García, F. Jiménez, J.J. Anaya, J.M. Armingol, J.E. Naranjo, A. de la Escalera, Distributed pedestrian detection alerts based on data fusion with accurate localization. Sensors **13**(9), 11687–11708 (2013)

Chapter 25
Context in Robotics and Information Fusion

**Domenico D. Bloisi, Daniele Nardi, Francesco Riccio
and Francesco Trapani**

Abstract Robotics systems need to be robust and adaptable to multiple operational conditions, in order to be deployable in different application domains. Contextual knowledge can be used for achieving greater flexibility and robustness in tackling the main tasks of a robot, namely mission execution, adaptability to environmental conditions, and self-assessment of performance. In this chapter, we review the research work focusing on the acquisition, management, and deployment of contextual information in robotic systems. Our aim is to show that several uses of contextual knowledge (at different representational levels) have been proposed in the literature, regarding many tasks that are typically required for mobile robots. As a result of this survey, we analyze which notions and approaches are applicable to the design and implementation of architectures for information fusion. More specifically, we sketch an architectural framework which enables for an effective engineering of systems that use contextual knowledge, by including the acquisition, representation, and use of contextual information into a framework for information fusion.

Keywords Context-awareness · Autonomous robotics · Context-dependent information fusion

D.D. Bloisi (✉) · D. Nardi · F. Riccio · F. Trapani
Department of Computer, Control, and Management Engineering,
Sapienza University of Rome, via Ariosto 25, 00185 Rome, Italy
e-mail: bloisi@dis.uniroma1.it

D. Nardi
e-mail: nardi@dis.uniroma1.it

F. Riccio
e-mail: riccio@dis.uniroma1.it

© Springer International Publishing Switzerland (outside the USA) 2016
L. Snidaro et al. (eds.), *Context-Enhanced Information Fusion*,
Advances in Computer Vision and Pattern Recognition,
DOI 10.1007/978-3-319-28971-7_25

25.1 Introduction

The ability of quickly recognizing the context and acting accordingly to it is a highly desirable skill for the development of robotic and intelligent systems. Robotic systems need to be robust and adaptable to multiple operational conditions, in order to be deployable in different application domains. In fact, the use of contextual knowledge can be a key factor for achieving greater flexibility and robustness to complete the required tasks. In this chapter, we survey several works about context in robotic systems, focusing on the acquisition, management, and deployment of contextual information. While there is a plethora of literature on the topic, we further refine the review to those concepts that can contribute creating a bridge between information fusion into robotic architectures.

There are two main ways to use context in robotics design. One is to use context holistically, i.e., by emphasizing its impact on the whole system. The approach we choose, instead, is to use context where needed, i.e., by analyzing its influence on the single parts of the system. The explicit representation of knowledge about context in the design phase of a system aims at improving its performance, by dynamically tailoring the functions of the system modules to the specific features of the situation at hand. Indeed, a clear separation of contextual knowledge leads to a design methodology that supports the definition of small specialized system components rather than complex self-contained sub-systems.

Our aim is to analyze which notions and approaches, among the several uses of contextual knowledge (at different representational levels) that have been proposed in the literature, are applicable to the design and implementation of architectures for information fusion. More specifically, we sketch an architectural framework which enables for an effective design of systems that use contextual knowledge. As a result, we formalize the acquisition, representation, and use of contextual information into a framework for information fusion.

The remainder of this chapter is organized as follows. Section 25.2 provides an overview about the use of context in robotics. In particular, a novel classification of existing methods, based on the context representation, is presented. In Sect. 25.3, a context-aware framework for information fusion applications is proposed and a context-based architecture for an application example is described in Sect. 25.4. Conclusions are drawn in Sect. 25.5.

25.2 Context in Robotics

Contextual knowledge can be defined in general as "the information that surrounds a situation of interest in the world" [1]. With specific reference to robotics, the interest for contextual knowledge is twofold [2]:

- Context is useful in the design and implementation of systems that are focused on cognition;

- The performance of robotic systems, as well as their scope of applicability, can be improved by formalizing different high-level features by means of context representation and contextual reasoning.

This section explores different methods and approaches for managing contextual information. First, we recall the taxonomy defined by Turner [3], and then we propose a novel classification that groups existing approaches according to the methodologies used for managing context. Finally, we discuss the advantages of our categorization.

25.2.1 Contextual Knowledge

The identification and exploitation of contextual knowledge plays a key role in robotic systems. Indeed, a robotic system requires high-level information fusion capabilities [4], responsiveness, and an appropriate level of awareness about the external environment, its mission, and its own status. In the robotics domain, data fusion techniques have been widely exploited (e.g., [5, 6]), as well as cognitive level fusion (e.g., [7]); however, a common and standard definition of context does not exist, and, in general, the formalization of "context" depends on the actual implementation.

In this work, we adopt the Turner's categories [3] as the main reference for the formalization of context knowledge in robotics applications. Turner defines *context* as an identifiable configuration of features which are meaningful to characterize the world state and useful to influence the decision process of a robotic system. Moreover, he characterizes context information (CI) as a tuple of three elements, namely *environmental information* (EI), *task-related information* (TI), and *self-knowledge* (SK). More specifically, Turner refers to contextual information as the sum of these three contributions (see Fig. 25.1).

Environmental knowledge. This kind of contextual information formalizes data that is environment-dependent and that does not directly depend on the robot

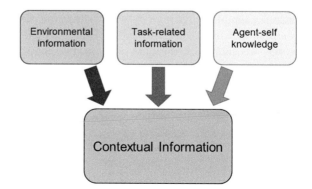

Fig. 25.1 Turner's context knowledge classification: (i) environmental information, (ii) task-related information, and (iii) agent self-knowledge [3]

actions. The robot perceives the world through its sensors and it infers the context according to the current status of the scenario (e.g., presence of obstacles or people). In a navigation system, the robot can tune its parameters depending on the terrain conditions, or its perception system, the information about the illumination conditions can be used to improve the perception or to discern the saliency of information as related to the task. In the case of a coordinated team of robots, e.g., unmanned aerial vehicles (UAVs) [8], having the task to search for a lost object, the robots may adapt their navigation parameters according to the detected conditions of the environment (e.g., terrain, trafficability, and constraints information).

Task-related knowledge. Task-related information is generally imposed by the mission specifications. Depending on the operating condition and on the task constraints (e.g., time constraints, priorities, and locations), the robot adapts its execution plan in order to increase robustness and efficiency. It is worth noting that the knowledge about a task does not modify the task outcome or requirements, but it is exploited to influence the execution of the task with the aim of improving the performance. Using again the example of multiple robot search, the team of robots can execute the task in different modalities by considering: (i) The current day time; (ii) The location where the robots are searching for the objects; (iii) The information processed by the other teammates; (iv) The known locations where a particular objects uses to be; and (v) Additional information gathered during the search (e.g., the robot can receive information about where the object of interest has been detected the last time).

In the above-discussed example, the contextual knowledge does not modify the goal of the task (which remains the localization of an object), but it drastically influences the task execution (e.g., ordering) such as sensor and mission management, and thus the performance of the system (e.g., timeliness, accuracy).

Self-knowledge. In this case, the robot infers context knowledge by relying on its own status and on the internal representation of the surrounding environment. In the multiple robot search example, for instance, it is possible that one of the teammates recognizes a self malfunctioning or has a low battery level. Then, it can communicate its status to the team. Consequently, the team can consider unreliable the information coming from that particular robot.

In the remainder of this section, we provide an analysis of some context-based systems in robotics. Our aim is not to provide a comprehensive survey. Rather, we reference sample works from the robotic literature, with the purpose of investigating connections with the use of context in information fusion. For each of the cited works, we emphasize the type of contextual information and the representation adopted in it. In addition to the Turner's categorization, we use an additional taxonomy based on the representation structures and methodology conceived for exploiting the concept of context.

25.2.1.1 Environmental Context

Environmental context formalizes the information about the external world that is not necessary for achieving the goals, but provides a more exhaustive and clear modeling of the typical scenarios. This kind of information is useful to recognize situations of interest and to adapt the behavior of the system on the basis of the situation at hand. As an example, Nüchter et al. [9] employ environmental knowledge to establish correspondences among objects of the environment by considering geometric information. The proposed system has static knowledge about the geometrical properties of well-known items. Whenever these properties are observed, the system makes assumption about the current scenario, and hence tunes its association procedures according to it, which results in a quicker and more reliable completion of the task.

The work by Rottmann et al. [10] exploits context-awareness to classify indoor scenarios into semantic classes. After an initial classification phase, based on the recognition of geometrical and visual features, the system makes use of its contextual knowledge to map the observed features to known classes of scenario types. To model this dependency, the system exploits an Hidden Markov Model, that is updated by sensory data and movements of the robot, and outputs the likelihood for the label of the environment.

Hawes et al. [11] exploit contextual knowledge about geometric and functional properties of known environments to accomplish recognition of spatial regions. Those properties are basically intended as the types of objects expected to be in a particular region and their location relative to each other. As an example, in the case of a classroom, contextual knowledge would predict the presence of desks, arranged in rows and facing a whiteboard. The context-dependent spatial regions are represented in terms of groups of anchor points, which are symbolic description of these salient objects. Through visual recognition techniques, the agent identifies and estimates the relative positions of the anchor points and hence proceeds in the labeling of the environment.

Triebel et al. [12] design a *multilevel surface map* (MLS) to inform the robot about the terrain conditions. The authors divide the environment into different cells and store in each cell the information related to the particular area covered by the current cell. This representation of contextual knowledge is useful in designing navigation and localization systems for outdoor scenarios.

Aboshosha and Zell [13] propose an approach for adapting robot behavior for victim search in disaster scenarios. The authors collect information about unknown indoor scenarios to properly shape the robot behavior. An adaptive controller regulates the robot velocity and gaze orientation depending on the environment of the mission and on the victim distribution within the environment.

Dornhege and Kleiner [14] introduce the concept of *behavior maps*. They represent the environment as a grid and collect meaningful information for each cell related to the current context. The key idea is to directly connect the map of the environment to the behavior of the robot. Using the information stored in each cell, they shape the behavior of the robot by means of fuzzy rules, in order to make the system *context-sensitive*.

25.2.1.2 Mission-Related Context

Context-driven choices are useful in robotic scenarios for adapting the robot behaviors to the different situations. Indeed, systems that use mission-related information aim at representing *task-related* features to influence the execution and to improve the system performance. For instance, Simmons and Apfelbaum [15] generate contextual information by characterizing a task at different levels of information. The authors enhance the task definition language (TDL) formalism with a new representation for the robot tasks, called *task trees*, that relates the information about the tasks and that is a suitable way for reasoning about it.

Saffiotti et al. [16] exploit the concept of multivalued logic to define task requirements and specifications. The authors propose an approach for integrating task planning and execution in a unified representation, named *behavior scheme*, which is context-dependent by definition. This approach allows the system to be efficient in characterizing and planning the task and to be as reactive as possible in executing the mission.

Mou et al. [17] describe a context-aware robotic system—a robotic walker for Parkinson's disease patients—able to adjusts its behavior according to the context of the task. The robot detects through its sensory system the type of gait and the kind of movement performed by the patient, e.g., "turning" or "going backward." Then, contextual information is represented with a vector of variables, which determines the law of motion of the walker through simple *if-else* structures.

Calisi et al. [2] employ a high level of Petri-Net formalism, the so-called *Petri-Net Plans* (PNPs), to represent the task design, execution, and monitoring. The authors deploy a robot in a multiobjective exploration and search scenario. The robot features a strategic level to adapt or modify the task execution according to the mission specifications.

25.2.1.3 Self-related Context

Self-knowledge is often an underestimated aspect in robotic systems. However, self-related contextual information is crucial to evaluate the status of the robot and the reliability of its decisions while performing a mission. For example, Newman et al. [18] exploit introspective, as well as environmental, knowledge using two different algorithms for incremental mapping and loop closure: An efficient incremental 3D scan matching is used when mapping open-loop situations, while a vision-based system detects possible loop closures.

Agent-related context directly refers to behavior actions and it can be adopted in behavior specialization routines, in order to optimize the task execution and the system adaptation to the environment. The use of contextual knowledge about the system status for behavior specialization is suggested by Beets et al. [19]. The authors exploit introspective knowledge to obtain smooth transitions between behaviors, in particular by applying sampling-based inference methods.

25.2.2 Context Representation

Environment, task information, and robot self-knowledge are the fundamental concepts for defining the Turner's contextual information taxonomy. Once the system gathers contextual knowledge, a common representation is needed to reason about the collected knowledge. Hence, we focus on the context representation criteria that allows the robot and, more in general, a context-aware system to exploit contextual information at different levels (e.g., at reasoning and sensory level).

A *context representation* has to provide a uniform view of the collected data and a robust reasoning process for state estimations, behaviors specialization, and task execution evaluations. In the rest of this section, we analyze the state of the art by emphasizing the differences between existing context representation methodologies and we present a novel classification that groups representation structures into three classes:

1. *Embedded*;
2. *Logic*;
3. *Probabilistic*.

25.2.2.1 Embedded Context Representation

Systems using *embedded context representation* represent context as sets of meaningful sensory features that characterize particular situations. Since this kind of representation works at a perceptive level, it is typical of reactive systems. Such systems focus on the recognition and labeling of the current context and adjust their behavior in accordance with the identified scenario, representing it at a sub-symbolic level. However, even if a reactive strategy can be effective for sensory driven recognition of known environments, such a methodology is highly system-dependent and not versatile. In fact, even if the contextual knowledge is formalized explicitly, it is inherently bonded to the perceptual structures, and hence it is specific of the particular system.

Context classification with different sets of features is used for robots relying on visual perception such as scouting mobile robots, and more generally, on systems performing visual recognition. Narayanan et al. [20] model reactive behaviors for a mobile robot according to a set of scenarios. Each scenario consists of traces of visual frames with the respective desired movements. During the execution of its tasks, the robot scans the environment and tries to build correlations between the sensed world and the demonstrated scenario frames. Once a correlation is established, the current context is identified and the robot actuators execute the requested motion law. Moreover, the authors describe another approach which substitutes the explicit movement commands with a set of neural networks, previously trained for a specific scenario. Hence, if the scenario has been recognized, then the corresponding network is triggered and commands the system.

When image classification or scene recognition techniques are involved, a priori knowledge about the geometrical and visual properties of known classes of objects can be gathered and used to direct the recognition process more efficiently [21]. These features can be encoded explicitly as desired values for functions representing particular visual features, or, implicitly, as collections of frames displaying the desired features. The detection of known features in a target image enables the system to recognize meaningful contextual elements, such as the presence of relevant objects, which are useful cues for the final classification of the image.

Buch et al. [22] exploit specific features for evaluating the alignment pose between objects in an image; the problem is addressed by defining descriptors that encode the geometrical features of the objects. In particular, context descriptors are used to represent the relative orientation of feature segments inside an Euclidean neighborhood around the feature of interest. Contextual descriptors are then used to perform alignment estimation with RANSAC.

Costante et al. [23] propose a visual classifier that clusters a target image with a *normalized-cut* based approach. In order to increase the efficiency of the system, a measure of similarity with respect to the other previously labeled sets of images is computed before the classification step. Whenever a correlation is found, the system clusters the set of images and exploits the labels of the known images to infer the classification of a new image. Here, contextual information is represented as a set of labeled images, without any further abstraction about the classes they symbolize.

Liu et al. [24] present a system for generating abstract graphs for *table-top* scenes from 6D object pose estimates. The system relies on the pose estimations for feature-driven recognitions, which are used to determine spatial objects relations (e.g., points of contact, relative disposition). The obtained relationships are encoded with reactive rules, which contribute to generate the abstract object graph of relations.

25.2.2.2 Logic-Based Representation

The most common choice in modeling contextual information is the use of *declarative knowledge representation languages*. Logic-based representations range from rule-based ontologies to first-order logic. The main advantage in using such a representation is that a symbolic framework implicitly provides *inference tools*, which supports planning and reasoning. In Laird et al. [25] cognitive architectures integrate sensory data and descriptive knowledge with contextual rules, directly into the *decision-making process* of the system. More in detail, Laird's decision procedure aims at modeling the current symbolic knowledge of the system, named *symbolic working memory*. The symbolic working memory communicates to the perception layer and to the *permanent memory* modules, and it provides relational representations of recent sensory data, current goals, and long-term memories. Contextual information is structurally defined within the permanent memory modules. More precisely, the context is represented as rules in the *procedural memory* and as scenarios (from past experience) in the *episodic memory*, respectively. The system can query the contextual database by loading the proper memory, which is continuously updated through reinforcement and episodic learning techniques.

The challenging problem for this type of architectures is in developing context modules able to dynamically update and increment their context knowledge. Indeed, turning experience into structured logical assertions needs a high level of abstraction, which is often difficult to achieve. Furthermore, logic-based models require an accurate grounding of semantics into the sensed world. Karapinar et al. [26] describe a learning method for expanding and correcting contextual knowledge in robotics systems. The authors represent knowledge by means of *linear temporal logic* formulas, which allow the system to analyze episodes of failures occurred in past experiences and to adjust its internal knowledge. Whenever a failure occurs, the system identifies the related configuration of *risks of failures*, which is context-dependent. Therefore, the system learns how to connect possible failures to a *risk of failure* scenario, which can anticipate the failure itself. Inherently, the system learns to avoid potential failure situations, if any, and to handle different routines in performing tasks.

A system based on *formal representation languages* can be easily understood by human operators, which is a main advantage when context information is directly provided by users or obtained through interactions. However, context-aware systems that use a formal representation generally require a high level of abstraction.

Scalmato et al. [27] employ *predefined logic ontologies* to formalize contexts and situation awareness. Concepts (in form of T-Boxes) are provided by humans, while the contingent knowledge (A-Boxes) is populated by the system. This kind of representation is highly flexible, since a knowledge base based on representation languages does not depend neither on the internal structure of the system nor on its domain. Therefore, the overall context knowledge can be easily shared and adapted to different systems. Turner et al. [28] introduce a novel methodology for defining *distributed context-mediated behaviors* for multiagent systems. In particular, their analysis focuses on the need of a common ontology and of expressing knowledge in a common representation, such as frame-based system or a description logic language. The authors suggest some strategy for the distributed development of contextual knowledge, as a set of comparison, fusion, and integration techniques of the ontologies built out of the experience of the single agents.

25.2.2.3 Probabilistic-Based Representation

A robotic system is affected at any level (i.e., perception, reasoning, and action) by some degree of error, or, more in general, of *uncertainty* in its processes. Therefore, a probabilistic representation of the system is often needed. Several contextual knowledge representations formalize relations between context and desired behaviors through probabilistic structures, e.g., Bayesian networks. Once the contextual variables are identified, Bayesian networks can model the *degree of belief* of the different scenarios and the most likely behavior quite effectively.

A preliminary analysis of the contextual knowledge (both task- and environment-related) needs to be carried out off-line, in order to learn and set the network dependencies.

Witzig et al. [29] describe a collaborative human–robot system that provides context knowledge to enable more effective robotic manipulation. Contexts are represented by probability density functions, covering task specifications, known object properties, or manipulator poses. Contextual variables are automatically computed by elaborating the perceptual information or they are specified by an external operator through a software interface. The contextual knowledge is then used to assess the internal Bayesian network, in order to model the grasp poses of the manipulator.

Probabilistic approaches are also used for object classification. In fact, they allow the system to estimate the likelihood of membership of a particular element with respect to each category present in the learning process. Held et al. [30] propose an algorithm for allowing intelligent cars to recognize other cars on the roadway. Vision-based object detection techniques are used to perform a preliminary recognition. Then, in order to remove the false positive perceptions, the probability of each candidate object is weighted with a contextual score, and the final likelihood for each item is computed. The contextual score is based on the object size and on the position in the scenario. Size score is high when the dimension of the object is compatible with the one of an actual vehicle. Position score is based on the global positioning system (GPS) information: such a score is close to the maximum if the object is positioned on the road consistently with a vehicle position.

25.2.3   Discussion

From the above sketch of recent developments in the use of context in robotic systems, it results that the contextual information is exploited and involved in many different ways. Here, we focus on a categorization based, respectively, on the representation of the contextual variables, but other approaches are also possible.

Table 25.1 shows a summary of the specific classes of representations used in the cited approaches. In addition to the type of encoding used for representing the contextual knowledge, we also indicate the Turner's categories involved, the application scenario, and the main task supported by context information. Figure 25.2 shows how different approaches can fit into our classification. It is worth noting that multiple representations can be exploited within the same system.

Since the way of representing contextual knowledge strongly influences the implementation of the system, a representation-based categorization highlights the differences between approaches. As emerges from Table 25.1, not all the reviewed methods involve all the categories of contextual information. Furthermore, the analysis of the literature shows that there are many representation approaches. Indeed, each approach has its own strengths and weaknesses and multiple approaches can be combined to improve the results.

Table 25.1 Summary of the surveyed approaches to context-awareness

Approach	Application	Task	T. C.			Repr.		
			S	E	T	E	L	P
Laird et al. [25]	Cognitive architecture	Navigation	✓	✓	✓	✓	✓	✓
Kurup et al. [31]	Cognitive architecture	Visual recognition		✓			✓	
Karapinar et al. [26]	Planning	Navigation and simple object manipulation	✓	✓	✓		✓	
Scalmato et al. [27]	Situation awareness	Classification		✓	✓		✓	
Turner et al. [28]	Distributed context assessment for multiagent systems	General decentralized multiagent tasks	✓	✓	✓		✓	
Narayanan et al. [20]	Mobile robots navigation	Navigation		✓	✓	✓		
Buch et al. [22]	Visual recognition	Alignment estimation		✓			✓	✓

Application the general field of application. *Task* the kind of task on which the system has been tested. *T. C.* (*Turner Classification*) the categories of context formalized by Turner (*Self, Environment,* or *Task* related) that are considered. *Repr.* the type of encoding used for representing the contextual information, i.e., *Embedded, Logic,* or *Probabilistic*

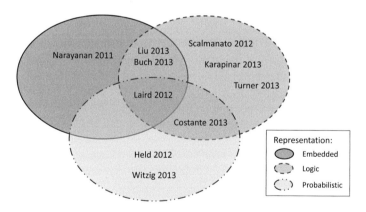

Fig. 25.2 Some recent approaches using knowledge representation grouped according to our classification

Logic and probabilistic representations both supply effective structures for describing effects and causes of contextual scenarios, the former focusing on the expressiveness of the language and the latter on the reliability of the estimates. However, logic representations alone fail in modeling inferential processes when they require complex computations. On the other hand, probabilistic encodings lack descriptive power for modeling complex environments.

Embedded representations rely on sub-symbolic structures for an effective mapping between the sensory data in input and the estimates for the contextual variables, but do not produce an easily interpretable knowledge.

The future challenge for context-aware systems will probably be to find a suitable way to combine effectively the different representation strategies, so that they can complement each other. For example, a system following a combined approach may have a layered modeling of the context: (i) A high-level layer, where logical structures describe the relationships and the hierarchies among the contextual variables; (ii) A middleware layer, made of probabilistic modules that provide reliable inference processes; (iii) A low-level embedded representation, for managing particular context configurations which require quick identification and a fast reactive behavior.

25.3 A Context-Aware Framework for Information Fusion Applications

In this section, we define a context-aware framework for information fusion systems. It has been sketched by extending an existing framework, in particular the one proposed by Llinas in [32]. Our aim is to embed ideas borrowed from the robotics literature into a state-of-the-art framework for information fusion.

The key insight is to exploit, beside the use of sensory data, additional information (i.e., context knowledge) to implement a more efficient and adaptable system. The perception system of the robot can be seen as a *Data Fusion system* that builds a representation of the world, which supports the robot operations. It is in charge of reading the sensor data, processing the information, and communicating the inferred knowledge to external entities. In our concept design, contextual knowledge is inherently assessed in the robotic system to influence the agent data acquisition routines and, eventually, its actions.

25.3.1 Framework Design

As stated above, the information fusion framework proposed by Llinas in [32] is our starting point for developing a context-based architecture. Even if the Llinas' framework includes a component for handling contextual information, the formalization in [32] does not explicitly foresee a feedback data flow that can influence the contextual data base. Our goal is to enhance the Llinas' framework by better defining the role of the contextual system within the information fusion one.

In particular, we aim at designing a system able to take advantage of the context representation, containing two components for contextual exploitation: a context middleware and a context reasoner. The former is in charge of modifying the contextual knowledge base; the latter infers contextual knowledge at a high level, independently from the robotic system deployed. This formulation allows to influence the robotic system at any layer and to accept feedback from the agent, in order to update the context data.

The use of a middleware is not novel and it has been proposed by the information fusion community for exploiting contextual information in high-level fusion architectures. For example, Gomez-Romero et al. [33] discuss the use of a middleware in "a priori frameworks," where contextual information is known at design time and can be incorporated to the fusion procedures (hard-wired). However, in our formulation, we generalize the contribution of the middleware modules, making every layer (i.e., acquisition, detection, and fusion) *context-dependent*.

Indeed, in addition to the use of context for influencing the fusion processes (as in the framework proposed by Llinas), we want to influence also the data acquisition and decision phases. The key insight is that any component of the system can be optimized by means of context. To this end, (i) a proper contextual knowledge, (ii) a coherent methodology for the reasoning, and (iii) a dedicated adaptation logic for each of the *context-dependent* component have to be defined. By defining a common representation modality, we impose a compact and coherent way for managing every kind of information generated by any of the layer within the framework.

25.3.2 Framework Scheme

The scheme of our context-aware framework for information fusion is shown in Fig. 25.3. In our concept design, the operation of the context-aware framework is structured into three main phases:

1. *Acquisition*;
2. *Reasoning*;
3. *Decision*.

Acquisition
In the acquisition phase, hard and soft sensor data are acquired. Hard sensor data refer to the system perceptions directly retrieved from the sensors of the system, while soft sensor data are information provided by human observers, such as reports from humans or context analysis by domain experts [34]. The system acquisition submodule is responsible for managing the hard sensor data. Soft information, instead, are analyzed by the *context information extraction* submodule, together with the current system status.

Context Middleware
Context information extraction constitutes the first process carried out by the so-called *context middleware* module, which is responsible for:

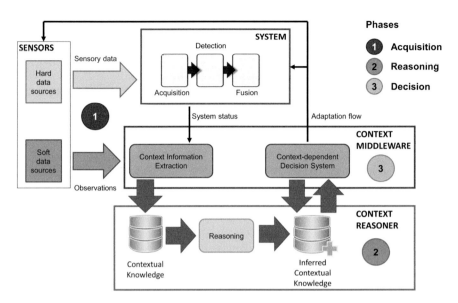

Fig. 25.3 A context-aware framework for information fusion

1. Extracting content information from the input data;
2. Adapting the system configuration in accordance to the context.

The context middleware constitutes the connection between the context reasoner and the system. In particular, the context middleware translates the inferred contextual knowledge, generated by the context reasoner, in a suitable format for the underlying system. The context middleware allows for creating a clear conceptual separation between the reasoning processes and the state estimation processes. This leads to a less coupled system. Indeed, the chosen representation of the context is totally independent with respect to the particular system implementation.

Reasoning
The reasoning phase relies on contextual knowledge produced by the context middleware. The *context reasoner* is responsible for informing contextual knowledge and for making it available back to the context middleware.

Decision
In the decision phase, the context-dependent decision system submodule uses the available contextual information to adapt the system configuration (e.g., the sensor parameters) in accordance with the current context. In such a way, contextual knowledge enhances the effectiveness of the whole system, by influencing its routines of data acquisition and processing. Accordingly, Fig. 25.3 illustrates the data flow between the context reasoner and context middleware modules. The context-dependent decision system generates the action policies for the robotic system, and simultaneously it allows the *context reasoner* to know taken decisions providing feedback information that is used to update contextual knowledge.

It is interesting to notice how this pattern is totally orthogonal to the actual representation of context. Indeed, the internal structure of the context middleware is independent of the structure of the whole system.

In order to give the reader a clear idea of our concept design and to highlight the features of our proposed framework, we want to describe the application of our framework to a concrete example. Hence, in the following section we illustrate the design of in an intelligent vehicle system within a context-aware framework.

25.4 Example of Context-Based Architecture with Information Fusion

In this section, an application example is exploited to illustrate how a context-based architecture can be designed by adopting the proposed context-aware framework. In particular, the example concerns the development of a context-aware architecture for an adaptive cruise control system mounted on an intelligent vehicle.

The application scenario is illustrated by providing a description of the available data acquisition devices for the vehicle. The system architecture is designed to allow for a shared acquisition and representation of the contextual knowledge, which can be used to improve the different processes needed for accomplishing the desired tasks.

25.4.1 Application Scenario: An Adaptive Cruise Control System for an Intelligent Vehicle

Our application scenario focuses on an intelligent vehicle. The goal is to develop an adaptive cruise control system for providing the vehicle with the ability of adjusting its speed according to the conditions of the road (environmental information), the needs of the driver (task-related information), and the vehicle status (agent self-knowledge). Figure 25.4 shows the different information sources available for the autonomous vehicle:

- Internet connection, two cameras, battery level indicator (hard data sources);
- Button console (soft data sources).

The hard data sources produce electronic and physics-based data. In this example, hard sensor information comes from two cameras, placed in the front part of the car with different fields of view. Moreover, the vehicle is connected to the Internet and websites can be accessed to extract information about weather forecast and traffic conditions. It is also possible to extract information about the charge level of the batteries that power the vehicle.

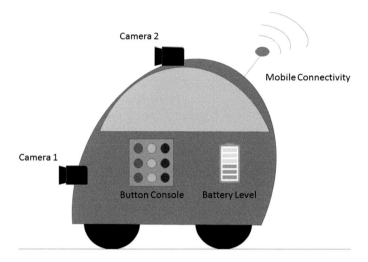

Fig. 25.4 The intelligent vehicle is equipped with two cameras, a mobile connection and a button console for interacting with the human driver. It is also possible to obtain the current level of the battery charge

Soft data sources acquire data from human observers. In the example, the passengers have a button console that serves to communicate with the vehicle.

Since the adaptive cruise control system has multiple heterogeneous information sources, it is necessary to adopt an architecture conceived for fusing both hard and soft sensor data. Furthermore, the status of the environment, the status of the vehicle, and the goals of the passengers (e.g., the final destination) influence the behavior of the system.

25.4.2 Problem Formalization

An autonomous vehicle, in its basic formalization, has the task of bringing a passenger from a starting location to a goal destination through a road network. In order to achieve this purpose, the system should plan and execute a sequence of actions (e.g., "turn right at the crossroad") respecting some constraints (e.g., "stop at the red light"), and possibly maximizing/minimizing some variables (e.g., the safety of the path or the duration of the journey).

In the case of a non context-aware autonomous vehicle, the path is generated according to the information stored in static maps and the plan is executed with the aid of a self-localization module (for instance, using the GPS signal). The topology of the road network and the position of the vehicle are the problem variables, and those variables have to be properly handled for the resolution of the problem.

A context-aware system can be seen as an extension of the above-sketched model. Although the tasks, the set of actions, and the constraints are identical, in such a case the system takes advantage of contextual knowledge, thus allowing for developing adaptive solutions. In our example, the described vehicle accesses the data representing the traffic probability distributions over the several roads of the map during the different periods of the day, or information about which roads have an accident rate over some fixed threshold. Moreover, the system has the ability to acquire and take into account observations from the passengers, as the requested driving mode (e.g., economy mode) or the preferred paths (e.g., "avoid toll roads"). Finally, the vehicle can benefit from an Internet connection, supplying streaming data about the weather or the traffic conditions, or it can have a reasoning system, which can infer information about the environment by analyzing the images from the cameras.

It is important to notice how all the contextual information does not influence directly the resolution of the task, which is actually solvable independently of it. The context, instead, provides a tool for evaluating the admissible sequences of actions by analyzing their characteristics and for selecting among them the ones that best fit the current scenario.

25.4.3   Taxonomy of Context

In order to organize effectively each piece of information inside the architecture of a system, it is worth to categorize the different nature of contextual data. Indeed, contextual information can be modeled by means of different types of structures.

A first category, called *logical and physical structures*, includes all the static data, usually provided off-line, organized in data sets or probability networks. Examples of information belonging to this group are constant-time data structures, like the rules of the road or the graphs representing the road network, and the knowledge, representable through probabilistic networks, about the relationships among events and contextual variables.

A second set is constituted by the *contextual data* fed to the system during the execution of the task, usually in the form of observations. These assertions might come from human users, as in the case of voice commands from a passenger, or from external systems, like a satellite location system, the web, or the connection to a weather forecast provider.

The *inferred context* represents the third category. The inferred context amounts to all the contextual information that derives from the processing of the system variables and the context data. An example is the estimate of the traffic in a given road, calculated on the basis of the information about weather conditions and past accidents. It is worth to notice, and this third category makes it clear, how several contextual data are reciprocally related and influence each other. For example, the detection of several cars within the same road alters the context variable that represents the intensity of traffic, which in turn can affect the risk of accident of the road.

25.4.4 Contextual Information Fusion

Some of the above-discussed relations between contextual variables follow a layered hierarchy: Contextual information can be obtained as a result of information fusion processes and contextual information can in turn influence the fusion processes themselves.

Each contextual variable, independently from its representation, can be used at different fusion layers as a source or as a parameter of the processing function.

In our architecture, we adopt the joint directors of laboratories (JDL) model [4] for information exploitation and consider contextual knowledge to actively influence the underneath system and to improve its performance. In particular, we consider the following levels of the JDL model:

- Level 0: features;
- Level 1: individual entities;
- Level 2: structures;
- Level 3: scenarios and outcomes;
- Level 4: aspects of the system itself.

Each of the above-listed levels is particularly suitable for addressing information management and exploitation, depending on the type of knowledge to be represented.

For example, visual features can be used at level 0 to help in detecting the objects of interest on the roadway (e.g., pedestrians or other vehicles). The information about the traffic, acquired through external or internal observations, contributes at level 2 to define a reliable estimation of the current scenario.

At level 4, the analysis of the status of the resources of the vehicle (e.g., battery level, fuel level, possible malfunctioning), can help in controlling the organization of the fusion processes, with the aim of minimizing the consumption of the resources, or reducing possible risks.

The context data, through the information fusion process, make the estimations of the state of the environment more complete and trustworthy and, consequently, they influence the fusion processes of the system variables (such as the vehicle localization, the selection of the path, and the detection of colliding objects), generating adaptive solutions. It should be kept in mind that the relationship between the fusion processes and the contextual data is not only from the bottom to the top, but it is indeed a two-way relation. For instance, the recognition of several machines increases the probability of being in a congested area; the awareness of being in traffic jam might result in a different a priori probability to detect a vehicle, thus influencing the fusion processes at level 0.

25.4.5 The Information Fusion Pipeline Following the JDL Perspective

Contextual information can affect different JDL levels [35]. Table 25.2 provides three examples of estimations of the *context variables* for the intelligent cruise control example.

Context variables are calculated by evaluating the available *input variables*, i.e., problem-related variables containing the information that can be useful to infer the context variables. According to the adopted information fusion framework, this inferring process includes three stages, namely the processes of *common referencing*, *data association*, and *situation estimation* that are usually indicated as the fusion node functions.

For the application example, we select three problem variables to cover each of the different levels of the JDL model [36] and to reflect the Turner's classification:

1. `presence_of_cars_on_the_roadway` for task-related information, JDL level 1;
2. `safe_following_distance` for environmental information, JDL level 2;
3. `operational_mode` for agent self-knowledge, JDL level 3;

It is important to point out that we consider the levels of JDL and the Turner's categories as two orthogonal concepts and we are not interested in finding a correspondence between them.

Table 25.2 Example of fusion node functions across the JDL level for the use case

JDL level	Context variables	Input variables	Fusion node functions		
			CR	DA	SE
L1 object assessment	Presence of cars on the roadway	Features detected by cameras 1 and 2	Correlation of feature points among cameras	Matching of features with car model	Classification
L2 situation assessment	Safe following distance	Presence of raindrops on cameras, weather forecast	Camera views alignment	Clustering	Thresholding
L3 impact assessment	Operational mode	User preferences, weather forecast, road type, battery level	Mapping of inputs on mode scores	Calculation of mode scores	Selection of mode with the highest score

Level 1

The object assessment (level 1) example considers the contextual variable representing the presence of another car in the field of views of the cameras. The information used as input for this estimate are the points of interest identified by a feature detector on the two cameras. During the common referencing and data association processes, the features detected by the two cameras are correlated and composed, i.e., the two views are aligned to produce a single view and the detections are grouped by means of an Euclidean clustering. The impact assessment task deals with the comparison of the obtained structure with the models of known cars, and the likelihood of the detected observation being a car is estimated. The output of the whole process is a Boolean variable representing the presence of vehicles in the area in front of the intelligent car.

Level 2

As an example of a situation assessment variable (level 2), we consider the safe following distance that the intelligent vehicle has to maintain with respect to other vehicles ahead. Indeed, variables at level 2 models situation comprising relationships among entities with their selves and/or with the environment.

A safe distance from the car ahead with good, dry roads can be calculated by the following so-called "three-second rule" [37]: This time-lapse method uses a mark on the road, such as a power or light pole, to estimate the distance from the vehicle ahead. When weather conditions are not ideal (e.g., in case of rain), the safe following distance increases and it should be doubled to achieve a time interval of six seconds, for added safety.

In our example, the data coming from the two cameras on the vehicle are used to infer meteorological conditions, with specific reference to the detection of rainy weather. A rain drop detection mechanism is used to derive the most appropriate value for the variable `safe_following_distance`, according to the weather conditions.

Input data in such a case are the results of raindrops detections on the two camera lens. For example, raindrops can be detected using a suitable photometric raindrop model (as in [38, 39]). Since there are two cameras, one on the lower and one on the upper part of the vehicle, it is possible to have different detection results. Thus, it is necessary to perform a projection of the camera detection results in a common reference space.

The CR task involves the alignment of the two camera views, e.g., from different scales to a common one. Information about context can be used to set the focus value of the camera. If a rainfall is expected (e.g., extracting such information from the Internet), then the focus of the cameras can be adjusted in order to better detect raindrops. Indeed a focused raindrop can be more easily detected due to its spherical form. The association task consists mainly in deciding which observations are true positives while discarding false positives. The observations from the two cameras can be grouped according to an Euclidean clustering carried out in the common reference space. The final state estimation is obtained by thresholding the detected number of raindrops onto the camera lens with respect to a predefined threshold. It is worth noting that, in this phase, soft information can be used to validate the estimation.

To set the current state of the context variable `safe_following_distance` requires to fuse the information about the number of raindrops with the weather forecast, because water drops on the camera lens can also be generated by events other than rain.

Level 3

An example of an impact assessment contextual variable (level 3) is the decision about the most convenient operational mode. The operational modes presented to the passengers can be, for example, "economy," "normal," and "performance." Input variables are the observations of the human passengers regarding their favorite driving mode, knowledge about the road type, and other useful data, such as information about the weather conditions. Soft input variables can be transmitted via the button console.

The common reference space is made of the possible operational modes in the internal representation of the system, for example: (1) electric-only with the engine disengaged; (2) hybrid charge-depletion; and (3) hybrid charge-sustaining [40]. Then each of the possible values for the input variables is mapped to scores on each of the driving modes.

The association task requires the computation of the final scores for each of the operational modes, among which the one with the highest score is selected. The situation assessment then outputs the most convenient mode.

Given the above description of the application scenario and the context-aware framework for information fusion applications discussed in Sect. 25.3, it is possible to sketch a context-aware architecture that models the intelligent vehicle use case. Figure 25.5 shows the proposed scheme.

The adaptation flow that origins from the context-dependent system configuration module is used to modify the parameters of the hard and soft sensor data sources, for influencing the detection, semantic labeling, and flow control, and to direct the fusion nodes functions.

By referring to the previous example, the adaptation flow can be used to change the focus parameter of the cameras, to better detect the raindrops. Moreover, the adaptation flow can be used to select a specific weather forecast website that is considered more reliable (e.g., on the basis of the GPS position).

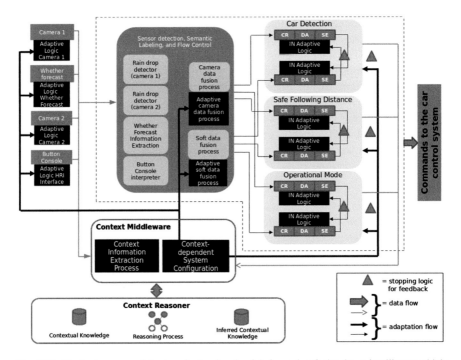

Fig. 25.5 Context-aware architecture for hard and soft information fusion in an intelligent vehicle system use case

25.5   Concluding Remarks

The use of contextual knowledge is a key feature in different application domains, where the acquisition, formalization, and exploitation of context information may substantially improve system performance under different operational conditions.

Throughout this chapter, our aim is to provide a general overview about the use of context information in the robotic domain, in order to discuss the possible connection with information fusion. To this end, we analyze the recent approaches in the literature according to the Turner's categories [3] to provide examples of use of contextual knowledge in robotics.

In addition, we highlight the manifold approaches to context representation, proposing, in particular, a novel classification for the considered methods. We categorize context knowledge as: probabilistic-based, logic-based, and embedded.

Furthermore, we sketched a context-aware framework for information fusion in a robotic scenario. The proposed framework is an extension of the information fusion proposed by Llinas et al. in [32] with the introduction of a more detailed implementation of the *contextual module*.

Our context module includes a *context middleware* and a *context reasoner*. Context information is extracted by the modules inside the in the context middleware, exploiting both soft and hard sensor sources. Then, the context reasoner infers contextual knowledge providing it back to the decision system, which is in charge of adapting the parameters of the system components according to the current contextual configuration.

In order to validate our insights, we provide an application example, concerning the design of a control system for an intelligent vehicle. The considered system may be able to modify its operation and driving policies according to its current contextual knowledge and the available hard and soft sources data.

Acknowledgements This work was supported by ONRG Grant N62909-14-1-N061.

References

1. L. Snidaro, J. García, J. Llinas, Context-based information fusion: a survey and discussion. Inf. Fusion **25**, 16–31 (2015)
2. D. Calisi, A. Farinelli, L. Iocchi, D. Nardi, Multi-objective exploration and search for autonomous rescue robots. J. Field Robot. Spec. Issue Quant. Perform. Eval. Robot. Intell. Syst. **24**, 763–777 (2007)
3. R.M. Turner, Context-mediated behavior for intelligent agents. Int. J. Hum Comput. Stud. **48**(3), 307–330 (1998)
4. E. Blasch, J. Llinas, D. Lambert, P. Valin, S. Das, C. Chee, M. Kokar, E. Shahbazian, High level information fusion developments, issues, and grand challenges: Fusion 2010 panel discussion, in *2010 13th Conference on Information Fusion (FUSION)*, 2010, pp. 1–8
5. R.C. Luo, M.G. Kay (eds.), *Multisensor Integration and Fusion for Intelligent Machines and Systems* (Ablex Publishing Corp., 1995)
6. M. Kam, X. Zhu, P. Kalata, Sensor fusion for mobile robot navigation. Proc. IEEE **85**(1), 108–119 (1997)
7. E. Blasch, Assembling a distributed fused information-based human-computer cognitive decision making tool. Aerosp. Electron. Syst. Mag. IEEE **15**(5), 11–17 (2000)
8. D. Shen, G. Chen, J.B. Cruz, E. Blasch. A game theoretic data fusion aided path planning approach for cooperative uav isr, in *Aerospace Conference, 2008 IEEE*, 2008, pp. 1–9
9. A. Nüchter, O. Wulf, K. Lingemann, J. Hertzberg, B. Wagner, H. Surmann, 3D Mapping with semantic knowledge, in *RoboCup 2005: Robot Soccer World Cup IX*, 2005, pp. 335–346
10. A. Rottmann, Ó. Martínez, M. Cyrill, S.W. Burgard, Place classification of indoor environments with mobile robots using boosting, in *Proceedings of the National Conference on Artificial Intelligence (AAAI)*, 2005, pp. 1306–1311
11. N. Hawes, M. Klenk, K. Lockwood, G.S. Horn, J.D. Kelleher, Towards a cognitive system that can recognize spatial regions based on context, in *AAAI*, 2012
12. R. Triebel, P. Pfaff, W. Burgard, Multi-level surface maps for outdoor terrain mapping and loop closing, in *Proceedings of the IEEE/RSJ International Conference on Intelligent Robots and Systems (IROS)*, 2006
13. A. Aboshosha, A. Zell, Adaptation of rescue robot behaviour in unknown terrains based on stochastic and fuzzy logic approaches, in *Proceedings of 2003 IEEE/RSJ International Conference on Intelligent Robots and Systems, (IROS'03)*, vol. 3, 2003, pp. 2859–2864
14. C. Dornhege, A. Kleiner, Behavior maps for online planning of obstacle negotiation and climbing on rough terrain. Technical Report 233, University of Freiburg, 2007
15. R. Simmons, D. Apfelbaum, A task description language for robot control, in *IROS, International Conference on Intelligent Robots and Systems*, vol. 3, 1998, pp. 1931–1937

16. A. Saffiotti, K. Konolige, E. Ruspini, A multivalued logic approach to integrating planning and control. Artif. Intell. **76**, 481–526 (1995)
17. W.II. Mou, M.F. Chang, C.K. Liao, Y.H. Hsu, S.H. Tseng, L.C. Fu, Context-aware assisted interactive robotic walker for parkinson's disease patients, in *2012 IEEE/RSJ International Conference on Intelligent Robots and Systems (IROS)*, 2012, pp. 329–334
18. P. Newman, D. Cole, K. Ho, Outdoor SLAM using visual appearance and laser ranging, in *Proceedings of the IEEE International Conference on Robotics and Automation (ICRA)*, 2006, pp. 1180–1187
19. M. Beetz, T. Arbuckle, M. Bennewitz, W. Burgard, A. Cremers, D. Fox, H. Grosskreutz, D. Hahnel, D. Schulz, Integrated plan-based control of autonomous service robots in human environments. IEEE Intell. Syst. **16**(5), 56–65 (2001)
20. K. K. Narayanan, L. F. Posada, F. Hoffmann, T. Bertram, Scenario and context specific visual robot behavior learning, in *2011 IEEE International Conference on Robotics and Automation (ICRA)*, 2011, pp. 1180–1185
21. Z. Liu, E. Blasch, Z. Xue, J. Zhao, R. Laganiere, W. Wu, Objective assessment of multiresolution image fusion algorithms for context enhancement in night vision: a comparative study. Pattern Anal. Mach. Intell. IEEE Trans. **34**(1), 94–109 (2012)
22. A.G. Buch, D. Kraft, J.K. Kamarainen, H.G. Petersen, N. Kruger, Pose estimation using local structure-specific shape and appearance context, in *2013 IEEE International Conference on Robotics and Automation (ICRA)*, 2013, pp. 2080–2087
23. G. Costante, T.A. Ciarfuglia, P. Valigi, E. Ricci, A transfer learning approach for multi-cue semantic place recognition, in *2013 IEEE/RSJ International Conference on Intelligent Robots and Systems (IROS)*, 2013, pp. 2122–2129
24. Z. Liu, D. Chen, K. M. Wurm, G. Von Wichert, Using rule-based context knowledge to model table-top scenes, in *2014 IEEE International Conference on Robotics and Automation (ICRA)*, 2014, pp. 2646–2651
25. J.E. Laird, K.R. Kinkade, S. Mohan, J.Z. Xu, Cognitive robotics using the soar cognitive architecture. Cognitive Robotics AAAI Technical Report WS-12-06. Accessed 27 July, 2012, pp. 46–54
26. S. Karapinar, S. Sariel-Talay, P. Yildiz, M. Ersen, Learning guided planning for robust task execution in cognitive robotics, in *Proceedings of the AAAI-13 Workshop on Intelligent Robotic Systems*, 2013, pp. 26–31
27. A. Scalmato, A. Sgorbissa, R. Zaccaria, Describing and classifying spatial and temporal contexts with owl dl in ubiquitous robotics, in *2012 IEEE International Conference on Robotics and Automation (ICRA)*, 2012, pp. 237–244
28. R.M. Turner, S. Rode, D. Gagne, Toward distributed context-mediated behavior for multiagent systems, in *Modeling and Using Context* (Springer, Berlin, 2013)
29. T. Witzig, J.M. Zollner, D. Pangercic, S. Osentoski, R. Jakel, R. Dillmann, Context aware shared autonomy for robotic manipulation tasks, in *2013 IEEE/RSJ International Conference on Intelligent Robots and Systems (IROS)*, 2013, pp. 5686–5693
30. D. Held, J. Levinson, S. Thrun, A probabilistic framework for car detection in images using context and scale, in *2012 IEEE International Conference on Robotics and Automation (ICRA)*, 2012, pp. 1628–1634
31. U. Kurup, C. Lebiere, A. Stentz, M. Hebert, Using expectations to drive cognitive behavior, in *AAAI*, 2012
32. J. Llinas, A survey and analysis of frameworks and framework issues for information fusion applications, in *Hybrid Artificial Intelligence Systems, Lecture Notes in Computer Science*, vol. 6076, 2010, pp. 14–23
33. J. Gomez-Romero, J. Garcia, M. Kandefer, J. Llinas, J.M. Molina, M.A. Patricio, M. Prentice, S.C. Shapiro. Strategies and techniques for use and exploitation of contextual information in high-level fusion architectures, in *13th Conference on Information Fusion*, 2010, pp. 1–8
34. S. Acharya, M. Kam, Evidence combination for hard and soft sensor data fusion, in *2011 Proceedings of the 14th International Conference on Information Fusion (FUSION)*, 2011, pp. 1–8

35. L. Snidaro, I. Visentini, J. Llinas, G.L. Foresti, Context in fusion: Some considerations in a JDL perspective, in *2013 16th International Conference on Information Fusion (FUSION)*, 2013, pp. 115–120
36. J. Llinas, C. Bowman, G. Rogova, A. Steinberg, F. White, Revisiting the JDL data fusion model ii, in *Proceedings of the Seventh International Conference on Information Fusion (FUSION 2004)*, eds. by P. Svensson, J. Schubert, 2004, pp. 1218–1230
37. CEDRs TG Road Safety. Safe distance between vehicles. Technical report, Conference of European Directors of Roads (CEDR), 2010
38. M. Roser, A. Geiger, Video-based raindrop detection for improved image registration, in *2009 IEEE 12th International Conference on Computer Vision Workshops (ICCV Workshops)*, 2009, pp. 570–577
39. S. You, R.T. Tan, R. Kawakami, K. Ikeuchi, Adherent raindrop detection and removal in video, in *2013 IEEE Conference on Computer Vision and Pattern Recognition (CVPR)*, 2013, pp. 1035–1042
40. M.S. Duvall, Battery evaluation for plug-in hybrid electric vehicles, in *Vehicle Power and Propulsion, 2005 IEEE Conference*, 2005, p. 6

Erratum to: System-Level Use of Contextual Information

Alan N. Steinberg and Galina L. Rogova

Erratum to:
Chapter 7 in: L. Snidaro et al. (eds.), *Context-Enhanced Information Fusion*, Advances in Computer Vision and Pattern Recognition, DOI 10.1007/978-3-319-28971-7_7

The book was inadvertently published with an incorrect order of authors in Chap. 7, the correct order should be "Alan N. Steinberg and Galina L. Rogova" rather than "Galina L. Rogova and Alan N. Steinberg".

The updated original online version for this chapter can be found at
DOI 10.1007/978-3-319-28971-7_7

A.N. Steinberg (✉)
2568 Fox Ridge Ct, Woodbridge, VA 22192, USA
e-mail: alaneilsteinberg@gmail.com

G.L. Rogova
State University New York at Buffalo, Buffalo, USA
e-mail: rogova@buffalo.edu

© Springer International Publishing Switzerland (outside the USA) 2016   E1
L. Snidaro et al. (eds.), *Context-Enhanced Information Fusion*,
Advances in Computer Vision and Pattern Recognition,
DOI 10.1007/978-3-319-28971-7_26

Index

© Springer International Publishing Switzerland (outside the USA) 2016
L. Snidaro et al. (eds.), *Context-Enhanced Information Fusion*,
Advances in Computer Vision and Pattern Recognition,
DOI 10.1007/978-3-319-28971-7